LEARN SPANISH MASTERY

Big Collection of Common Phrases & Words from Beginners to Intermediate Level to Learn How to Speak a New Languages in Less Than 3 Weeks. Spanish Short Stories to Enjoy

Miguel González

TABLE OF CONTENTS

CHAPTER 1

LEARN SPANISH FOR BEGINNERS

INTRODUCTION

L earning Spanish is a great idea for anyone who wants to be able to speak fluently in another language. It opens up many opportunities and cultures from Spain, Latin America, and the U.S. Spanish speakers will often find themselves in high demand in the workforce. Get started today!

In our modern culture, you'll often find yourself surrounded by many people who speak Spanish due to its prevalence in American culture and throughout Latin America.

We'll also go over how to pronounce each language in more detail.

In Spain, the language is called Castilian Spanish in which they typically speak with a very strong accent. In South America and Central America, Spanish is mostly spoken in formal or informal environments as it is associated with other countries like Mexico and Portugal.

Andalusian Spanish is the form of Spanish that generally gives off a rural vibe as it is spoken in the southern parts of Spain like Andalusia. This is a type of Spanish that some people may find hard to understand because it's so different when compared to other forms of Spanish.

Cuban Spanish is also another variation that you can learn as well. This type of speech has challenged many speakers in the northern parts of Latin America and throughout Spain. Most Cuban speakers speak with an even thicker accent, have their own unique slang words, and favor certain constructions with words when compared to traditional Spanish speakers.

A quick understanding of the differences between each form of Spanish can be found below:

- **Castilian Spanish:** The Standard Form of Spanish. It is spoken throughout most of Spain and forms the basis for most other forms of Spanish throughout Latin America and other areas of the world. If you learn Castilian, you will have very little trouble learning any other form of Spanish as it's very similar to each other - especially if you've lived in different parts of Spain (like Madrid vs. Barcelona, etc.).
- **Andalusian Spanish:** The Form of Spanish spoken in Andalusia. It is very similar to Castilian Spanish but with a more rural flair and general lack of proficiency because of the geographical location of Andalusia. It's also the most popular form of Spanish in Cuba due to its historical ties to Spain.
- **Cuban Spanish:** The Form of Spanish that has typically been associated with Cuba for decades. It's also known as "Spanglish" as it has both Latin American and Caribbean influences on it. It is often said that the Spanish spoken in Cuba is the most difficult to understand.

What Is the Best Way to Learn Spanish?

One of the best ways to learn new languages is by actually traveling to that particular country and living there for a period of time. This can be very costly but if you really want to learn Spanish, it's an important step before moving elsewhere.

Alternatively, you can also try learning online as this will give you instant access to a wide range of resources depending on your level of fluency with previous languages. One of our favorite resources is the SpanishPod101 website as they have excellent audio and video content that is specifically made to help you learn Spanish.

There are many different online programs such as Rosetta Stone and Babbel. However, there are also some programs that aren't very reputable and may not help you learn as effectively as they claim to. This is basically a type of interactive game which makes learning much more fun!

Learning a new language is always challenging but it can also be very rewarding as well. In our modern culture, you'll often find yourself surrounded by many people who speak Spanish due to its prevalence in American culture and throughout Latin America.

Learning a new language can seem daunting, and there are few things more intimidating than trying to pick up a foreign tongue for the first time. But luckily, millions of people worldwide have taken on the challenge and learned how to communicate in Spanish—or any other language—in just a short amount of time. Learning strategies such as immersion learning techniques will make it easier for you to learn quickly. You can also motivate yourself by remembering that it will be easy to create a network of people interested in helping you learn a new language. After you have heard about many of the ways people learn Spanish, you will realize this is the best possible way to "check out" on the language and become one of those people who can converse easily in a new language. Of course, there are other methods that work as well. Research shows that using an audio CD or cassette tape is one way people learn their new language quickly and effectively. Make sure that you use a good quality recording where the instructor speaks clearly and completely.

The best way to find a good audio cassette is to ask someone knowledgeable about the subject. Asking a native of the Spanish-speaking country is a great way to go. Knowing what you will be learning before you begin is also helpful. This means knowing how to conjugate verbs, and understanding how the language works within the structure of grammar rules and phrases. It is also important to know about Spanish pronunciation, reading comprehension, and even writing in Spanish. In addition, there are other methods that will help you learn your new language quickly. For instance, learning with a friend or with family members can be an excellent strategy. It is also good to use a method of relaxation that will allow you to focus your attention on the language, such as meditation or yoga. Finally, you can get more than the basics by reading books and watching educational videos. These will give you a good insight into the language, although sometimes it is hard to follow when you are done. However, if you prepare yourself with all of this information before starting, you can learn Spanish quickly—even if it takes a while to complete the study sessions.

Types of Learning

It all depends on what kind of learner you are. Common forms of learning include formal education (in traditional settings), self-directed learning, and informal learning (through experience). The main distinction among these three forms of learning is that in formal education, the learner is in a group and is taught by a teacher or through books. Self-directed learning means that the learner controls his or her own learning process. For example, this method might include using a language program and choosing your own method of reading a book or listening to an audio cassette. Informal learning occurs when you learn from your own experience by watching television, reading newspapers, listening to music, etc.

As you can see there are many different methods for learning Spanish with audio cassettes and CDs. The fact remains that you must learn up-to-date information on the language in order to get the most from your course. This means that your learning may also include the Internet, a language lab, or attending a seminar on the topic. Whatever method you use, you must practice what you have learned in order to become proficient in Spanish. Studying must be done on a regular basis so that it will improve your skills and help you learn Spanish quickly. Once you have integrated all of these methods into your approach for learning, it is important to remember that many experts agree that motivation comes from within. Therefore, in addition to following an effective course and reading books about speaking Spanish or attending lectures, you should find a reason for learning this new language. This might be traveling to Latin America or living in an area with many native speakers of Spanish.

SPANISH BASICS

Business involves a lot of communication. Shy people don't usually get very far in making money on the higher end of things, because the need for meetings and encounters ends up usually being crucial for the big-money deals and projects. There's just something more valuable about meeting in person and deciding something face-to-face that no computer program has yet managed to replicate, so we're still closing business deals the old-fashioned way: with smiles and handshakes.

For this reason, you need to dominate the way you open up to a conversation in Spanish and start chatting with them. A grasp of greetings and introductions will be crucial if you want to make a great first impression and win your new friend over. In fact, confidence and self-belief are pillars in these types of encounters, and you will realize this soon as the conversation advances.

To begin a conversation with a greeting, many will use the expression "Hola" (Oh-la), which means "Hi" in English. This is a common mistake to make in many contexts because you don't actively say "Hi" in Spanish when talking in formal or semi-formal situations. Business, especially, doesn't welcome this type of greeting, and it could earn you a frown or strange look.

Spanish has the habit of putting an emphasis on greeting somebody according to the time of day, which will be illustrated as follows:

Buenos (Buey-nose) / Buenas (Buey-nas) + Time of day. In this sense, Buenos and Buenas are masculine and feminine plural versions of "Good." You may follow these by the time of day in which you are currently situated, in the sense of Buenos días (dee-az) for the morning, Buenas tardes (tar-dez) for the afternoon, and Buenas noches (no-ches) for the evening or night.

It is important to note that Buenas noches may also be used as a farewell for someone leaving or going to sleep; it is also important to observe that días is a masculine word and that both tardes and noches are feminine. Be wary with these genders, as they are very important when talking or writing in Spanish, and misgendering somebody is considered a big mistake.

Examples of these greetings:

- Buenos días, estimado (ess-tee-mah-do). = Good morning, dear sir.
- Buenas tardes, compañero (com-pa-nie-ro). = Good afternoon, co-worker (masculine).
- Buenas noches, jefa (hef-ah). = Good evening, boss (femenine).

You may follow up on these greetings with a "How are you?" or similar expression, further cementing the trust in this initial exchange. For example:

- Buenas tardes, señora (se-nio-ra), ¿qué hace (ah-se)? = Good afternoon, madame, what are you doing?
- Buenos días, profesor, ¿cómo está? = Good morning, professor/teacher, how are you?

As you may see when writing in Spanish, questions (and exclamations) require an opening question or exclamation mark to identify where you'll be asking or exclaiming something, and (despite not being very useful) must be written when you're creating a body of text.

Furthermore, you're going to want to keep an eye on accents (or tildes) when pronouncing or writing words because these will indicate where a vowel is stressed. Entire meanings can be changed from the writing of a stressed vowel, as in the case of "este" and "esté," for example.

The next tool to identify is the introduction, or basically when you offer your name or identity to the person you're talking to. In other situations, this is kind of informal and may be considered a friendly afterthought; in business, however, you have to use this correctly and concisely if you want to accomplish anything.

In this sense, you can tell them who you are and what your occupation or role is in the following manner:

- Buenas tardes, señor, mi nombre es… = Good afternoon, sir, my name is…
- Buen día, amigo, me llamo… = Good morning, friend, my name is…

- Buenas noches, señora, yo soy… = Good evening, madame, I am (followed by either your profession or role)
- Buenos días, joven (ho-ven), yo me dedico a… = Good morning, young person, I am a (followed by your profession)

A note to consider is that mi nombre es and me llamo are completely interchangeable for this purpose.

If you want to ask someone use the following questions:

- ¿Cuál es tu nombre? = What is your name?
- ¿Cómo te llamas? = What's your name?
- ¿A qué te dedicas? = What do you do for a living?
- ¿En qué trabajas? = What do you do for work?

Questions and Requests

We've all had the need to find out more about something we don't know about. Similarly, asking for something is a delicate subject, since you have to ask nicely and politely to avoid causing any disrespect.

To ask a question, there are several ways, but let's limit ourselves for now to the basic questions—what, where, when, why, and how? These are illustrated in the following examples:

1. What? = ¿Qué?
    - ¿Qué significa eso? = What does that mean?
    - ¿Para qué se utiliza (oo-tee-lee-za) eso? = What is that used for?
    - Señor, ¿qué sucedió (sue-seh-dio) aquí? = Sir, what happened here?
2. Where? = ¿Dónde?
    - ¿Dónde es el encuentro (en-coo-en-troh)? = Where is the encounter/meeting?
    - ¿Para dónde va el jefe? = Where is the boss going?
    - ¿Dónde estamos ahora? = Where are we now?
3. When? = ¿Cuándo?
    - Cuándo llegaste aquí (a-key)? = When did you arrive here?

- ¿Puedes decirme cuándo vamos a decidir? = Can you tell me when we're going to decide?
- Me gustaría saber algo, ¿cuándo tendrás respuesta? = I would like to know something, when will you have an answer?

4. Why? = ¿Por qué?
- ¿Por qué no ha llegado aún? = Why hasn't he/she arrived yet?
- Dime (dee-meh), ¿por qué han bajado (ba-ha-do) las ventas? = Tell me, why have sales gone down?
- Quiero saber, ¿por qué llegaste tarde? = I want to know, why did you arrive late?

5. How? = ¿Cómo?
- ¿Cómo podemos mejorar nuestros resultados? = How can we improve our results?
- ¡Increíble! ¡¿Cómo lo hiciste (ee-sees-teh)?! = Incredible! How did you do it?!
- Tengo que preguntar, ¿cómo vamos a seguir (seh-gear) adelante? = I have to ask, how are we going to continue forward?

Obviously, there are many more expressions to be used in this situation, but these are the bread and butter of all your question needs, and the ones you will be using most of the time.

As for requests, these will vary depending on who you are talking to and what you're asking for, but we will go over them briefly to help you out with these tools of Spanish. ¿Puedes? And ¿Podrías? Usually start the request, followed by a por favor at the end, as you will see in the following examples:

- ¿Puedes (pueh-des) venir a mi oficina, por favor? = Can you come to my office, please?
- Hola, ¿podrías (poh-dree-ass) cerrar la puerta? Quiero conversar sobre algo delicado. = Hello, can you close the door? I want to talk about something delicate.
- ¿Podrías decirme cómo manejar (ma-neh-har) este problema, por favor? = Can you tell me how to manage this problem, please?

The next of these guidelines will provide you with farewells, so you can say goodbye and hope for the next meeting.

Farewells

Every conversation or meeting must come to an end, and this means that you will begin preparing your farewell while hoping for a future encounter. In this particular sense, Spanish isn't all too different from English, and you should manage without having to learn too many things. Only the vocabulary itself is different, but the experience will be enough to discover just how exactly you say "so long" in Spanish:

- Adiós = Goodbye.
- ¡Chao! = Bye!
- Hasta (az-tah) luego (loo-eh-go) = See you later.
- Nos vemos pronto, señor = See you soon, sir.
- Hasta la próxima = Until next time.
- Fue un placer = It was a pleasure.

These are basically it, as you probably won't need other manners of saying goodbye to the people you work with (or for), as well as the fact that they will take you far on their own. Don't be afraid to use new vocabulary, though, and know that some people don't really mind if you're a bit too friendly with them. This can actually be well-received among some people, in fact, but be sure to get to know them before you overreach your limits!

Basic Terms and Vocabulary

Remember the more words you know of a language, the more you know the language, and the quicker you will learn. In fact, the amount of vocabulary you're familiar with has been linked with the amount of a language you know, as well as the level of fluency you possess when reading, writing, or speaking the tongue.

They may be simple, but many of these words and phrases will help get you out of trouble and allow you to let your new friends know what exactly you want or need, so don't discount them. You're going to need every single one if you want to succeed in business around Spanish speakers!

35 DAYS OF SPANISH EXPRESSION

Week 1

Day 1

Expression of the day: Ser pesado (Mexico)

Literal meaning: To be heavy

What it means in English: To be rude

Spanish example: No quiero ser pesada pero no me gusta tu estilo

English example: I don't want to be rude but I don't like your style.

Day 2

Ser un plasta (Santo Domingo)

To be a pain

To be annoying

Spanish example: Sabes que puedes ser un plasta, ¿verdad?

English example: You realize that you can be really annoying, right?

Day 3

Estar molido (Mexico)

To be ground

To be very tired; worn out; knackered

Spanish example: Necesito un descanso, la carrera me dejó molido.

English example: I need to take a break, that race left me worn out.

Day 4

Estar hecho polvo (Spain)

To be made dust

To be very tired, exhausted, beat

Spanish example: Me alegro de estar en casa. Estoy hecha polvo.

English example: It's good to be home. I'm beat.

Day 5

De pe a pa (Mexico)

From pe to pa

From the beginning to the end; end to end; inside out

Spanish example: Conozco todos los temas de pe a pa.

English example: I know all the issues inside and out.

Day 6

Ni de coña (Spain)

Not in a joke

No way

Spanish example: No estoy ni de coña preparado para algo así.

English example: There's no way I'm ready for something like that.

Day 7

Estar de coña (Spain)

To be joking

To be joking; to be kidding

Spanish example: Debes de estar de coña, colega.

English example: You gotta be kidding me, buddy.

Week 1 Quiz

1. Explain the Spanish expression "Estar hecho polvo" in English.
2. Can you translate "To be annoying" in Spanish?

Answers:

1. Estar hecho polvo
   To be very tired
   Spanish example: Me alegro de estar en casa. Estoy hecha polvo
   English example: I'm glad to be home I'm very tired
2. Ser un plasta

Week 2

Day 8

Estar algo patas arriba (Spain)

To be something with the legs up

To be something very untidy, chaotic

Spanish example: Lo siento, he dejado la habitación patas arriba.

English example: Sorry, I messed up the room.

Day 9

Ahogarse en un vaso de agua (Spain)

To drown in a glass of water

To be extremely worried about things that are not very important; to make a big deal out of nothing.

Spanish example: Gary, te ahogas en un vaso de agua.

English example: Gary, you're making a big deal out of nothing.

Day 10

Echar una mano (Spain)

To throw a hand

To help someone, to lend a hand

Spanish example: Sólo estoy aquí para echar una mano.

English example: I'm just here to lend a hand.

Day 11

Costar un ojo de la cara (Spain)

To cost an eye from the face

Spanish example: Editel nos cobró un ojo de la cara por ese software.

English example: Editel charged us an arm and a leg for the software.

Day 12

Costar un riñón (Spain)

To cost a kidney

To be very expensive; to cost a fortune.

Spanish example: Nos va a costar un riñón.

English example: It's going to cost a fortune.

Day 13

Cruzarse los cables a alguien (Spain)

To cross the cables of someone

To get mad for a moment, or to blow a fuse

Spanish example: A Nick se le cruzaron los cables y se fue a la ciudad.

English example: Nick blew a fuse and drove into town.

Day 14

Dejar plantado (Mexico)

To leave planted

To stand up

Spanish example: Ayer tenía una cita, pero me dejó plantada.

English example: I had a date yesterday, but I got stood up.

Week 2 Quiz

1. Explain the Spanish expression "Ahogarse en un vaso de agua" in English.
2. Can you translate "To help someone" in Spanish?

Answers:

1. Ahogarse en un vaso de agua
   To sink in a glass of water
   To be extremely worried about things that are not very important
2. Echar una mano
   To help someone
   Spanish example: Sólo estoy aquí para echar una mano.
   English example: I'm just here to lend a hand.

Week 3

Day 15

En un abrir y cerrar de ojos (Spain)

In a blink of an eye

Very fast

Spanish example: Podemos desaparecer tu pequeña aldea en un abrir y cerrar de ojos.

English example: We could wipe out your little village here in the blink of an eye.

Day 16

Hacer la vista gorda (Mexico)

To make the sight fat

To not give attention to some facts or details; to look the other way

Spanish example: A la mayoría les pagan por hacer la vista gorda.

English example: Most people in this town just get paid to look the other way.

Day 17

Ponerse las pilas (Spain)

To put the battery to shape up and get a move on.

Spanish example: Todo lo que digo es que si deseas realmente algo, hay que ponerse las pilas.

English example: All I'm saying is that if you really like something, you've got to get a move on it.

Day 18

Tener algo en la punta de la lengua (Mexico)

To have something on the tip of the tongue

When you don't remember something but you feel you will do soon

Spanish example: Tenía su nombre en la punta de la lengua, pero no lograba recordarlo.

English example: I had his name on the tip of my tongue, but I couldn't remember it.

Day 19

Pagar a escote/a pachas (Spain)

To pay by the neckline

To split the bill; to share the cost of something; to go Dutch

Spanish example: ¡Bebe lo que puedas, pero vamos a pagar a escote!

English example: Drink as much as you can, but we're going Dutch!

Day 20

Hacerse el sueco (Spain)

To do the Swede

To pretend you haven't heard or know something because you don't want to do it, play dumb

Spanish example: Acusé al moderador de hacerse el sueco.

English example: I accused the moderator of playing dumb.

Day 21

Ser pan comido (Spain)

To be eaten bread

To be very easy; a piece of cake

Spanish example: Escalar aquella montaña fue pan comido.

English example: Climbing that mountain was a piece of cake.

Week 3 Quiz

1. Explain the Spanish expression "Ponerse las pilas" in English.
2. Can you translate "To be very easy" in Spanish?

Answers:

1. Ponerse las pilas
   To put the battery
   To shape up and get a move on.
   Spanish example: Todo lo que digo es que si deseas realmente algo, hay que ponerse las pilas.

English example: All I'm saying is that if you really like something, you've got to get a move on it.

2. Ser pan comido
   To be eaten bread
   To be very easy; piece of cake
   Spanish example: Escalar aquella montaña fue pan comido.
   English example: Climbing that mountain was a piece of cake.

Week 4

Day 22

Consultar algo con la almohada (Mexico)

To consult something with the pillow

To need time to think about an important decision, usually when you go to bed; to sleep on (something).

Spanish example: ¿Vas a prestarme el dinero? No sé, lo voy a consultar con la almohada.

English example: Are you going to lend me the money? I don´t know, Iĺl sleep on it.

Day 23

Irse el santo al cielo (Spain)

The saint goes to the sky

To forget something or to be distracted; to lose track of time

Spanish example: Perdona, se me fue el santo al cielo.

English example: Sorry, I totally lost track of time.

Day 24

Matar el gusanillo (Spain)

To kill the little worm

To eat something (a snack, for example) when you're too hungry to wait for the food

Spanish example: El producto ideal para disfrutar entre horas y matar el gusanillo.

English example: The ideal product to enjoy between meals and to keep you going.

Day 25

Estar como una cuba (Spain)

To be like a barrel or a vat

To be drunk, plastered

Spanish example: Si sigues bebiendo Tequila, en diez minutos estarás borracho como una cuba

English example: If you keep drinking Tequila, in 10 minutes, you'll be plastered.

Day 26

Comerse a alguien con los ojos (Spain)

To eat someone with the eyes

To look deeply into someone, usually with desire or lust

Spanish example: Nos quieren comer con los ojos.

English example: They are ogling at us.

Day 27

Comerse el coco (Spain)

To eat your own head

To think too much about something, usually a problem; to obsess about an issue

Spanish example: Aunque te comas el coco, nunca sabrás por qué no te quiere.

English example: There's no point obsessing about it, you will never know why she doesn't love you.

Day 28

Comerse un marrón (Spain)

To eat a brown

To receive/solve a problem that isn't yours and nobody wants to take care of because it's complicated/delicate.

Spanish example: No me voy a comer el marrón yo sola.

English example: I won't deal with this by myself.

Week 4 Quiz

1. Explain the Spanish expression "Matar el gusanillo" in English.
2. Can you translate "To look deeply into someone, usually with desire or lust" in Spanish?

Answers:

1. Matar el gusanillo
   To kill the little worm

To eat something (a snack, for example) when you're too hungry to wait for the food

Spanish example: El producto ideal para disfrutar entre horas y matar el gusanillo.

English example: The ideal product to enjoy between meals and to keep you going.

2. Comerse a alguien con los ojos

To eat someone with the eyes

To look deeply into someone, usually with desire or lust

Spanish example: Nos quieren comer con los ojos.

English example: They want to eat us with their eyes.

Week 5

Day 29

A bulto (Spain)

By package

At first glance; to estimate based on a first look

Spanish example: No puedo ver bien la caja, pero asi, a bulto, estimo que hay unas 30 unidades.

English example: I can't see the box, but by the looks of it, there could be 30 units.

Day 30

A la vuelta de la esquina (Spain)

Around the corner

Very near; just round the corner

Spanish example: Las oportunidades están a la vuelta de la esquina.

English example: Opportunities are just around the corner.

Day 31

A ojo de buen cubero (Spain)

By the eye of good cooper

To do something in an approximate way, without accuracy and without measuring tools; to estimate

Spanish example: A ojo de buen cubero, calculamos que caja mide 1 pie y medio.

English example: By a rough estimation, we calculate that each box is about a foot and a half

Day 32

A otro perro con ese hueso (Spain)

To another dog with that bone

When you don't believe what someone is telling you, and you suggest telling that story to another person.

Spanish example: ¡A otro perro con ese hueso!

English example: Go try that on someone else.

Day 33

A palo seco (Spain)

By a dry stick

To eat/drink something by itself. (For example, an alcoholic drink without any mix)

Spanish example: Camarero por favor, ponme un ron a palo seco

English example: Bartender, please, a glass of rum, straight in, no water.

Day 34

Ahuecar el ala (Spain)

To scoop out the wing

To leave

Spanish example: Si eso es lo que hace, ya puede ahuecar el ala.

English example: If that's what you're doing, get out of here.

Day 35

Al tun tun (Spain)

By the "tun tun."

Something made in a random way

Spanish example: Uno no se abalanza sobre este tipo de cosas al tun tun.

English example: You don't just randomly jump into these sorts of things.

Week 5 Quiz

1. Explain the Spanish expression "Ahuecar el ala" in English.
2. Can you translate "To do something in an approximate way, without accuracy and without measuring tools" in Spanish?

Answers:

1. Ahuecar el ala

   To scoop out the wing

   To go from somewhere

   Spanish example: Si eso es lo que hace, ya puede ahuecar el ala.

   English example: If that's what you're doing, get yourself right out of here.

2. A ojo de buen cubero

   By eye of good cooper

   To do something in an approximate way, without accuracy and without measuring tools.

   Spanish example: A ojo de buen cubero, calculamos que cada euro diputado británico cuesta a los contribuyentes del ReinoUnido cerca de 1,2 millones de libras cada año.

   English example: By a rough estimation, we calculate that each British MEP costs the UK taxpayers about £1.2 million annually

ARTICLES, CONJUNCTIONS, PREPOSITIONS, AND PRONOUNS

Articles

1. The= El (Masculine singular)
   a. I didn't pick up the phone= No contesté el teléfono.
2. The= La (Feminine singular)
   a. I am heading back to the house= Estoy volviendo a la casa.
3. The= Lo (Neuter)
   a. The nice thing about living here is the sunsets= Lo más lindo de vivir acá son los atardeceres.
4. The= Los (Masculine plural)
   a. I brought the shoes you told me about= Traje los zapatos que me dijiste.
5. The= Las (Feminine plural)
   a. And I also have socks that match with them= Y también tengo las medias que van con ellos.
6. A/An= Uno (Masculine singular)
   a. You can use a pencil if it is easier for you= Puedes usar un lápiz si se te hace más fácil.
7. A/An= Una (Feminine singular)
   a. He is inside an empty cardboard box= Él está dentro de una caja de cartón vacía.

Conjunctions and Prepositions

8. For= Para
   a. I was told to leave this package for María= Me dijeron que dejara este paquete para María.
9. And= Y
   a. I asked my father about you and the answer was no= Le pregunté a mi padre sobre ti y la respuesta fue que no.

36

10. Nor= Ni
    a. I cannot stand your sister, nor that puffy little dog of hers= No puedo soportar a tu hermana ni a ese perrito peludo de ella.
11. Neither= Ninguno (Masculine)
    a. Neither of them had any clue of what was going on= Ninguno de ellos tenia idea de lo que estaba pasando.
12. Neither= Ninguna (Feminine)
    a. Neither of the two choices suits me= Ninguna de las dos opciones me convence.
13. But= Pero
    a. I would invite you to the beach, but it is too cold to go= Te invitaría a la playa, pero hace mucho frío para ir.
14. Then= Entonces
    a. If you want more fries, then bring me more potatoes= Si quieres más papas fritas, entonces tráeme más papas.
15. Or= O
    a. Do you want juice or soda?= ¿Quieres un zumo o una soda?
16. So= Así que
    a. They didn't bring their homework, so I told them to do it here= No trajeron la tarea, así que les dije que la hicieran aquí.
17. Although= Aunque
    a. Although I was in a hurry, I took the time to read the instructions= Aunque estaba apurado, me tomé el tiempo de leer las instrucciones.
18. As= Mientras
    a. As we sit here talking, they have already arrived at their destination= Mientras nos sentamos aquí a hablar, ellos ya llegaron a su destino.
19. As if= Como si
    a. It's not as if it is my fault= No es como si fuera mi culpa.
20. As long as= Mientras que
    a. You can stay here as long as you help me with the store= Puedes quedarte aquí mientras que me ayudes con la tienda.
21. As much as= Tanto como
    a. I would like to earn as much as possible= Me gustaría ganar tanto como sea posible.
22. As soon as= Tan pronto como

a. We will leave as soon as my daughter arrives= Nos iremos tan pronto como venga mi hija.

23. As good as – Tan Bueno como
    a. You are never going to be as good as your master= Nunca vas a ser tan Bueno como tu maestro.

24. As though= Como si
    a. It feels as though as if I had lifted a weight from my shoulders= Se siente como si hubiese levantado un peso de mis hombros.

25. Why= Por qué
    a. Why did you leave the door open?= ¿Por qué dejaste la puerta abierta?

26. Because= Porque
    a. He went home because he felt tired= Se fue a casa porque se sintió cansado.

27. Because of= A causa de
    a. We couldn't go because of the weather= No pudimos ir a causa del clima.

28. By the time= Para cuando
    a. It's going to be too late by the time we get there= Va a ser muy tarde para cuando lleguemos allá.

29. However= Sin embargo
    a. This car is expensive; however, it's worth it= Este auto es caro; sin embargo vale la pena.

30. Even if= Incluso si
    a. I will finish the course even if it takes me four hours= Terminaré la pista incluso si me toma cuatro horas.

31. Even when= Incluso cuando
    a. My cat is beautiful even when he sleeps= Mi gato es hermoso incluso cuando duerme.

32. Even though= A pesar de
    a. Even though he got there on time, the door was already closed= A pesar de que llegó a tiempo, la puerta ya estaba cerrada.

33. If= Si
    a. I cannot let you in if you don't show me your documents= No te puedo dejar pasar si no me muestras tus documentos.

34. In order that= Para que

a. You must learn how to walk in order that you can learn how to run= Debes aprender a caminar para que puedas aprender a correr.

35. In case= Por si
   a. Let's fill the tank here in case we don't find any more gas= Llenemos el tanque aquí por si no encontramos más gas.

36. Once= Una vez
   a. Once we reach the island, we will continue on foot= Una vez que lleguemos a la isla continuaremos a pie.

37. Only if= Solo si
   a. Only if you close your eyes you will be able to hear it= Solo si cierras los ojos podrás escucharlo.

38. Provided that= Siempre y cuando
   a. I can wash the dishes provided that you cook= Puedo lavar los platos siempre y cuando cocines.

39. Since= Desde
   a. I haven't played that game since 1992= No había jugado ese juego desde 1992.

40. So that= Con el fin de que
   a. I bought this pillow so that my cat can sleep in it= Compré esta almohada con el fin de que mi gato duerma en ella.

41. Than= Más que
   a. John is taller than Mike= John es más alto que Mike
   b. Today is sunnier than yesterday= Hoy está más soleado que ayer.

42. That= Que
   a. Here is the t-shirt that I bought for you= Aquí está la camisa que compré para ti.

43. Although= Aunque
   a. Although the sun was bright, the weather was pleasant= Aunque el sol estaba brillante, el clima estuvo agradable.

44. Until= Hasta
   a. We will wait for them until tomorrow morning= Esperaremos por ellos hasta mañana por la mañana.
   b. The power will be off until next week. La electricidad estará cortada hasta la próximasemana.

45. Unless= A menos que
   a. Don't open the door unless they knock three times= No abras la puerta a menos que toquen tres veces.

39

46. Whenever= Siempre que
   a. We should feed stray dogs whenever possible= Deberíamos alimentar a los perros callejeros siempre que sea possible.
47. Where= Donde
   a. That's the factory where he works= Esa es la fábrica donde él trabaja.
48. Wherever= Donde sea que
   a. They have to find the victims wherever they are= Tienen que encontrar a las víctimas donde sea que se encuentren.
49. While= Mientras
   a. The sun was rising while I was driving= El sol estaba saliendo mientras conducía.
50. Of= De
   a. This cabin is made of wood= Esta cabaña está hecha de madera.
51. At= En
   a. Tell them that we meet at the airport= Diles que nos veamos en el aeropuerto.
52. With= Con
   a. I decided to go with my mother= Decidí ir con mi madre.
53. Into= En
   a. I loaded the boxes into the truck= Cargué las cajas en la camioneta.
54. From= De
   a. She comes from a different planet= Ella viene de un planeta diferente.
55. From= Desde
   a. He was able to see the boat from the shore= Él pudo ver el barco desde la orilla.
56. During= Durante
   a. The baby cried during the entire game= El bebé lloró durante todo el partido.
57. Including= Incluso
   a. All dogs are beautiful, including stray dogs= Todos los perros son hermosos, incluso los callejeros.
58. Against= Contra
   a. The Pirates play against the Rangers today= Los Piratas juegan contra los Rangers hoy.
59. Among= Entre

a. I am sure the traitor is among us= Estoy seguro de que el traidor está entre nosotros.

60. Throughout= durante todo

   a. You drove throughout the whole trip= Tú manejaste durante todo el viaje.

61. Despite= A pesar de

   a. Despite the traffic jam, we managed to arrive early= A pesar del tráfico, pudimos llegar temprano.

62. Upon= Al

   a. The packages will be checked upon arrival= Los paquetes serán revisados al llegar.

63. Concerning= Con respecto a

   a. I have something to say concerning your decision= Tengo algo que decir con respecto a tu decisión.

64. Of= De

   a. Here are the keys of your car= Aquí tienes las llaves de tu auto.

65. To= Para

   a. I have to get up to get to work= Tengo que levantarme para ir a trabajar.

   b. Tell your brother to go with you to the store= Dile a tu hermano que vaya contigo a la tienda.

66. Regarding= Sobre

   a. I need information regarding my documents= Necesito información sobre mis documentos.

67. Regardless= Independientemente

   a. I rather go regardless of your decision= Prefiero ir independientemente de tu decisión.

68. By= Por

   a. These houses were built by natives= Estas casas fueron construídas por nativos.

69. About= Acerca de

   a. The movie is about a robot who meets a human girl= La película es acerca de un robot que conoce a una chica humana.

70. Like= Como

   a. He is tall like your father= Él es alto como tu padre.

71. Over= Sobre

   a. Pass the bike over the fence= Pasa la bici sobre la cerca.

41

72. Between= Entre
   a. There is almost no space between the houses= Casi no hay espacio entre las casas.
73. Without= Sin
   a. I feel useless without my car= Me siento inútil sin mi auto.
74. Along= A lo largo
   a. We met a lot of people along the way= Conocimos a muchagente a lo largo de el camino.
75. Following= Siguiente
   a. She told me she would call the following week= Ella me dijo que llamaría la semana siguiente.
76. Plus= Además
   a. I think he is the perfect fit for the job, plus he has experience= Creo que es la opción perfecta para el trabajo, además tiene experiencia.
77. Except= Excepto
   a. I never oversleep, except for Sundays= Nunca duermo de más, excepto los domingos.

Pronouns

78. I= Yo
   a. I ride my bike every day= Yo monto en bicicleta todos los días.
79. You= Tú
   a. You should drive tonight= Tú deberías manejar esta noche.
80. You= Usted (Indicates respect)
   a. You are one of the best professors I ever had= Usted es uno de los mejores profesores que he tenido
81. You= Ustedes (Plural)
   a. You will be responsible for the equipment provided= Ustedes serán responsables de el equipamento otorgado.
82. He= Él
   a. He is the son of the Minister= Él es el hijo del Ministro.

AVOID PLUS MISTAKES

he following is a list of common mistakes people make when they start learning Spanish and the best way to avoid them.

T 1.**Forgetting that words have genders in Spanish:** -o and -a are for masculine nouns, and -a is for feminine nouns. Make sure you know which gender a word belongs to before using it, or your sentence will not make sense.

2.**Forgetting that verbs change based on who they're talking about:** If you want to be polite, use usted instead of tú; if you want to be informal, use tú instead of usted (though this may not always be appropriate).

3. **Forgetting to use tú before a verb.** In Spanish, the verb always comes first.

4. **Believing that Spanish is gender-neutral:** Just as in English, there are no words such as "she" or "he" for people of all genders. However, one of the most common mistakes made by beginning learners is using masculine terms to refer to women and/or feminine terms when referring to men (for example yo te lo di , no lo juzguen , ojalá vaya).

5. **Exposing your ignorance regarding the gender of certain nouns and other pronouns:** For example, saying "I have a problem with my teacher" or "I am looking for my house." In Spanish, "teacher" and "house" are both feminine nouns.

6. **Trying to speak too quickly:** If you can't understand the person you're speaking to, it's not likely that he/she will be able to understand you either.

7. **Making mistakes in verb conjugations**: For example, me gusta tu camisa, no me gustas tú.

8. **Avoiding informal speech:** While it may be tempting to go with formal conjugations all the time, using informal speech is often necessary in conversations among friends and family members; and using formal conjugations when speaking informally is also incorrect (for example I speak English, no hablo inglés).

9. **Thinking that all nouns in Spanish end in -o:** For example, thinking that the word for "manger" is marido, and the word for "father" is padre.

10. **Not knowing how to use adjectives properly:** In Spanish, adjectives are expressed after the noun (they modify it). For example, tiene una camisa azul: "he has blue shirt." (Also see No. 8.)

11. **Using tú in place of "usted."** Verbs and other forms of address are never pluralized in Spanish.

12. **Not knowing how to conjugate verbs:** Spanish verbs have to be conjugated according to who's performing the action, whether it's "I," "you" (singular), or "we." See a list of common verbs for more information.

13. **Believing that you shouldn't use usted until you know someone well:** This is not an issue of trust; it's just good manners.

14. **Using le instead of les:** The substitutions le for les and les for le are grammatically incorrect in almost all cases except when an object pronoun is a direct object (example: Me gusta la comida - I like the food).

15. **Confusing the preterite and imperfect tense:** The preterite, or "simple past," is used in written Spanish to refer to past events that have already occurred; the imperfect, or "present continuous," is used in spoken Spanish in a narrative sense. In other words, spoken language is used to describe ongoing events in the present.

16. **Skipping verbs and conjugations:** In Spanish, verbs change their forms depending on who they are talking about: If you're talking about yourself, use—como form. If you're talking about someone else, use—como hace. If you're talking about both yourself and someone else, use—como hable.

17. **Thinking that Spanish grammar is the same as English grammar:** For example, thinking that "I speak Spanish" is the same as "I speak English" (if you don't remember why, reread No. 15).

18. **Not knowing how to say things like "I am looking for my house:"** In Spanish, it's no sé donde está mi casa, not no sé mi casa.

19. **Forgetting to use pronouns in sentences:** For example, saying "Yo te amo" instead of "Te amo a ti." (Also see No. 12.)

20. **Listening to bad Spanish language lessons:** As Ben Yabes, General Coordinator of the Ministry of Education and Science in Spain states, "Spanish language instruction (which includes language classrooms, radio and television broadcasts, university language programs, etc.) belongs to the education system. It's not something that can be supplied by private companies (television stations and classes). The state must provide information about the usefulness of this teaching method."

21. **Not knowing about alternate ways to say things.** If you don't know what construction to use with a word or phrase, you can often use an alternative. For example: yo soy un amigo: "I am a friend." Me gusta tu camisa: "I like your shirt." (More informal) tú no me gustas: "You don't like me."

22. **Not enjoying the grammar of Spanish:** Contrary to what you may read elsewhere, Spanish grammar is similar to English grammar. The majority of language students who come from an English-speaking background find that the grammar of Spanish is much easier than that of their native tongue.

23. **Using accents (sounds) incorrectly:** Some varieties of Spanish have different accents, which can cause all kinds of confusion when you try to understand them. To make things worse, not all Spanish accents are correctly pronounced; and not all people speak with a correct accent in any variety they speak.

24. **Not knowing the correct pronunciation of a word.** Pronunciation is extremely important in Spanish, and it's difficult and time-consuming to learn the correct pronunciation of each word. For this reason, most Spanish language students tend to ignore this area, instead choosing to memorize lists of words that are familiar from their native tongue.

25. **Believing that one should not write about Spain:** Picking up a Spanish newspaper or visiting the Internet will invariably lead you to some sort of article written by someone who is either stationed in Spain or has had extended contact with Spaniards while living abroad. As Ben Yabes points out, such articles are "a very valuable source of information because they provide new insights into the culture."

26. **Not realizing that many Spaniards are not native speakers:** In the following example, the "I" is probably a non-native speaker of Spanish.
    - Para mí es importante no olvidar que la mejor forma de despertar el interés de la gente en nuestra cultura es enseñándola, y que no hay nada como mostrarla.

27. **Thinking that Spanish is spoken only in Spain:** Although Spain has a large concentration of native Spanish speakers, other countries have their own languages and cultures and do have Spanish-speaking minorities.

28. **Not knowing whether the group you're talking to is made up of native or nonnative Spanish speakers:** In comparison with other European languages, Spanish has few words that sound or are spelled differently in different countries. However, a non-native speaker may hesitate to mention that he speaks only basic Spanish unless he's with other non-native speakers.

29. **Assuming that all Hispanics are Mexican:** Although a significant percentage of America's Hispanic population is Mexican, most are not (for example, they come from Argentina, Puerto Rico, Cuba, and Spain).

30. **Believing that teaching students English is the same as teaching them Spanish:** Because of immigration and globalization, many people in Spain speak at least some English. Therefore, "teaching" them Spanish is not necessarily the correct approach.

31. **Constantly correcting students:** This should be left to a professional Spanish teacher and not someone who's just a native speaker of the language for the simple reason that students learn better when their own mistakes are corrected in class.

32. **Using English phrases:** For example, asking for "two sugars and a coke."

33. **Not being open to new ideas about language:** It's important to remember that even though you speak Spanish, your way of speaking may not be the best way to learn it. For example:
    - **Learning Spanish is a process, not an event.** The learning doesn't stop when you learn how to pronounce a word, or how to translate a sentence from Spanish into English. If anything, it's just the beginning of the hard part.

34. **Not wanting to make any changes in your way of speaking:** This is not just as a general rule; it also applies to your native language. It can be hard to accept those other ways of speaking are not inferior, and if you feel that you've succeeded in making Spanish your primary language, others may feel that their own way of speaking is inferior (especially if they speak with proper pronunciation).

35. **Not using the right Spanish words:** To get the most out of Spanish, one needs to learn not only new Spanish vocabulary but also the correct usage.

36. **Thinking that all Spanish learners are similar:** This may be a good generalization for Spain, but it's absolutely incorrect when studying other countries and their languages. Just as you will find many different kinds of people in any country who speak different ways of speaking, you will find that each country and its people have traits that make them unique.

37. **Choosing not to speak Spanish at home:** When you make the decision to choose another language for your home, you need to make sure that your children are acculturated to their new language.

38. **Not being flexible when learning Spanish:** This includes keeping one's mind open as well as being ready and willing to learn and adapt to change from

time to time, which is the only way that any language can be learned or spoken correctly.

39. **Not believing that Spanish is difficult:** Because it's similar to English in so many ways, many students assume that they'll pick up Spanish easily by simply watching movies or television shows in the language and listening closely with English subtitles. However, without a comprehensive program that focuses on pronunciation and speaking as well as reading and writing, you'll have a difficult time mastering the language.

40. **Not knowing when to switch to Spanish:** This is another area where you need to be able to be flexible. If you're in Spain for just a short time, it's probably better to use English rather than risk not being understood. In fact, if you're planning on staying in Spain for more than two months, you should start learning the language from day one.

BATHROOM—THINGS YOU WILL FIND IN A BATHROOM

Petra: Hola Martin. ¿Cómo estuvo tu fin de semana? *

Petra: Hello Martin. How was your weekend?

*Martin: No tan mal, gracias. ¿Cómo estuvo el tuyo? *

Martin: Not too bad, thanks. How was yours?

Petra: Estuvo bien. Llevé a los niños a visitar a sus abuelos. ¿Qué hiciste tú?

Petra: It was good. I took the boys to visit their grandparents. What did you do?

*Martin: El sábado fui a una barbacoa en casa de un vecino. Ayer pasé todo el día instalando un baño nuevo. Fue un trabajo duro, pero lo hice.

Martin: On Saturday, I went to a barbecue at a neighbor's house. Yesterday, I spent the whole day putting a new bathroom in. It was hard work, but I got it done.

*Petra: ¡No sabía que te gustaba el bricolaje! *

Petra: I didn't know you liked DIY?

*Martin: No puedo decir que lo disfrute, pero odio pagar a la gente para que haga trabajos que yo mismo podría hacer. *

Martin: I cannot say I enjoy it, but I hate paying people to do jobs that I could do myself.

*Petra: Entonces, ¿qué hiciste exactamente? *

Petra: So what exactly did you do?

48

***Martin:** Bueno, no lo hice yo solo. Mi cuñado me ayudó. Primero sacamos el fregadero, la ducha y el armario en el que guardamos la pasta de dientes, los cepillos de dientes y otras cosas. Luego quitamos las baldosas del suelo. *

Martin: Well, I didn't do it on my own. My brother-in-law helped. First, we took out the old sink, shower, and the cabinet in which we keep the toothpaste, toothbrushes, and other things. Then we took up the floor tiles.

***Petra:** Eso suena a trabajo duro. *

Petra: That sounds like hard work.

***Martin:** Esa parte sólo tomó un par de horas. Luego tomó otra hora colocar más baldosas en el suelo. La parte difícil fue poner la ducha nueva, pero me alegro de que mi esposa no quisiera una bañera nueva o un inodoro nuevo también. *

Martin: That part only took a couple of hours. It then took another hour to lay more floor tiles. The hard part was putting in the new shower, but I am pleased my wife didn't want a new bath or new toilet as well.

***Petra:** ¿Está todo terminado? *

Petra: Is everything finished?

***Martin:** Lo único que queda es poner unos estantes en la ducha para el jabón y el champú. Sólo me llevará unos minutos hacerlo esta noche. *

Martin: The only thing left is to put up some shelves in the shower for the soap and shampoo. It will only take a few minutes for me to do that tonight.

***Petra:** Me encantaría que mi esposo pudiera hacer ese tipo de cosas. *

Petra: I wish my husband could do things like that.

***Martin:** Estoy seguro de que podría si alguien le mostrara qué hacer. No es tan difícil. *

Martin: I am sure he could if someone showed him what to do. It is not that difficult.

*Petra: Si compráramos un mueble de baño nuevo, ¿podrías ayudar a mi esposo? *

Petra: If we bought a new bathroom unit, would you help my husband?

*Martin: Si tengo tiempo. *

Martin: If I had time.

*Petra: De acuerdo. Lo recordaré. *

Petra: OK. I will remember that.

*Martin: No hay problema. *

Martin: No problem.

Bedroom—Things You Will Find in a Bedroom

Cosas que encontrarás en un dormitorio:

*Mamá: Barry, ¡ven aquí ahora mismo! *

Mum: Barry, get here now!

*Barry: Está bien. ¿Qué sucede? *

Barry: OK. What is it?

*Mamá: Mira tu dormitorio. Es un desastre. ¿Cuándo fue la últimavez que lo limpiaste y por qué no has hecho tu cama? *

Mum: Look at your bedroom. It is a disaster. When was the last time you cleaned it and why have you not made your bed?

*Barry: Normalmente hago la cama, pero esta mañana estaba ocupado.

Barry: I usually do make the bed, but I was busy this morning.

*Mamá: Además, tienes un armario y unos cajones para la ropa. ¿Es tan difícil para ti guardar la ropa en vez de dejarla en la silla? *

Mum: Also, you have a wardrobe and some drawers for your clothes. Is it so difficult for you to put your clothes away instead of leaving them on the chair?

*Barry: Iba a hacerlo más tarde.

Barry: I was going to do it later.

*Mamá: No puedo creer que pases tiempo aquí. ¿Cómo puedes estudiar en tu escritorio si está cubierto de libros y revistas? Tampoco estoy segura de cuándo fue la última vez que vaciaste tu cubo de basura. *

Mum: I cannot believe you spend time in here. I am also not sure when you last emptied your trash can.

*Barry: Lo hice ayer. *

Barry: I did it yesterday.

*Mamá: ¡De verdad! No huele como si lo hubieras hecho. Lo que hay en él apesta. *

Mum: Really! It does not smell like it. The stuff in it stinks.

*Barry: Está bien. Lo haré ahora mismo. *

Barry: OK. I will do it now.

*Mamá: Además, ¿por qué siguen cerradas las cortinas? La gente normal abre las cortinas por la mañana. *

Mum: In addition, why are your curtains still drawn? Normal people open their curtains in the morning.

51

*Barry: Simplemente lo olvidé está mañana. Te prometo que lo haré mañana. *

Barry: I just forgot this morning. I promise I will do it tomorrow.

*Mamá: Me aseguraré de que así sea. *

Mum: I will check to make sure you have.

*Barry: De hecho, ya que estamos hablando de mi escritorio, ¿puedes pedirle a papá que ponga unos estantes en la pared? No tengo suficiente espacio para todos mis libros. También necesito una cama nueva. Soy demasiado grande para una cama individual. Necesito una doble. *

Barry: I also need a new bed. I am too big for a single bed. I need a double one.

*Mamá: Hablaré con tu padre sobre los estantes. *

Mum: I will talk to your dad about the shelves.

*Barry: ¿Y la cama? *

Barry: And the bed?

*Mamá: Si mantienes tu habitación ordenada durante los próximos seis meses, también lo discutiré con tu padre. *

Mum: If you keep your room tidy for the next six months, I will discuss that with your dad as well.

*Barry: Está bien. Trato hecho. *

Barry: OK. You have a deal.

Colors — Examples of Colors

Ejemplos de los colores:

*Julie: Mamá, ¿has visto mi top blanco? Aquel que compré en España el año pasado. *

Julie: Mum, have you seen my white top? The one I got from Spain last year.

*Mamá: Sigue en la pila de lavar. Iba a poner toda la ropa sucia en la lavadora antes de irnos. *

Mum: It is still in the wash. I was going to put all the dirty clothes in the machine before we left.

*Julie: Pero quería ponérmela para la boda. Queda bien con mis jeans negros. *

Julie: But I wanted to wear it for the wedding. It goes well with my black jeans.

*Mamá: No puedes ponerte unos jeans para una boda. No sería respetuoso. Creo que deberías ponerte ese vestido rojo que llevaste a la boda de tu hermana el año pasado. Me pareció que estabas muy guapa en él. *

Mum: You cannot wear jeans for a wedding. It would not look respectful. I think you should wear that red dress that you wore at your sister's wedding last year. I thought you looked nice in that.

*Julie: No puedo llevar el mismo vestido en dos bodas. Si no puedo usar jeans, llevaré una falda y un top. Creo que me pondré mi falda negra y mi top morado. *

Julie: I can't wear the same dress for two weddings. If I can't wear jeans, I will wear a skirt and a top. I think I will wear my black skirt and my purple top.

*Mamá: No estoy segura de que el negro y el morado combinen. ¿Tienes algo más claro? *

Mum: I am not sure black and purple go together. Do you have something lighter?

Julie: Podría usar la blusa amarilla que Peter me dio en mi cumpleaños.

Julie: I could wear the yellow blouse that Peter got me for my birthday.

Mamá: Pienso que te quedaría bien. *

Mum: I think that would look nice.

*Julie:** Pero, ¿está limpia? *

Julie: Is it clean though?

*Mamá:** Sí, pero hay que plancharla. *

Mum: Yes, but it needs ironing.

*Julie:** ¿Puedes hacerlo por mí? Necesito ducharme antes de irnos. *

Julie: Can you do it for me? I need to take a shower before we leave.

*Mamá:** Está bien. Tengo que planchar la camisa de tu padre, así que puedo planchar el top al mismo tiempo. ¿Sabías que tiene pensado llevar una camisa naranja con una corbata dorada? *

Mum: OK. I have to iron your father's shirt, so I can do your top at the same time. Did you know he plans to wear an orange shirt with a gold tie?

*Julie:** Al menos no es esa camisa negra que llevó la semana pasada. No me gustó para nada. *

Julie: At least it is not that green shirt he wore last week. I didn't like that at all.

*Mamá:** A mí tampoco. *

Mum: Nor me.

*Julie:** ¿Qué te vas a poner? *

Julie: What are you wearing?

*Mamá:** Ayer me compré un vestido lila. Estaba de oferta. *

Mum: I bought a lilac dress yesterday. It was on sale.

*Julie: Estoy segura de que todos estaremos guapísimos. *

Julie: I am sure we will all look good.

Daily Routines—The Simple Things You Do Every Day

Rutinas diarias:

*Simon: Hola, Lisa. ¡Cuánto tiempo sin verte! ¿Cómo estás? *

Simon: Hello, Lisa. Long time no see. How are you?

*Lisa: Hola Simon. Estoy bien, pero un poco aburrida de todo. *

Lisa: Hello Simon. I'm fine, but a little bored with everything.

*Simon: Lamento escuchar eso. ¿Te está desanimando el trabajo? *

Simon: I am sorry to hear that. Is work getting you down?

*Lisa: En realidad, me gusta lo que hago. Es solo que me levanto a la misma hora todos los días. Desayuno lo mismo. Veo a las mismas personas cuando tomo el autobús para ir al trabajo. Termino a la misma hora. ¿Sabes a lo que me refiero? *

Lisa: Actually, I like what I do. It is just that I get up at the same time every day. I have the same thing for breakfast. I see the same people when I take the bus to work. I finish at the same time. Do you know what I mean?

*Simon: Sé exactamente a lo que te refieres. ¿Qué haces por las tardes? *

Simon: I know exactly what you mean. What do you do in the evenings?

*Lisa: Ese es el problema. Tiendo a hacer las mismas cosas. Cocino la cena, lavo los platos, quizás hago alguna tarea doméstica y veo la televisión. *

Lisa: That's the problem. I tend to do the same things. I cook dinner, wash the dishes, maybe do some housework, and watch TV.

A GUIDE TO SPANISH PRONUNCIATION

s with English, the Spanish language has five vowels, A, E, I, O, and U.

Each vowel has a distinct sound. It is always pronounced the same way, and it's worth remembering if you want to perfect your accent, that vowels in Spanish have a set length, and are usually shorter than their English counterparts. Also, if there is an accent on any vowel, this vowel should be emphasized in your pronunciation.

Let's take a closer look at vowels:

- **A**—The vowel A is pronounced "ah," like the -a in "father."
- **E**—E is pronounced as "eh," like the -e in "bed."
- **I**—The letter I is pronounced as "ee" as in "see."
- **O**—O is simply pronounced as "oh," just like "know," so now you know how to pronounce O.
- **U**—U is pronounced as a short "uu." Like the -u in "put."

Tackling the Consonants

Many consonants in Spanish are pronounced very similarly to how they are pronounced in English, but there are several exceptions. It's worth learning the more common ones to really help you get your phrases across clearly.

Here are some of the consonant sounds that are rather different from how you might expect…

- **H**—The letter H is nearly always silent. There is no sound for the letter H in Spanish, so you would never have a word such as 'hat', it would be pronounced as 'at'. However, some words from other languages have been brought into common use and for these, the letter H is pronounced like the Spanish letter J.

56

- **J**—On the other hand, the letter J is pronounced like the letter H in English. So if English followed the same rules, the name Jack would be pronounced as Hack.
- **G**—The pronunciation of the letter G is dependant on the letter that follows it. If G is before either E or I then it is pronounced like the letter H. When followed by any other letter, then you simply pronounce it as you would the G in "garden."

Some more subtle differences...

- **B**—The letter B is pronounced the same as in English, but it is always said softly, resulting in a sound similar to the letter V.
- **R**—R is also pronounced very softly, sometimes almost sounding like the letter D.
- **D**—The letter D should be pronounced with your tongue further forward in your mouth than you would usually have it to pronounce the letter D.

The resulting sound is something close to a "th" sound.

- **Q**—Q is always pronounced like the letter K in English.
- **Z**—The letter Z is pronounced like the letter S in English. I.e.: the word "zoo" would sound like "soo."

There are also some consonants that are not present in the English alphabet...

- **LL**—This letter is often pronounced like the letter Y, as in "yoga," however in some countries, such as Argentina, Uruguay, and parts of Chile, it is pronounced as "sh."
- **Ñ**—Similar to N, but with more of a "nyer" sound, Ñ is pronounced like the letters NY in the word "canyon."
- **RR**—RR only occurs in the middle of a sentence and is simply pronounced like the letter R in "red."

Questions

Just like in English, questions in Spanish may be answered with a Yes or No.

You'll realize when this is the case when the speaker raises the pitch of their voice at the end of the question.

1. ¿Hablas español?
   Do you speak Spanish?
   - Sí
     Yes
   - No
     Noh

Here are the words that form questions that require an answer beyond Yes or No. By learning them, you'll be able to find your way around in Spanish-speaking countries.

- Who?
  ¿Quién? (Kee-ehn)
- What?
  ¿Qué? (Keh)
- When?
  ¿Cuándo? (Coo-ahn-doh)
- Where?
  ¿Dónde? (Dohn-deh)
- Why?
  ¿Por qué? (Pohrkeh)
- How?
  ¿Cómo? (Cohm-mo)

Common Questions

- Who are you?
  ¿Quién eres? (¿Kee-ehn eh-rehs?)
- What is your name?
  ¿Cuál es tu nombre? (¿Coo-ahl ehs too nohm-breh?)
- Whose is (it)?
  ¿De quién es (eso)? (¿Dehkee-ehnehs [eh-soh]?)
- What is it?
  ¿Qué es eso? (¿Kehehs eh-soh?)

58

- What are you doing now?
  ¿Qué haces ahora? (¿Keh ah-sehs ah-oh-rah?)
- When are you coming?
  ¿Cuándo vienes? (¿Coo-ahn-doh vee-eh-nehs?)
- When is your birthday?
  ¿Cuándo es tucumpleaños? (¿Coo-ahn-doh ehs too coom-pleh-ah-nyos?)
- Where do you live?
  ¿Dónde vives? (¿Dohn-deh vee-vehs?)
- Where do you go?
  ¿A dónde vas? (¿Ah dohn-dehvahs?)
- Where are you from?
  ¿De dónde eres? (¿Dehdohn-deh eh-rehs?)
- Where do you work?
  ¿Dónde trabajas? (¿Dohn-dehtrah-bah-hahs?)
- Why did you come here?
  ¿Por qué viniste aquí? (¿Pohrkeh vee-nees-teh ah-kee?)
- How are you doing?
  ¿Cómo estás? (¿Coh-mohehs-tahs?)
- How did you get here?
  ¿Cómo llegaste hasta aquí? (¿Coh-moh yeh-gahs-tahahs-tah ah-kee?)
- How many hours until your next flight?
  ¿Cuántas horas faltan para el próximo vuelo? (¿Coo-ahn-tahs oh-rahsfahl-than pah-rah ehlprohx-see-mohvoo-eh-loh?)
- How much is a bottle of water?
  ¿Cuánto sale una botella de agua? (¿Coo-ahn-tohsah-lehoo-nah boh-teh-yah deh ah-wa?)
- Can I ask you a question?
  ¿Puedo hacerte una pregunta? (¿Pwe-doh ah-sehr-tehoo-nah pre-goon-tah?)

Days of the Week

- Monday
  Lunes (Loo-nehs)
- Tuesday
  Martes (Mahr-tehs)

- Wednesday
  Miércoles (Mee-ehr-coh-lehs)
- Thursday
  Jueves (Hoo-eh-vehs)
- Friday
  Viernes (Vee-ehr-nehs)
- Saturday
  Sábado (Sah-bah-doh)
- Sunday
  Domingo (Doh-meen-goh)

Months

- January
  Enero (Eh-neh-roh)
- February
  Febrero (Feh-breh-roh)
- March
  Marzo (Mahr-soh)
- April
  Abril (Ah-breel)
- May
  Mayo (Mah-yoh)
- June
  Junio (Hoo-nyo)
- July
  Julio (Hoo-lee-oh)

- August
  Agosto (Ah-gohs-toh)
- September
  Septiembre (Sehp-tee-ehm-breh)
- October
  Octubre (Ohs-too-breh)
- November
  Noviembre (Noh-vee-ehm-breh)
- December
  Diciembre (Dee-see-ehm-breh)

Numbers

Cardinal Numbers

- 0
  Cero (Seh-roh)
- 1
  Uno (Oo-no)

- 2
  Dos (Dohs)
- 3
  Tres (Trehs)
- 4
  Cuatro (Coo-ah-troh)

- 5
Cinco (Seen-coh)
- 6
Seis (Seh-ees)
- 7
Siete (See-eh-teh)
- 8
Ocho (Oh-cho)
- 9
Nueve (Noo-eh-veh)
- 10
Diez (Dee-ehs)
- 11
Once (Ohn-she)
- 12
Doce (Doh-seh)
- 13
Trece (Treh-seh)
- 14
Catorce (Cah-tohr-seh)
- 15
Quince (Keen-seh)
- 16
Dieciséis (Dee-eh-see-seh-ess)
- 17
Diecisiete (Dee-eh-see-see-eh-teh)
- 18
Dieciocho (Dee-eh-see-oh-choh)
- 19
Diecinueve (Dee-eh-see-noo-eh-veh)
- 20
Veinte (Veh-een-the)
- 21

- Veintiuno (Veh-een-tee-oo-noh)
- 22
Veintidos (Veh-een-tee-dohs)
- 23
Veintitres (Veh-een-tee-oo-trehs)
- 30
Treinta (Treh-een-tah)
- 40
Cuarenta (Coo-ah-rehn-tah)
- 50
Cincuenta (Seen-coo-ehn-tah)
- 60
Sesenta (Seh-sehn-tah)
- 70
Setenta (Seh-tehn-tah)
- 80
Ochenta (Oh-chen-tah)
- 90
Noventa (Noh-vehn-tah)
- 100
- Cien (See-ehn)
- 200
Doscientos (Dohs-see-ehn-tohs)
- 1000
Mil (Meal)

Ordinal Numbers

- First
Primero (Pree-meh-roh)
- Second
Segundo (Seh-goon-doh)
- Third
Tercero (Tehr-seh-roh)

- Fourth
  Cuarto (Coo-ahr-toh)
- Fifth
  Quinto (Keen-toh)
- Sixth
  Sexto (Sex-toh)
- Seventh
  Séptimo (Sehp-tee-moh)
- Eighth
  Octavo (Ohc-tah-voh)
- Ninth
  Noveno (Noh-veh-noh)
- Tenth
  Décimo (Deh-see-moh)

Telling the Time

- What time is it?
  ¿Qué hora es? (¿Keh oh-rah ehs?)
- Can you tell me what time it is?
  ¿Puedes decirme la hora? (¿Pwe-dehsdeh-seer-meh lah oh-rah?)
  - It's 4 pm.
    Son las 4 de la tarde. (Sohn lahs coo-ah-trohdehlahtahr-deh.)
  - O' clock…
    … en punto (… ehn poon-toh)
  - Half past…
    … y media/y treinta (… e meh-dee-ah/ e treh-een-tah)
  - Quarter past…
    … y cuarto (… e coo-ahr-toh)
  - A quarter to…
    … menos cuarto (… meh-nos coo-ahr-toh)
  - Midnight
    Medianoche (Meh-dee-ah-noh-cheh)
  - Morning
    Mañana (Mah-nya-nah)
  - Noon
    Mediodía (Meh-dee-oh-dee-ah)
  - Afternoon
    Tarde (Tahr-deh)
  - Evening
    Noche (Noh-cheh)
- At what time do you have class?
  ¿A qué hora tienes clase? (¿A keh oh-rah tee-ehn-ehsclah-seh?)
  - My classes start at 7:00 in the morning.
    Mis clases empiezan a las 7:00 de la mañana. (Mees clah-sehsehm-pee-eh-sahn ah lahs see-eh-tehdehlahmah-nya-nah)
- Could we have lunch at 2:30 in the afternoon?
  ¿Podríamos almorzar a las dos y media de la tarde? (¿Poh-dree-ah-mohs ahl-mohr-sahr ah lahsdohsee meh-dee-a dehlahtahr-deh?)
- I go to sleep around 11:00 at night.
  Yo me duermo alrededor de las 11:00 de la noche. (Yoh meh doo-ehr-moh ahl-reh-deh-dohrdehlahsohn-sehdehlahnoh-cheh)
- Her appointment is at noon.

Sucita es al mediodía. (Soo see-tahehs al meh-dee-oh-dee-ah)

- We'll go hiking tomorrow. Mañana iremos de excursión. (Mah-nya-nah ee-reh-mohsdehehx-coor-see-ohn)

- I couldn't sleep last night. No pude dormir anoche. (Noh poo-dehdohr-meer ah-noh-cheh)

Popular Colors

- Green
  Verde (Vehr-deh)
- Yellow
  Amarillo (Ah-mah-ree-yoh)
- Blue
  Azul (Ah-sool)
- White
  Blanco (Blahn-coh)
- Light blue
  Celeste (Seh-lehs-teh)
- Gold
  Dorado (Doh-rah-doh)
- Gray

  Gris (Grees)
- Brown
  Marrón (Mah-rohn)
- Orange
  Naranja (Nah-rahn-hah)
- Black
  Negro (Neh-groh)
- Red
  Rojo (Roh-hoh)
- Pink
  Rosa (Roh-sah)
- Purple
  Púrpura (Poor-poo-rah)

Examples:

1. What color is the car?
   ¿De qué color es el coche? (¿Dehkehcoh-lohrehsehlcoh-che?)
   a. The car is gray.
      El coche es gris. (Ehlcoh-cheehsgrees)
2. What is your favorite color?
   ¿Cuál es tu color favorito? (¿Coo-ahl ehstucoh-lohr fah-voh-ree-toh?)
   a. My favorite color is red.
      Mi color favorito es el rojo. (Mi coh-lohr fah-voh-ree-tohehsehlroh-hoh.
3. What is the color of your hair?
   ¿De qué color es su pelo? (¿Dehkehcoh-lohrehssoopeh-loh?)

64

    a. Her hair is black.

       Su pelo es negro. (Soo peh-lohehsneh-groh)

4. Do you like the green or the yellow shirt?

    ¿Te gusta la camisa verde o la amarilla? (¿Tehgoos-tahlahcah-mee-sahvehr-deh oh lah a-mah-ree-yah?)

    a. I like the green one.

       Me gusta la verde. (Me goos-tahlahvehr-deh)

5. This is a red pen.

    Es un bolígrafo rojo. (Ehsoonboh-lee-grah-fohroh-hoh)

Greetings

- Hello.
  Hola. (Oh-lah)
- How are you?
  ¿Qué tal? (¿Keh tahl?)
- What's up?
  ¿Qué pasa? (¿Kehpah-sah?)
- How're you doing?
  ¿Cómo te va? (¿Coh-mohtehvah?)
- How is your day?
  ¿Qué tal tu día? (¿Kehtahl too dee-ah?)
- How is everything?
  ¿Cómo va todo? (¿Coh-mohvahtoh-doh?)
- How is life?
  ¿Cómo va tu vida? (¿Coh-mohvah too vee-dah?)
  - ➢ I'm great.
    Estoy estupendo. (Ehs-toy ehs-too-pehn-doh)
  - ➢ I'm very well.
    Estoy muy bien. (Ehs-toy mooy bee-ehn)
  - ➢ I'm okay.
    Estoy bien. (Ehs-toy bee-ehn)
  - ➢ I'm unwell.
    Estoy mal. (Ehs-toy mahl)
  - ➢ I feel terrible.
    Estoy fatal. (Ehs-toy fah-tahl)

- I'm tired.
  - Estoy cansado. (Ehs-toy cahn-sah-doh)
- I'm exhausted.
  - Estoy exhausto. (Ehs-toy ex-sah-oos-toh)
- I'm sick.
  - Estoy enfermo. (Ehs-toy ehn-fehr-moh)

- And you?
  ¿Y tú? (¿Ee too?)
- Goodbye.
  Adiós. (Ah-dee-ohs)
- See you tomorrow.
  Nos vemos mañana. (Nohsveh-mohsmah-nya-nah)
- See you later.
  Hasta luego. (Ahs-tah loo-eh-goh)
- See you soon, friend.
  Hasta pronto, amigo. (Ahs-tahprohn-toh, ah-mee-goh)
- I have to go.
  Tengo que irme. (Tehn-go keheer-meh)
- I need to get going.
  Necesito irme. (Neh-ceh-see-toheer-meh)
- It's time for me to go!
  ¡Es hora de que me vaya! (Ehs oh-rah dehkeh meh vah-ya)
- Speak soon.
  Hablamos pronto. (Ah-blah-mohsprohn-toh)
- See you later!
  ¡Nos vemos! (¡Nohsveh-mohs!)
- It was so nice to meet you!
  ¡Me encantó conocerte! (Meh ehn-cahn-tohcoh-noh-sehr-teh)
- I hope to see you soon.
  Espero verte pronto. (Ehs-peh-rohver-tehprohn-toh)
- May I introduce you to my friend?
  ¿Puedo presentarte a mi amigo? (¿Pwe-doh preh-sehn-tahr-teh ah mee ah-mee-goh?)

Emotions

66

- I'm happy.
  Estoy contento/a. (Ehs-toy cohn-tehn-toh/ah)
- I'm sad.
  Estoy triste. (Ehs-toy trees-teh)
- I'm scared.
  Tengo miedo. (Tehn-goh mee-eh-doh)
- I'm excited.
  Estoy emocionado/a. (Ehs-toy eh-moh-see-oh-nah-doh/ah)
- I'm bored.
  Estoy aburrido/a. (Ehs-toy a-boo-ree-doh/ah)
- I'm angry.
  Estoy enojado/a. (Ehs-toy eh-noh-hah-doh/ah)
- I love it.
  Me encanta. (Meh ehn-cahn-tah)
- I like it.
  Me gusta. (Meh goos-tah.)
- I don't like it.
  No me gusta. (Noh meh goos-tah)
- I hate it.
  Lo detesto. (Lohdeh-tehs-toh)
- Cool!
  ¡Genial! (¡Heh-nee-ahl!)
- I don't care.
  Me da igual. (Meh da ee-goo-ahl)
- As you wish.
  Como quieras. (Coh-mohkee-eh-rahs)
- It bothers me.

- Me molesta. (Meh moh-lehs-tah)
- I'm nervous.
  Estoy nervioso/a. (Ehs-toy nehr-vee-oh-soh/ah)
- I'm sleepy.
  Tengo sueño. (Tehn-gohsoo-eh-nyo)
- I'm embarrassed.
  Estoy avergonzado/a. (Ehs-toy ah-ver-gohn-sah-doh/dah)
- I'm calm.
  Estoy tranquilo/a. (Ehs-toy trahn-kee-loh/ah)
- I'm jealous.
  Estoy celoso/a. (Ehs-toy ceh-loh-soh/ah)
- I'm worried.
  Estoy preocupado/a. (Ehs-toy preh-oh-coo-pah-doh/ah)
- I'm overwhelmed.
  Estoy agobiado/a. (Ehs-toy ah-goh-bee-ah-doh/ah)
- I'm uncomfortable.
  Estoy incómodo/a. (Ehs-toy een-coh-moh-doh/ah)
- I'm depressed.
  Estoy deprimido/a. (Ehs-toy deh-pree-mee-doh/ah)
- I'm busy.
  Estoy ocupado/a. (Ehs-toy oh-coo-pah-doh/ah)
- I'm shy.
  Soy tímido/a. (Soy tee-mee-doh/ah)
- I'm sensitive.

Soy sensible. (Soy sehn-see-bleh)

Common Sayings

- Well dressed for a special occasion
  - ➢ De punta en blanco (Deh poon-tahehnblahn-coh)
- To be right, to be assertive
  - ➢ Dar en el blanco (Dahrehnehlblahn-coh)
- To look for the perfect man
  - ➢ Buscar el príncipe azul (Boos-cahrel preen-see-peh ah-sool)
- To belong to a royal or very rich family
  - ➢ Tener sangre azul (Teh-nehrsahn-greh ah-sool)
- To find the perfect or ideal partner
  - ➢ Encontrar tu media naranja (Ehn-cohn-trahr too meh-dee-ah nah-rahn-hah)
- To feel very embarrassed about something
  - ➢ Ponerse rojo como un tomate (Poh-nehr-sehroh-hohcoh-mohoontoh-mah-teh)
- There is no comparison
  - ➢ No hay color (No I coh-lohr)
- To have bad luck
  - ➢ Tener la negra (Teh-nehr la neh-grah)
- To have excellent vision
  - ➢ Tener vista de lince (Teh-nehr bees-tahdehleen-seh)
- To have a bad memory
  - ➢ Tener memoria de pez (Teh-nehr meh-moh-ree-ah dehpez)
- To be good for nothing
  - ➢ Ser la oveja negra (Sehr la oh-beh-hah neh-grah)
- To be a coward
  - ➢ Ser un gallina (Sehr oon gah-yee-nah)
- To trick someone, to rip someone off
  - ➢ Dar gato por liebre (Dahr gah-tohpohr lee-eh-breh)
- To be crazy
  - ➢ Estar como una cabra (Ehs-tahrcoh-mohoo-nah cah-brah)
- To be a very lucky person

68

- Tener más vidas que un gato (Teh-nehrmahs vee-dahs kehoon gah-toh)
- To be cunning and sharp in practical matters
  - Ser más astuto que un zorro (Sehr mahsahs-too-tohkehoon soh-roh)
- To be a piece of cake
  - Ser pan comido (Sehr pan coh-mee-doh)
- To be eye candy
  - Ser un bombón (Sehr oonbohm-bohn)
- To be from another era
  - Ser del año de la pera (Sehr dehl a-nyodehlahpeh-rah)
- To turn the tables
  - Dar la vuelta a la tortilla (Dahrlahvoo-ehl-tah a la torh-tee-yah)
- Do not care, couldn't care less
  - No importar un pepino/rábano (Noh eem-pohr-tahroonpeh-pee-noh/rah-bah-noh)
- To be a blockhead
  - Ser un melón (Sehr oon meh-lohn)
- To be here, there and everywhere
  - Estar hasta en la sopa (Ehs-tahrahs-tahehnlah soh-pah)
- To eat (one's) lunch
  - Comer la papa (Coh-mehrlahpah-pah)
- To put your foot in it
  - Meter la pata (Meh-tehrlahpah-tah)
- Without rhyme or reason
  - No tener pies ni cabeza (No teh-nehr pee-ehs nee cah-beh-sah)
- Without sleeping a wink
  - No pegar un ojo (Noh peh-gahroonojo)
- To walk on eggshells
  - Andar con pies de plomo (An-dahrcohn pee-ehsdehploh-moh)
- To not mince your words
  - Sin pelos en la lengua (Seen peh-lohsehnlahlehn-wa)
- To be spot on
  - Dar en el clavo (Dahrehnehlclah-voh)

ORDERING AT RESTAURANT

Synopsis

esús walks into a restaurant and the waitress, Luna attends to him.

J He orders coffee, food, and even mentions her excellent service at the end. You'll learn some things to say when you're at a restaurant and ready to place an order.

-Un hombre entra en un restaurante-

-A man enters a restaurant-

Luna: Buenas tardes señor, bienvenido al restaurante estrella. ¿Cómo puedo ayudarle?

Luna: Good evening sir, welcome to the star restaurant. How may I help you?

Jesús: Gracias, muchacha, buenas tardes a usted también. Tengo tanta hambre; ¿puedo ver el menú?

Jesús: Thanks, young lady, good evening to you as well. I am so hungry; may I see the menu?

Luna: Claro, ¿para cuántas personas?

Luna: Of course, for how many people?

Jesús: No hay nadie más, solo yo.

Jesús: There's no one else, just me.

Luna: Está bien, puede sentarse allí por la ventana. ¿Le gustaría tomar algo? Tenemos algunas especial es increíbles.

70

Luna: Okay, you may have a seat over there by the window. Would you like something to drink? We have some amazing Specials.

Jesús: No, ahora no, es demasiado temprano para beber alcohol. Un café está bien, con muy poca azúcar, por favor.

Jesús: No, not now, it's too early to drink alcohol. Coffee is fine with very little sugar, please.

Luna: ¿Quiere leche con su café, señor?

Luna: You want milk with your coffee, sir?

Jesús: Sí, pero no mucha, solo un poco. Me gustaría pan con el café también.

Jesús: Yes, but not a lot, just a little bit. I would like bread with the coffee too.

Luna: No hay problema, suena bien, ¿algo más? ¿Quiere algo para comer del menú?

Luna: No problem, sounds good, anything else? Do you want something to eat from the menu?

Jesús: Hmmmm, me gustaría una ensalada. ¿Cuánto cuestan_el arroz y el pollo? No tienen un precio.

Jesús: Hmmmm, I would like a salad. How much are the rice and chicken? It does not have a price.

Luna: Ohhh perdón, están aquí al reverso.

Luna: Ohhh sorry, they're here on the back.

Jesús: Ok, muy bien, me gustaría el arroz y el pollo, por favor.

Jesús: Okay, very well, I would like the rice and the chicken, please.

Luna: Ok, señor, vamos a preparar esto para usted ahora mismo. ¿Algo más?

Luna: Ok, sir, we are going to prepare this for you right now. Anything else?

Jesús: Eso es todo por ahora. Gracias por su excelente servicio.

Jesús: That's all for now. Thanks for your excellent service.

Luna: No hay problema, señor, es un placer. Buen provecho.

Luna: No problem, sir, it's a pleasure. Enjoy your meal.

-Fin de la historia-

-End of story-

Breaking It All Down

Buenas Tardes: This is how you say good afternoon. It's "Buenas" and not, "Buenos" because the word, "Tardes" (afternoons/evenings) is feminine.

Note: In English, you usually use the singular, but in Spanish, the plural is more common. In some places, you might hear the singular too. It is usually a matter of regional/personal preference.

Buenos días (plural)/Buen día (singular) = Good morning

How to say good morning and good night in Spanish:

- "Buenos días, señor. ¿Quiere desayunar? " = "Good morning, sir. Do you want some breakfast? "
- "Buenas tardes, señora."= "Good afternoon, ma'am."
- "Buenas noches. ¿Tiene reservación? "= "Good evening. Do you have a reservation? "
- "Buenas noches, mamá. ¿Quieres algo de la tienda? " = "Good night, mom. You want something from the store? "

Puedo ayudarle: Puedo comes from the verb, "Poder" (to be able to/can). Puedo is the "Yo" form (first person singular) of the verb used in the present indicative tense.

So, let's talk about the next word, the infinitive/nonconjugated verb, "Ayudar." This verb means, "To help." Noticed that she added the "le" to it?

That "le" is an indirect object pronoun.

The le is considered the third person, but she is talking directly to him (because, as you can see in the table below, it is used with the formal you, "usted"). An easy rule of thumb when you're are speaking in the usted form is to pretend as if you're speaking about someone or something else.

Subject	Singular	Plural
First person	me (to/for me)	nos (to/for us)
Second person	te (to/for informal you)	os (to/for formal you)
Third person	le (to/for it, him, her, formal you)	les (to/for them, formal you)

Le can also be, "him/her."

If she was speaking using the "tú" form, she would have been more direct and said, "Puedoayudarte" instead.

Here is a table of Spanish indirect pronouns.

I mentioned that she is speaking to him using the usted/formal form. If she was speaking to him using the Tú form, which pronoun do you think she would have used?

I said before that she would have said, "Puedoayudarte" instead, so it would have been "te."

This is how the verb, "Poder" (to be able to/can) is conjugated in the present indicative tense.

- Yo puedo= I can

- Tú puedes=You can
- Él/ella puede=He/She can
- Usted puede=You (formal) can
- Nosotros/nosotras podemos=We can
- Ustedes pueden=You all can
- Ellos/ellas pueden=They can
- Vosotros podéis=You all (informal) can

Only use in Spain examples:

- "We can be friends."
- "Podemos ser amigos."
- "You can come with me."
- "Puedes venir conmigo."

And here is how the infinitive verb, "Ayudar" (to help) in the sentence is conjugated in the present indicative tense:

- Yo ayudo= I help
- Tú ayudas= You help
- Él/ella ayuda= He/she helps
- Usted ayuda= You (formal) help
- Nosotros/nosotras ayudamos= We help
- Ustedes ayudan= You all help
- Ellos/ellas ayudan= They help
- Vosotros ayudáis= You all (informal) help. Only use in Spain.

And here are some examples of how to use "Ayudar" (to help) in the present indicative tense.

- "Quiero ayudar" = "I want to help"
- "Quieren ayudarte" = "They want to help you."
- "¿Puedes ayudarme?" = "Can you help me?"
- "¿Puedes ayudarnos?" = "Can you help us?"

Noticed how the object pronouns, te, me, and nos are joined to the infinitive verb?

The cool thing is those object pronouns can also be placed before the conjugated verb.

For example, if you wanted to say "Can you help me," it can be, "Puedes ayudarme" or "me puedes ayudar."

- "Nos puedes ayudar?" = "Can you help us?"
- "Can you help us?" = "Puedes ayudarnos"

Muchacha: A Term that is used to address a young woman. Muchacho would be a young man. The young lady here is old enough to be referred to as, senorita as well.

You can use the word muchacha/muchacho for young people. If you say it to an older person, they may take offense to it. But when speaking, always remember, it's all about context.

Older people like to use the term, "muchacha/muchacho" a lot. So, someone in their 70s might use the word "muchacho/a" when referring to someone in his/her 20s, 30s or even 40s.

Old people aside, it is reasonable to call someone in his/her teens- 20s "muchacho/a."

"Muchacha" can also mean "cleaning lady/maid." Again, the context determines the meaning.

Puedo ver: The conjugated word, "Puedo" is from the verb, "Poder" (to be able to/can) and it's used in the present indicative tense. "Ver" is the nonconjugated/infinitive verb and it means, "To see."

Making it, "I can see" (Puedo ver).

Again, this is how the verb "Poder" (to be able to/can) is conjugated in the present indicative tense.

- Yo Puedo—I can
- Tú Puedes—You can

75

- Él/ella Puede= He/She can
- Usted Puede= You (formal) can
- Nosotros/nosotras Podemos= We can
- Ustedes Pueden= You all can
- Ellos/Ellas Pueden= They can
- Vosotros Podéis= You all (informal) can.

Only use in Spain examples:

- "Podemos ir a la playa." = "We can go to the beach."
- "Puedes ver el cielo." = "You can see the sky."
- "Pueden verte." = "They can see you."

See how the object pronoun "te" was added to the infinitive in this last example?

Remember it can also be, "Te pueden ver" and means the exact same thing.

It all depends on how you'd like to write/speak.

No hay: The word hay is super useful when you want to say, there is, there are, is there, are there. You may walk into a supermarket, for example, and ask a person working there, "¿ Hay manzanas aquí?" (Are there apples here?), they may simply respond, "No hay" (There aren't any) or they may say, "Yes, there are apples" (Sí, hay manzanas).

You'll hear "hay" when people say, "No hay problema" (no problem or there's no problem).

Where did it come from? The verb, "Haber."

The verb "haber" is a very important auxiliary verb, meaning, "to have," used with a past participle, as in, for example, "He has gone," "Él ha ido." (This is of course not to be confused with the regular transitive verb, "tener," which means "to have."

For example, "I have a wife" (tengo una esposa).

But "haber" also has another meaning. It is the impersonal verb that means "to be," used in a specific way, as in, for example, "there is rain," "Hay lluvia."

Notice that in the second example above, the word "hay" is used, (not "ha").

It is a special conjugation, used when "haber" is in its "to be" form in the present tense.

Furthermore, "hay" is used for both singular and plural nouns, that is, when saying "there is," or "there are."

As you advance with your Spanish, the verb "Haber" will be used to create all kinds of sentences, no doubt about it, but in this version of Gritty Spanish, you'll not hear it used in all those forms, which is a good thing since this is meant to be a "Basic" version of Gritty Spanish.

Other examples of how to use "Hay."

- "Hay muchos carros en la calle." = "There are many cars on the street."
- "Hay una bicicleta afuera." = "There is a bicycle outside."

Remember, you can use, "Hay" if you wanted to ask, "Is there/are there" in Spanish too!

- "¿Hay un hotel en la cuidad?" = "Is there a hotel in the city?"
- "¿Hay libros aquí?" = "Are there books here?"

Puede sentarse: She is still speaking to him using a formal tone. She starts off with the verb, "Poder" (to be able to/can" and conjugated it to, "puede." "Puede is the 3rd person: Él/ella/usted form of the verb used in the present/indicative tense.

She then follows up with the infinitive/nonconjugated verb, "Sentar," which means, "to sit."

Noticed that she added the "Se" at the end of the nonconjugated verb, "Sentar?"

Remember in the first story, when we were talking about the verb, "llamar" (to call) and how we can use it in a reflexive manner to say, "What you call yourself? What's your name?" or "¿ Cómo te llamas?" in Spanish?

This is kind of using the same concept, "Puede sentarse" is like saying, "You can sit yourself down." But see, she is speaking to him in a formal manner, this is why she didn't say, "Puedes sentarte…"

When you're asking someone their name in a formal manner, you'd say, "¿Cómo se llama?" instead of "Cómo te llamas." When you say, "¿Cómo se llama?" It can also be, "What's his/her name."

Here, the young lady could have also used the reflexive pronoun first and said, "Se puede sentar." Makes sense?

PREGNANT WOMAN ON THE TRAIN

Summation

The spunky Puerto Rican lady, Medellín is on a Queens-bound F-train with a long-lasting companion of hers. She is right now seven months pregnant. She regularly gets offered a seat at whatever point she is on the transport or the train. Toward the beginning of today, she isn't offered a seat and is a little fomented.

-Anuncio de tren-

-Train declaration-

Medellín: ¡No sé qué está mal con los hombres estos días! No tienen ninguna consideración en absoluto.

Medellín: I don't have the foggiest idea what's up with the men nowadays! They don't have any thought whatsoever.

Andriena: Sí, ya sé Medellín, estos días los hombres no son buenos. ¿No ven que estás embarazada? ¡Mira ese de allá!

Andriena: Yes, I know Medellín, nowadays, men are nothing but bad. They don't see that you are pregnant? Take a gander at that one around there!

Medellín: Sí, lo veo. No quiere ceder su asiento, ¿verdad?

Medellín: Yes, I see him. He would not like to surrender his seat, isn't that so?

Andriena: No te preocupes por eso. Entonces, ¿Cuántos meses tienes?

Andriena: Don't stress over it. Anyway, how long would you say you are?

Medellín: Tengo siete meses. No puedo esperar a tener a mi niñita. Sé que será tan hermosa. ¡No puedo esperar para vestirla!

Medellín: I am 7 months. I can hardly wait to have my daughter. I realize she'll be so excellent. I can hardly wait to dress her up!

-El mismo tipo del que están hablando se levanta para ofrecer su asiento-

-A similar person they are discussing, gets up to offer his seat-

Joel: Oh, señora, señora, perdón, disculpe… Siento haber sido tan grosero, no la vi. ¿Le gustaría tomar un asiento?

Joel: Oh, miss, miss, pardon me… I sincerely apologize for being so inconsiderate, I didn't see you. Might you want to grab a chair?

Medellín: Oh es muy amable, siéntese, no necesito un asiento, voy a bajar en un standard de paradas.

Medellín: Oh you are excessively kind, plunk down, I needn't bother with a seat, I will get off a few stops.

Joel: ¿Está segura señora? ¿Está segura de que no quiere sentarse?

Joel: Are you certain Miss? You sure you would prefer not to sit?

Medellín: Estoy segura, usted es un caballero, el mundo necesita más hombres como usted.

Medellín: I am certain, you are a refined man, the world requirements more men like you.

Joel: Gracias, señora. Mi madre me educó bien. Que tenga un día maravilloso.

Joel: Thanks, ma'am. My mom showed me well. Have a brilliant day.

-Fin de la historia-

-End of story-

Return to Episode List

Separating everything:

Yasé: You might inquire, "when Spanish talking individuals use, 'Yasé,' has gone against 'lo sé,' is there a motivation behind why they do this?"

On the off chance that you simply use "sé" alone, that would not bode well; you need to add "what" you know:

- "Sé tu nombre"= I know your name.
- "Lo sé" and "ya lo sé" are generally utilized conversely "Lo sé" = "I know it"

A strict interpretation of "Ya lo sé" could be "I definitely know it" (yet by and by, it's likewise utilized the same way as "lo sé." Possibly you can say "ya lo sé" is more earnest, something like: "I know, I know."

Remember that while in English, adding "as of now" to "I know" can infer or pass on a disturbance at the speaker for telling the audience something he/she definitely knows; this isn't the situation in Spanish.

¿No ven que estás embarazada? Where "No" signifies "Don't they" and "ven" is "they see." "Ven" is the current demonstrative type of the action word "ver" (to see) that you use for the pronouns "ellos (they; manly)/ellas/they, feminine)/ustedes (all of you)." "Estás" is "you are" and "embarazada" is "pregnant."

Ese: "Ese" signifies, "That," yet when you are alluding to "that someone or something" then, at that point it likewise signifies, "that one." Assuming she was alluding to a lady, saying, "that one," it would be "esa."

Lo veo: "veo" (I see) comes from the action word, "ver" (to see). Veo is utilized in the current demonstrative tense and it's utilizing the "Yo" type of the action word, "Ver." The "lo" was said before "veo" in light of the fact that she is saying, "I see him." Here, "Lo" is him. "Lo" can likewise signify, "it," if that IT is a manly word, as, "elteléfono" (the phone).

No quiere ceder: They are discussing the person not having any desire to surrender his seat. Quiere (he/she needs) is the él/ella/usted type of the action word, "Querer" (to need) in the current demonstrative tense.

Ceder is an action word that signifies, "to offer up/to surrender." ¿Verdad? Depending on the unique circumstance, this word can signify "right," "valid," and "truly."

Models:

- Mañana es la celebration, ¿verdad? = The party is tomorrow, correct?
- ¡Es verdad! = It is valid!
- Yo vi todo= I saw everything
- De verdad extraño a mi mam= I truly miss my mother

No te preocupes por eso: The word, "Preocupes" comes from the action word, "Preocupar" (to stress). On the off chance that you provide somebody an order, and advise them, "Stress," then, at that point it's, "preocupa" in the "tú" structure. Here, a negative order is given, however, the reflexive pronoun was added before the action word to make it, "Try not to stress yourself."

Here are two or three simple instances of how to utilize negative orders:

- No compres la manzana= Try not to purchase the apple.
- No aprendas español= Try not to learn Spanish.
- ¡No escribas en la plateau! = Try not to compose on the table!

In case you are providing an order, saying exactly the same thing as above, it would be:

- Compra la manzana= Purchase the apple.
- Aprende español= Learn Spanish.
- ¡Escribe en la plateau! = Compose on the table!

Do you see the change?

No puedo esperar: Puedo comes from the action word, "Poder" (to be ableto/Can). "Puedo" is the "Yo" type of the action word utilized in the current characteristic tense. Esperar is an action word that signifies, "to hang tight for/to trust."

Niñita: This is from "Niña" (young lady). You can add diminutives, "ito" (manly) or "ita" to certain words to demonstrate littleness or show fondness. Actually like in English when you would say "kitty" rather than "feline" or "pup" rather than "canine."

Models:

- (Gato) Gatito= kitty (male)/gatita (female)
- (Casa) Casita= little house
- (Abuela) Abuelita= grandmother
- (Face) Carita= little face, etc…

Será: This word is from the action word, "Ser" (to be) and it's utilized later on tense. "Será" is the él/ella/usted type of the action word in that strained since they are discussing the unborn child young lady in that line. You utilize the future tense when you need to discuss what you will do.

To shape the basic future tense, basically, add the right consummation of the infinitive of the action word. All action word formations (-ar, -er, and -ir) have similar endings in the basic future tense.

Spanish Simple Future

Se levanta: "levanter" comes from the action word, "Levantar" (to raise, to lift).

At the point when it's utilized reflexively, then, at that point it's "levantarse" and it becomes, "to stand up." The pronoun "se" was added first, since it addresses a third individual, the man in the scene, "Joel." "Levanta" alone is the "él/ella/usted" type of action word. This resembles saying, "He/she stand himself up."

Señora: It can be incredibly precarious in Spanish to settle on "señorita" (miss) and "señora" since the "socially right" method of utilizing these terms is diverse relying upon the country.

Overall:

- **Señorita:** Traditionally alludes to a youthful unmarried woman or young lady.
- **Señora:** Married ladies regardless of how youthful they might be or it tends to be extremely old women, regardless of whether they never have been hitched.

In Spain:

- **Señorita:** A wedded 25-year-elderly person would be completely glad to be called "señorita" all over the place, without fail, aside from while anticipating convention.
- **Señora:** As age increments, "señorita" begins getting hostile. A 50-year-elderly person could believe you're deriding her, paying little mind to conjugal status.

Note: Spain has been having something of a sexual orientation uniformity mindfulness arousing as of late, and, essentially in certain spots, there is a pattern toward calling all grown-up ladies Señora.

In any case, in Mexico, hitched ladies are consistent "señoras" and singles are "señoritas;" yet the older women, regardless of whether they are single are called "señoras." In case you are in Mexico and you don't know what the conjugal status is, the vast majority like to say: "Señorita" until told something else. The more "develop" ladies will snicker and appear to be complimented.

Nonetheless, in case you don't know about the conjugal status and call a young woman, "señora," she may get vexed on the grounds that you are inferring "she looks old for her age." I called a 29-yr. an old companion of mine from Honduras, "Señora," she immediately answered, "I'm not a Señora."

Along these lines, as should be obvious, while in Spain "señora" might draw you nearer to the protected side, in Mexico is by and large the reverse way around.

To keep away from this in Mexico and some different nations of Latin America, individuals simply say "seño".

In all cases, if the lady has an expert title, for example, "doctora" (specialist) or "profesora" (teacher), they liked to be called as such: Doctora Mariana (rather than señorita/señora Mariana)

Siento haber sido: This makes an interpretation of in a real sense to, "sorry to have been."

"Siento" is from the action word, "Sentir" (to feel). At the point when you say "Lo siento" alone in Spanish, it signifies, "I'm heartbroken," which in a real sense signifies, "I feel it."

The action word haber (to have) is regularly utilized with the past participle of another action word to frame the current wonderful tense. Here, "sido" is the previous participle of the action word, "ser" (to be).

- Haber sido= to have been
- He sido= I have been
- Has sido= you have been
- Han sido= they have been, etc.

The compound action word, "haber" was utilized since "Siento" (I feel) from the action word, sentir (to feel) was just before it.

No la vi: Let us start with the final word, "Vi" (I saw). "Vi" comes from the action word, "Ver" (to see). It's utilized here in the preterite past tense in the "Yo" structure. "La" signifies, "Her." He is talking officially, this is the reason he isn't addressing her straightforwardly, else, he would have said, "no te vi," where, "te" signifies "you."

You can say, "no la vi" to say, "I didn't see Her" when alluding to a third individual or thing, like an apple, "La manzana."

In case it was one apple, it would be, "no la vi" (I didn't see It). In the event that they were various apples, it's, "No las vi."

Es muy amable: She is talking in a deferential, formal way, so she utilized "es," which is from the action word, "Ser" (to be). "Es" is the "él/ella/usted" type of the action word utilized in the current demonstrative tense. By her idiom, "es," as far as we might be concerned, it resembles she is discussing another person, isn't that so? However, this is the manner by which it's done when talking officially in Spanish.

- Muy= Very
- Amable= Nice

Assuming you needed to tell somebody "You are exceptionally decent" in a casual way, you'd say, "eres muy amable." "Eres" is the tú type of the action word, "Ser" (to be) utilized in the current characteristic tense.

Siéntese: This comes from the action word "sentar" (to sit). Recollect whether you need to simply say, "Sit" you utilize the order/basic state of mind of the action word, "Sentar," which is, "siente" in the él/ella/usted structure. "Sienta" is the tú type of that action word utilized in a similar order/basic structure.

THE MAIN PRINCIPLES

There are three main principles involved in what I call "memory amplification." I use this term because memory techniques do seem to "turn up the volume." This means that the memory palaces themselves become a kind of like storage units for our roaring Spanish words.

The three principles we will learn in this chapter are location, imagery, and activity. Along with these principles, we have preparation and predetermination.

Keep in mind that each of these principles is individually important and each is interrelated. Use them independently, and they will still help improve your memory. Use them together and your memory skills will soar beyond belief.

Joshua Foer's recent book Moonwalking with Einstein: The Art and Science of Memory are also fantastic, but please be advised that this book covers more cultural history than specific guidance when it comes to building memory palaces for language acquisition. But if you're serious about improving your memory in ways that will directly impact your ability to learn Spanish, then you have everything to gain by reading all that you can on the topic.

Location

Location is part of, but not the entire picture of the memory palace concept.

Locations are used to store imagery. The reason we use locations is that we tend to remember places we've been without exerting any effort, and this is one of the key principles of memory work: eliminate everything that you don't have to work at remembering and build natural associations.

When thinking about locations for storing memories, try doing something that I did for myself. I once determined that I have lived in eight cities, twenty-five houses (or apartments), and sixteen neighborhoods within those cities. I have yet to count all the houses I remember that belong to my friends and extended family members, but surely the number is exponential because it gets expanded all the time. There are even hotel rooms that I remember very well in cities that I have visited. The path I took from an apartment in Paris to the Louvre, for instance, has served me very well over the years.

We all have more territory in our minds than we could ever possibly hope to use for storing memories. The best part is that we can then sub-divide locations into individual stations. So if you consider an apartment a "location," then each individual room will be a station within that location.

As I'm going to discuss further on, I like to combine indoors and outdoors locations, places that I know very well.

I think you'll be impressed by the power of location in storing memories.

However, for memorizing Spanish vocabulary effectively, I suggest that you always use locations you are familiar with. It can't be said enough: the more you use places you already know, the less you have to remember. The less you have to take note, the more you can associate. And the more you can associate, the more you can remember. It's an awkward equation, I know, but it works.

But for now, let's move on to...

Imagery

Imagery is … well, imagery. Mental pictures that you build in your mind. For the purposes of memorization, these pictures need to be big and colorful. The larger and the more colorful, the better. Essentially, you want to exaggerate the size and colors because that will make the image more memorable. This will in turn strengthen the association.

Some of the students I've taught tell me that they are not particularly visual in their imaginations and I completely understand this. In fact, when I read a novel, I rarely see images in my mind. It's always conceptual. It's possible that I have something called Imagination Deficit Disorder or IDD.

Whether I suffer from this condition or not, because I have a low visual threshold in my mind, I am able to give my non-visual students a few suggestions based on my own experiences.

First, if you can't think in color, don't force. However, try thinking in black and white, taking care to exaggerate the black and white. How black is the black and how white is the white? Is there an opportunity to use gray in some memorable way?

Whatever happens, do not allow a lack of imagination for intense imagery to be a barrier. I know that you can incorporate images into your memory work because as I mentioned, I am not particularly visual myself. This surprises people a great deal because I have spent a great deal of my career teaching Film Studies. I teach theory and concepts, however, and am absolutely lost when anyone asks me about how individual shots are composed.

In the event that black and white patterns are not useful for you, another tactic, one that I have used to great comes up, is to associate certain prefixes with actors or fictional characters. For instance, the Spanish prefix cachi- is associated in my mind with Charles "Chachi" Arcola, who was played by Scott Baio on the popular television series, Happy Days. The words don't sound exactly the same, but I am able to visualize Chachi and make the association cachi. Thereafter, every word that begins with cachi gets automatically linked with Chachi.

Another option is to use paintings that you are familiar with in your imagery.

The more you are aware of their intricacies, the better. The next moment you are in an art museum or looking through an art book, pay closer attention to what you are looking for. The material could become fodder for better associations with the Spanish vocabulary you will be memorizing.

I must mention a small problem with artwork, however. Paintings and statues tend to be static. They don't move. That said, if you can imagine the Mona Lisa walking like an Egyptian outside of her frame, or Michelangelo's David doing the Moonwalk, then you should have no problem.

Finally, you could use toys that you remember. GI Joe, Barbie, My Little Pony… anything goes. As with paintings, the most important factor here is that you can put these figures into action.

So without further adieu, let's turn our attention to…

Action

By now, you will have thought about different locations you are familiar with, sub-locations or stations within those locations, and different ways that you can use exaggerated imagery.

The next step is to give your images a bit of movement.

More than a bit, actually. Just as you want to exaggerate the size and color of your images, you also want to exaggerate their actions.

It's not an entirely nice way to think of things, but something that will work wonders for you is to make the action violent. Highway accidents serve as the perfect example of how memorable scenes of violence can be—even in their aftermath. If after seeing an accident or accident site you could not shake the memory of your mind, then you know how powerful violent images can be.

This is not to suggest that lives need to be lost. Cartoon violence will work just as well. Wile E. Coyote, for instance, provides a strong example of someone willing to savage himself in some pretty hilarious ways when trying to make the Road Runner his dinner.

Again, the object is to create something so potently memorable that working hard to recall the image is unnecessary. It will instantly come to mind when you look for it because you've given yourself no other choice. You've made the image impossible to forget.

Now, you may be thinking that using this technique is going to lead to a brain cluttered with bizarre images. This may happen in the beginning when you are

90

first learning the techniques. With practice, however, the images you have used will ultimately fall away. You'll still wander your palaces and have a hankering of what the images were that you used, but they will be secondary.

The word and its meaning will be the central artifact on display.

Preparation and Predetermination

Like the memory palace system itself, I'll be revealing later on, Preparation and Predetermination are two memory skills that I have not seen talked about in any other memory book. I feel that both of these are essential elements to memorization success, be it a language or anything else you might like to remember.

Preparation, to begin, involves relaxing the mind. This does not mean that you won't be able to remember anything. It only means that your mind won't be in the most receptive state possible. When your mind is open and relaxed, you'll be amazed by how these techniques will double, triple, and even quadruple your effectiveness.

Predetermination, on the other hand, involves charting out the memory locations and stations in your memory palace system before making any single attempt to place the words you want to memorize. I must stress that before populating your memory palaces for Spanish, you will need to have built the entire system first. Having tried to make up my palaces as I went along, I can tell you that this leads to little more than frustration and impoverished results. Please spend the necessary time to predetermine the locations that you want to use and label the individual stations within them.

Before continuing, I want to stress that perfection is not the goal here. It's important not to harm your forward movement by being too particular about every little detail. You just want to get the basic layout in place so that you can work relatively quickly with the words you want to memorize. I will also give you samples of how I memorized those words so that you can model the procedure on your own.

Preparing Your First Location

It helps a great deal to draw a map of the locations you will be using and have some system for labeling the individual stations. Alternatively, you can list them in a Word document or catalog them in an Excel file. Some students I've had like to actually draw the different rooms or use computer architectural programs to create digital layouts. Although I personally don't go that far, I tend to do all three of the former in order to maximize the strength of the associations I'll be making. Let's face it: If I'm going to spend time learning a language, I want the vocabulary to stay in my head. Learning grammar is pointless if you haven't got plenty of words to fit into the equations.

The first Memory Palace I ever created was my first apartment in Berlin. It had 8 stations, though I now recommend and always make sure a new memory palace I've started working with has at least 10.

This particular apartment was on the Feurigstraße, which means "fiery street." The name came from the fact that a fire station was located just a few blocks north of me, but that was fine because the firemen had the lovely habit of only turning the sirens on after they had left the street.

earning a new language can be fun!

You can use your Spanish vocabulary to try to guess the words. There are also other clues provided as hints, to help you!

Two hints have been provided for every puzzle. One of them gives the second letter of the word, and one of them gives its meaning (in English).

For the shorter words, the answer may not be unique. However, longer words usually have only one unique solution.

Guess the word in each case; some of the letters have been hidden by the underscore (_) sign.

Exercise 1

1. d_s_ñ_
2. m_j_r_s
3. e_c_i_o
4. e_c_j_r
5. s_g_i_i_a_á

Hints:

1. The second letter of the answer is *i*
   The meaning of this word (in English):
   design
2. The second letter of the answer is *u*
   The meaning of this word (in English):
   women
3. The second letter of the answer is *s*
   The meaning of this word (in English):

written

4. The second letter of the answer is *n*
   The meaning of this word (in English):
   fit

5. The second letter of the answer is *i*
   The meaning of this word (in English):
   mean

Exercise 2

1. c_d_n_
2. s_g_i_i_a_o
3. c_b_a_
4. a_c_n_o
5. o_c_r_

Hints:

1. The second letter of the answer is *a*
   The meaning of this word (in English):
   string

2. The second letter of the answer is *i*
   The meaning of this word (in English):
   meant

3. The second letter of the answer is *o*
   The meaning of this word (in English):
   charge

4. The second letter of the answer is *s*
   The meaning of this word (in English):
   climb

5. The second letter of the answer is *s*
   The meaning of this word (in English):
   dark

Exercise 3

1. i_t_rés
2. H_l_r
3. p_s_r
4. p_e_s_
5. c_m_r_b_r

Hints:

1. The second letter of the answer is *n*
   The meaning of this word (in English):
   interest
2. The second letter of the answer is *a*
   The meaning of this word (in English):
   pull
3. The second letter of the answer is *a*
   The meaning of this word (in English):
   spend
4. The second letter of the answer is *r*
   The meaning of this word (in English):
   press
5. The second letter of the answer is *o*
   The meaning of this word (in English):
   check

Exercise 4

1. l_n_a
2. síl_b_
3. l_n_
4. b_q_e
5. a_a_o

Hints:

1. The second letter of the answer is *e
   The meaning of this word (in English):
   slow

2. The second letter of the answer is *í*
   The meaning of this word (in English):
   syllable
3. The second letter of the answer is *u*
   The meaning of this word (in English):
   moon
4. The second letter of the answer is *u*
   The meaning of this word (in English):
   ship
5. The second letter of the answer is *b*
   The meaning of this word (in English): *down*

Exercise 5

1. m_e_t_a_
2. s_p_r_a_
3. t_p_
4. d_n_a
5. t_d_

Hints:

1. The second letter of the answer is *i*
   The meaning of this word (in English):
   while
2. The second letter of the answer is *o*
   The meaning of this word (in English):
   bear
3. The second letter of the answer is *i*
   The meaning of this word (in English):
   type
4. The second letter of the answer is *a*
   The meaning of this word (in English):
   dance
5. The second letter of the answer is *o*
   The meaning of this word (in English):
   whole

In this puzzle format, you still have to guess common Spanish words, but there is a twist.

Here are the key details of the format: your main clue contains the letters of the word you have to guess, but all the letters of that word are jumbled up.

You have to decode the clue by rearranging the letters so they make a meaningful word. Multiple hints (the first letter of the word, and the meaning of the word in English) are also provided.

Here are your puzzles:

Exercise 6

1. Mtaiolsen
2. Ididerc
3. Olad
4. Amigo
5. Aponrse

Hints:

1. The answer starts with the letter *a*
   The meaning of this word (in English): *food*
2. The answer starts with the letter *d*
   The meaning of this word (in English): *decide*
3. The answer starts with the letter *l*
   The meaning of this word (in English): *side*
4. The answer starts with the letter *a*
   The meaning of this word (in English): *friend*
5. The answer starts with the letter *p*
   The meaning of this word (in English): *person*

Exercise 7

1. Ridmenetar
2. Iinrmgaa
3. Oadldso
4. Rctana
5. Iscelpea

Hints:

1. The answer starts with the letter *d*
   The meaning of this word (in English):
   determine
2. The answer starts with the letter *i*
   The meaning of this word (in English):
   imagine
3. The answer starts with the letter *s*
   The meaning of this word (in English):
   soldier
4. The answer starts with the letter *c*
   The meaning of this word (in English):
   sing
5. The answer starts with the letter *e*
   The meaning of this word (in English):
   special

Exercise 8

1. Culoríc
2. Raoc
3. Ortrfa
4. Sascatnui
5. Dpíoa

Hints:

1. The answer starts with the letter *c*

The meaning of this word (in English):
circle

2. The answer starts with the letter *r*
   The meaning of this word (in English):
   rock

3. The answer starts with the letter *f*
   The meaning of this word (in English):
   rub

4. The answer starts with the letter *s*
   The meaning of this word (in English):
   substance

5. The answer starts with the letter *p*
   The meaning of this word (in English):
   could

Exercise 9

1. Anntoerdoc
2. Btou
3. Iarnlieogs
4. Savuntsiot
5. Alranz

Hints:

1. The answer starts with the letter *e*
   The meaning of this word (in English):
   found

2. The answer starts with the letter *t*
   The meaning of this word (in English):
   tube

3. The answer starts with the letter *o*
   The meaning of this word (in English):
   original

4. The answer starts with the letter *s*
   The meaning of this word (in English):
   noun

5. The answer starts with the letter *l*

The meaning of this word (in English):
throw

COMMON SPANISH WORDS

Colors—Los colores

- Red= Rojo
- Orange= Naranja
- Yellow= Amarillo
- Green= Verde
- Blue= Azul
- Purple= Púrpura
- Black= Negro
- White= Blanco
- Grey= Gris
- Brown= Marrón
- Pink= Rosa
- Clear= Transparente
- Golden= Dorado
- Silver= Plateado
- Sky blue= Celeste
- Cherry= Cereza
- Chocolate= chocolate
- Coffee= Café
- Emerald= Esmerelda
- Multi-colored= Multicolor
- Smokey= Humo
- Mauve= Malva
- Mustard= Mostaza
- Turquoise= Turquesa
- Violet= Violeta
- Dark= Oscuro
- Light= Claro
- Plaid= A cuadros
- Striped= Rayado

Examples:

1. The car is black= El auto es negro.
2. The bananas are Green= Los plátanos son verdes.
3. I need black pants= Necesito pantalones negros.

Numbers—Los números

- Zero= Cero
- One= Uno
- Two= Dos
- Three= Tres
- Four= Cuatro
- Five= Cinco
- Six= Seis
- Seven= Siete
- Eight= Ocho
- Nine= Nueve
- Ten= Diez
- Eleven= Once
- Twelve= Doce
- Thirteen= Trece
- Fourteen= Catorce
- Fifteen= Quince
- Sixteen= Dieciséis
- Seventeen= Diecisiete
- Eighteen= Dieciocho
- Nineteen= Diecinueve
- Twenty= Veinte
- Twenty-One= Veintiuno
- Twenty-Two= Veintidós
- Twenty-Three= Veintitrés
- Twenty-Four= Veinticuatro
- Twenty-Five= Veinticinco
- Twenty-Six= Veintiséis
- Twenty-Seven= Veintisiete

- Twenty-Eight= Veintiocho
- Twenty-Nine= Veintinueve
- Thirty= Treinta
- Thirty-One = Treinta y Uno
- Thirty-Two= Treinta y Dos
- Thirty-Three= Treinta y Tres
- Thirty-Four= Treinta y Cuatro
- Thirty-Five= Treinta y Cinco
- Thirty-Six= Treinta y Seis
- Thirty-Seven= Treinta y Siete
- Thirty-Eight= Treinta y Ocho
- Thirty-Nine= Treinta y Nueve
- Forty= Cuarenta
- Forty-One= Cuarenta y Uno
- Forty-Two= Cuarenta y Dos
- Forty-Three= Cuarenta y Tres
- Forty-Four= Cuarenta y Cuatro
- Forty-Five= Cuarenta y Cinco
- Forty-Six= Cuarenta y Seis
- Forty-Seven= Cuarenta y Siete
- Forty-Eight= Cuarenta y Ocho
- Forty-Nine= Cuarenta y Nueve
- Fifty= Cincuenta
- Fifty-One= Cincuenta y Uno
- Fifty-Two= Cincuenta y Dos
- Fifty-Three= Cincuenta y Tres
- Fifty-Four= Cincuenta y Cuatro
- Fifty-Five = Cincuenta y Cinco
- Fifty-Six= Cincuenta y Seis
- Fifty-Seven= Cincuenta y Siete
- Fifty-Eight= Cincuenta y Ocho
- Fifty-Nine= Cincuenta y Nueve
- Sixty= Sesenta
- Sixty-One= Sesenta y Uno
- Sixty-Two= Sesenta y Dos
- Sixty-Three= Sesenta y Tres
- Sixty-Four= Sesenta y Cuatro

- Sixty-Five= Sesenta y Cinco
- Sixty- Six= Sesenta y Seis
- Sixty-Seven= Sesenta y Siete
- Sixty-Eight= Sesenta y Ocho
- Sixty-Nine= Sesenta y Nueve
- Seventy= Setenta
- Seventy-One= Setenta y Uno
- Seventy-Two= Setenta y Dos
- Seventy-Three= Setenta y Tres
- Seventy-Four= Setenta y Cuatro
- Seventy-Five = Setenta y Cinco
- Seventy-Six= Setenta y Seis
- Seventy-Seven= Setenta y Siete
- Seventy-Eight= Setenta y Ocho
- Seventy-Nine= Setenta y Nueve
- Eighty= Ochenta
- Eighty-One= Ochenta y Uno
- Eighty-Two= Ochenta y Dos
- Eighty-Three= Ochenta y Tres
- Eighty-Four= Ochenta y Cuatro
- Eighty-Five= Ochenta y Cinco
- Eighty-Six= Ochenta y Seis
- Eighty-Seven= Ochenta y Siete
- Eighty-Eight= Ochenta y Ocho
- Eighty-Nine= Ochenta y Nueve
- Ninety= Noventa
- Ninety-One= Noventa y Uno
- Ninety-Two= Noventa y Dos
- Ninety-Three= Noventa y Tres
- Ninety-Four= Noventa y Cuatro
- Ninety-Five= Noventa y Cinco
- Ninety-Six= Noventa y Seis
- Ninety-Seven= Noventa y Siete
- Ninety-Eight= Noventa y Ocho
- Ninety-Nine= Noventa y Nueve
- One Hundred= Cien
- Two Hundred= Doscientos

- Three Hundred= Trescientos
- Four Hundred= Cuatrocientos
- Five Hundred= Quinientos
- Six Hundred= Seiscientos
- Seven Hundred= Setecientos
- Eight Hundred= Ochocientos
- Nine Hundred= Novecientos
- Thousand= Mil
- Thousand and one= Mil Uno
- Two Thousand= Dos Mil
- Two Thousand and Six= Dos Mil Seis
- Hundred Thousand= Cien Mil
- Million= Millón

Examples:

1. I am 37 years old= Tengo treinta y siete años.
2. It costs 200 dollars= Cuesta doscientos dólares.

Ordinals—Los ordinales

- 1st= Primero
- 2nd= Segundo
- 3rd= Tercero
- 4th= Cuarto
- 5th= Quinto
- 6th= Sexto
- 7th= Séptimo
- 8th= Octavo
- 9th= Noveno
- 10th= Décimo
- 11th= Undécimo
- 12th= Duodécimo
- 13th= Decimotercero
- 14th= Decimocuarto
- 15th= Decimotercero
- 16th= Decimosexto

- 17th= Decimoséptimo
- 18th= Decimoctavo
- 19th= Decimonoveno
- 20th= Vigésimo
- 21th= Vigésimo primero
- 30th= Trigésimo
- 33rd= Trigésimotercero
- 40th= Cuadragésimo
- 47th= Cuadragésimoséptimo
- 50th= Quincuagésimo
- 60th= Sexagésimo
- 70th= Septuagésimo
- 80th= Octogésimo
- 90th= Nonagésimo
- 100th= Centésimo
- 1000th= Milésimo
- Millonésimo= one millionth

Examples:

1. You are second in line= Eres segundo en la fila.
2. I am the 1st person= Yo soy la primera persona.
3. The 1st house= La primera casa.
4. She is attending the 2nd grade= Ella está en Segundo grado.

Days and Months - Los días y los meses

- Monday= Lunes
- Tuesday= Martes
- Wednesday= Miércoles
- Thursday= Jueves
- Friday= Viernes
- Saturday= Sábado
- Sunday= Domingo
- January= Enero
- February= Febrero
- March= Marzo

- April= Abril
- May= Mayo
- June= Junio
- July= Julio
- August= Agosto
- September= Setiembre
- October= Octubre
- November= Noviembre
- December= Diciembre
- The day before yesterday= Anteayer
- Yesterday= Ayer
- Today= Hoy
- Tomorrow= Mañana
- The day after tomorrow= Pasado mañana
- Dawn= Madrugada
- Midnight= Medianoche
- Noon= Mediodía
- Afternoon= Tarde
- Evening= Noche
- Century= El siglo
- Decade= La década
- Year= El año
- Month= El mes
- Week= La semana
- Day= El día

Examples:

1. Today is Tuesday= Hoy es martes.
2. The first day of the week is Monday= El primer día de la semana es el lunes.
3. We met in December= Nos conocimos en diciembre.

Seasons

- Spring= La primavera
- Summer= El verano
- Fall= El otoño

- Winter= El invierno

People—La gente

- Adolescent= Adolescente
- Baby= El bebé
- Boy= El chico
- Girl= La chica
- Children= Los niños
- Friend= El amigo
- Gentleman= El señor
- Lady= La señora
- Man= El hombre
- Old man= El anciano
- Old woman= La anciana
- People= La gente
- Woman= La mujer
- Young boy= El niño
- Young girl= La niña

Family and Relatives—La familia y los parientes

- Grandmother= La abuela
- Grandfather= El abuelo
- Married= Casado
- Sister-in-law= La cuñada
- Brother-in-law= El cuñado
- Divorced= Divorciado
- Twin= Gemelo
- Sister= La hermana
- Brother= El hermano
- Daughter= La hija
- Stepchild= El hijastro
- Son= El hijo
- Orphan= Huérfano
- Stepmother= La madrastra

- Mother= La madre
- Husband= Marido
- Wife, woman= Mujer
- Granddaughter= La nieta
- Grandchild, grandson= El nieto
- Daughter-in-law= La nuera
- Stepfather= El padrastro
- Father= El padre
- Parents= Los padres
- Cousin= El primo
- Niece= La sobrina
- Nephew= El sobrino
- Nephews and nieces= Los sobrinos
- Mother-in-law= La suegra
- Father-in-law= El suegro
- Aunt= La tía
- Uncle= El tío
- Uncles and aunts= Los tíos
- Widow= La viuda
- Widower= El viudo
- Son-in-law= El yerno
- Boyfriend= El novio
- Girlfriend= La novia
- Extended family= Parientes lejanos
- Great great grandfather= El tatarabuelo
- Great great grandmother= La tatarabuela
- Great grandfather= El bisabuelo
- Great grandmother= La bisabuela
- Grandparents= Los abuelos
- Grandchildren= Los nietos
- Grandson= El nieto
- Granddaughter= La nieta
- Great grandson= El bisnieto
- Great granddaughter= La bisnieta

Directions—Las direcciones

- Right= A la derecha
- Left= A la izquierda
- Straight ahead= Derecho
- At the corner= En la esquina
- North= Norte
- South= Sur
- East= Este
- West= Oeste
- Here= Aquí
- There= Allí

Example:

1. Turn right= Dobla a la derecha
2. Go straight ahead= Siga recto
3. Go west and then turn left= Ve al oeste y luego gira a la izquierda

Animals—Los animales

Farm Animals—Animales de granja

- Bull= Toro
- Cow= Vaca
- Chicken= Pollo
- Chick= Pollito
- Donkey= Burro
- Goat= Cabra
- Horse= Caballo
- Pig= Cerdo
- Rabbit= Conejo
- Sheep= Oveja
- Turkey= Pavo

Sea Animals—Animales del mar

- Crab= El cangrejo
- Dolphin= El delfín

- Shark= El tiburón
- Eel= La anguila
- Gray whale= La ballena gris
- Jellyfish= La medusa
- Killer whale= La orca
- Lobster= La langosta
- Manta ray= La mantarraya
- Octopus= El pulpo
- Oyster= La ostra
- Seal= La foca
- Turtle= La tortuga
- Sealion= El león marino
- Squid= El calamar
- Seahorse= El caballito de mar
- Starfish= La estrella de mar
- Seagull= La gaviota
- Carp= La carpa

Forest Animals—Animales del bosque

- Beaver= Castor
- Bird= Pájaro
- Boar= Jabalí
- Chameleon= Camaleón
- Cipmunk= Ardilla listada
- Deer= Ciervo
- Dove= Paloma
- Eagle= Águila
- Falcon= Halcón
- Goose= Oca
- Snake= Serpiente
- Hawk= Halcón
- Hummingbird= Colibrí
- Koala= Koala
- Mouse= Ratón
- Rat= Rata
- Owl= Búho

- Racoon= Mapache
- Skunk= Mofeta
- Squirrel= Ardilla
- Armadillo= Armadillo
- Bat= Murciélago
- Bear= Oso
- Weasel= Comadreja
- Moose= Alce
- Pheasant= Faisán
- Tick= Garrapata
- Lizard= Lagarto
- Wolf= Lobo
- Fox= Zorro
- Rooster= Gallo
- Hen= Gallina
- Starling= Estornino
- Hedgehog= Erizo
- Raven= Cuervo
- Insects= Insectos
- Butterfly= Mariposa
- Dragonfly= Libélula
- Fly= Mosca
- Grasshopper= Saltamontes
- Ladybug= Mariquita
- Mosquito= Mosquito
- Moth= Polilla
- Praying mantis= Mantis religiosa
- Snail= Caracol
- Scorpion= Escorpión
- Spider= Araña
- Hornet= Avispa
- Ant= Hormiga
- Bee= Abeja
- Beetle= Escarabajo
- Stag beetle= Ciervo volante
- Bed bug= Chinche
- Cockroach= Cucaracha

- Cricket= Grillo

Jungle Animals—Animales de la jungla

- Ape= Mono
- Baboon= Babuino
- Cobra= Cobra
- Chimpanzee= Chimpancé
- Gorilla= Gorila
- Panda bear= Oso panda
- Sloth= Perezoso
- Parrot= Loro
- Tiger= Tigre

House Pets—Mascotas

- Goldfish= Pez de color oro
- Hámster= Hámster
- Parrot= Loro
- Cat= Gato
- Dog= Perro
- Ferret= Hurón
- Guinea pig= Cobaya

Animals of the Savannah—Los Animales de la sabana

- Buffalo= Búfalo
- Cheetah= Guepardo
- Elephant= Elefante
- Giraffe= Jirafa
- Hyena= Hiena
- Kangaroo= Canguro
- Ostrich= Avestruz
- Rhinocerous= Rinoceronte
- Zebra= Cebra
- Antelope= Antílope
- Jackal= Chacal

Swamp Animals—Los animales de los pantanos

- Flamingo= Flamenco
- Frog= Rana
- Hippopotamus= Hipopótamo
- Crocodile= Cocodrilo
- Duck= Pato

Animals of the Desert and Arctic—Los animales del desierto y del arctico

- Camel= Camello
- Penguin= Pingüino
- Polar bear= Oso polar
- Seal= Foca

Examples:

1. The giraffe is white and Brown= La jirafa es blanca y cafe
2. The bird is Green= El pájaro es verde
3. The dog likes to bark= Al perro le gusta ladrar
4. What a ginormous snake!= ¡Qué serpiente más enorme!
5. I love cats= Amo a los gatos
6. I see a bear!= Veo un oso

Adjectives and Attributes—Los adjetivos y atributos

- Open= Abierto
- Boring= Aburrido
- Lucky= Afortunado
- Pleasant= Agradable
- High= Alto
- Tall= Alto
- Friendly= Amable

- Bitter= Amargo
- Wide= Ancho
- Mean= Antipático
- Tight= Apretado
- Athletic= Atlético
- Adventurous= Atrevido
- Low= Bajo
- Cheap= Barato
- Soft= Blando
- Pretty= Bonito
- Good= Bueno
- Hot= Caliente
- Funny= Cómico
- Expensive= Caro
- Near= Cerca
- Closed= Cerrado
- Correct= Correcto
- Short= Corto
- Curious= Curioso
- Thin= Delgado
- Weak= Débil
- Unlucky= Desafortunado
- Unpleasant= Desagradable
- Unorganized= Desordenado
- Difficult= Difícil
- Fun= Divertido
- Sweet= Dulce
- Hard= Duro
- Polite= Educado
- Excited= Emocionado
- Angry= Enojado
- Wrong= Equivocado
- Narrow=Estrecho
- Stupid= Estúpido
- Excellent= Excelente
- Easy= Fácil
- False= Falso

- Happy= Feliz
- Ugly= Feo
- Thin= Fino
- Cold= Frío
- Strong= Fuerte
- Generous= Generoso
- Fat= Gordo
- Big= Grande
- Thick= Grueso
- Beautiful= Hermoso
- Loose= Holgado
- Important= Importante
- Intelligent= Inteligente
- Interesting= Interesante
- Useless= Inútil
- Young= Joven
- Long= Largo
- Far= Lejos
- Slow= Lento
- Light= Ligero
- Clean= Limpio
- Full= Lleno
- Crazy= Loco
- Bright= Luminoso
- Rude= mal educado
- Bad= Malo
- Wet= Mojado
- Many=- Muchos
- Dead= Muerto
- New= Nuevo
- Organized= Ordenado
- Dark= Oscuro
- Patient= Paciente
- Dangerous= Peligroso
- Small= Pequeño
- Lazy= Perezoso
- Heavy= Pesado

- Short= Corto
- Poor= Pobre
- Few= Pocos
- Popular= popular
- Worried= Preocupado
- Deep= Profundo
- Cautious= Prudente
- Fast= Rápido
- Relaxed= Relajado
- Rich= Rico
- Loud= Ruidoso
- Dry= Seco
- Safe= Seguro
- Unimportant= Sin importancia
- Sincere= Sincero
- Dirty= Sucio
- Shallow= Superficial
- Stingy= Tacaño
- Late= Tarde
- Early= Temprano
- Terrible= Terrible
- Shy= Tímido
- Hard working= Trabajador
- Quiet= Tranquilo
- Sad= Triste
- Useful= Útil
- Empty= Vacío
- True= Verdadero
- Old= Viejo
- Alive= Vivo

Example:

1. The woman is blonde= La señora es rubia.
2. My mom is very intelligent= Mi mamá es muy inteligente
3. My stepfather is very kind= Mi padrastro es muy amable.
4. You are friendly and fun= Eres amistoso y divertido

5. He is sad= Él está triste
6. She is a hard worker= Ella es una trabajadora ardua
7. My cup is empty= Mi taza está vacía

PERSONAL PRONOUNS

Personal pronouns in Spanish with their English counterparts.

- Yo= I
- Tú (or vos)/usted= You
- Él= He
- Ella= She
- Nosotros (masc.) Nosotras (fem.)= We
- Vosotros (masc.)/Vosotras (fem.) Ustedes= You
- Ellos (masc.)/Ellas (fem.)= They

"Tú"/"Vos" or "Usted?" Tú and vos are merely geographical variants. It is out of the scope of this book to cover the peculiarities of their use. You should simply know that they are exact equivalents but usually take different verb forms (conjugations).

What is, however, interesting to us is the difference between tú (or vos) and usted. Even when some countries prefer to use 'usted' extensively and some others scarcely use it, there is a general rule.

"Usted" is the formal way of address in Spanish. Again, considerations of formality and informality are subject to social and geographical variables.

Still, usted is generally used when the other person is a stranger, when they are older (especially if they are not an acquaintance), or when they are superior in hierarchy. For example, we might say to a stranger in the street, "¿Puede usted decirme la hora, por favor?"' (Literally, "May you tell me the time, please?" Meaning, "What time is it, please?"), and to a friend, "Me dices la hora?" (Literally, "Will you tell me the time?")

Dropping the Pronoun

Because Spanish has many more verb forms than English, it is possible (and highly advisable) to drop the pronoun at the beginning of the sentence. The addition of the pronoun will probably change the implication of the sentence if it is not obligatory in the context.

Let us see some examples:

- Eres mi amigo. (You are my friend, no implication).
- Tú eres mi amigo (Either emphatic or expressing contrast as in, "and she isn't").
- No vas a la fiesta. (You are not going to the party, no implication)
- Tú no vas a la fiesta (Possibly meaning that the person is not allowed to go, or I don't want them to go)

Hence, the lesson is this. Do away with the pronoun unless you have a clear reason to use it. Clear reasons to use the pronoun are Potential Ambiguity. Imagine a setting where there are three people. You need to address one of them using "usted." It so happens that the conjugation for "usted" is normally the same as for "él/ella." That context calls for the addition of the pronoun to clarify to whom you are referring.

- **Wrong:** ¿Va a la fiesta? (Ambiguous: Are you/is he going to the party?
- **Right:** ¿Él va a la fiesta? (Is he going to the party)
- ¿Usted va a la fiesta? (Are you (formal) going to the party?)

Emphasis

- ¡Tú sí que me tienes harta! (Literally, "You do make me fed up!" meaning "I'm so fed up with you!")
- Tú eres muy inteligente. No les hagas caso (You are very intelligent. Don't listen to them)

Contrast

- Te digo que tú no vas. Voy yo. (I'm telling you that you are not going. I'm going)
- Él me lo dijo. Tú me lo ocultaste. (He told me. You hid it from me)

120

"Vosotros" or "Ustedes"?

A word of comfort: whichever you use, you will be understood. However, the use of "vosotros" is mainly restricted to Spain as an informal way of address to two or more people (the plural of "tú"). Elsewhere, the most likely pronoun is 'ustedes' (which is restricted to formal contexts in Spain).

Practice Text

Por fin, el domingo, Marisa encuentra al párroco. Le preguntasi hay algún registro de la muerte de un hombre llamado Alejandro Torres. Él no le responde, sino que la invita a sentarse.

—*Alejandro era muy querido por aquí. Sé que estuvo preguntando por él en la estación de policía. ¿Lo conocía usted?*

— En realidad, no…

— *¡Discúlpeme! Qué descortés. Olvidé preguntarle su nombre.*

—Marisa Torres.

-El viejo sacerdote suspira-

— *¿Usted tiene con él algún parentesco?*

—Yo… No lo sé.

—*Mire, él era un buen hombre…*

—Sé lo que le dijo a usted. -interrumpió Marisa-. No se preocupe; sé que usted no puede decirme nada.

—*¿Qué es lo que sabe?

—Él era mi padre. -Ella no estaba segura de lo que decía, pero tenía que conseguir información de algún modo. Era una estrategia un poco sucia, pero no tenía alternativa-. Dicen por aquí que era muy devoto. Sé que usted escuchó su confesión. Más de una vez.

-Una vez más, él suspira, temblando de nervios esta vez-

—*Mire…*

—No, no me diga nada. Basta con su silencio.

—*¿Puedo ayudarla con algo?*

—Muchas gracias. Usted no puede ayudarme.

Translation:

Finally, on Sunday, Marisa finds the parishioner. She asks him if there is any record of the decease of a man called Alejandro Torres. He doesn't reply but invites her to take a seat.

"Alejandro was very appreciated around here. I know you have been asking about him at the police station. Did you know him?"

"In fact, no."

"Excuse me! How uncourteous. I forgot to ask you your name."

"Marisa Torres."

-The old priest sights.-

"Are you related to him?"

"I… I don't know."

"Look, he was a good man…"

"I know what he told you," interrupted Marisa. "Don't worry—I know you can't tell me anything."

"What do you know?"

"He was my father." She wasn't sure of what she was saying, but she had to get information somehow. It was a bit of a dirty strategy, but she had no alternative. "They say here that he was very devout. I know you heard his confession. More than once."

-Once again, he sighs, trembling with nerves this time.-

"Look…"

"No, don't say anything. Your silence is enough."

"May I help you with anything?"

"Thank you very much. No, you can't help me."

Practice!

1. Go back to the text. Underline the personal pronouns with red.
2. Why are they using "usted" rather than "tú"?
3. Go back to the text again. With the help of the translation, underline the sentences with dropped pronouns. Hint: a sentence always contains a verb.

Key:

Points 1 and 3:

Por fin, el domingo, Marisa encuentra al párroco. Le pregunta si hay algún registro de la muerte de un hombre llamado Alejandro Torres. Él no le responde, sino que la invita a sentarse.

—*Alejandro era muy querido por aquí. Sé que estuvo preguntando por él en la estación de policía. ¿Lo conocíausted?

—En realidad, no…

—*¡Discúlpeme! Qué descortés. Olvidé preguntarle su nombre.*

—Marisa Torres.

-El viejo sacerdote suspira-

—*¿Usted tiene con él algún parentesco?*

—Yo… No lo sé.

—*Mire, él era un buen hombre…*

—Sé lo que le dijo a usted. -interrumpió Marisa-. No se preocupe; sé que usted no puede decirme nada.

—*¿Qué es lo que sabe?*

—Él era mi padre. -Ella no estaba segura de lo que decía, pero tenía que conseguir información de algún modo. Era una estrategia un poco sucia, pero no tenía alternativa-. Dicen por aquí que era muy devoto. Sé que usted escuchó su confesión. Más de una vez.

-Una vez más, él suspira, temblando de nervios estavez-

—*Mire…*

—No, no me diga nada. Basta con su silencio.

—*¿Puedo ayudarla con algo?*

—Muchas gracias. Usted no puede ayudarme.

Point 2:

Marisa is using "usted" for three reasons—the priest is a stranger, he is old, and he has a higher status or hierarchy. The priest is using "usted" for one main reason: he doesn't know Marisa. On the other hand, it is quite possible that, in a conversation with an adult, not even a senior priest would use "tú" since doing so would emphasize the difference in status.

BASIC VERBS

Customary—AR Verbs

L ikewise, in English, Spanish action words are either customary or sporadic.

There are three sorts of ordinary action words in Spanish: those closure in—AR, those completion in—ER, and those consummation in—IR.

Instances of the infinitives of action words in these three classes are:

- Hablar= to talk
- Comer= to eat
- Vivir= to live

We should focus on the principal bunch—standard action words finishing off with—AR, for example, hablar—and figure out how to form it in the Present Indicative Tense.

If you somehow managed to form the action word to express in the Present Tense in English, it would be this way:

- To talk (infinitive)
- I talk
- You (singular) talk
- He/she/it talks
- We talk
- You (plural) talk
- They talk

You've as of now found out about Spanish Personal Pronouns and how to utilize them.

Presently, you simply need to know the action word endings.

The Present Tense of hablar—and all customary action words finishing off with—AR—would be as per the following:

Singular:

- Yo hablo= I talk
- Tú hablas= you (natural) talk
- Él/ella/ habla= he/she/you (formal) talk/s

Plural:

- Nosotros/as hablamos= we talk
- Vosotros/as habláis= you (natural) talk
- Ellos/ellas/ hablan= they/you (formal) speak

You form ordinary—AR action words by taking the infinitive (ie to talk) which, for this situation is hablar furthermore, eliminating the—AR finishing off with a request to get the root, which would be: habl (= hablar-ar)

To this root, you then, at that point add the accompanying endings:

- o
- as
- a
- amos
- áis
- an

In spite of the fact that we've utilized hablar as our model, a similar guideline would apply to any standard action words which end in—AR.

Customary—ER Verbs

How about we currently take a gander at customary action words finishing off with—ER, taking comer (to eat) as the model, and figure out how to form that in the Present Tense.

Above all else, we'll take the infinitive (to eat)—comer—and discover the foundation of the action word by knocking off the—ER finishing: Com (= comer-er)

To this root, add the endings for the Present Tense of standard - ER action words, as follows:

- o
- es
- e
- emos
- éis
- en

Thusly, the Present Indicative Tense of the action word comer would be:

Singular:

- Yo como= I eat
- Tú comes= you (recognizable) eat
- Él/ella/ come= he/she/you (formal) eat/s

Plural:

- Nosotros/as comemos= we eat
- Vosotros/as coméis= you (recognizable) eat
- Ellos/ellas/ comen= they/you (formal) eat

These equivalent endings don't simply apply to comer however to all customary—ER action words.

Normal—IR Verbs

You realize how to form normal—AR and—ER action words in the Present Indicative Tense. Presently how about we take a gander at the last gathering—action words finishing off with—IR. We'll take vivir (to live) as our model.

Indeed, discover the base of the action word by eliminating its consummation which, for this situation, will leave you with: viv (=vivir-ir)

Then, at that point, contingent upon the individual you wish to address, add the endings:

- o
- es
- e
- imos
- ís
- en

All in all, the full Present Tense of the action word vivir would be:

Singular:

- Yo vivo= I live
- Tú vives= you (natural) live
- Él/ella/ vive= he/she/you (formal) live/s

Plural:

- Nosotros/as vivimos= we live
- Vosotros/as vivís= you (natural) live
- Ellos/ellas/ viven= They/you (formal) live

Again, the above rules apply to any normal action word finishing off with—IR.

You currently realize how to decay all standard action words in the Present Indicative Tense!

Utilizing Spanish Verbs

1. Because action word endings shift a great deal more in Spanish than they do in English, it's not generally important to utilize the Personal Pronoun. For instance, you could say:
   a. Hablas español= you communicate in Spanish

b. Como mucha fruta= I eat a lot of organic product

c. Vivimos en España= we live in Spain

Nothing unless there are other options sentences needs Personal Pronouns since it's conspicuous from the completion of the action word who the subject is.

2. It is, be that as it may, some of the time important to remember the Personal Pronoun for the request to explain what its identity is we're discussing, as on account of vive. Whenever left all alone, it could mean he/she daily routines or you experience.

   In this manner, you'd incorporate the Personal Pronoun:
   a. Él vive
   b. Ella vive
   c. Ellos viven

In any case, frequently in the discussion, it's undeniable who the subject is and, if so, the Personal Pronoun is excluded.

3. Sometimes, Personal Pronouns are incorporated simply to add accentuation:
   a. Yo como carne y tú comes pescado= I eat meat and you eat fish
4. When utilizing two action words in succession, the first is formed, and the second comes in the infinitive:
   a. Deseo comer paella= I wish to eat paella
5. In Spanish, in the event that you wish to suggest invalidation, you basically place the word no before the action word:
   a. El niño no come= the kid doesn't eat
   b. No hablo español= I don't communicate in Spanish
6. If you wish to utilize the inquisitive frame and pose an inquiry, you should make sure to put a switched question mark toward the start of the sentence. On the off chance that utilizing the action word alone, without the Personal Pronoun, this is all you need to do to shape an inquiry in the Present Tense. For instance:
   a. ¿Hablas español? = Do you communicate in Spanish?
      While including the Personal Pronoun, you simply turn around the typical situation of the action word and the pronoun. For instance:
   b. ¿Habla el/ella español? = Do you speak Spanish?

As opposed to el/ella habla español, which would mean you speak Spanish.

Common Regular—AR Verbs

As you now know how to decline the Present Tense of regular -AR verbs, here's a list of 25 for you to practice with them!

- Alquilar= to rent
- Ayudar= to help
- Bailar= to dance
- Buscar= to look for
- Comprar= to buy
- Contestar= to answer
- Dejar= to allow, to leave
- Entrar (in) = to enter (into)
- Enviar= to send
- Esperar= to hope, to wait for
- Ganar= to earn, to win
- Gastar= to spend
- Llegar= to arrive
- Llevar= to wear, to carry
- Mirar= to look at, to watch
- Necesitar= to need
- Olvidar= to forget
- Pagar= to pay, to pay for
- Preguntar= to ask
- Preparer= to prepare
- Regresar= to return
- Tomar= to take, to drink
- Trabajar= to work
- Viajar= to travel
- Visitar= to visit

Common Regular—ER Verbs

And, here's a list of 25 regular—ER verbs with which to experiment!

- Aprender= to learn
- Beber= to drink
- Ceder= to give in
- Comer= to eat
- Cometer= to commit
- Comprender= to understand
- Correr= to run
- Creer= to believe
- Deber= to have to, to owe
- Depender (de)= to depend (on)
- Esconder= to hide
- Exceder= to exceed
- Leer= to read
- Meter (en)= to put (into)
- Ofender= to offend
- Poseer= to possess
- Proceder= to procede, to come from
- Prometer= to promise
- Proveer= to provide
- Responder= to reply
- Romper= to break
- Sorprender= to surprise
- Temer= to fear
- Vender= to sell

Common Regular—IR Verbs

To finish off with, here you have 25 regular—IR verbs.

- Abrir= to open
- Admitir= to admit
- Asistir (a)= to attend (to)
- Confundir= to confuse
- Cubrir= to cover
- Decidir= to decide
- Describir= to describe
- Descubrir= to discover

- Discutir= to argue, to discuss
- Dividir= to divide
- Escribir= to write
- Evadir= to evade
- Existir= to exist
- Fundir= to melt
- Hundir= to sink
- Imprimir= to print
- Ocurrir= to happen
- Omitir= to omit
- Partir= to leave, to divide
- Permitir= to allow, to permit
- Recibir= to receive
- Subir= to go up, to come up
- Unir= to unite
- Vivir= to live

In the following exercises, you have to complete either the conjugated verb or the corresponding pronoun:

Example: I am Anaś best friend= soy la mejor amiga de Ana

1. You are a great boss= Usted … un gran jefe
2. He is a very smart boy= Él … un muchacho muy inteligente
3. We are the best= ……… los mejores
4. You guys are always fighting= Ustedes ……… siempre peleando.
5. They are the greatest scientists in their generation= ……… son las mejores científicas de su generación
6. I'm tired= ………cansado
7. You are prettier each day= ……… más lindo cada día
8. She's sad= ……… está triste
9. We are in danger= ……… en peligro
10. You are crazy= Vosotros ……… locos
11. They are coming= ……… están viniendo
12. I'm cold= ……… frío
13. Do you have a lighter? = ¿……… un encendedor?
14. He's afraid= ……… miedo

15. We have what it takes= Nosotros ……… lo necesario
16. I'm OK, but you always have a problema= Yo estoy bien, pero ……… Tienen siempre algún problema
17. They have a secret= Ellas ……… un secreto
18. I live alone= ……… solo
19. We live two blocks away= ……… a dos cuadras
20. You say she's lying? = ¿……… que ella está mintiendo?
21. They say it's too late= Ellos ……… que es demasiado tarde
22. I'm going to ask you to leave= ……… a pedirte que te marches
23. Let's go dancing! = ¡……… a bailar!
24. I do what I can= ……… lo que puedo
25. You do the right thing= ……… hace lo correcto
26. We do everything! = ¡Nosotros ……… todo!
27. I love you= Te ………
28. We love Peruvian food= ……… la comida peruana
29. I can't go= No ……… ir
30. He sees what's going on= Él ……… lo que sucede
31. I give you everything I have= Yo te ……… todo lo que tengo
32. We give our lives for art= ……… nuestras vidas por el arte
33. I want to eat something spicy= ……… comer algo picante
34. Do you want to dance with me? = ¿……… bailar conmigo?
35. They want to travel= Ellas ……… Viajar

GREETINGS AND BASIC VOCABULARY

Era un día como cualquier otro para Juan. Juan es un muchacho alto, de cabello corto y de tez muy blanca. A Juan no le gusta levantarse temprano pero tiene que hacerlo, ya que él tiene que ir a la escuela. Sus padres siempre lo animan a ser puntual y responsable, pero Juan a veces no los escucha. Bostezando y estirándose, se sienta en la cama. Unos instantes después, él baja las escaleras hacia el baño para tomar una ducha, cuando de repente ve a su madre.

La mamá de Juan se levanta mucho más temprano que Juan. Ella va a trabajar a las 10 de la mañana, pero ella se levanta más temprano para tener listo el desayuno. El abuelo de Juan también se levanta temprano. Los fines de semana, cuando Juan no va a estudiar, él ayuda en la cocina a hacer el desayuno. Hoy día Juan tiene que ir a estudiar.

"¡Buenos días, hijo!" – Dice su mamá con voz muy alta. – "! Me alegro que te hayas levantado a tiempo!

"¡Buenos días, mamá! – responde Juan.

"El desayuno ya está listo en la mesa" – Anuncia su mamá.

"Gracias, pero tomaré una ducha primero"

Juan camina hacia el baño. El baño de la casa se encuentra en el segundo piso y el dormitorio de Juan se encuentra en el tercer piso. Cuando Juan finalmente llega al baño, él intenta abrir la puerta. Pero Juan no se había dado cuenta que la luz del baño estaba encendida y que también había ruidos que salían del baño. Eran ruidos familiares, como la de una voz cantando.

Era la hermana de Juan que había entrado a tomarse una ducha mucho antes de que Juan se levantara.

La hermana de Juan se llama Luisa. Luisa es una muchacha joven. Ella es mayor que Juan por tres años. Ambos asisten a la misma escuela, pero Luisa está en tres grados más adelante que Juan.

"¿Vas a tardar?" – Juan pregunta a su hermana.

Pero Juan no escucha ninguna respuesta. Tal parece que su hermana no lo puede escuchar. Juan puede escuchar que hay música que viene dentro del baño. La hermana de Juan trajo la radio al baño. Eso puede ser peligroso. La hermana de Juan tiene una pequeña radio en su habitación que ella puede llevar a cualquier lugar. Es por eso que ella no puede escucharlo. Entonces Juan decide tocar la puerta del baño con fuerza y pregunta una vez más:

"¿Cuánto tiempo vas a estar en el baño? Yo también quiero tomar una ducha"

Finalmente su hermana responde:

"Juan, dame unos 15 minutos más"

"¡¿15 minutos?! ¡Pero no puedo esperar 15 minutos, se me va hacer muy tarde para la escuela!" – dice Juan.

Juan no tiene otra opción más que esperar a que su hermana salga del baño antes que sea muy tarde para la escuela. Pero Juan sabe muy bien que, en ocasiones, su hermana toma una ducha por más de 15 minutos.

Su hermana puede llegar tarde a la escuela pero tal parece que eso no le importa. Sus padres le han dicho ya varias veces que ella debe tomar una ducha en sólo 10 minutos. En ocasiones, su novio viene a recogerla. Tal vez por eso ella se está tomando más tiempo de lo usual. Normalmente, cuando su novio viene a recogerla, ellos van a ala escuela en el auto de su novio. De esa manera, ellos llegan rápido a la escuela.

Juan decide sentarse en las escaleras a esperar a que su hermana acabe de bañarse. Mientras Juan está sentado esperando por su hermana, él escucha la voz de su papá que le dice:

"Tendrás que irte a la escuela sin ducharte hoy día, hijo"

"¡Buenos días, papá!" – dice Juan.

"Felizmente, yo ya tomé una ducha. ¿Por qué no vas a cambiarte de ropa y desayunas?"

"Pero papá, yo quería tomar una ducha primero" – Se queja Juan

"Tendrás que esperar a tu hermana, entonces" – dice jocosamente el papá de Juan.

Es obvio que Juan tendrá que ir a la escuela sin ducharse. Juan no está acostumbrado a ir a la escuela sin ducharse. Derrotado, Juan sube a su habitación, se cambia de ropa y luego baja las escaleras nuevamente para ir al comedor dónde su desayuno le espera. Es un desayuno que a él le encanta. Avena con cereal y gofres con mucha miel.

Su mamá sabe cómo levantarle el ánimo. Gofres es el desayuno favorito de Juan. A Juan le gusta tanto los gofres que en ocasiones él ha pedido a su mamá que ponga gofres en su lonchera. Ahora, en el desayuno, Juan le pide que ponga bastante miel a los gofres.

"Buenos días, Juan" – dice la abuela de Juan.

"Buenos días, abuela" – responde Juan – ¡Muchas gracias por los gofres, mamá, son mis favoritos!

"De nada, hijo" – responde su mamá.

Juan come tan rápido como puede su desayuno y se alista para ir a la escuela. Él sabe que si no llega temprano, puede meterse en problemas.

Pero no se preocupa mucho ya que hoy día su papá lo llevará en su auto.

El auto que su papá tiene es uno nuevo. A Juan le parece muy bonito el carro de su papá. Su papá compró ese auto hace sólo unos meses. Juan también sueña con comprarse un auto cuando él crezca. Pero antes de eso, él tiene que aprender a conducir. Todo eso es lo que piensa mientras toma su desayuno.

Después de unos minutos, su mamá le dice que se apure porque puede llegar tarde.

"Ya terminé, mamá"

"Entonces entra al auto de tu papá ya" – responde la mamá de Juan.

Juan sale corriendo del comedor. Sale tan rápido que se olvida su lonchera.

Pero felizmente, su mamá le avisa y Juan regresa para coger su lonchera.

Con un beso, se despide de su mamá y de su abuela.

"Adiós, mamá"

"Adiós, hijo, pórtate bien" – responde su mamá

"Nos vemos luego" – grita su abuela

"Entra al auto, hijo" – le dice su papá.

"Ahí voy" – dice Juan

Juan abre la puerta, entra al auto, se abrocha el cinturón y se pone cómodo.

Su papá hace lo mismo pero además pone música. Juan conoce muy bien esa canción. Es una canción que el papá de Juan siempre pone cuando va a trabajar.

"Sube el volumen, papá"

"Claro, hijo"

A Juan también le gusta mucho la canción, por eso le dice a su papá que suba el volumen. Ir en el auto de su papá es también algo que le encanta Juan.

Desde que él era pequeño, su papá llevaba a toda la familia de paseo a la playa en el auto. Hoy día, él no está en camino a la playa. Lo mejor de todo es que cuando él va a la escuela en al auto de su papá, el viaje no toma más de 20 minutos, lo que asegura que Juan llegará no sólo a tiempo a la escuela, pero también mucho más temprano que sus compañeros.

La escuela a la que Juan va es una escuela muy grande. La escuela también es antigua. En la escuela de Juan, los profesores enseñan muy bien y a Juan le gusta ir a esa escuela. Él tiene muchos amigos en esta escuela. Una de las cosas que a Juan le gusta de esta escuela es que hay bastantes cosas que hacer, tiene un campo de futbol enorme y sus amigos siempre le ayudan con su tarea si él necesita tarea.

Finalmente, Juan y su papá llegan a la escuela. Su papá lo dejaen la escuela pero antes le dice:

"¡Hasta pronto, hijo! ¡Nos vemos en la casa!"

A lo que Juan responde: "¿Vendrás a recogerme después de clases?"

"No podré, hijo. ¿Puedes tomar el bus?" – responde su papá.

"Claro, papá" – dice Juan.

"¿Tienes suficiente para el pasaje de bus?" – pregunta el papá de Juan.

"Sí, mi mamá me dio dinero para el bus"

Juan se despide de su papá y entra a la escuela. Como era de esperarse, no hay muchos alumnos aún, pero Juan sabe que pronto sus compañeros de clase llegarán. Él sabe que será un día divertido en la escuela.

La hora de entrada en la escuela de Juan es a las 8:30 de la mañana. Juan llegó hoy día media hora antes de la hora de entrada. Normalmente, no hay nadie a esa hora más que algunos profesores y a veces, algunos alumnos que les gusta llegar temprano. Juan tiene toda la escuela para él. Mientras él espera a que las clases comiencen, él se pone a jugar en el campo de fútbol.

De repente, él ve una figura que viene de adentro de la escuela.

"Juan, ¿qué haces aquí tan temprano?"

Juan escucha una voz que viene desde dentro de la escuela. Es su mejor amigo, Andrés.

"Vine en el auto de mi papá y él me dejó aquí en la escuela" – responde Juan

"¿Quieres venir a jugar conmigo mientras esperamos a los demás?" – le dice Andrés

"Claro, ¡Vamos ya!"

Resumen de la historia:

Un muchacho de 14 años llamado Juan empieza su día queriendo tomar una ducha pero se da cuenta que su hermana está en baño y tomará demasiado tiempo, así que decide salir a la escuela sin tomarse una ducha. Después del desayuno, Juan sube al auto de papá. El viaje en el auto de su papá es tan rápido que Juan llega a la escuela mucho antes que sus otros compañeros de clase. Finalmente, él escucha a un compañero llamándolo, por lo que Juan entra a jugar con él.

Summary of the story:

A 14-year-old boy called Juan starts his day wanting to have a shower but he realizes that his sister is in the bathroom and will take a long time, so he decides to go to school without taking a shower. After breakfast, Juan gets into his father's car. The trip in his dad's car is so fast that Juan arrives at school way earlier than his other classmates. Finally, he hears one of his classmates calling him, so Juan enters to play with him.

- Día= day
- Como cualquier otro= Like any other
- Muchacho= Boy
- Alto= Tall
- Cabello= Hair
- Corto= Short
- Tez= Skin
- Blanca= White
- Gusta= Like

- Levantarse= Get up
- Temprano= Early
- Escuela= School
- Padres= Parents
- Siempre= Always
- Puntual= Punctual
- Responsable= Responsible
- Escucha= Listen
- Bostezando= Yawning
- Estirándose= Stretching
- Cama= Bed
- Baja= Go down
- Escaleras= Stairs
- Baño= Bathroom
- Tomar una ducha= Take a shower
- De repente= Suddenly
- Buenos días= Good morning
- Hijo= Son
- Voz= Voice
- Alta= High
- Me alegro= I'm glad
- A tiempo= On-time
- Mamá= Mother
- Responde= Answers
- Desayuno= Breakfast
- Listo= Ready
- Mesa= Table
- Anuncia= Announces
- Gracias= Thank you
- Primero= First
- Dado cuenta= Realized
- Luz= Light
- Baño= Bathroom
- Encendida= On
- Había= There were
- Ruidos= Noises
- Familiares= Familiar

- Cantando= Singing
- Hermana= Sister
- Tardar= Take long
- Pregunta= Ask
- Respuesta= Answer
- Puede= Can
- Tocar la puerta= Knock on the door
- Una vez más= One more time
- Cuánto tiempo= How long
- También= Also
- Quiero= Want
- Dame= Give me
- Minutos= Minutes
- Esperar= Wait
- Opción= Option
- Papá= Dad
- Felizmente= Thankfully
- Cambiarte= Change
- Ropa= Clothe
- Desayunas= Have breakfast
- Queja= Complain
- Jocosamente= Jokingly
- Obvio= Obvious
- Acostumbrado= Used to
- Derrotado= Defeated
- Habitación= Bedroom
- Nuevamente= Again
- Comedor= Dining room
- Encanta= Love
- Avena= Oatmeal
- Cereal= Cereal
- Gofres= Waffles
- Mucha= A lot
-

HISTORY OF SPAIN

A t a time as unclear as when the Phoenicians landed there, the Iberians and Celts invaded Spain. The latter founded Gades (Cadiz) there, which was the warehouse to exploit the gold and silver mines for all the colonies they produced in Bétique. The Greeks visited the eastern coast, where only a small number of permanent establishments were founded. The Carthaginians, a people descending from the Phoenicians, extended their rule over much of the country; but the Romans, who completed their conquest by taking Gades in 206 BC, dispossessed them. JC, And until the fifth century AD, masters persisted, rendering Spain a province called Hispania.

Spain endured a fate close to that of other countries under Roman rule when the Roman Empire collapsed. While Gallo-Roman rule was replaced by that of three Germanic peoples from the Rhine to the Pyrenees: the Franks, the Burgundians, and the Visigoths, in the south of the Pyrenees, the Roman control was replaced by that of the Suevi, the Vandals, and the Alans, who conquered it in 409. In 585, Leovigilde, King of the Visigoths, destroyed the kingdom established by the Suevi in Galicia, Lusitania, and Bétique. The Vandals remained in Baetica for just a short time and went to Africa. The Alans, some of whom had pursued the Vandals of Africa, succumbed to the blows of Wallia, king of the Visigoths, in 418.

Present in Spain from 415 to restore Roman authority there, the Visigoths, under their kings Theodoric II, 453–466, and Euric, 466–484, made themselves masters of the land. The latter is the author, under the name Fuero Juzgo, of the compilation of laws called Forum Judicum, which King Ferdinand translated into Castilian. The Visigoths had arrived in Spain, but their King Recarède's conversion to Catholicism in 587 decided the entire nation's conversion. The renowned councils of Toledo and the teachings of the Bishops of Seville, Saint Leander, and his companion, Saint Isidore, made a powerful contribution to the establishment in the nation of this Christian religion. The Visigoth monarchy, whose seat was established in Toulouse in 419, was moved to Narbonne in 508 and Toledo in 512. (Spain in the middle Ages).

By the end of the fifth century, Spain was already in possession of the Visigoths almost entirely, except for the northwestern portion. The conquest was accomplished by the end of the next century. The Romance language was embraced by the new masters of the land, who thus founded a sort of unitary empire in Spain. It was the age of splendor of the Visigoths' kingdom.

But then their control split up to make way for feudalism to be fragmented; after that, another unitary state was seen to reappear. However, the domination of the Arabs, who came from Africa in 712, disrupted this creation. Victors of Rodrigue (Roderic), the last king of the Visigoth dynasty, the Arabs completed the conquest of Spain in the battle of Jerez de la Frontera in three years, which became a province of the Umayyad Caliphs' empire (Muslim Spain).

The Arab rule was going to throw a harsh glare, to make the arts and sciences flourish, to differentiate it even by its religious freedom, but it was to be disputed easily. The country's old rulers, the Christian Visigoths, who were forced back to the north into the mountains of Asturias by the Muslims, retained a kind of independence there. Don Pelagius (Pelayo) was proclaimed king in 718 by the Visigothic chiefs and the communities that accompanied them. The first King of Asturias, who died in 737, inaugurated a long period of time with a first victory, called the Reconquista, which would last seven centuries and during which the Arabs were to be forced back to the South (Christian kingdoms in the Middle Ages).

The Reconquista

Pelage was succeeded by Favila, his son. The son of the Duke of the Cantabrians and the son of Pelagius was Alfonso I, who was given the nickname Catholic. He took advantage of the divisions that paralyzed the Arab powers to reconquer much of Galicia, part of Leon and Castile's kingdom, Portugal and Navarre. In 756, Abderrahman I first founded an Umayyad Empire in Spain, independent of the Abbasid Caliphs of the East and whose capital was Cordoba. He took the title of Emir-al-Mouménin, the chief of the believers, that is to say. Froila, son and successor of Alfonso I, conquered 760 Arabs and founded the city of Oviedo, which he made his capital, with the proceeds of the booty that they took. But the murder of his brother made him despised, and he was murdered by the great kingdoms, who had installed his first cousin Aurele on the throne of Oviedo.

Bermuda I, Aurelius's brother, while Deacon, raised the crown from 788 to 791, but he returned it to Alfonso II, recognized as Froila's chaste son, who won a great victory over Caliph Hescham's army in 794—forced all his Christian subjects to speak and write the Arabic language to the exclusion of theirs, this caliph, who waged a merciless war on Christianity. Al-Hakkam, his son and heir, spent his life in his voluptuous Cordoba gardens (Muslim Spain).

To use the very partisan term of a Spanish historian, Abderrahman II, son of Al-Hakkam, only liked to hurt Christians. Ramiro, I st and Ordoño I er, her uncle, Alfonso, the Chaste's worthy successors, were characterized by their piety and exploits against the Arabs and against the Vikings. Alfonso III, revered as the Mighty, compelled to abdicate by the pretensions to the crown of his eldest son Garcia, shared his States after a glorious reign and gave Galicia to his second son Ordoño with his conquests of Portugal. Imitated by his successors, the example of this division became fatal for Spain. In 914, Ordoño transferred the seat of government from Oviedo to Leon, and the Spanish rulers have since been called Kings of Leon. Froila II, his brother, was a tyrant. In 924, Alfonso IV, son of Ordoño II, ascended to the throne, ceded it in 927 to his brother Ramire II, and withdrew to the Sahagun monastery.

In 928, he tried to take back the throne, but his brother forced his eyes out and locked him in a dungeon, where he died in 932. In 938, Ramire II won a resounding victory against Caliph Abderrahman III, credited by the Spaniards to the intercession of Saint James, and the name of this apostle became their war cry from then on. Ordoño III, Ramire II's son, defeated the Arabs and, in 953, took Lisbon from them.

Another son of Ramiro II, Sancho I, took the throne vacated by the death of Ordoño III. Ordoño the Poor, the son of Alfonso IV, contested it with him.

Ramiro III, Sancho I's son and successor lost the war against the kingdom's great rebellion and died in 982. Under Bermuda II, son of Ordoño III. In 996, Almanzor, king of the Cordoba Empire, ravaged the peninsula's Christian states, took and burned the city of Leon to the ground. But Bermude, Garcia IL, King of Navarre, the State established in 831, and the Count of Castile, forgetting the differences that favored the Arab achievements, united against Almanzor, and defeated him in 998 in the fields of Calatañazor. The city of Leon was rebuilt by Alfonso V, son of Bermude II, and fatally wounded by the siege of Viseu in 1027. Bermudo III succeeded his father, Alfonso V, and his sister married Ferdinand I, the second son of Sancho III, regarded as the Great King of Navarre, to whom his father gave Castile, erected in 1033 in the kingdom. In 1035, Sancho III left the Kingdom of Navarre to die in Garcia, the eldest of his sons, the third in the State of Sobrarbe in Gonzalo, and Aragon to his natural son, Ramire.

Soon, the State of Sobrarbe was incorporated into the Kingdom of Aragon, the roots of which date from this split. In 1037, Bermudo III was killed in a war against Ferdinand I, who tried to take the seats that his sister had handed him. The male posterity of the world died in him. Ferdinand, I was his successor, and he met Leon and Castile with the crowns. Since Mahmoud al-usurpation Mahadi's of the throne of Cordoba in 1000, many ambitious ones have aspired to the sovereignty of the Arab Kingdom, of which bloody chaos hastened the ruin. Hescham III, a prince of the Umayyad dynasty, held the throne of the Caliphs for the last time from 1027 to 1038 and was slaughtered by his subjects. The Umayyad Caliphate in Spain ended, and as many separate and rival principalities (emirates) were established by the dismemberment of the Cordoba Empire as there were important cities (Zaragoza, Valencia, Toledo, Seville, etc.).

His kingdom became divided between his 1st, 2nd, and 3rd sons and two daughters by Ferdinand I er; but Sancho the Powerful, who shared Castile, wanted to rob his brothers and sisters of their inheritance and, by treason, was killed in 1072 in front of Zamora, the dominion of his sister Urraca. In 1075, Garcia, who had gained Galicia and Portugal, was locked up by his brother Alfonso VI, King of Leon, who united the three crowns in the castle of Lima.

With the arrival in Spain of the Almoravids from Morocco, from where the Arabs of the Peninsula had named them, the powers of Islam increased in 1086. The marriage of Infanta Urraca, the only daughter of Alfonso VI, to Count Raymond of the French house of Burgundy, by the accession to the throne of Alfonso VIII, born of this union, passed through the Crown of Castile and Leon in that house in 1126. Alfonso VIII backed the colors of Christianity against the Arabs after the blows struck on Islam by Alfonso the Battler, King of Aragon. Under his rule, the religious order of Alcantara was born, and that of Calatrava under Sancho, his uncle. Founded on the ruins of the Templar order, this religious knighthood is deeply involved in undertaking the Reconquista (Christian kingdoms in the Middle Ages).

About the same time, with a victory over the Muslims in 1139, Alfonso Henriquez gained the title of King of Portugal. But the division between his two sons, Sanche III, King of Castile, and Ferdinand II, King of Leon, of the States of Alfonso VIII, weaken the influence of Christians. Taking some places away from the Muslims, Ferdinand II repopulated the cities of his empire that had been left abandoned by the battle. He also appeased the troubles of Castile, ruled by his nephew Alfonso IX, son of Sancho III, as his tutor, and died in 1188. Pope Innocent III was excommunicated by his son and successor, Alfonso IX, for having married his cousin Bérengère, daughter of Alfonso IX, King of Castile, without dispensation. In 1230, he gained a major victory over the Arabs and died that same year. The Almohads at Alarcos defeated Alfonso IX, King of Castile, one of the greatest princes who ruled in Spain, in 1193. But he won the battle of Las Navas de Tolosa, so-called by the name of the plains (Navas in Spanish) where it took place, in the Sierra Morena in 1212.

"SER"

Present Simple of the Verb "Ser"

The verb "ser" (to be) is used to talk about the permanent state of something. For example, this could be personal information. Personal information includes name, address, nationality, origins, occupation, and so on. In this conversation, we are going to look at two university students, Fernando and Diego, exchange information about themselves along with some other interesting language you can use when you first meet someone.

Here is a quick rundown of how the verb "ser" is conjugated:

- Yo soy= I am
- Tú eres= You are (singular)
- Él es= He is
- Ella es= She is
- Nosotros somos= We are
- Ustedes son= You are (plural)
- Ellos son= They are (masculine, plural)
- Ellas son= They are (feminine, plural)

Conversation:

-Two new friends-

-Dos nuevos amigos-

Fernando: Hi! My name is Fernando. And you?

Fernando: ¡Hola! Mi nombre es Fernando. ¿Y tú?

Diego: Hello, my name is Diego. It's nice to meet you.

Diego: Hola, mi nombre es Diego. Es un gusto conocerte.

147

Fernando: It is nice to meet you too. I am a student.

Fernando: Es un gusto conocerte también. Soy estudiante.

Diego: I am a student too. I am a medical student. And you?

Diego: Yo también soy estudiante. Soy estudiante de medicina. ¿Y tú?

Fernando: I am a law student. Where are you from?

Fernando: Yo soy estudiante de leyes. ¿De dónde eres?

Diego: I'm from Madrid. And where are you from?

Diego: Soy de Madrid. Y tú, ¿de dónde eres?

Fernando: I am from Barcelona. I am not from Madrid.

Fernando: Soy de Barcelona. No soy de Madrid.

Diego: So, we are Spanish.

Diego: Entonces, somos españoles.

Fernando: Yes! We are Spanish.

Fernando: ¡Sí! Somos españoles.

Diego: Is your family also from Barcelona?

Diego: ¿Tu familia también es de Barcelona?

Fernando: My father is from Barcelona, but my mother is from Seville.

Fernando: Mi padre es de Barcelona, pero mi madre es de Sevilla.

Diego: Oh, interesting.

Diego: Oh, interesante.

Fernando: And you? Is it your family from Madrid?

Fernando: ¿Y tú? ¿Es tú familia de Madrid?

Diego: Yes, my family is from Madrid. But my grandparents are from Barcelona.

Diego: Sí mi familia es de Madrid. Pero mis abuelos son de Barcelona.

Fernando: Oh, what a coincidence!

Fernando: ¡Oh, qué coincidencia!

Diego: Yes, it is!

Diego: ¡Sí, lo es!

Occupations with the Present Simple of the Verb "Ser"

Since the verb "ser" can be used to express permanent states, it is commonly used to describe occupations. These occupations are not jobs since jobs can be considered temporary action. A job could be considered as a permanent action when the speaker has no intention of changing jobs at any point. If the speaker is intending to change jobs at any point, then they may choose to use the present continuous form to indicate a temporary condition.

As such, here is a list of occupations and professions.

- Abogado= Lawyer
- Bombero= Firefighter
- Cajero= Cashier
- Carpintero= Carpenter
- Conductor= Driver
- Constructor= Builder
- Contador= Accountant
- Doctor= Doctor
- Electricista= Electrical technician

- Enfermera= Nurse
- Gerente= Manager
- Ingeniero= Engineer
- Jardinero= Gardener
- Maestro= Teacher
- Mecánico= Mechanic
- Mesero= Waiter
- Oficial de policía= Police officer
- Oficinista= Office worker
- Plomero= Plumber
- Recolector de basura= Garbage collector

Note: The feminine version of these professions generally ends in "a" as in "enfermera," whereas the masculine version usually ends in "o" or a consonant as in "enfermero."

Conversation:

-En una conferencia-

-At a conference-

Fernando: Hi, how are you?

Fernando: Hola, ¿Cómo estás?

Blanca: Very well, and you?

Blanca: Muy bien, ¿y tú?

Fernando: My name is Fernando. What is your name?

Fernando: Me llamo Fernando. ¿Cómo te llamas?

Blanca: My name is Blanca. It's nice to meet you.

Blanca: Mi nombre es Blanca. Es un gusto de conocerte.

Fernando: Thank you, you too.

Fernando: Gracias, igualmente.

Blanca: Are you coming to the conference?

Blanca: ¿Vienes a la conferencia?

Fernando: Yes. Are you also here for the conference?

Fernando: Sí. ¿Tú también vienes a la conferencia?

Blanca: Yes. I am an accountant.

Blanca: Sí. Soy contadora.

Fernando: Oh, good. I'm a lawyer.

Fernando: Oh, qué bien. Yo soy abogado.

Blanca: My father is a lawyer.

Blanca: Mi padre es abogado.

Fernando: And my sister is an accountant!

Fernando: ¡Y mi hermana es contadora!

Blanca: See you at the conference.

Blanca: Nos vemos en la conferencia.

Fernando: Yes, see you later.

Fernando: Sí, nos vemos luego.

Physical Characteristics with the Present Simple Form of the Verb "Ser"

Given that the verb "ser" is used to indicate permanent states, physical characteristics are expressed using this tense. Of course, there are physical characteristics that can be changed. Nevertheless, these are usually expressed in the present simple as they are considered permanent.

Physical characteristics are also subject to the masculine-feminine agreement.

Also, each characteristic is subject to the plural and singular agreement. For example, "altos" refers to "tall males," which is plural whereas "altas" refers to "tall females."

Here is a list of physical characteristics.

- Alto= Tall
- Bajo= Short
- Blanco= Fair (skin)
- Bonita= Pretty
- Calvo= Bald
- Castaño= Brunette
- Delgado= Thin
- Estatura media= Average height
- Flaco= Skinny
- Gordo= Fat
- Guapo= Handsome
- Moreno= Dark (skin)
- Pelirrojo= Redhead
- Robusto= Well built
- Rubio= Blonde

Conversation:

-Getting to know each other better-

-Conociéndonos mejor-

Blanca: Hi Diego. How are you?

Blanca: Hola, Diego. ¿Qué tal estás?

Diego: Hi, Blanca. I am fine, how are you?

Diego: Hola, Blanca. Muy bien, ¿y tú?

Blanca: I'm very good. You look great with short hair.

Blanca: Estoy muy bien. Te ves muy bien con el cabello corto.

Diego: Thank you. I like short hair.

Diego: Gracias. Me gusta el cabello corto.

Blanca: You look good. My hair is long.

Blanca: Se te ve bien. Mi cabello es largo.

Diego: But it's pretty.

Diego: Pero es bonito.

Blanca: Thank you. You look handsome with your short brown hair.

Blanca: Gracias. Te ves guapo con tu cabello castaño corto.

Diego: And you look pretty with your long blond hair.

Diego: Y tú te ves bonita con tu cabello rubio largo.

Blanca: You are tall, too.

Blanca: También eres alto.

Diego: And you are short.

Diego: Y tú eres baja.

Blanca: Yes, I know. But I am thin.

Blanca: Sí lo sé. Pero soy delgada.

Diego: Yes, and I'm fat.

Diego: Sí, y yo soy gordo.

Blanca: No, you are not fat. You are well built.

Blanca: No, tú no eres gordo. Eres robusto.

Diego: My brothers are tall and fat.

Diego: Mis hermanos son altos y gordos.

Blanca: My sisters are thin and brunette.

Blanca: Mis hermanas son delgadas y morenas.

Diego: My father is bald.

Diego: Mi padre es calvo.

Blanca: My mother is white and redhead.

Blanca: Mi madre es blanca y pelirroja.

Diego: Our families are very different.

Diego: Nuestras familias son muydiferentes.

Blanca: Yes, they are!

Blanca: ¡Sí, lo son!

Personality Traits with the Present Simple Form of the Verb "Ser"

Just like physical characteristics, personality traits can be expressed using the verb "ser" in the present simple tense. Personality traits are considered to be permanent and are part of a person's description. As such, you can use this form in order to describe yourself and others. Also, please bear in mind that they are subject to the masculine-feminine agreement in addition to the singular plural agreement. For instance, "reservados" would indicate "reserved" for males in the plural while "reservadas" would indicate the same for females in the plural.

Here is a list of personality traits:

- Active= Active
- Amable= Nice
- Ambicioso= Ambitious
- Amistoso= Friendly
- Aventurero= Adventurous
- Confiado= Naïve
- Cuidadoso= Careful
- Despistado= Forgetful
- Divertido= Fun
- Generoso= Generous
- Independiente= Independent
- Inteligente= Smart
- Optimista= Optimistic
- Pesimista= Pessimistic
- Práctico= Practical
- Reservado= Reserved
- Sensible= Sensitive
- Sereno= Serene
- Simpatico= Sympathetic
- Sociable= Sociable

Conversation:

-What is your family like?-

-¿Cómo es tu familia?-

Blanca: Diego, What is your father like?

Blanca: Diego, ¿cómo es tu padre?

Diego: My father is very kind. He is friendly and serene.

Diego: Mi padre es muy amable. Es amistoso y sereno.

Fernando: My father is very different. He is forgetful. But, he is nice.

Fernando: Mi padre es muy diferente. Es despistado. Pero es simpático.

Blanca: My mother is also forgetful. She always forgets something.

Blanca: Mi madre también es despistada. Siempre olvida algo.

Fernando: Yes, I understand.

Fernando: Sí, lo entiendo.

Diego: My mother is generous and sociable. She really enjoys being with her friends.

Diego: Mi madre es generosa y sociable. Ella disfruta mucho estar con sus amigas.

Fernando: Blanca, tell me. What is your sister like?

Fernando: Blanca dime. ¿Cómo es tu hermana?

Blanca: She is intelligent and careful. She is a good student. Diego, what is your brother like?

Blanca: Ella es inteligente y cuidadosa. Es buena estudiante. Diego, ¿cómo es tu hermano?

Diego: He is ambitious. He likes to work and money. We are very similar.

Diego: Él es ambicioso. Le gusta el trabajo y el dinero. Somos muy similares.

Fernando: Yes! But they are also optimistic.

Fernando: ¡Eso sí! Pero también son optimistas.

Blanca: My sister and I are practical.

Blanca: Mi hermana y yo somos prácticas.

Diego: I am not practical. But I am fun!

Diego: Yo no soy práctico. ¡Pero soy divertido!

Blanca: Yes, we are fun!

Blanca: ¡Sí, somos divertidos!

Describing a Place with the Present Simple Form of the Verb "Ser"

Just like people, the present simple of "ser" can be used to describe places.

Cities, towns, houses, and so on can be described in this manner.

Consequently, you can use the masculine form to describe places as the default gender for places and objects is the masculine form. Unless the object or place is considered feminine, it is best to use the masculine form. For example, "casa" (house) is considered feminine. But a place such as "restaurante" (restaurant) is considered male. The singular-plural agreement also applies if a place is considered plural such as "Los Estados Unidos de América" (The United States of America).

Here is a list of adjectives used to describe places:

- Abierto= Open
- Aburrido= Boring
- Barato= Cheap
- Bueno= Good
- Callado= Quiet
- Caluroso= Hot
- Caro= Expensive
- Cerrado= Closed

- Divertido= Funny
- Feo= Ugly
- Frío= Cold
- Grande= Big
- Limpio= Cleansed
- Lindo= Cute
- Malo= Bad
- Nuevo= New
- Pequeño= Small
- Sucio= Dirty
- Tranquilo= Quiet
- Viejo= Old

Conversation:

-Where are you from?-

-¿De dónde eres?-

Fernando: Hey Diego, you're from Madrid, aren't you?

Fernando: Oye Diego, ¿tú eres de Madrid, no?

Diego: Yes, and you are from Barcelona?

Diego: Sí, ¿y tú eres de Barcelona?

Fernando: Yes, that's it. Tell me, what do you think of Madrid?

Fernando: Sí, así es. Dime, ¿qué piensas de Madrid?

Diego: It's a very big city. There are many people and also many cars.

Diego: Es una ciudad muy grande. Hay muchas personas y también muchos autos.

Fernando: Yes, it's true. It seems to me that it is a very beautiful city. There are historical monuments everywhere.

Fernando: Sí, es cierto. A mí me parece que es una ciudad muy linda. Hay monumentos históricos por todos lados.

Diego: There are also new buildings.

Diego: También hay edificios nuevos.

Fernando: It is also a clean city.

Fernando: También es una ciudad limpia.

Diego: And it's quiet. It's a little cold sometimes.

Diego: Y es tranquila. Hace un poco de frío algunas veces.

Fernando: Barcelona is a hot city.

Fernando: Barcelona es una ciudad calurosa.

Diego: Yes, Barcelona also has many impressive monuments.

Diego: Sí, también Barcelona tiene muchos monumentos impresionantes.

Fernando: You're right. Barcelona has monuments made by Gaudí.

Fernando: Tienes razón. Barcelona tiene los monumentos hechos por Gaudí.

Diego: Yes, I want to visit Barcelona. I would very much like to know these places.

Diego: Sí, quiero visitar Barcelona. Me gustaría muchísimo conocer estos lugares.

Fernando: Then, we must go soon.

Fernando: Entonces, debemos ir pronto.

Diego: I think it's excellent.

Diego: Me parece excelente.

Fernando: When do you have a vacation?

Fernando: ¿Cuándo tienes vacaciones?

Diego: In a couple of months.

Diego: Dentro de un par de meses.

Fernando: We can go then.

Fernando: Podemos ir entonces.

Diego: Great!

Diego: ¡Genial!

GENERAL GRAMMAR—GRAMÁTICA

Phonetics—Fonética

Spanish is known to be a pretty easy-to-pronounce language due to the fact that it always is pronounced as it is written when it comes to letters.

In Spanish, there are only five vowel sounds (a, e, i, o, u, they are pronounced in their basic form, don't try to put some of them together as we do in English).

You can find the case that, when you are reading Spanish, you will find some words that you don't know what they mean, but you will be able to pronounce.

This phenomenon is due to the fact that Spanish is a "phonetic" language. What that means is that once you learn the sounds that are produced by individual letters, then you will be able to take that pattern and apply it to any words that use such letters.

On the contrary, languages such as French and English, use a number of letter combinations that produce various sounds. In fact, it is quite common to see combinations of two, three, or even four letters that produce a single sound. Moreover, it is very common to use silent letters in English.

This can be really tricky for anyone who is learning to read English.

In addition, it is important to note that Spanish vowels are all pronounced. As we will see later, when there are two, or even three vowels next to one another, they must all be pronounced with their corresponding sounds. This can be somewhat tricky, but it gets really easy when you recognize the straightforward nature of Spanish consonant and vowel sounds.

In Spanish, there are accents, acute accents to be exact, and they are only situated on vowels, and it will vary depending on which syllable is located the strongest sound of a word. Thanks to this, we know on which part of the word we should make an emphasis. However, there are some rules and names for these acute accents.

The names of the words according to where its strongest syllable is located are: "Agudas, graves y esdrújulas."

Let's use the word "Canción," which means "song" in English. As we can see, there is a little mark above the "O" letter, which is called "tilde" because it is shown. If we separate by syllables that word, it would be Can-ci-ón.

Then, as the tilde is on the last syllable, the word is aguda.

At last, let's use "Esdrújula." The syllable separation will result in Esdrú-ju-la. As you can see, is above the "U" located on the antepenultimate syllable, and that is why the word is esdrújula.

Words will not always have a tilde, but they will have always one strong syllable (only one). If the word does not have a tilde, we will follow the next rules:

- Piano. If we separate it by syllables, we will get pi-a-no. As it ends in a vowel and lacks tilde, the strongest syllable will be the penultimate, and it will be pronounced piano.
- The same goes for Computadora, which means computer. If we separate it: Com-pu-ta-do-ra. As it ends in a vowel and doesn't have a tilde, it will be pronounced: ComputaDOra.

If the word ends on any consonant except for "n" or "s," the strong syllable will be the last one. For example:

- Comer. This means to eat, separating it we will have co-mer. As it ends on a consonant that is neither "n" nor "s," the strong syllable will be the last; hence, it will be pronounced.

Another important thing about Spanish's phonetics is that the letter h is the only silent letter, but this is only for certain cases like hola (hello), helado (ice cream), hueco (hole), búho (owl), almohada (pillow), zanahoria (carrot) this is when the "H" doesn't have a letter C or S previous to it. When we have C+H it is pronounced CH, pretty similar to when we say CHerry.

Some words may be:

- Chile
- Chocolate
- Chernobyl.

In Spanish there are no apostrophes and only two contractions as we will see:

- El helado es de el bebé/El helado es del bebé= The ice cream is from the baby.
- Voy a el colegio/Voy al colegio= I go to school.

Please bear in mind that practice does make perfect. So, the more you are able to practice through listening, you will be able to not only recognize the sounds as they are spoken, but this will also help you hone in on your own speaking and pronunciation skills. At the end of the day, this will enable you to make the most of your efforts in learning the language. There are plenty of resources that you can use to practice your listening and pronunciation skills. YouTube is filled with such resources in addition to television and movies. Thus, you can take advantage of the abundance of resources available to you.

Verbs—Verbos

One of the most important things to know about every language is the verbs because thanks to them we are able to communicate about what we are doing, what we did, or what we will do. That is why learning verbs is the core of effective communication and building fluency. As you gain more experience, you will find that your knowledge of verbs is essential to your communication efforts. Once you reach a point where you feel comfortable with the most common verbs, you can then begin to branch out into a larger number of verbs in the various tenses.

Generally speaking, we tend to think about verbs in terms of their "tense," that is, the time that these verbs represent. There are three main "times" that we commonly use when talking about verbs: past, present, and future. When we see these tenses, we immediately begin to talk about the time in which actions happen. As a result, languages use conjugation to determine the proper form of the verb that needs to be used in order to reflect this "time."

Spanish verb tenses essentially work the same as most European languages.

However, the mechanics of this conjugation change rather significantly when compared to English. What this means is that you need to pay close attention to the patterns that lead to proper conjugation. But fear not, you will find all the information you need to know right here.

There are different forms of verbs depending on the time the actions were done or are being done or will be done. This is what we mean by the "past," "present," and "future." As such, your understanding of these tenses ought to reflect what you mean to say when communicating with your Spanish interlocutors.

These different forms of verbs are known as verb tenses. In Spanish, they would be "Tiempos verbales." Just like English, or any other language for that matter, verb tenses can get somewhat tricky, especially when you begin to combine them in conversation. But fear not, we will be covering all bases in this book. So, you won't have to scour all across the internet looking for the proper conjugation of verbs or how to build them appropriately.

Before that, we get into the "Tiempos verbales" we will see the infinitive form of the verbs and the "Conjugacion de las formas no finitas" which are certain forms of the verbs really important. It should be noted that the infinitive form means that the verb lacks a tense, which means it doesn't have present, past, nor future. This form is widely used especially when one verb follows another in the same sentence.

Infinitive — Infinitivo

- Correr= to run
- Cantar= to sing
- Reir=to laugh
- Comer= to eat.

In this "Tiempo verbal," the verbs always end with "AR," "ER," or "IR." This is important to note at the ending in the infinitive form will determine the proper ending of the verb once conjugated.

For example:

Spanish/English

- Ser= To Be
- Nadar= To Swim
- Estar= To Be
- Ir= To Go
- Traer= To Bring
- Bailar= To Dance
- Caer= To Fall
- Hacer= To Do
- Cortar= To Cut
- Pensar= To Think
- Amar= To Love
- Llamar= To Call
- Escribir= To Write
- Manejar= To Drive
- Leer= To Read
- Preguntar= To Ask

Examples:

1. Yo quiero bailar= I want to dance
2. Me gusta escribir= I like to write.
3. Samantha quiere correr= Samantha wants to run.

In the examples above, there is one verb, which is the main verb of the sentence. Then, another follows it. This second verb must be in the infinitive form as it is considered to be the "object" of the verb. By definition, all objects must be nouns. What this means is that the infinitive form of the verb acts as a noun. This ensures that you maintain proper structure since a sentence can only have one properly conjugated verb.

It is essential to mention that this is the only case in Spanish, where the verb is not modified in spite of the subject that is doing the action. As such, please bear in mind that whenever you are looking into conjugating all verbs, it is the subject (the person or thing doing the action) that is responsible for determining the proper ending to the verb according to the tense it is representing.

Now, the "Conjugacion de las formas no finitas" are:

Gerund — Gerundio

This form of the verb is used when we want to express some kind of continuity of action. This would be something similar to the –ing verbs. In addition, please note that a "gerundio" is considered a noun. It is used in conjunction with auxiliaries and takes the "object" position of the verb. This position can be easily identified as it is the position that comes after the main verb of the sentence.

- Corriendo= Running
- Comiendo= Eating.

Examples:

1. He is running= El esta corriendo.
2. He was running= El estaba corriendo
3. He will be running= El estara corriendo.

For regular verbs, we have this little tip:

If the infinitive form of the verb ends in "ar" the "Gerundio" will end on "ando" (Nadar/Nadando), and, if it ends in "er" or "ir" it will end on "iendo" (Com er/Com iendo; Dorm ir/ Durm iendo)

Participle — Participio

- Corrido= ran
- Cantado= sung
- Reido= laughed
- Comido= eaten.

Also, please note that the participle form can also be used as an adjective. So, it can be used to describe nouns in addition to being combined with auxiliaries in the object position.

In Spanish, the regular verbs in participle end on "-ado" for "ar" and "-ido" for "er" and "ir"

1. Yo había cocinado= I had cooked.
2. Ella había comido= She had eaten.

This verbal form needs an auxiliary verb. These forms of verbs are used in some "Tiempos verbales" as we will see in a bit.

UNDERSTANDING THE SPANISH

I t's not that they are extremely different; it's that they all have something particular that sets them apart.

There are many varieties of spoken Spanish you'll find all over the Americas and Europe. Amazingly, Spanish speakers can easily understand each other as long as they speak without "regionalisms," that is, without words that can only be understood by speakers of only one area and nobody else. Particular words aside, Spanish is also, surprisingly, a very uniform language thanks in part to one institution: The RAE.

RAE (Real Academia Española, in Spanish or Spanish Royal Academy in English) is the institution that deals with all that concern the Spanish language as a whole. Thanks to it, Spanish speakers have a comprehensive and very useful understanding of the language. Each year, this institution adds new terms to the Spanish language, subtracts old ones who have fallen into disuse, or modifies words that have changed with time. RAE has also the last word when it comes to the pronunciation of the Spanish language.

What should you have in mind when beginning to learn Spanish? Take a look at these tips:

Similar, Yet Different

How many variations of Spanish are there? All you need to know is that there are many and that all of them are particular to one geographical area. So, if you travel to Mexico, you will hear how Mexicans pronounce words. If you keep traveling farther south to another Spanish-speaking country, then you'll find out that Argentines and Chileans have another peculiar way of saying words. You might even find out that you have never heard of certain words and phrases. What's going on?

Those are accents. Simply put, accents are the way people pronounce words in a language. You might feel people from Spain pronounce words very fast. Or you might think that Chileans speak very softly. These differences don't make learning the language a barrier or a difficulty; rather, they make it unique and very special. Each accent has a different "story" to tell and has its place among the people who possess it.

Don't come to think that they are extremely different. They all are understandable to every Spanish speaker. Thanks to the standard provided by the RAE, all Spanish speakers can understand each other without much trouble. Similar to the way Americans can understand Australians as long as they don't use Americanisms, Spanish speakers can understand other such speakers if they don't use a very colloquial type of the language or many regionalisms.

Do you need to learn all the accents that there are among Spanish speakers?

Not necessarily. While it's a very commendable effort if you ever decide to learn a little of all the Spanish accents, it's better if you just focus on one accent and then learn all you can about it. At the same time, don't be afraid to expose yourself to other accents; your vocabulary might be enriched greatly!

Spanish Language Lessons will focus on a standard variation of the language that you can use with any Spanish speaker, no matter the situation.

The Spanish Vowels

They are just five. They are:

- A, as the English letter a when it appears in words like a cat.
- E, as the English letter e when it appears in words like an elephant.
- I, as ee in words like feet and teeth.
- O, as a when it appears in words in English like all.
- U, as oo when it appears in words like foot and tooth.

The Spanish Consonants

The consonants are actually the same as in English, except for one additional consonant:

- B, as it appears in the word boat
- C, has two different pronunciations. Before the vowels a, o, and u, it's pronounced as the letter k when it appears in words like koala and Kurt. Before the vowels e and i, it's pronounced as the letter s when it appears in words like sincere, celebrate, and circus.
- D, as it appears in the word dad.
- F, as it appears in the word fail.
- G, it has two pronunciations. Before the words a, o, and u, it's pronounced as the letter g when it appears in words like game, goal, and gut. Before the vowels e and i, it's pronounced as the letter h when it appears in words like hero or hill. On the other hand, if you write the vowel u before the letters g and e or i, you'll have the same pronunciation as it appears in words like gender, general, guitar, and gift.
- H is a "mute" letter; that is, it doesn't have any pronunciation. It's still used to separate diphthongs, and you'll see it in words like alcohol. Also, it can also be used after the letter c to produce a sound similar to ch when it appears in English words like chocolate, change, choose, and check.
- J, the letter h when it appears in English words like hotel and herb.
- K, as it appears in kilo and koala.
- L, as it appears in Lisa and lab. Also, the double letter
- Ll is pronounced as y when it appears in words like yes and yeast.
- M, as it appears in mom.
- N, as it appears in no.
- Ñ, a special letter that only appears in Spanish and other indigenous languages. It's pronounced as nee.
- P, as it appears in potato.
- Q, only used before ue and ui. The sound it produces is similar to the sound of the letter k when it appears in words like a kilo and keeps.
- R, as it appears in words like rat and Romeo.
- S, as it appears in some.
- T, as it appears in take.
- V, as it appears in Veronica.
- W, as it appears in whisky and wine.
- X, as it appears in words like exact
- Y, as it appears in yes.
- Z, the last letter of the Spanish Alphabet, pronounced as it appears in zebra.

Written Accents

Unlike English, Spanish has written accents. The most common of them is called tilde, or acute accent.

The Acute Accent

This type of accent is by far the most used in the Spanish language. You'll see it only once in a word. It's only used to denote stress in a word. In the meantime, see how some words have written accents and why they're important:

Papá (dad) is not similar to papa (potato, or Pope) Tomó (past tense of the verb take) is different from tomo (present tense of the verb take)

Más (more) doesn't have the same meaning as mas (but) Cómo (how) can easily be confused with como (eat).

Él (he), which is a pronoun, is not the same as el (the), which is an article.

The Diaresis

If you see two points above a letter, then you've seen the diaresis. It's very uncommon to see the diaresis since it's only used in certain words like:

- Antigüedad= Antiquity
- Bilingüe= Bilingual
- Desagüe= Drain
- Pingüino= Penguin
- Vergüenza= Shame

What is it used for? Simply put, it's used to indicate that the letter u and the vowels e or i that follow them have to be pronounced separately.

Word Stress

Simply put, stress is when a syllable or group of syllables is emphasized.

This means that this syllable or group of syllables is pronounced louder or longer. The English language, like any other language, uses stress liberally.

The difficult part is that the English language doesn't really indicate where exactly the stress is in the word. That's not the case in Spanish.

Since Spanish is regulated and has a very uniform pronunciation across all varieties, it's actually very easy to identify how to stress a word. Take a look at some general rules:

1. If you don't see an acute accent on a word that ends in a vowel, an n or an s, then you need to stress the last-but-one syllable:
   a. Como (Koh-moh)
   b. Adulto (Ah-dool-toh)
   c. Teclado (Teh- klah-doh)
   d. Hombre (Hom-bre)
2. If you don't see an acute accent on a word that ends in a consonant other than n or s, then you need to stress the last syllable:
   a. Hablar (Ah-blahr)
   b. Borrar (Boh-rahr)
   c. Continental (Kohn-tee-nehn-tahl)
3. If the word has an acute accent, then you'll have to forget all of the above rules and just stress the syllable where the acute accent is on. In other words, the acute accent is the exception to all other rules:
   a. Francés (Frahn-ses)
   b. Empezó (Ehm-peh-só)
   c. Televisión (The-leh-vee -seeohn)
   d. Jóvenes (Ho-veh-nehs)

Also, have in mind that all the question words in Spanish have written accents on it:

- ¿Qué?
- ¿Dónde?
- ¿Cómo?
- ¿Cuándo?
- ¿Por qué?

172

- ¿Cuál?
- ¿Quién?

How can you read the phonetic transcription you'll see here in this book?

Many of the sounds will be written in a way that's very simple to understand for an English speaker. Double vowels will indicate sounds produced by some vowels in Spanish, like in these examples:

- Ir (eer)
- Tú (too)
- Hoy (oh-eeh)

Most consonants in Spanish have the same pronunciation as in English. Some sounds you'll see are:

- No (noh)
- Papa (pah-pah)
- Amigo (ah-mee-goh)

As you may have also noticed in these examples, the stressed syllable is in bold. This will help you see when exactly to stress the word to have the right pronunciation. Remember that some words in Spanish are monosyllabic which means that they only have one syllable, so you won't see them in bold since all of them are already stressed.

Advance Spanish Rules

Since English and Spanish are Indo-European languages, they have a common origin that goes back over several thousands of years from some places in Eurasia. They are more alike than just their shared vocabulary that is based in Latin. Spanish isn't that hard for native English speakers to figure out if you compare it with Swahili or Japanese.

Spanish might not be all that difficult to learn for native English speakers, but some things are contrary, a bit strange, or hard to comprehend.

Spanish and English use the various parts of speech in much of the same way.

Preposiciones or as, we know them, prepositions, are called this because they get placed before the object. Different languages have circumpositions and postpositions that English and Spanish don't.

Here is a peek at some absurd concepts like why are certain words capitalized and others aren't? Why do they place a comma there rather than a period?

Why isn't there a subject in every sentence? Why is a bra considered to be masculine?

These small differences might cause someone who isn't familiar with the language to be thrown for a loop. When you are learning Spanish, you have to recognize the differences and similarities between Spanish and English.

VERBS LIKE "HACER" AND INTERROGATIVE WORDS

I. New Vocabulary—Vocabulario nuevo

- Hacer= to make, to do
- Ganar= to win, to earn
- Poner= to put
- Salir= to leave, to go out
- Traer= to bring
- Explicar= to explain
- ¿Cómo está Carla? = How is Carla?
- El ejercicio= exercise
- La fiesta= party
- La temperatura= temperatura
- Los grados= degrees
- ¿Qué tiempo hace? = What's the weather like?
- Hace buen tiempo= It's good weather.
- Hace mal tiempo= It's bad weather.
- Hace sol= It's sunny.
- Hace viento= It's windy.
- Hace frío= It's cold.
- Hace calor= It's hot.
- Hace fresco= It's cool.
- Está a veinticinco grados= It's twenty-five degrees.
- Hay tormenta=There's a storm.
- Caen rayos= It's lightning.
- La puntuación= punctuation
- El signo de puntuación= punctuation mark
- El punto= period, point
- Dos puntos= colon
- La coma= comma
- Hacer ejercicio= to exercise
- Hacer una pregunta= to ask a question

- Hacer una fiesta= to throw a party
- ¿Cómo es Carla? = What is Carla like?
- La cama= bed
- La radio= radio
- El huracán= hurricane
- La precipitación= precipitation
- Truena= It's thundering.
- Estánublado= It's cloudy.
- Estádespejado= It's clear (cloudless).
- Llueve= It's raining.
- Está lloviendo= It's raining.
- La lluvia= rain
- Hay niebla= It's foggy.
- Llovizna= It's drizzling.
- Nieva= It's snowing.
- Hay hielo= It's icy.
- El punto y coma= semicolon
- Los signos de interrogación= question marks
- Los signos de exclamación= exclamation marks
- Si= if

II. General Review—Repaso general

Hacer and Expressions with Hacer

The verb hacer means "to make" or "to do," and it's one of the most commonly used verbs in Spanish. Beyond its normal use (e.g., "I always do my work" is Siemprehago mi trabajo), hacer is used in a number of expressions, such as hacer una pregunta, which is "to ask a question," and hacer una fiesta, which is "to throw a party." Hacer is also used with many of the weather expressions (e.g., ¿Qué tiempo hace? is "What is the weather like?" Hacesolis "It's sunny"; Hace mal tiempo is"It'sbadweather"). If you consult the website ofSpain'sAgenciaEstatal de Meteorología (State Meteorological Agency), at aemet.es, you can see a meteorologist giving a weather report. All present tense endings for hacer are regular; the only unusual form of the verb is the "yo" form (hago), which has a g.

Verbs Conjugated Like Hacer

Verbs conjugated like hacer (meaning that they also use regular endings and have a g in the "yo" form) include poner (to put), salir (to leave, to go out), and traer (to bring). The "yo" forms for these verbs are pongo, salgo, and traigo.

Interrogatives

The meaning of cómo is different when used with estar than it is when used with ser because estar expresses a state or condition, while ser expresses an inherent characteristic of someone or something. ¿Cómo están las chicas? Asks "How are the girls?" while ¿Cómo son las chicas? asks "What are the girls like?"

The interrogative qué (what) is used directly before a noun (e.g., ¿Qué clases tomas este semestre? is "What classes are you taking this semester?"). The interrogatives cuál and cuáles (which or what) are often used before the preposition de, as in ¿Cuáles de las camas es tucama? , which is "Which of the beds is your bed?" You use qué when asking for a definition or explanation (e.g., ¿Qué pasa aquí? is "What's happening here?" ¿Qué significa salir? is "What does salir mean?"). The interrogatives cuál and cuáles are used when you want someone to tell you some information, not explain it (e.g., ¿Cuál es la fecha de hoy? is "What is today's date?" ¿Cuál es el nombre de la profesora del curso? Is "What is the name of the professor of the course?").

Punctuation

In Spanish, it is never correct to put a comma after the second-to-last item in a list (e.g., "I'm going to bring many books, a notebook, and a computer" is Voy a traer muchos libros, un cuaderno y una computadora).

Questions in Spanish begin with an inverted question mark, which could be at the start of a sentence or at the start of a clause in the middle of a sentence (e.g., ¿Dónde están las camas? Is "Where are the beds?" Si tenemos tiempo, ¿debemos salir después de la clase? Is "If we have time, should we go out after the class?"). An exclamation must begin with an inverted exclamation mark and end with an exclamation mark (e.g., ¡Que día fantástico! is "What a fantastic day!" Después del examen, ¡qué fiesta vamos a hacer! is "After the exam, what a party we're going to throw!").

III. Activities—Actividades

1. Contesta las siguientes preguntas sobre el pronóstico del tiempo en Buenos Aires y Guadalajara= Answer the following questions about the weather forecast in Buenos Aires and Guadalajara.

   Buenos Aires, Argentina Guadalajara, México

   a. **Hoy:** 31°
      Soleado: 18°
      Temperatura mínima: 0%
      Probabilidad: de lluvia

   b. **Mañana**: 31°
      Parcialmente nublado: 18°
      Probabilidad: de lluvia

   c. **Viernes:** 41°
      Soleado: 25°
      Temperatura mínima: 0%
      Probabilidad: de lluvia

   d. **Sábado:** 41°
      Parcialmente nublado: 26°
      Temperatura mínima: 0%
      Probabilidad: de lluvia

   e. **Domingo:** 33°
      Tormenta: 21°
      Temperatura mínima: 80%
      Probabilidad: de lluvia

   1.1 ¿Cuándo y dónde hay probabilidad de lluvia?

   1.2 ¿Cuál es la temperatura mínima en Buenos Aires el domingo?

   1.3 ¿Cuál es la temperaturamáximaelviernesen Buenos Aires?

   1.4 ¿Cuál es la probabilidad de lluviaen Buenos Aires elsábado?

   1.5 ¿Cuándo y dónde hay probabilidad de tormenta?

   1.6 ¿Qué tiempo hace en Buenos Aires hoy?

   1.7 ¿Qué tiempo va a hacer en Guadalajara el sábado?

1.8 ¿Cuál es la temperatura máxima de hoy en Guadalajara?

1.9 ¿Cuál es la temperatura mínima el sábado en Guadalajara?

2. Diana quiere ir a la piscina de Villa Celeste. Erica va a revisar el pronóstico del tiempo= Diana wants to go to the pool in Villa Celeste. Erica is going to check the weather forecast.

Lee el siguiente diálogo y contesta las preguntas= Read the following dialogue and answer the questions.

Diana: ¡Mami, quiero (I want) ir a la piscina!

Erica: Sí, está bien, pero tenemos que llevar a tu hermana Mariana con nosotras.

Diana: Está bien, mami, pero ¡vamos a la piscina!

Erica: Muy bien, pero primero (first) voy a mirar el pronóstico del tiempo.

Erica: Diana, ¿puedes (can you) poner la televisión, por favor?

Diana: ¡Sí, mami!

Erica: Diana, hoy no vamos a ir a la piscina porque va a llover.

Diana: No, mami, ¡hace sol!

Erica: Sí, hace sol ahora, pero en una hora va a llover mucho.

Diana: Pero yo quiero ir a la piscina.

Erica: Yo sé (I know), pero no vamos a salir porque va a llover.

Erica: Mañana sí vamos con tu amiga Valeria, ¿está bien?

Diana: ¡Sí, mañana!

2.1 ¿Por qué Erica y sus hijas no van hoy a la piscina?

2.2 ¿Qué tiempo hace ahora?

2.3 ¿Cuándo va a llover?

2.4 ¿Cómo se llama la amiga de Diana?

2.5 ¿Cuándo van a ir a la piscina?

3. Completa las frases con la opción apropiada= Complete the sentences with the appropriate option.

   a. Hoy quiero ejercicio a las seis y media de la tarde.
      - ✓ Hacemos… hacer ejercicio con Victoria a las cinco de la tarde.
      - ✓ Hacer…vais a hacer
      - ✓ Hacer…voy a hacer

   b. ¿Cuál el nombre de tu nuevo vecino?
      - ✓ Está
      - ✓ Es
      - ✓ Ser

   c. ¿Cómo la personalidad (personality) de tu vecino?

179

- ✓ Está
- ✓ Es
- ✓ Ser

d. Yo la radio todos los días, pero no
- ✓ Pongo…ponéis la
- ✓ Pongo…poner
- ✓ Pongo…pongo

e. ¿Cuáles los ingredientes (ingredients) que necesitas comprar en el supermercado?
- ✓ Están
- ✓ Eres
- ✓ Son

f. ¿Vecinos tienes?
- ✓ Cuántos
- ✓ Cuántas
- ✓ Cuál

g. Marisol y Valeria todos los fines de semana con sus amigos.
- ✓ Salgan
- ✓ Salen
- ✓ Salimos

h. ¿Y tú? ¿Cuándo con tus amigos?
- ✓ Sale
- ✓ Sales
- ✓ Salgo

i. ¿Y ustedes? ¿Cuándo los libros para estudiar?
- ✓ Traigo
- ✓ Trae
- ✓ Traen

IV. Correct Answers—Respuestas correctas

Exercise 1:

1.1 Hay probabilidad de lluvia el domingo en Guadalajara.

1.2 La temperatura mínima en Buenos Aires el domingo es de 18 grados.

1.3 La temperatura máxima el viernes en Buenos Aires es de 31 grados.

1.4 No hay probabilidad de lluvia en Buenos Aires el sábado.

1.5 Hay probabilidad de tormenta el domingo en Guadalajara.

1.6 Hoy hace buen tiempo en Buenos Aires. /Hoy en Buenos Aires está soleado. /Hoy en Buenos Aires hace sol.

1.7 El sábado en Guadalajara va a estar parcialmente nublado.

1.8 La temperatura máxima de hoy en Guadalajara es de 41 grados.

1.9 La temperatura mínima el sábado en Guadalajara es de 26 grados.

Exercise 2:

2.1 No van a la piscina porque va a llover.

2.2 Hace sol ahora.

2.3 Va a llover en una hora.

2.4 La amiga de Diana se llama Valeria.

2.5 Van a ir a la piscina mañana.

Exercise 3.

1. Hacer… voy a hacer
2. Es
3. Es
4. Pongo… pongo
5. Son
6. Cuántos
7. Salen
8. Sales
9. Traen

Lesson the Verbs Saber and Conocer

- Saber= to know facts, to know how to do something
- Traducer= to translate
- Conocer= to know a person, place, or thing
- Conducir= to drive
- Producer= to produce
- Manejar= to drive
- Reducir= to reduce
- Ofrecer= to offer

- Parecer= to seem
- Rápido= fast
- La respuesta= answer
- Con= with
- Para= for, to, in order to
- Por= for, by, through
- Sin= without
- Entre= between, among
- Encima de= on top of, over
- Sobre= on, about
- Debajo de= under
- Dentro de= inside of
- Detrás de= behind
- Delante de= in front of
- Enfrente de= across from
- La lámpara= lamp
- El sillón= armchair
- La puerta= door
- La ventana= window
- El techo= roof
- Visitar= to visit
- Saludar= to greet
- Comunicarse= to communicate
- Que= that
- Hacia= toward
- Hasta= until
- Contra= against
- Desde= from, since
- Cerca de= near to
- Lejos de= far from
- Al lado de= next to
- A la derecha de= to the right of
- A la izquierda de= to the left of
- Alrededor de= around, about
- La cómoda= bureau
- La alfombra= rug
- El escritorio= desk
- El estante= bookshelf

EDUCATION

School vs. Online Education—Escuelas vs educación en línea

Part 1

a educación es importante? Creo que todo el mundo diría Sí, pero ¿se piensa lo mismo de las escuelas? ¿La escuela es importante? En el pasado, el mejor lugar para aprender era en la escuela, pero ahora Internet ha cambiado todo. Existen cursos en línea para todo. Tú puedes estudiar casi cualquier tema o materia que desees. Incluso puedes conseguir que un profesor te enseñe por Skype.

English:

Is education important? I think everyone would say yes. But what about school? Is school important? In the past, the best place to learn was in school.

But now the internet has changed everything. You can even get a teacher to teach you on Skype.

Vocabulary:

- Educación= Education.
  - ➢ Example: La educación es importante porque ayuda a las personas a tener una buena vida.
  - ➢ Example: Tú puedes aprender mucho de la lectura. (You can learn a lot from reading.)
- Curso= A course.
  - ➢ Example: Yo hice un curso de ciencia en línea. (I did an online science course.)
- Estudiar= To study.

> Example: Yo estudio ciencias en la escuela. (I study science at school.)
- Tema/Materia= A topic/subject.
    > Example: Ciencias es mi materia favorita. (Science is my favorite subject.)
- Profesor= A teacher.
    > Example: A mí me agrada mi profesor de ciencias. (I like my science teacher.)
- Enseñar= To teach.
    > Example: Voy a enseñarle a mi amiga a conducir porque ella aún no sabe. (I will teach my friend how to drive because she doesn't know how.)

Part 2

Incluso puedes hacer grados universitarios en línea. Puedes realizar el plan de estudios completo sin necesidad de entrar en un aula. La única diferencia es que no hay periodos o semestres. Así que puedes estudiar tan rápido o tan lento como desees. Sin embargo, tal vez tendrás que hacer el examen en la universidad.

English:

You can even do university degrees online. You can do the full curriculum without even going into a classroom. The only difference is that there are no terms or semesters. So you can study as quickly or slowly as you want. You may have to take the exam at the university though.

Vocabulary:

- Universidad= University.
    > Example: Yo estudié ciencias en la universidad. (I studied science at university.)
- Grado universitario= (A university) degree.
    > Example: Yo tuve un grado universitario en ciencias. Ahora voy a hacer mi maestría. (I got a degree in science. Now, I'm going to do a Masters degree.)
- Plan de estudios= A (school) curriculum.

184

- Example: El plan de estudios es algo difícil porque hay muchas materias. (The curriculum is quite difficult because there are many subjects.)
- Aula= A classroom.
  - Example: El profesor se para enfrente del aula.
- Periodo (académico)= A term.
  - Example: Hay 3 periodos en el año. (There are 3 terms in a year.)
- Semestre= A semester.
  - Example: Las universidades generalmente tienen 2 semestres, en otoño y en primavera. (Universities usually have two semesters, autumn and spring.)
- Examen= An exam.
  - Example: Al final del curso hice un examen. (At the end of the course I took an exam.)

HOW TO WRITE IN SPANISH

Writing and speaking are very similar to each other in that they require a lot more active participation from the learner. You have to create your own speech, generate your own grammatical awareness, and focus on little things like word order and spelling.

Writing and speaking, however, take that input you've received and turn it into your own personal output, therefore helping to solidify the concepts and vocabulary in your mind.

Writing in Spanish is a wonderful tool and will help improve various other skills you've been working on. When you write, you have to read what you're writing (practice your reading). You can read it out loud (practice your speaking) and focus on your pronunciation and how the words sound (practice your listening).

Benefits of Writing in Spanish

Writing can be tedious and it's not always the most enjoyable of activities, especially when thinking about writing in Spanish. It is, however, a very important skill to have. We use writing every day, way more often than we may even realize. All those text messages and emails you send are written.

Are those reminders you put in your phone or scribble onto post-it notes? These little, casual ways of writing are precisely where you can start when looking for chances to practice this skill in Spanish.

If you can't find a Spanish conversation partner, you should try to find a pen pal. Maybe someone in one of your Spanish classes you can send text messages to or email back and forth with. You can write out your to-do lists or leave reminders in Spanish.

Writing in Spanish is beneficial, not only because it's something that draws on the other areas of the language that you will want to work on, but also because it is a daily part of life. If you plan on using your Spanish for work, you'll need to write emails. If you're learning Spanish for pleasure, you'll surely find yourself wanting to meet and communicate with native speakers, via Facebook, email, WhatsApp, etc.

Let's take a look at ways that you can practice and perfect your writing ability.

Write to Other People

As you may have discovered when we were talking about speaking, having a network of Spanish speakers (or Spanish language learners) around you is extremely beneficial. Well, this is also true when talking about writing.

Write to Yourself

What's that word we keep using when talking about learning Spanish? A habit? Well, surprise, surprise, here it comes again! Creating a habit of writing in Spanish on a regular basis can be the key to success when mastering this specific skill. A writing habit can be created by writing little things in Spanish every day. This doesn't mean it has to be full sentences.

Maybe it's a to-do list. Maybe it's a quick reminder to yourself to pay the gas bill. Whatever it is, writing in Spanish is a great way to commit vocabulary to memory and to ensure that you're using what you've learned on a regular basis.

Keep a Journal

This doesn't mean you have to write a daily "Dear Diary" entry. What we're talking about here is just a small notebook and a daily habit of writing down a handful of things. Start by writing the day of the week, the month, etc. to practice with that basic vocabulary. Then, write out three little bullet points.

What did you do that day? What good thing happened (everyone can benefit from some positive reflection at the end of every day)?

Write Yourself Daily Reminders

Do you live in a sea of post-it notes? Why not make that a sea of Spanish?

Similarly, do you find yourself typing out a lot of reminders on your phone?

Type them out in Spanish. The things that we need to do every day. If you start keeping track of those things in Spanish, you already have a built-in habit in the making.

Put Your Phone, Calendar, Facebook in Spanish

On the surface, this tip is something that will help with your reading. When you're penciling in your dinner with friends on your calendar write it down in Spanish. Setting your alarm for the morning? Type in a quick note to yourself in Spanish reminding you of anything important that you're doing that day.

Write Your Lists in Spanish

This is a wonderful way to really put all that vocabulary you've been studying into practice. Writing out your to-do lists in Spanish will help you review daily chores and household items vocabulary. Food vocabulary is something that you will want to be familiar with, especially if you plan on traveling in a Spanish-speaking country (being able to read a menu may save you some interesting experiences you'd rather not have). Write out your shopping list in Spanish.

Read, Then Write

We've talked a little about taking notes when reading. At that point, we talked about how it will help to check your reading comprehension. What we didn't say was how much it will help with other areas of your language learning, as well.

When you read something in Spanish, you may not realize it, but you are being exposed to a whole slew of useful, beneficial, and necessary input—word order, masculine/feminine, verb conjugations, object pronouns, etc.

Being familiar with all of these things will not only make reading easier and speaking more natural, but they will surely help your writing as well.

After you read a passage, find a sentence or phrase that really "speaks to you." This doesn't mean it has to move you on an emotional level. Maybe it's something that contains one of those tricky verb conjugations you've been working with or perfectly puts that one vocabulary word into a context you feel you would actually use it in in the future. Then, take the time to write out this chunk of text. The best way to do this, honestly, is the good old-fashioned pen and paper method. This is simply because it has been proven that the muscle memory that comes with writing helps the brain absorb and retain the information better than simply typing it up on a computer or into a "page" on our phone.

Don't just stop with writing out that one sentence or phrase, however.

This doesn't have to just be limited to passages from a book. You could find a song that you really like or a scene from a movie that really drew you in.

Copying or writing things out is a good idea because it pulls on several different skills at the same time (reading or listening or both, then writing).

Here are some ideas for things you may find yourself wanting to write down:

- Song lyrics
- Passages from a favorite book/poem
- Inspirational quotes
- Recipes

Information about things that interest you--fun facts or statistics, sports terminology or medical terms.

TIPS

Tip #1: The Dialect Dilemma

A common misconception about the Spanish language is that each and every Spanish-speaking country speaks it the same. The sooner you realize that this is completely false, the better. The first important step is to separate Spanish from Spain from the rest of the Spanish-speaking world. Having Spanish roots, I can attest that I speak quite differently than my many friends from Latin America. For example, I speak Spanish with a lisp that is rumored to have been caused by a Spanish king with a speech impediment. Supposedly, this is why Spaniards have the accent that we find today. That being said, in Latin America, people will instantly be able to tell if you are Spanish due to the difference in not only accent but also verb tenses and vocabulary. For example, in Spain, we use an entirely different verb tense called "Vosotros," which is equivalent to saying "you all" or "y'all" in English.

If one ventures to Argentina and Uruguay, they are going to hear an accent that has a heavy Italian influence due to the plethora of Italian immigrants that went there. Chilean Spanish has many German roots as heard in their accent; and as you travel North in Latin America, the accent changes dramatically due to the exposure of the Spanish to the indigenous people in countries such as Perú, Bolivia, Venezuela, Columbia, Panamá, Costa Rica, Nicaragua, Guatemala, Honduras, El Salvador, Dominican Republic, Cuba, México, Equatorial Guinea, and Puerto Rico. Each and every one of these places has shown a substantial influence from the local population that was there when the Spanish arrived. From this, came entirely different dialects.

Where the dialects have the most profound effect is in familiar conversations and the business culture. Thus, if you are planning on being in one specific Spanish-speaking country for a substantial amount of time, then it is wise to immerse yourself in the local Spanish dialect before you go so that you are able to communicate with the locals. Additionally, another important aspect of the Spanish-speaking world is the class system. Many countries in Latin America have different accents based on their educational level and socioeconomic status. By having an awareness of these fundamental differences, you will be able to differentiate between different types of speaking.

Tip #2: The Components of Language Learning

Language learning is a very complex skillset that many people attempt to acquire through a means that makes them unable to have a conversation successfully. The reason for this is that many schooling methods make the mistake of having language learning courses that are derived from the principle that translating literally is the way to learn languages. This is a fundamental error that causes the individual to fail to have a grasp of the language they are learning. An example of this can be said when I use my two native languages of Spanish and English. The only way that I can be the translator that I am today is that I have to separate my "English mind" and my "Spanish mind" when I am speaking, listening, reading, or writing in either language. If I try to convert between the two languages, the method does not work and I make translation errors as a result. This is a pivotal point that any language learner needs to apply to their language learning methods.

When studying languages, my uncle used to always say that speaking comes last and I could not agree more with him. Upon studying languages, it is pivotal to develop one's "ear" first before you can ever hope to have a conversation. The key to developing one's ear is to listen to the radio or movies in Spanish, let's say in order to develop the listening comprehension portion of language learning. With movies, it is important to have subtitles in English while listening to Spanish at first because it allows the language learner to not only associate how the Spanish thought process is different than English, but also how to formulate proper sentence structures in the Spanish language. This method can also be used in reverse by watching a movie in English with Spanish subtitles in order to see how Spanish sentences are formed grammatically. By using the listening comprehension and sentence structure method, one is taking the first important steps to develop the fundamental building blocks of the language they are trying to learn.

Grammar and vocabulary building is the next natural step; however, it is important not to translate these aspects literally as they have different meanings in their respective languages. By knowing to separate one's mind from English to Spanish or vice versa, they will be able to develop their Spanish mind as a separate entity from their English one and, in turn, speak correctly in both languages. Developing sentence structure and verb conjugations comes from the traditional flashcard methods and verb conjugation charts; however, it also comes from watching the news and reading articles more advanced than one's level every day. This is the best way to challenge your mind to understand the language. For example, when I was learning French, I would read the newspaper in French every day by reading one article and study the sentence structure and vocabulary. This is how I developed my French mind. Additionally, by listening to the news, one's "ear" is challenged because newscasters tend to talk faster than everyday speakers. This gives the language learner a great advantage because they will be accustomed to faster speech and this will make the everyday conversation far simpler to absorb.

Another key component to language learning is that there is something to be said by allowing your mind to begin thinking in the language independently from speaking. One of the best ways to develop this skill is to write essays in Spanish, for example. Conduct your brainstorming sessions entirely in Spanish so that your mind begins to think fluidly in Spanish. This will be a great asset to you as you converse down the road.

Lastly, as your level advances, you should be eliminating the subtitles from the movies you are watching and allow your ear to be challenged further.

While this may drive you crazy at first, start with ten to fifteen minutes a day and allow your Spanish mind to have a workout. This will allow you to associate emotions and actions with vocabulary words and accents and create a visual memory with your Spanish-speaking mind.

All of these components combined create your Spanish-speaking mind. This is the best way to build a foundation as you study to give you more than what we like to call "Textbook Spanish." "Textbook Spanish" is not what is going to get you to converse with locals and have unique travel experiences. In fact, it is going to limit you when you enter the Spanish-speaking world a great deal.

Tip #3: Ditch the Dictionary!

Language learning is a science complete with viable formulas. That being said, it is important to take note that the dictionary is your enemy and that you should not use it along with automatic translate applications such as Google. There is a specific way to find out the meaning of words when you are learning Spanish, and the answer is in looking up the definition of words in Spanish and in Spanish only.

What this trick does for your "Spanish mind" is that it allows your "Spanish mind" to derive the meaning of the word you are trying to research in Spanish rather than translating literally from English. In the long term, this is going to make you a more effective Spanish speaker because you will be able to think in Spanish as you are studying and conversing with Spanish speakers. Those who use these methods also turn into the best translators because rather than translating word by word, they are able to take a sentence and translate the context and meaning of the sentence, which will lead to less awkward and incorrect phrasing in translated texts.

An important note to understand about dictionaries, in general, is that they are quite detrimental for the business and legal worlds where there are certain formalities to maintain. This is precisely why using a dictionary in Spanish is far more effective because there are different contexts for the word and how it is effectively used. These are a great source of guidance that will not lead to embarrassment in a business meeting. Regarding formal correspondence, be sure to invest in a book on Spanish business etiquette because there are certain formalities originally from Spanish customs that are still used in many business practices in Latin America.

Relating to the different dialects, it is also important to understand that if you do invest in an etiquette book or a Spanish dictionary entirely in Spanish, it is essential to ensure which dialect the book is geared towards. The differences between the various dialects in Spanish have become so pronounced that there have been specific books published in Spanish from Spain or Spanish from Venezuela, for example.

Dictionaries are something helpful; however, they are not the best tool to use when learning Spanish. By merely opting to use a dictionary in Spanish rather than using an English dictionary that translates from English to Spanish, you will be a leg up in how you approach learning the Spanish language. In the long term, this will do a great deal for your conversational skills.

Tip #4: Avoid Programmed Conversations

Many language learning courses have standard conversational scripts to learn in order to be able to communicate effectively in a foreign language. I personally greatly dislike this method because when you interact with native Spanish speakers in the real Spanish-speaking world, you are not going to have one possible response to the question you are asking. This is why it is essential to study many different conversations with multiple answers so that you are prepared to converse with authentic individuals in the everyday Spanish-speaking world.

COMMON SPANISH ADJECTIVES TO DESCRIBE THE WORLD AROUND YOU

- Lindo (pretty)
- Feo (ugly)
- Feliz (happy)
- Triste (sad)
- Alto (tall)
- Bajo (short)
- Grande (big)
- Pequeño (small)
- Simple (simple)
- Complicado (complicated)

Let's hear them one more time:

- Lindo (pretty)
- Feo (ugly)
- Feliz (happy)
- Triste (sad)
- Alto (tall)
- Bajo (short)
- Grande (big)
- Pequeño (small)
- Simple (simple)
- Complicado (complicated)

Now, how do you translate these Spanish words to English?

- Lindo... That's right, pretty
- Feo... That's right, ugly
- Feliz... That's right, happy
- Triste... That's right, sad
- Alto... That's right tall
- Bajo... That's right, short

- Grande… That's right, big
- Pequeño… That's right, small
- Simple… That's right, simple
- Complicado… That's right, complicated.

Well done! Now, how do you translate these English words to Spanish?

- Pretty… That's right, lindo
- Ugly… that's right, feo
- Happy… That's right, feliz
- Sad… That's right, triste
- Tall… That's right, alto
- Short… That's right, bajo
- Big… That's right, grande
- Small… That's right, pequeño
- Simple… That's right, simple
- Complicated… That's right, complicado

Well done! Let us continue with the same format for the next Spanish words.

- Divertido (fun)
- Aburrido (boring)
- Rico (rich)
- Pobre (poor)
- Delicioso (delicious)
- Repugnante (disgusting)
- Inteligente (intelligent)
- Tonto (stupid)
- Nuevo (new)
- Viejo (old)

One more time:

- Divertido (fun)
- Aburrido (boring)
- Rico (rich)
- Pobre (poor)

- Delicioso (delicious)
- Repugnante (disgusting)
- Inteligente (intelligent)
- Tonto (stupid)
- Nuevo (new)
- Viejo (old)

Now how do you translate these Spanish words to English?

- Divertido… That's right, fun
- Aburrido… That's right, boring
- Rico… That's right, rich
- Pobre… That's right, poor
- Delicioso… That's right, delicious
- Repugnante… That's right, disgusting
- Inteligente… That's right, intelligent
- Tonto… That's right, stupid
- Nuevo… That's right, new
- Viejo… That's right, old

Well done! And now, how do you translate these English words to Spanish?

- Fun… That's right, divertido
- Boring… That's right, aburrido
- Rich… That's right, rico
- Poor… That's right, pobre
- Delicious… That's right, delicioso
- Disgusting… That's right, repugnante
- Intelligent… That's right, inteligente
- Stupid… That's right, tonto
- New… That's right, Nuevo
- Old… That's right, Viejo

Well done! Let's continue with more words.

- Abierto (open)
- Cerrado (closed)

- Cansado (tired)
- Despierto (awake)
- Caluroso (hot)
- Frío (cold)
- Caro (expensive)
- Barato (cheap)
- Rápido (fast)
- Lento (slow)

How do you translate these Spanish words into English?

- Abierto… That's right, open
- Cerrado… That's right, closed
- Cansado… That's right, tired
- Despierto… That's right, awake
- Caluroso… That's right, hot
- Frío… That's right, cold
- Caro… That's right, expensive
- Barato… That's right, cheap
- Rapido… That's right, fast
- Lento… That's right, slow

How do you translate these English words to Spanish?

- Open… That's right, open abierto
- Closed… That's right, cerrado
- Tired… That's right, cansado
- Awake… That's right, despierto
- Hot… That's right, caluroso
- Cold … That's right, frío
- Expensive… That's right, caro
- Cheap… That's right, barato
- Fast… That's right, rápido
- Slow… That's right, lento

Well done! Here are another ten adjectives.

- Loco (crazy)
- Tranquilo (tranquil)
- Fuerte (strong)
- Débil (weak)
- Enfermo (sick)
- Sano (healthy)
- Dulce (sweet)
- Salado (savory)
- Limpio (clean)
- Sucio (dirty)

How do you say these Spanish words in English?

- Loco… That's right, crazy
- Tranquilo… That's right, tranquil
- Fuerte… That's right, strong
- Débil… That's right, weak
- Enfermo… That's right, sick
- Sano… That's right, healthy
- Dulce… That's right, sweet
- Salado… That's right, savory
- Limpio… That's right, clean
- Sucio… That's right, dirty

How do you say these English words in Spanish?

- Crazy… That's right, loco
- Tranquil… That's right, tranquilo
- Strong… That's right, fuerte weak… That's right, débil
- Sick… That's right, enfermo
- Healthy… That's right, sano
- Sweet… That's right, dulce
- Savory… That's right, salado
- Clean… That's right, limpio
- Dirty… That's right, sucio

Now onto the last ten adjectives.

- Seco (dry)
- Mojado (wet)
- Injusto (unfair)
- Justo (fair)
- Vacío (empty)
- Lleno (full)
- Delgado (thin)
- Gordo (fat)
- Bueno (good)
- Malo (bad)

Last exercise. How do you translate these Spanish words into English?

- Seco… That's right, dry
- Mojado… That's right, wet
- Injusto… That's right, unfair
- Justo… That's right, fair
- Vacío… That's right, empty
- Lleno… That's right, full
- Delgado… That's right, thin
- Gordo… That's right, fat
- Bueno… That's right, good
- Malo… That's right, bad

Lastly, how do you translate these English words to Spanish?

- Dry… That's right, seco
- Wet… That's right, mojado
- Unfair… That's right, injusto
- Fair… That's right, justo
- Empty… That's right, vacío
- Full… That's right, lleno
- Thin… That's right, Delgado
- Fat… That's right, gordo
- Good… That's right, Bueno
- Bad… That's right, malo

Great Job! You have now gone through 50 of the most regularly used adjectives in the Spanish language. I recommend that you go through them more than once in order for the words to truly stick.

Now let us continue with colors!

- Amarillo= Yellow
- Verde= Green
- Rojo= Red
- Morada= Purple
- Azul= Blue
- Naranja= Orange
- Blanco= White
- Negro= Black
- Marrón= Brown
- Rosado= Pink

Once more:

- Amarillo= Yellow
- Verde= Green
- Rojo= Red
- Morada= Purple
- Azul= Blue
- Naranja= Orange
- Blanco= White
- Negro= Black
- Marrón= Brown
- Rosado= Pink

When comparing with the English language, there is one major difference when it comes to conjugation. In the English language, you always use personal pronouns in conjunction with the verb to describe which person the verb is referring to. For example, "to talk" is conjugated like this in the present tense:

- I talk
- You talk
- He/she/it talks
- We talk
- You talk
- They talk

The Spanish language works in a slightly different manner. Instead of using personal pronouns, you simply change the ending of the verb itself in order to denote which person the verb concerns.

And, depending on which house a verb belongs to, you should use specific endings.

- The house of Ar has its own set of endings
- The house of Er has its own set of endings

And now, we will begin by looking at how you conjugate verbs that belong to the house of AR.

Conjugating Verbs in the House of AR—Present Tense

Let us use "to talk" as an example in Spanish.

"To talk" translates to hablar and its conjugation in the present tense is as follows:

- Yo hablo
- Tu hablas
- Él/Ella usted habla
- Nosotros hablamos
- Vosotros habláis
- Ellos/Ellas ustedes hablan

Now, I did include the subject pronouns before the verb, but in general, this is not something you include when you are communicating. Instead, you simply say:

- Hablo
- Hablas
- Habla
- Hablamos
- Habláis
- Hablan.

What I want you to notice is that the way you conjugate the verb Hablar is simply to take away the -ar in the word hablar and replace it with a different ending to denote which person that is doing the talking.

The following is the rule you should take away with you.

For every verb in the house of AR such as Hablar, Trabajar (to work), preguntar (to ask) you will conjugate them in the exact same way.

If it refers to I, the verb ends with -o, hablo, trabajo, pregunto. If it refers to you, the verb ends with -as, hablas, trabajas, preguntas. If it refers to he/she/it, the verb ends with -a, habla, trabaja, pregunta. If it refers to we, the verb ends with -amos, hablamos, trabajamos, preguntamos.

If it refers to you (second person plural), the verb ends with -áis, habláis, trabajáis, preguntáis. And if it refers to they (third person plural) the verb ends with -an, hablan, trabajan, preguntan.

It is as simple as that!

Now, we will do a short exercise. I want you to repeat out loud the following.

- O
- As
- A
- Amos
- Áis
- An.

Say them several times out loud

- O
- As
- A
- Amos
- Áis
- An
- O
- As
- A
- Amos
- Áis
- An
- O
- As
- A
- Amos
- Áis
- An

By saying them out loud like this, you are creating a sound association in your brain, making it easier for you to remember how to conjugate the verbs.

Say them a couple of times more in order for the conjugations to stick.

- O
- As
- A
- Amos

- Áis
- An
- O
- As
- A
- Amos
- Áis
- An.

Well done!

Now, I want you to conjugate the following verbs on your own. Let us start with 'to practice'= Practicar

Follow the exact same rules and conjugate the verb practicar. Do that now, please. If you said:

- Practico
- Practicas
- Practica
- Practicamos
- Practicáis
- Practican

You were right! Well done!

You have now learned how you conjugate verbs that belong to the house of Ar.

Below you can go through the most common verbs that are in this house.

- Pasar= to pass or spend time with
- Quedar= to stay, remain
- Hablar= to talk or speak
- Llevar= to bring
- Dejar= to leave
- Llamar= to call
- Tomar= to take, or drink
- Tratar= to treat, or to handle

- Mirar= to look at or watch
- Esperar= to wait
- Trabajar= to work
- Terminar= to finish

I suggest you practice conjugating these verbs by yourself. Simply follow the rule of:

- O
- As
- A
- Amos
- Áis
- An

And you will manage!

This concludes the house of Ar in the present tense. Next up follows the House of Er.

CONJUGATING VERBS IN THE HOUSE OF ER—PRESENT TENSE

By now you should understand that it is the ending of the verb that changes in order to denote which person a verb is referring to.

The logic for the House of Er is exactly the same as for the house of Ar.

Knowing this we will directly learn how you conjugate verbs that belong to the House of Er.

The verb we will use is "to learn" which is aprender in Spanish.

You conjugate aprender like this:

- Yo aprendo
- Tu aprendes
- Él/Ella/ usted aprende
- Nosotros aprendemos
- Vosotros aprendéis
- Ellos/ellas ustedes aprenden.

The verbs that belong to the house of Er follow the exact same conjugation principle as the House of Ar.

The first person singular (meaning I) remains the same and for every other subject, you simply change the "a" to an "e" in the ending of the word.

Compare these two verbs, you talk and you learn:

- You talk is hablas
- You learn is aprendes.

Notice that the ending of aprendes consists of es instead of as.

We will now go through only the endings in order to make them stick.

For every verb that belongs to the house of Er, such as aprender, responder (to respond), comprender (to understand) you conjugate them like this: If it refers to I, the verb ends with -o, aprendo, respondo, comprendo

If it refers to you, the verb ends with -es, aprendes, respondes, comprendes. If it refers to he/she/it, the verb ends with -e, aprende, responde, comprende. If it refers to we, the verb ends with -emos, aprendemos, respondemos, comprendemos

If it refers to you (second person plural), the verb ends with -éis, aprendéis, respondéis, comprendéis. And if it refers to they (third person plural) the verb ends with -en, aprenden, responden, comprenden.

Well done! Let us create another sound association for the house of Er with your brain.

- O
- Es
- E
- Emos
- Éis
- En
- O
- Es
- E
- Emos
- Éis
- En
- O
- Es
- E
- Emos
- Éis
- En
- O

- Es
- E
- Emos
- Eis
- En.

Now, I want you to follow this principle and conjugate the verb: correr (meaning to run).

Do it now please!

If you said:

- Corro
- Corres
- Corre
- Corremos
- Corréis
- Corren

Well done! You have now learned how to conjugate verbs in the house of Er.

THE USE OF GENDER

The grammatical genre does not have a definition that can be used globally, since within each language the number of genres and their use varies greatly. For instance: Danish has four grammatical genres; in German, there are three and in Spanish, there are two, which are the traditional masculine and feminine genres.

Gender is a characteristic that nouns possess and only other words such as adjectives match the noun referred to, but this does not mean that the adjectives or the article have their own gender, since this possibility depends entirely on the noun.

Neutral

Previously, before Spanish existed, its predecessor language Latin had three genders: feminine, masculine and neutral. In Latin, nouns existed in a neutral gender and could be declined, that is, a noun could be transformed to adapt to another characteristic, gender for instance.

In Spanish, nouns have no gender, the only one that has retained its neutral character has been the article "Lo" which also cannot be used together with any nouns. This neutral article can only appear next to the qualifying adjectives and some possessives. Example:

- This is the beauty of living= Esto es lo hermoso de vivir.
- This is my thing= Esto es lo mio.

Female

Nouns ending in "a" are feminine. With some exceptions: el día, el mapa.

The letters of the alphabet are feminine.

To convert a masculine word into feminine, the most common suffixes are: "Esa, Isa, and Triz." Examples:

- Mayor= Alcalde/alcaldesa
- Priest= Sacerdote/sacerdotisa
- Emperor= Emperador/emperatriz

The differences in suffix A and O are not only used to distinguish between feminine and masculine in nouns but also between large and small. Example:

- Cesto (large) cesta (small)
- Manzano (tree) manzana (fruit)

Male

- **Nouns ending in "o" are male.** With some exceptions such as la mano.
- **Nouns ending in "ma" are masculine:** el telegrama, el problema.
- The months and days of the week are masculine.
- **The cardinal points are masculine:** norte, sur, este, and oeste.

Heteronymous Nouns

Refers to the variant of a noun when it is feminine and masculine, these words change several characters in their form, for example:

- Mother/father= Madre/padre
- Bull/cow= Toro/vaca
- Gentleman/lady= Caballero/dama.

Indistinct or Common

The gender of the noun, which corresponds to the sex of the referent, is indicated by the determinants and adjectives with generic variation: el testigo/la testigo.

At the moment, the form of the word varies according to gender, Example:

- El primer ministro/la primera ministra.

- **Nouns formed with the suffix ISTA.** Example: el/la pianista.
- **Nouns ending in "a" work in their vast majority as common nouns:** el/la guía, el/la terapeuta.
- **Nouns ending in "and" tend to function as common:** el/la cantante.
- **Nouns ending in "ante" or "ente."** Example: el/la estudiante.

Epicenity

These have a unique form, which corresponds to a single grammatical genre in order to refer, indistinctly, to individuals of one sex or the other. The grammatical gender is independent of the sex of the referent. A couple of examples:

- Male epicens (vástago, tiburón).
  The shark turned out to be female and was pregnant= El tiburón, resultó ser hembra y estaba embarazada.
- Female epicens (víctima, hormiga).
  The victim was an elderly man= La víctima fue un hombre anciano.

Ambiguous

These are usually used to designate inanimate beings. This does not differentiate between masculine and feminine, it could be said that these are nouns that have no defined gender. Some examples of this type of noun can be:

- El mar
- La mar
- El sartén
- La sartén.

ACCENTUATION

his is a process that occurs in Spanish and other languages.

Accentuation occurs when there is a phonetic emphasis or stress on some syllable of the word. This emphasis is represented by some words graphically with the presence of an accent mark (´) on one of the vowels. The tildes can only appear at the top of the vowels and each word can carry a maximum of accent marks.

The Accent and the Accent Mark

As you have already noticed, there are two terms that can generate some confusion when it comes to accentuation. The accent and the accent mark, similar but not the same. The accent is that emphasis that is done phonetically when saying a word. All words have a particular accent in Spanish since in all of them there is an emphasis on a particular syllable.

This does not mean that all words in Spanish carry an accent mark, which is the graphic representation of the accent.

You will be wondering now, why not all words carry accent marks if they all have an accent. Then we will talk about the accentuation rules that will help you know when a word should be accentuated and when not. For this, there is something you must learn to handle very well and it is the syllabic separation.

The Syllable

The syllable is made up of a phoneme or set of two or several phonemes or letters. Those are phonological units in which any word is divided, according to the minimum grouping of its sounds articulated, which means the union of a vowel and one or several consonants, that is, the syllables, are the sound fragments in which we can split a word, without altering the logic of its pronunciation.

All words are composed of syllables, from the longest to those with only one, and each syllable also has a core, which in Spanish is always the vowel, since its sound receives a greater emphasis on pronunciation. The number of syllables of a word can be classified into syllables or monosyllables, two syllables or bisyllable, three syllables or trisyllable, four syllables or tetrasyllable, and polysyllable that contain five or more syllables.

And how does this help you with accentuation? Well, depending on the number of syllables a word has, its accentuation, and the placement of the accent mark will change.

Atonic and Tonic Syllables

Within the same word, syllables are pronounced with different intonations. Some receive a common intonation and others have a more intense intonation, becoming the sound the center of the word, thus being the tonic syllable of the word. It is important to remember that the tonic syllable will not always carry the accent mark. These tonic syllables, depending on their location within the word, can be classified as acute, severe, and esdrújulas, a classification which we will go into further detail.

Next, we will see some examples of the syllabic separation:

- Perro separates: Pe-rro.

This word, which means dog, has two syllables since there are two voice strokes.

- Casa separates: Ca-sa
- Hola separates Ho-la
- Ajo separates A-jo

Monosyllable Words

The words that are made up of a single syllable are those that are pronounced with a single voice stroke and usually have one, two, and even up to four letters, one of them must necessarily be a vowel. Remember that the vowel is the core of the syllable. These types of words are not accentuated, however, there is a phenomenon called diacritical accent mark that we will see in a few moments. Example of monosyllables:

- Dos
- Luz
- Mar
- Mes
- Bar

None of these are separated, they are made up of a single whole syllable.

Polysyllable Words

Polysyllable words are those that are separated into two or more syllables. These, as we already mentioned, have a classification that is based on the number of syllables that each word has, from this classification and its rules it is known how to accentuate and whether or not to put the accent mark.

- Acute:
  - ➤ The tonic syllable is the last: Canción
- Severe:
  - ➤ Tonic syllable is the penultimate: Puerta and azúcar
- Esdrújula:
  - ➤ It is the last to last syllable: Sábado and catálogo
- Sobreesdrújula:
  - ➤ Any place before the last: Cuéntamelo

The syllabic separation also does not depend only on where the tonic syllable is, for there are certain rules that govern the division of syllables. In Spanish, we can find several words that create conflict with the basic statement of the syllabic separation that is any unit that has a vowel that may or may not is linked to a constant. But what happens when there are two vowels or several consonants in a row? We'll see.

Diacritical Accent Mark

The accent mark is placed in words that have a tonic variety to differentiate it from its unstressed variety and thus give them a grammatical category. Normally diacritical accent mark appears in monosyllable words that should not be accentuated. You may be wondering now: then they should not be accentuated but they are accentuated? In some cases: yes. What are these cases?

Remember that words with diacritical accent marks are those that have a twin word that means something else, this accent mark is placed to differentiate meanings. Keeping this in mind, we see this:

- TE (personal pronoun)/TÉ (noun)
- EL (pronoun)/ÉL (pronoun)
- SE (pronoun)/SÉ (conjunction of the verb saber)
- DE (preposition)/DÉ (conjunction of the verb dar)

The Diphthong

This is nothing more than the presence of two consecutive vowels in the same words. If one of the vowels carries an accent mark it will keep the accent mark. When a diphthong is formed, the syllabic separation occurs by keeping these two vowels together: APLAU-SO. The diphthong only occurs when:

- Opened tonic vowel + unstressed closed vowel: Bonsái (bon-sái)
- Unstressed vocal closed + Tonic vowel opened: Canción (can-ción)
- Two different vowels: City (ciu-dad)

The Triptongo

The triptongo is the appearance of three consecutive vowels in one syllable. It is triptongo when:

- Atonic vowel closed + Tonic vowel opened + Atonic vowel closed: Uruguay (u-ru-guay), miau (miau)

The Hiatus

The hiatus is when two consecutive vowels that belong to different syllables coincide. It is hiatus when:

- Two equal vowels: Microondas (mi-cro-on-das)
- Two opened vowels: Héroe (hé-ro-e)
- Tonic vowel closed + Unstressed vowel opened: Río (rí-o)
- Atonic vowel opened + Tonic vowel closed: Reír (re-ír)

Practical Exercises

Now you will have a box where you must separate the words by syllables.

Syllabic separation:

Example: Animal (A-ni-mal)

- Cosa
- Nada
- Hola
- Adiós
- Como
- Día
- Mano
- Pie
- Estrecho
- Aceite
- Plato
- Cebolla
- Tomate
- Bombillo
- Luz
- Crema
- Talco

In this second exercise, you will find a table with a list of words and you must place next to what type of word is that: diphthong, triptongo, or hiatus.

Type of word:

- Uruguay
- Semi-Triptongo
- Semiautomático
- Podéis
- Craís
- Paraguas
- Mío
- Cuota
- Navío
- Guau

- Cuidar
- Ahorrar
- Buey
- Paraguay
- Oír
- Despeinar
- País
- Peine
- Frío

EXERCISES ABOUT THEORY

1. Identify what kind of tense belongs to the following conjugation:
   a. Yo he hablado
   b. Tú has hablado
   c. Él ha hablado
   d. Nosotros hemos hablado
   e. Ellos han hablado.
   f. Yo hablo
   g. Tú hablas
   h. Él habla
   i. Nosotros hablamos
   j. Ellos hablan
   k. Yo hablaba
   l. Tú hablabas
   m. Él hablaba
   n. Nosotros hablábamos
   o. Ellos hablaban
   p. Yo había hablado
   q. Tú habías hablado
   r. Él había hablado
   s. Nosotros habíamos hablado
   t. Ellos habían hablado

2. Now, place the following verbs in their previous verb form: Caminar-Querer
   a. Yo
   b. Tú
   c. Él
   d. Nosotros
   e. Ellos

3. Identify in the following text the verbal tenses that exist.
   *Entre las modificaciones celulares que conducen al cáncer, los cambios en el metabolismo de la célula son notorios. Conocer dichos cambios abre una ventana de oportunidades para el desarrollo de terapias selectivas y eficientes que puedan atacar específicamente cada tipo de tumor.

Conocemos por cáncer a una familia de enfermedades, de espectro y pronóstico muy amplio, caracterizadas por un crecimiento descontrolado y acelerado de células de determinados tejidos. Aunque en un origen se abordó el cáncer como una única enfermedad, nuestro conocimiento a nivel molecular y celular del cáncer nos permite hoy entender que, en realidad, se trata de fenómenos celulares con un origen muy diverso, y con unas características moleculares y celulares muy complejas y diferentes de unos tipos a otros, quedando pocas propiedades que se puedan aplicar comúnmente a todos los diferentes tipos de cáncer. Ello nos lleva ineludiblemente a la "medicina personalizada": el conocimiento pormenorizado de las características moleculares y celulares específicas de cada tumor, para poder aplicar terapias específicas que den resultado en cada paciente.*

Among the cellular modifications that lead to cancer, changes in cell metabolism are noticeable. Knowing these changes opens a window of opportunities for the development of selective and efficient therapies that can specifically attack each type of tumor.

We know cancer as a family of diseases, with a very broad spectrum and prognosis, characterized by uncontrolled and accelerated growth of cells of certain tissues. Although cancer was originally approached as a single disease, our knowledge at the molecular and cellular level of cancer allows us today to understand that, in reality, these are cellular phenomena with a very diverse origin, and with very complex molecular and cellular characteristics in which they are different from one type to another, leaving few properties that can be commonly applied to all different types of cancer. This inevitably leads us to "personalized medicine": detailed knowledge of the specific molecular and cellular characteristics of each tumor, in order to apply specific therapies that work for each patient.

4. Read and analyze if the use of the following verb tenses is correct according to its statement:

   a. Futuro perfecto:
      - ✓ Yo habré querido
      - ✓ Tú habrás querido
      - ✓ Él habrá querido
      - ✓ Nosotros habremos querido
      - ✓ Ellos habrán querido

   b. Condicional perfecto:

- ✓ Yo quería
- ✓ Tú querías
- ✓ Él quería
- ✓ Nosotros queríamos
- ✓ Ellos querían

  c. Presente:
- ✓ Yo habría querido
- ✓ Tú habrías querido
- ✓ Él habría querido
- ✓ Nosotros habríamos querido
- ✓ Ellos habrían querido

5. Identify what kind of verbal tense belongs to the following conjugations:
   a. Yo haya amado
   b. Tú hayas amado
   c. Él haya amado
   d. Nosotros hayamos amado
   e. Ellos hayan amado
   f. Yo hubiera amado
   g. Tú hubieras amado
   h. Él hubiera amado
   i. Nosotros hubiéramos amado
   j. Ellos hubieran amado

6. In the following text, highlight all the verbs you find.

   *Las vacunas son uno de los avances médicos más importantes de la humanidad. Aprovechando las propiedades de nuestro sistema inmunitario, previene eficazmente la propagación de las enfermedades infecciosas y sus graves efectos en nuestra salud y en la sociedad. Frente a los movimientos anti vacunación debemos reivindicar con firmeza su uso, porque las vacunas salvan vidas.

   Todos hemos oído hablar de las vacunas. Cuando éramos niños, quizás nos asaltaba una cierta ansiedad en el momento de visitar al médico para recibir áquel pequeño pinchazo, pero sabíamos que era por nuestro bien. Ya de adultos, si somos padres responsables, estaremos muy pendientes del calendario vacunal y de las recomendaciones de los pediatras para proteger a nuestros hijos de las enfermedades infecciosas.

   La vacunación es uno de los avances médicos más importantes de la humanidad. Las vacunas son útiles y salvan vidas. Y somos afortunados por disponer de esta fenomenal herramienta para no sufrir los males que hacían estragos en nuestros antepasados, en épocas no tan lejanas.*

Vaccines are one of the most important medical advances in human history. Taking advantage of the properties of our immune system effectively prevents the spread of infectious diseases and their serious effects on our health and society. In the face of anti-vaccination movements, we must firmly claim their use, because vaccines do save lives. We have all heard of vaccines. When we were children, perhaps we were assaulted by certain anxiety when visiting the doctor to receive that little jab. But we knew it was for our good. As adults, if we are responsible parents, we will be very aware of the vaccination calendar and the recommendations of pediatricians to protect our children from infectious diseases. Vaccination is one of the most important medical advances in human history. Vaccines are useful and save lives. And we are fortunate to have this phenomenal tool to avoid suffering the evils that wreaked havoc on our ancestors, in not-so-distant times.

7. You must identify what type of discursive connector has been used from the following sentences.
    a. Quédate. Además, ya es tarde
    b. Mañana lloverá, en cambio, hoy hizo sol
    c. Quiero algo frío, mejor dicho, quiero helado
    d. Ella lo quiere, aun así lo dejó ir
    e. Quiero una caja, por ejemplo, una como esa
    f. En resumen, hoy fue un gran día
    g. Él correrá pido, por lo tanto ganó el torneo.

Answers to the Exercises

Answers for 1:

- Perfect past compound= Pasado perfecto compuesto
- Present tense= Presente
- Past tense= Pasado
- Past perfect Past= Pasado perfecto

Answers for 2:

- I had wanted= Yo había querido
- You had wanted= Tu habias querido
- He had wanted= Él había querido
- We had wanted: Nosotros habíamos querido
- They had wanted= Ellos hubiésen querido
- I had walked= Yo había caminado
- You had walked= Tu has caminado
- He had walked= Él habia caminado
- We had walked= Nosotros habíamos caminado
- They had walked= Ellos habían caminado

Answers for 4:

a. Perfect future:
   - ✓ I will have wanted
   - ✓ You will have loved
   - ✓ He will have wanted
   - ✓ We will have wanted
   - ✓ They will have wanted
b. Futuro perfecto:
   - ✓ Yo habré querido
   - ✓ Tu habrás amado
   - ✓ Él habrá amado
   - ✓ Nosotros habríamos querido
   - ✓ Ellos habrían querido
c. Present:
   - ✓ I want
   - ✓ You want
   - ✓ He wants
   - ✓ We want
   - ✓ They want
   - ✓ Yo quiero
   - ✓ Tu quieres
   - ✓ Él quiere
   - ✓ Nosotros queremos
   - ✓ Ellos quieren
d. Conditional perfect:

- ✓ I would have wanted
- ✓ You would have wanted
- ✓ He would have wanted
- ✓ We would have wanted
- ✓ They would have wanted
- ✓ Yo habría querido
- ✓ Tu habrías querido
- ✓ Él habría querido
- ✓ Nosotros habríamos querido
- ✓ Ellos habrían querido

Answers for 5:

- Past subjunctive compound= Pasado compuesto subjuntivo
- Past perfect subjunctive= Pasado perfecto subjuntivo

Answers for 7:

a. Stay, it's too late (ADDITIVE)
b. Tomorrow it will rain, instead, today it was sunny (COUNTER ARGUMENTATIVE)
c. I want something cold, rather, I want ice cream (RECTIFICATIVE)
d. She wants it, yet she let it go (CONCESSIVE)
e. I want a box, for example, one like that (EXEMPLIFICATIVE)
f. In short, today was a great day (CONCLUSIVE)
g. He runs fast, therefore he won the tournament. (ILLATIVE)

CONCLUSION

Learning Spanish is an excellent choice for anyone. The benefits are many, and it is a skill that will develop your intellect and flexibility in thinking.

Learning Spanish isn't for everyone, but it seems that those who do pursue this lifelong journey are glad they did! From expanding your horizons to becoming a citizen of the world to boosting your career prospects… All reasons to consider adding this incredible language to your academic repertoire!

Spanish is a Romance language. It originated from the Latin language, which was spoken in ancient Rome from the 3rd through to the 5th century A.D. Roman rulers brought Latin to many areas they conquered, and the language later evolved into different languages including Italian, French, Portuguese and Spanish. The Spanish language is very similar to its sister languages French and Portuguese because of their shared roots in Latin.

That is why it is sometimes called Castilian Spanish (Castellano). It has evolved over time, but it maintains strong ties with its roots. In fact, it has been referred to as "one of the most conservative Romance languages."

As mentioned, the Spanish language is the root of several other languages. It has had an influence on them, and they have in return influenced it. For instance, Latin was the base for many of today's languages including Spanish, Italian, French, and Portuguese. All European languages have Latin roots!

Spanish is used by over 500 million people worldwide. This means that it has been able to spread throughout many countries and continents as well as global communities which speak different languages such as Chinese and Arabic. As a result, Spanish is spoken in Spain itself (of course), but also in Mexico, South America (including places like Argentina), Central America, and even parts of Africa.

The Spanish language has a lot of variations. There are dialects, accents, and slang words that differ from region to region. One of the most famous dialects is Mexican Spanish. This is mainly because it is spoken in the country where it originated: Mexico! It differs from other types of Spanish in that it makes use of the Nahuatl language, which was spoken by the Aztecs who ruled the land during the 400s to 500 A.D.

Another example is Argentinean Spanish which is also known as Castellano Rioplatense, being that it shares its roots with Castilian. It also takes its cues from South American languages such as Quechua and Aymara.

As you can see there are a lot of variations to the Spanish language. It is an excellent choice for people who want to learn a good skill that will provide them with so many opportunities!

The history of the Spanish language started from the Latin language, which was spoken in ancient Rome. It was brought there by wealthy Roman citizens. After the fall of Rome, the Spanish nation conquered and added many other cultures into its military campaigns including those in Spain itself (this is where we get our name "Spanish"). After this period, it began to develop into different languages such as French and Italian. These languages had strong roots in both Latin and Spanish but also added different words, structures, and rules.

The Spanish language is sometimes referred to as Castellano which comes from the fact that it was created in Castile, Spain. In fact, many of its rules are formed by the country's customs such as marriage and inheritance laws—although these have changed over time!

The history of the Spanish language has most recently been influenced by its links to other languages such as Arabic. This is because it has spread across South America. Even Mexico which uses a lot of Spanish words still has a lot of influence from African civilizations like the Maya and Inca.

It's likely that the Spanish language is set to continue on and evolve in different ways since its influence continues to go around the world.

There is also the Basque language, which is native to the region in far Northern Spain. However, this language does not have a lot of influence from Spanish and

French because like I said earlier its roots are in Latin. The Spanish language has many different dialects and speech patterns which all vary depending on where they are found. These differences among dialects can be seen in the different accents and slang we use on a daily basis.

If you are interested in learning the Spanish language, check out our website! We offer all different levels of courses and because we specialize in education, we will be able to teach you everything you need to know!

Now that we've got the basics out of the way, let's talk a bit more about the differences between Spanish and English. You might be thinking: hello I already know that Spanish is different than English! But hear me out.

What Is Spanish and English?

It's all about communication.

One of the biggest differences between languages is how people use them. This is because the language has changed over time, and with that comes different ways of saying things. For example, if someone was talking about a car in English, he might say: "He drives a blue car." whereas a Spanish speaker would say: "Cíe un coche azul."

This is where the communication and the culture of Spain comes into play and why it's important to learn both Spanish and English. When people hear "Cie, ee un coche azul" they instantly know what he's going to say, whereas if they hear "He drives a blue car" there's a good chance that he means a vehicle that isn't blue or that is not actually driven by a human being. It might sound like this: "He drives an invisible car."

Both Spanish and English are spoken in different parts of the world and to a different degree by people who live there. That said, it might sound a bit odd or funny if you hear a Spaniard talk about a car as if it's an animal. This is because they just don't have that mindset at all when doing so! On the other hand, English might seem like Spanish to a foreigner living in Spain since some of the words are similar.

What Is the Difference Between Spanish and English?

A language by itself does not make a person who speaks it any better than someone else who speaks it. It's more about how people use their language and the culture they're exposed to. This is why we've put together this short guide to help you get a better idea of what it means to speak Spanish in Spain!

Spanish and English are very similar because they both come from Latin, which has been around for over 2000 years. That said, over time there have many differences between them. This is why it can sometimes be hard to understand one or the other.

Differences in Modifiers

Words are important for language. This is why they can be broken down and studied to figure out if they actually mean something or not. In English, words can be categorized into a word class that has different levels of meaning. For example, there are words that can only mean one thing whereas others can be used with other words to make new meanings. For instance, the word: "centrifuge" means something completely different from "centrifuge!" Because of this, it's important to know how to use modifiers correctly in both Spanish and English.

For example, if you're from Spain and you haven't lived in a Spanish-speaking country for a long time, it might sound strange to hear someone say: "Espero que se esté bien." It's clear that the speaker meant that the person he's talking about hopes everything goes well. However, both words are being used incorrectly because "Está" is a verb of the second person singular while "Se" is an impersonal pronoun that changes depending on what it's describing. This is why it might come off as a bit odd to someone from Spain.

CHAPTER 2

LEARN SPANISH MASTERY

INTRODUCTION

Learning Spanish isn't as easy as you think. It doesn't come naturally in a few days (unless you've been studying for years) and there are a lot of hurdles along the road to fluency. But if you're determined and willing to put the time in, I'm here to prove that language learning is totally possible — even with limited Spanish knowledge or practice.

The first step to learning a new language is understanding the basics. If you've already spent enough time learning English, then it shouldn't be hard to understand these essential grammar points.

Have you ever heard people (like me) say that they don't need to learn Spanish if they're not in a Spanish-speaking country? Wrong! A lot of Spanish speakers expect you to speak Spanish so if you don't, then there's a chance that they'll be disappointed in you. Don't disappoint people!

Learning Spanish can be useful even if you're not planning on living in Mexico or Spain. You never know when it will come in handy, and I've found some ways that this knowledge can help you even outside of a Spanish-speaking country.

I think everyone should learn at least some basic Spanish skills because it's such a beautiful, romantic language. Although sometimes brutal (because it's not an easy language), Spanish is one of the most interesting languages around.

Learn to laugh at mistakes, and don't get discouraged if you don't progress as quickly as you want to. Take things slowly, one step at a time, and stick with it!

Say "Buenos días" and "Adiós" whenever you leave or enter your apartment! Go ahead — be nice to your neighbors — everyone will love you for it.

Wow, this was an emotional ride. I hope that somewhere between laughter and tears you learned something new about our relationship with Spanish. Now, go out and conquer your fears!

Spanish isn't easy, but with the right tools and the right attitude, you can learn Spanish. Don't hesitate to stand up for yourself, and don't be afraid to ask for help when you need it.

There's a lot of work involved in learning a new language, but nothing is impossible — especially with the help of a few friends. There are plenty of good reasons to learn Spanish! Until next time, keep on studying!

ESTAR

The Verb "Estar"

Before, you learned about the verb "ser." "Estar" is another verb that means to be. However, the two have distinct meanings. Once you have learned how to conjugate "estar," you will learn the differences between the two.

Conjugation of "Estar"

Let's review the people you have learned. Write the pronoun in Spanish beside each of the following English pronouns.

- You (when talking to a friend) - Tú
- They -Ellos
- I - Yo
- He - Él
- We - Nosotros
- She - Ella
- You (when talking to a respected person) - Usted
- You all (formal) - Ustedes

Here is the conjugation of "estar"

- Yo estoy
- Nosotros estamos
- Tú estás
- Vosotros estáis
- Él/ ella/ usted está
- Ellos/Ustedes están

Emotions Vocabulary

One of the ways you can use "estar" is with emotions. In order to talk about how you feel, you need to memorize some emotions. Use your vocabulary notebook to draw a picture related to each emotion. If the emotion is happy, you can draw a happy memory or something that you associate with happiness. For some people, that might be a certain restaurant or a favorite person.

- Feliz /feh-lees/ - happy
- Triste /trees-tay/ - sad

- Enojado /en-oh-ha-do/ - angry
- Emocionado /ee-mo-see-oh-nah-do/ - excited
- Asustado /ah-soo-stah-do/ - scared
- Aburrido /ah-bore-ee-do/- bored
- Preocupado /preh-aw-coo-paw-do/ worried
- Cansado /cahn-saw-do/ tired
- Bien /bee-in/ - good
- Mal /mahl/- bad

Even though "bien" technically means "good," it is also used to mean "okay" or "fine." Also, for the emotions ending with "o," they need to be changed to match the gender of the speaker. For example, if the speaker is a female and she feels scared, she would say "asustada" with an "a," instead of the letter "o." For the emotions that end in a different letter, they remain the same for male and female.

Just as with other adjectives, these words need to match the subject in number as well as gender. You can make these adjectives plural if you are describing multiple people. For example, "triste" would become "tristes."

"Asustado" would become "asustados." Feliz is strange because it ends with a 'z'. "Feliz" becomes "felices." "Bien" adds "es" to become "bienes." "Mal" can become "malas" or "malos" depending on the gender of the group. If a group is mixed with boys and girls, then the male version is used.

Read the following sentences aloud and determine how the person is feeling.

- Estoy asustada /Eh-stoy ah-soo-stah-duh/
- Estoy bien /Eh-stoy bee-en/
- Ella está feliz /Ay-yuh es-tah feh-lees/
- Nosotros estamos bien. /No-so-tros es-tah-mos bee-in/

Read the following situations and determine how you would feel in each situation. Say a full sentence in Spanish to describe your feelings. Below you will see some possible answers. Your answer does not have to match.

1. You win a free trip to visit Italy.
2. You can't find your car keys.
3. You woke up five minutes before your alarm.
4. You have just worked a thirteen-hour shift.
5. Your friend lied about what she was doing yesterday.
6. Your grandpa is very sick.

Possible answers:

1. Estoy emocionada.

232

2. Estoy preocupada.
3. Estoy bien.
4. Estoy cansada.
5. Estoy enojada.
6. Estoy triste.

Ser vs. Estar

"Ser" and "Estar" both mean "to be." So how do you know which one to use?

Here is a basic chart of the reasons. Below, you will find examples and explanations of each reason.

- Characteristics
- Emotions
- Identification
- Location
- Possession
- Progressive Tense
- Profession
- Price
- Origin

The easiest way to differentiate the two is to remember "ser" as a more permanent verb while "estar" is a more temporary verb. For example, you will not always be in the same location. You will not always feel the same way, and you will not always be doing the same action. However, your characteristics will not change. If you are blonde, for example, then even if you dye your hair, you are still a blonde.

Here are some example sentences for each of the reasons under "ser."

- Characteristics - Soy gordo. (I am fat)
- Identification - Él es un hombre. (He is a man)
- Possession - El libro es de Alfredo. (The book is Alfred's). See the note below on possession.
- Profession - Yo soy un doctor.
- Price - Son treinta dolares.
- Origin - Soy de los Estados Unidos.

*Note on possession. In English, we often use an apostrophe and an 's' to show possession. However, in Spanish, we say "de Bob" or "de Jorge." The object is of or from them.

- La bolsa es de Jorge.

233

- El libro es de mi amigo.

Here are some example sentences for each of the reasons under "estar."

- Emotions - Ella está muy triste.
- Location - Estoy en el parque. (I am in the park).
- Progressive Tense - Estoy caminando en el parque. (I am walking in the park).

The progressive tense shows an action in progress. We will work on creating this later. However, just know when that comes that "estar" will be the verb to use.

Read the following sentences and determine why each one uses the verb it does. The answers are below.

1. Ellos son de Inglaterra.
2. Mi amiga está en mi casa.
3. Yo estoy feliz.
4. Nosotros somos rubios. (rubio-blonde)
5. El es gordo.
6. La silla es de Matilda (silla- chair)
7. Tu estás asustado.
8. Usted es una maestra (maestra- teacher)

Answers

1. Origin
2. Location
3. Emotions
4. Characteristics
5. Characteristics
6. Possession
7. Emotions
8. Profession

There are a few unexpected instances where you use neither "ser" nor "estar."

If you want to say "I am thirsty," you actually will use a version of "tener"- I have.

- Tengo hambre - I am hungry. Literally, it translates to I have hunger, but we don't say that in English.
- Tengo sed - I am thirsty.
- Tengo sueño - I am tired.

These phrases take a little time to accustom yourself to using "tener" instead of a "to be" verb. Practice these phrases. In the weather section, you will learn two more situations that also use "tener."

Descriptions – Describing People Vocabulary

Now that we know which verb would be used to describe someone (which one is it?), you need to learn some adjectives. A few were listed above.

Adjectives are fun to illustrate in your vocabulary notebook.

Remember that, as explained earlier, your adjectives should match the person being described in both gender and number. Below, all adjectives are listed in the singular male form.

- Alto /all-to/- tall
- Bajo /bah-ho/- short
- Gordo /gor-do/- fat
- Delgado /del-gah-do/- thin
- Viejo /vee-eh-ho/- old
- Joven /ho-ven/- young
- Inteligente /in-tell-ee-hen-tay/- smart or intelligent
- Estupido /es-too-pee-do/- stupid
- Amable /ah-mah-blay/- kind
- Hablador /ah-bluh-door/- talkative
- Bonita /bo-nee-tuh/- beautiful
- Guapo /gwah-po/- handsome
- Feo /fay-oh/- ugly
- Grande /grahn-day/- big
- Pequeño /pe-ken-yo/- small
- Divertido /dee-vare-tee-do/- fun
- Aburrido /ah-bore-ee-do/- boring (remember that this can also mean bored as a feeling)
- Rico /ree-co/- rich
- Pobre /poh-bray/- poor
- Rubio /roo-bee-oh/- blonde
- Castaño /cas-tahn-yo/- brunette

That is a lot of vocabulary. Please take your time studying the words and drawing your illustrations. Making flashcards with pictures on one side and the Spanish word on the other can also help you. Once you have studied them thoroughly, complete the following exercises.

Adjectives Rules

With adjectives, you must keep two rules in mind.

1. Adjectives come after the objects they describe. If the adjective is a number, a version of la, el, las, or los, or "bien" or "mal," then it can come before the object. For example, you can say "Tengo cuarenta carros," but you cannot say "Tengo gordos carros." Cuarenta is a number. Gordo is a regular adjective.
2. Adjectives must match in gender and in number. Most adjectives simple have an "s" added on to make them plural. With "hablador" and "joven," since they end in a consonant, you will add "es." Habladores and jóvenes.

Descriptions Practice

Activity 1:

Select the correct adjective for each of the following sentences.

1. La mujer (woman) es (gordo/ gorda/ gordos).
2. Ellos son (rica/ rico/ ricos).
3. Mi padre es (alto/ alta/ altos).
4. Penelope es (inteligente/ inteligenta/ inteligentes).
5. Nosotros somos (viejo/ vieja/ viejos).
6. Mis perros (dogs) son (joven/ jovens/ jovenes).

Answers

1. Gorda
2. Ricos
3. Alto
4. Inteligente (there is no female version of this adjective)
5. Viejos
6. Jovenes (remember you need 'es' to make this plural because the adjective ends with a consonant)

Activity 2:

Read the following descriptions and draw a picture of the person.

Try to illustrate each adjective in the picture.

*   El hombre es muy alto. Tiene pelo rubio y es rico. Él no es feo y es guapo. Él es un poco (a little) viejo.

236

- La mujer es muy vieja. Ella es gorda y baja. Ella es inteligente y habladora.
- El niño es bajo y joven. Es guapo y divertido. No es gordo.

Activity 3:

Take a moment to describe your best friend. Try to describe both their physical characteristics and their personality. Use full sentences. Read your description aloud.

Weather and Temperature Vocabulary

Temperature vocabulary can get a little complicated because you cannot simply put together sentences about the weather following the English format. Once you have practiced the vocabulary, you will learn how to know which verb to use to talk about the weather.

- Calor /cah-lore/- heat or hot
- Frío /free-oh/- cold
- Sol /sole/- sun or sunny
- Fresco /fres-co/- fresh or cool
- Viento /vee-en-to/- wind
- Nieve /nee-eh-veh/- snow
- Lluvia /yoo-vee-uh/- rain
- Nubes /noo-bes/- clouds
- Lloviendo /yo-vee-en-do/- raining
- Nevando /nay-vahn-do/- snowing
- Nublado /noo-blah-do/- cloudy
- Relámpago /ree-lamp-ah-go/- lightning (it says lamp in the middle, so it's easy to remember lightning)
- Trueno /tray-no/- thunder (it looks like trumpet at the beginning)

Spend time drawing pictures for each of the above vocabulary words.

¿Hace o Está?

How do you ask about the weather?

- ¿Qué tal el clima?
- ¿Qué tiempo hace?

Both of these questions are commonly used to ask about the weather. Both "clima" and "tiempo" refer to the weather, though "tiempo" can also double and talk about time.

To make the above vocabulary into sentences, you need three main verbs.

"Hay" is the easiest one. Hay, pronounced "ay," or like the long letter /i/, means "there is or there are." If something is a noun, you can use it with "hay." For example:

- Hay relámpago. There is lightning.
- Hay lluvia. There is rain
- Hay nieve. There is snow.

However, when talking about the heat and cold, you will use "hace." "Hace" comes from the verb "hacer" which means to do or to make. You will say:

- Hace calor.
- Hace frio.

Even though this is not a direct translation of what you would say in English, you need to memorize these two phrases.

"Está" comes from what verb? Yes, "estar." It is the more temporary version of "to be," so it makes sense that it would be used for weather since the temperatures change often. Any "ing" verbs in English will be used with "estar." For example:

- Está lloviendo.
- Está nevando.
- Está nublado.

Read the following sentences and decide if they are correct or wrong. If they are correct, make a check mark. If they are wrong, cross out what is wrong and fix it.

1. Hay lloviendo.
2. Hace calor.
3. Está nevando.
4. Hay frío.
5. Hay trueno.
6. Hace lluvia.
7. Hace frío.
8. Hay nieve.

Answers

1. Está lloviendo. (The 'iendo' ending on here indicates "ing" in English. You must use "estar" with these verbs).

2. Correcto
3. Correcto
4. Hace frío. (This is one of the phrases you just have to memorize.)
5. Correcto
6. Hay lluvia.
7. Correcto
8. Correcto

Now, how do you talk about weather-related concepts in reference to yourself? If you want to say "I am hot" or "I am cold," you will not use "ser" or "estar." In this case, you will use "tener"- I have.

- Tengo frío- Literally, this phrase means "I have a cold," but it translates to "I am cold."
- Tengo calor- I am hot.

STRESSES AND ACCENTS

Knowing the way letters get pronounced is only one part of learning Spanish.

Another important part of pronunciation is knowing what syllables need to be stressed or which one gets the most emphasis.

There are some rules that govern using stresses and accent marks in the Spanish language. The good news is that Spanish only has three rules of stress with only a few exceptions.

Written Accent

These are known as tildes and will be on top of specific letters in the Spanish language. They are seen as a short line that is in a diagonal direction going from bottom left to top right. They will only be seen over the vowels. This means you won't ever see a Spanish word that has an accent over consonants.

Accents have three functions inside the language:

- They are used to show the difference in words that are spelled the same.
- They are used to show questions.
- They help show what syllable within the word needs to be emphasized or stressed when spoken.

Word Stress

Any stressed syllable could be defined as any syllable that has more emphasis than the syllables around it.

You can stress this through pronunciation in various ways like change in pitch, increased loudness, and increased vowel length. Every Spanish word will have no less than one stress.

Stress is functional in the Spanish language. This means that where stressed syllables are placed could change the meaning of words that were spoken.

The words célebre and celebré do have meanings that are different. Célebre means famous while celebré means celebrated. The difference in pronunciation gets differentiated by where the stressed syllable is within the word.

Rules

The Spanish language uses the acute accent mark. They don't use circumflex and grave marks. The accent mark gets used only if after you have followed the rules below, and you still haven't shown which syllable gets stressed:

If a word doesn't have an accent mark, and it has an "s," "n," or a vowel on the end, the next to last syllable is stressed. Look at these words: zapatos, joven, computadora, and toro. All of these words are stressed on the syllable for the last. You will find that most Spanish words fall into the category.

You will stress the last syllable if a word doesn't have an accent mark but ends in letters beside "s," "n," and a vowel. Look at these words: virtud, matador, hablar, and hotel. The last syllable is stressed in all of these words.

Any words that don't fall into these two categories will have the accent placed over the vowel in the syllable that is stressed. Look at these words: ojalá, inglés, médico, lápiz, común. All of these words have a stress mark on a certain syllable.

Within the Spanish language, about 79.5 percent of all words will fall into this category. Words that have their final syllable stressed are called oxytone.

Words that break these rules and have the third-to-last syllable are called proparoxytone.

Camino, meaning path, as you can see, ends with a vowel. This makes the word paroxytone and the penultimate syllable gets stressed. Animal, meaning "animal," has a consonant for its ending, and it isn't an "s" or "n." This means this is an oxytone word, and the last syllable is stressed.

The word propósito, meaning purpose, does end with a vowel but breaks all the rules because the stress is put on the third-to-last syllable. This makes it a proparoxytone. We begin to see how using written accents in the Spanish language works to show the location of where a word should be stressed.

When you finally understand these two rules about stress, using accent marks begins to make more sense. Basically, accents are used to show where the stress is within a word that breaks one of the rules above.

Let's look at some examples:

Débil, meaning weak does end in a consonant that isn't "s" or "n", so looking at the second rule, the stress needs to be on the ending syllable. Rather, the stress gets put on the first syllable, as you can see with the accent mark above the "e."

Compró, meaning buy, does end in a vowel, so looking at rule one, the stress needs to be on the next to the last syllable. Rather, the stress has been put on the last syllable, as you can see by the accent mark above the "o."

Exámenes, meaning exams, does end with an "s," so looking at rule one, the stress needs to be on the next to last syllable. Rather, the stress is put on the second syllable as you can see by the mark above the letter "a."

Now that you know why they are in words, you can begin looking at accent marks as being a helpful guide to help you pronounce the word, instead of viewing it as an alien concept. The main thing to remember is that these accents will only be above vowels, and they show the syllable that needs to be stressed and this breaks the rules.

The main exception of these rules is with words that were not originally Spanish but came from other languages. Normally, when words get adopted from the English language, they will retain their normal spelling, and sometimes, the same pronunciation. When it comes to the place and personal names that came from foreign origins, they are typically written without the use of accents unless the original language writes them with accents Signs and publications won't use accent marks over any capitalized letter even though, to clarify, it would be best to use them whenever possible.

Making Plural Words Changes Accent Marks

Since words that end in "n" or "s" will be accented on the syllable before last, and sometimes, an "es" gets used to make words plural; changing a word from singular to plural could change the accent mark. This can have an effect on adjectives and nouns.

If a word is more than two syllables, it doesn't have an accent mark and ends with an "n". If you add an "es" to the word, it will need to have an accent mark added to it. Adjectives and nouns that don't have a stressed vowel and end in "s" will have the same plural and singular forms. Words within this category aren't frequent.

- Aborigen (singular); aborígenes (plural) = indigenous
- Cañón (singular) = canon; cañones (plural) = cannons
- Crimen (singular) = crime; crímenes (plural) = crimes
- Joven (singular) = young or youth; jóvenes (plural) = youths

The most common are singular words ending in "s" or "n" will have the accent on the last syllable. When these words have two syllables or more, they get changed to plural by adding an "es," the accent marks won't be needed anymore.

- Comunes (plural); común (singular) = common

242

- Afiliaciones (plural) = affiliations; afiliación (singular) = affiliation
- Talismanes (plural) = lucky charms; talismán (singular) = lucky charm
- Almacenes (plural) = warehouses; almacén (singular) = warehouse

Orthographic Accent Marks

As stated above, another use for accent marks is to help you figure out the difference between words that are pronounced and spelled the same but have different meanings. These words are called homonyms. The words él meaning "he" and el meaning "the" are pronounced the same but they have very different meanings. There are some words like quién or quien that use accent marks only when they are in questions. When accents don't change the pronunciation, they are called orthographic accents.

Here are some words that get changed by the orthographic accent:

- Sí = yes
- Si = if
- Sé = form of "saber"
- Se = reflexive pronoun
- Qué = what
- Que = that
- Dé = form of "dar"
- De = of
- Cómo = how
- Como = I eat or as
- Aún = yet or still
- Aun = including
- Mí = my
- Mi = me
- Más = more
- Mas = but
- Sólo = only
- Solo = alone

There are some rules that govern the types of words that are given accents to show their difference from their homonym counterpart. You just need to simply learn them as a different vocabulary. Not all homonyms get distinguished by using accents.

Question Words

Accent marks can be used to show question words. To give you an example, the word "which," if it is used as a connective word, is "cual" in the Spanish language. But if "which" is being used as a question, it gets written as "¿cuál?"

This same pattern can be seen in other words, too:

- Quien = who
- ¿Quién? = who?
- Donde = where
- ¿Dónde? = where?
- Cuando = when
- ¿Cuándo? = when?

Accent marks are important because:

- They will help you find where stresses need to be in words.
- They are used to show the difference between homonyms.
- They are used to show you there is a question being asked.
- They are used to show that the stress is on a syllable where the normal rules aren't followed.
- Spanish words that don't have any will put the stress on the last syllable if the words don't end in "no," or "s." If this is the case, you will put the accent on the next to the last syllable.
- They are very helpful for both comprehension and pronunciation purposes.

ONE WORD, SEVERAL MEANINGS

There are some words in Spanish that may have several meanings. The differentiation depends on the context. Here are some of them:

1. Cuadro can mean Painting or a Geometric figure (Square shaped).

That is a beautiful painting by Picasso

In Spanish this is said:

Ese es un hermoso cuadro de Picasso

My dad has a squared shirt.

In Spanish this is said:

Mi padre tiene una camisa a cuadros.

2. Vino can mean Wine or Third person of the verb "venir" (Come).

He came to my house

In Spanish this is said:

Él vino a mi casa.

She loves wine.

In Spanish this is said:

A ella le encanta el vino.

3. Planta can mean Plant or Synonym of factory.

I have a plant in my living room

In Spanish this is said:

Tengo una planta en mi sala de estar.

He works at a recycling plant.

In Spanish this is said:

Él trabaja en una planta de reciclaje.

4. Banco can mean Bank or Bench.

We go to the bank

In Spanish this is said:

Nosotros vamos al banco

She sits on the bench

In Spanish this is said:

Ella se sienta en el banco.

5. Cura can mean Cure or Priest.

They found a cure for varicella

In Spanish this is said:

Ellos encontraron una cura para la varicela.

There is a new priest in our Church.

In Spanish this is said:

Hay un Nuevo cura en nuestra iglesia.

6. Capital can mean Capital of a country or Capital of a company (money).

Canberra is the capital of Australia

In Spanish this is said:

Canberra es la capital de Australia

The company has enough capital for new investments.

In Spanish this is said:

La compañía tiene suficiente capital para nuevas inversiones.

7. Café can mean Coffee or Brown color.

I love coffee

In Spanish this is said:

Me encanta el café

He has brown eyes.

In Spanish this is said:

Él tiene los ojos color café.

8. Chile can mean Country or fruit.

Santiago de Chile is the capital of Chile

In Spanish this is said:

Santiago de Chile es la capital de Chile.

Jalapeños are very spicy chilies.

In Spanish this is said:

Los jalapeños son chiles muy picantes.

9. Cólera can mean Anger or Cholera.

You have to learn to calm your anger.

In Spanish this is said:

Debes aprender a calmar tu cólera.

Cholera is a disease

In Spanish this is said:

El cólera es una enfermedad.

10. Derecho can mean Right or University degree.

Education is a fundamental right.

In Spanish this is said:

La educación es un derecho fundamental.

She studies Law at the university

In Spanish this is said:

Ella estudia Derecho en la Universidad.

11. Destino can mean Destiny or Destination.

We make our own destiny

In Spanish this is said:

Hacemos nuestro propio destino.

Our new destination for this trip is Hawaii

In Spanish this is said:

Nuestro nuevo destino para este viaje es Hawai.

12. Entrada can mean Entrance or Ticket.

The airport has many entrances.

In Spanish this is said:

El aeropuerto tiene muchas entradas.

I buy the tickets for the concert.

In Spanish this is said:

Yo compro las entradas para el concierto.

13. Gato can mean Cat or Mechanical Jack.

Sophia has a cat.

In Spanish this is said:

Sophia tiene un gato.

Robert has a new mechanical jack for his car.

In Spanish this is said:

Robert tiene un nuevo gato mecánico para su coche.

14. Bajo can mean Musical instrument (bass) or Short.

Tim plays the bass

In Spanish this is said:

Tim toca el bajo.

Edgar is very short

In Spanish this is said:

Edgar es muy bajo.

15. Barra can mean Bar's table or piece of metal.

He likes to drink at the bar of the restaurant

In Spanish this is said:

A él le gusta beber en la barra del restaurante.

They found a metal bar in the backyard.

In Spanish this is said:

Ellos encontraron una barra de metal en el patio.

16. Bota can mean Boots or the Third person of the verb "botar" (Throw away).

I have new boots

In Spanish this is said:

Tengo botas nuevas.

She throws away the trash every morning

In Spanish this is said:

Ella bota la basura todas las mañanas.

17. Busto can mean Breast or Bust.

Women have breasts.

In Spanish this is said:

Las mujeres tienen busto.

The museum has a new bust of Napoleon.

In Spanish this is said:

El museo tiene un nuevo busto de Napoleón.

18. Canino can mean Dog or Fangs.

Dogs are canines.

In Spanish this is said:

Los perros son caninos.

The girl lost one of her fangs.

In Spanish this is said:

La niña perdió uno de sus caninos.

19. Carrera can mean Race or Career.

My boyfriend runs in a race.

In Spanish this is said:

Mi novio corre en una carrera.

¿What career do you study?

In Spanish this is said:

¿Qué carrera estudias?

20. Carta can mean Letter or Card.

The soldier writes letters to his family.

In Spanish this is said:

El soldado escribe cartas a su familia.

We like to play cards.

In Spanish this is said:

Nos gusta jugar a las cartas.

21. Clave can mean Key or Password.

Her statement was key to the case.

In Spanish this is said:

Su declaración fue clave para el caso.

You must create a new password.

In Spanish this is said:

Debes crear una nueva clave.

22. Visto can mean Check mark or Seen.

Right answers get a checkmark.

In Spanish this is said:

Las respuestas correctas obtienen un visto.

I have already seen this movie.

In Spanish this is said:

Ya he visto esta película.

23. Arco can mean Bow or Arch.

You need a bow to throw the arrow.

In Spanish this is said:

Necesitas un arco para lanzar la fleche.

The Arch of Triumph is in Paris.

In Spanish this is said:

El Arco del Triunfo está en París.

24. Blanco can mean White or Target.

His favorite color is white.

In Spanish this is said:

Su color favorito es el blanco.

They aim at the target.

In Spanish this is said:

Ellos apuntan al blanco.

25. Libra can mean the British pound or Zodiac's sign.

That cost 35 pounds.

In Spanish this is said:

Eso cuesta 35 libras.

Their zodiac sign is Libra.

In Spanish this is said:

Su signo zodiacal es Libra.

26. Corredor can mean Corridor or Runner.

The corridor is very long.

In Spanish this is said:

El corredor es muy largo.

Africans are excellent runners.

In Spanish this is said:

Los africanos son corredores excelentes.

27. Goma can mean Bubble gum or Eraser.

Some lollipops have bubble gum inside

In Spanish this is said:

Algunos chupetes tienen goma de mascar adentro.

May I borrow your eraser?

In Spanish this is said:

¿Me prestas tu goma de borrar?

28. Mango can mean Fruit or Handle.

My favorite fruit is mango.

In Spanish this is said:

Mi fruta favorita es el mango.

The teacup has a broken handle

In Spanish this is said:

La taza de té tiene el mango roto.

29. Pico can mean Peak or Beak.

He likes to climb snowy peaks.

In Spanish this is said:

A él le gusta escalar picos nevados.

That bird has a broken beak.

In Spanish this is said:

Esa ave tiene el pico roto.

30. Pie can mean Unit of length (feet)/ Part of the human body.

That has 20 feet long.

In Spanish this is said:

Eso tiene 20 pies de largo.

I have small feet.

In Spanish this is said:

Tengo pies pequeños.

31. Placa can mean Badge, Plate or Vehicle number plate.

Police officers have a badge.

In Spanish this is said:

Los oficiales de policías tienen una placa.

Tectonics plates are always moving.

In Spanish this is said:

Las placas tectónicas siempre se mueven.

What's your vehicle's number plate?

In Spanish this is said:

¿Cuál es el número de placa de tu vehículo?

32. Tienda can mean Store or Tent.

I like the new store.

In Spanish this is said:

Me gusta la nueva tienda.

We need a tent to go camping.

In Spanish this is said:

Necesitamos una tienda para ir a acampar.

33. Regla can mean Ruler, Rules or Menstruation.

May I borrow your ruler?

In Spanish this is said:

¿Me prestas tu regla?

You have to respect de rules of the game.

In Spanish this is said:

Debes respetar las reglas del juego.

Menstruation changes women's moods.

In Spanish this is said:

La regla cambia el estado de ánimo de las mujeres.

34. Ratón can mean Mouse (Animal) or A Computer Mouse.

Mickey is a mouse.

In Spanish this is said:

Mickey es un ratón.

My computer's mouse is blue.

In Spanish this is said:

El ratón de mi computadora es azul.

35. Timbre can mean Doorbell or Stamp.

Ring the doorbell, please.

In Spanish this is said:

Toca el timbre, por favor.

You need another stamp for this document.

In Spanish this is said:

Necesitas otro timbre para este documento.

36. Portero can mean Doorman or Goalkeeper.

Rick is the new doorman.

In Spanish this is said:

Rick es el nuevo portero.

The goalkeeper protects the football goal.

In Spanish this is said:

El portero protege la portería.

37. Palo can mean Stick or Cards Suit.

Throw the stick and the dog will bring it back

In Spanish this is said:

Lanza el palo y el perro lo traerá de vuelta.

All my cards are of the same suit.

In Spanish this is said:

Todas mis cartas son del mismo palo.

38. Masa can mean Dough, Pastry or Mass.

Donuts dough should be smooth.

In Spanish this is said:

La masa de los donuts debe ser suave.

I prepared the pastry for the pie.

In Spanish this is said:

Preparé la masa para el pastel.

There is a big mass of people there.

In Spanish this is said:

Hay una gran masa de gente ahí.

39. Llave can mean Key, Spanner or Grappling.

He always loses his keys.

In Spanish this is said:

Él siempre pierde sus llaves.

He fixes the machine with a spanner.

In Spanish this is said:

Él repara la máquina con una llave.

In the martial arts, they use many grappling.

In Spanish this is said:

En las artes marciales, se usan muchas llaves.

40. Juego can mean Game or First person of the verb "jugar" (play).

I love this game.

In Spanish this is said:

Me encanta este juego.

I play volleyball with my friends

In Spanish this is said:

Yo juego vóleibol con mis amigos.

41. Sumo can mean Sport (Sumo) or First person of the verb "sumar" (Sum).

He practices sumo.

In Spanish this is said:

Él practica sumo.

I add with the calculator.

In Spanish this is said:

Yo sumo con la calculadora.

42. Yema can mean Fingertips or Yolk.

The egg has yolk and white.

In Spanish this is said:

El huevo tiene yema y clara.

In volleyball, you hit the ball with your fingertips.

In Spanish this is said:

En vóleibol se golpea la pelota con la yema de los dedos.

43. Villano can mean Villain or Peasants.

He is the villain of the story.

In Spanish this is said:

Él es el villano de la película.

They are peasants from the village.

In Spanish this is said:

Ellos son villanos de la villa.

THE INDICATIVE MOOD (EL MODO INDICATIVO)

Presente del indicativo

This is the simpler verbal tense, and it's equivalent to the English simple present: I love, I fear, I live.

To love (amar)

- yo amo
- tú amas / vos amás / usted ama
- él/ella ama
- nosotros amamos
- ustedes aman / vosotros amáis
- ellos/ellas aman

To fear (temer)

- yo temo
- tú temes / vos temés / usted teme
- él/ella teme
- nosotros tememos
- ustedes temen / vosotros teméis
- ellos/ellas temen

To live (vivir)

- yo vivo
- tú vives / vos vivís / usted vive
- él/ella vive
- nosotros vivimos
- ustedes viven / vosotros vivís
- ellos/ellas viven

Exercises

1. Martín (abandonar) .... la escuela
2. Los abuelos (ofrecer) .... un regalo a sus nietos
3. La película (aburrir) .... a los niños

Pretérito perfecto simple

This verbal tense is a past tense equivalent to the English simple past: I loved, I feared, I lived.

To love (amar)

- yo amé
- tú amaste / vos amaste / usted amó
- él/ella amó
- nosotros amamos
- ustedes amaron / vosotros amasteis
- ellos/ellas amaron

To fear (temer)

- yo temí
- tú temiste / vos temiste / usted temió
- él/ella temió
- nosotros temimos
- ustedes temieron / vosotros temisteis
- ellos/ellas temieron

To live (vivir)

- yo viví
- tú viviste / vos viviste / usted vivió
- él/ella vivió
- nosotros vivimos
- ustedes vivieron / vosotros vivisteis
- ellos/ellas vivieron

Exercises

1. Yo (comprar) .... un auto
2. Martina y Juana (comer) .... toda la pizza
3. Nosotros (escribir) .... un libro

Pretérito perfecto compuesto

This past tense is widely used and it is equivalent to the English present perfect: I have loved, I have feared, I have lived. Instead of using the verb to have, in

Spanish, we use a special verb that is only used in this occasion: haber. While haber is conjugated, the verb remains the same.

To love (amar)

- yo he amado
- tú has amado / vos has amado / usted ha amado él/ella ha amado
- nosotros hemos amado
- ustedes han amado / vosotros habéis amado ellos/ellas han amado

To fear (temer)

- yo he temido
- tú has temido / vos has temido / usted ha temido él/ella ha temido
- nosotros hemos temido
- ustedes han temido / vosotros habéis temido ellos/ellas han temido

To live (vivir)

- yo he vivido
- tú has vivido / vos has vivido / usted ha vivido él/ella ha vivido
- nosotros hemos vivido
- ustedes han vivido / vosotros habéis vivido ellos/ellas han vivido

Exercises

1. ¿Quién (tomar) ....mis cosas?
2. Sin darnos cuenta (beber), ... toda la botella
3. Mis padres nos (prohibir) .... salir

Pretérito imperfecto

This verbal tense is sometimes confusing to English-speaking people because it is also equivalent to the English simple past, but it also works as the past continuous: I was loving, I was fearing, I was living. It is a bit of both since it expresses a continuity in a past action.

To love (amar)

- yo amaba
- tú amabas / vos amabas / usted amaba
- él/ella amaba
- nosotros amábamos

- ustedes amaban / vosotros amabais
- ellos/ellas amaban

To fear (temer)

- yo temía
- tú temías / vos temías / usted temía
- él/ella temía
- nosotros temíamos
- ustedes temían / vosotros temíais
- ellos/ellas temían

To live (vivir)

- yo vivía
- tú vivías / vos vivías / usted vivía
- él/ella vivía
- nosotros vivíamos
- ustedes vivían / vosotros vivíais
- ellos/ellas vivían

Exercises

1. De niña, (amar) .... los dibujos animados
2. Mis abuelos siempre (recorrer) .... el parque de la mano
3. Siempre (recibir) .... el mismo regalo en Navidad: ¡medias!

Futuro simple

This verbal tense is equivalent to English simple future: I will love, I will fear, I will live.

To love (amar)

- yo amaré
- tú amarás / vos amarás / usted amará
- él/ella amará
- nosotros amaremos
- ustedes amarán / vosotros amaréis
- ellos/ellas amarán

To fear (temer)

- yo temeré
- tú temerás / vos temerás / usted temerá
- él/ella temerá
- nosotros temeremos
- ustedes temerán / vosotros temeréis
- ellos/ellas temerán

To live (vivir)

- yo viviré
- tú vivirás / vos vivirás / usted vivirá
- él/ella vivirá
- nosotros viviremos
- ustedes vivirán / vosotros viviréis
- ellos/ellas vivirán

Exercises

1. Cuando yo sea grande, (trabajar) .... de abogada
2. Si el niño se acerca más, el perro (morder) .... su mano
3. Pase lo que pase, tú (partir) .... al amanecer

Estar + gerundio (presente)

This construction of the present conjugation of verb estar + the gerund of the verb is very similar to the English present continuous: I am loving, I am fearing, I am living. While the English gerund always ends with -ing, the Spanish gerund ends in -ando or -endo.

To love (amar)

- yo estoy amando
- tú estás amando / vos estás amando / usted está amando él/ella está amando
- nosotros estamos amando
- ustedes están amando / vosotros estáis amando ellos/ellas están amando

To fear (temer)

- yo estoy temiendo
- tú estás temiendo / vos estás temiendo / usted está temiendo él/ella está temiendo

- nosotros estamos temiendo
- ustedes están temiendo / vosotros estáis temiendo ellos/ellas están temiendo

To live (vivir)

- yo estoy viviendo
- tú estás viviendo / vos estás viviendo / usted está viviendo él/ella está viviendo
- nosotros estamos viviendo
- ustedes están viviendo / vosotros estáis viviendo ellos/ellas están viviendo

Exercises

1. Ahora que vivimos en el campo, finalmente (respirar)........................... aire puro
2. Los vecinos (vender) .... su casa
3. Ella ya tiene todo resuelto, pero yo todavía (decidir)........................... qué hacer

Estar + gerundio (pasado)

This construction of the pretérito imperfecto conjugation of verb estar + the gerund of the verb is very similar to the English past continuous: I was loving, I was fearing, I was living.

To love (amar)

- yo estaba amando
- tú estabas amando / vos estabas amando / usted estaba amando él/ella estaba amando
- nosotros estaba amando
- ustedes estaban amando / vosotros estabais amando ellos/ellas estaban amando

To fear (temer)

- yo estaba temiendo
- tú estabas temiendo / vos estabas temiendo / usted estaba temiendo él/ella estaba temiendo
- nosotros estábamos temiendo
- ustedes estaban temiendo / vosotros estabais temiendo
- ellos/ellas estaban temiendo

To live (vivir)

- yo estaba viviendo
- tú estabas viviendo / vos estabas viviendo / usted estaba viviendo él/ella estaba viviendo
- nosotros estábamos viviendo
- ustedes estaban viviendo / vosotros estabais viviendo ellos/ellas estaban viviendo

Exercises

1. Cuando me llamaste (pensar) ....en ti
2. Antes de contratarnos, usted (correr) .... muchos riesgos
3. Nosotros (definir) .... nuestro futuro

Ir + infinitivo (futuro)

This construction with the conjugated present tense verb ir (to go) + the infinitive form of the verb is a ver, a usual alternative to the simple future.

To love (amar)

- yo voy a amar
- tú vas a amar / vos vas a amar / usted va a amar él/ella va a amar
- nosotros vamos a amar
- ustedes van a amar / vosotros vais a amar ellos/ellas van a amar

To fear (temer)

- yo voy a temer
- tú vas a temer / vos vas a temer / usted va a temer él/ella va a temer
- nosotros vamos a temer
- ustedes van a temer / vosotros vais a temer ellos/ellas van a temer

To live (vivir)

- yo voy a vivir
- tú vas a vivir / vos vas a vivir / usted va a vivir él/ella va a vivir
- nosotros vamos a vivir
- ustedes van a vivir / vosotros vais a vivir ellos/ellas van a vivir

Exercises

1. Yo siempre (contar) .... contigo
2. Tus regalos lo (sorprender).....................................

3. Hasta que no se enfrente a sus miedos, ella (sufrir)...........................

THE SUBJUNCTIVE MOOD (EL MODO SUBJUNTIVO)

The Subjunctive Mood (El Modo Subjuntivo) is a grammatical mood that's used in Spanish to talk about hypothetical or conditional situations. In this post, I'll teach you the basics of the Subjunctive Mood and provide some helpful examples to help you get started.

Subjunctive sentences use ser (to be) + past participle of verb + el/la/los/las + subjunctive form of pronoun: Sería bueno que vinieras. (It would be good if you came.)

Seré feliz si me invitas para tu cumpleaños. (I'll be happy if you invite me for your birthday). Let's go over the lists of verbs and their various past participles:

Verb Past Participle -er -ir -ar -ir y ser -er, ir:

- atender and asomarse (to peek)
- toc (to touch) tocar (to play) tocar-se
- acordar-se (to remind oneself of...) acordar-se de algo (by reminding oneself about it. In other words, to become aware of it again)
- estar-se (to be tired of...)
- estar harto de (to be sick and tired off... by being sick and tired of... or bored with...)
- estar-se en un sitio (to be in a place)
- ¡estar de gira! (to be on tour!)
- estar de más (¡estar de sobra!) (to be surplus to requirements. to be more than enough.)
- acostumbrarse a ver... (To get accustomed to seeing....)
- acostumbrarse a viajar (To get accustomed to traveling.)
- acostumbrarse a hablar inglés (To get accustomed to speaking English.)
- practicarse en algo (to practice doing something...)
- practicarse para algo (to practice for..., to practice for... etc.)
- practicarse en la escuela (To practice in the schoolyard.)
- ¡no lo hago nunca! (I never do anything!)
- ¡no lo hago! (I'll never do it!)
- no lo hago (I can never do it.)
- acostumbrarse a hablar con gente (to get used to talking with people.)
- vamos mejorando (we go on getting better.)

*IMPORTANT NOTE: We know that the verbs vamos and yo voy are conjugated as follows: yo voy (I go.) nosotros vamos (we go.) papá y mamá van (my parents go.)

- Yo vivo (I live) en Miami.
- Yo vivo en España (I live in Spain.)
- Ella vive en Alemania (She lives in Germany.)

How do we use the Subjunctive Mood to make suggestions?

- ¿Quieres que te acompañe? [If you want me to accompany you.]
- ¿Querrías que te portara en el avión? [Would you like me to take you on the plane?]
- ¿Podrías grabar una parte de mi música? [Could you record a part of my music?]
- ¿Quieres que vayamos al cine a ver la película? [Do you want me to take us to see the movie?]

If we want something done, we can say it as a suggestion by using the verb ser (to be). We don't follow the word order of the main clause, but rather use, Is it possible for you to perform this task. For example:

- ¿Fue posible para ti hacer eso?
- ¿Necesita usted ayuda?
- ¿Es posible me lo enseñe?

Is it possible for you to perform this task? Is there anything I can do to help you? Is there anything you can show me?

It's good if you came. It would be good if you came. It's a pity that I didn't come. (...) it's too bad that (...) It's a pity that we didn't ask him to come with us. (...it is a pity that we didn't invite him.) ¡Qué lamentable que (...!) He's a good singer. He doesn't speak much English.

¿Necesita usted ayuda? ¡Qué lamentable que no viniera!

[Do you need help? What a pity that he couldn't come!]

¿Necesita usted ayuda? ¡Qué lástima que no pudió venir!

[Do you need help? What a pity (...!) that he couldn't come!]

¡Qué lamentable que (...) (What a pity....)

270

¡Qué lástima que (...) (What a pity...!)

THINK IN SPANISH

To speak Spanish, you have to think Spanish. You already have enough words to express most of your thoughts in Spanish. In this lesson, you're going to train yourself to think in Spanish by changing your habits. Let's start forcing our minds to turn English thoughts into Spanish thoughts.

"You can never get one language until you understand at least two." - Geoffrey Willans

"Listen to your heart, listen to the rain, and listen to the voices in your brain." - Becky and Joe

Now that you have mastered Lessons 1-6 of this course, you might be congratulating yourself: "I know 50% of Spanish! I'm in my process of becoming a true Spanish speaker." But "knowing" Spanish words isn't the same thing as thinking in Spanish. Don't get too comfortable yet; you are now faced with the difficult task of helping your mind make the switch.

Right away, let's try two quick tests to see what your current level is of thinking in Spanish.

(1) Can you say this phrase out loud and think the meaning, without thinking about English?

- Mis cosas están en tu casa.

This is pretty easy to translate, word by word; it means "my things are at your house". But when you say this sentence, do you translate each word one by one? Or do you actually know what it means, in your mind, in Spanish... without translating the words into English?

- "Mis cosas están en tu casa."

Say it several times, thinking about the heart of what each word means, but not thinking about the English versions of those words.

(2) Next, try this sentence:

- Para entonces, se habrán ido.

Wow, that's a lot harder.

In English, the sentence means "By that time, they will have left." Sorry, but you can't translate it word by word! If you try, you get something like "for then, themselves they will have gone"... nope, doesn't work.

- "Para entonces, se habrán ido."

Say this several times, and make sure you know what you're saying. This is the only way to genuine fluency: Starting to think in Spanish phrases. True Spanish speakers know exactly what para entonces means as soon as they hear it. They don't translate word by word and figure it out.

This isn't unique to Spanish, of course; English is the same: If I say "he's here as well", you aren't going to puzzle over these two words: "as... well? Why are these two words being used together?" Instead, you immediately know that this phrase means "also" ("he's here also"). And that's for a simple reason: If you're a native English speaker, you've been using the phrase "as well" your entire life. It's like its own word, one you've used every day. You never even think about it; "as well" and "also" are used interchangeably. In your conscious mind, the thought behind the phrase "as well" is more important than the individual words you use to put that meaning into your sentence.

So that's our goal with Spanish. You need to be able to THINK Spanish, using idiomatic phrases without consciously puzzling through the individual words. The sooner you do this, the sooner you'll be able to jump into even the most advanced Spanish conversations.

Labels vs. Syntax

Imagine that you accidentally stumble into a classroom where you don't belong. You're a first-year medical student, and you happen to enter a forum where two surgeons are describing the analgesic protocols for use during atlantoaxial stabilization procedures. If you're like me, you'll probably walk out of the room in a daze, saying, "That was all Greek to me."

What's funny is that they weren't speaking Greek; they were speaking English. But they were using a lot of words you don't know: Specifically, words we call labels.

Labels are different from syntax. Those doctors were speaking with completely English syntax that you would understand; their articles ("the", "a", "an"), pronouns ("it", "they", "their"), prepositions ("of", "at", "with"), and other essential connectors are all entirely within your comfortable vocabulary. It was just the labels, certain big nouns, verbs, etc., that you couldn't understand. The syntax itself was English.

"So what?" you might ask. "I still didn't understand a thing."

Well, that's because you weren't participating in the conversation. If you had asked a few questions, you might have clarified what some of those labels meant. This would be easy for you to do if you're fluent in English syntax. Once you were talking with them, it would be very clear that you and they were essentially speaking the same language, just with some labels that you would have to clarify.

How does the difference between labels and syntax help you with thinking in Spanish? Let's imagine that you have this English thought:

"My suitcase is very full, and I'm not sure if I can carry it."

There are plenty of words in there that you probably don't know yet in Spanish, such as "suitcase" and "carry". But you can still work out the syntax of this sentence:

"Mi suitcase está muy full, y no estoy sure si lo I can carry."

That's a Spanish sentence. It just happens to be missing a few labels. But if you can think that sentence, you're still thinking in Spanish. Once you're thinking that way, and speaking that way, you'll very soon be able to participate in Spanish conversations, no matter how advanced they are. At that point, Spanish conversation on ANY topic will be very much like English conversation where you simply don't know some of the labels.

Using your Spanish syntax, you could even jump into the conversation with the surgeons! Or into any other conversation. You would just have to be willing to ask questions; you'd have to be humble and admit that although you CAN speak Spanish, you don't know everything. Imagine that you're working in an office in Chile, and you know all the syntax that is necessary for conversation, but you're missing some important labels for your everyday office work.

One day the printer runs out of ink, and you need to let the techs know what the problem is so they can fix it. At first, you'll be confronted with unfamiliar words like impresora and amarillo and cian, but once you learn those few new labels, it will start to make sense. Since you understand the syntax, all you'll need to clarify are a few labels. And at any point, if you need to indicate something that you don't know the label for, you can improvise with terms like esta cosa and cuando esté mejor. Let's look at some practical ways to make this a part of your life.

The Spanish Zone

Remember, you've arrived at 50%. That means that at this point, you really have a lot of things you can say that are entirely in Spanish. De verdad, ya tienes muchas cosas que son sólo de español. Wait, what did I just do? I took this sentence: "At this point, you really have a lot of things you can say that are entirely in Spanish."

274

And then I modified it to simpler, more accessible terms: "Really, now you have many things that are only of Spanish:" De verdad, ya tienes muchas cosas que son sólo de español.

Theoretically, you could do this with every single thought that you have! But that would get tiring very quickly. So let's implement The Spanish Zone. Choose a place in your house, or maybe an hour of the day, to be your Spanish Zone where you must force yourself to think in Spanish. There's just one rule: While in The Spanish Zone, all of your English thoughts must turn into Spanish thoughts.

It's a three-step process:

1. Express the thought clearly, using English words. (Maybe even write it down.)
2. Rephrase it and translate it into a Spanish sentence.
3. *Think* that thought again, this time using your Spanish sentence.
4. Bonus: Now write down the Spanish version (and, ideally, send it to a native Spanish teacher to see if you're on the right track).

To make this work, it's important that you start with your English thoughts and then translate those into Spanish. English has to come first. If you start with the Spanish words, you will probably gravitate towards topics and structures that you're already familiar with. In real life, if you're in a situation where you need to speak Spanish, it's likely that what you need to express won't fit naturally within the patterns you've practiced. They'll require some creative thinking to get the ideas across.

Imagine that you're sitting at your desk and this phrase occurs to you: "I want to get up and get some coffee." You don't have the words for "want", "get up", or "coffee", so let's modify this. Simply point at the coffee and change your sentence to "I don't have that": Yo no tengo eso. Or maybe even "There is something that I don't have": Ahí está algo que no tengo. Another phrase that might commonly occur to you is "I'm bored; I want to go do something else." We can change this to "I have to leave; I have to have something else now." Yo me tengo que ir, tengo que tener algo más ahora.

But then you might tell yourself, "But I can't leave; I have to be here." Pero no hay que ir, tengo que estar aquí. Sure, these sentences don't perfectly express your thoughts. But they're getting close. You're turning your English thoughts into Spanish thoughts. And at the same time, you're giving yourself extensive practice with Spanish grammar. Instead of creating simple sentences, you'll be forced to turn complex English sentences (the type that you think all the time) into complex Spanish sentences.

There will still be a lot of English sentence structures that you have difficulty converting into Spanish, but fortunately, the vocabulary and grammar that we're about to learn in Lesson 7 will greatly expand your capabilities.

Vocabulary:

Yol (Joel's World)

This lesson's vocabulary will involve a survey of Joel's entire world, besides verbs.

Fruit Amusement

Joel comes to the amusement park extremely early on a Monday morning, just before the sun comes up.

Of course, Joel likes the light. We've seen before that he feels like he belongs to the "day". So when he picks a ride in the early morning, he wants to pick the ride that looks closest to the rising sun.

To help him with this task, he uses a piece of fruit that he found in the marketplace. This fruit's colors look a lot like the colors of the rising sun. As Joel stands next to the park binoculars, he compares the different parts of the sky with the fruit he's holding, insisting, "I want to go where the dawn is", or "I want to go donde the dawn is".

The word donde means "where" as a conjunction. You'll notice that this is similar to a word in the marketplace, but there it had an accent mark (dónde), whereas now it doesn't. ("It's not in the market, so don't mark it.") Instead of asking questions, this word donde is used to join phrases, just like other conjunctions. So we'll leave this little slice of "dawn-day melon" next to the binoculars, along with the pero pear and the porque pig.

There's another new item here at the conjunction paths. Joel realizes that he has spent a lot of money at this amusement park. He is a wealthy bee, but it seems that his wealth is being partly redistributed to the people who own the different rides. As he sits at the intersection pondering this, he starts placing Yen bills on the different branches of the path, based on how many times he has gone to each ride in the last week, trying to determine who has gotten the most money from him.

FIND YOUR VOICE

"Learning another language is not only learning different words for the same things but learning another way to think about things." - Flora Lewis

"I enjoy translating; it's like opening your mouth and hearing someone else's voice emerge." - Iris Murdoch

One of my earliest memories happened at a park when I was about five years old. Two women on a bench were speaking with each other in a foreign language. I was amazed: They seemed to be communicating, and yet to my young English-speaking ears, it sounded like complete gibberish.

In the car heading home, I proposed a theory to my parents. Perhaps to those foreign women, English also sounds like complete gibberish, with the exact same sonic effect on their ears. If this were true, languages would be like radio stations, each one sounding like indefinite, neutral static to someone who is not tuned in. But this isn't quite true. To Spanish speakers, English doesn't sound like Portuguese or German. It sounds like English. Rather than sounding like random nonsense, it actually has a voice of its own, even to people who don't understand it.

In fact, every language has its own distinct sound. For example, even if you don't know a word of Mandarin or Arabic, you can easily learn to tell the two apart just by the way they sound. This Spanish "sound" is part of the foundation we'll be laying here at the beginning of Lesson 1. But we won't be able to talk about the sound of the language without also covering the personality of the language.

I moved to Argentina a year after I started learning Spanish. While there, I made new friends with whom I only spoke in Spanish. But during the first three months, I didn't feel like myself.

The version of me that my Argentinian friends knew was a brand-new creation. They saw a different side of me, a different voice and personality, that none of my friends at home had ever known. This was the Spanish-language version of me. It forced me to express myself very differently than I was used to doing.

When I speak Spanish, many of the quirky idiosyncrasies of my own personality are lost. Since I was raised speaking English, my personality is intertwined with the English language. But the Spanish rendition of myself is not a lot like my English-speaking personality. At first, it was like bad movie subtitles that don't really express the original meaning. But at the same time, the Spanish language has its own idiosyncrasies.

During my time in Argentina, I began to develop new stories, jokes, and personality traits in this language, all of which were entirely separate from my English-speaking personality. I had opened up a new side of my mind that I never knew existed. By learning Spanish, I discovered a whole new amazing world that I could live in, entirely hidden from my native tongue.

It's time for you to start building that world. And speaking of your native tongue, the "tongue" is a good place to start. Let's do a quick exercise to demonstrate. Here I've listed a few names that are quite common in Spanish-speaking countries and are also well-known to English speakers. We'll work on that Spanish voice soon, but we have to go a little deeper. Before we can produce accurate Spanish sounds, we need to think about Spanish more deeply than that. A new language doesn't just sound different. It thinks differently.

"Named Must Your Voice Be Before Brandish It You Can."

Look again at the names listed above. If you were to hear a bilingual person reading them over and over, first in a Spanish voice and then in an English voice, it would sound as if she were two different actors reading the same script. There are other aspects of communication that require a different mindset. If you've worked on learning a language before, you may be used to studying grammar, vocabulary, and idioms separately. But what you're about to learn will turn them all into one entity.

Let's imagine for a second that you decide to talk like Yoda from Star Wars. If you start imitating Yoda on purpose, you might find that you start to think differently as well. Your personality will change slightly based on what you're saying. But for efficiency, we're going to go the opposite direction: We're going to change our personality first. For the Star Wars fans, I'm afraid Yoda isn't quite going to do the job. We need to create a very unique personality, something that really encompasses everything about the Spanish language. It has to be a person separate from yourself, but you have to be able to switch back and forth between your own personality and that separate personality.

For the rest of this book, our Spanish personality is a bee named Joel.

Joel talks kind of like Yoda, but he follows his own strange rules about it. This confuses a lot of English speakers. Even after they've learned the grammar and memorized loads of phrases, it can be all too easy to make a silly mistake with this verb. Joel doesn't want to be the one doing the action; instead, he wants the thing itself to do the action. He wants the tea to do the work for him. Notice how Joel makes it sound like the tea is the one that's doing the action. Now you have to become the bee.

You need to associate everything you learn about Spanish with Joel. Each time you come across a new Spanish word, idiom, or grammar rule, you can associate it with Joel, and it will become a part of your developing Spanish personality. Let's begin by learning some more things about Joel.

Putting On Your Wings

When you get your Joel character on, you'll want to understand everything about Joel, including the world that he lives in. So before we can become the bee, we have to stop and get to know him really well. For the next few pages, pay close attention and try to remember every detail of his personality.

First of all, Joel is no mere human bee. He's not even from Earth.

He lives on a planet called "Yol". If you think about it, "Yol" sounds kind of like "Joel", and in fact, Joel sometimes gets his own name confused with the name of the planet he lives on because they sound kind of similar.

Joel is a mischievous bee. While he tries to appear attractive and charming, he really just uses his wealth for his own selfish purposes, and he tries to get everyone else to do work for him because he's extremely lazy.

It's important to note that Joel's tastes are pretty strange: He loves drinking tea, and he'll do almost anything to get a nice hot cup. But he has a strong distaste for all mammals (that is, animals with fur such as dogs, horses, bears, and giraffes); in fact, he's generally frightened of all such animals.

However, his best friend is a lizard. He has no problem with him because he's a reptile, not a mammal. As you'll see in future stories, this lizard has no name, can't talk, and likes to spend time in dark caves.

Joel also hangs out with a group of stuffed pandas. They're OK because they aren't real pandas; they're living stuffed animals, which is not a problem by Joel's strange standards. Since the pandas are clumsy and simple-minded, Joel loves causing mischief to these stuffed pandas. He thinks it's funny when they get dizzy or blown around by the wind, which happens pretty often.

Also be aware that Joel has a tendency to get into a strange sort of mood and to talk with an old-fashioned, almost formal British mode of speech. This especially happens when he's about to do something mischievous, so be on the lookout for that. If he starts speaking in a pompous voice, it usually means that he's up to no good.

Another funny thing about the way that Joel talks is that he can be extremely redundant. He'll say the same thing more than once in a sentence, sometimes even to the point of bad logic, such as double negatives, like "I didn't see nothing".

We absolutely must imitate this kind of thing if we want to speak like Joel authentically. It may be uncomfortable or feel wrong, but just remember that you aren't the one saying "I didn't see anything"; it's just Joel, and it makes perfect sense for him.

GIVING GOOD NEWS TO YOUR EMPLOYER

Nuestra suerte ha cambiado – Our Luck Has Turned

Vocabulary List

- recibirme = receiving me
- departamento de Ventas = sales department
- buena noticia = great news
- me encantaría oírla = I would love to hear it
- hacer contacto = make contact
- fabricante de plásticos y adhesivos = manufacturer of plastics and adhesives
- contratar nuestros servicios = hire our services
- se hará efectivo = will be made effective
- nuestro esfuerzo y el talento que tenemos = our efforts and the talent we have
- punto crítico = critical point
- menor punto en años = lowest point in years
- la sede de la empresa = the headquarters of the Company
- nuestra filosofía = our philosophy
- materiales ecológicos con tecnología de punta = ecological, cutting-edge materials
- mejorar la calidad = improve the quality
- proteger el ambiente = protect the environment
- seguir los estándares y las regulaciones = adhere to the standards and regulations
- sus actuales proveedores = their current suppliers
- otros competidores = other competitors
- bono importante = important bonus
- pago adicional por empleados de excelencia = extra payment for employees of excellence
- el reconocimiento que tanto mereces = the recognition that you deserve so much
- estrategia para concretar futuros contratos = a strategy to work
- generando estrategias = generating strategies
- ¡enhorabuena! = congratulations!

281

Spanish

Liliana: Buenas tardes, Francisco.

Francisco: Buenas tardes, señora Liliana. Gracias por recibirme en su oficina.

Liliana: Me cuenta el Departamento de Ventas que tiene una buena noticia que darme el día de hoy. Me encantaría oírla.

Francisco: Es cierto, señora. He logrado hacer contacto con una empresa importante, fabricante de plásticos y adhesivos.

Liliana: ¿Y? ¿Qué dijeron? ¿Están listos para contratar nuestros servicios?

Francisco: Sí, señora. Acabamos de firmar un contrato por más de cien mil dólares con ellos. ¡Se hará efectivo a partir de este fin de semana!

Liliana: ¿Cien mil dólares? ¿Estoy escuchando bien? ¡Espero que esto no sea una broma!

Francisco: No, señora Liliana. Gracias a nuestro esfuerzo y el talento que tenemos en nuestro departamento, hemos logrado concretar este enorme contrato.

Liliana: ¡Eso es increíble! ¡Felicidades, Francisco! Estábamos llegando a un punto crítico, ya que nuestras ventas estaban en su menor punto en años, pero... De verdad que ustedes hicieron magia. ¿Cómo lo lograron?

Francisco: Pues, mis compañeros y yo estuvimos hablando con ellos por dos semanas, y ayer viajé hacia la sede de la empresa.

Liliana: ¿Qué tal te trataron allá? Y, ¿qué hiciste para lograr que firmaran?

Francisco: Pues les expliqué sobre nuestra filosofía, además de los materiales ecológicos con tecnología de punta que usamos en nuestra empresa. Les dije que no solo iban a poder mejorar la calidad de sus productos, sino también proteger el ambiente y seguir los estándares y las regulaciones. Pero aún no estaban convencidos.

Liliana: ¿No? ¿Cómo hiciste para que se convencieran de contratarnos?

Francisco: Muy fácil: les hablé de precios. Cuando comparé nuestros precios con los de sus actuales proveedores, además de otros competidores, terminé de empujarlos a lo que quería. Diez minutos después, estaban firmando el contrato.

Liliana: Vaya... creo que esto merece una celebración. Pero no solo una celebración; creo que tú y tu equipo ya merecen un bono importante. Este mes recibirán el pago adicional por empleados de excelencia. Es el mejor bono que ofrece la empresa, y me aseguraré de que lo recibas por dos.

Francisco: ¿Doble? ¡Muchas gracias! ¡Eso para mí es un honor! No tiene idea de cuántas horas de trabajo invertimos para que esto saliera como lo deseábamos. Incluso, pasé toda la noche de ayer preparando la presentación de hoy. Ni siquiera pude dormir bien.

Liliana: Pues este bono demuestra que nuestra empresa, y yo, te estamos dando el reconocimiento que tanto mereces. Espero que te sirva de mucho.

Creo que estás entre nuestros mejores empleados, Francisco. Gracias.

Francisco: No hay problema, señora Liliana. Todo con tal de ver a nuestra compañía triunfando en el mercado. Es mi mayor deseo.

Liliana: Perfecto, tienes la actitud de un ganador y de alguien que realmente quiere vernos crecer. Ahora, ¿qué viene? ¿Ya tienes una estrategia para concretar futuros contratos o estás trabajando con improvisación?

Francisco: Definitivamente voy a seguir generando estrategias. Gracias por los cumplidos, señora Liliana. Seguiré siendo un ganador, ya verá. Bueno, regresaré al trabajo. ¡Gracias por recibirme!

Liliana: ¡Gracias a ti por la buenísima noticia y tu excelente trabajo!

¡Enhorabuena!

English

Liliana: Good afternoon, Francisco.

Francisco: Good afternoon, Mrs. Liliana. Thanks for receiving me in your office.

Liliana: The sales department has told me that you have great news for me today. I would love to hear it.

Francisco: It's true, madame. I have managed to make contact with an important manufacturer of plastics and adhesives.

Liliana: And? What did they say? Are they ready to hire our services?

Francisco: Yes, ma'am. We've just signed a contract for over one hundred thousand dollars with them. It will be made effective from this weekend onwards!

Liliana: One hundred thousand dollars? Am I hearing correctly? This better not be a joke!

Francisco: No, Mrs. Liliana. Thanks to our efforts and the talent we have within our department, we've managed to make this enormous contract a reality.

Liliana: That's incredible! Congratulations, Francisco! We were arriving at a critical point since our sales were at their lowest point in years, but... You guys really made magic. How did you accomplish it?

Francisco: Well, my team members and I were discussing with them for two weeks, and yesterday I traveled to the headquarters of their company.

Liliana: How were you treated there? And, how did you manage to get them to sign?

Francisco: Well I explained about our philosophy, as well as the ecological, cutting-edge materials that we use at our company. I told them that they weren't only going to be able to improve the quality of their products, but also protect the environment and adhere to the standards and regulations. But they still weren't convinced.

Liliana: No? How did you convince them to hire us?

Francisco: Very easily – I talked about the prices. When I compared our prices to their current suppliers, as well as other competitors, I finished pushing them to where I wanted them. Ten minutes later, they were signing the contract.

Liliana: Wow... I think this deserves a celebration. But not just a celebration; I believe that you and your team deserve an important bonus.

This month you all will receive an extra payment for employees of excellence. It is the best bonus the company offers, and I'll make sure you receive it twice over.

Francisco: Double? Thanks a lot! That is an honor to me! You have no idea how many hours of work we invested for this to come out as it did. I even spent all of last night preparing today's presentation. I couldn't even sleep well.

Liliana: This is why the bonus demonstrates that our company, and I, are giving you the recognition that you deserve so much. I hope it serves you well. I believe you're among our best employees, Francisco. Thank you.

Francisco: There's no problem, Mrs. Liliana. Anything as long as I can watch our company triumph in the market. It's my greatest wish.

Liliana: Perfect, you have the attitude of a winner, and of somebody who truly wants to see us grow. Now what? Do you have a strategy to work out future contracts, or are you working on improvisation?

Francisco: I'm definitely going to continue generating strategies. Thanks for the praise, Mrs. Liliana. I will continue being a winner, you'll see. Well, I'll get back to work. Thanks for seeing me!

Liliana: Thank you for the amazing news and your excellent work! Congratulations!

CLARIFYING IRREGULAR VERBS

It's time to put regular verbs to one side and start on those pesky irregular verbs!

The downside to learning irregular Spanish verbs is that several of the most commonly used verbs are irregular.

But, there are upsides:

1. many verbs only have minor irregularities, such as spelling changes, or accents added;
2. frequently, once you've learned one irregular verb, several others will follow the exact same pattern;
3. often, there's a logical reason for the irregularity, or it falls within a recognized and common category.

Step 5 lays out and explains several of the irregularities which occur with Spanish verbs. This knowledge should ease your path when it comes to actually memorize irregular Spanish verbs — which will be your next step.

Meanwhile, gently read through Step 5, going back over anything you've not quite understood. Don't worry if you can't assimilate every single thing ... it will all fall into place when you start learning them.

Once again, go at your own pace — and enjoy yourself!

YOUR GOALS FOR STEP 5

1. Assimilate deviations likely to occur in the Present Simple Tense.
2. Memorize the 3 verbs with an irregular Imperfect Tense.
3. Understand Past Tense.
4. Study the 13 verbs with abnormal Future and Conditional stems.
5. Take in Present Subjunctive irregularities.
6. Absorb peculiarities in the Imperfect Subjunctive.
7. Get the hang of deviant Gerunds.
8. Peruse non-conforming Past Participles.
9. Get to grips with Imperative abnormalities.

Present Simple Tense Irregularities Uncovered

Several verbs come under the heading of being irregular because of changes in their stems. In other words, the irregularity takes place in the middle of the verb, not at the end. These verbs are sometimes known as radical-changing verbs or stem-changing verbs.

The actual ending of the verb is usually the same as for regular verb conjugations. Also, the nosotros/nosotras and vosotros/vosotras forms are not normally affected.

Present Simple Tense Stem Change -E to -IE

With the following list of -AR, -ER, and -IR verbs:

1. the letter -E in the stem or root of the verb, changes to -EI when conjugated in the Present Tense
2. the nosotros/nosotras and vosotros/vosotras forms are not affected
3. the endings are the same as regular verbs
- cerrar – to close
- comenzar – to begin, commence
- pensar – to think
- defender – to defend
- entender – to understand
- tender – to spread, stretch out, hang up
- convertir – to convert
- hervir – to boil
- preferir – to prefer

As an example, we'll decline cerrar in the Present Simple Tense:

- cierro
- cierras
- cierra
- cerramos
- cerráis
- cierran

Present Simple Tense Stem Change -O to -UE

With this group of -AR, -ER, and -IR verbs:

1. the letter -O in the stem of the verb changes to -UE
2. the nosotros/nosotras and vosotros/vosotras forms are not affected 3) the endings are the same as regular verbs
- acordar – to decide, agree upon
- encontrar – to find, to meet
- volar – to fly

287

- doler – to hurt
- mover – to move
- volver – to return
- dormir – to sleep
- morir – to die

Here you have volver conjugated in the Present Simple Tense.

- vuelvo
- vuelves
- vuelve
- volvemos
- volvéis
- vuelven

Present Simple Tense Stem Change -E to -I

This stem change only happens with -IR verbs, never with -AR or –ER verbs:

1. the letter -E in the stem changes to -I
2. the nosotros/nosotras and vosotros/vosotras forms are not affected 3) the endings are the same as regular verbs
- competir – to compete
- despedir – to say good-bye
- medir – to measure
- pedir – to ask (for), request
- servir – to serve
- vestir – to dress

Take pedir as your example:

- pido
- pides
- pide
- pedimos
- pedís
- piden

Present Simple Tense Change - Accent Added -I to -Í

Some verbs are considered irregular purely because an accent is added to an -I. The reason for this addition is, basically, to retain the pronunciation of the verb throughout its conjugation, and to avoid a diphthong. This only happens with verbs ending in -IAR and, again, the nosotros/nosotras and vosotros/vosotras forms are unaffected.

- confiar – to confide, trust, rely
- criar – to raise, rear, breed
- desviar – to deviate, deflect
- enfriar – to cool, make cold, chill
- esquiar – to chill

Take a look at confiar:

- confío
- confías
- confía
- confiamos
- confiáis
- confían

Present Simple Tense Change - Accent Added -U to -Ú

With the majority of verbs ending in -UAR, you'll need to add an accent to the -U, again for reasons of pronunciation and to avoid a diphthong. The first and second persons plural are not affected.

- continuar – to continue
- evacuar – to evacuate, empty, vacate
- evaluar – to evaluate
- graduar – to graduate
- insinuar – to insinuate

Let's use graduar as our example:

- gradúo
- gradúas
- gradúa
- graduamos
- graduáis
- gradúan

Present Simple Tense Spelling Change - Adding -Y

-IR verbs ending in -UIR add an extra -Y to maintain stress and pronunciation, the exception, once again, being the first and second person plural.

- atribuir – to attribute
- concluir – to conclude
- constituir – to constitute
- construir – to build
- destruir – to destroy
- distribuir – to distribute
- incluir – to include

Check out the verb construir:

- construyo
- construyes
- construye
- construimos
- construís
- construyen

Present Simple Tense Spelling Change - From -G to -J

For reasons of pronunciation, and in order to keep the soft sound that the –G has throughout the remainder of the conjugation, the following -ER and –IR verbs have -JO at the end of the first person singular (i.e., yo form) of the Present Simple Tense:

- coger – to catch, grasp, take
- escoger – to choose, pick
- recoger – to pick up
- afligir – to afflict
- corregir – to correct (also a stem change -e to -i)
- dirigir – to direct, to run
- elegir – to elect, vote (also a stem change -e to -i)
- exigir – to demand

Coger is a good example:

- cojo
- coges
- coge
- cogemos
- cogéis
- cogen

Present Simple Tense – First Person Singular Ends -ZCO

Some -ER and -IR verbs ending -CER and -CIR have -ZCO at the end of the first person singular, mainly for better-sounding pronunciation:

- aparecer – to appear
- conocer – to know (a person rather than a fact)
- crecer – to grow
- establecer – to establish
- parecer – to seem, appear
- conducir – to drive
- deducir – to deduce
- introducir – to introduce
- producir – to produce

Conocer is a very commonly-used verb of this type:

- conozco
- conoces
- conoce
- conocemos
- conocéis
- conocen

Present Simple Tense – First Person Singular Ends -GO

Although there is no good explanation, some very common, and therefore very important, verbs have a -GO ending added to their stem in the first person singular:

- hacer – to do, to make
- poner – to put
- tener – to have (also stem change -e to -ie) valer – to be worth
- decir – to say (also stem change -e to -i) salir – to go out
- venir – to come (also stem change -e to -ie)

All of these are very important verbs, which you'll learn later, but let's take hacer as our example:

- hago
- haces
- hace
- hacemos
- hacéis
- hacen

NOTE: Do you remember, when studying the Present Subjunctive, you learned you had to remove the -O ending from the first person singular of the Present Tense in order to form it? Well, because of this, the alterations in the first person singular of the above verbs are carried through to the Present Subjunctive.

Unorthodox Imperfect Tense Verbs

Only three verbs are irregular in the Imperfect Tense – ser, ver, and ir – and you'll find these conjugated later in the book.

Preterite Tense Irregularities Revealed

Preterite Tense – Spelling Change in -CAR Verbs from -C to -Q

With the following verbs, the -C changes to a -QU in the first person singular of the Preterite. This is purely to avoid incorrect pronunciation.

- acercar – to approach, get near
- atacar – to attack
- buscar – to look for, seek
- clasificar – to classify
- dedicar – to dedicate
- educar – to educate
- identificar – to identify
- sacar – to take out

Let's take sacar as an example:

- saqué
- sacaste
- sacó
- sacamos
- sacasteis
- sacaron

Preterite Tense – Spelling Change in -GAR Verbs: U Added

With verbs ending in -GAR, a -U needs to be introduced into the first person singular of the Preterite, again to avoid incorrect pronunciation:

- ahogar – to drown
- cargar – to load, burden
- castigar – to punish
- encargar – to charge, entrust, order (goods etc) investigar – to investigate

- llegar – to arrive
- pagar – to pay, pay for
- pegar – to hit
- tragar – to swallow

The verb llegar is a very common example:

- llegué
- llegaste
- llegó
- llegamos
- llegasteis
- llegaron

Preterite Tense – Spelling Change In -ZAR Verbs

A -Z followed by an -E (-ZE) is rarely used in Spanish, so verbs ending in -ZAR have their -Z replaced by a -C in the first person singular of the Preterite.

- abrazar – to hug, embrace
- analizar – to analyze
- bostezar – to yawn
- cazar – to hunt
- cruzar – to cross
- enfatizar – to emphasize
- gozar – to enjoy
- organizar – to organize

Take a look at cruzar:

- crucé
- cruzaste
- cruzó
- cruzamos
- cruzasteis
- cruzaron

Preterite Tense – Y In 3rd Person Singular and Plural

-ER and -IR verbs with stems ending in a vowel often need a strong -Y to replace the -I in the third person singular and the third person plural.

They also accent the -I in all other forms if the preceding vowel is strong, in order to avoid a diphthong. Verbs that fall into this category are:

- caer – to fall
- creer – to believe
- leer – to read
- proveer – to provide
- construir – to build
- destruir – to destroy
- excluir – to exclude
- oír – to hear

Accordingly, this is how you'd decline the Preterite of caer: caí

- caíste
- cayó
- caímos
- caísteis
- cayeron

Preterite Tense – Stem-Changing -IR Verbs

1. Some irregular -IR verbs containing an -E in their stem, change that -E to an -I in the third persons singular and plural, including:
- advertir – to warn, notice
- competir – to compete
- consentir – to allow, permit
- convertir – to convert
- hervir – to boil
- medir – to measure
- mentir – to lie
- pedir – to ask for
- preferir – to prefer
- repetir – to repeat
- seguir – to follow
- sentir – to feel, to be sorry
- sugerir – to suggest

As in:

- mentí
- mentiste
- mintió
- mentimos
- mentisteis

- mintieron
2. And the following -IR verbs change the final -O of the stem to -U in third person forms:
- dormir – to sleep
- morir – to die

As in:

- dormí
- dormiste
- durmió
- dormimos
- dormisteis
- durmieron

Preterite Tense – Verbs with Irregular Preterite Stems

You'll discover that some verbs have unusual stems in the Preterite. Here's a list of these verbs, including the irregular stem you must use when conjugating the Preterite:

-AR Verbs:

- andar (to walk) – anduv-
- estar (to be) – estuv-

-ER Verbs:

- haber (to have – auxiliary verb) – hub-
- hacer (to do, to make) – hic-
- poder (to be able to) – pud-
- poner (to put) – pus-
- querer (to want, to love) – quis-
- saber (to know) – sup-
- satisfacer (to satisfy) – satisfic-
- tener (to have) – tuv-
- traer (to bring) – traj-

-IR Verbs:

- decir (to say, to tell) – dij-
- venir (to come) – vin-
- Verbs ending in -ducir (eg reducir – to reduce) – duj-

Atypical Future and Conditional Tense Stems

Some verbs do not use the Infinitive to form the Future Tense, but use an irregular stem (listed below) along with the normal Future Tense endings.

These irregular stems are also used to form the Conditional Tense.

-ER Verbs:

- caber (to fit) – cabr-
- haber (to have – auxiliary verb) – habr-
- hacer (to do, to make) – har-
- poder (to be able to) – podr-
- poner (to put) – pondr-
- querer (to want, to love) – querr-
- saber (to know) – sabr-
- satisfacer (to satisfy) – satisfar-tener (to have) – tendr-
- valer (to be worth) – valdr-

-IR Verbs:

- decir (to say, to tell) – dir-
- salir (to go out, to leave) – saldr-
- venir (to come) – vendr-

Present Subjunctive Irregularities Spelt Out

As you're aware, the Present Subjunctive is formed by knocking off the -o ending of the first person singular of the Present Simple Tense of the verb, and using what remains as the stem for forming the Present Subjunctive.

Some Spanish verbs – decir, hacer, poner, salir, tener, venir, etc – have extremely irregular yo forms in the Present Simple Tense, and these are reflected in the stem for the Present Subjunctive.

Stem-changing verbs in the Present Tense generally have this change carried through to the Present Subjunctive, eg entender, pensar, poder, querer, volver.

Also, you'll occasionally find that the stem of the nosotros/vosotros forms isn't the same as the Present Tense, eg dormir, morir, pedir, seguir, sentir.

Imperfect Subjunctive Irregularities Explained

You'll remember that you work out the correct stem for the Imperfect Subjunctive by removing the -aron or -ieron endings of the third person plural of the Preterite Tense. Once again, verbs with an irregular Preterite have this reflected in the stem for the Imperfect Subjunctive, eg dar, estar, hacer, poner, tener, venir.

Another thing to watch, is that irregular -IR verbs which don't have an -I in the third person plural of the Preterite, (eg decir, ir, ser) have the following endings in the Imperfect Subjunctive:

- -era
- -eras
- -era
- -éramos
- -erais
- -eran

OR

- -ese
- -eses
- -ese
- -ésemos
- -eseis
- -esen

OPPOSITES - ADJECTIVES - DIFFERENT ADJECTIVES WITH THEIR OPPOSITES

Opuestos - Adjetivos - Diferentes adjetivos con sus opuestos

Sunita: ¿puedo hacerte una pregunta personal?

Sunita: May I ask you a personal question?

Jose: Puedes preguntar. Sin embargo, no estoy segura de poder responderla.

Jose: You can ask. I am not sure if I will be able to answer it though.

Sunita: Alguien dijo que tenías seis hijos. ¿Es eso cierto?

Sunita: Someone said you had six children. Is that true?

Jose: Sí. Tuve dos niños. Luego tuve gemelos: un niño y una niña. Luego tuve dos chicas. Y todos son diferentes.

Jose: Yes. I had two boys. Then I had twins, a boy and a girl. Then I had two girls. And they are all different.

Sunita: ¡En serio! ¿En qué sentido?

Sunita: Really! In what way?

Jose: Ben, mi hijo mayor, es muy alto, pero todos los demás niños son bastante bajos, como yo.

Jose: Ben, my oldest, is really tall, but all of the other kids are quite short, like me.

Sunita: ¿Tu esposo es alto?

Sunita: Is your husband tall?

Jose: Sí. Además, Dempsey, mi gemelo mayor, es muy extrovertido, pero James, su gemelo es muy tranquilo. Sin embargo, James es super inteligente, mientras que Dempsey no es inteligente para nada.

Jose: Yes. Also, Dempsey, my oldest twin is really outgoing, but James, her twin is really quiet. However, James is super smart, while Dempsey is not clever at all.

Sunita: Es extraño cómo sucede eso.

Sunita: It is strange how that happens.

Jose: Además, a Lizzy, mi hija menor, le encanta cualquier color que sea brillante, mientras que Sophia, que es sólo un año mayor, prefiere los colores oscuros. Sophia también se esfuerza mucho en la escuela, pero Lizzy es un poco perezosa.

Jose: Also, Lizzy, my youngest, loves any color that is bright, while Sophia, who is only a year older, prefers dark colors. Sophia also works hard at school, but Lizzy is a little lazy.

Sunita: ¿Tú y tu esposa sois diferentes?

Sunita: Are you and your wife different?

Jose: Mucho. Sus padres son bastante ricos, pero los míos son relativamente pobres. A veces esto puede crear problemas.

Jose: Very. His parents are quite wealthy, but mine are relatively poor. It can create problems sometimes.

Sunita: Me lo puedo imaginar.

Sunita: I can imagine.

Jose: Además, mi esposa es muy organizada. Planea todo antes de hacerlo. Yo, por otro lado, soy bastante desorganizado.

Jose: Moreover, my wife is really organized. He plans everything before he does it. I, on the other hand, am quite disorganized.

Sunita: Supongo que eso vuelve loco a tu esposa. Mi esposo es como tú y a veces me enoja tanto. Me enfado fácilmente, pero mi marido se lo toma todo con mucha tranquilidad.

Sunita: I guess that drives your wife crazy. My husband is like you and it makes me so angry sometimes. I do get angry easily, but my husband is calm about everything.

Jose: Yo era como tú, pero cuando llegaron los niños, tenía que asegurarme de mantener la calma por ellos. Tal vez te pase lo mismo que a mi después de tener hijos.

Jose: I was like you, but when the kids came along, I had to make sure I remained calm for them. Perhaps you will be the same after you have given birth.

Sunita: Tal vez. Supongo que tendremos que esperar y ver qué pasa.

Sunita: Maybe. I think we will have to wait and find out.

Opposites - Verbs - Different verbs with their opposites

Verbos opuestos

Max: Oye, me quedé "despierto" toda la noche después de la fiesta.

Max: Hey, I stayed "awake" all night after the party.

Phoebe: Wow. ¿Cómo es posible? Me quedé "dormida" casi inmediatamente cuando llegué a casa.

Phoebe: Wow. How come? I fell "asleep" almost immediately after I got home.

Max: No es de extrañar que hayas "llegado" temprano a la escuela esta mañana.

Max: No wonder you "arrived" at school early this morning.

Phoebe: Sí. Te quedaste demasiado tiempo en la fiesta. Deberías "haberte ido" antes.

Phoebe: Yes. You stayed too long at the party. You should have "left" earlier.

Max: De todos modos, has "completado" esa difícil tarea de Matemáticas.

Max: Anyway, have you "completed" that difficult Mathematics assignment.

Phoebe: ¿Me estás tomando el pelo? Confiaba en ti. Ni siquiera la he "empezado".

Phoebe: Are you kidding me? I was relying on you. I've not even "started" at all.

Max: Uf... Estoy muy "preocupado" ahora mismo porque nos podrían castigar.

Max: Phew... I'm very "worried" right now because we could be punished.

Phoebe: Mantén la "calma", todo irá bien.

Phoebe: Keep "calm", everything will be fine.

Max: Tenemos que encontrar una solución. Quiero "aprobar" mi tarea.

Max: We have to find a solution. I want to "pass" my assignment.

Phoebe: Me estás haciendo entrar en pánico. No podemos "suspender", confía en mí.

Phoebe: You're making me panic. We cannot "fail," trust me.

Max: Ni siquiera tenemos las respuestas. ¿Conoces a alguien que pueda "enseñarnos"?

Max: We don't even have the answers. Do you know anyone who can "teach" us?

Phoebe: El tema es realmente interesante. Podemos "aprender" por nuestra cuenta.

Phoebe: The topic is actually interesting. We can "learn" it on our own.

Max: Es una gran idea. Me "sentaré" allí.

Max: That's a great idea. I will "sit" over there.

Phoebe: Genial. Yo me quedaré "de pie".

Phoebe: Cool. I will just "stand."

(Ambos completaron la tarea en 15 minutos).

(Both complete the assignment in 15 minutes)

Max: Esto ha sido realmente "duro".Deberíamos descansar un poco.

Max: That was really "tough." We should rest a little.

Phoebe: Para mi ha sido bastante "simple". Deberías mejorar tus matemáticas.

Phoebe: It was kind of "simple" for me. You should really improve on your mathematics.

Max: Vamos a "dárselo" a alguien para que lo entregue por nosotros.

Max: Let's "give it" to someone to submit it for us.

Phoebe: Si me preguntas, creo que es mejor que el maestro lo "reciba" directamente de nuestras manos.

Phoebe: If you ask me, I think it's better the teacher "receives" it right from our hands.

Max: Muy bien, entonces, "vamos" nosotros mismos a entregarlo.

Max: Okay then, let's "go" ourselves to hand it in.

Phoebe: Así se habla. Pero por favor, "deja" de tararear. Odio cuando haces eso.

Phoebe: Now you're talking. But please "stop" humming. I hate it when you do that.

Max: Por eso es exactamente por lo que somos amigos. Siempre "terminamos" las cosas.

Max: That's exactly why we're friends. We always "get" things done.

Phoebe: Espera a que le "pida" mi bolígrafo a Ben antes de que nos vayamos a casa.

Phoebe: Wait for me to "collect" my pen from Ben before we start going home.

Diferentes partes del cuerpo

Esther: El tipo con el mejor "cabello" de la escuela...Hola.

Esther: The guy with the best "hair" in school... Hi.

303

Aaron: ¿Qué tal Esther? Gracias por el cumplido. Tus "ojos" también son muy hermosos.

Aaron: What's up Esther? Thanks for the compliment. Your "eyes" are also very beautiful.

Esther: Gracias. Es mi mejor característica.

Esther: Thank you. It's my best feature.

Aaron: (Risas). No puedes culparlo. Espero que sus "ojos" y "oídos" no se hayan lastimado en el proceso porque eso sería muy malo.

Aaron: (Laughs). You really can't blame him. I hope his "eyes" and "ears" didn't also get hurt in the process because that would be really bad.

Esther: No. La única otra complicación fue su "tobillo" que se torció.

Esther: Nope. The only other complication was his "ankle" which got twisted.

Aaron: Gracias a Dios. Espero que se mejore pronto porque he oído que una lesión en el tobillo puede provocar dolores en los "pies".

Aaron: Thank God. Hope he gets better soon because I heard an "ankle" injury can lead to pains on the "feet."

Esther: Eso es cierto. Se pondrá mejor. Pero en serio, Aaron, ¿cómo te las arreglas para mantener tu "cabello" y tus "cejas" tan geniales todo el tiempo?

Esther: That's true. He'll get better. But seriously, Aaron, how do you manage to keep your "hair" and "eyebrows" this cool all the time.

Aaron: (Sonríe) Noté que los rasgos de mi cara como mi "nariz" y mi "boca" no eran muy bonitos. Así que decidí que tener un gran "cabello" compensaría mis malos rasgos faciales.

Aaron: (Smiles) I noticed the features on my face like my "nose" and "mouth" weren't really very good. So I decided that having great "hair" would compensate for my bad facial features.

Esther: Wow. Ese plan funcionó a la perfección porque toda tu "cara" ahora luce perfecta.

Esther: Wow. That plan worked to perfection because your whole "face" now looks perfect.

Aaron: Gracias. ¿Te enteraste del accidente de anoche que hirió a 10 personas, a la mayoría de ellas en sus "dientes"?

Aaron: Thank you. Did you hear about the accident last night that injured 10 people, most of them on their "teeth"?

Esther: Oh, sí. Es realmente triste. Los internaron a todos en el hospital de mi padre. Mi papá es un dentista, uno que cuida los "dientes" y las "encías" de la "boca".

Esther: Oh yes. It's really sad. They were all admitted to my dad's hospital. My dad is a dentist, someone who looks after the "teeth" and "gums" of the "mouth."

Aaron: ¡Oh, Dios mío! No sabía que tu padre trabajaba en medicina. Yo mismo espero llegar a ser óptico en el futuro, alguien que cuida de los "ojos".

Aaron: Oh my God! I never knew your dad was in the medicine line. I, myself, hope to become an optician in the future, someone who looks after the "eyes."

Personal Information - Talking about yourself in English

Información personal

María: Hola, mi nombre es María. ¿Cuál es tu nombre?

Maria: Hi, my name is Maria. What's your name?

Brandon: Mi nombre es Brandon. Es un gusto conocerte María.

Brandon: My name is Brandon. It's nice to meet you, Maria.

Maria: Es un gusto también conocerte. ¿De dónde eres?

Maria: It's nice to meet you, too! Where are you from?

Brandon: Vengo de NuevaYork. ¿De dónde eres tú?

Brandon: I'm from New York. Where are you from?

María: Vengo de Texas. ¿Alguna vez has estado en Texas?

Maria: I'm from Texas. Have you ever been to Texas?

Brandon: No, no he estado en Texas, pero siempre he querido ir. ¿Qué estás haciendo en Washington?

Brandon: No, I haven't, but I've always wanted to go. What are you doing in Washington?

María: Me mude aquí por trabajo. Soy profesora de inglés en Arlington.

Maria: I moved here for work. I'm an English teacher in Arlington.

Brandon: ¡Vaya!, eso está genial. Yo soy enfermero en Alexandria. ¿Cuánto tiempo has vivido aquí?

Brandon: Wow, that's great. I'm a nurse in Alexandria. How long have you lived here?

Maria: Me mudé aquí hace tres años después de terminar la universidad. ¿Y tú?

Maria: I moved here three years ago after I finished college. What about you?

Brandon: Me mude aquí hace dos meses. Vivía en Siracusa, Nueva York antes de mudarme aquí. ¿Tienes 25 (veinticinco) años?

Brandon: I moved here two months ago. I lived in Syracuse, New York before moving here. Are you 25 years old?

María: Sí, tengo 25 (veinticinco) ¿Cuántos años tienes tú?

Maria: Yes, I'm 25. How old are you?

Brando: Tengo 28 (veintiocho), casi 29 (veintinueve). Mi cumpleaños es el próximo mes. El 13 (trece) de diciembre. ¿Cuándo es tu cumpleaños?

Brandon: I'm 28, almost 29. My birthday is next month. December 13. When is your birthday?

María: Mi cumpleaños en el 23 (veintitrés) de marzo.

Maria: My birthday is March 23.

THE VERBS SABER AND CONOCER

Vocabulario nuevo / New Vocabulary

- saber – to know facts, to know how to do something
- conocer – to know a person
- producir – to produce
- reducir – to reduce
- ofrecer – to offer
- parecer – to seem
- rápido – fast
- la respuesta – answer
- con – with
- para – for, to, in order to
- por – for, by, through
- sin – without
- since entre – between, among
- encima de – on top of, over
- sobre – on, about
- debajo de – under
- dentro de – inside of
- detrás de – behind
- delante de – in front of
- enfrente de – across from

Repaso general / General Review

Saber and conocer

Let's approach these verbs by asking the three questions we ask about any new verbs.

1. What do they mean?
2. How do you use them?
3. How do you conjugate them?

What do they mean? Both saber and conocer mean "to know."

How do you use them? The verb saber expresses "to know" in the sense of knowing information or knowing how to do something (e.g., Ellos saben que Marta es simpática is "They know that Marta is nice"; ¿Sabes hablar italiano? is "Do you know how to speak Italian?"). The verb conocer expresses "to know" in the sense of being familiar with someone or with a place or thing (e.g., No conocemos a Arturo is "We don't know Arturo"; Mis amigos conocen una buena biblioteca is "My friends know a good library").

How do you conjugate them? Both saber and conocer have irregular yo forms: yo sé and yo conozco. The other five forms for both verbs are regular.

The Personal a

When the direct object of a verb is a specific person or group of people, the word a must precede the direct object. In the world of grammar, this is called the "personal a," or the a personal in Spanish (e.g., Conozco a Julia, pero no conozco a sus padres is "I know Julia, but I don't know her parents"; ¿A quién buscas? is "Whom are you looking for?").

If the person or group is not specific, no personal a is needed (e.g., Necesitamos unos nuevos amigos is "We need some new friends"). The personal a is generally not used with tener or hay (e.g., Tengo cuatro tíos is "I have four uncles"; Hay un chico al lado de mí is "There's a boy next to me").

Verbs like conocer

The verbs producir [to produce], reducir [to reduce], ofrecer [to offer], parecer [to seem], traducir [to translate], and conducir [to drive] are conjugated like conocer, meaning that they all have a z before the c in the yo form while the other five verb forms in the present are regular. The present tense of the yo forms for these verbs are produzco, reduzco, ofrezco, parezco, traduzco, and conduzco.

Using en and a

The preposition en [in, at] is used when there is no motion expressed (e.g., Estamos en el parque is "We are in the park"; Ella estudia en la universidad is "She studies at the university"). If what you're talking about involves motion, use the preposition a [to], which is often used with ir [to go] and llegar [to arrive] (e.g., Vamos a la tienda is "We are going to the store"; Siempre llegan a la estación de trenes is "They always arrive at the train station").

Understanding Spoken Spanish

When listening to spoken Spanish, make use of context, cognates, and conjecture. You're more likely to understand what you're hearing if, as the other person is speaking, you focus on context while listening for possible cognates. Conjecture is an opinion or conclusion formed on the basis of incomplete information.

When you hear something beyond your current level of comprehension, you must work to make sense of what's being said on the basis of incomplete information because there are gaps in your understanding. Conjecture simply means that at times you should guess what's being said. In fact, what beginning language learners often consider a wild guess is often an informed guess. Making use of context, cognates, and conjecture will help maximize your understanding of what you hear.

Actividades / Activities

a. Un cliente de Luis Cortés quiere viajar a El Salvador. El cliente le está pidiendo información sobre la ciudad. / A customer of Luis Cortés wants to travel to El Salvador. The customer is asking him for information about the city.

Escoge la respuesta correcta. / Choose the correct answer.

1. ¿Dónde está el Gimnasio [gymnasium] Adolfo Pineda?

   a) El gimnasio está en la carretera Panamericana.
   b) El gimnasio está entre la 4 Avenida Norte y la carretera Panamericana.
   c) El gimnasio está entre la carretera Panamericana y la 2 Avenida Sur.

2. ¿Dónde está la Parroquia Inmaculada Concepción?

   a) La parroquia está en el Parque Daniel Hernández.
   b) La parroquia está entre la 4 Avenida Norte y la 2 Avenida Sur.
   c) La parroquia está en la carretera Panamericana.

3. ¿Dónde está el Hotel El Portal?

   a) El hotel está en la 8 Avenida Norte.
   b) El hotel está lejos de la Parroquia Inmaculada Concepción.
   c) El hotel está cerca del Parque Daniel Hernández.

4. ¿Dónde está el Liceo Antonio Machado?

   a) El liceo está detrás de la Iglesia El Carmen.
   b) El liceo está al lado del Gimnasio Adolfo Pineda.
   c) El liceo está entre la 2 Avenida Sur y la 4 Avenida Norte.

5. ¿Dónde está el Centro Comercial Kukulkán?

a) El centro comercial está lejos del Gimnasio Adolfo Pineda.
b) El centro comercial está en la calle Daniel Hernández.
c) El centro comercial está delante del Minicentro Express La Libertad.

b. El cliente de Luis no sabe exactamente dónde están los países en América Central o América del Sur. / Luis's customer doesn't know exactly where the countries of Central America or South America are located.

Escoge la respuesta correcta. / Choose the correct answer.

1. ¿Dónde está El Salvador?

   a) El Salvador está al oeste de México.
   b) El Salvador está en América del Norte.
   c) El Salvador está al sur de Guatemala.

2. ¿Dónde está Ecuador?

   a) Ecuador está cerca de Argentina.
   b) Ecuador está entre Bolivia y Paraguay.
   c) Ecuador está cerca de Colombia.

3. ¿Dónde está Bolivia?

   a) Bolivia está entre Brasil y Chile.
   b) Bolivia está cerca de Guatemala.
   c) Bolivia está al sur de Paraguay.

4. ¿Dónde está Uruguay?

   a) Uruguay está cerca de Perú.
   b) Uruguay está al este de Argentina.
   c) Uruguay está entre Brasil y Bolivia.

5. ¿Dónde está la República Dominicana?

   a) La República Dominicana está oeste de Puerto Rico.
   b) La República Dominicana está al oeste de Cuba.
   c) La República Dominicana está entre Venezuela y Colombia.

c. Rogelio está buscando trabajo. Hoy tiene una entrevista de trabajo en la agencia de viajes de Luis Cortés. / Rogelio is looking for a job. Today he has a job interview in Luis Cortés's travel agency.

Completa el siguiente diálogo entre Rogelio y Luis. / Complete the following dialogue between Rogelio and Luis Cortés.

Luis: ¡Buenos días, Rogelio! Yo 1. _____ (ser) Luis Cortés.

Rogelio: ¡Mucho gusto, señor Cortés!

Luis: Bueno [Well], Rogelio, ¿usted 2. _____ (tener) experiencia [experience] en otros trabajos?

Rogelio: No, señor. No 3. _____ (tener) experiencia.

Luis: ¿Por qué está buscando trabajo en una agencia de viajes?

Rogelio: 4. _____ (estudiar) administración en turismo y recreación [Tourism and Recreation Management] y 5. _____ (necesitar) dinero para la universidad.

Luis: ¡Muy bien! 6. ¿_____ (saber) mucho sobre tecnología [technology]?

Rogelio: Sí, señor. 7. _____ (saber) trabajar con Photoshop, y eso [that] es importante para la publicidad [advertising] en una agencia de viajes.

Luis: Sí, 8._____ (tener) razón. 9. ¿_____ (saber) organizar [organize] eventos [events]?

Rogelio: Sí, señor. Yo 10. _____ (saber) organizar eventos. Por ejemplo, yo 11. _____ (organizar) todos los eventos en mi familia. También, yo 12. _____ (ofrecer) muchas fiestas en mi casa.

Luis: 13. ¿_____ (saber) hablar otras lenguas?

Rogelio: Sí, señor. Yo 14. _____ (saber) hablar alemán y francés. Yo 15._____ (traducir) muchos documentos [documents] para mis amigos.

Luis: 16. ¿_____ (conocer) otros países?

Rogelio: Sí, señor. 17. _____ (conocer) otros países — por ejemplo, España, Francia, Chile y Panamá.

Luis: ¡Muy bien, Rogelio! ¡Gracias por hablar conmigo [with me]!

d. Escoge la respuesta correcta. No olvides conjugar el verbo. / Choose the correct answer. Don't forget to conjugate the verb.

Conocer / Saber

1. Esteban y Luisa _____ sus vecinos.

2. Diana no _____ manejar su bicicleta [bicycle].

3. Luis _____ la cuñada de Ana.

4. Luis _____ muchos países de Europa y Asia.

5. Elena no _____ cocinar.

6. Alberto, Diego y Javier _____ jugar [to play] ajedrez [chess].

7. ¿ (Tú) _____ un buen restaurante para ir a comer con tu familia?

8. ¿ (Usted) _____ dónde está la estación de trenes?

9. Yo no _____ una buena universidad para estudiar administración en turismo.

e. Contesta las siguientes preguntas. / Answer the following questions.

Entre / a la izquierda / encima / enfrente / a la derecha / debajo

1. La lámpara está _____ del sillón.

2. El periódico está _____ de la mesa.

3. El televisor está _____ del sillón.

4. El teléfono está _____ la puerta y la ventana.

5. La alfombra está _____ de la mesa.

Respuestas correctas / Correct Answers

a. 1. a)

4. a)

2. b)

5. a)

3. c)

b. 1. c)

4. b)

2. c)

5. a)

3. a)

c. 1. soy

10. sé

2. tiene

11. organizo

3. tengo

12. ofrezco

4. Estudio

13. Sabe

5. necesito

14. sé

6. Sabe

15. traduzco

7. Sé

16. Conoce

8. tiene

17. Conozco

9. Sabe

d. 1. conocen a

6. saben

2. sabe

7. Conoces

3. conoce a

8. Sabe

4. conoce

9. conozco

5. sabe

e. 1. a la derecha

4. entre

2. encima

5. debajo

3. a la derecha

Stem-Changing Verbs

Vocabulario nuevo / New Vocabulary

- cambio – change
- raíz – root, stem of a verb
- conjugación – conjugation
- sin mí – without me
- contigo - with you
- hacia ti – toward you
- próximo – next
- conmigo – with me
- comprender – to understand
- poder - to be able
- tocar – to play an instrument, to touch
- pensar – to think
- cerrar – to close
- almorzar – lunch
- comenzar – to begin
- tener – to have
- empezar – to begin
- entender – to understand
- recordar – to remember
- perder – to lose
- querer – to want, to love
- mentir – to lie
- mostrar - to show
- preferir – to prefer
- volver - to return

- encontrar – to find
- costar – to cost
- devolver – to return
- algo - something
- dormir - to sleep
- morir - to die
- jugar – to play
- servir - to serve
- pedir - ask for
- repetir - to repeat
- ¡Qué elegante! – How elegant!

Repaso general / General Review

Stem-Changing Verbs in the Present Stem-changing verbs in the present tense have regular endings but change stem in all the singular forms and in the third-person plural form (there is no stem change for the nosotros or vosotros forms). The four possible stem changes are e à ie, o à ue, e à i, and u à ue (jugar is the only verb with a u à ue stem change). Conjugations of stem-changing verbs in the present include the following.

querer [to want, to love]

encontrar [to find]

e - ie

o à-ue

- quiero
- queremos
- encuentro
- encontramos
- quieres queréis
- encuentras encontráis
- quiere
- quieren
- encuentra encuentran

servir [to serve]

jugar [to play]

e - i

u - ue

- sirvo servimos
- juego jugamos
- sirves servís
- juegas
- jugáis
- sirve
- sirven
- juega juegan

What's easy about stem-changing verbs is remembering that all endings are regular and that the stem change happens only in the boot (in all forms except the nosotros and vosotros forms). What's difficult about stem-changing verbs is remembering which verbs change stem and what the stem change is for each verb.

A commonly used stem-changing verb is costar, meaning "to cost" (e.g., ¿Cuánto cuesta la computadora? is "How much does the computer cost?"; ¿Cuánto cuestan los zapatos? is "How much do the shoes cost?").

Prepositional Pronouns

Pronouns used after a preposition (also known as prepositional pronouns) are the same as the subject pronouns, with two exceptions: The first-person singular form is mí and the second-person singular, informal form is ti. The prepositional pronouns are as follows.

- mí
- nosotros, nosotras
- ti
- vosotros, vosotras
- usted
- ustedes
- él
- ellos
- ella
- ellas

Two forms that are irregular are conmigo, which means "with me," and contigo, which means "with you" (using the informal, singular form of "you").

MOTIVATION AND HABIT

Surprising as it may sound, these two things are probably the most important elements of learning Spanish. While a "knack" for languages or an ability to memorize vocabulary is nice, any person who has the motivation and the dedication to make learning Spanish a daily habit can be successful at attaining a very high, if not fluent, level.

Motivation

Motivation is a funny thing. It's something we all have, but that doesn't mean it's something we all share. Each person reading this book has his or her own reasons for deciding to learn Spanish. Perhaps you need it for work. Maybe you're planning a trip to Spain or Latin America and you don't want to make a complete fool out of yourself. Or maybe you simply love the culture and want to immerse yourself into it more.

Whatever your reasons may be, they brought you to this point. The road ahead of you may be a long one, but if you keep your motivation in mind, it doesn't have to be arduous! Finding a reason to learn Spanish is easy. The problem is maintaining that motivation that got you started. Learning a language can be frustrating and keeping hold of that initial spark of desire throughout the entire process may seem a little difficult at times.

True, personal dedication can't be found in carefully charted out study schedules. It's not in forcing yourself to sit in front of a desk for hours, staring at textbooks and hoping that the words will somehow come to mean something to you.

It's something much more than that--at least, it should be. Your reasons for learning Spanish should be fun and exciting. They should be something that you really desire and something that can and will keep you going through the rough patches that will inevitably come as you dive deeper into your newfound adventure.

"But I have to learn Spanish for work," you might say. "How can that be fun and exciting when I'm being forced to do it?"

I'm so glad you asked! Just because you're being obligated to learn a language doesn't mean that you can't still have fun in the process.

Don't believe me? Check out the following points to see what I mean.

Passion

Without passion, doing just about anything can become a chore. Think about your everyday life. Do you enjoy cooking? If you do, then you probably don't mind making your meals. If you don't, you probably don't get a high level of satisfaction from the process. Do you work out? Do you enjoy it? If you do, then great! If you don't but do it anyways (good for you!), then it probably takes a lot of self-discipline to continue going to the gym. The same could be said about anything--your job, your responsibilities around the house, etc. The point I'm trying to make here is simple--if we don't have a passion for what we're doing, then doing whatever it is probably isn't the most enjoyable experience. Bearable? Maybe. But fun? Definitely not.

Learning a foreign language is the same. If you think of learning Spanish as something you have to do instead of something you want to do, then you're in for a very long, very exhausting, and not very enjoyable experience.

What you have to do to avoid this is simple--find your passion! Draw on elements of your daily life. Make your language-learning journey your own.

Learning Spanish doesn't have to mean pouring over textbooks non-stop. It can mean incorporating things you love into your education and using them as your reason to keep going.

Are you a sports fan? Do you love music? What about books? No matter what it is that you have a passion for, you can make it an element in your Spanish-learning experience.

- **Sports fans** — Follow your favorite sports team online.
- **Music lovers** — Listen to Spanish music or learn a Spanish dance. Try a Spanish channel on YouTube or check out this playlist created by the mydailyspanish.com team.
- **Film fanatics** — Watch a movie in Spanish. There are tons of great options.
- **Art lovers** — Learn about famous Spanish artists, like Picasso or Dalí. Read about their lives and the impacts they had on culture and history.
- **Bookworms** — Spanish-language literature is rich, extensive, and very much worth your time. There are countless books you can pick up, no matter what level you're at.
- Advanced students have a very large selection of wonderful literary works of art. Of course, there's Cervantes' Don Quijote de la Mancha. But you could also check out Carmen Laforet's Nada for a more modern piece. And we can't forget Gabriel Garcia Marquez's world-famous Cien años de soledad.

- There's also the great option of reading some of your long-time favorites in Spanish. Pick up a Spanish copy of Harry Potter or Dan Brown's Da Vinci Code. No matter what you love, you'll surely be able to find a Spanish copy.

These are just a few examples to show you have you can take your passions and use them to keep you motivated when you feel like you just can't keep going.

Immersion

Immersion is yet another way to keep your passions and motivations at the forefront of your language learning. As we have seen, staying motivated is a very crucial part of learning Spanish.

Sometimes sitting down with your book to study just doesn't seem appealing.

That's where immersion comes in. Turn on a Spanish TV show or movie.

Listen to Spanish music while you're going about your daily routine. Read in Spanish or find a Spanish recipe to make. These will still give you exposure to the language. Doing these little things each week and studying for a solid period of time (when you're in the right mindset) will make your Spanish learning experience much more enjoyable.

Variety

As we mentioned before, there is more than just one cookie-cutter form of motivation. Keeping in line with that, you shouldn't feel like you have to stick with just one pattern of motivation. Your reasons for wanting to learn Spanish may change as you dive deeper into the language and that's fine!

Through learning a language, you have the opportunity to learn so many other things. You will learn about culture and cuisine, history and cinema, and so much more. You never know what you might discover and what passions or interests you might find suddenly surfacing.

Let's Look at Two Forms of Motivation...

What you may not know is that your very unique and personal reasons for learning Spanish can be categorized into one of two different types of motivation.

- **Integrative motivation:** This is when you go about learning a language for the purpose of immersion, i.e., becoming integrated into a Spanish-speaking environment. This occurs when learning Spanish is motivated by a desire to move to Spain or Mexico, for example, or when you have an extended vacation planned to Costa Rica, or any other place where Spanish is the primary language spoken.
- **Instrumental motivation:** This is motivation derived from practical or pragmatic purposes, i.e., when you need Spanish as an instrument to achieve a specific goal. This could be to fulfill your foreign language requirements in order to graduate from high school or college. Or perhaps your chances of getting your dream job increase when you add "Spanish" to your resume.

Both types of motivation are valid reasons to learn a foreign language. In some cases, you may even find that your motivation fits into both categories.

Let's say your job has asked you to move to a Spanish-speaking country.

Well, in this case, your motivation is both integrative (since you will be immersed into a Spanish-speaking environment) and instrumental (since you need it for work).

Generally speaking, someone learning Spanish for Integrative reasons will tend to focus more on the basics of communication. They want to go out and explore the Spanish-speaking world and, in order to do so, they want to be able to speak. A person who is learning a language for Instrumental reasons will usually focus more on the grammatical side of things. This is because, if they are using Spanish for work, for example, they want to be able to fill out forms and reports accurately.

The best environment for learning a foreign language can be created when you find a way to balance the two forms of motivation, letting them work in tandem. Basically, this means don't just throw out your grammar books and stick to a completely communicative approach. But at the same time, don't focus so much on the little details that you don't actually get out and put your language learning into practice!

Quality vs Quantity

When you begin your journey into language learning, you're usually bright-eyed and bushy-tailed, ready to take on the Spanish-speaking world, one verb conjugation at a time. However, this enthusiasm generally wears off right about the time that you reach your tenth verb conjugation. Things start to get overwhelming—vocabulary lists that go on and on with no clear end in sight and grammar rules that seem just as long and daunting.

The best way to learn Spanish is to remember—quality over quantity! Write that down, internalize it, and hold it close to your heart.

Let's say, for example, that you decide to set a somewhat lofty goal for yourself-- study Spanish for 2 hours a day. That's all well and good, but you'll quickly find that by day three or four, you're already feeling a little burnt out.

Here's why that method isn't working for you:

- Time-frame goals are nowhere near specific enough.
- Two hours a day is not realistic and almost completely unachievable for most people.

Life happens—it happens to all of us. Our busy schedules get in the way and before you know it, it's late and you're trying to keep your eyes open long enough to cram whatever you can into your mind before you collapse in bed.

More than likely, you do this cramming with a textbook, which, let's face it, isn't exciting enough to hold your interest after a long day of work, family responsibilities, etc., especially when your nice, cozy bed seems to literally be calling your name.

For the best results when learning Spanish, time is key. You not only need time to learn the information, but you also need time to absorb it and time to let your brain rest. Instead of forcing yourself to study at a time that you would really much rather be doing anything else, wait until you are genuinely interested and ready to take in the information.

You may think that doing this means that you aren't going to be investing the time it takes to master a language. I mean, come on--it's a foreign language!

THE ORIGIN OF SPANISH SPEAKERS

You will agree with me that, as one of the most popular and oldest languages, the Spanish language bears a vibrant and exciting history. Apart from that, it enhances communication in many parts of the world, and its richness brings about happiness among the human race at large. Without further ado, let's dig into the roots of Spanish for you to appreciate some of the milestones the language has overcome and, more importantly, generate some interest in you.

The Spanish language has its underlying foundations in 210 BC. It was gotten from Latin and began being spoken in Burgos, north-focal Spain, during the ninth century and was of the bygone sort. Because of some common exercises, like conflicts, exchange, and intermarriages occurring at that specific time, it had the option to advance toward the south heading.

Toward the start of the eleventh century, it had shown up in the southern side of Spain and urban communities, like Madrid and Toledo. Its initially composed organization was created in Madrid City during the fourteenth century. Other composed types of lingo were made in Toledo around a similar time.

Spanish or Castilian, as alluded by the Spaniards, was first introduced as an authority language in Spain at the finish of the fifteenth century. A similar happened in the wake of joining the Aragon and Leone realms, which at last prompted the spread of the language to various pieces of the globe. A portion of the prominent nations that were impacted by this language incorporates the Americas, Morocco, and different nations lining Spain. Among them were a few pieces of the Mediterranean Sea, particularly the southern piece of it.

The previous type of language was known as old Spanish, which was archived during the fifteenth century. From that point forward, a more up-to-date form has appeared. These components are, for the most part, alluded to as "old-style Spanish." The equivalent is attached to the way that there's the modernization of the language and its different accomplishments in the contemporary fields, like the scholastic world.

Castilian, which is a variety of the first type of the language, begins from the northern and focal locales of Spain and is generally spoken around their state-of-the-art. The agreement of fostering the composed type of the language was arrived at when various adaptations of the language began springing up with no specific request. These achieved the normalization of the language. Then again, it ruled different lingos due to the huge adventures by the Castilians during the conflicts, like the Reconquista.

Essentially, the Reconquista was likewise persuasive in the northern pieces of Spain and furthermore moved southwards. Its words were vigorously Arabic, and because of it traveling south, it supplanted numerous neighborhood dialects found inside this piece of the country. Afterward, the language becomes terminated inside Spain's borders because of individuals embracing different varieties of the Spanish language.

The Glosas Emillanenses were generally accepted to have been in presence during the previous hundreds of years. It contained plenty of Spanish compositions of that time and was counseled for different reasons. Lord Alfonso x Castile normalized the past duplicates of the Castilian by growing generally satisfactory structures. What he did was to gather a few journalists in his office and afterward supervised their creative cycle. Therefore, a great deal of well-off information was produced in a few fields. It is accepted that gaining from those sources was used to run the Spanish domain. For example, laws composed by these creators were utilized to decide cases in the domain. The cosmic information was utilized in the progression of the specialized field in the domain, among other huge abundance of assets used to run the country.

Additionally, another person by the name of Antonio de Nebrija made the clench hand sentence structure for the language. It framed the grammar for composing the language, which was of extraordinary assistance to the two essayists and perusers as it made a reason for composing and comprehension. He ultimately offered it to Queen Isabella in the year 1942 in view of her adoration for it. She accepted that it was an important resource that achieved authority.

Similitudes are there between the bygone and current types of Spanish. This implies that the perusers can comprehend it from the two perusers. A current Spanish speaker can rapidly flip through the old Spanish writing and have the option to fathom what is being said.

Following quite a long while of relying upon the composed configurations of the language, the primary Spanish institute opened up its entryways in the late eighteenth century and concocted a normalized variety of the language. These achieved a lot of understanding between the various parts of the field. All things considered, authors might foster their work dependent on a uniform norm; in this manner, it empowered consistency and general comprehension inside their crowd.

The foundation then, at that point created its first sort of Spanish language word reference. Similarly empowered both the journalists and perusers to foster new jargon concerning the Spanish language. In case one was in question with respect to a specific word, they could rapidly search for it in the word reference. It additionally created sentence structure for the language, which recommended they compose grammar, syntactic standards, and articulations that ought to be utilized in regards to the Spanish language.

Right now, the foundation keeps on delivering more up-to-date versions of the word reference and sentence structure rules. At last, you can get to the said word reference through the web.

On a worldwide scale, the Spanish language can be ordered as the second most communicated in language after English and is likewise an authority language of somewhere around thirty nations. Something else to note about the language is that it is primarily spoken in Mexico, which is home to the most dynamic clients of this tongue.

Different nations with a critical number of Spanish speakers incorporate Spain, Argentina, and America. The Spaniards allude to it as Espanola to differentiate it from the remainder of the dialects and call it Castilian while separating it from the other standard lingos found inside Spain.

The Advent of Spanish in the U.S.

This language gained entry into the United States as a result of colonizing Spain. Due to the constant interaction between the citizens of the two countries, the Spanish language infiltrated further into the American territory and almost influenced all its states. After the end of the colonization period, the inhabitants of these states continued enforcing their use and even made it the national language through the enactment of policies that expanded the use of the language.

Also, immigrants from Spanish colonies found their way into the US mainland and continued to spread the language. And those who lived in the southwestern parts of America did not see the need for adopting English as the language since they believed that the American government had forcefully taken their land. Therefore, in retaliation, they maintained their culture and language and even spread it to other people around them.

Similarly, inhabitants of the US welcomed the idea of learning a new language, which brought in new changes. Also, a result of intermarriages between the American citizens and those from Spanish-speaking countries led to multi-racial communities that were bilingual in nature, which further spread the language to places it had never reached.

Spanish in Other Parts of the World

Its Establishment in Africa

Its presence was first felt in Africa during the 18th century. The language was established in Guinea during a particular period when it became a Spaniard colony. Consequently, it was recognized as the national language after the country got liberated. It is also common in western parts of the Sahara because of its colonization by the Spanish.

In the Jew Population

After the Spanish government repatriated the Jewish community from its country in the year 1492, a new version of the Spanish language, known as Ladino, was born within them. It started and spread to other areas on its own and is still used by a declining number of speakers of Jewish origin.

In the Pacific

The pacific, being part of Chile Island, made people speak Spanish from 1888, particularly the Easter Island.

In Spain

Spain is the homeland of the Spanish language. It is here that language was conceived, brought up, and spread. This makes the language continue to receive unwavering support and popularity. People here literary wake in it and sleep in it. The government and a majority of the private institutions use it as an official language of communication.

Other variations of the language have been allowed by parliament to be used in provinces, depending on their familiarity with them. The early forms of written Spanish in this country were witnessed as early as the 11th century.

They comprised of texts borrowed from the Castile and Rioja. Literacy works done in Leones existed until the 14th century while that of the Aragonese stayed until the 15th century.

The Roots of the Spanish Dialects

Apart from Spain, the Spanish language has infiltrated a lot of countries on a global scale. Such include the Americas, the Philippines, and Mexico, among other popular nations; thus, developing different regional dialects with a common denominator based on Castilian. However, these dialects disagree on various instances of their phonology.

An example is a difference in the pronunciation of nouns that produce different sounds while speaking the language. Many of the native Spanish speakers use the

Catalina variation of the language. It might sound a bit different from the Spanish expressed in the US.

Spain also has other forms of language that can be used depending on which province one comes from.

4 FACTORS TO BETTER UNDERSTAND SPOKEN SPANISH

Do we really speak Spanish so fast? When you talk to someone in Spain, you always end up thinking: "But what's wrong with them? Are you in a hurry or something? "Ok, I admit it. Sometimes we can talk pretty fast. But many other times, it is not so bad, it just seems so to you.

The problem is that when you listen to someone you try to capture ALL the words they say. And if you don't understand a word or phrase well, you think "what did he just say?" And you lose the thread. That person keeps talking, and all of a sudden, you realize that you have missed the rest of the conversation. Pfff, wow! And because of that, you think again, "my mother, how fast these Spanish speak! ".

"Well then, what do I have to do to understand them better?"

Try to grasp the basic idea of what is being said. And keep listening. And though there is anything that you have not learned. In the end, you can end up learning more and quicker than if you concentrate on each term.

The more words and expressions you know, the more you understand, of course. But knowing how to recognize the sounds of spoken Spanish is essential.

Yes, the sounds.

You probably learned the alphabet when you went to your first Spanish class a looooong time ago. The typical class on the alphabet and how each letter sounds. This was your first or second Spanish class. Very elementary. But have you ever had a class on sounds again? A class exclusively on pronunciation? Probably not. The correct and/or natural pronunciation of Spanish does not seem to be that important in most Spanish schools.

Grammar and vocabulary continue to be the true protagonists of these classes. Do you agree with me?

1. Know and Recognize Spanish Sounds

It will seem very obvious and maybe even a waste of time. "I already know the alphabet, why do I have to pay so much attention to sounds? "Well, because there are usually small differences between the sounds when we say them separately and when we say them in a word or in a sentence.

Also, the sounds of your mother tongue do not leave you. It's hard for them to leave you. You know that V and B have the same sound in Spanish.

However, it is difficult for you not to distinguish between them. It seems unnatural to you, it is uncomfortable. So, if you want to say "let's go," you say [famous] instead of [bamos]. And if you say "valencia," it seems that you say [falencia] instead of [balencia].

Try to forget how sounds are written in your language. Surely the V doesn't sound like a B in your language. Listen well to Spanish sounds. Let your brain analyze them, recognize them, and welcome them. Now listen again.

And imitate them.

And now it's time to practice a little...

Take your mobile and open the recorder application. If you don't have one, download anyone. And record yourself as you naturally read these sentences out loud:

I'm going to live in Valencia all summer.

The truth is, he has never seen a cow kiss another cow.

Wow, I got a pretty weird phrase! Well, never mind, it's perfect for practicing.

Listen to your recording. Read them again, but now focus more on the correct sounds.

Is there a difference between the 2 recordings? If the difference is very big, you will have to gain confidence and believe more in yourself. If there is little difference and you think the sounds are correct congratulations!

2. Recognize Words within a Spoken Passage

Where does a specific word start and end? Careful. Some sounds may change slightly under the influence of "neighboring" sounds. If you don't believe me, compare the sound / a / of the words "tree" and "Antonio." The influence of the / n / is evident.

How would you say this phrase at normal speed?

Tomorrow morning we are going to the field with Antonio's son.

When we speak in Spanish we join the last consonant of a word with the first vowel of the next or with similar consonants. The same happens between the last vowel of one word and the first of the next.

330

This sentence would look like this:

[Tomorrow morning, we will go to the field with Antonio's son].

"Oh my! But how can I think about all this when I listen to a conversation or speak to someone?"

There's no need. It is good that you know why and how the words come together when speaking. But the important thing here is practice. Listen and speak in Spanish. You will recognize words without thinking. The more you use Spanish, the better. So you can differentiate words and identify them more easily.

3. The Intonation

Are you asking, exclaiming, or just stating something? Intonation is essential for this. Sometimes, we can even know if the person speaking is happy, nervous, angry, afraid, etc. And this will also help us better understand the message.

For example, it is very different to say:

Maria is coming to dinner tonight.

Record yourself while you read those phrases out loud. Do not be embarrassed. Bring out your inner actor/actress and overreact a bit. It is fun and you will notice the difference between one phrase and another better.

And now for good news. Spoken Spanish offers you an advantage. In general, Spaniards are quite expressive when we speak. We love to help us with gestures to tell something and we express a lot with our faces and hands.

Sometimes we even use our arms and legs. How about? This is also very useful when it comes to understanding each other.

The tone, the expression, the gestures. All of this will help you understand the general meaning of what they are saying to you.

4. Variants of Spanish

Surely you already know. In each region of Spain, and even in each province, you can find a somewhat different accent. I love this. But I understand that it can be an added difficulty for someone who wants to learn to speak like us.

You can always learn to speak with a more neutral accent. But you should also know the accent of the region that you usually visit the most in Spain.

You don't have to speak with that accent, but it is good to know how they speak to better understand the people around you. In the end, that accent will be part of your experiences in Spain, part of your Spanish self.

They say that the most neutral accent in Spain (if it exists) is in Valladolid.

For example, the Galician accent (from Galicia) is vastly different from the Andalusian accent (from Andalusia) and the Madrid accent (from Madrid).

The Catalan accent is also very different from Asturian. The Canarian accent (from the Canary Islands) is more like the Andalusian and the Cuban accent (Cuba) than the accent from the north of Spain.

I am Andalusian. I love my accent. But when I talk to someone who is not from the South, I always try to neutralize him a little. It is a matter of respect.

Make it easy for another person to understand you without any problem.

Here I give you my most neutral version first and then my most Andalusian version of the same phrases.

It's that I'm not here tomorrow.

Come on, don't be like that.

By the way, Spanish is not the only language with variants. It's not easy for a Spanish woman like me to learn to speak flamenco (from Flanders). In flamenco, there are many different dialects and this makes learning difficult.

Now I can distinguish dialects very well. I do not speak them, but I feel closer to me the way of speaking of East and West Flanders because it is where I live.

Different sensations (perceptions) of the student if you are studying Spanish (or any other foreign language), your feelings and, accordingly, your ability to "understand" and "speak," most likely, will not be the same.

— Perhaps you think that you are good at understanding Spanish, that you have an excellent auditory perception, which is able to perfectly distinguish the words pronounced by your interlocutor carrier, and you also have a subtle intuition that allows you to determine the meaning of unfamiliar expressions from just one context.

Or maybe you're sure you really feel like a fish in the water as you verbally express yourself in Spanish. You have an excellent vocabulary and you use it rationally, you also have a clear command of verb form schemes, and therefore feel that you can express yourself with confidence in many situations.

From the teacher's perspective and the student's opinion, everyone understands what is good for him and what is worse, and this is obvious. What about the Spanish language? What causes the greatest difficulties for a Russian student, apart from his own feelings and intuition: to speak Spanish or understand Spanish speech?

The Spanish teacher, who perfectly knows the "problem points" of his students, has a definite answer that does not coincide at all with their opinion.

Understanding Spanish Speech by Hearing

Correct auditory perception is a real obstacle, a wall in front of which a Russian person finds himself studying Spanish here in Moscow, far from Spain and Latin America, without the opportunity to listen to native speakers in his daily life.

A Russian student who studies Spanish with great desire and from a good teacher will be able to learn to speak in just 2-3 months. However, he has a long process to go before he learns to understand the spoken language of Spanish or Latin Americans.

Positive and negative aspects

a) Speaking

There is a big difference between speaking and understanding. The ability to speak is closely related to intelligence, the ability to think. An intelligent person actively learning Spanish can learn to speak it in record time.

Therefore, the ability to freely express one's thoughts is a great advantage for such a person.

b) The ability to understand

However, the same intelligent person, despite all his efforts, no matter how carefully and tensely he listens to Spanish speech, he will not be able to achieve perfect auditory perception as quickly, and the speed of development of this skill will rather slow, which is a kind of negative aspect in this case.

About the ability to speak and understand Spanish, listening comprehension is not as much of intelligence as the ability to express yourself in the foreign language you are learning, in this case, Spanish.

Many people with mental disabilities are able to perfectly understand others who speak the same language. However, such people have serious problems with self-expression both orally and in writing.

On the one hand, understanding spoken language is more difficult for Spanish learners than speaking. On the other hand, learning to speak Spanish fluently requires more mental resources than understanding Spanish by ear.

Sounds a bit paradoxical, doesn't it? Perhaps this fact made you think.

How to develop good hearing as quickly as possible the process of oral expression involves a lot of intellectual activity.

However, listening to speech requires a calmer attitude.

To learn to speak a foreign language, you must assimilate new information, process it and present it (express your opinion). To understand a foreign speech, you need something else: get used to the sounds and melodies of a language that is new to you, which, unfortunately, depends only on time and requires a lot of patience.

Whether you're ready to understand Spanish on the radio or on TV, your intellect will be equally effective at processing the sounds you hear, slowly but continuously. The most important thing is the duration of the effect on your hearing, i.e., time.

IR AND THE FUTURE

Ir

The verb "ir" (to go) is rather straightforward. It is used any time you are referring to going to a place. As such, you can combine it with the preposition "a" to indicate the place, or direction, in which you are headed. It can also be used in the present simple to indicate a future intention. For example, "voy al banco" would mean "I go to the bank". However, if you say, "voy al banco mañana" (I am going to the bank tomorrow) then you are making reference to a future event by adding a future time expression.

Conversation:

My favorite place / Mi lugar favorito

Fernando: Diego, where are you going on weekends?

Fernando: Diego, ¿a dónde vas los fines de semana?

Diego: I go to several places. On Saturday I go to the gym in the morning. Then, I go to the mall in the afternoon.

Diego: Voy a varios lugares. El sábado voy al gimnasio por la mañana. Luego, voy al centro comercial por la tarde.

Fernando: Great! Where do you go on Sundays?

Fernando: ¡Qué bien! ¿A dónde vas los domingos?

Diego: I go to church and then I go to the movies with my friends.

Diego: Voy a la iglesia y luego voy con mis amigos al cine.

Fernando: Interesting. Do you like movies?

Fernando: Interesante. ¿Te gusta el cine?

335

Diego: Yes, a lot. And you, where do you go on weekends?

Diego: Sí, mucho. Y tú, ¿A dónde vas los fines de semana?

Fernando: On Saturday I go to university. My friends go to an art course.

Fernando: El sábado voy a la universidad. Mis amigos van a un curso de arte.

Diego: Oh, interesting. What do you do on Saturday afternoons?

Diego: Oh, interesante. ¿Qué haces los sábados por la tarde?

Fernando: My friends and I go to the gym. It is a fun activity after a long week.

Fernando: Mis amigos y yo vamos al gimnasio. Es una actividad divertida después de una semana larga.

Diego: Yes, it is. Where do you go on Sundays?

Diego: Sí, lo es. ¿A dónde vas los domingos?

Fernando: My older brother goes to golf. I'm going with him.

Fernando: Mi hermano mayor va al golf. Voy con él.

Diego: Golf? Interesting.

Diego: ¿Golf? Qué interesante.

Fernando: We are going next weekend.

Fernando: Vamos el próximo fin de semana.

Diego: Thank you! I love the idea.

Diego: ¡Gracias! Me encanta la idea.

Future Tense

Well, it's time now to start with the future tense. Let's start with the simple future. The "futuro simple" expresses a forthcoming action, an intention or a probability. We can use the future tense to express:

❖ An intention regarding the future:

- Mañana ordenaré mi habitación (Tomorrow I will tidy up my bedroom)

❖ A supposition about the future:

- No lo acabarás en un día (You won't finish in one day)

❖ A supposition about the present:

- Me imagino que tu habitación todavía estará desordenada (I suppose your bedroom is still messy)

Once I know when we use the simple future, let's see how to form this tense for the regular verbs. For this tense, instead of separating the ending from the infinitive, we have to add to the full infinitive the corresponding ending for each person. But the good news is that all three conjugations have the same endings for each subject.

Let's see some other verbs:

COMPARAR (to compare): yo compararé, tú compararás, él/ella comparará, nosotros/nosotras compararemos, vosotros/vosotras comparareís, ellos/ellas compararán.

BARRER (to sweep): yo barreré, tú barrerás, él/ella barrerá, nosotros/nosotras barreremos, vosotros/vosotras barrereís, ellos/ellas barrerán.

COMPARTIR (to share): yo compartiré, tú compartirás, él/ella compartirá, nosotros/nosotras compartiremos, vosotros/vosotras compartireís, ellos/ellas compartirán.

Now that we know how to form the future simple with regular verbs, let's see some sentences to practice the different uses of the tense:

❖ An intention regarding the future:

- El mes que viene empezaré a estudiar español (Next month I will start to learn Spanish)
- Mañana llevarás el coche al mecánico (tomorrow you will bring the car to the garage)
- El año que viene ella comprará un piso (Next year she will buy a flat)
- Él vendrá pronto mañana (He will come early tomorrow)
- Nosotros actuaremos en el concierto (We will act in the concert)
- Nosotras traeremos bebida y aperitivos para la fiesta (We will bring drinks and snacks for the party)
- Vosotros compartiréis habitación durante el viaje (You will share a room during the travel)
- Vosotras viajaréis mañana en el tren de las dos (You will travel tomorrow by train at 2)
- Ellos comerán con nosotros la semana que viene (They will have lunch with us next week)
- Ellas vivirán en Roma el próximo curso (They will live in Rome next course)

❖ A supposition about the future:

- No lo acabarás en un día (You won't finish in one day)
- Creo que llegarás tarde, como siempre (I think you will be late, as always)
- No vendrá a cenar porque saldrá tarde (He won't come to dinner because he'll finish late)
- Supongo que ellas traerán los regalos que compramos (I suppose they will bring the presents we bought)
- Imagino que aprobaré el examen (I imagine I will pass the exam)

❖ A supposition about the present:

- Me imagino que tu habitación todavía estará desordenada (I suppose your bedroom is still messy)
- Supongo que todavía estará de camino (I suppose he's still on his way)
- Creo que la reunión acabará en breve (I think the meeting is nearly finished)
- Imagino que vendrás a comer a casa hoy, ¿no? (I imagine you are coming to have lunch at home today, don't you?)
- Supongo que estarás arreglada ya (I suppose you are ready)

Now you know how to form the simple future. Practice to conjugate the following verbs:

EXISTIR (to exist): yo existiré, tú existirás, él/ella existirá, nosotros/nosotras existiremos, vosotros/vosotras existiréis, ellos/ellas existirán

BUCEAR (to dive): yo bucearé, tú bucearás, él/ella buceará, nosotros/nosotras bucearemos, vosotros/vosotras bucearéis, ellos/ellas bucearán

LEER (to read): yo leeré, té leerás, él/ella leerá, nosotros/nosotras leeremos, vosotros/vosotras leeréis, ellos/ellas leerán.

Great! We know the simple future so let's learn now the future perfect, the "futuro perfecto."

Let's put the explanation in context:

- ¿Por qué está cambiando una rueda Belén? (Why is Belen changing the tire?)
- Se habrá pinchado la rueda (The tire must have been punctured)
- ¡Oh, no! En una hora queríamos ir al cine y necesitamos el coche (Oh, no! We would like to go to the cinema in an hour and we need the car)
- ¡No te preocupes! Para entonces ya la habrá cambiado (Don't worry! It will be changed by then)

To conjugate the perfect future we have to use the auxiliary verb "HABER" (to have) in future tense plus the past participle. Do you remember how we form the past participle?

If the infinitive ends in AR, we change the ending for ADO

- Comprar – comprado (to buy – bought)
- Hablar – hablado (to speak – spoken)

If the infinitive ends in ER or IR, we change the ending for IDO.

- Beber – bebido (to drink – drank)
- Aprender – aprendido (to learn – learnt)
- Vivir – vivido (lo live – lived)
- Compartir – compartido (to share – shared)

And also remember the verbs that has irregular forms for the past participle:

Verb – perfect participle – translation

- abrir – abierto – open
- decir – dicho – say
- escribir – escrito – write
- hacer – hecho – do/make
- freír – frito/freído – fry
- imprimir – impreso/imprimido – print
- morir – muerto – die

- poner – puesto – place/set
- proveer – provisto/proveído – provide
- suscribir – suscrito/suscripto – sign/subscribe
- ver – visto – see
- volver – vuelto – return

Once this has been refreshed, let's conjugate the perfect future:

Person – haber – past participle

- yo habré hablado / aprendido / vivido
- tú habrás hablado / aprendido / vivido
- él/ella/usted habrá hablado / aprendido / vivido
- nosotros/-as habremos hablado / aprendido / vivido
- vosotros/-as habréis hablado / aprendido / vivido
- ellos/ellas/ustedes habrán hablado / aprendido / vivido

NEXT STEPS IN IMPROVING YOUR SPANISH – VOCABULARY

Find below some new and old words

- profesión – profession
- maestro – teacher
- abogado – lawyer
- hombre de negocios -businessman
- mujer de negocios – businesswoman
- arquitecto – architect
- sitio web – website
- página web – web page
- blog – blog
- correo electrónico – e-mail
- mensaje de texto – text message
- tecnología – technology
- enfermero – nurse
- director de escuela – school principal
- trabajador social – social worker
- policía – police officer
- usuario – user
- enlace – link
- conexión – connection
- buscador – search engine
- contraseña – password
- internet – internet
- conexión inalámbrica – wireless connection
- teléfono inalámbrico – cordless phone
- teléfono celular/ celular/ móvil – cell phone

General Review

Verbs Followed by a Preposition

You have already learned several verbs that are followed by a preposition: asistir a is "to attend"; salir de is "to leave"; jugar a is "to play a sport." Other verbs that are followed by a preposition include tratar (which is followed by de) and entrar (which is followed by a or en).

Siempre trato de estudiar antes de un examen is "I always try to study before an exam." As for entrar, Latin Americans tend to follow it with a, while Spaniards tend to follow it with en. So, to say "At times, we enter the building late," a Latin American would say A veces entramos al edificio tarde, and a Spaniard would say A veces entramos en el edificio tarde.

Verbs That Need a Preposition before an Infinitive

You've learned in general that in Spanish if you place one verb directly after another, the first verb is the one that is conjugated, and the second verb needs to be in the infinitive form:

- Ellos quieren navegar por la red is They want to surf the Internet.
- No puedes hablar conmigo ahora is You can't talk to me now.

But there are some verbs that must be followed by a preposition before an infinitive. Two examples of this you've seen already are acabar de [to have just done something] and ir a [to be going to do something].

- Elena acaba de dormir is Elena just slept.
- Vamos a chatear is We are going to chat online.

Four other verbs that need a preposition before an infinitive (and specifically the preposition a) are empezar [to begin], comenzar [to begin], aprender [to learn], and enseñar [to teach]. Consider these examples:

- Es hora de empezar a trabajar is It's time to begin to work.
- Al mediodía, los abogados empiezan a llegar al restaurante is At noon, the lawyers begin arriving at the restaurant.
- Pedro debe aprender a manejar is Pedro should learn to drive.
- Su hermano lo enseñó a mentir is His brother taught him to lie.

Immersing Yourself in Spanish

One good way to improve your Spanish is to force yourself to speak it. So, if you have someone you can speak Spanish with, meet and decide that you will speak only Spanish for an hour, a dinner, or a certain event—you decide. Of course, more time is better, but no matter how much time you spend speaking Spanish, the important thing is to continue with it. The impossibility of using English really forces you to try to (tratar de) figure out how to express yourself in Spanish. And your companion doesn't need to be a native speaker; he or she could be another Spanish language learner like you.

Know that when you have difficulties expressing yourself, it's okay. Often, a problem in communication will lead a learner to study a bit more—maybe grammar, maybe vocabulary. But the learner tends to be motivated because the studying is designed to solve a real communication problem that occurred during the immersive experience.

The Learning Curve of a Language Learner

Sometimes language learners imagine that their progress in studying a language will be a steadily ascending curve, starting with a baseline knowledge of zero and gradually but steadily moving upward toward communicative competence. The reality, however, is that while the progress of a language learner has many ups, it also has some downs. And there are definitely periods when your skills plateau and you seem not to be improving at all.

So, you need to know that it's entirely normal—to be expected, even—that there will be times when you feel stuck, and you think that you've stopped improving or even gotten worse with your Spanish skills. When this happens, don't give up. Continue your studies and keep in contact with the language as much as possible. The more you hear, speak, read, and write Spanish, the more quickly you'll notice that your Spanish really is getting better.

Actividades - Activities

Lee el párrafo y contesta las preguntas que siguen. / Read the paragraph and answer the questions that follow.

Luisa está planeando [planning] una reunión de vecinos. Ella quiere hacer la reunión en su casa. Además, quiere ver a sus nietas Diana y Mariana, y por eso también invitó a la reunión a su hija Erica y a su yerno Javier. Ella envió [sent] un correo electrónico la semana pasada, pero no todos enviaron una respuesta. Luisa va a mandarles otro mensaje a sus vecinos. La reunión va a ser mañana a las 6:30 de la tarde. Luisa quiere hablarles mañana sobre la necesidad [need] de tener un servicio de policía privado [private] en el vecindario. Ella también está preocupada porque últimamente [lately] alrededor del vecindario hay mucha basura [trash]. Algunos de los vecinos le dijeron a Luisa que estos son asuntos [issues] importantes de discutir [discuss]. Ella les dijo a todos que pueden llevar sus iPads para tomar notas [notes], y además [moreover] todos pueden usar su conexión inalámbrica. Luisa está enviándole un mensaje de texto a su hija para recordarle sobre la reunión.

Exercise:

1. ¿Cuáles son dos expresiones que hablan de acciones en el futuro? _____ .

2. ¿Cuáles son tres verbos conjugados en el pretérito? _____ .

3. ¿Cuál es un ejemplo del uso del presente progresivo (que expresa algo que ocurre ahora mismo)? _____ .

4. ¿Cuáles son tres ejemplos del uso del objeto indirecto? _____ .

5. ¿Cuál es un uso de estar para expresar una emoción? _____ .

Answers:

1. va a mandarles / va a ser

2. invitó / envió / enviaron / dijeron / dijo

3. está planeando / está enviándole

4. va a mandarles / quiere hablarles / le dijeron / les dijo / está enviándole / recordarle

5. está preocupada

Completa las oraciones usando el pretérito - Complete the sentences using the preterite.

1. Cuando Diego 1. _____ (empezar) su compañía [company], 2. _____ (pedir) un servicio de Internet con conexión inalámbrica. Él 3. _____ (comprar) una computadora, un teléfono celular y otro inalámbrico. Al principio, 4. _____ (tener) problemas para acceder a Internet y la conexión no 5. _____ (ser) la mejor, y por eso 6. _____ (llamar) a la compañía de Internet para solicitar [ask for] una conexión más rápida. En la compañía, ellos le 7. _____ (ayudar), y Diego 8. _____ (obtener) [to get] una mejor conexión. Cuando él 9. _____ (cerrar) su empresa, 10. _____ (vender) todas las cosas de su oficina.

Answers:

1. empezó

2. pidió

3. compró

4. tuvo

5. fue

6. llamó

7. ayudaron

8. obtuvo

9. cerró

10. vendió

Exercise:

Escoge la opción correcta - Choose the correct option:

1. Luisa _____ un blog para hablar de nutrición desde hace cinco años.

    a) tuvo
    b) va a tener
    c) tiene

2. En este momento, Luisa y Esteban _____ tener una página web con información sobre medicina y nutrición.

    a) quisieron
    b) van a querer
    c) quieren

3. Luisa _____ a todos los vecinos del vecindario, y por eso la reunión va a ser en su casa.

    a) conoció
    b) va a conocer
    c) conoce

4. Elena y su esposo _____ a la reunión de mañana.

    a) fueron
    b) van a ir
    c) van

5. Alejandra _____ directora de escuela por unos años, antes de casarse [to get married].

    a) fue
    b) va a ser
    c) es

6. A Alejandra le gusta mucho su nuevo teléfono celular y todos los días _____ mensajes de texto.

   a) mandó
   b) van a mandar
   c) manda

7. El primer año de universidad, Pablo _____ en estudiar enfermería [nursing], pero ahora no _____ estudiar enfermería.

   a) pensó...quiere
   b) van a pensar...quiso
   c) piensa...quiere

8. Ahora tú _____ dos correos electrónicos.

   a) Tuviste
   b) vas a tener
   c) tienes

9. Ayer, tú y tus amigos _____ en el mejor restaurante de la ciudad.

   a) comieron
   b) van a comer
   c) comen

10. Tus amigos y tu _____ muchos correos electrónicos ayer durante el trabajo.

   a) enviaron
   b) van a enviar
   c) envían

Answers:

1. c) tiene

2. c) quieren

3. c) conoce

4. b) van a ir / c) van

5. a) fue

6. c) manda

7. a) pensó...quiere

8. b) vas a tener / c) tienes

9. a) comieron

10. a) enviaron

STEM-CHANGING VERBS

Repaso general / General Review

A. Stem-Changing Verbs in the Present

Stem-changing verbs in the present tense have regular endings but change stem in all the singular forms and in the third-person plural form (there is no stem change for the nosotros or vosotros forms). The four possible stem changes are e → ie, o → ue, e → i, and u → ue (jugar is the only verb with au → ue stem change). Conjugations of stem-changing verbs in the present include the following.

- querer [to want, to love] e → ie
- encontrar [to find] o → ue

Quiero, queremos, quieres, queréis, quiere, quieren, encuentro, encontramos, encuentras encontráis, encuentra, encuentran

- servir [to serve] jugar [to play] e → i u → ue

Sirvo, servimos, juego, jugamos, sirves, servís, juegas, jugáis, sirve, sirven, juega, juegan

What's easy about stem-changing verbs is remembering that all endings are regular and that the stem change happens only in the boot (in all forms except the nosotros and vosotros forms). What's difficult about stem-changing verbs is remembering which verbs change stem and what the stem change is for each verb.

A commonly used stem-changing verb is costar, meaning "to cost" (e.g., ¿Cuánto cuesta la computadora? is "How much does the computercost?"; ¿Cuánto cuestan los zapatos? is"How much do the shoescost?").

B. Prepositional Pronouns

Pronouns used after a preposition (also known as prepositional pronouns) are the same as the subject pronouns, with two exceptions: The first-person singular form is mí and the second-person singular, informal form is ti. The prepositional pronouns are as follows.

Mí, nosotros, nosotras, ti, vosotros, vosotras, usted, ustedes, él, ellos, ella, ellas

Two forms that are irregular are conmigo, which means "with me," and contigo, which means "with you" (using the informal, singular form of"you").

C. Knowing Where to Place Spoken Stress

Spanish has three rules that determine where to place the stress in a word when speaking.

1. When a word ends with a vowel or with the letter n or s, you stress the second-to-last syllable (e.g., comen, cervezas, trabajadora).
2. When a word ends with a consonant that is not the letter n or s, you stress the last syllable (e.g., entender, pared, accidental).
3. When a word does not follow the first two rules, an accent mark is used to show which syllable should be stressed (e.g., francés, Ángela, república).

Actividades / Activities

a. Pronuncia cada una de las palabras en esta lista. Para cada palabra, subraya la sílaba acentuada—es decir, la sílaba que lleva énfasis a la hora de hablar. / Pronounce each one of the words on this list. For each word, underline the accented syllable—in other words, the syllable that is emphasized when speaking.

1. chocolate

2. hospital

3. café

4. universidad

5. palabra

6. Honduras

7. instrumento

8. ciudad

9. veintidós

10. almorzar

11. contigo

12. lecciones

13. dormir

14. actividad

15. Málaga

b. Pablo y sus amigos Sebastián y Guillermo están hablando con Felipe. Ellos quieren convencer a Felipe de ir a la universidad. / Pablo and his friends Sebastián and Guillermo are talking with Felipe. They want to convince Felipe to go to college.

Completa el diálogo con la conjugación correcta del verbo indicado. / Complete the dialogue with the correct conjugation of the indicated verb.

Pablo: Debes tomar clases el próximo semestre [semester].

Felipe: 1._____ (preferir) tener solo mi trabajo. No 2._____ (querer) estresarme [stress out] por las clases y las notas [grades].

Sebastián: Sí, nosotros 3._____ (saber) que no quieres estresarte, pero la universidad no es mala idea.

Guillermo: Nosotros 4._____ (estudiar) juntos [together] en la biblioteca. Si nosotros no 5._____ (entender) algo, 6._____ (poder) estudiar más. Los lunes, miércoles y viernes 7._____ (almorzar) juntos en la cafetería. Los martes y jueves yo 8._____ (almorzar) con mi novia.

Felipe: Yo 9._____ (trabajar) todos los días, entonces [so] 10._____ (preferir) tomar clases por la noche.

Pablo: Yo 11._____ (creer) que es una buena idea tomar clases por la noche.

Felipe: La universidad 12._____ (costar) mucho dinero, y no sé si ahora mismo 13._____ (poder) pagar tanto dinero [so much money].

Sebastián: Sí, es mucho dinero, pero vale la pena [it's worth it].

Felipe: Yo 14._____ (jugar) al fútbol con mis amigos los sábados y domingos.

Sebastián: En la universidad también [also] 15._____ (poder) jugar al fútbol.

Felipe: Voy a 16._____ (pensar) en mis opciones [options], gracias. ¡Nos vemos!

Pablo, Guillermo, Sebastián: ¡Nos vemos!

c. Escoge la preposición o el pronombre preposicional correcto para las oraciones siguientes. / Choose the correct preposition or prepositional pronoun for the following sentences.

ti – mí – detrás de – entre – para – conmigo – contigo – de – hasta – sobre – con

1. Los lunes tengo clases _____ las nueve de la mañana y las cinco menos diez de la tarde.

2. En la clase hablamos _____ la situación política Cuba.

3. Hablo _____ mis amigos todos los días.

4. ¿Quieres ir _____ al seminario [seminar] de esta noche ?

5. Esta tarea [homework] es _____ la clase de inglés.

6. Quiero ir a la fiesta, pero sin _____ no voy a ir.

7. Todos los días duermo _____ las ocho de la mañana.

8. Shhhh, la profesora está _____ nosotros.

d. Completa las respuestas de las siguientes preguntas. No olvides conjugar el verbo. / Complete the answers to the following questions. Don't forget to conjugate the verb.

1. ¿Juegas mucho al fútbol los fines de semana? No,
_____.

2. ¿Generalmente mientes a tus amigos? No,
_____.

3. ¿Pierdes las llaves [keys] de tu carro frecuentemente [frequently]? Sí,
_____.

4. ¿Cuánto cuesta un buen diccionario? por lo menos [at least] veinte dólares.
_____.

5. ¿A qué hora almuerzas? al mediodía.
_____.

6. ¿Entiendes los verbos con cambio de raíz en el presente? Sí,
_____.

Respuestas correctas / Correct Answers

a. 1. chocolate

351

2. hospital

3. café

4. universidad

5. palabra

6. Honduras

7. instrumento

8. ciudad

9. veintidós

10. almorzar

11. contigo

12. lecciones

13. dormir

14. actividad

15. Málaga

b. 1. Prefiero

2. quiero

3. sabemos

4. estudiamos

5. entendemos

6. podemos

7. almorzamos

8. almuerzo

9. trabajo

10. prefiero

11. creo

12. cuesta

13. puedo

14. juego

15. puedes

16. pensar

c. 1. entre

2. sobre / de

3. con

4. conmigo 5. para

6. ti

7. hasta

8. detrás de

d. 1. No, no juego mucho al fútbol los fines de semana.

2. No, no miento a mis amigos.

3. Sí, pierdo las llaves de mi carro frecuentemente.

4. Un buen diccionario cuesta por lo menos veinte dólares.

5. Almuerzo al mediodía.

6. Sí, entiendo los verbos con cambio de raíz en el presente.

PRACTICE MAKES PERFECT

We've established that you will need to create a learning program for yourself that includes immersion into both the Spanish language and culture. You already know that you should read, write, and speak in Spanish every day to keep yourself on pace to meet your deadline. At this point, you should focus on getting to a point where you can communicate effectively. Be sure to break out of the self-imposed isolation that is common when studying Spanish. Once you've built up an arsenal of common and personalized phrases, it's time to practice them in the real world! If you haven't located a Spanish language partner, you'll want to find someone fast.

Practicing your Spanish will improve your functional ability to use the skills you've learned so far. Interacting with native Spanish speakers regularly can improve your new language skills dramatically. You'll hear authentic pronunciations, expansive vocabularies, and accurate grammar. Finding a consistent language partner can help you to avoid getting discouraged by not finding informational content that's exactly at your pace since you'll be able to communicate with them if something is too easy or advanced.

Traditional Methods of Practice

If you already know any Spanish speakers, reach out to them directly and ask if they would be able to go over a few things with you. Set up a video chat date with them once or twice a month, or if they are local, meet up for coffee.

Being able to speak with a native Spanish speaker in person is best.

You may not know anyone personally that speaks Spanish, but there are plenty of other ways to practice. For example, there are lots of people online that you can have anything—from quick chats to full-length discussions with—entirely in Spanish. There are websites dedicated to helping you break down the barriers that typically prevent people from really understanding Spanish.

Language Exchange

In addition to typical language partners, there are Language Exchange opportunities as well. A language exchange partner is what it exactly sounds like. These are people looking for someone to practice English with, and they can be super helpful with your Spanish. You might be able to find an exchange partner that will work with you one-on-one in exchange for your help. Be sure to set up a defined time frame for your conversations and work on English half of that time, and the other half in Spanish. There are language exchange boards and forums all over the world that you can search for. Some people will be upfront with what they need help with and how much of a time commitment they are able to dedicate. Make a post yourself and let prospective language exchange partners know what you'd like to work on and your availability.

Ask a Stranger

Don't be afraid to talk to strangers and try and grow a thick skin. If you hear people talking Spanish when you're out and about, be brave enough to ask them for the time or even directions. Chances are most people are more than happy to answer your question. It's quite possible that they will respond to you quickly and that you may not understand; don't worry and don't get defensive! Getting defensive is way more likely to make the exchange uncomfortable than simple Spanish slip-ups. Just tell them that you're new to Spanish and ask if they can repeat what they said slowly or help you understand what they meant. While this can be a difficult thing to ask of strangers, it's a great way to get out of your comfort zone, and once you've been corrected in a real-world scenario, the chances that you'll remember the correct words for next time are very high.

Unconventional Approaches

Call restaurants and bakeries

There are plenty of unconventional approaches to practicing your Spanish as well. Make a list of Mexican or any Spanish-speaking restaurants anywhere in the country. For example, you can call them and ask if you would need to make a reservation if you have a group of 7 people wanting to dine next weekend on Saturday at around 7:30 p.m. Have a script prepared for yourself before you call. Be sure to greet the person and then follow your script. There are a few different ways that you can ask this, so have those options ready to go and try them out on different phone calls. If they don't speak Spanish, simply move on to another number. Mix up the number of people on the reservation, the day, and the time that you're asking about. You could even actually make a reservation, and then call back later that day or week and cancel it.

You could also simply call to ask what hours they are open, or if they have vegetarian options. Another great way to get real-world practice is to look up Latin grocery or bakeries in your area. You could make up a scenario where you call or go in and ask if they make custom birthday cakes and get pricing and details.

Get on the Phone

Try calling 1-800 numbers that have Spanish menus. Look up numbers for banks, airlines, internet providers, or any company you assume would have Spanish-speaking clientele. Again, have a scenario picked out, or if you're feeling bold, improvise something based on the menu options. Before going into a call, pretend that while you may just be learning Spanish, your native language isn't English. "Lo siento, no hablo ingles" (I'm sorry, I don't speak English) will help them continue to attempt communication with you in Spanish. Some companies have an online option for a live chat. This can be a great way to practice both writing and reading.

Take it to the Kitchen

If you like to cook, you can find a wealth of Spanish cookbooks that will test out your reading comprehension and give your palate a new way to branch out. Watch a Spanish cooking show and attempt to recreate a dish you are interested in. You can search for recipes in Spanish by dish, or find a recipe you love and translate it yourself. Make a list of items you need and go to a Hispanic grocery store so that you can reinforce the language you're learning.

When you're preparing the meal, read every step out loud so that you can get verbal practice.

Help Others

Volunteer organizations hold opportunities to interact with Spanish speakers as well. Perform a quick search for organizations that are active in your community and find out what kind of help they're looking for where you may get exposure to Spanish speakers. Some excellent volunteer programs focus on improving language skills while volunteering time towards a good cause.

Make a few calls and ask the organizers if they are familiar with anything in line with your needs. Of course, giving back to underprivileged people in your community can be an advantageous experience in and of itself.

Remember to keep things light-hearted and fun. If you can learn to relax and go with the flow, you will naturally fall into the rhythm of the Spanish language. Commit to getting the most out of every opportunity you must practice, and you'll move from beginner to intermediate, and to advanced in no time.

HOW INTERACTIONS BUILD SPANISH LANGUAGE MASTERY

We communicate every day through conversations, phone calls, social media, text, and emails. Interaction is how we communicate and exchange ideas. So you might say that language is inherently interactive. We may define interaction as two people or things that have an influence or affect each other. In this context, it is two or more people exchanging ideas and information and influencing each other positively.

Interacting with other people and our environment is how we learn our native languages as babies. Also, listening and interacting with those around us help form our vocabulary and knowledge. The reason that interaction works when learning a new language is that it is simple, and it's natural. There is a theory in language that when learning a new language as an interactive process between a learner and a native speaker, communication and fluency are easily achieved. It is because the native speaker modifies the language and makes it easier for you as a beginner to learn the language. The proficient speaker will use known vocabulary, speaking slowly and clearly.

The native speaker will adjust the topic, avoid idioms, and use simpler grammatical structures. In this way, the input facilitates you with a better understanding of the Spanish language. When interacting with a proficient speaker, you get a chance to ask questions in areas that you haven't understood. It helps you in the comprehension of the language. Interactions of this kind help in language facilitation, and evidence will be seen in the long run as your grammar accuracy and Spanish fluency improve.

Let us look at some ways in which you can start interacting to become a master in the Spanish language.

Different Ways to Interact to Improve Your Spanish Language

Through Social Interaction

Speaking verbally is the most common form of human communication and a great social activity. This claim is supported by evidence coming across all fields, which intrinsically states that social interaction influences people's communication and, more specifically, in mastering a new language.

When you socialize with people who can speak Spanish fluently, it will help you to speak the language effortlessly in no time. It is because, through people, you can learn the different pronunciations that will not be taught in books.

Speaking and interacting with native speakers will do wonders for your Spanish proficiency journey. You will get to learn pronunciations and the colloquiums of the Spanish language that will help you in comprehension. It's also fun and more natural to learning a new language through interactions. Do it with people who speak it as their mother tongue because you will get real-time feedback.

Speaking may be tough, and you can start by practicing a lot. When you are alone, and if you do come across a word that you don't understand, you can always look it up in your Spanish dictionary. If you feel uncomfortable speaking Spanish in the first instances of interacting with native speakers, then it's okay not to speak too soon. It would be advisable to find someone who sympathizes with you and is patient enough to take you slowly through the learning process. However, you shouldn't take a long time to practice speaking, or you might delay your chances of learning and comprehension.

It's a slow learning process, so take baby steps and be consistent with what you are doing. Try to accept the fact that you will make mistakes along the way, and that is allowed. The goal here is to keep going and visualize that, in the future, you will be speaking fluently almost as good as the natives.

Through Language Websites

For those who are not that lucky to live in a Spanish-speaking country to interact with the natives, you can try joining an online exchange program.

You will find people willing to teach you Spanish, and in return, you can teach them English or a language you are fluent in. It will enable you to form a mutually beneficial relationship. You can both create a schedule, where half the time, you are teaching them your language, and the other half, you are learning Spanish. They will be your link to the Spanish world, so make an effort to maintain contact until you feel you have mastered the language. These free language websites work by connecting you to someone via text, audio, or video service to facilitate communication. After being linked by the website, you will both decide on the type of connection you are comfortable using.

Conversion Exchange. This site provides a simple platform for you to meet someone to help you learn Spanish. There are options where you can precisely find a partner that you can communicate through videos or audio calls. You can also opt to meet with the person physically.

The mixxer. You create a user account through the site. Once you find someone you can interact with and learn Spanish with, you can exchange Skype details for video calls. This site has the option of posting your writings in Spanish, and you can have people proficient in the language correct you. So you build your Spanish language prowess, both in speech and written form.

Easy language exchange. It has thousands of users and also has tests that help you with your Spanish.

Papora. This website is easy to use and navigate and has the option of joining groups where you can interact as a group and help each other learn.

Speaky. This is a great website because, other than interacting with Spanish natives, it has an automated tool that will help you in translations where you don't understand.

Through Social Media

Another awesome way to interact and learn Spanish is through social media.

We spend many hours a day on social media, chatting with friends and family. You could also spend this time learning and mastering your Spanish language. Here are a few ways you can optimize your time spent on social media and still learn Spanish at the same time.

1. Subscribe to pages and people who are proficient in Spanish

To learn Spanish on social media, start by following people who are Spanish speakers. Whether it's on Twitter, Facebook, or Instagram, it doesn't matter. And, of course, try as much as possible to interact with them. It's free, and your brain already sees this as a habit you are used to. You can practice speaking and interacting with them and get used to speaking in Spanish.

These changes will have a significant impact on your language mastery skills, without realizing you will be creating a Spanish language immersion environment.

You can still keep up with your interests and hobbies like cooking or whatever you are interested in. But at the same time, you will get to improve your language skills. Remember, the key here is to interact so that your learning experience is more active and not passive.

2. Follow language enthusiasts and experts

You can follow Spanish natives or specialists in the language. You can also follow some people who teach the language or polyglots who speak Spanish fluently. These are people like Benny Lewis, on Facebook, Twitter, and Instagram. You can get a ton of advice from these language enthusiasts.

YouTube is also a great platform that you can use because you can work on your listening comprehension skills while you learn. There is really good content online that can help you in mastering your Spanish language skills.

3. Join language groups on Facebook

If you prefer to interact on Facebook, there are groups you can join to learn Spanish. Be sure to join as many groups as you can that are Spanish-oriented. This way, every time you visit Facebook, you will find one or two interesting posts to read in Spanish. You are also being exposed to the language every time you log in.

To top that, joining Spanish learning language groups is a great way to make new friends who speak the language. Interacting with other learners keeps you motivated and spikes your interest to continue learning. You can also post your learning goals in your group, and other members can hold you accountable and even keep motivating and pushing you. Remember to support other learners, too, and create a mutually beneficial interaction.

You can also send messages and videos with your new friends as ways of interaction. It's a great way to put your progress into practice and gauge your language prowess.

4. Watching YouTube videos

Watch whatever you like watching on YouTube, but do it in Spanish. Learning to make tacos from scratch is way more fun and more authentic if the teacher is showing the instructions in Spanish.

YouTube is also another great way you can use to master your pronunciations. When subscribing to these videos, you will familiarize yourself with the accents. Watch how they speak and try to repeat after them as much as possible. An excellent channel to check out on YouTube is Easy Languages; this is one of the easiest ways to learn Spanish as a beginner.

They interview natives, so you have access to fresh content. It also comes with subtitles to help you understand and translate what you don't understand.

5. Spanish speaking with Twitter users

Twitter is an awesome place where you can experience sarcasm and, at the same time, interact with other users. Following key people will improve your Spanish language capabilities. If you don't understand some tweets in Spanish, no worries. Twitter has a feature for translations. Under each tweet, you will see an icon that says 'translate.' Click on it, and you will read the translation in English or your native language.

6. Blogs

Reading blogs in Spanish is also another exciting way to start your interactive Spanish learning process.

Through Socializing

Go out and meet people who are learning Spanish or can speak the language fluently. Clubs, music concerts, and local cultural events offer a great platform for language practice and growth. Just think about it; these events offer an entire interactive process with people who speak and also those who are learning the language.

It can be intimidating being in a crowd of people, but you should take the opportunity to go out and mingle. Use the opportunity to the fullest to speak with natives, listen to sing songs, or even sample the Spanish cuisine. Learn how to order in Spanish and interact with natives in Spanish restaurants.

Strike up a conversation with other diners or the waiter at the restaurant; your aim here is to interact and socialize.

SPANISH PRACTICES

Exercise #1

Below you have a text written entirely in Spanish and its corresponding English translation below. This text is an excerpt from the first pages of "The Little Prince" written by Antoine de Saint, a children's story.

What you should do now, even if it seems crazy to you, will be to read the text in Spanish and English several times until you feel confident about what you just read. You must begin to relate the words to their meaning and necessarily relate to the language in a more authentic way than with a boring grammar lesson. This means that you have to constantly and consistently consume information written in Spanish, whether it be movies, music, news, online videos...etc.

Until you feel confident enough to try and talk to a native Spanish speaker. Only then you will actually feel pushed to figure out somehow how to speak Spanish properly. Remember: the necessity to establish communication will be your fuel to boost your learning curve for any language! Learning a language is all about being in contact with it. This story was chosen because, apart from the fact that he is a jewel literature, an easy-to-understand and entertaining text.

Let's read!

Exactly when I was six years old, I found in the book about the virgin wild:

Unmistakable stories, a remarkable picture. It tended to be a boa snake eating a beast. Here is a copy of the drawing. The book communicated: "The boa snake gulps down its entire prey, without gnawing it. Then, as it can't move, he rests during the half year that his retention continues onward". I reflected an extraordinary arrangement around then on the endeavors of the wild and sorted out some way to fan out my first drawing with concealed pencils.

"La serpiente boa que digiere un elefante. Entonces dibujé el interior de la serpiente boa para que las personas mayores pudieran comprender. Los mayores siempre tienen necesidad de explicaciones."

I showed my show-stopper to the more established and asked with regards to whether my drawing terrified them. - Why may a cap freeze me? - They reacted to me. My drawing was not a cap. It tended to be a boa snake that measures an elephant. Then I drew inside the boa snake so more settled people could grasp. More settled people reliably need explanations.

More settled people urged me to quit drawing boa snakes, whether or not boas were opened or closed, and put more interest in geology, history, math and sentence structure. Subsequently, I abandoned a fantastic occupation as a painter being six years old.

Exercise #2

By and by you ought to organize the sentence according to the praiseworthy development showed around the beginning of the book, review?

A. Es de ella Buenos Aires.

B. Caminamos por nosotros la calle.

C. Aeropuerto llegue al.

D. ¿Hora es qué?

E. Voy me mañana.

F. ¿Llego a dirección cómo?

G. Ir que tengo al baño

H. ¿Queda dónde la policía?

I. Hablo yo no español

J. Siento me mal

K. Enfermo estoy

L. Nombre es mi María

M. Ayuda necesito

N. Ella gusta a le bailar

O. Hambre nosotros tenemos

P. Salir quieres noche esta

Q. Camino estoy en

R. Mañana almorzaré ciudad en la

S. Quiero casa irme a

T. María a José quiere

U. ¿Llego cómo a la salida?

V. Compro mañanas todas las

W. Quiero chocolate comer

X. Mi mamá mucho quiero a

Y. José gusta le correr a

Z. Como tardes en las

Exercise #3

The going with movement is in like manner about sentences, you will remember that we talk about the sentences and the subordinate sentences, since now it will be your opportunity to recognize the accompanying sentences which are subordinate and which are not.

A. Juan, who is my carpenter, made that family thing.

Juan, quien es mi carpintero, hizo ese mueble.

B. I need to buy various things.

Necesito comprar muchas cosas.

C. Make an effort not to cook if you don't have all of the trimmings.

No cocines si no tienes errands los ingredientes.

D. My sidekicks need to go out today.

Mis amigos quieren salir hoy.

E. I'm going, considering the way that I trust it's the best thing to do.

Voy an ir, porque me parece lo correcto.

F. I need to see you, yet I was unable to say whether I can today.

364

Quiero verte, pero no sé si pueda hoy.

G. I question he appreciated.

Tengo la duda de que haya entendido

H. Every day they go for a run.

Todas las mañanas ellos salen a correr

I. The shower you credited me is broken.

La regadera que me prestaste está rota.

J. I dropped the phone, it was seriously situated.

Se cayó el teléfono, estaba mal colocado.

K. We need to talk.

Tenemos que hablar.

L. Tomorrow I go anyway not today.

Mañana voy pero hoy no.

M. I have a lot of work.

Tengo mucho trabajo.

N. I will need support at home.

Necesitaré ayuda en la casa

O. She isn't eager, yet I am.

Ella no tiene hambre, pero yo sí

P. The time is nice today, disregarding the way that I can't leave.

El clima está lindo hoy, aunque no puedo salir

Q. I need to eat frozen yogurt, anyway it broke down.

Quiero comer helado, pero se derritió

R. The jelly is delightful but amazingly sweet.

La mermelada esta sabrosa aunque muy dulce

S. I need to tidy up whether or not is cold water.

Me tengo que bañar así esté fría el agua.

T. We can go to the coastline notwithstanding the way that I like the mountain.

Podemos ir a la playa aunque me gusta la montaña.

U. She sings pretty.

Ella canta bonito.

V. That child is astoundingly tall.

Ese niño es muy alto.

W. Tomorrow we will go running.

Mañana saldremos a correr.

X. I have a canine and a cat as well.

Tengo un perro y un gato también.

Y. They will manage their hair, yet not today.

Ellas se cortaran el cabello, pero no hoy.

Z. I got you, at this point represent yourself better.

Te entendí, pero explain mejor

Exercise #4

Area 8 of "The Little Prince".

"mañana y morían por la tarde... Pero aquella flor time distinta, había surgido de una semilla llegada quién sabe de dónde, y el principito había vigilado cuidadosamente aquella ramita tan diferente de las que él conocía. Podía ser una nueva especie de Baobab, pero el arbusto cesó right now de crecer y comenzó a brotar la flor."

I sorted out some way to understand that bloom. There had been ordinary blooms on the planet of the little sovereign, with a lone section of petals that hardly happened and no one was attracted to it. They punched through the grass one morning and kicked the pail in the early evening ... Regardless, that sprout was one of a kind, it had ascended out of a seed who knows from where, and the little sovereign had meticulously watched that branch so not exactly equivalent to those he knew. It might be another sort of Baobab, anyway the brier after a short time quit creating and the bloom began to develop.

"El principito observó cómo crecía un enorme capullo y presentía que de allí habría de salir una aparición milagrosa; la flor tardaba en definir su forma y en completar su belleza al abrigo de su verde envoltura. Poco a poco escogía sus colores y ajustaba sus pétalos. No quería salir fea; quería aparecer en pleno esplendor de su belleza ¡Era coqueta desde pequeña y su misteriosa preparación le tomó varios días!"

"¡Una mañana, al salir el sol, por balance se mostró espléndida! La flor, que había trabajado con tanta precisión, dijo bostezando: – ¡Oh, acabo de despertar... perdón por estar tan despeinada... !El principito no pudo contener su embeleso: – ¡Qué hermosa eres! – ¿Verdad? – Respondió dulcemente la flor–. Además, ha nacido al mismo tiempo que el sol."

The little prince watched as a huge cocoon grew and sensed that a miraculous shape would emerge from there; the flower was slow to define its shape and complete its beauty under the cover of its green envelope. Piece by piece it chose its colors and adjusted its petals. It didn't want to sprout being ugly; it wanted to appear in the full splendor of its beauty. It was flirtatious since she was little and her mysterious preparation took several days! One morning, at sunrise, she finally looked splendid! The flower, which had worked with such precision, said yawning: "Oh, I just woke up ... sorry for being so disheveled ...!" The little prince could not contain his trance: - How beautiful you are! -Right? The flower sweetly answered. Also, it was born at the same time as the sun.

Exercise #5

In this exercise, you must identify and place the correct verb of SER or ESTAR in each sentence. On this occasion, you will not have any English translation so you can try and complete these exercises the best way possible.

Do not be desperate if you miss it at first, you need to be patient in order to learn.

A. Yo _____ alto

B. Mañana _____ ocupado

C. Yo _____ feliz

D. Yo _____ mexicano

E. Lo siento, no _____ listo

F. _____ muy amable

G. Necesito _____ tranquila

H. Ellos _____ molestos

I. _____ aprendiendo francés

J. vamos a _____ felices

K. Yo _____ pronto en Inglaterra

L. Yo _____ aprendiendo español

M. _____ apurados

N. _____ una estrella de rock

O. Ella _____ mi mejor amiga

P. Mi mamá _____ en el trabajo

Q. Mi papá _____ chef profesional

R. Nosotros _____ estudiantes

S. Yo _____ de España

T. _____ arrepentido

U. Yo _____ adicto al celular

V. Ella _____ bailarina

W. Mañana _____ cansados

X. _____ jugando

Y. _____ médico cuando crezca

Exercise #6

Now, you will have to identify the interrogative, exclamatory and imperative sentences.

A. ¿Tienes la hora?

B. Qué hora es

C. ¡Nos vemos mañana!

D. Llévate eso de aquí

E. ¡Vamos amiga!

F. ¿Por qué hace frío?

G. Termina ya tu tarea

H. ¿En cuánto tiempo llegamos?

I. Levántate de la cama

369

J. ¿Puedo comenzar hoy?

K. ¡Ayudame!

READING FOR PRACTICE

Texts for Reading Practice (PDF, EPUB, MOBI formats): Day 1-12; Day 13-25.

Day 1 - 12 are the original texts and days 13 - 25 are the new texts! It is important to make sure you have read day 12 before reading day 13 and so on and so forth! Don't worry if you don't understand everything or anything at all really! That's why it is important to get used to some of the Spanish sounds before moving onto more complicated sentences. I would recommend you to read the original text first, listen to it and then read the new one.

You know everything.

There's nothing to learn.

You're trying too hard.

If you're worried about learning Spanish, then you won't be able to learn Spanish.

The only way to learn Spanish is by seeing and hearing it used naturally in real conversations and interactions.

If you always have a grammar book in your hand or a dictionary on your lap, then you're going to be staring at one for the rest of your life.

You need to learn how to hold an intelligent conversation with someone in Spanish and that can only be done by practicing what you already know.

Here are some Spanish phrases that are good for beginner students. You don't have to memorize them but it will help you get used to the sounds. This is where most people fail when learning Spanish because they don't use the language enough. Once you hear someone say these things, then try saying them back!

"Soy nuevo en esto." - I'm new at this.

"¿Cómo se llama usted?" - How are you called?

To say goodbye in Spanish

To say hello in Spanish

To ask for something to write down in a book: "¿Me puedo tener su nombre?" - May I have your name?

Listening comprehension - 1st audio file (5 minutes)

Listening comprehension - 2nd audio file (13 minutes)

Talking about yourself: "I'm new at this." "I don't speak French." To give compliments: "You look nice today." "You are very intelligent." "I like your mobile phone. It's very smart." "It's a nice color." "I like your bag." "What do you do for a living?"

Listening comprehension - 1st audio file (8 minutes)

Listening comprehension - 2nd audio file (9 minutes)

Talking about being hungry. Talking about drinks. Talking about food. To make a suggestion: "Why don't we go to that restaurant?"

To talk about knowing someone. To talk about the weather. To complain about the price of something in Spanish: "¿A cuánto es esto?"

"¡Está too expensive!" etc.

To say the date in Spanish. To talk about time: "We have half an hour to do this now."

To say goodbye. Oral exercises - 1st audio file (6 minutes)

Talking about things. To ask where something is: "Where can we buy milk?" "I forgot my passport."

To ask for the price of something in Spanish: "¿Cuánto cuesta eso?"

"A cuánto es esto?" etc.

To say a telephone number in Spanish. To give directions in Spanish.

Listening comprehension - 1st audio file (9 minutes)

Listening comprehension - 2nd audio file (4 minutes)

To say you will do something. To say you want to do something. To state your opinion: "I want to learn Spanish." "I don't want to go shopping."

To ask for permission to do something: "May I come in?" "May I have a look at that book?"

To ask someone if they are employed: "Are you working today?" To mention that it is a holiday today: "It's Sunday today."

Or the day of the week and then the actual date.

To say you will be away for a period of time. To talk about going away for a period of time: "I'm off to Los Angeles next week." "I'm off to America next month."

"¿Me puedo ir mañana?" - Can I go tomorrow? To ask someone if they are free to do something.

To ask how much something costs in Spanish. To ask someone if they need something or if they want something: "Do you need any help?" "Do you want a drink?" etc.

To say you want to do something in Spanish: "I want to go on a trip" etc.

To say you don't have something or you don't know something in Spanish: "I don't have any money." "I don't know what he said."

"No sé nada de eso." - I don't know anything about it.

Listening comprehension - 1st audio file (10 minutes)

To give directions in Spanish. To talk about future plans: "The weather is going to change tomorrow." "It's going to rain tomorrow." etc. To talk about the months of the year. To talk about something in the future: "We're going to Mexico next week."

"I'm getting married next month." To mention that the weather was nice or terrible today.

Listening comprehension - 1st audio file (5 minutes)

Listening comprehension - 2nd audio file (7 minutes)

To complain that you have been waiting for a long time. To ask someone if they are free today: "Are you free this afternoon?" To say what you are doing in Spanish. To be so excited: "What a surprise!" etc.

To say what you want to do today: "I want to go to the beach today.

To ask how much something costs and then to say you are happy with the price. To do something if money is tight: "I don't have any money now."

"It's a bit expensive, but I'll pay for it." To say you don't want something: "No quiero nada." - I don't want anything.

To ask someone what they would like to eat. To request that someone is free to help you with something. To ask someone if they have something or if they could get something: "May I use your phone?" or "Would you give me a lift to the supermarket?" etc.

To mention that it's very cold today or hot today.

To mention that it's very urgent today.

Listening comprehension - 1st audio file (7 minutes)

Listening comprehension - 2nd audio file (3 minutes)

To say something in Spanish or to produce something as a result of speaking Spanish. To call people to come to something: "Come on, the movie starts in ten minutes." To mention that it's an emergency today: "It's an emergency today, so we've got to go to the hospital."

"It's an emergency now, so let's go and see if my car is still here."

To ask someone if they would like a drink. To ask someone if they want to sit down. To tell someone to sit down. To tell a waiter that your food is not very good.

To ask for the bill in Spanish: "Can I have the bill, please?"

Listening comprehension - 1st audio file (11 minutes)

Listening comprehension - 2nd audio file (11 minutes)

To ask someone about their job. To talk about one's job.

To make a suggestion to someone. To accept or refuse an invitation: "I'd love to come!" "No, thank you."

"¿Está enfermo?" - Are you ill? "Yes, I'm ill."

"No, no me duele nada. - I'm not in any pain.

To ask someone to explain something. To ask someone about their plans for the future. To ask someone why they are late: "When are you coming?"

To mention that something will happen soon. To talk about when something happened.

"I don't know when it happened, but it did." "It happened last month." "It's happening now." To talk about how long it will take to do something or that something will take a long time: "It's going to take us a long time to get there."

"This is going to cost a lot of money.

Listening comprehension - 1st audio file (4 minutes)

Listening comprehension - 2nd audio file (9 minutes)

To be happy to meet someone. To speak about someone who is not here today: "He'll be sorry that he missed you."

"He could have come with us today." "She didn't come with us because she had no petrol."

To make a suggestion or an offer: "Why don't we go to the beach?" "I'll help you if I can." To state an opinion in Spanish. To state something in Spanish: "The weather is terrible today." / "The weather is good today.

To make a joke in Spanish. To make a remark about someone's appearance in Spanish: "Hola, qué bonito que hayas venido!" – Hello, what a nice surprise that you have come!

Listening comprehension - 1st audio file (7 minutes)

Listening comprehension - 2nd audio file (8 minutes)

To ask if something is true or to ask about something. To talk about something in Spanish: "Do you think it's true?"

"I don't believe it." "I don't know anything about it." To say why you reject the truth.

To ask for the bill in Spanish.

To ask something in Spanish. To ask if a person would like something: "Would you like a drink?" etc.

To say something in Spanish and to produce something as a result of speaking Spanish. To ask about the weather: "Is it warm today?"

"¿Qué pasó ahora?" - What has happened now?

To say that someone is polite or well-mannered in Spanish. To talk about what someone is wearing: "That's a nice shirt. Where is it from?"

To talk about one's family in Spanish. To talk about one's health in Spanish. To mention that something is not expensive: "It's not expensive." "It's cheap."

To make a suggestion to someone: "Let's go there instead of here."

To refuse to do something: "No, I don't want to speak now." / "No, I cannot speak now.

"No puedo hablar ahora. Estoy trabajando" - I'm working right now. / "No, I'm not busy."

Listening comprehension - 1st audio file (5 minutes)

375

Listening comprehension - 2nd audio file (4 minutes)

To complain that you are very tired. To complain about the weather: "The weather is terrible today."

"It's too cold today / hot today." To say to someone that they've made a mistake. To talk about somebody who is absent: "He's not here today."

To ask someone if they can help you and to say what will happen if you don't get help: "Could you please phone my friend?"

"If I don't phone him now, he'll be angry with me.

Listening comprehension - 1st audio file (3 minutes)

Listening comprehension - 2nd audio file (4 minutes)

To tell someone that you don't know. To ask someone to repeat themselves because you weren't listening: "I couldn't hear you, I'm sorry."

"I didn't hear what you said." "Could you speak more slowly?"

To say that something is very impressive or impressive. To say that something is not difficult: "It's easy!" / "It's not difficult."

To mention an opinion in Spanish: "I like it / I don't like it." / "I prefer it this way... / I prefer it this way instead." / "To me, that's not as good..."

To tell someone that you don't understand what they're saying in Spanish. To be surprised that a negative opinion can be expressed in Spanish. To ask if a person is well: "Are you well?"

To say something in Spanish and to produce something as a result of speaking Spanish. To ask about the weather: "Is it cold today?" / "Is it hot today?"

"I'm afraid the rain will start soon.

Listening comprehension - 1st audio file (4 minutes)

Listening comprehension - 2nd audio file (6 minutes)

To make a suggestion or an offer: "Why don't we go there instead?"

"I'd like to go to the beach." / "I'd like to go swimming."

To ask something in Spanish; to ask for something in Spanish. To say something in Spanish and produce something as a result of speaking Spanish. To make a joke in Spanish: "Say something in Spanish!"

"Say something in Korean!" "I can say a Spanish word." / "I can say a Korean word."

To talk about what someone is wearing: "That's a nice shirt." To mention that something is not expensive.

SPEEDING UP THE PROCESS

We covered how you can start learning Spanish by reading and listening to native materials starting from day one but with a somewhat heavier emphasis on listening over reading. After all, reading in a foreign language can be so overwhelmingly difficult at first, and listening to the foreign language is just much more beginner-friendly in comparison.

But if you're using the Spanish subtitles to learn from things like TV shows and YouTube videos, you are learning Spanish not only through listening but reading as well. Reading does not always have to mean reading from dusty, old books. In fact, it can be done in all sorts of non-traditional ways like when we use Spanish subtitles to learn specific lines and moments from shows we are watching. And it can be even more useful when done in larger quantities.

The challenge lies in figuring out how to get yourself to read more Spanish every day.

After studying comes to an end for the day, why read when you can listen for hours on end? For starters, it will help you to quickly convert more of that incomprehensible stream of Spanish gibberish into a language you can understand. Secondly, it provides another fun and holistic way to keep engaged in learning and ultimately living through Spanish for hours every day. Third, some of the world's most skilled polyglots like Alexander Arguelles, Luca Lampariello, and Steve Kaufmann are major advocates of reading as a means to learn foreign languages. And finally and most importantly, extensive reading is perhaps one the most effective ways to build and easily maintain a massive range of vocabulary in a foreign language.

Reading native Spanish materials can be tremendously slow and difficult as a beginner, so when exactly should you start reading things other than Spanish subtitles? As soon as possible is ideal if you're looking to get really good at Spanish within a few years. The more you expose yourself to written Spanish the better. The more early attempts at reading you make, the faster you will learn.

So let's say you did decide to do some extensive reading, for example, by playing a video game in Spanish. Do you always stop to look up every unfamiliar word the entire game? When do you just relax and play the game?

Handling such a large amount of text in any foreign language can be completely overwhelming at first, and you can be left completely drained and discouraged after just a day or two. This is where smart language learning strategies can come in handy.

Intensive vs. Extensive Reading

To answer these, we need to understand the difference between intensive and extensive reading. In intensive reading, the goal is to break down and look up every single new word and grammar point in a selected text of relatively short length. This kind of reading is only intended to last around 20-45 minutes.

You can only study a small number of pages of a difficult text before your mind starts giving out, but when you read a text that is easy for your level, you can read a much larger quantity of pages for several hours with only a few breaks in between.

Unfortunately, the problem is that it's very tough to find extensive reading materials for your level when you are in the beginner and intermediate stages. It's estimated that you need 98% comprehension of a text before you are able to do true extensive reading.

Ideally, you're supposed to rely on mostly context alone to learn new words in extensive reading. But in reality, no matter what material you choose to start with, there will be a ton of words that you have never seen or heard before. It's very likely that you will have to go through your first reading material heavily with a dictionary or English translation in order to understand what's happening in the text.

Just like how there's no magical point where you're ready for native Spanish materials, there's also no magical point where you're ready for extensive reading. In order to successfully bridge between intensive reading and extensive reading, a long series of efforts at reading must be made. There are principles of extensive reading, however, that you can use at any level to make this process much more enjoyable and faster overall.

Although when you feel ready to try something new, extensive reading is here to help speed up the rate at which you progress towards fluency.

Limiting Anki Reviews

The next step is to make sure you actually have enough time to read by making a few small adjustments to Anki's schedule so that you aren't stuck reviewing cards for more than two hours every day. Regardless of how much time you can devote every day to learning Spanish, lengthy Anki review sessions are completely unnecessary. There comes a point where your time is much better spent doing things like extensive reading.

Anki audit meetings include doing new cards (shading coded blue in Anki) and survey cards (shading coded green in Anki). New cards are practices that have been made however not yet seen during So an Anki meeting with 10 new cards, what's more, 10 audit cards will be alluded to here as a 10/10 meeting, which would be 20 activities inside and out.

In Anki, you can set the number of activities to be finished each day to 10/10 or to whatever numbers you might want. This should handily be possible by opening Anki, tapping on the stuff to one side of your deck, and choosing 'Choices'. Set 'New cards/day' to 10, and afterward, click the 'Audits' tab and set 'Greatest surveys/day' to 10.

Our beginning proposal is set at 10/10 audit meetings, and an alert is encouraged if you could get a kick out of the chance to expand those numbers. Assuming you need to join more Anki surveys, a bigger number like 20/20 should conceivably be possible whenever broken into at least two more modest meetings for the duration of the day. Doing a huge number each day will be a massively troublesome propensity to keep up with, yet in case you are feeling especially persuaded to accomplish more Anki on certain days, pull out all the stops.

100 "Greatest audits/day" is the current default setting in Anki at the hour of composing this book, however, in the event that you keep this setting, Anki survey meetings alone can rapidly begin surpassing an hour and a half day by day when the surveys start to stack up. This does exclude the time it takes to make cards from new material not to mention peruse and pay attention to it.

Doing an unnecessarily high measure of Anki cards for quite a while can be more negative than supportive. More Anki doesn't mean really learning and progress in the event that it causes your inside inspiration meter to plunge and move toward nothing. There's no compelling reason to prepare for the Agony Olympics with unpleasantly long ultra-long distance races of Anki surveys.

You can do dramatically more Anki cards in the long haul by staying away from burnout just by doing little meetings reliably as a propensity. To assemble this consistency with Anki, hold meetings under an hour and don't compel yourself to help out the purpose of quicker advancement. Stop just before you get exhausted and keep yourself hungry for the following meeting.

If you have trouble focusing during 10/10 sessions, start with 5/5 sessions. Train to grow stronger in both your Spanish proficiency and ability to deeply focus. If you have a habit of waking up and going straight to social media in the morning, chances are that you will have great difficulty in trying to maintain focus while studying or reading and listening to raw Spanish.

You might find that you have more focus and energy when you start your day with things like morning walks, meditation, inspirational audiobooks, and exercise.

Their importance should not be underestimated in the slightest. How you start your day can determine whether your time and energy will be sapped by all the distractions of the world or will be channeled 100% into doing the things that matter the most to you.

Principles of Extensive Reading

Now that you have enough time available to start extensive reading, let's take a look at five principles to help make reading a much more pleasurable and overall effective learning experience. The more pleasurable it is the more time you'll naturally want to spend doing it which equates to you learning faster.

While reading aloud can certainly be beneficial to pronunciation, it is a telltale sign of intensive reading. But in extensive reading, it's completely unnecessary for the most part. Continuously reading aloud makes reading painfully slow and unnatural which in fact pushes you further away from extensive reading.

Think about reading in your native language. Have you been moving your lips to form the words with your mouth? If English is your native language, the answer to these questions is most likely no. The reason we can read so well in our native language is not because we practice reading everything aloud. It's because of the massive volume we have read extensively throughout the years, and the overwhelming majority of it was read silently.

For Spanish, try aiming to read silently 95% of the time and save the other five percent for speaking new words aloud with proper pronunciation.

In this way, it will be more akin to how you learned to read so well in your native language. You already have more than enough new words to say aloud as a beginner or intermediate learner, and reading aloud anymore than this is just going to slow you down.

The second principle of extensive reading is to read for general meaning, pleasure, and curiosity rather than 100% complete comprehension.

In general, once you understand the overall meaning of a sentence, move right along to the next. Don't try to read it aloud or re-read it in an attempt to memorize new vocabulary and grammar structures. These are short-term memory tactics that have little impact on what is stored in your long-term memory. You naturally learn faster when you allow yourself to naturally read. Forgetting words means that you are learning them.

Extensive reading is most effective when it is the means to an end and not the other way around. The end goal in mind should be the content you're really interested in. And when Spanish is the means to that end, you get really good at the language as a result of the sheer volume of comprehensible input you receive through reading.

Our third principle of extensive reading is to find something to read that is not the news. Reading the news from time to time can be quite beneficial in learning the geography, politics, and current events of Spanish-speaking countries, but you may not find this information compelling enough to do it extensively.

ENGLISH-SPANISH GLOSSARY

A

accent – acento

action movie – película de acción

actor/actress – actor, actriz

adding machine – sumadora

Africa – África

african – africano

airport – aeropuerto

alarm clock – despertador

almonds – almendras

american – americano (north + south)

american – estadounidense (united states)

anchovy - anchoa

and - y

and you? - ¿y tú?

angry – enojado

ankle – tobillo

annoyed - enfadado

ant – hormiga

appetizer – aperitivo

apple – manzana

apricot – albaricoque

april - abril

arabic - árabe

arch - un arco

argentine - argentino

arm - brazo

arrivals - llegadas

art - arte

artichoke - alcachofa

artista - artista

asian - asiático

asparagus - espárragos

athletic - atlético

attic - desván

August - agosto

aunt - tía

australian - australiano

autumn – otoño

B

baby - bebé

back - espalda

backgammon - backgammon

backpack - mochila

baggage - equipaje

baggage claim - reclamo de equipaje

baker - panadero, panadera

bakery - panadería

balcony - balcón

ballet - ballet

ballroom dancing - baile de salón

banana - plátano

bank - banco

barber - barbería

baseball - béisbol

basement - sótano

basketball - baloncesto

basketry - cestería

bathing suit - traje de baño

bathroom - baño

bathtub - bañera, baño

beans - judías

beauty shop - peluquería

bed - cama

bedroom – dormitorio

beef - carne de res

beer - cerveza

belt – cinturón

bicycle – bicicleta

biking – ciclismo

bikini – biquini

biology – biología

bird – pájaro

birthday – cumpleaños

birthday cake – torta, pastel de cumpleaños

birthday card – tarjeta de cumpleaños

birthday party – fiesta de cumpleaños

birthday present – regalo de cumpleaños

black – negro

black hair – cabello o pelo negro

blackberry – zarzamora

blizzard – ventisca

blond hair – cabello o pelo rubio

blouse – blusa

blue – azul

blueberry – arándano

blues – blues

board game – juego de tablero

boarding pass – tarjeta de embarque

boat – barco

book – libro

bookshelf – estantería

boots – botas

bored – aburrido

boring – aburrido

bottle – botella

bowl – bol

box – caja

boxer shorts – calzones

boxing – boxeo

boy – niño, chico

boyfriend – novio

bra – sostén

bracelet – brazalete

brave – valiente

Brazil – Brasil

Brazilian – brasileño

bread – pan

breakfast – desayuno

bridge – puente

briefcase – maletín

brother – hermano

brown – marrón

brown hair – cabello, pelo marrón

bus – autobús

butcher – carnicería

butter – mantequilla

buttermilk – suero de leche

bye – chao

bye-bye – adiosito

C

cake – torta, pastel

calculator – calculadora

can – lata

Canada – Canadá

Canadian – Canadiense

candy – dulce, golosinas

candy store – confitería

car – coche, auto

card game – juego de cartas

carpenter – carpintero, carpintera

carpet – moqueta

carrot – zanahoria

carry-on luggage – equipaje de mano

cartoon – dibujos animados

cashews – anacardos

cashier – cajero, cajera

cat – gato, gata

Catalan – catalán

Catch you later! – ¡Nos vemos!

CD-ROM – CD-ROM

ceiling – techo

celery – apio

chair – silla

chalk – tiza

chalkboard – pizarra

check, bill – cuenta

checked luggage – equipaje registrado

checkers – damas

check-in desk – mostrador de registro

cheek – mejilla

cheese – queso

chemistry – química

cherry – cereza

chess – ajedrez

chest – pecho

chicken – pollo

Chilean – chileno

Chinese – chino

Chinese checkers – damas chinas

chocolate – chocolate

Christmas – Navidad

Christmas Eve – Nochebuena

circle – círculo

civics – educación cívica

class – clase

classic movie – película clásica

classical music – música clásica

classroom – aula

closet – clóset, armario empotrado

clothesline – cuerda para la ropa

clothing store – ropería

coat – abrigo

coffee – café

cold – frío

collage – collage

collecting – coleccionismo

college – universidad

Colombian – colombiano

comedy – comedia

computer – computadora

cone – cono

cook – cocinero, cocinera

cookie – galleta

cookie sheet – bandeja de horno

cooking – cocina

copy machine – copiadora

corn – mazorca

Costa Rican – costarricense

cottage cheese – requesón

couch – canapé

country music – música country

cousin – primo, prima

crayons – lápices de colores

cream – crema

crescent – media luna

crocheting – hacer ganchillo

cube – cubo

cucumber – pepino

cup – taza

curly hair – cabello, pelo rizado

currency exchange – cambio de moneda

curtain – cortina

curve – curva

custard – natilla, flan

customs – aduana

cylinder – cilindro

D

dancing – baile

dark hair – cabello, pelo oscuro

dark purple – violeta oscuro

dark red – rojo oscuro

darts – dardos

database – base de datos

daughter – hija

December – diciembre

den – salón

dentist – dentista

department store – grandes almacenes, tiendas por departamentos

depressed – deprimido

desk – escritorio

dessert – postre

diamond – diamante

dictionary – diccionario

dining room – comedor

dinner – cena

dishwasher – lavavajillas

disk drive – unidad de disco

dizzy – mareado

doctor – doctor, doctora

documentary – documental

dog – perro, perra

doghouse – casa del perro

dominoes – dominó

don't mention it – no hay de qué

donut – rosquilla, dónut

door – puerta

down – abajo

Dr. – Doctor, Dr.

drama – drama

drawing – dibujo

dress – vestido

dresser – tocador

driver – conductor

driveway – entrada

drought – sequía

drum – tambor

dry cleaner – tintorería

dryer – secadora

Dutch – neerlandés

E

ear – oreja

earrings – aretes

east – este

Easter – Pascua

economy (coach) class – clase económica

Ecuadoran – ecuatoriano

eggplant – berenjena

Egypt – Egipto

Egyptian – egipcio

eight – ocho

eighteen – dieciocho

eighty – ochenta

elbow – codo

electrician – electricista

eleven – once

email – correo electrónico

email address – dirección electrónica

embarrassed – avergonzado

embroidery – bordado

employee – empleado, empleada

enemy – enemigo, enemiga

engineer – ingeniero, ingeniera

England – Inglaterra

English – inglés

eraser – borrador

espresso – café exprés

Europe – Europa

European – europeo

excited – entusiasmado

excuse me – con permiso –

eye – ojo

eye doctor – optometrista

F

face – cara

far – lejos

fat – gordo

Father's Day – Día del Padre

fax machine – máquina de fax

fear – miedo

February – febrero

fence – valla

ferret – hurón

ferry – transbordador

fifteen – quince

fifty – cincuenta

file – fichero

file folder – carpeta

filing cabinet – fichero

finger – dedo

fingernail – uña

fireman – bombero, bombera

first class – primera clase

fish – pez

fish (to eat) – pescado

fishing – pesca

five – cinco

flight – vuelo

flight attendant – auxiliar de vuelo

flood – inundación

floor – suelo

flower – flor

flute – flauta

folk music – música folklórica

foot – pie

football – fútbol americano

forgive me – perdóneme, discúlpeme

fork – tenedor

forty – cuarenta

four – cuatro

fourteen – catorce

France – Francia

French – francés

French fries – papas fritas

Friday – viernes

friend – amigo

friendly – amistoso

fritter – buñuelo

frog – rana

fruit – fruta

fruit stand – frutería

frying pan – sartén

funny – divertido

G

garage – garaje

garden – jardín

gardening – jardinería

garlic – ajo

gate – verja

gate (at airport) – puerta

geography – geografía

gerbil – gerbo

German – alemán

Germany – Alemania

gin rummy – gin rummy

girl – niña, chica, muchacha

girlfriend – novia

glass – vaso

glasses – gafas

gloves – guantes

glue – cola

golf – golf

Good afternoon – Buenas tardes

Good evening – Buenas noches

Good night – Buenas noches

Goodbye – Adiós

good-looking – guapo, guapa

granddaughter – nieta

grandfather – abuelo

grandmother – abuela

grandson – nieto

grape – uva

grapefruit – toronja

gray – gris

green – verde

grocery store – tienda de comestibles

guinea pig – cobayo

guitar – guitarra

gym, physical education – educación física

H

hair – cabello, pelo

hall – pasillo

ham – jamón

hammock – hamaca

hamster – hámster

hand – mano

happy – feliz, alegre

Happy birthday! – ¡Feliz cumpleaños!

hard drive – disco duro

hardware – hardware

hardware store – ferretería

hat – sombrero

Have a nice day – Que tenga(s) un buen día

He is... – Él es...

head – cabeza

heart – corazón

hearts – corazones

heavy metal – heavy metal

helicopter – helicóptero

Hello – Hola

Her name is... – Ella se llama...

hermit crab – cangrejo ermitaño

hexagon – hexágono

Hi – Hola

high school – colegio

high-heeled shoes – zapatos de tacones altos

highlighter – marcador

hiking – excursionismo

hip hop – hip hop

His name is... – Él se llama...

history – historia

hockey – hockey

home economics – ciencia del hogar

homework – tarea

horror movie – película de terror

horse – caballo

hose – manga

hospital – hospital

hot – calor

hot chocolate – chocolate caliente

hotel – hotel

how – cómo

How are you? – ¿Cómo está(s)?

How do you say_____in spanish? – ¿Cómo se dice_____en español?

How do you spell_____? – ¿Cómo se escribe_____?

how much – cúanto

How's it going? – ¿Qué tal?

huge – enorme

hungry – hambre

hunting – caza

hurricane – huracán

husband – esposo

I

I can't eat... – No puedo comer...

I don't know – No sé

I don't like... – No me gusta...

I have a question – Tengo una pregunta

I live in – Vivo en

I live near – Vivo cerca de

I thank you – Le doy gracias

I want – Quiero, Deseo

I was born in – Nací en

I would like – Quisiera

ice cream – helado

iced tea – té helado

I'm a vegetarian – Soy vegetariano, soy vegetariana

I'm allergic to... – Tengo alergia a...

I'm from – Soy de

I'm going... – Yo voy...

I'm good – (Estoy) bien

I'm great – (Estoy) muy bien

I'm sorry – Lo siento

I'm very sorry – Lo siento mucho

immigration – inmigración

impatient – impaciente

in back of – detrás de

in front of – enfrente de

index card – ficha

Indian – indio

interesting – interesante

Internet – Internet

Internet browser – motor de búsqueda

Internet café – cibercafé

Italian – italiano

Italy – Italia

itchy – comezón

It's bad weather – Hace mal tiempo

It's cloudy – Está nublado

It's cold – Hace frío

It's cool – Hace fresco, Está fresco

It's foggy – Hay neblina

It's hot – Hace calor

It's nice out – Hace buen tiempo

It's nice to meet you – Mucho gusto

It's sunny – Hay sol, está soleado

It's windy – Hace viento

It is... – Está...

J

jacket – chaqueta

jam – mermelada

January – enero

Japan – Japón

Japanese – japonés

jar – pote

jazz dance – jazz-ballet

jazz music – jazz

jealous – celoso

jet ski – moto acuática

jigsaw puzzle – rompecabezas

Judaism – judaísmo

juggling – malabarismo

juice – jugo, zumo

July – julio

June – junio

K

keyboard – teclado

kind – amable

kitchen – cocina

knee – rodilla

knife – cuchillo

knitting – tejer

Korean – coreano

L

lamb – cordero

lamp – lámpara

laptop (computer) – computadora portátil

large – grande

Latin – latín

laundromat – lavandería

lawyer – abogado, abogada

layover – escala

lazy – perezoso

left – a la izquierda

leg – pierna

lemon – limón

lemonade – limonada

lettuce – lechuga

light blue – azul claro

light green – verde claro

lime – lima

line – línea

lip – labio

long – largo

long hair – cabello o pelo largo

lunch – almuerzo

M

macrame – macramé

magic – magia

maid – criada

mail – correo

mail carrier – cartero, cartera

mailbox – buzón

main course – plato principal

man – hombre

manager – gerente

map – mapa

March – marzo

market – mercado

math – matemáticas

May – mayo

May I... ? – ¿Puedo... ?

mayonnaise – mayonesa

Me too – Yo también

meal – comida

mean – mezquino

mechanic – mecánico, mecánica

medium – mediano

menu – carta

Mexican – mexicano

Mexico – México

milk – leche

milkshake – batido

miniseries – miniserie

mirror – espejo

Miss – Señorita

mittens – mitones

modern dance – baile moderno

Monday – lunes

monitor – monitor

Mother's Day – Día de la Madre

motorbike – moto

motorboat – lancha a motor

motorcycle – motocicleta

mouse – ratón

mouth – boca

movie – película

movie theater – cine

Mr. – Señor

Mrs. – Señora

muffin – magdalena

museum – museo

mushroom – champiñón

music – música

mustard – mostaza

My address is – Mi dirección es

my best friend – mi mejor amigo

My email address is – Mi dirección electrónica es

My name is... – Me llamo...

My phone number is – Mi número de teléfono es

N

napkin – servilleta

narrow – estrecho

near – cerca

neck – cuello

necklace – collar

needlepoint – cañamazo

neighbor – vecino, vecina

nephew – sobrino

nervous – inquieto, nervioso

New Year's – Año Nuevo

New Year's Eve – Nochevieja

next to – junto a

nice – simpático

niece – sobrina

nightgown – camisón

nine – nueve

nineteen – diecinueve

ninety – noventa

no – no

north – norte

nose – nariz

notebook – cuaderno

Nothing (is new) – Nada, sin novedad

Nothing much – Nada de particular

November – noviembre

nurse – enfermero, enfermera

O

octagon – octágono

October – octubre

offended – ofendido

office – oficina

oil – aceite

OK – de acuerdo

old – viejo

olive – aceituna

omelet – tortilla (in Spain)

one – uno, una

one hundred – cien

one million – un millón

one thousand – mil

one-way ticket – billete sencillo

onion – cebolla

or – o

orange (color) – anaranjado

orange (fruit) – naranja

orange juice – jugo, zumo de naranja

outgoing – abierto

oval – óvalo

oven – horno

overseas – extranjero

P

painting – pintura

pajamas – pijama

panties – bragas

pants – pantalones

paper – papel

paper clip – clip

parcheesi – parchís

pardon me – perdón, dispense

park – parque

parking space – aparcamiento

passenger – pasajero

passport – pasaporte

path – camino

patient – paciente

patio – patio

peach – melocotón

peanuts – cacahuetes

pear – pera

peas – guisantes

pen – pluma

pencil – lápiz

pentagon – pentágono

pepper – pimienta

Persian – persa

pharmacy – farmacia

photography – fotografía

piano – piano

pie – tarta, pastel

pilot – piloto

pinball – pinball

ping pong – tenis de mesa, ping-pong

pink – rosado

pistachios – pistachos

plane – avión

plane ticket – billete de avión

plate – plato

playful – guasón

please – por favor

plum – ciruela

plumber – plomero, plomera

poker – póquer

Poland – Polonia

police officer – policía

police station – comisaría

Polish – polaco

pool (for swimming) – piscina

pool (game) – billar americano

porch – veranda

pork – cerdo

Portuguese – portugués

post office – oficina de correos

poster – cartel, póster

pot – cazuela, olla

potato – patata, papa

pottery – alfarería

pretty please – porfis, por favorcito

printer – impresora

Professor – profesor

Puerto Rican – puertorriqueño

purple – violeta

purse – bolsa

pyramid – pirámide

Q

quilting – hacer adredones –

R

rabbit – conejo, coneja

radish – rábano

raincoat – impermeable

rap – rap

rare – poco cocido

raspberry – frambuesa

rat – rata

reading – lectura

receptionist – recepcionista

rectangle – rectángulo

red – rojo

red hair – cabello o pelo rojo

refrigerator – refrigerador, nevera

restaurant – restaurante

rice – arroz

rice pudding – arroz con leche

right – a la derecha

ring – anillo

road – calle

roast beef – rosbif

rock and roll – rock and roll

romance movie – película romántica

romantic comedy – comedia romántica

room – cuarto, pieza

round trip ticket – billete de ida y vuelta

rubber band – goma

rubber stamps – estampillas de goma

rug – tapete

rugby – rugby

ruler – regla

rummy – rummy

running – correr

Russia – Rusia

Russian – ruso

RV – caravana pequeña

S

sad – triste –

sailboat – barco de vela

sailing – navegación a vela

salad – ensalada

salt – sal

same here – igualmente

sandals – sandalias

sandbox – cajón de arena

sandwich – bocadillo, sándwich

Saturday – sábado

saucer – platillo

sausage – salchicha

saxophone – saxofón

scarf – bufanda

school – escuela

science – ciencia

scissors – tijeras

scooter – scooter, ciclomotor

scrapbook – álbum de recortes

screen door – puerta con mosquitera

sculpture – escultura

seafood – mariscos

search engine – motor de búsqueda

secretary – secretario, secretaria

security check – control de seguridad

See you later – Hasta luego, Hasta pronto, Hasta la vista

See you next week – Hasta la semana próxima

See you tomorrow – Hasta mañana

September – septiembre

serious – serio

seven – siete

seventeen – diecisiete

seventy – setenta

sewing – costura

397

shirt – camisa

shoes – zapatos

short – bajo

short hair – cabello o pelo corto

shorts – pantalones cortos

shoulder – hombro

shower – ducha

shuttle – servicio de autobús

shy – tímido

sick – enfermo

sidewalk – acera

sink (in kitchen) – fregadero

sink (in bathroom) – lavabo

sister – hermana

sitcom – comedia de situación

six – seis

sixteen – dieciséis

sixty – sesenta

skateboard – monopatín

skateboarding – monopatinaje

skates – patines

skating – patinaje

skiing – esquiar

skirt – falda

slide – tobogán

slippers – zapatillas

small – pequeño

smart – inteligente

smoothie – licuado (de frutas)

snake – serpiente

sneakers – deportivos

snobbish – esnob

soap opera – telenovela

soccer – fútbol

social studies – estudios sociales

socks – calcetines

soda/pop – refresco

software – software

solitaire – solitario

son – hijo

soup – sopa

south – sur

spades – picas

Spain – España –

Spaniard – español, española

Spanish – español

spatula – espátula

spell checker – corrector ortográfico

spelling – ortografía

sphere – esfera

spinach – espinacas

spoon – cuchara

sports jacket – chaqueta sport

spring – primavera

square – cuadrado

stairway – escalera

staple – grapa

stapler – grapadora

star – estrella

stationery store – papelería

steak – bistec

stereo – estéreo

stomach – estómago

stove – estufa, cocina

straight ahead – todo seguido

straight hair – cabello o pelo liso

strawberry – fresa

strong – fuerte

student – estudiante

student desk – pupitre

studious – estudioso

study – despacho

stupid – estúpido

subway – metro

sugar – azúcar

suit – traje

summer – verano

Sunday – domingo

sunglasses – gafas de sol

supermarket – supermercado

sweater – suéter

swimming – natación

swing – columpio

Swiss – suizo

Switzerland – Suiza

T

table – mesa

tall – alto

tanned – bronceado

tap dance – claqué

tape – cinta adhesiva

tarantula – tarántula

taxi – taxi

tea – té

teacher – profesor, profesora

teenager – joven

telephone – teléfono

television – televisión

ten – diez

tennis – tenis

terminal – terminal

test – examen

thank you – gracias

Thank you so much! – ¡Cuánto se (te) lo agradezco!

thank you very much – muchas gracias

theater – teatro

thin – delgado

thirsty – sed

thirteen – trece

thirty – treinta

This is... – Este es...

three – tres

thumb – pulgar

Thursday – jueves

tie – corbata

tights – pantimedias

tiny – pequeñito

tip – propina

tip included – servicio incluido

tired – cansado

to be hungry – tener hambre

to be thirsty – tener sed

to board – embarcar

to brush (hair, teeth) – cepillarse

to buy a ticket – comprar un billete

to comb (hair) – peinarse

to cook – cocinar

to do laundry – lavar la ropa

to do the dishes – lavar los platos

to do the shopping – hacer las compras

to drink – beber

to eat – comer

to fall asleep – dormirse

to get dressed – vestirse

to get ready – arreglarse

to get tired – cansarse

to get up – levantarse

to go to bed – acostarse

to land – aterrizar

to make a reservation – hacer una reservación

tomake the bed – hacer la cama

to mop the floor – fregar el suelo

to mow the lawn – cortar el césped

to print – imprimir

to put on clothes – ponerse ropa

to put on makeup – maquillarse, pintarse

to put the house in order – arreglar la casa

to read – leer

to save – archivar

to shave – afeitarse

to straighten up – poner en orden

400

to sweep the floor – barrer el suelo

to take a bath – bañarse

to take a shower – ducharse

to take off – despegar

to take off clothes – quitarse la ropa

to take out the garbage – sacar la basura

to type – escribir a máquina

to vacuum – pasar la aspiradora

to wake up – despertarse

to wash (up) – lavarse

to write – escribir

to write in cursive – escribir en cursiva

toast – pan tostado

toe – dedo del pie

tomato – tomate

tooth – diente

tornado – tornado

trail – pista

train – tren

tree – árbol

triangle – triángulo

tricycle – triciclo

truck – camión

trumpet – trompeta

T-shirt – camiseta

Tuesday – martes

turkey – pavo

turtle – tortuga marina

TV show – programa de televisión

TV station – cadena de televisión

twelve – doce

twenty – veinte

two – dos

typewriter – máquina de escribir

U

ugly – feo

uncle – tío

undershirt – camiseta

underwear – calzoncillos

United States – Estados Unidos

up – arriba

V

Valentine's Day – Día de San Valentín

van – camioneta

vanilla – vainilla

veal – ternera

video game – videojuego

Vietnamese – vietnamita

violin – violín

visa – visado

volleyball – vóleibol

W

waiter, waitress – camarero, camerera

walking – a pie

wall – pared

wallet – cartera

walnuts – nueces

washer – lavadora

watch – reloj

water – agua

wavy hair – cabello o pelo ondulado

weak – débil

weaving – tejido

Web page – página web

Web site – sitio web

Wednesday – miércoles

well done – bien hecho

west – oeste

what – qué

What does_____mean? – ¿Qué quiere decir_____?

What's new? – ¿Qué hay de nuevo?

What's your name? – ¿Cómo te llamas?

when – cuándo

where – dónde

Where are you from? – ¿De dónde eres?

Where are you going? – ¿Adónde vas?

Where do you live? – ¿Dónde vives?

Where is the...? – ¿Dónde está...?

whisk – batidor

white – blanco

who – quién

Who are you? – ¿Quién eres?

why – por qué

wide – ancho

wife – esposa

window – ventana

wine – vino

winter – invierno

woman – mujer

wooden spoon – cuchara de madera

woodworking – carpintería

word processor – procesador de textos

wrestling – lucha

wrist – muñeca

writer – escritor, escritora

writing – escritura

Y

yard – jardín

yellow – amarillo

yes – sí

yogurt – yogur

young – joven

you're welcome – de nada

Z

zero – cero

BUILD YOUR OWN SENTENCES

"Whatever beneficial things we develop end building us." - Jim Rohn

"The face is an image of the psyche with the eyes as its mediator." - Cicero

Imagine that is no joke "Spanish Zone," as depicted in the past section.

At the present time, this zone may feel little and awkward. How are you expected to say and think everything in Spanish... when your own Spanish sentences are so restricted?

There are two different ways to enhance your capacity to think in Spanish:

1. Expand your jargon.
2. Expand how you can manage your vocabulary.

At this moment, the second alternative is our main concern.

We're going to contemplate Spanish sentence structure in more detail than we at any point have.

Up until this point, you've been learning sentences as a visual demonstration. Rather than making your own sentences word by word, you've been doing what local speakers do: Using existing sentences and marginally altering them to cling to your own importance.

That is the most solid approach to shape sentences in Spanish effectively.

Be that as it may, imagine a scenario where you need to say more. Imagine a scenario where you need to add phrases, change the request for the words, or consolidate different sentences. Local speakers do that effectively, so for what reason right?

That is what's going on with this exercise.

You'll presumably be alluding back to them pretty regularly as you develop sentences in Spanish without any preparation.

How about we delve into the hypothesis of how Spanish sentences work.

Formed Verbs

Since all language learning is by impersonation, we need in the first place the way that we realize local speakers talk. So we'll begin with stock sentences that you're as of now alright with.

Here are a few sentences that you know, all organized from numerous points of view:

- Yo no lo soy.
- Quizá sea muy tarde.
- Me fui a una nueva casa.
- Es muy seguro de sí mismo.

Albeit these sentences are altogether different from one another, there's one thing that every one of these total sentences shares practically speaking... indeed, one thing that ALL Spanish sentences share for all intents and purpose:

A formed action word.

No pretty much than ONE for each sentence.

- Yo no lo soy.
- Quizá sea muy tarde.
- Me fui a una nueva casa.
- Es muy seguro de sí mismo.

Recollect in Lesson 2 that we contrasted Spanish sentences with potato head toys, where you can change out the various parts however keep up with a similar design. Indeed, obviously, there is a wide range of sentence structures, actually like there is a wide range of potato head mixes. However, they'll all make them think in like manner.

Look at the different potato heads that you see in several areas. What's the shared belief between every one of them?

Believe it or not: A couple of eyes. No pretty much than one for every potato.

It bodes well; potatoes consistently need eyes. Else they wouldn't actually be potato heads; they'd simply be exhausting old potatoes. You can add or eliminate whatever else, however, the eyes must be there for it to appear to be a face.

Spanish sentences are the same way. You can add or eliminate subjects, articles, intensifiers, and prepositional expressions, yet every total sentence has a solitary formed action word.

As a fast update, formed action word structures are the ones that we find on the ground of any action word shop, regardless of whether inside or outside.

In any case, unconjugated action word structures are found over the ground, like the infinitive (for example ser), the participle (sido), or the "ing" word (siendo).

A sentence can have various unconjugated action words. However, it will in any case have only one formed action word.

For instance, look at this sentence:

Task va a haber estado bien.

In a real sense, "Everything will have been fine."

There is just one formed action word: va (from the current state of Ir). Be that as it may, there are two unconjugated action words: haber, an infinitive, and estado, the participle of Estar.

This little stunt is truly enjoyable to mess with. You can make pretty long, long-winded sentences, even with only one formed action word.

We should begin playing with this by finding out about the few different ways to decorate a potato's eyes.

Articles

Obviously, the most immediate approach to adjust a potato's eyes is basically to give it eyebrows.

At the point when you consider eyebrows, consider object pronouns.

Similarly, as eyebrows are constantly connected to the eyes, object pronouns are ALWAYS straightforwardly appended to the action word in a Spanish sentence.

Here are a few models:

- Lo soy.
- La tienen.
- ¿Los tenemos?

Every one of these sentences is essentially made of an action word (eyes) and an article pronoun (eyebrows). We can generally change the action word out for an alternate one, and we can pretty effectively change the item pronoun out, similarly as it's not difficult to change the eyes and eyebrows on the potato head. However, you can't change the request. The eyebrows are constantly appended to the eyes, right "previously" them (above them).

Truth be told, the center of Spanish sentence structure is depicted as [obj][verb].

Make that the core of each sentence you talk in Spanish. The [obj] and [verb] are hitched to one another, as indivisible as the eyebrows and the eyes on our potato head.

When you handle this, you can do anything you need with the remainder of the potato head. All the other things in a Spanish sentence are adaptable and can basically do anything it desires. Yet, the formed action word is consistently the center of the sentence, and the item pronouns consistently have a place just before the action word. This is a sacrosanct association that can never be abused.

Subjects

Look at the potato head we made in the past segment. Eyes and eyebrows are quite cool. Also, they're too's important for a Spanish sentence.

Be that as it may, stand by a moment. Doesn't each sentence have a subject? In the event that an action word demonstrates an activity, shouldn't there be an individual or thing doing that activity?

Indeed, in Spanish, the subject is frequently inferred. Since you don't see it, that doesn't mean it isn't there. Contemplate a reptile's ears: You can't see them, however, they're there at any rate.

Similarly, we can add ears to the potato head assuming we need them. In any case, regardless of whether we don't, the ear openings are still there. These address the subject of the sentence: It's there if it's really apparent.

Rethink this sentence: La tienen. We could change this to Ellos la tienen, expressing unmistakably "They have it", however, the ellos is now suggested in the first sentence.

How about we address the subject of the sentence utilizing sheep ears since the animals from the sheep field scene address subject pronouns for us (él, ella, yo, tú, and so forth)

So you may say that there are two different ways to treat subjects in Spanish: Add sheep ears, or essentially let the potato coexist with earholes, which is additionally fine.

As a fascinating point, it's in reality OK to put the subject either previously or after the [obj][verb] structure, and as you can find in the image, the ears are portrayed "previously" and "after" the eyes. Here are a few models that follow this construction, with a [obj][verb] just as an unmistakably expressed subject:

- Ella lo es.
- Yo lo soy.
- ¿Los tenemos nosotros?
- ¿Nosotros los tenemos?
- Las mujeres se fueron.
- Se fueron las mujeres.

As should be obvious, sometimes we've utilized subject pronouns, for example, nosotros also, ella, and in others, we've utilized whole things, for example, las mujeres. These capacity the same way as the subject of a sentence, regardless of whether previously or after the fundamental [obj][verb] "eyebrow-eye" structure.

Intensifiers and Prepositional Phrases

Utilizing only an action word, an article pronoun, and a subject, you can make a Spanish sentence that is around four or five words in length.

However, here comes the part where we begin designing: Adverbs (from the court) and relational words (from the carnival rides) add tone and detail.

For instance, we should envision that verb modifiers are carrots (from the monkey's vegetable substitute the square). They can be stuck anyplace in the sentence, and they add intriguing data.

- Yo siempre lo soy.
- ¿Nosotros los tenemos hoy?
- Se fueron las mujeres así.

You can stick a carrot (verb modifier) in the potato any place you need. But, obviously, between the eyebrows and the eyes.

Relational words are comparable, however, they have a standard: You need to follow a relational word with a thing. Here are some normal relational words, with an illustration of a thing that may follow them:

- en la casa
- en verdad
- de ese lugar
- por eso
- por muchos años

These kinds of expressions are amazingly adaptable, actually like intensifiers. They can go anyplace in a sentence, and they add fascinating data.

- En verdad, yo siempre lo soy.
- ¿Nosotros los tenemos en la casa hoy?
- Se fueron las mujeres así de ese lugar.

As should be obvious, it's feasible to eliminate these prepositional expressions from the sentences. They actually work as complete sentences, regardless of whether you strip them down to the [obj][verb] structure:

- Lo soy.
- ¿Los tenemos?
- Se fueron.

Be that as it may, the subjects, intensifiers, and prepositional expressions give additional data, detail, and shading to these fundamental sentences.

I like to consider prepositional expressions clothing that can be added to the potato head. Envision a brilliant scarf. You can dress the potato head up in a scarf, doing it in any capacity you like, as long as you don't conceal its eyes.

Conjunctions

Prior I said that all Spanish sentences have one formed action word, no pretty much than one for each sentence. In any case, "sentence" is somewhat deceptive, on the grounds that it's really conceivable to consolidate different "sentences" together into one bigger sentence.

Take this model:

- She has a house yet I don't have a house.
- Ella tiene una casa pero yo no tengo una casa.

LEARN IN PHRASES

"Impersonation isn't only the sincerest type of adulation; it's the sincerest type of learning." - George Bernard Shaw

"Interpretation is the specialty of disappointment." - Umberto Eco

We've now learned 15 of the most utilized words in Spanish. These words help to shape the constructions of sentences.

Yet, we forgot about a single word.

There's an explanation we've put this word off. It's difficult to examine this word without opening Pandora's case of befuddling data about Spanish action words. Es is muddled, on the grounds that it's only one of the numerous signs of a greater, seriously threatening word: Ser.

We should handle this venture head-on and talk about Spanish action words. These are the words that enable us to talk whole sentences. Also, as you might have speculated, Spanish sentences don't work the same way that English sentences do.

In Spanish, action words are a greater arrangement than they are in English. A solitary action word, without help from anyone else, can be a whole idea. A few sentences are only single words, and that word will be an action word.

"Action word, no doubt about it."

Action words don't interpret between English and Spanish.

For instance, the Spanish word es can mean different things. It could just signify "is", which works in these cases:

- He is a tall man.

- She is an unusual lady.

- It is a lovely day.

However, as often as possible, this word means "it is", or "he is", or "she is", without requiring the additional word toward the start by any stretch of the imagination.

- Es un hombre alto.

- Es una inusual dama.

410

- Es un adorable día.

Indeed, it's considerably more typical not to incorporate "he", "she", or "it".

This drives English speakers nearly as insane as it drives Spanish instructors since it's extremely difficult to clarify. How would you realize if to incorporate the subject pronoun? What's the standard?

It's extremely challenging to think of rules for this. All things being equal, here's the directing principle that will work in all circumstances: Learn in phrases.

Indeed, this is fundamental expertise that will apply to each part of your language learning. It's never enough to learn words and formations. You ought to gain proficiency with all your jargon inside Spanish phrasal builds.

That is on the grounds that Spanish words don't straightforwardly convert into English, and English words don't make an interpretation straightforwardly into Spanish.

This is the reason interpretation apparatuses don't actually work except if they're extraordinarily modern. To make an interpretation of it appropriately into Spanish, it must be totally re-worked into a Spanish sentence structure.

Mr. Sentence Head

Developing a sentence resembles assembling a "Mr. Potato Head" face.

On the off chance that you've at any point played with a Potato Head toy, you think about the evolving parts, like the hair, eyes, nose, and mouth. You can supplant the hair with a cap, you can exchange the open eyes for shut eyes or irate eyes, or you can switch the typical mouth for a stood-out tongue.

Obviously, you're not actually expected to put eyes where the mouth goes (except if you're a cubist). The face has a design you're required to follow: Hair on top, then, at that point eyes, then, at that point nose, then, at that point mouth.

Sentences are the same way. On the off chance that you know what you can exchange around, it's enjoyable to supplant the various parts.

For instance, we should utilize this basic English sentence:

"This is a sentence."

There are four words. I've represented them as four pieces of a face ("this" is the hair, "is" is the eyes, "a" is the nose, and "sentence" is the mouth).

We should begin modifying this sentence. Assume we supplant the principal word, "this", with another word: "that."

Since those two words are syntactically the same, it works impeccably.

"That is a sentence."

How about we get more imaginative. On the off chance that "this" can be supplanted with "that", what can "is" be supplanted by? We can transform it out for "was," "will be," or some other action word. To illustrate, I've picked "changed."

We can likewise supplant "a" with "the" since they're the same. So presently our sentence is "That changed the sentence."

As should be obvious, it's as yet precisely the same sentence structure! Yet, it's been adjusted fundamentally to make another importance, similar to changing out Potato Head parts to make our own face.

Presently we'll go much further. How about we exchange "that" for a fascinating thing:

"Dolphins."

How about we likewise supplant our action word "changed" with "broke."

Furthermore, our last thing will change from "sentence" to a whole expression that works as a thing: "neighborhood transit regulations."

"Dolphins violated neighborhood transit regulations." This is still an unchanged sentence structure that we began with: "This is a sentence." We just changed each word for something syntactically the same.

Fundamental Phrase Units

Lamentably, making an interpretation of from English to Spanish is just about as abnormal as moving pieces from a Potato Head face to a honey bee's face. Joel doesn't have any spot to put the nose, and how are you expected to manage the radio wires? The constructions essentially aren't something similar. Spanish expressions work uniquely in contrast to English expressions.

Rather than interpreting word-by-word (which much of the time prompts calamity), we should figure out how Spanish expression structures work without any preparation.

Luckily, there aren't an excessive number of designs to learn. Before the finish of Lesson 6, you will have adapted essentially the entirety of the sentence structures utilized in Spanish.

Look at this illustration of a total Spanish sentence that is just two words: "Es tall."

This sentence could signify "he is tall," "she is tall," or "it is tall" (contingent upon the unique situation). A phrasal unit can be utilized much of the time, and it's a finished sentence. Syntactically, there's no requirement for any more data.

However, now and again we need to explain the unique situation. Assume we're within the sight of both a kid and a young lady, and we need to discuss one of them explicitly.

The arrangement is essential to add a thing to the start: "The young lady es tall."

All things considered, we remembered a subject for the sentence. However, a ton of the time, Spanish doesn't require the subject to be named. "Es tall" is finished without help from anyone else. "The young lady" is additional data that can be added to the start.

On the off chance that you get familiar with the expression "es tall," you can utilize it differently. Without anyone else, you can allude to any individual you need. Or, on the other hand, assuming you need to be explicit, you can just name the individual toward the start: "(individual) es tall." Either way, you're utilizing a similar fundamental two-word state.

Presently we should go above and beyond: Suppose we would prefer not to say "he is tall." Imagine a scenario where we need to say "I'm tall."

You'll, in any case, utilize the fundamental sentence structure: "es tall." But you'll change the action word from "he is" to "I am," and you'll wind up with "soy tall." (Soy signifies "I am," as you'll learn to some degree B of the exercise.)

These two expressions, "es alto" and "soy alto", are something very similar, however, with a single word changed. We didn't develop an entirely different sentence. We just changed a single word from our essential expression unit.

To talk wonderful Spanish, you'll never make up sentences without any preparation. As a general rule, you've never made up a sentence in English by the same token. You've been utilizing minor departure from similar few sentences for as long as you can remember. You're simply changing a portion of the words to make your own importance.

Spanish (and each and every other language) works the same way: You generally utilize the expression structures that you learned in your developmental days, yet when you talk or compose, you inventively change out specific words to make your own importance, very much like changing out the pieces of a Potato Head face.

Two Sentences

As we learn jargon for this exercise, we'll present each word with regards to one of two fundamental expression structures. How about we get acquainted with everyone.

(1) Es tall.

This fundamental design will be altered in two or three different ways. To start with, we could alter the action word:

- They are tall.
- We were tall.
- He will be tall.

Or then again we could change the data after the action word:

- Es a tall individual.
- Es snide.

As should be obvious, these are altogether straightforwardly dependent on the fundamental sentence structure

"Es tall," with all things considered "Es" or "tall" supplanted by something different.

(2) I trust que he be tall.

This sentence is more muddled, yet it's a critical Spanish construction.

Most importantly, notice the que in the sentence. This partitions two separate expressions: "I expectation" and "he be tall."

You'll get familiar with the meaning of this sentence structure soon. For the present, practice it a tad: "I trust que he be tall." Keep this precise phrasing at the top of the priority list.

When you're OK with both of these fundamental sentences, you're prepared to start learning this present exercise's jargon.

A short time later, to some extent C of the exercise, we'll jump a lot further into the development of Spanish expressions.

THE TRUTH ABOUT LEARNING SPANISH

Commonly, on the off chance that you tell somebody that you are learning an unknown dialect, yet that you are explicitly learning Spanish, you might be met with an assortment of reactions. They might go from "Amazing, that is great!" to "For what reason do you have to learn Spanish? Everybody communicates in English at any rate..."

Many individuals even have the discernment that learning Spanish can be a somewhat troublesome undertaking or that every one of the assortments of Spanish is comparative, if not indistinguishable. In this part, we will examine one familiar way of thinking (fantasy) about learning Spanish, and afterward examine, in somewhat more detail, a few of the interesting little subtleties about learning Spanish. The objective of this part is to diagram a portion of the parts of Spanish that might entangle students, particularly toward the start of their Spanish-learning venture.

Legend: All Spanish is something similar. (If by some stroke of good luck it were that basic!)

Spanish is the authority language in more than 20 unique nations! Mexico, Spain, Venezuela, Argentina... they all communicate in Spanish. This is valid. However, expecting that there are no contrasts between the assortments of Spanish you'll discover spoken all throughout the planet is extremely, wrong.

This resembles saying that individuals from the US, Britain, and Australia all talk the same way since they all communicate in English. Not exclusively are there shifting accents (even inside the nations referenced, for instance, the southern emphasis found in Texas versus the northern complement found in New York) however even phrasing changes. On the off chance that you go to England and request "chips," you're not requesting the firm potato chips you would hope to get in the United States. You're really requesting what Americans would call "fries."

The equivalent is valid in Spanish. In certain spots, certain words are utilized to mean a certain something while, in others, they mean something totally different.

Accents, slang, and surprisingly set articulations will change dependent on what nation you're in.

There is the thing that can be thought of as "standard Spanish." This is the Spanish expressed in D.F. (Mexico City), Mexico or Lima, Peru. It is not necessarily the case that in those spots there aren't some special and recognizing components to the language however simply that speakers from those two urban areas will make some simpler memories speaking with and being perceived by Spanish speakers from other Spanish-talking nations.

What's the significance here for you as a Spanish language student?

Particularly when beginning, this reality mustn't have a lot of bearing on your language-learning experience. The fundamentals (for example action word formations and significant jargon) will quite often be similar regardless of where you go.

Nonetheless, as you plunge further into the language and your level starts to expand, you might need to give careful consideration to things.

For instance, the utilization of "vosotros" in the focal and northern locales of Spain or the "vos", which is utilized in numerous Southern and Central American nations. Except if you plan on investing broad measures of energy in one of the nations that utilizes one of these pronouns, you don't have to stress over remembering them for your own discourse. Be that as it may, on the off chance that you mean to submerge yourself in the language (through perusing, sitting in front of the TV shows or motion pictures, and so forth) you will need to know about this reality.

This is valid for a significant number of the shifting components found inside the enormous umbrella that is the Spanish language and something you'll need to remember.

Except if you plan on turning into a Spanish etymologist or devoting your life to examining the Spanish language, odds are you won't ever have the option to completely gain proficiency with the entirety of the distinctions that range the 20+ Spanish-talking nations.

The most ideal approach to move toward something is this, when you believe you have a firm comprehension of the language, discover the assortment of the language that best accommodates your own advantages.

In the event that you end up inspired by the set of experiences, culture, writing, music, and so forth of a particular area, you'll presumably need to acclimate yourself with their particular method of talking so your submersion interaction goes all the more easily.

Regardless assortment of Spanish you choose to go with, when you have functioning information on the language, you will not battle with utilizing it no matter who you're talking with. Of course, there might be some snapshot of misconception (take the "chip" model referenced before when communicating in English) yet eventually, correspondence can and will occur.

Those precarious little subtleties...

Regardless assortment of Spanish you're learning, there are sure realities that will consistently be available - the seemingly insignificant details that make Spanish, all things considered, Spanish.

Commonly, these things I'm going to list and examine momentarily can be hard for English-speakers in light of the fact that, basically, they don't exist in our language.

Articulation

In contrast to different dialects, Spanish articulation isn't really that troublesome. Spelling (something that can be disappointing and befuddling in dialects like French and surprisingly English) shouldn't be an issue when learning Spanish.

Each letter in the Spanish letters in order has a particular sound. They will ALWAYS make that sound. This reality WILL NOT change. Dissimilar to in English when we have long vowels and short vowels and peculiarities like the notorious - ough finishing (genuinely - what's with that? For what reason do words like through, however, and harsh, all having a similar closure, must be said as much in an unexpected way?), you will not go over these things in Spanish.

In the event that you give careful consideration to this reality when you begin learning Spanish, seeing words like estacionamiento or murcielago (the two words that appear to be long and fairly scary) shouldn't hit you with dread. Just solid out the letters as you see them and the writing is on the wall!

For more data on the Spanish letters in order, look at this astonishing site with sound examples: http://studyspanish.com/articulation/

Diphthongs

There is one component of the Spanish language that is vital to recollect when discussing articulation. It's something we don't have in English- - the diphthongs.

Without getting too specialized here, this interaction will happen when you have two vowels put together (in a similar syllable — this is vital). The sounds they make will kind of mush together to make one, consolidated sound.

To improve comprehension of what I'm saying with this present, how about we start little.

Take the accompanying two words for instance:

- Bailar
- Tiene

Separating these, you'll see that they each just have TWO syllables.

- Bai·lar
- Tie·ne

In the primary word (bailar-significance to move), we have the main syllable contains two vowels ("a" and "I"). The "a" in Spanish is articulated "ah" also, the "I" is articulated like "ee". If we somehow managed to say these two sounds exclusively, the word would sound fairly off-kilter and uneven.

- Bah/ee·lar

Actually, the "a" and the "I" in the principal syllable will meet up to make the "ay" sound. Henceforth the articulation will be:

- Bay(sounds like "bye")·lar

The equivalent can be said with the subsequent word (tiene-meaning he/she/it/you [singular/formal] have). The "I" again would be articulated "ee" and the "e" is articulated like "eh." Since the two vowels are together in a similar syllable, we need to push them together, with the goal that they structure one, slurred together solid - "ee-eh."

- Tee-eh·ne

The site referenced before will likewise give you some incredible data about these slight peculiarities.

Action Word Conjugations

This is something that numerous English-speakers battle with. As a general rule, we do have formations in English—the lone thing is they're a lot less complex and in reality exceptionally essential. Do you realize that senseless little "s" that is added to the finishing of action words when we use them in the third individual solitary (I run, he runs)?

This is that way, just in view of significantly more to keep. In English, it's quite often necessitated that you incorporate both the subject and the action word when expressing. For instance, you can't say "have a canine." Who has a canine? I, you, we, they? In Spanish, nonetheless, including the subject isn't generally fundamental, and here's the reason.

A fast introduction to the formation cycle

This graph is something I have used to show subject pronouns, just as formations, for quite a long time and it is in reality ordinarily utilized in Spanish homerooms all throughout the planet.

- I
- We
- You
- You plural
- He/She
- They

As should be obvious, there are two sections on the diagram. The first (to one side) addresses the solitary pronouns. Going down the lines, you will find that they go all together (plunging) from first to third individual. In like manner, the right segment contains your plural types of similar first third individual pronouns.

At whatever point we utilize an action word in English, we pick the fitting pronoun to oblige the action word, so as not to create any turmoil.

In Spanish, nonetheless, as I will before long clarify, the utilization of the subject pronoun isn't generally fundamental. This is on the grounds that the action word will form, generally, to contain the subject too.

As you will learn, in the event that you haven't as of now, there are three fundamental action word endings in Spanish. This implies that when an action word is in its infinitive structure (to + action word), it will end in either - ar, - er, or - ir.

- Hablar-to talk
- Comer-to eat
- Vivir-to live

CONCLUSION

Learning Spanish can have many benefits, from improved communication skills to a more versatile resume. However, as many people realize it too late, it can be difficult to find the time and motivation necessary to learn a new language. This is why this guide is here for you! We've got all sorts of valuable information about the benefits of learning Spanish plus tons of tips for how you can study and keep your motivation high.

Learning Spanish isn't always easy but there are still ways that you can reap the rewards of speaking this beautiful language every day!

Tip #1: Learn Spanish Online

Online language learning tools are some of the best ways to advance your skills no matter what level of Spanish you're studying. They're almost always free and they'll help you develop better reading, writing, pronunciation, and comprehension skills. If you want to learn a little faster or even get "college credit" for the course, consider taking an online class through a reputable language provider like Rosetta Stone.

Tip #2: Get a Personal Tutor!

Many people make the mistake of thinking that they don't need to pay attention in class.

Tip #3: Watch Movies In Spanish

Watching movies in your target language is an excellent way to expose yourself to the new language without putting any pressure on yourself. You don't need to have conversations with anyone or even go out of your way to understand everything that's happening in the movie. The beauty of watching movies in your target language is that you don't have to focus on the actual dialogue at all! You can relax and enjoy the movies in your target language, without worrying about understanding everything.

Tip #4: Learn a New Skill Every Day

If you're using a learning tool like FluentU or Rosetta Stone, you can make it part of your weekly schedule to learn a new skill each weekday. For example, if you're using FluentU, every weekday start off by selecting something from the list of topics that you find interesting. Then, watch the video and take a quiz to see how much you've learned.

Tip #5: Record Yourself Spreading Info to Others

Practice makes perfect! The best way to improve your Spanish is by constantly speaking it, so make sure you're doing this as often as possible. One of the best ways to keep improving is to record yourself speaking Spanish and then listening back afterward. If you're using FluentU or Rosetta Stone, both of these programs have built-in features to help you listen back and keep improving your Spanish skills!

Tip #6: Learn More Than Just Talking Spanish!

Sure, there are many dialects and variations of the Spanish language that will suit your needs depending on where you're visiting, but it's important to learn all of these aspects.

Tip #7: Don't Forget to Learn the Grammar Rules!

It can be tempting to study grammar rules last since they can be tough to learn. However, it's important not to wait until you're almost done with your learning plan before moving onto grammar. The sooner you start learning your target language's grammar rules, the easier they'll be to master! FluentU turns fun videos like music videos, movie trailers, news and inspiring talks into Spanish learning experiences.

Tip #8: Listen to Spanish Music in the Target Language

Did you know that listening to music in your target language will help you speak better? Why not add some Spanish reggaeton, cumbia or salsa into your rotation? There are lots of popular songs that are over 10 years old and still being played on the radio today.

Tip #9: Don't Forget to Follow Through with Your Spanish Goal

We all have idealistic visions of what we want to achieve, but it's easy to get distracted and lose sight of them. If your goal is learning Spanish, then commit yourself 100% and keep following through with your daily routine. Before you know it, you'll be having conversations with native speakers!

Tip #10: Don't Get Discouraged!

Don't let the challenges discourage you, though, because it will only make you push yourself harder.

CHAPTER 3

EASY AND FUN WAYS TO LEARN SPANISH

INTRODUCTION

S panish language is spoken in a variety of countries and territories worldwide, most notably Mexico, Spain, Argentina, Colombia, Peru and Equatorial Guinea.

You will learn the origins of the language as well as how it evolved over time to what it is today.

This book will give you a checklist of words that are all important when speaking in Spanish. You can use the words in sentences as well as practice them to improve your pronunciation and understanding. Additional information is also provided on proper grammar and other important aspects of speaking Spanish correctly.

As the language is spoken, the vocabulary of each nation changes slightly. It is still very similar overall but there are some modes, pronunciations, and sentence structures that are exclusive to certain regions only.

The Spanish language is varied on a global scale, from Spain to Argentina, Ecuador, Brazil and other countries where Spanish is spoken.

Spanish is a complex language with a vast vocabulary that changes from region to region [or even country to country]. This will be useful for travelers who wish to speak in Spanish but do not want to sound foolish or stilted when conversing with locals.

The language of Spain is one of the most spoken languages in the world.

This book offers you an insight into the history of Spanish as well as how it has evolved to its present state. There are a few misconceptions you need to be aware of when studying the history of Spanish and some background information about how this language evolved from Latin to Castillian as well.

There are a variety of different accents for Spanish. You are not limited to the regions listed here, there is a wide range of people who speak with distinctive accents and dialects.

This book talks about words that are commonly used in everyday Spanish. Many times these words are universal but other times they have different meanings depending on who you speak to. These Spanish words can be useful when traveling or in daily conversation as well.

This book will teach you how to construct sentences correctly when speaking Spanish. You will learn how to make a subject and verb agree and how to change tenses in a sentence. You will also learn about conjunctions, prepositions and other rules that are important when speaking Spanish.

Your ability to speak Spanish fluently is paramount in order for you to meet local people, practice your Spanish language skills, and travel more freely throughout the world. Most of us can speak little or no Spanish but when you can speak it fluently then you are well on your way toward learning this language.

This book will teach you some basic grammar rules as well as the correct pronunciation of words when speaking Spanish. If you are traveling to Latin America, you will want to learn this information so that your pronunciation is correct.

It offers general global information about Spanish and its expansion around the world. You will also learn more about how it has evolved through time and how it is different from other languages in the region.

Are you looking to improve your Spanish language skills? There are no strict requirements to become fluent in Spanish, but it can be helpful if you have some basic skills already.

This book provides you with a checklist of important Spanish words that you should be able to use when speaking. You will learn the different ways of saying things well as well as expressions and phrases for more sophisticated conversation.

This book will teach you some basic grammar rules and how to construct sentences in good and correct Spanish. In order to build on your vocabulary, you must have a firm grasp of the basic grammar rules so that you can construct better sentences.

This book will provide you with some important grammar rules that can be used when speaking Spanish.

This book will give you an insight into the history of Spanish as well as how it has evolved over time to what it is today. There are a few misconceptions that native speakers have about the language and some background information about how this language evolved from Latin to Castillian. This is useful for students of Spanish who need additional background information on the history of the language.

This book gives you an introduction to Spanish as a world language. It offers global information about Spanish and its expansion around the world. It offers some background information on how this language evolved through time and how it is different from other languages in the region

This book will teach you some basic grammar rules for Spanish as well as showing you how to construct sentences in correct Spanish. Knowing the grammatical rules is crucial for building vocabulary and sentence structure.

ADVERBS AND VERBS

Adverbs and Verbs Adverbs

Adverbs of Place / Time

There – Ahí

- The documents you asked me for are there on the desk.
- Los documentos que me pediste están ahí sobre el escritorio.

There – Allí

- They told us to take off our shoes and wash our feet right there.
- Nos dijeron que nos quitáramos los zapatos y nos laváramos los pies allí mismos.

Here – Aquí

- They will bring the pets here later on during the day.
- Traerán a las mascotas aquí más tarde durante el día.

Here – Acá

- Get over here as soon as you can!
- ¡Ven para acá en cuanto puedas!

Ahead – Adelante

- We will find more small towns and villages up ahead.
- Encontraremos más pueblitos y caseríos adelante.

Behind – Detrás

- You should get behind me and let me lead.
- Deberías ponerte detrás de mí y déjame dirigir.

Up – Arriba

- There were many different types of planes, up in the sky.

- Había muchos tipos de aviones diferentes, arriba en el cielo.

Above – Encima

- Planes usually fly above the clouds.
- Los aviones generalmente vuelan por encima de las nubes.

Below – Bajo

- Temperatures in the highest parts can reach up to forty degrees below zero.
- Las temperaturas en las partes más altas pueden alcanzar los cuarenta grados bajo cero.

Under – Debajo

- Water flows under the ground in this area.
- El agua fluye por debajo de la tierra en esta zona.

Underneath – Debajo

- That noise came from underneath the bed.
- Ese ruido vino de debajo de la cama.

On – Sobre

- The car keys and the tools are on the table.
- Las llaves del auto y las herramientas están sobre la mesa.

Beyond – Más allá

- What you are asking me to do goes beyond my skills.
- Lo que me estás pidiendo que haga va más allá de mis habilidades.

Down – Abajo

- They seemed to be having a bit of a discussion down on the first floor.
- Parecía que estaban teniendo una discusión abajo en el primer piso.

Close – Cerca

- John lives very close to my apartment.
- John vive muy cerca de mi apartamento.

Near – Cerca

- If you could leave me near the train station, that would be fine.
- Si pudieras dejarme cerca de la estación del tren estaría genial.

Far – Lejos

- The gas station was actually pretty far, we ended up pushing the car for miles.
- La estación de servicio quedaba demasiado lejos, terminamos empujando el auto por millas.

Away – Lejos

- Keep your claws away from my cake!
- ¡Mantén tus garras lejos de mi tarta!

Over – Encima

- My cats are over me all the time.
- Mis gatos se la pasan encima mío todo el tiempo.

Out – Fuera

- Please tell the children to stay out of my gaming room.
- Por favor, dile a los niños que se queden fuera de mi cuarto de juegos.

Outside – Afuera

- I had to stay outside the house during the day so that they could finish the work.
- Me tuve que quedar afuera de la casa durante el día para que pudieran terminar el trabajo.

In – En

- I told you we would be in the waiting room.
- Te dije que estaríamos en la sala de espera.

Inside – Dentro

- The money is inside the bag in the kitchen.
- El dinero está dentro de la bolsa en la cocina.

Through – A través

- We were able to see through the windows and we are sure he wasn't there.
- Pudimos mirar a través de las ventanas y estamos seguros de que él no estaba ahí.

Around – Alrededor

- The Earth spins around the Sun, and the Moon spins around the Earth.
- La Tierra gira alrededor del Sol y la Luna gira alrededor de la Tierra.

Across – Alrededor

- We went across the planet looking for this particular flower.
- Estuvimos alrededor del mundo buscando ésta flor en particular.

Beneath - Debajo

- Every tree has roots beneath its trunk.
- Todo árbol tiene raíces debajo de su tronco.

Where – Donde

- That's the small town where I was born.
- Ese es el pueblito donde nací.

Next to – Junto a

- The socks were next to the shoes.
- Los calcetines estaban junto a los zapatos.

In front of – Frente a

- I dream to have an apartment in front of the sea.
- Sueño con tener un apartamento frente al mar.

Adverbs of Time / Frequency

Now – Ahora

- Now I would like you to remain quiet while I continue the explanation.
- Ahora me gustaría que permanecieran callados mientras continúo con la explicación.

Right away – Ya mismo

- Tell them to bring the accused to this room right away.
- Dígales que traigan al acusado a esta sala ya mismo.

Yet – Aún

- We have not received a proper invitation yet.
- No hemos recibido una invitación adecuada aún.

Today – Hoy

- I thought you were supposed to finish today.
- Pensé que se suponía que ibas a terminar hoy.

Late – Tarde

- It is a little late to open another bottle, I'd rather leave.
- Es un poco tarde para abrir otra botella, preferiría irme.

Early – Temprano

- I told you to come back early, don't blame it on me if there is no food left.
- Te dije que volvieras temprano, no me eches la culpa si no queda comida.

Soon – Pronto

- Don't worry, we'll get to the beach soon and forget about this cold.
- No te preocupes, llegaremos a la playa pronto y nos olvidaremos de este frío.

Still – Todavía

- There's still time to obtain your driver's license this month.
- Todavía hay tiempo de que obtengas tu carnet de conducir este mes.

Yesterday – Ayer

- I almost bought that truck yesterday, now I've decided to go for another car.
- Casi compro esa camioneta ayer, ahora me decidí a ir por otro auto.

Just – Recién

- I've just finished my lunch, give me a couple of minutes to get there.
- Recién terminé de almorzar, dame un par de minutos para llegar.

Never – Nunca

- Never send a dog to do a cat's work.
- Nunca envíes a un perro a hacer el trabajo de un gato.

Always – Siempre

- I always thought Argentina was a nice country to live in.
- Siempre pensé que Argentina era un lindo país para vivir.

Ever – Alguna vez

- If I ever go to Japan, I sure will eat a whole puffer fish.
- Si alguna vez voy a Japón, seguro que me comeré un pez globo entero.

Later – Luego

- I will call you later to provide you more information.
- Te llamaré luego para darte más información.

Currently – Actualmente

- I currently work as a waitress, although I may get a better job soon.
- Actualmente trabajo como mesera, aunque tal vez consiga un mejor trabajo pronto.

Constantly – Constantemente

- My dog looks for attention constantly.
- Mi perro busca atención constantemente.

Last night – Anoche

- I ended up having pizza for dinner last night.
- Terminé comiendo pizza para cenar anoche.

Before – Antes

- My nose used to look huge before the surgery.
- Mi nariz se veía gigante antes de la cirugía.

After – Después

- I always drink a lot of water after I finish my cardio.
- Siempre bebo mucha agua después de terminar mi cardio.

Usually – Usualmente

- It usually doesn't take this long to wait for a cab.
- Usualmente no toma tanto tiempo esperar un taxi.

When – Cuando

- This is the medal they gave me when I finished school.
- Esta es la medalla que me dieron cuando terminé la escuela.

Immediately – Inmediatamente

- I immediately had cold sweats and I knew they were caused by the pill.
- Inmediatamente comencé a tener sudor frío y supe que era a causa de la pastilla.

This morning – Esta mañana

- I took a shower this morning, so I don't need to take another one.
- Tomé una ducha esta mañana, así que no necesito tomar otra.

This afternoon – Esta tarde

- I was told to visit the doctor this afternoon.
- Me dijeron que fuera al doctor esta tarde.

Tonight – Esta noche

- Ibiza's biggest party will take place tonight.
- La fiesta más grande de Ibiza se celebrará esta noche.

Prior – Antes

- Make sure you go to the restroom prior to our meeting.
- Asegúrate de ir al baño antes de nuestra reunión.

Frequently – Frecuentemente

- The trains pass by frequently.
- Los trenes pasan frecuentemente.

Recently – Recientemente

- There has been a drop in the price of oil recently.
- Ha habido una bajada en el precio del petróleo recientemente.

Every day – Todos los días

- I ride my bike to work every day.
- Yo voy al trabajo en bici todos los días.

Indefinitely – Indefinidamente

- All flights have been canceled indefinitely.
- Todos los vuelos han sido cancelados indefinidamente.

Hourly – Cada hora

- We have to check his vital signs hourly.
- Tenemos que revisar sus signos vitales cada hora.

Tomorrow – Mañana

- I'll have to take the bus to get to work tomorrow.
- Tendré que tomar un bus para ir al trabajo mañana.

Often – A menudo

- I try to go for a walk often.
- Trato de ir a caminar a menudo.

Adverbs of Quantity / Manner

All – Todo (singular)

- All the time I wasted would have been useful to do something else.
- Todo el tiempo que desperdicié hubiera sido útil para hacer otra cosa.

All – Todos (plural)

- All the papers you found on the table were mine.

- Todos los papeles que encontraste en la mesa eran míos.

Any – Algún

- If you have any problems regarding our service, you can always contact Customer Service.
- Si tiene algún problema con respecto a nuestro servicio, siempre puede consultar en Atención al Cliente.

Any – Alguno

- I wouldn't be here if I had any doubts.
- No estaría aquí si tuviera alguna duda.

Both – Ambos (Masculine)

- Both parents are responsible for the development of the child.
- Ambos padres son responsables del desarrollo del niño.

Both – Ambas (Feminine)

- I thought about it and both choices seem reasonable.
- Pensé sobre ello y ambas opciones parecen razonables.

Each – Cada

- I have to change the hen's water each day.
- Debo cambiar el agua de la gallina cada día.

Every – Cada

- Every time I ask for a burger I ask for extra pickles.
- Cada vez que pido una hamburguesa, pido pepinillos adicionales.

Again – Nuevamente

- I had to write the report again after my dog ate it.
- Tuve que escribir el reporte nuevamente después de que mi perro se lo comiera.

Little – Poco (singular)

- I thought it would take them a little time to talk about the event.

434

- Pensé que les tomaría poco tiempo hablar sobre el evento.

Lots of – Bastante

- I hope they bring lots of beer to the party.
- Espero que traigan bastante cerveza a la fiesta.

A lot – Mucho

- I usually work out a lot during weekdays.
- Generalmente entreno mucho durante los días de semana.

LEVERAGE ESSENTIAL VOCABULARY

Active Ignorance

"We first make our habits, and then our habits make us."

- John Dryden

"One who is faithful in a very little is also faithful in much."

- Jesus

You now know about 300 words. But how well can you use them?

Not long ago, I received an email from a student whom we'll call

"Nate". Nate was dissatisfied with his small vocabulary.

He had recently tried to converse with a 5-year-old who was a native Spanish speaker. This kid was talking about what he'd had for breakfast that morning, and Nate couldn't understand the items that the kid described.

Nate wrote to me:

"I can't express very much without more nouns, adjectives, and adverbs... I would like you to introduce common words of basic conversation."

I get this kind of complaint a lot. Students like Nate don't really like relying on pronouns such as *esto* and *eso,* or on vague verbs like *hacer*. They'd rather have more colorful words like "oatmeal" and "slurping".

The reasoning is simple: "If I had just had the vocabulary from that conversation, I would have understood everything!"

Well, yes. Maybe.

If you train for one specific conversation, sure, you might be able to understand that one specific conversation. But where does that lead you?

Conversation Training Is a Dead End

Which of the following sentences do you think you'll find yourself saying more often?

(A) "The eggs and milk are in the kitchen, with the apples and carrots."

(B) "I want you to do it as soon as you can."

Each of these sentences requires approximately the same amount of vocabulary. But the second one will obviously be useful in many, many more situations.

And yet many second-year Spanish students can easily say the first sentence, but they have no idea how to assemble the second one in Spanish.

Why do most people make this mistake?

It's a simple temptation: The first example is visual and physical, while the second one is abstract. But that's exactly why the second one is SO much more valuable.

Let's think about Nate again for a second. If Nate had just happened to study the exact words that the 5-year-old kid was going to use in the short conversation about breakfast, he could have understood him. That vocabulary list would probably include about 20 obscure words like "blueberries", "stuffed", and "sloppily". And this specific knowledge would have prepared Nate for a grand total of one conversation.

However, there are BILLIONS of potential conversations you might have.

You can't specifically prepare for each one. As soon as the other person goes off-script, you'll be lost.

Instead, if you want to talk about anything and everything, you need to begin with the vocabulary that will allow you to talk about anything and everything.

This means learning the words that are used all the time every day in Spanish, the top 600 words by frequency.

It means perfecting those words until they're second nature, until you can say them without thinking about them, and until you can perfectly understand them in a conversation with a native speaker.

It means learning to stretch each word that you know to its maximum potential until you know every function that you can get out of it.

And although it's counterintuitive, it means temporarily avoiding learning words outside that essential realm, until you've perfected this critical core of your Spanish knowledge. These incredibly foundational skills must come first, with exclusive priority.

Syntax: Essential Skills

One of the fundamental rules of accelerated language learning is very simple: Until a certain point in your language journey, restrict your knowledge to a very small amount of vocabulary.

Instead of entertaining ourselves with shiny objects like foods and animal names, we need to focus on clear, perfect communication. And this actually requires us to ignore certain information for a while.

One day, after a certain point in your language learning journey, you'll be ready to expand your horizons. Then you can confidently absorb every single thing that you find important… And it will work! But ONLY because of the foundations you've laid first.

We've learned almost all the essential syntax of the Spanish language, and in this lesson, we're going to be learning a lot more labels (especially descriptive labels).

It's easy to learn new labels. You've been doing it your whole life. Learning labels in Spanish is no different than learning labels in English; learning to call the bathroom the baño or the aseo is just like learning to call it the "loo" or the "water closet". It's a simple, entertaining way to learn new names for things.

And when you focus on entertaining yourself, you'll find that you can move very fast without getting anywhere.

Let's imagine you want to improve your baseball game. You're terrible at hitting, you can't pitch, and you're really bad at throwing and catching the ball.

But your favorite part of the game is running between bases.

So every afternoon, your 1-hour practice schedule looks like this:

- — 4:00: Practice running from home to 1st base.
- — 4:15: Practice running from 1st to 2nd.
- — 4:30: Practice running from 2nd to 3rd.

- 4:45: Practice running from 3rd to home.

Does that look like productive practice? Of course not. When you practice running from one base to another, you aren't practicing baseball at all.

You're just practicing running, which is a basic skill common to most sports, not baseball specifically.

Labels are just unproductive to learn Spanish. If you're practicing animal names or memorizing lists of action verbs, you're not practicing

Spanish. You're just learning lists of labels, which is a skill common to all languages.

What's a better baseball practice schedule?

- 4:00: Practice hitting the ball in a batting cage.
- 4:15: Practice throwing the ball at a vertical line, learning from errors to perfect your aim.
- 4:30: Play catch with a friend, standing at a distance just at the edge of your comfort zone.
- 4:45: Practice with a friend who is slightly better than you, focusing on hitting and pitching.

If you practice like this, you'll actually improve your baseball skills.

That's because you're actually focusing on the essential skills inherent to the game, which are the most difficult skills.

Strangely enough, you don't get better at baseball simply by playing the whole game. You get better by restricting yourself to a small set of essential skills and focusing on those.

It's true of other sports as well. Professional basketball players don't spend most of their time playing. They focus on very specific skills: Shots and ball handling. Sure, practicing basketball is more fun when you're playing a game. But if you're a professional player, you know to spend most of your time focused on the essential skills inherent to the game.

Every basketball player looks forward to passing the ball across the court in a real game.

Every baseball player is excited to make an epic, game-winning home run.

Every language learner is excited to use hundreds of nouns and verbs in a passionate conversation on a personal topic.

But in all of these cases, the fastest way outward is inward. The more focus you put inside the realm of essential skills, the faster you'll be able to explode outward from there.

In a language, the "essential skills inherent to the game" are syntax: Mastering the top few hundred words that hold the entire language together.

So When Do We Get Labels?

The good news is that if you focus on this most essential vocabulary, you can learn the language much more quickly. Instead of spending time and attention on learning new vocabulary but not knowing exactly how to use it, you'll direct that effort toward using your core vocabulary as effectively as possible, like a native speaker.

One day, after a certain point in your language learning journey, you'll be ready to expand your horizons. After you've truly mastered everything in this book, you can confidently absorb every single thing that you find important… And it will work! But ONLY because of the foundations you've laid first.

Recall what I mentioned about the doctors' forum in Lesson 7? A native English speaker is able to integrate new, obscure vocabulary, even in complex sentence structures, because of a strong existing foundation.

So when, exactly, will you be ready for more colorful vocabulary?

After you're basically fluent.

Until then, you should outright refuse to learn any words other than the minimum amount to make you fluent.

This is extremely important. If you set yourself the goal of only mastering the top 600 words of Spanish, in all of their possible uses, you can make tangible progress. With each lesson in this book, you'll know that you're closer to your goal.

But if your goal is to learn "everything", you'll end up going in circles... which is sadly what most people do. They think that just learning more words, like "strawberries" and "yummy", will make them fluent. But they would serve themselves much better by focusing on the core essence of the language and not moving beyond there until it's mastered.

The more comfortable you make your essential vocabulary, the more easily you'll be able to learn thousands more words and express yourself fluently in Spanish.

Don't Get Distracted

I have to emphasize this warning: It's essential that we stick with this core vocabulary for a while, even when it hurts.

The temptation is strong. Sometimes it's a lot easier to learn a new word instead of finding a way to describe something with your current vocabulary.

But in order to master the language, it's critical that we fully conquer all the most frequent vocabulary.

You should especially plan to practice sticking to these essentials while in your "Spanish zone".

Recall Lesson 7, where we started training ourselves to think exclusively in

Spanish, for example by using words like "esta cosa" instead of more specific nouns.

You can also use "hacer" instead of most verbs, and "así" instead of most adjectives or adverbs.

Instead of saying "I don't really plan to play many sports", you can say "No voy a hacer muchas cosas de esas." It conveys the same meaning, though in a more abstract way.

Here's what all of this means: If you've made it through the first eight lessons of this course, you've come a long way. In fact, a whole year of classroom Spanish would normally teach very little of what has been taught so far, and you've learned more grammar than some fourth-year Spanish students. Ultimately, you should congratulate yourself for a strong knowledge of how the language works.

Now it's time to move forward with our vocabulary, learning more words in this lesson than we've ever learned before. But even so, don't get distracted with outside vocabulary! There will be time to explore later, but for now, we'll continue focusing on the most frequent words.

FOCUS ON LOCATION

Meanwhile, you don't want your brain to become a junk heap of disorganized information. As you learn more and more Spanish, you must keep all the vocabulary and phrases clearly organized in your head.

There's a method to this, and you're about to learn it.

So before we learn any more words, I'm going to prove that even now, you do NOT have a horrible, disorganized memory. You actually have a phenomenally organized mind. You just have to use it the way it wants to be used.

Let's see how amazing your brain is, and how you can use it to its fullest potential, not only for Spanish vocabulary but for any information you want to learn.

"Rolling in the deep kitchen sink", or "how to lose everything you own"

The following story is not true.

Last Tuesday morning I woke up late, surprised to see the sun shining in my window. I panicked and looked at my phone. It wouldn't turn on. When I flipped open my computer to check the time, I saw that it was 8:30; I had slept in by over 3 hours. Apparently, my phone had died during the night so the alarm never went off.

Oops.

My calendar told me that I had a meeting at 9:00 at a nearby coffee shop. I plugged in my phone, hoping it would charge quickly enough to give me time to request an Uber. Meanwhile, I ran to the kitchen to prepare some breakfast.

I'm such an addict that I always have to have a cup of coffee, even before leaving the house to join a friend for more caffeine. (Otherwise, I'm a complete zombie when I meet them.) So my mission was clear: I was about to see how quickly I could make coffee and fry eggs at the same time. What could possibly go wrong?

First I went to the kitchen sink and fished around for a coffee filter. I found one under a pile of spoons and forks, shook the dust off of it, and dropped it in the coffee maker.

Then I dug to the bottom of the sink and scooped out a handful of coffee beans with my left hand (scraping my finger slightly on a knife). I dropped the beans into the grinder and then ran to the bedroom to check on my phone.

It was just then booting up. After waiting a few seconds I sent out an Uber request, then rushed back to the kitchen to fry some eggs.

Fortunately, I had used the frying pan recently and found it near the top of the sink. A stick of butter happened to be just underneath it.

But eggs were a little harder to come by… at least, unbroken eggs were. Raw egg and shell pieces were scattered all throughout the sink, not really usable.

Eventually, I found three non-cracked specimens rolling around under an upside-down saucepan in a hard-to-reach corner.

I quickly fried them up, then wolfed down the result while clawing around in the sink for my hat. After hastily washing the frying pan in the bathroom, I tossed it and everything else back into the kitchen sink on the way out the door.

As I stepped out I saw my Uber arriving. But unfortunately, when I turned around to lock the house, I realized that I'd forgotten something. I shouted to my driver that I'd be right back, then flew back inside to dig desperately around in the kitchen sink for my keys.

end of fictional story

Obviously, I don't really keep everything I own in the kitchen sink.

It turns out that cabinets, shelves, and drawers are a good idea. It's much easier to find things if we know where they are.

This demonstrates how powerful the human mind is. I bet that if I mention just about any household item to you, you'll know where it is normally kept in your house.

Spoons? In the silverware drawer, next to the forks.

Mugs? In the cabinet to the right of the kitchen sink.

Carrots? In a drawer in the refrigerator.

Scissors? In the bedroom, on the left side of the desk.

The notion of keeping everything we own in a single pile (or in the kitchen sink) is completely ridiculous.

But here's a serious question: Why do we do that with the things that we learn?

Why do we dump hundreds of facts, vocabulary words, and names into our heads, all in one pile… and then expect to find the right piece of information when we need it?

Hmm. If only there was a process to organize your brain the way that your house is organized…

The Mental Matrix: Hack into your brain's universe.

Your mind is incredible. If it can store information about most of the locations in your house, it can do basically anything.

Try to imagine the different pieces of information in your house that you know. Assuming there are 10 rooms, and then each of those rooms has a few shelves and several pieces of furniture, the math says that you have hundreds of locations already stored in your memory, and you can access them with your mind pretty quickly.

But this can apply to more houses as well. Think back to any other house you've lived in. If you lived in just one other house for a significant amount of time, that's already hundreds of more facts stored.

It doesn't end there. You also probably know your way around the houses of a few friends, as well as several dozen public buildings such as libraries, schools, and restaurants. Then there are larger outdoor areas such as parks (with details like benches and trees), streets you've driven down or walked along, and train stations. Not to mention fictional locations such as the workspace from The Office or Marty's house from Back to the Future.

If you can shut your eyes and imagine yourself walking around some of these places, it's clear that the universe in your head is incredibly vast.

It doesn't end there. I'm betting that you have some sort of memory attached to almost any of these locations, even down to some of the tiny information. When I think of the front left burner of my sister's stove, I remember that that's where I burned a pot of lentil soup. When I think of a particular platform in a subway station in Buenos Aires, I remember giving directions to someone who walked by.

These memories can be thought of as "facts". As you can see, we have millions of these facts stored in our heads. The steps for remembering them are simple: Just think of a particular location, and the memory comes back.

So you actually have an incredible memory! That's millions of pieces of information already in your brain, sorted and filed by location for easy access.

When you have trouble remembering something, it's often because you don't associate that thing with a unique location. If you have a location for something, you can remember it much more easily.

Maybe you lose your keys all the time. But that's not a problem with your memory; that's just because your keys don't have a consistent place where you can always find them. There are always dozens of places they could possibly be. But you never have trouble finding them if they're in the right pocket, in the proper drawer, or hanging on the hook where they belong.

Facts and memories are just like your keys. You'll lose them if you don't put them in a place that's easy to find.

Let's take this a step further. Maybe you think it's smart to leave your keys close to other things that you need when you go out of the house. You might hang them near your coat and hat, or perhaps you leave them on a table next to your wallet and cell phone.

That's a great habit. You're categorizing your keys with other items that you carry around. This is kind of like keeping your forks with the knives and spoons: You're categorizing them with the silverware.

You habitually know that it's good to have an organized system: Forks/knives/spoons the silverware drawer, keys/wallet/phone on the nightstand,

and clothing in the bedroom closet. Ultimately, hundreds of household items are sorted by category.

Let's go back to the subject of Spanish vocabulary.

Pretty soon we'll be learning hundreds of words. We can't afford to dump them all in the kitchen sink.

This whole book is designed as a manual to help you build a geographic world of vocabulary. A world where no word gets lost. A world so big that Joel can live in it and fly around it all day, picking different Spanish words based on what he needs at the time.

These words are intentionally placed in very specific locations for a carefully planned reason.

During this lesson, as well as the rest of the book, really try to immerse yourself. Make yourself truly at home in Joel's world. Get know it as well as you know your own house.

Lesson 3 Vocabulary: Plaza (The Neighborhood Marketplace)

All throughout this lesson, we're going to revisit most of the locations that we used in Lesson 1, but we'll be adding more details to them.

Before we start, I strongly suggest that you do a little exercise. We need to ensure that you can remember your way around Joel's world just like you can remember your own house.

Look at the list of places that I've put below. For each one, close your eyes and mentally explore it. Make sure you can remember the words that belong to each area.

- amusement park: paths (1 word) and power lines (1 word)
- amusement park: carousel (2 words)
- amusement park: water slide (2 words)
- countryside: sheep pastures (5 words)
- countryside: tree scene (3 words)
- countryside: swamp (1 word)
- marketplace (1 word)

Flip through the Lesson 1 images and make sure each word is concretely stored in its location.

Meanwhile, for this lesson, make sure to focus and visualize everything even better than you did in Lesson 1. Immerse yourself in the environments until they feel almost as real as your own world.

Con Man (connectors)

When Joel returns to the amusement park today, he is resolved to have more fun than last time.

In Lesson 1, you might have noticed that Joel spent a lot of time between the rides, but he didn't seem to do much on the rides themselves. When gave the pandas a tour of the park, using the word y between each ride, he wasn't actually riding anything. It was the same with the word 'que.' That was when he was between rides, choosing which one to go on.

The only ride that he actually rode on was the carousel, the one he doesn't like. There, he got stuck 'en' (at) the ride, went away de (from) it as quickly as possible, flew a (to) the water slide, and cleaned the horse hair off his body by sitting in the water 'por' (next to) the slide for a while.

The four words 'en,' de, a, and 'por' are in a special category. Instead of being between the rides, they occur at the rides themselves, usually when Joel is sitting on the rides. Grammatically speaking, these words are considered prepositions. These words happen at the rides, usually when you're sitting down, and "sit" sounds similar to the stressed syllable of the word preposition.

CONFIDENT INTERVIEWS

Vocabulary List

- Soy el mejor para el cargo – I'm the Best Guy for the Job
- proceso de captación de talento – Talent recruitment process
- Directora de Recursos Humanos – Director of Human Resources
- Inmediatamente comenzaremos con la entrevista – Immediately begin with the interview
- parece estar entusiasmado – You look enthusiastic
- leyendo tus documentos – I'm reading your documents
- ¿qué te ha traído hoy a esta empresa? – What has brought you to this company today?
- Existen muchas oportunidades para trabajadores de mi perfil en el mercado – there are currently many existing opportunities for workers of my profile
- Esta empresa tiene una filosofía, una misión y una visión que se asemejan a lo que yo quiero para mi carrera – This company has a philosophy, a mission and a vision that are extremely similar to what I want for my career
- Aportar mucho – Bring a lot
- Me gusta tu actitud – I love your attitude
- te sientes a gusto – Feel comfortable
- ¿qué experiencia tienes...? – What experience do you have...?
- Qué tipo de proyectos has llevado a cabo – What type of projects have you undertaken
- Me irá muy bien aquí si soy contratado – I will have a great time here if I'm hired
- He trabajado para una gran variedad de empresas Fortune 500 – I've worked for a large number of Fortune 500 companies
- La última empresa para la cual trabajé – The last company I worked for was
- Industria bancaria – Banking industry
- Cumpliendo con los objetivos. Me fui en busca de un nuevo reto – While fulfilling objectives. I left in search of a new challenge

449

- La recomendación de mis superiores – The recommendation from my superiors
- Muy reconocida – World-famous
- ¿En qué ambiente de trabajo te desempeñas mejor? – In what work environment do you perform best?
- Me gusta que me dejen hacer lo mío – I like to be left to do what I know
- Instrucciones iniciales – Initial instructions
- Luego me dejen trabajar sin problema – Then be left to work without issues
- Soy bueno trabajando en equipo – I'm good at working in team
- Solo en mi cubículo – Alone in my cubicle
- Acá trabajamos en equipo – Here we work in teams
- ¿Sería un problema para ti acostumbrarte a eso? – Would it be a problem for you to get used to that?
- Estoy abierto a nuevas posibilidades y métodos – I'm open to new possibilities and methods
- Asociarse a nuestro Departamento de Mercadeo – Work alongside our marketing department
- Podrías incrementar los resultados logrados en ingresos – You could enhance our results in sales revenue
- He trabajado a fondo – I've worked in depth
- podríamos hacer una campaña de mercadeo por correo electrónico – We could do an email marketing campaign
- Me gustaría que acordáramos los términos de tu contrato y procediéramos a la firma del mismo – I would like us to arrange your contract terms and sign it
- Comenzar a trabajar apenas pueda – Start working as soon as I can
- ¡Gracias por la oportunidad, Mary! – Thanks for the opportunity, Mary!

Spanish

– **Mary:** Bienvenido a nuestro proceso de captación de talento, señor… ¡Daniel González! Mi nombre es Mary Pérez y soy la directora de Recursos Humanos en esta empresa. Puede sentarse, ya que inmediatamente comenzaremos con la entrevista.

– **Daniel:** ¡Hola, Mary! Bueno, me parece excelente. Estoy muy emocionado por esto, de verdad.

– **Mary:** Sí, parece estar entusiasmado, y eso siempre es bueno. De acuerdo, comencemos ya, ahora que estoy leyendo tus documentos. ¿Qué te ha traído hoy a esta empresa?

– **Daniel:** Pues, la verdad es que actualmente existen muchas oportunidades para trabajadores de mi perfil en el mercado de la tecnología de información, pero esta empresa tiene una filosofía, una misión y una visión que se asemejan a lo que yo quiero para mi carrera. Pienso que podría aportar mucho a esta ambiciosa compañía.

– **Mary:** Vaya, me gusta tu actitud. Bueno, me encanta que te sientas a gusto aquí en esta empresa. ¿Qué experiencia tienes como diseñador de UX y qué tipo de proyectos has llevado a cabo antes de llegar aquí?

– **Daniel:** Sí, creo que me irá muy bien aquí si soy contratado. En cuanto a mi experiencia, he trabajado para una gran variedad de empresas Fortune 500, como podrá ver en mi currículo. La última empresa para la cual trabajé estaba en la industria bancaria y estuve con ellos por dos años, cumpliendo con los objetivos. Me fui en busca de un nuevo reto, pero aquí puede ver la recomendación de mis superiores. También he diseñado numerosos sitios web, incluyendo el de una empresa manufacturera de automóviles muy reconocida.

– **Mary:** Impresionante, parece que todos tus empleadores anteriores te recomiendan para diferentes cargos, incluso fuera del campo del diseño. Eso es muy buena señal. ¿En qué ambiente de trabajo te desempeñas mejor?

– **Daniel:** Buena pregunta. La verdad es que me gusta que me dejen hacer lo mío, que me den instrucciones iniciales y luego me dejen trabajar sin problema. Soy bueno trabajando en equipo, pero soy aún mejor cuando me dejan solo en mi cubículo y con completa concentración.

– **Mary:** Bueno, acá trabajamos en equipo prácticamente todo el tiempo, es algo de nuestra filosofía. ¿Sería un problema para ti acostumbrarte a eso?

– **Daniel:** No, no creo. Estoy abierto a nuevas posibilidades y métodos. No quiero ir en contra de lo que ustedes hacen acá, ¡para nada!

– **Mary:** Perfecto, me gusta esa actitud. Bueno, y estoy viendo acá que tienes experiencia en ventas. ¿Podrías contarme sobre eso? Tenemos un tiempo buscando a alguien con tu perfil para asociarse a nuestro Departamento de Mercadeo. Trabajando junto a ellos podrías incrementar los resultados logrados en ingresos por ventas de nuestros productos digitales y suscripciones. Sería lo ideal.

– **Daniel:** He trabajado a fondo con suscripciones y modelos de monetización digital antes; no sería un problema para mí. Podríamos hacer una campaña de mercadeo por correo electrónico que probablemente generaría grandes ingresos.

– **Mary:** Vaya, Daniel, parece que sabes exactamente qué es lo que necesitamos y buscamos en este momento. ¿Puedes venir mañana? Me gustaría que acordáramos los términos de tu contrato y procediéramos a la firma del mismo, si estás interesado, una vez hayamos terminado. ¿Está Bien?

– **Daniel:** Me parece genial, vendré mañana y traeré un bolígrafo para firmar ese contrato. Sí sería bueno acordar los términos y comenzar a trabajar apenas pueda. ¡Gracias por la oportunidad, Mary!

English

– **Mary:** Welcome to our talent recruitment process, Mister... Daniel Gonzalez! My name is Mary Perez, and I'm the director of Human Resources at this company. You can sit, as we will immediately begin with the interview.

– **Daniel:** Hello Mary! Well, that seems excellent. I'm very excited about this, to be honest.

– **Mary:** Yes, you look enthusiastic, and that is always good. All right, let's begin now since I'm reading your documents. What has brought you to this company today?

- **Daniel:** Well, the truth is that there are currently many existing opportunities for workers of my profile in the information technology market, but this company has a philosophy, a mission and a vision that are extremely similar to what I want for my career. I believe I could bring a lot to this ambitious company.

- **Mary:** Wow, I love your attitude. Good, I love how you feel comfortable here at this company. What experience do you have as a UX designer, and what type of projects have you undertaken before arriving here?

- **Daniel:** Yes, I believe I will have a great time here if I'm hired. As for the experience, I've worked for a large number of Fortune 500 companies, as you can see on my resume. The last company I worked for was in the banking industry, and I was with them for two years while fulfilling objectives. I left in search of a new challenge, but here you can see the recommendation from my superiors. I've also designed numerous websites, including one for a world-famous auto manufacturing company.

- **Mary:** Impressive, it seems that all of your previous employers recommend you for various roles, including outside of the designer field. That is a very good sign. In what work environment do you perform best?

- **Daniel:** Good question. The truth is that I like to be left to do what I know, that I receive initial instructions and then be left to work without issues. I'm good at working in teams, but I'm even better when I'm left alone in my cubicle and with absolute concentration.

- **Mary:** Well, here we work in teams practically all the time, as it is something within our philosophy. Would it be a problem for you to get used to that?

- **Daniel:** No, I don't think so. I'm open to new possibilities and methods. I don't want to go against how you do things here, not at all!

- **Mary:** Perfect, I like that attitude. Okay, and I'm seeing here that you have experience in sales. Can you tell me more about that? We've been looking for someone with your profile to work alongside our marketing department for a while. Working within them, you could enhance our results in sales revenue through our digital products and subscriptions. It would be the most ideal approach.

- **Daniel:** I've worked in depth with subscriptions and digital monetization models before; it wouldn't be a real problem for me. We could do an email marketing campaign that would probably generate great revenue.

- **Mary:** Wow, Daniel, it seems that you know exactly what it is that we need and what we're seeking at this moment. Could you return tomorrow? I would like us to arrange your contract terms and sign them if you're interested once we're finished. Good?

- **Daniel:** It sounds great, I will come tomorrow and bring a pen so that I can sign that contract. It would be great to arrange the terms and start working as soon as I can. Thanks for the opportunity, Mary!

CASTILIAN VERSUS LATIN AMERICAN SPANISH

Is this book suitable for learning both Castilian verbs and Latin American verbs?

The answer to this is Yes, and for two main reasons:

1) First of all, the difference between Castilian and Latin American verb usage is only minor and tends to be centered on the use and translation of the 'you' form of the verb.
2) Verb usage is not uniform in all Latin American countries anyway. For example, the rules of Mexico differ from those of Argentina.

Below, you will find an explanation of how its shape differs between Spain, Latin America and Argentina.

If, as yet, you don't have much knowledge of Spanish verbs—Castilian or otherwise—you may find this explanation rather difficult to understand.

Don't worry! It will all fall into place as you work your way through the book.

Most Central and South American Countries

1) In both Spain and most South/Central American countries, the informal, 2nd Person Singular form is "tú"
2) However, outside Spain, the 2nd Person Plural – in other words the "vosotros/vosotras" form – is not used at all, the "ustedes" (3rd Person Plural) form being used instead

In other words, in Spain you'd say:

- Vosotros habláis español – you (informal, plural) speak Spanish Whereas, in most Central or South American countries you'd say:
- Ustedes hablan español

Argentina

In Argentina, unlike Spain and other Central and South American countries, the Personal Pronoun tú is not used, being replaced by the Personal Pronoun *vos*.

The Present Simple form of *vos* is formed by chopping off the final r of the Infinitive, replacing it with an *s*, and adding an accent to the final syllable, to make:

- Hablás
- Comés
- Vivís

This means that, whereas in Spain and many other Latin American countries you'd say:

- Tú hablas español – you speak Spanish

In Argentina you would say:

- Vos hablás español

The only irregular vos form you'll encounter in the Present Tense is with the verb 'ser' (to be) where, instead of the Castilian 'eres,' you would say 'sos.' In other tenses, such as the Past, Future, Conditional, Subjunctive etc., the Argentinian 'vos' form is conjugated in exactly the same way as the Castilian 'tú' form. However, to form the Argentinian Imperative mood, you need to remove the d from the 'vosotros' Imperative form and add an accent, as in: *hablad* (vosotros) ... *hablá* (vos).

Practice Makes Perfect

I hope that, one day, you'll come and visit this country and put all you've learned into practice, for Spain is a rich and varied land, with something to appeal to all tastes... But, for now, it's time to concentrate on learning those Spanish verbs.

Are you ready to take the Spanish Verb Perfect Challenge? Then jump on in and enjoy!

Step 1: Ready to Take the Plunge?

First and foremost, you must get the hang of Personal Pronouns and Reflexive Pronouns.

You also need to understand – though not necessarily learn at this point – the various Spanish verbs for to be and to have. These verbs are irregular, but we'll take a look at them now for two reasons:

1) They play a part in conjugating certain tenses of both regular and irregular verbs.
2) There are two different ways of translating both to be (ser, estar) and to have (haber, tener), and it's best to grasp these differences as early as possible.

We'll also take a look at the useful Spanish word 'hay', which in English can be there is or there are.

YOUR GOALS FOR STEP 1

1. Read through at your own pace.
2. Pop along to the How to Use Your Flash Cards section, and download appropriate flash cards.
3. Learn Personal/Subject Pronouns with the help of flashcards.
4. Get the hang of Reflexive Verbs.
5. Memorize Reflexive Pronouns with the help of flashcards.
6. Grasp when to use SER and when to use ESTAR.
7. Assimilate when to use HABER and when to use TENER.
8. Learn the Spanish word HAY – THERE IS or THERE ARE.

FLASH CARDS FOR STEP 1

1. Personal Pronouns (zip folder 1, pronouns plus passive document).
2. Reflexive Pronouns (zip folder 1, pronouns plus passive document).

Let's kick off with Personal Pronouns...

What Are Personal Pronouns?

Do you know what Personal Pronouns are? They're also known as Subject Pronouns, and they're words like I, you, he, she, we, they. In other words, you use them to replace nouns, and you need to learn them in order to conjugate verbs. Here's a list of Spanish Personal Pronouns:

Singular Pronouns

- To I
- Tú .... you (familiar/informal form)
- Él .... he
- Ella .... she
- Usted ..... you (polite/formal form)

Plural Pronouns

- Nosotros... we (used with an all-male or mixed-gender group of people) nosotras... we (used with an all-female group of people)
- Vosotros... you (familiar/informal form and used with an all-male or mixed-gender group)
- Vosotras... you (familiar/informal form used when addressing females) ellos... they (when referring to an all-male or mixed-gender group) ellas... they (feminine, used when referring to an all-female group) ustedes... you (polite/formal form, used for all-male, all-female, or mixed-gender groups)

Clarifying the Use of Spanish Personal Pronouns

As you can see, Spanish Personal Pronouns are a little more complex than English ones. Some have masculine and feminine forms, and there are a variety of ways of saying the English you. Let's take a closer look at them ...

Nosotros/Nosotras

In other words, there are two ways of saying we in Spanish: nosotros – we (masculine or mixed group) nosotras – we (purely female group)

Ellos/Ellas

The same rule applies to the Spanish equivalent of 'they':

Ellos – they (when referring to a masculine or mixed group) ellas – they (when referring to an entirely female group)

You

Let's take a look at the various ways of saying you in Spanish.

Firstly, the Spanish language has polite (or formal) and familiar (or informal) forms of the word you:

1) **Usted** is the polite (singular) form, and would be used when addressing a male or female who is a stranger/older person/employer etc., in order to show a certain amount of respect;

2) **Tú** is the familiar (singular) form, and would be used when talking to a male or female who is a family member/friend/work companion/younger person, etc.

These two ways of saying you also have their plural forms: 1) ustedes is the plural form of usted, and should be used when addressing more than one person to whom you should show respect, irrespective of their gender;

The plural form of tú has both masculine and feminine versions – vosotros (when addressing a familiar, all-male or mixed group), and vosotras (when addressing a familiar, all-female group).

To recap on the Spanish equivalents of YOU:

1. one friend/family member, etc. – tú
2. one stranger/older person, etc. – usted
3. more than one friend/family member – vosotros/vosotras 4) more than one stranger/older person – ustedes

NOTE: These rules differ slightly in Central and South American countries … Check out the explanation provided in the Introduction.

The role of personal pronouns in declining Spanish verbs further on in this book, you'll see that most Spanish verb tenses are conjugated with six different endings, and they'll be laid out in the following way:

Singular

- Yo + verb
- Tú + verb
- Él/Ella/Usted + verb

Plural

- Nosotros/Nosotras + verb

- Vosotros/Vosotras + verb
- Ellos/Ellas/Ustedes + verb

The first three in the list (yo, tú, él/ella/usted) are all singular forms of the verb, and the last three (nosotros/nosotras, vosotros/vosotras, ellos/ellas/ustedes) are all plural forms.

They're arranged in this way because the third person singular will normally be the same when used with he, she or you (polite), and the third person plural the same for they or you (polite).

Difference in Spanish and English Personal Pronoun Usage

The Personal Pronoun can be added before the verb in order to clarify who it is you're talking about. For example, you may need to include it when using the third person singular, or the third person plural, for the same verb endings could apply to he/she/you and they/you.

Another reason for including the Personal Pronoun is for emphasis.

Reflexive Verbs and Pronouns

I wash myself, José talks to himself, They look at themselves in the mirror.

What do the above phrases have in common?

1) They all have pronouns ending in self/selves.
2) The subject/s and object/s of the verb refer to the same person.
3) The action reflects back on the subject.

In other words, these are Reflexive Verbs.

In Spanish, Reflexive Verbs are accompanied by the following Reflexive Pronouns (the related Personal Pronoun is placed alongside in brackets):

Singular Reflexive Pronouns

- Me (yo)
- Te (tú)
- Se (él, ella, usted)

Plural Reflexive Pronouns

- Nos (nosotros, nosotras)
- Vos (vosotros, vosotras)
- Se (ellos, ellas, ustedes)

When conjugating a Reflexive Verb, you normally place the Reflexive Pronoun after the Personal Pronoun and before the verb. For example:

- Él se habla
- He talks to himself.

- José se habla.
- José talks to himself.

You'll also come across other tenses where the Reflexive Pronoun is placed at the verb ending, but you'll learn about these later. Also, some Spanish verbs exist solely or frequently in the Reflexive form.

Understand the Spanish Verbs for TO BE

These are both irregular, and are: *estar / ser*

The reason we're introducing them at this point, is because *estar* is used as an auxiliary verb when declining the Present Continuous Tense, and *ser* is used as an auxiliary verb in the Passive Voice.

Very basically, *estar* tends to be used with temporary states or locations. And, *ser* tends to be used when identifying permanent or lasting attributes or situations.

When to Use ESTAR

You'll be learning this verb later on. For the time being, you just need to be aware that estar would be used:

1) To describe an ongoing action (i.e. in the Present Continuous Tense), e.g.:

- Estoy estudiando español.
- I'm studying Spanish.

2) To describe location, emotion, and condition, e.g.:

- Mi hermana está en Inglaterra, y está triste porque está enferma.

461

- My sister is in England, and she's sad because she's ill.

When to Use SER

Again, you'll learn ser later in the book. For now, it's sufficient to understand that you'd use it in the following situations:

1) With the Passive Voice, e.g.

- El vino es bebido en España.
- Wine is drunk in Spain.

2) Permanent descriptions of a person, e.g.

- Es Victoria, y es alta y rubia.
- She is Victoria, and she is tall and blond

3) When describing a person's occupation, e.g.

- Mi madre es maestra.
- My mother is a teacher.

4) Days, dates, and hours, e.g.

- Hoy es viernes, y es la una.
- Today is Friday, and it's one o'clock.

DAYS, MONTHS & SEASONS - DAYS OF THE WEEK, MONTHS OF THE YEAR AND THE SEASONS

Días, meses y estaciones

- **Jane:** Hola Ben, la escuela terminará el "lunes" de la semana que viene. Estoy tan feliz.
- **Jane:** Hey Ben, school will be over next "Monday". I'm so happy.

- **Ben:** Sí, lo sé. Esta es la primera vez que las vacaciones empiezan en "junio".
- **Ben:** I know right. This is actually the first time school will be starting vacation in "June."

- **Jane:** Eso es cierto. He oído que nos podemos ir el "viernes" de esta semana para tener suficientes vacaciones de "primavera" antes de volver a empezar durante el "invierno".
- **Jane:** That's true. I heard we are even free to leave this "Friday," so that we have enough "Spring" break before coming back for "Winter."

- **Ben:** ¿Qué importa eso? Tengo clases de "verano" a partir del primer "martes" de "julio".
- **Ben:** What does it even matter? I have "summer" classes starting on the first "Tuesday" in "July."

- **Jane:** Ayyy... Eso significa que probablemente te perderás el concierto de Ariana Grande en "agosto".

– **Jane:** Aww… So that means you'll probably miss the Ariana Grande concert coming up in "August."

– **Ben:** Es una pena. Todo lo que sé es que nunca me perdería el estreno de El Rey León el 2 de "octubre" este "otoño".

– **Ben:** It's such a shame. All I know is that I won't miss the 2nd "October" premiere of The Lion King this "Fall" for anything.

– **Jane:** ¿Qué tiene de especial esa película? Preferiría pasar el "otoño" haciendo otra cosa.

– **Jane:** What's so special about that movie? I'd rather spend the "Autumn" doing something else.

– **Ben:** Por lo menos, la escuela de "verano" estará de vacaciones el 4 de "Julio", el día de la Independencia. ¿Cuáles son tus planes?

– **Ben:** At least "summer" school will be on holiday on 4th "July", Independence Day. What are your plans?

– **Jane:** Planeo ir a ver un partido de tenis con mi papá. Sólo espero que Serena Williams gané después de haber perdido el título en "marzo" del año pasado.

– **Jane:** I plan to go to see a tennis game with my Dad. I just hope Serena Williams wins after losing the title last "March."

– **Ben:** Guao. Disfruta del partido y no te olvides de ponerme al día. Creo que el partido es un "miércoles", ¿verdad?

– **Ben:** Wow. Enjoy the game and don't forget to give me updates. I think the game is on a "Wednesday," right?

– **Jane:** No, en realidad es un "sábado".

- **Jane:** Nope, it's actually on a "Saturday."

- **Ben:** ¡Oh, Dios mío! Estas clases de "verano" van a ser muy aburridas. ¡Reza por mí, Jane!
- **Ben:** Oh my God! These "summer" classes are going to be so boring. Pray for me, Jane!

- **Jane:** (Risas) No te preocupes, estaré en la ciudad hasta finales de "junio". Te hare compañía.
- **Jane:** (chuckles) Don't worry, I'll still be in town till the end of "June." I'll keep you company.

- **Ben:** ¿En serio? Eso significaría mucho para mí. Eres una buena amiga. Recuérdame que te compré un regalo en Best Buy el "jueves".
- **Ben:** Really? That would mean the world to me. You're such a good friend. Remind me to give you a treat at Best Buy on "Thursday."

Dining Room - Things you will find in a dining room

Comedor

- **James:** Hola John, ¡estoy aquí para ver tu nuevo comedor!
- **James:** Hello John, I am here to see your new dining room!

- **John:** Sí, ¡por favor, pasa!
- **John:** Yes, please come in!

- **James:** Me gusta la mesa azul nueva.
- **James:** I like the new blue table.

— **John:** Gracias, James, compré la mesa porque combinaba con las sillas que me gustaron.
— **John:** Thank you, James, I bought the table as it matched the chairs I liked.

— **James:** Sí, veo que combinan, ¿Cuántas personas caben en la mesa?
— **James:** I can see they do match. How many people can fit around the table?

— **John:** 6 personas. Sin embargo, podemos hacer la mesa más grande cuando tengamos una cena con invitados, ¡y caben hasta diez personas!
— **John:** 6 people. However, we can make the table bigger when we have a dinner party and fit up to 10 people!

— **James:** ¿Estás planeando tener una cena con invitados pronto?
— **James:** Are you planning to have a dinner party soon?

— **John:** ¡Sí! Pero no tengo todo lo que necesito. El comedor aún no está listo.
— **John:** Yes! But I don't have everything I need. The dining room isn't finished.

— **James:** ¡Espero con ansias esa cena con invitados! ¿Qué quieres comprar para el comedor?
— **James:** I am looking forward to the dinner party! What do you want to buy for the dining room?

—

— **John:** La mesa es cara, así que quiero comprar unos manteles para mantenerla limpia.
— **John:** The table is expensive, so I want to buy placemats to keep the table clean.

— **James:** ¡Esa es una gran idea! ¿Dónde guardas los platos y los cubiertos?
— **James:** That's a great idea! Where do you hide your plates and cutlery?

- **John:** Los guardo en la alacena. No tengo suficientes cubiertos, así que tengo que comprar algunos más.
- **John:** I keep them in the cupboard. I don't have enough cutlery, so I need to buy some more.

- **James:** Está bien, ¿qué cubiertos te faltan?
- **James:** Okay, what cutlery is missing?

- **John:** Necesito 3 cucharas más, dos tenedores y un cuchillo.
- **John:** I need three more spoons, two forks and one knife.

- **James:** Sí, ¡no puedes tener una cena sin ellos!
- **James:** Yes, you can't have a dinner party without those!

- **John:** ¡Sí James! ¡Tienes razón! ¿Crees que necesito comprar nuevos platos?
- **John:** Yes James! You are right! Do you think I need to buy new plates?

- **James:** No, ¿para qué necesitas nuevos platos?
- **James:** No, why do you need new plates?
- **John:** Estos platos son rosas. Quiero unos azules para que combinen con la mesa y las sillas.
- **John:** These plates are pink. I want blue ones to match the table and chairs.

- **James:** Sí, sería una buena idea. Tengo que irme a casa ahora, aunque espero con ansias esa cena con invitados. Hasta luego John.
- **James:** Yes, that would be a good idea. I need to go home now, but I am looking forward to the dinner party. Bye, John.

- **John:** Gracias. Te veré pronto en la cena. Hasta luego James.
- **John:** Thank you. I will see you soon at the dinner party. Bye, James.

REGULAR -ARVERBS IN THE PRESENT

Vocabulario nuevo / New Vocabulary

- Cubano – Cuban
- Salvadoreño – Salvadoran
- Venezolano – Venezuelan
- Paraguayo – Paraguayan
- Dominicano – Dominican
- Hondureño – Honduran
- Colombiano – Colombian
- Argentino – Argentine
- Puertorriqueño – Puerto Rican
- Nicaragüense – Nicaraguan
- Ecuatoriano – Ecuadorian
- Uruguayo – Uruguayan
- Norteamericano (North) – American
- Costarricense – Costa
- Peruano – Peruvian
- Español - Spanish
- Mexicano – Mexican
- Panameño – Panamanian
- Boliviano – Bolivian
- Ecuatoguineano – Equatoguinean
- Guatemalteco – Guatemalan
- Chileno – Chilean
- El café – Coffee
- El trabajador – Worker
- Hablar – To speak, to
- Comprar – To buy
- Trabajar – To work
- Cocinar – To cook
- Bailar – To dance
- Preparar – To prepare
- Llegar – To arrive
- Indicar – To indicate
- Tomar – To take, to
- Escuchar – To hear
- Estudiar – To study
- Ordenar – To order
- Ayudar – To help
- Viajar – To travel
- Cantar – Tosing
- Dedicar – To dedicate
- Fuerte – Strong
- Tímido – Timid
- Contento – Happy
- Malo – Bad
- Egoísta – Selfish
- Terrible – Terrible
- Famoso – Famous
- Mucho – A lot
- Trabajador – Hard-working
- Fenomenal – Phenomenal
- Formal – Formal
- Muchos – Many
- Hablador – Talkative
- Paciente – Patient
- Informal – Informal
- Poco – Little
- Ideal – Ideal
- Impaciente – Impatient
- Bueno – Good

- Pocos – Few

Conjugating Verbs in Spanish

As you learned in an earlier lesson, the infinitive form of a verb is the form that appears in the dictionary and is a non-conjugated verb form. All Spanish verbs have infinitive forms ending either in -ar, -er, or -ir, so the three kinds of verbs in Spanish are -ar verbs, -er verbs, and -ir verbs.

The infinitive form of the verb has two parts: the stem of the word (which is everything before the ending) and the ending itself (which is either -ar, -er, or-ir). For example, the stem of viajar ("to travel") is viaj-, and the verb's ending is -ar. Once you've identified the stem of a verb, you conjugate the verb by adding the appropriate ending to the stem for the given subject.

Conjugating Regular -ar Verbs in the Present. The present tense endings for regular -ar verbs are -o, -as, -a, -amos, -áis, and-an. The following is an example of a regular -ar verb conjugated in the Present tense.

- Ayudar [to help]
- Yo ayudo
- Nosotras, nosotros ayudamos
- Tú ayudas
- Vosotras, vosotros ayudáis
- Él, ella, usted ayuda
- Ellos, ellas, ustedes ayudan

The verb form *ayudamos*, for example, can mean "We help," "We do help,"

"We are helping," or even—in certain contexts— "We are going to help."

When to Use Subject Pronouns before Verbs

Because the ending of a verb indicates the verb's subject, most often Spanish speakers do not include a subject pronoun before the verb. There are, however, two common cases in which subject pronouns are used. They are often used before verbs in the third-person singular and plural because there can be many possible subjects for these verb forms. *Trabaja mucho*, for example, could mean

"You work a lot" (with the subject being *usted*), or it could be "He works a lot," or "She works a lot." To clarify, then, it's common to include a subject with a third-person form of the verb and say, for example "Usted estudia mucho."

Another time to use a subject pronoun is to emphasize the subject. If, for example, people around you are saying that they don't sing much, and you actually do, it would be appropriate to say *"Yo canto mucho,"* emphasizing "I do sing a lot."

More Agreement of Adjectives with Nouns

Adjective sending in -dor in the masculine singular have four forms, as can be seen with the adjective meaning "talkative": hablador, habladora, habladores, habladoras. Any adjective of nationality that ends in a consonant also has four forms, as seen in the adjective meaning "French": francés, francesa, franceses, francesas. Except for adjectives ending in -o, -dor, and ones ending in consonants that express nationality, almost all other adjectives in Spanish have two forms (e.g., fenomenal, fenomenales; terrible, terribles).

Placement of Adjectives

Adjectives in Spanish almost always follow the noun modified (e.g., las doctoras ideales). To modify a noun with two adjectives, put the adjectives after the noun and put y ("and") between them (e.g., el pianista famoso y egoísta). Bueno and malo can go before or after the modified noun. Before masculine nouns, both of these adjectives drop the-o (e.g., el buen hombre; el mal día). Adjectives of quantity precede the modified noun (e.g., muchos estudiantes; poca agua).

Pronunciation of Consonants

The double-r sound requires that you roll your *r*, creating a sound that does not exist in English. The sound is required when a word has the letter combination *rr*, when a word starts with *r*, and after the letters *l*, *n*, and *s* (e.g., carro, Raúl, alrededor, Enrique, Israel). You make the sound corresponding with rr by having your tongue vibrate up against the center of the roof of your mouth.

At the start of a word or after the letters n and l, you pronounce d as you would in English. After a vowel, the sound of the d should be like the *th* sound of the English word "this." When saying the name David, for example, you should pronounce the first *d* similar to the *d* sound made in English and the second *d* similar to the *th* of "this."

There are variations by country, but in many places, both y and *ll* are pronounced similar to the way y is pronounced in English.

Actividades / Activities

1. Cecilia Ruiz Ramírez es una secretaria ejecutiva en un banco muy importante de su ciudad. Ella está explicando lo que hace generalmente durante la semana. / Cecilia Ruiz Ramírez is an executive secretary at a major bank in her city. She is explaining what she usually does during the week.

a. **Completa las frases siguientes con la conjugación del verbo en presente. / Complete the following sentences with the present tense conjugation of the verb.**

Todos los días [Every day], yo 1. _____ (tomar) café con mi esposo [my husband] Luis. Mi esposo y yo 2. _____ (llegar) al trabajo [at work] a las 8:00 de la mañana. Mis colegas [my colleagues] 3. _____ (llegar) a las 8:50. Nosotros 4. _____ (tomar) café a las 10:50. En mi trabajo, (yo) 5. _____ (escuchar) a muchas personas que [that] 6. _____ (hablar) en las reuniones [meetings]. Yo a veces [at times] 7. _____ (hablar) también [also], pero generalmente [generally] yo 8. _____ (tomar) las notas [notes] importantes de las reuniones. Mi asistente [My assistant] también 9. _____ (tomar) notas en las reuniones. Todos los días, mi asistente y yo 10. _____ (llamar) a muchas personas. También, yo 11. _____ (viajar) a dos simposios [symposiums] cada año [every year]. En casa, mi esposo y yo 12. _____ (preparar) la cena [dinner] juntos [together]. Alberto, mi hijo [son], no 13. _____ (llegar) a cenar [to have dinner] con [with] nosotros porque [because] él 14. _____ (trabajar) muy tarde [late]. Diego, mi otro [other] hijo y sus [his] amigos a veces 15. _____ (llegar) a cenar con nosotros. Ellos 16. _____ (cocinar) el postre [dessert].

b. **De la historia anterior, escribe la forma negativa de los siguientes verbos. / From the previous story, write the negative form of the following verbs.**

1. Mis colegas y yo _____ (tomar) café a las 11:50 de la mañana.

2. Ellos _____ (llegar) a las 7:50 de la mañana.

3. Yo _____ (hablar) nunca [never] en las reuniones.

4. Diego, mi hijo y su profesora _____ (llegar) a comer con nosotros.

c. **Responde a las preguntas de forma afirmativa. / Answer the questions affirmatively.**

1. ¿Bailas mucho? _____

2. ¿Clara y Roberto bailan tango? _____.

3. ¿Estudias en la universidad? _____.

4. ¿Tú y tu [your] familia preparan la cena juntos? _____.

5. ¿Tomas agua todos los días? _____.

6. ¿Isabel compra la comida en el supermercado [supermarket]? _____.

7. ¿Andrea Bocelli a veces canta en español? _____.

8. ¿Cocinas pizza con amigos? _____.

9. ¿Las chicas miran el fútbol [soccer]? _____.

10. ¿Escuchan ustedes música en el carro [car]? _____.

2. Cecilia Ruiz Ramírez está en un simposio esta semana. Ella está impresionada por la organización del simposio. / Cecilia Ruiz Ramírez is at a symposium this week. She is impressed by the organization of the symposium.

a. **Escoge el adjetivo de cantidad correcta. / Choose the correct adjective of quantity.**

1. En la mesa hay _____ (mucho, mucha, muchos, muchas) comida [food].

2. En la recepción [reception desk] hay _____ (mucho, mucha, muchos, muchas) programas [programs] del simposio.

3. En el salón [meeting room] norte hay _____ (poco, poca, pocos, pocas) café.

4. En el salón oeste hay _____ (poco, poca, pocos, pocas) personas.

5. En el salón sur hay _____ (mucho, mucha, muchos, muchas) personas.

6. En la recepción hay _____ (mucho, muchas, muchos, muchas) bebidas [drinks] pero

7. _____ (poco, poca, pocos, pocas) servilletas [napkins].

3. Luis e Cortés Navarro es el dueño de un agencia de viajes. El conoce a muchas personas de distintas nacionalidades. Él está mirando un álbum de fotos y está recordando las nacionalidades de sus amigos y amigas. / Luis Cortés Navarro is the owner of a travel agency. He knows many people of different nationalities. He is looking at a photo album and is remembering his friends' nationalities.

a. **Escoge el adjetivo correcto. / Choose the correct adjective.**

1. Gerardo Martínez es muy _____ (simpático, simpática, simpáticos, simpáticas). Él es de la ciudad [city] de Guadalajara, México. Él es _____ (mexicano, mexicana, mexicanos, mexicanas).

2. Hagen Hoffmeiter y su esposa [wife] Brigitte son de Núremberg. Ellos son
_____

(activo, activa, activos, activas) y son _____ (alemán, alemana, alemanes, alemanas).

3. El Rey [King] Felipe VI es de Madrid y es muy _____ (alto, alta, altos, altas). Su esposa Letizia Ortiz es de Oviedo, Asturias. Ellos son _____ (español, española, españoles, españolas).

4. Pierre Duboises de Dijon y su familia es de Toulouse. Él es _____ (francés, francesa, franceses, francesa). Él es _____ (estudiante, estudiantes) de medicina [medicine].

5. Juan Manuel Ríos es de Buenos Aires. Él y su hermano son _____ (profesor, profesora, profesores, profesoras). Ellos son _____ (argentino, argentina, argentinos, argentinas).

6. La familia Flores Quispees de Lima. Ellos son _____ (peruano, peruana, peruanos, peruanas).

7. Graciela Mercedes Ramírez Villalba es _____ (dentista, dentistas). Ella trabaja en Capiatá. Ella es _____ (paraguayo, paraguaya, paraguayos, paraguayas).

b. Respuestas correctas / Correct Answers

a. 1. tomo

9. toma

2. llegamos

10. llamamos

3. llegan

11. viajo

4. tomamos

12. preparamos

5. escucho

13. llega

6. hablan

14. trabaja

7. hablo

15. llegan

8. tomo

16. cocinan

b.

1. no tomamos

3. no hablo

2. no llegan

4. no llegan

d.

1. mucha

5. muchas

2. muchos

6. muchas

c.

3. poco

1. Sí, bailo mucho.

7. pocas

7. Sí, Andrea Bocelli a veces canta en español.

4. pocas

2. Sí, Clara y Roberto bailan tango.

8. Sí, cocino pizza con amigos.

e.

/ Sí, mis amigos y yo

1. simpático / mexicano

3. Sí, estudio en la universidad. cocinamos pizza.

5. profesores / argentinos

2. activos / alemanes

4. Sí, preparamos la cena juntos.

6. peruanos

9. Sí, las chicas miran el fútbol.

3. alto / españoles

5. Sí, tomo agua todos los días.

7. dentista / paraguaya

10. Sí, escuchamos música en el carro.

4. francés / estudiante

Indefinite Articles and Numbers to 100

Vocabulario nuevo / New Vocabulary

- un – a, an [masculine, singlar]
  una – a, an [feminine, singular]
- unos – some [masculine]
- unas – some [feminine]
- el estudiante [masculine] – student
- la estudiante [feminine] – student
- zapato – shoe
- béisbol – baseball
- kilo – kilo
- deporte – sports
- examen – exam
- cerveza – beer
- águila – eagle
- kilómetro – kilometer
- católico – catholic
- caminar – walk
- extra – extra
- llevar – to wear, to carry
- enseñar – teach
- buscar – to look for
- mirar – to look at
- necesitar – to need
- ¿cuánto? – How much?
- ¿cuántos? ¿cuántas? – How many?
- Cómo? – How?
- para – for

- por favor – please
- cero – zero
- uno – one
- dos – two
- tres – three
- cuatro – four
- cinco – five
- seis – six
- siete – seven
- ocho – eight
- nueve – nine
- diez – ten
- once – eleven
- doce – twelve
- trece – thirteen
- catorce – fourteen
- quince – fifteen
- dieciséis – sixteen
- diecisiete – seventeen
- dieciocho - eighteen
- diecinueve – nineteen
- veinte – twenty
- treinta – thirty
- cuarenta – forty
- cincuenta – fifty
- sesenta – sixty
- setenta – seventy
- ochenta – eighty
- noventa – ninety
- cien – one hundred

GETTING TO KNOW SOMEONE

- My name is…
- Me llamo…
  Meh yah-moh…

- What's your name?
- ¿Cómo te llamas?
  ¿Coh-mohteh yah-mahs?

- Nice to meet you.
- Mucho gusto.
  Moo-chohgoos-toh

- A pleasure.
- Un placer.
  Oonplah-sehr

- Likewise.
- Igualmente.
  Ee-gooahl-mehn-the

- Where are you from?
- ¿De dónde eres?
  ¿De dohn-deh eh-rehs?

- I'm from…
- Soy de…

478

Soy deh…

- How old are you?
- ¿Cuántos años tienes?
  ¿Coo-ahn-tohs a-nyos tee-eh-nehs?

- I'm … years old.
- Tengo… años.
  Tehn-goh … a-nyos

- I am American / an Englishman / an Englishwoman.
- Soy estadounidense / inglés(a).
  Soy ehs-tah-doh-oo-nee-dehn-seh/een-glehs(a)

- What do you do (for work)?
- ¿A qué te dedicas?
  ¿A kehtehdeh-dee-cahs?

- I'm a teacher / student / doctor.
- Soy profesor(a) / estudiante / doctor(a).
  Soy proh-feh-sohr(a)/ehs-too-dee-ahn-teh/doh-tohr(ah)

- What do you like to do in your free time?
- ¿Qué te gusta hacer en tu tiempo libre?
  ¿Kehtehgoos-tah ah-sehrehn too tee-ehm-poh lee-breh?

- I like to watch movies / to read / to dance.
- Me gusta ver películas / leer / bailar.

Meh goos-tahvehr pee-lee-coo-lahs / lehr / bah-ee-lahr

- What's your favorite movie / book / band?
- ¿Cuál es tu película favorita / libro favorito / banda favorita?
  ¿Coo-ahl ehs too pee-lee-coo-lah fah-voh-ree-tah / lee-broh fah-voh-ree-toh / bahn-dah fah-voh-ree-tah?

- My favorite movie / book / band is….
- Mi película favorita / libro favorito / banda favorita es…
  Mee pee-lee-coo-lah fah-voh-ree-tah / lee-broh fah-voh-ree-toh / bahn-dah fah-voh-ree-tahehs…

- What is your take on this?
- ¿Cuál es tu opinión sobre…?
  ¿Coo-ahl ehs too oh-pee-nee-ohn soh-breh…?

- What do you think?
- ¿Qué opinas?
  ¿Keh oh-pee-nahs?

- What are your thoughts on this?
- ¿Qué te parece esto?
  ¿Kehtehpah-reh-cehehs-toh?

- Where do you live?
- ¿Dónde vives?
  ¿Dohn-deh vee-vehs?

- Is it a very large city?
- ¿Es una ciudad grande?
  ¿Ehsoo-nah see-oo-dahdgrahn-deh?

- What city are you from?
- ¿De qué ciudad eres?
  ¿Dehkeh see-oo-dahd eh-rehs?

- Were you born here?
- ¿Naciste aquí?
  ¿Nah-sees-teh ah-kee?

- I'm looking for temporary work.
- Busco un trabajo temporal.
  Boos-cohoontrah-bah-hohtehm-poh-rahl

- I'm the general manager.
- Soy el gerente general.
  Soy ehl heh-rehn-teh heh-neh-rahl

- Do you have a business card?
- ¿Tienes una tarjeta profesional?
  ¿Tee-eh-nehsoo-nah tahr-heh-tahproh-feh-see-oh-nahl?

- What company do you work for?
- ¿En qué compañía trabajas?
  ¿Enkehcohm-pah-nyatrah-bah-hahs?

- I'm an independent contractor.
- Soy un trabajador independiente.
  Soy oontrah-bah-hah-dohreen-deh-pehn-dee-ehn-the

Relationships

- Let's be on first-name terms.
- Tutéame.
  Too-teh-ah-meh

- I'm glad to be your friend.
- Me alegra ser tu amigo/a.
  Meh ah-leh-grah ser too ah-mee-goh/ah

- You're very likable.
- Me caes bien.
  Meh cah-ehs bee-ehn

- You're cool.
- Eres Buena onda.
  Eh-rehs boo-eh-nah ohn-dah

- I think we're going to get along well.
- Creo que vamos a llevarnos bien.
  Creh-oh que vah-mohs ah ee-eh-vahr-nosh bee-ehn

- Will you go with me?
- ¿Me acompañas?
  ¿Meh ah-cohm-pah-nyas?

- Would you like to get dinner with me?
- ¿Quisieras cenar conmigo?
  ¿Kee-see-eh-rahsceh-nahrcohn-mee-goh?

- I want to invite you to…
- Quiero invitarte a…
  Kee-eh-roheen-vee-tahr-teh a…

- What would you prefer to do now?
- ¿Qué prefieres hacer ahora?
  ¿Kehpreh-fee-eh-rehs ah-sehr ah-oh-rah?

- Where do you want to go tonight?
- ¿A dónde vamos esta noche?
  ¿Ah dohn-dehvah-mohsehs-tahnoh-cheh?

- I'll wait for you in an hour.
- Te espero en una hora.
  Tehehs-peh-rohenoo-nah oh-rah

- Where shall I wait for you?
- ¿Dónde te espero?
  ¿Dohn-dehtehehs-peh-roh?

- I can pick you up at 6.
- Puedo pasar a buscarte a las seis.
  Pwe-doh pah-sahr a boos-cahr-teh ah lahsseh-ees

- I'll meet you at the hotel.
- Te encuentro en el hotel.
  Tehehn-coo-ehn-trohehnehl oh-tehl

- You look very pretty.
- Te ves muy bonita.
  Tehvehsmooyboh-nee-tah

- Wow, how handsome!
- ¡Ay, qué guapo!
  ¡Ay, kehwah-poh!

- I had a nice time with you.
- La he pasado muy bien contigo.
  Lah eh pah-sah-doh mooy bee-ehncohn-tee-goh

- I'd like to keep in touch with you.
- Me gustaría seguir en contacto contigo.
  Meh goos-tah-ree-ah seh-geerehncohn-tahc-tohcohn-tee-goh

- Let's not lose touch, okay?
- No perdamos el contacto, ¿eh?
  Noh pehr-dah-mosh ehlcohn-tahc-toh, ¿eh?

- I'll send you a message when I get to the hotel.
- Te mandaré un mensaje cuando llegue al hotel.
  Tehmahn-dah-reh oonmehn-sah-heh coo-ahn-doh ee-eh-gueh al oh-tehl

484

- Give me a call.
- Dame una llamada.
  Da-meh oo-nah ee-ah-mah-dah

- This is my phone number.
- Este es mi número de teléfono.
  Ehs-tehehs mee noo-meh-rohdehteh-leh-foh-noh

- Leave me a voice message.
- Déjame un mensaje de voz.
  Deh-hah-meh oonmehn-sah-jehdehvoss

- Do you use social media?
- ¿Usas alguna red social?
  ¿Usas al-goo-nah rehd soh-see-ahl?

- Would you give me your phone number?
- ¿Me darías tu número de teléfono?
  ¿Meh dah-ree-ahs too nuh-meh-rodehteh-leh-foh-noh?

- I'll call you for a next date.
- Te llamaré para una próxima cita.
  Tehee-ah-mah-reh pah-rah lahproh-xee-mah see-tah

- I can't wait to see you again.
- No puedo esperar a verte otra vez.
  Noh pwe-doh ehs-peh-rarh ah vehr-teh oh-trahvehs

485

- I'll pay for dinner tonight.
- Esta noche yo pagaré la cena.
  Ehs-tahnoh-chehyopah-gah-reh lahceh-nah

- You look amazing.
- Te ves increíble.
  Tehvehseen-creh-ee-bleh

- We can go to my hotel.
- Podemos ir a mi hotel.
  Poh-deh-mohseer ah mee oh-tehl

- I'll pick you up tonight.
- Te recogeré esta noche.
  Teh reh-coh-heh-reh ehs-tahnoh-cheh

- What time does the party start?
- ¿A qué hora empieza la fiesta?
  ¿A keh oh-rah em-pee-ehs-ah la fee-ehs-tah?

- May I hold your hand?
- ¿Puedo tomarte de la mano?
  ¿Pwe-doh toh-mahr-tehdehlahmah-noh?

- I'll give you a ride.
- Te daré un aventón.
  Teh dah-reh oon ah-vehn-tohn

- Are you free tonight?
- ¿Estás libre esta noche?
- ¿Ehs-tahs lee-brehehs-tahnoh-cheh?

- Can I hug you?
- ¿Puedo darte un abrazo?
  ¿Pwe-doh dahr-tehoon ah-brah-soh?

- Shall we split the bill?
- ¿Dividimos la cuenta?
  ¿Dee-vee-dee-mohslah coo-ehn-tah?

Being Polite

- Thank you.
- Gracias.
  Grah-see-ahs

- You're welcome.
- De nada.
  Deh nah-dah

- No problem.
- No hay de qué.
  Noh I dehkeh

- Excuse me. (when sorry)
- Disculpe.

- Dees-cool-peh

- I'm sorry.
- Lo siento.
  Loh see-ehn-toh

- Excuse me. (when being
- Permiso.
  Pehr-mee-soh

Polite

- I'm sorry to interrupt.
- Lamento interrumpir.
  Lah-mehn-toheen-teh-room-peer

- That's a shame.
- Es una lástima.
  Ehsoo-nah lahs-tee-mah

- Good luck!
- ¡Suerte!
  ¡Soo-ehr-the!

- Cheers/Bless you.
- Salud.
  Sah-lood

- Don't worry.
- No te preocupes.
  Noh tehpreh-oh-coo-pehs

- Allow me to introduce you to my friend…
- Quiero presentarte a mi amigo…
  Kee-eh-rohpreh-sehn-tahr-teh ah mee ah-mee-goh

- I'm sorry for your loss.
- Lamento tu pérdida.
  Lah-mehn-toh too pehr-dee-dah

- How can I help you?
- ¿Cómo puedo ayudarte?
  ¿Coh-mohpwe-doh ah-yoo-dahr-the?

- I apologize for being late.
- Perdón por la tardanza.
  Pehr-dohnpohrlahtahr-dahn-sah

- That was my fault.
- Fue mi culpa.
  Foo-eh mee cool-pah

- It won't happen again.
- No volverá a suceder.
  Noh vohl-veh-rah ah soo-seh-dehr
- Having a Conversation It's been a long time.
- Ha pasado mucho tiempo.
  Ah pah-sah-doh moo-choh tee-ehm-poh

- Home, sweet home.
- Hogar, dulce hogar.
  Oh-gahr, dool-ceh oh-gahr

- I'm going to have to have a think about that.
- Tengo que pensarlo.
  Tehn-gohkehpehn-sahr-loh

- Let me think about it.
- Déjame pensarlo.
  Deh-hah-meh pehn-sahr-loh

- Give me a moment.
- Dame un momento.
  Dah-meh oonmoh-mehn-toh

- Now that's a good question.
- Esa es una buena pregunta.
  Eh-sahehsoo-nah boo-eh-nah preh-goon-tah

- I'm not really sure.
- No estoy muy seguro.
  Noh ehs-toy mooyseh-goo-roh

- I don't have a clue.
- No tengo ni idea.
  Noh tehn-goh nee ee-deh-ah

- Who knows.
- Quién sabe.
  Kee-ehnsah-beh

- I don't know for sure.
- No lo sé con seguridad.
  Noh lohsehcohnseh-goo-ree-dahd

- How interesting!
- ¡Qué interesante!
  ¡Keheen-teh-reh-sahn-teh!

- Fantastic!
- ¡Fantástico!
- ¡Fahn-tahs-tee-coh!

- This is fascinating
- Me fascina esto.
  Meh fah-see-nah ehs-toh

- How boring!
- ¡Qué aburrido!
  ¡Keh ah-boo-ree-doh!

- You don't say
- No me digas
  Noh meh dee-gahs

- That's how it is.

- Así es.
  Ah-see ehs

- Isn't that right?
- ¿No es cierto?
  ¿Noh ehs see-ehr-toh?

- Seriously?
- ¿En serio?
  ¿Ehnseh-ree-oh?

- Really?
- ¿De veras?
  ¿Dehveh-rahs?

- In fact…
- De hecho…
  Deh eh-choh…

- By the way…
- A propósito…
  Ah proh-poh-see-toh…

- You are right.
- Tienes razón.
  Tee-eh-nehs rah-sohn

- Certainly.

- Claro que sí.
  Clah-rohkeh see

- Absolutely not.
- En lo absoluto.
- Ehnahb-soh-loo-toh

- It seems fine to me.
- Me parece muy bien.
  Meh pah-reh-cehmooy bee-ehn

- Do tell all.
- Cuéntamelo todo.
  Coo-ehn-tah-meh-lohtoh-doh

- I want to know everything.
- Lo quiero saber todo.
  Lohkee-eh-rohsah-behrtoh-doh

- I think you're mistaken.
- Creo que te equivocas.
  Creh-oh kehteh eh-kee-voh-cahs

- How funny!
- ¡Qué gracioso!
  ¡Kehgrah-see-oh-soh!

- You're exaggerating!

- Estás exagerando.
  Ehs-tahsehx-sah-heh-rahn-doh

- Please be quiet.
- Por favor, haz silencio.
  Pohr fah-vohr, ahs see-lehn-see-oh

- Don't interrupt me while I'm talking.
- No me interrumpas cuando estoy hablando.
  Noh meh een-teh-room-pahs coo-ahn-doh ehs-toy ah-blahn-doh

- Don't be rude.
- No seas grosero.
  Noh seh-ahsgroh-seh-roh

- Could you lower your voice?
- ¿Podrías bajar la voz?
  ¿Poh-dree-ahs bah-hahrlahvohs?

- Don't yell at me.
- No me grites.
  Noh meh gree-tehs

- When did you arrive?
- ¿Cuándo llegaste?
  ¿Coo-ahn-doh yeh-gahs-teh?

- It was a pleasant flight.

- Fue un vuelo agradable.
  Foo-eh oonvoo-eh-loh ah-grah-dah-bleh

- I have jetlag, I need to lie down.
- Tengo jetlag, necesito recostarme.
  Tehn-goh jetlag, neh-seh-see-toh reh-cohs-tahr-meh

- Do you have a lighter?
- ¿Tienes un encendedor?
  ¿Tee-eh-nehsoonehn-sehn-deh-dohr?

- I'll be working late tonight.
- Trabajaré hasta tarde esta noche.
  Trah-bah-hah-reh ahs-tahtahr-dehehs-tahnoh-cheh

- How was your trip?
- ¿Cómo estuvo el viaje?
  ¿Coh-mohehs-too-vohehl vee-ah-heh?

Tourism

- There is a free concert in the central park
- Hay un concierto gratuito en el parque central
  I ooncohn-see-ehr-tohgrah-too-ee-tohehnehl par-kehcehn-trahl

- Are there any seats available?
- ¿Aún hay asientos disponibles?
  ¿Ah-ooni ah-see-en-tohsdees-poh-nee-blehs?

- Are there movie theaters with movies in English?
- ¿Hay cines con películas en inglés?

495

¿I cee-nehscohnpeh-lee-coo-lahsehneen-glehs?

- What movies are they showing now?
- ¿Qué películas dan ahora?
  ¿Kehpeh-lee-coo-lahsdahn ah-oh-rah?

- Can you get me a ticket?
- ¿Puedes conseguirme una entrada?
  ¿Pwe-dehscohn-seh-geer-meh oo-naehn-trah-dah?

- Is it dubbed or does it have subtitles?
- ¿Es doblada o tiene subtítulos?
  ¿Ehs doh-blah-dah oh tee-eh-nehsoob-tee-too-lohs?

- We would like two tickets to the movie...
- Quisiéramos dos entradas para la película...
  Kee-see-eh-rah-mohsdohsehn-trah-dahs pah-rah lahpeh-lee-coo-la...

- Are there any tourist attractions for children?
- ¿Hay alguna atracción turística para niños?
  ¿I ahl-goo-nah ah-trahk-thee-ohn too-rees-tee-cahpah-rah nee-nyohs?

- Where do local people go for fun?
- ¿A dónde va la gente de la zona para divertirse?
  ¿Ah dohn-dehvahlahhhen-tehdehlah soh-nah pah-rah dee-vehr-teer-seh?

- Is there a mall nearby?
- ¿Hay una plaza comercial cerca?
  ¿I oo-nah plah-zahcoh-mehr-ceeahlcehr-cah?

- What kinds of activities are there for teens?
- ¿Qué actividades hay para adolescentes?
  ¿Keh ack-tee-bee-dah-dehsipah-rah ah-doh-leh-sehn-tehs?
- Are there amusement parks?
- ¿Hay parques de diversiones?
  ¿I pahr-kehsdeh dee-vehr-seeoh-nehs?

- Is there a national park nearby?
- ¿Hay un parque nacional cerca de aquí?
  ¿I oonpahr-keh nah-cee-oh-nahlcer-cahdeh ah-kee?

- Are there tours to see places of historical interest?
- ¿Hay excursiones para ver lugares de interés histórico?
  ¿I ehx-coor-seeoh-nehspah-rah vehr loo-gah-res deheen-teh-rehs ees-toh-ree-coh?

- Are there museums here?
- ¿Hay museos aquí?
  ¿I moo-seh-ohs ah-kee?

- What is the best tour for families?
- ¿Cuál es la mejor excursión para una familia?
  ¿Cooahlehslah meh-horehx-coor-seeohnpah-rah oo-nah fah-mee-leeah?

- Can you take our picture, please?
- ¿Puedes tomarnos una foto, por favor?
  ¿Pwe-dehstoh-mahr-nohsoo-nah foh-toh, porh fah-vohr?

- Where is the zoo?

- ¿Dónde se encuentra el zoológico?
  ¿Dohn-dehsehehn-cooehn-trahehlzoh-loh-hee-coh?
- What kind of animal is that?
- ¿Qué tipo de animal es?
  ¿Keh tee-pohdeh ah-nee-mahlehs?

- Is that animal dangerous?
- ¿Es un animal peligroso?
  ¿Ehsoon ah-nee-mahlpehlee-groh-soh?

- Are kids allowed?
- ¿Se admiten niños?
  ¿Sehahd-mee-tehn nee-nyohs?

- Can I smoke in this area?
- ¿Puedo fumar aquí?
  ¿Pwe-doh foo-mahr ah-kee?

- Where can I find an internet café?
- ¿Dónde hay un cyber café?
  ¿Dohn-deh I oon cee-behrcah-feh?

- The keyboard isn't working correctly.
- El teclado no funciona.
  Ehl the-clah-doh nohfoon-ceeoh-nah

- Where can I get a map of the area?
- ¿Dónde consigo un mapa de la zona?
  ¿Dohn-dehcohn-see-gohoonmah-pahdehlahzoh-nah?
- Are there any hiking trails?

- ¿Hay rutas de excursionismo?
- ¿I roo-tahsdehehx-coor-seeoh-nees-moh?

- Are there any trails for mountain biking?
- ¿Hay rutas de ciclismo de montaña?
  ¿I roo-tahsdeh cee-clees-mohdehmohn-tah-nyah?

- Which route is the easiest?
- ¿Cuál es la ruta más fácil?
  ¿Cooalhehslahroo-tahmahs fah-ceel?

- Is this track well marked?
- ¿Está bien marcada la ruta?
- ¿Ehs-tah bee-ehnmahr-cah-dah lahroo-tah?

- Is there a cabin to spend the night?
- ¿Hay una cabaña donde pasar la noche?
  ¿I oo-nah cah-bah-nyahdohn-dehpah-sahrlahnoh-cheh?

- We're lost.
- Nos perdimos.
  Nohs per-dee-mohs

- What is that building?
- ¿Qué es ese edificio?
  ¿Kehehs eh-seh eh-dee-fee-see-oh?

STUDY METHOD: IMPROVING

L istening is such an important aspect of learning a language. At the same time, it's often one of the most intimidating and frustrating parts. When you take your language skills out into the real world, you seem to suddenly realize "hey, all of these people speak a lot faster than my Spanish teacher" or "whoa… why aren't they enunciating everything like that guy I saw on YouTube?"

The ability to listen in Spanish, for obvious reasons, comes before being able to speak it. Very often, Spanish students find themselves becoming frustrated that they can't speak Spanish as well as they wished they could. A common reason for this is simply that their listening skills are not quite developed enough.

The good news is that improving your listening ability is something that can be done in a number of ways. In order to really take your listening ability to the next level, you have to practice Active Listening (something we'll discuss further). Passive Listening (putting on Spanish TV and music in the background while you go about your daily routine, for example) is a great way to continue with your language-learning habit. But if your goal is to improve your listening abilities, you'll need to add in a fair amount of Active Listening activities. There is an immense amount of resources available and they can help to make the process simpler—enjoyable even!

Let's look closer at a few things you can start doing NOW to improve your listening comprehension:

Focus on the Pronunciation

If you haven't noticed yet, this is a very important aspect of learning a language. And, as has been mentioned before, it isn't something that's overly difficult when learning Spanish. As a Spanish language student, you have the advantage of working with a phonetic language (i.e. words sound like they're written).

This doesn't mean that pronunciation is something that should be pushed to the back-burner. It means that it's something that you shouldn't have a problem working on and addressing early on.

While you go through your day listening to your Spanish-language materials, pay attention to how the words are pronounced.

- Focus on the vowels sounds. There are only five of them, but it's very important that you get them down and dedicate them to memory.
- Listen for the diphthongs. Make sure you understand how they work and how they will change the pronunciation of a word.
- Notice where the accents fall. There's a big difference in the meaning of words such as *pápa* (pope) and *papa* (dad). But the only thing that changes when saying these words is where the emphasis is placed.

Your abilities will be limited at first. This means you should find materials that are appropriate for your level. Starting out with something too advanced can be frustrating and may just lead to feeling discouraged and overwhelmed.

Choosing a listening piece that is too easy for you may leave you feeling bored or like you're not actually gaining anything from the experience.

Start small. Find a listening piece that fits your level and, after you feel you've mastered that, choose another and another.

Find the Right Resources and Know What to Do With Them

Figuring out what is the right listening resource for you is completely up to you. No one knows your level better than you do.

Try following the steps listed below to make sure you get the most out of your listening practice:

- If you don't understand it after a few attempts, go back to the beginning of the recording and start the whole thing over. See if, through paying attention to the context surrounding the sentence or section, you're able to understand it better.
- If you find a few words you don't understand, make a note of them.
- Write them out phonetically (how they sound). Try playing the recording again, making a mental note of when those words come up and see if you

can glean their meaning through context. If you still don't understand the word after doing this a few times, look it up and make a note of what it means.

- After doing all of the above-mentioned steps, listen to the entire recording again. See if you can understand it better.
- If you can't (don't get discouraged!), listen to the translation or find the tapescript to see how much of what you heard you really were able to comprehend.

If you make this process part of your listening-learning routine, you'll find that your abilities will improve greatly over time. As you become more advanced, you'll discover that some of the above-mentioned steps are no longer needed for you. And, eventually, you'll discover that you're understanding what you hear the first time around with no problem.

Active Listening

Active listening is the process of participating actively in the listening process. This is something you should do constantly, no matter what level of Spanish you're at. Active listening means that you don't just have Spanish going on in the background. That form of listening is considered passive listening and, while it's a wonderful way to reinforce different things you've learned (and any exposure to Spanish will be useful in one way or another), in order to acquire new skills, vocabulary, etc., you will need to make active listening an integral part of your learning experience.

Here are a few ways to ensure that you're actively listening to what you're hearing in Spanish:

Listen and Repeat

No matter what level you're at, take the time to pause the recording you're listening to and repeat what you've heard. This doesn't mean that you have to repeat it word for word. Focus on being able to reproduce the general gist of what you've heard. Try to incorporate any new vocabulary you may have learned from the listening activity. What's important here is checking your comprehension.

Listen and Write (dictations)

This may seem like a somewhat tedious task but it's actually very beneficial.

As you listen to your Spanish recordings, keep a notebook handy. Write down what you hear as you listen. This will help you with your vocabulary and be really useful when checking your comprehension.

At first, start out small—work with individual sentences or short phrases. As you progress, increase this to a paragraph or two. Write what you hear the first time through. Listen to the recording again, adding in anything you may have missed. Then, check it to see where you might have misunderstood something or where you're comprehension got a little foggy.

Listen and Read

Listening to audiobooks is a great way to be able to read and listen at the same time. This is extremely useful, as you'll not only hear the pronunciation of the words, but the visual aid of seeing them written out will help you dedicate new words to memory faster.

Improve Your Conversational Abilities in Spanish

The end goal for almost every Spanish student is to be able to reach a level of being conversational in Spanish. Being able to speak is, obviously, a very large part of this. However, if you are unable to understand what is being said to you, you'll find that your conversations are very short and probably somewhat awkward and uncomfortable.

If you want to be able to understand conversational, colloquially spoken, normal-paced, real-life Spanish, you're going to have to work at it. But working at it doesn't have to be a chore. In addition to working with your listening activities (following the steps outlined above), a daily dose of immersion will go a long way in helping you take what you've learned and implement it in a realistic way.

Try adding in one (or more) of the following immersion-based tools to your study routine and see how much your listening skills take off.

Watch Spanish TV

There are normally Spanish-talking stations recorded on digital TV and satellite TV, just as on ordinary stations that are accessible for nothing on any TV.

This is an extraordinary method to pay attention to Spanish being spoken by locals. Put on a telenovela or watch the news in Spanish while you're approaching your day-by-day schedule. Any smidgen of openness makes a difference.

Pay attention to Spanish Music

There are numerous popular Spanish artists. It doesn't make any difference in the event that you like an old-style guitar or cutting-edge hip jump. You can appreciate salsa or mariachi music or significantly more current rowdy groups. The Spanish-talking world has huge loads of artists who are continually making incredible music. You'll certainly discover something you love. Look at YouTube or iTunes to perceive what you find.

Watch Spanish Movies

This is an incredible method to hear Spanish being spoken by locals as well as a superb method to find out about the culture. You'll hear a ton of everyday articulations and slang, just as a wide range of accents and plenty of new jargon. Keep a journal close by to write down any new words you might go over.

Watch Movies in Spanish

This is marginally not the same as the point referenced previously. On pretty much every DVD you run over, you'll discover the alternative to watch the film in Spanish.

The distinction between watching motion pictures in Spanish and watching Spanish films is that the named forms aren't for the most part as real with regards to language. Everyday articulation isn't as normal and the general talking is by all accounts a little slower. This is as yet an extraordinary method to get on new jargon and secure an ear that is more acclimated with paying attention to Spanish being spoken.

Look at YouTube

YouTube offers so many Spanish channels. You can discover anything from hair and cosmetics instructional exercises to those irregular, amusing recordings that are intended to be simply amusement. Look at it. You'd be astounded at what you'll discover.

Discover Native Speakers to Speak With

Discovering a discussion or trade accomplice is extremely helpful. Having the option to watch somebody's lips move as they talk will make understanding simpler. Furthermore, you'll have the option to hear their articulation better than you would on a tune or over a recording.

Try not to Be Afraid to Use Subtitles... in Spanish!

In case you're watching a film in Spanish (or a Spanish film) or TV or YouTube, or whatever, don't be hesitant to utilize the captions in the event that you need to.

Ensure you put them in Spanish, however. That way you can consider to be as they're being spoken and acquaint yourself with how they sound. Try not to turn out to be excessively reliant upon this, however. Attempt to comprehend without perusing however, in the event that you need to, recall this is an extremely valuable instrument.

DIRECTIONS

ynopsis

S Camila is out in the street, heading to a clothing store but she is a bit lost. She stops Juan and asks him for directions. This episode will help you when you're out and about in a Spanish-speaking country and need some help getting where you have to go.

— Camila: Hola señor, discúlpame. Estoy buscando una tienda de ropa, pero no puedo encontrar la tienda.
— Camila: Hi sir, excuse me. I am looking for a clothing store, but I can't find the store.

— Juan: Puedo ayudar. ¿Cuál es el nombre de la tienda? ¿Conoces la dirección?
— **John:** I can help. What is the name of the store? Do you know the address?

— Camila: El nombre de la tienda es "Fabulosa"; está en la calle doce.
— Camila: The name of the store is called "fabulous"; it's located on twelve street.

— Juan: Ah, conozco esa tienda muy bien, mi madre siempre hace compras allí. Está apróximamente a media hora de aquí.
— **John:** Ah, I know that store very well, my mom always shops there. It's approximately half an hour away from here.

— Camila: ¿Dónde queda exactamente? ¿Cómo llego allá?
— Camila: Where is it located exactly? How do I get there?
— Juan: Bueno, puedes tomar un Uber para allá, si quieres. ¿Tienes la aplicación de Uber en tu teléfono?

- **John:** Well, you can take an Uber there if you want. Do you have the app for Uber in your Phone?

- Camila: No uso Uber; ¿puedo tomar el autobús? Prefiero tomar el autobús.
- Camila: I don't use Uber; can I take the bus? I prefer to take the bus.

- Juan: Sí, claro… Puedes tomar el autobús número catorce en la próxima manzana.
- **John:** Yes, of course… You can take the number fourteen bus on the next block.

- Camila: ¿Tengo que cruzar la calle y caminar para llegar allí?
- Camila: Do I have to cross the street and walk there?

- Juan: Así es. Puedes preguntarle al conductor del autobús también.
- **John:** That's right. You can ask the bus driver too.

- Camila: Entiendo. Gracias por tu ayuda.
- Camila: Got it. Thanks for your help!

- Juan: No hay problema, de nada.
- **John:** No problem, you're welcome.

—Fin de la historia—

—End of story—

Go Back To Episode List

Breaking it all down

Discúlpame: If you're out and about and wanted to tell someone, "Excuse me", you'd say, "discúlpame," You can also say, "disculpa" (informal) or "disculpe" (formal). Where does this come from? Let's break it down. Let's start with the verb, "Disculpar" (to forgive/to excuse). She is using a command, "Excuse" in the present tense, so she says, "Disculpa," but added the "Me" to it, making it, "discúlpame"(excuse me.) This can also mean, "forgive me."

Estoy buscando: Estoy comes from the verb, "Estar" (to be). Estoy is the Yo form (First-person singular) of the verb used in the present indicative tense. "Estoy buscando" means, "I am searching for." It comes from the verb, "buscar" (to look for/to search for). You know when we say in English, "Search-ING" or "Look-ING"? This is a great example of using the Present Participle, Busca-ndo. This is a more advanced Spanish than you'll see in this version of Gritty Spanish, but still good to keep in the back of your mind.

The present participle in Spanish is a verb form used to express continuous or ongoing actions.

Study the following chart:

No puedo encontrar: The "no" here, of course, makes it negative statement. Puedo comes from the verb, "Poder" (to be able to /can). It's conjugated using the "Yo" form (First-person singular) of the verb in the present indicative tense. "Puedo" by itself means, "I can," "No puedo" means, "I can't." The non-conjugated verb, "Encontrar" means, "to find." So, together, it means, "I can't find."

Sabes: This means, "You know." The word, "Sabes" comes from the verb, "Saber" (to know). Sabes is the *Tú* form (Second-person singular) of the verb used in the present indicative tense.

Here is how the verb, "Saber" (to know) is conjugated in the present indicative tense.

- Yo Sé – I know
- Tú Sabes – You know
- Él/Ella Sabe- He/She /knows
- Usted Sabe – You (formal) know
- Nosotros/Nosotras Sabemos – We understand

- Ustedes Saben- You all know
- Ellos/Ellas Saben – They know

Examples:

- "Yo sé su nombre."
- "I know his name."
- "¿Eres de Perú?"
- "Are you from Peru?"

There is another verb that means, "To know" in Spanish, it's "Conocer." Conocer is utilized to communicate commonality or associate (or scarcity in that department) with an individual, spot, or thing. For instance, you can know, or be familiar with a book, a film, a nation, or someone in particular.

Examples:

- "Conozco a tu hermano."
- "I know your brother."

- "No me conoces."
- "You don't know me."

- "¿Me conoces?"
- "Do you know me?"

Dónde queda: The word, "Dónde" means, "Where". The word, "Queda" comes from the verb, "Quedar" (to stay). Queda is the 3rd person singular/usted (formal second person singular) form of the verb in the present indicative tense. Quedar is one of the Spanish verbs that has so many different meanings depending on the context, and this is one of them.

Llego: Llego comes from the verb, "Llegar" (to arrive). Llego is the "yo" form (First-person singular) of the verb used in the present indicative tense.

If you ever want to ask someone, "how do I get there," you can say what the character said, "Cómo llego allá," it's like saying, "How do I arrive there," no?

Here is how the verb, "llegar" (to arrive) is conjugated in the present indicative tense in Spanish:

- Yo Llego – I arrive
- Tú Llegas – You arrive
- Él/Ella Llega – He/she/arrives
- Usted Llega- You (formal) arrive
- Nosotros/Nosotras Llegamos – We arrive
- Ustedes Llegan- You all arrive
- Ellos/Ellas Llegan – They arrive

Looking at the conjugation above, to say, "How do THEY get there" will be, "Como llegan allá." Remember, you can use the word, "allá" or "Allí" when you want to say "There" or "over there." In theory, "allá" implies/denotes a greater distance, but in practice, they are often used interchangeably. There are also regional preferences. Examples:

- You take a bus allá.
- Tomas un autobus there.

- "Podemos tomar un autobús mañana."
- "We can take a bus tomorrow."

Tengo que cruzar: When you're speaking or writing in Spanish, and want to express having to do something, you can use the verb, "Tener" (to have). So here, the character uses the following formula... Conjugated verb + que + a non-conjugated verb.

So the conjugated verb is, tengo (I have). Then, he used the word, "Que"... Followed by the non-conjugated verb, "cruzar" (to cross).

Here are other examples:

- Tengo que comprar algo para mi esposa.
- I have to buy something for my wife.

- Tienes que estar allí.
- You have to be there.

- No puedo hablar contigo; tengo que ir a la casa de mi madre.
- I can't talk with you; I have to go to my mom's house.

Entiendo: Entiendo means, "I understand" and it comes from the verb, "Entender" (to understand). "Entiendo" is the Yo form (First-person singular) of the verb used in the present indicative tense. When speaking to a Spanish-speaking person who does not understand something, they'll say, "no entiendo" (I don't understand). You'll also say this as well when you don't understand something. This is how *Entender* (to understand) is conjugated in the present indicative tense.

- Yo Entiendo – I understand
- Tú Entiendes – You understand
- Él/ella Entiende – He/she understands
- Usted Entiende – You (formal) understand
- Nosotros/Nosotras Entendemos – We understand
- Ustedes Entienden – You all understand
- Ellos/Ellas Entienden – They understand

Examples:

- ¿Entiendes inglés?
- Do you understand English?

- Quiero entender el inglés mejor.
- I want to understand English better.

- ¿Entienden mi español?
- Do they understand my Spanish?

MOVING INTO NEW APARTMENT

ynopsis

S Sofía just got a huge promotion at her job at a prestigious Law firm, she is now an executive secretary. She has spent years living in a tiny studio apartment in Spanish Harlem and finally found a new apartment in the Greenwich Village area. This episode is about her moving into her new apartment.

— Sofía: Me encanta mi nuevo departamento, tiene tanto espacio.
— Sofía: I love my new apartment, it has so much space.

— Antonio: Señora Martínez, ¿dónde puedo poner este sofá?
— Antonio: Ms. Martinez, where can I put this sofa?

— Sofía: ¡¿Qué clase de pregunta es esa?! Ponlo en la sala, ¡cretino!
— Sofía: What kind of question is that?! Put it in the living room, jerk!

— Antonio: Está bien, no se estrese, solo estaba preguntando. ¿En dónde puedo poner el microondas?
— Antonio: OK, don't stress yourself out, just asking. Where can I put the microwave?

— Sofía: Ponlo en la cocina. Espera, no compré un microondas. ¡Mañana lo voy a devolver!
— Sofía: Put it in the kitchen. Wait, I didn't buy a microwave. Tomorrow I am going to bring it back!

- Antonio: El jefe dijo que es gratis. Es un regalo por gastar tanto y ser una valiosa clienta.
- Antonio: The boss said it's free. It's a gift for spending so much and being a valued customer.

- Sofía: Ay, ¡qué lindo de su parte! Compré cortinas de ducha y tapetes para el baño. ¿Dónde está la televisión? ¿Todavía está en el camión?
- Sofía: Awwww, how nice of him! I purchased shower curtains and mats for the bathroom. Where is the TV? Is it still in the truck?

- Antonio: Sí, el resto de las cosas está abajo en el camión. Voy a subir las alfombras, la cama, y la cómoda también.
- Antonio: Yes, the rest of the stuff is downstairs in the truck. I am going to bring up the rugs, the bed, and the dresser too.

- Sofía: Está bien, gracias. Entonces, apresúrate y pon el sofá en la esquina de allí.
- Sofía: OK thank you. So, hurry up and put the sofa in the corner over there.

- Antonio: Está bien, eso haré, señora Martínez.
- Antonio: Okay, will do, Ms. Martinez.

Antonio sale del departamento

Antonio leaves the apartment

- Antonio: ¡Oh Dios mío! Es así que es una mujer desagradable. ¡Jamás volveré a hacer otra entrega para ella otra vez!
- Antonio: Oh my god! That is one mean lady. I'll never deliver anything for her ever again!

513

—Fin de la historia—

—End of story—

Go Back To Episode List

Breaking it all down

Me encanta: Encantar is a verb meaning, "to love" or "to be enchanting". Similar to the verb, *gustar*, which means, "to like" or "to be pleasing". The verb has a unique property, it is considered a backward verb. A backward verb like *encantar* uses an indirect object pronoun and it usually comes in front of the subject. In this Episode, the lady says, "Me encanta mi "nuevo departamento" (I love my new Apartment) or literally, "My new apartment enchants me". What enchants her? Her new apartment, this is why the él/ella/usted version of the verb in the present tense was used.

Notice that while the English sentence has a direct object, the Spanish sentence has an indirect object.

The room is pleasing to me.

me = Indirect Object

I love the apartment.

Apartment = Direct object

Keep in mind that In Spanish, you have different options to express "love": The first thing you need to know is that the English word "Love", as you know it, doesn't quite exist in the Spanish language. In English, "love" is very broad. It covers filial love, romantic love, platonic love and endearment to things and activities.

In Spanish:

Yo amo: (from the verb "amar" (to love)) is usually reserved for very personal, intimate moments. Like the word "love", it doesn't automatically translate to romantic feelings, but most of the time "amar" is used in that fashion. So basically, you use the word "amar"/"amo" when you want to convey that you don't just

514

"like" something; you absolutely love it. This is a sentimental and deep word. When you say to someone "Te amo" that means you are in love with that person.

Me encanta: From the verb "encantar": Can be more or less used how you'd use the word "love" colloquially. It is used to express "love" in the sense of liking something a whole heck of a lot. This conveys a strong feeling but is not as serious as love. When you say to someone "Me encantas", it means that you really like that person, but it doesn't necessarily mean that you are in love with him/her.

Querer: (Can be either "want" -something- or "love"). *Querer* can be used to express love to friends, family, etc., but it doesn't carry any heavy feelings.

This word is a lot less strong than "encantar"

Me gusta: (Form the verb gustar): You use this when you just like something.

Example:

- Me gusta la pizza = I like pizza.
- Me gusta Juan = I like Juan (romantically).

- However, if you like a person in a non-romantic way, don't say "me gustas".
- "Me agradas" or "Me caes bien" are better options that won't generate confusions.

Here are some other backward verbs similar to "Gustar" and "Encantar" in the table below.

Dónde puedo poner: Dónde means, "Where". The word, "Puedo" (I can) is the present tense (Indicative) form of the verb, "Poder" (to be able to). The compound verb, "Poner" means, "To put." When you combine those three words it means, "Where can I put". In the story, he says, "este sofa" (this sofa).

Cretino: There are a lot of "soft insults" that you can use in Spanish. If you want to say "jerk" you can use "cretino" or "tonto". Just keep in mind that some other insults like "idiota" (idiot) or "estúpido" (stupid) sound slightly more aggressive in Spanish.

No se estrese: If you ever want to tell someone, "Don't stress yourself out", this is how you would say it. The "se" was added before the verb, "estresar"(to stress out) as you can see. He is speaking to her using the "usted" form of that verb, this is why he used, "se". The command/imperative form of the verb is used, estrese, which is the "él/ella/usted" form in that mood,

If he was NOT speaking to her in the usted form, then it would be, "no te estreses". Two things were changed, the "te" was added and "estreses". Remember the command *tú* form of this verb, "estresar" is "estresa", but since it's a negative command in the "tú" form, then the word changes to, "estreses".

Solo estaba preguntando: You can also say, "Yo solo estaba preguntando" if you want to emphasize, but remember that in Spanish you don't always have to say the pronoun because it is revealed by the verb conjugation and the context. So "Solo" would be "only" (or just); "estaba" would be "I was" and "preguntando" would be asking; but the order of structural elements is backwards if you compare it to English.

So, you have:

- I was just asking (English)
- Yo solo estaba preguntando (Spanish)

The word, "Estaba" comes from the verb, "Estar" (to be). "Estaba" is the first person "Yo" form of the imperfect tense. If this was used in the present tense, then it would be, "Solo estoy preguntando" (I am only asking).

A Quick definition of the Imperfect tense:

The Spanish imperfect tense is used to describe past habitual actions or to talk about what someone was doing when they were interrupted by something else. To conjugate a regular verb in the imperfect tense in Spanish, simply remove the infinitive ending (-ar, -er, or -ir) and add the imperfect ending that matches the subject.

Check out the table of regular imperfect endings below:

En dónde: *Dónde* means "where". In Spanish, you can usually use either "Dónde" or "en dónde", where "en" is a preposition used to express location, and no movement.

Lo voy a devolver: This starts with, "lo" and in this instance, means, "IT", what's IT? The microwave (el microondas). *Voy* (I am going) comes from the verb, "ir"

516

(to go). "Voy" is the "Yo" form of the verb used in the present indicative tense. The compound verb, "Devolver" is "To return" an item such as a book, a dress, shoes, etc. This is THE verb to use when you would like to return something to a store. She could have also placed the "lo" (it) at the end of the compound verb, "Devolver", like so, "voy a devolverlo" and it would have meant the same thing.

Although technically incorrect, I've also heard people use "Regresar" instead of "Devolver" in some informal situations when talking about returning something to a location. They would say, "Lo voy a regresar". The verb, "Regresar" is used more when you want to talk about someone returning to a place.

For example:

- "No quiero regresar allí"
- "I don't want to go back there"

She could have also placed the "lo"(it) at the end of the compound verb, "Regresar", like so, "voy a regresarlo" or "voy a devolverlo" and it would have meant the same thing.

Ponlo: "Pon" is from the verb "Poner" (to put). "Pon" is the *tú* command/imperative mood of the verb "poner". If you are telling someone to "PUT" something somewhere, then you say, "pon", but what? She added the "lo" to "Pon" because she is referring to the sofa which is a masculine word, "el sofa". If she was talking about a bottle (Una botella), then it would be "Ponla", because she is talking about "La botella" (The bottle).

Valiosa clienta: You say "valiosa clienta" because she is a woman, if you were talking to a man, you say "valioso cliente". In plural, this would be "valiosas clientas" (if all of them are female) or "valiosos clientes" if at least one of them is male.

In Spanish, when you are talking about a group of people such as, "valiosos clientes" (valued customers)… If there are a hundred women and one man, it would still be "valiosos clientes". Notice how it's still masculine? Funny, right?

Niños = Boys

Niñas = Girls

- A Group of boys is "Los niños" (the boys)

517

- A Group of girls is "Las niñas" (the girls)

But let's say, there is ONE boy with that group of "Niñas" (girls), then when referring to them as a group, it automatically becomes, "Los Niños".

Compré: This word is from the verb, "Comprar" (to buy). Compré (I bought) is the "Yo" form of that verb used in the preterite tense. The preterite tense is frequently associated with phrases that pinpoint a particular occasion or specific time frame.

Examples:

In the event that the activity is previously, and you can decide correctly when it happened, or how often it happened, then, at that point, you will utilize the preterite tense.

There are just two arrangements of endings for ordinary preterite action words, one for - ar action words and one for both - er and-ir action words. To form an ordinary action word in the preterite tense, essentially eliminate the infinitive closure (- ar, - er, or - ir) and add the preterite finishing that coordinates with the subject. Investigate the table of ordinary preterite endings underneath.

Unpredictable Preterite Verb Conjugations

Four of the most well-known action words with unpredictable preterite structures are ser, ir, dar, and ver.

**Note that 'ser' and 'ir' have the same forms in the preterite.

NOTES ON THE CREATION AND MANAGEMENT OF YOUR SPANISH LANGUAGE MEMORY PALACES

An easy and fun way to learn Spanish is to purchase a memory palace. A memory palace is an artificial structure that becomes the physical representation of an idea, concept, or memory. This allows you to remember things in a more concrete manner by storing memories in a way similar to how we store objects such as furniture or other possessions. The memory palace is typically located indoors so that the memories can be stored on a consistent basis and stored in a manner that makes them more permanent.

The layout of any memory palace depends on the idea or concept you are trying to memorize. If, for example, you are studying complex mathematical concepts, you may want to create a building with multiple floors. This would allow you to organize mathematical concepts by levels and by multiple different subject areas, such as geometry, algebra, and calculus. Since all of these different subjects do not fit in one building, this would require several different buildings within your palace if they were all taught in the same way. If you find it easier to organize mathematical concepts in your mind, then you can simply design one building that houses all the different areas or topics. This building would contain everything you need to study the math topics and would become your real-world equivalent of a memory palace.

Another idea is to create very large memory palaces. This allows you to save a bunch of ideas or memories and create very large structures or rooms for them so that they will be easier to remember. To create an effective palace, there are several different elements that need to be included. Each of these elements is designed to help you remember the particular subject that you are learning as well as to help you remember all of your other memories.

Memory Palaces can be used at any level, but they typically work best for beginners, intermediate speakers, and advanced speakers. This is because the use of a memory palace makes it easier to learn complex information in both grammar and vocabulary. Once you have learned the language in context, then being able to store it with all of its terms into a single building will make it easier to remember individual terms or words in the future and for longer periods of time.

Another advantage that a memory palace offers is that many people find them fun when learning languages. If you were to try to study on your own without the use of a memory palace then it would be very difficult to remember all of the information. By using a memory palace, you are creating a sense of fun when studying and this makes it easier to remember the information. You become more interested in what you are studying and this helps it stick in your mind in a much more natural way that is easier for anyone to learn new languages or concepts.

A memory palace is also very easy to create. This is because you will be using your mind's ability to store and recall information onto a physical structure that can contain thousands of different ideas, subjects, or memories. All you need to do is spend some of your time designing a structure that contains the things that you want to memorize. The design and layout of the memory palace will be uniquely suited to what you want it to contain.

Remembering information becomes much easier if you use a memory palace because all of the memories will become more permanent and more concrete. This is because it can stick in your mind and become more real as opposed to being just random static images or words that you might recall from time to time. To be able to remember things like this it is necessary to store them in a way that can make them more permanent, but that is very difficult without a memory palace.

A memory palace also helps you remember vocabulary and grammar in context because of the idea of using it as a reference. For example, if you were studying some elements of grammar, you could make it into a memory palace by creating buildings or rooms for each of these subjects within your palace along with every other object that needs to be included. If you wished to include anything regarding nouns, verbs, adjectives, and adverbs then you would have several different rooms for each subject as well as many other rooms that represent the different parts of speech. You could then link each of the rooms to a specific topic or idea, so that you would be able to remember them much more effectively.

To make learning a language easy and fun, you should purchase a memory palace today. With these notes and instructions, you will be able to learn how to create your own palace so that you can learn the Spanish language more easily and have more fun doing it.

Here is the process you will need to follow to successfully use a memory palace.

Buy or find pictures of every object that you need to memorize.

Select a location for the memory palace that is quiet and comfortable. An indoor location is preferred over an outdoor one. This helps create your own little world for learning and gives you a place to escape where you can concentrate on what you are trying to learn.

Think about all of the different things that need to be memorized and imagine storing all of these things within your memory palace room as though it were an actual building with rooms and hallways.

Lay out the room however you like, labeling all of the objects that are important on the map and stick to it.

Put these things on the floor or choose a table or desk and place all of your items in it with their proper names written out within the location they are supposed to be placed.

Once you have them laid out as they should be, start going through each item and label each one as being in the room where it needs to be written down. You will do this a few times but then you will start to get a mental picture of what everything is supposed to look like inside of your palace.

Organize the items that you want to remember in a logical and natural order. Create a logical way of organizing them by using the different rooms that you have created for each subject.

Use the objects that are in your memory palace to help you remember all of the words, grammar, and vocabulary as well as helpful hints and tips that you will need when studying. By creating these things into buildings, you will be able to memorize much more than if they were just random images or pictures of objects or rooms that needed to be memorized. When putting objects within your palace, it is best to think about how these objects relate to each other and how they essentially function together.

Start creating a story or timeline that links the objects and makes it easy to remember them all. If you have an object that is used as a verb, noun, adjective, or adverb you could create a room for each one of these types of words. You want to link these objects within the palace so that they are all connected.

When you are done memorizing all of the things that need to be memorized in your memory palace simply close the doors and walk away from it for a few months. Then later in your life when you want to study Spanish again open up your memory palace and try to remember everything as though you were just reading through it from start to finish once again.

It is also possible to take a picture of the buildings and objects that you have created and upload them to a place like Evernote so that you can always go back and look at your palace later on when you want to remember something else. Learning Spanish will be easier when you create your own memory palace so that all of your information will stick in your mind more effectively instead of just being random mental pictures.

You can use this process in a variety of different ways. You can use it as described above to memorize vocabulary or grammar studies, or maybe just study vocab words along with declensions and conjugations. You can also use it for medical studies the same way that you would use a memory palace to memorize vocabulary lists. This is an excellent method for learning because it not only improves your memory, but also makes you feel really better about yourself because you can create something so beautiful and artistic.

If you are serious about learning Spanish, then you should try to create a memory palace today. It will be an incredible experience to create something that works so nicely and effectively. You will be able to remember much more than if you just relied on memorizing random images. Using a memory palace will also improve your reading skills because by accessing these memories, you will be able to remember specific words that will help you read much better. This is also one of the best activities for children and they too can make some of the best memory palaces.

Study the vocabulary list and create objects, places, or things that remind you of those words. For example, if the word is "naranja" then a picture of an orange would be a good idea. You can do this for every part of speech that needs to be studied. It is important to make sure that your memory palace makes sense because this will increase its effectiveness when using it later on. If the objects are not in order and linked together, then you shouldn't use it.

Creating a memory palace is a great way to learn new vocabulary and improve your reading skills. It is an activity that you should try on your own or with friends so that everyone can create his own memory palace and learn Spanish in a fun and beautiful way. Be creative with this process and come up with lots of different styles for your memory palaces so that they look amazing. You will be able to learn much more than if you were just memorizing random pictures of things.

When learning Spanish, sometimes it is difficult to remember important vocabulary because too many words are similar to each other or sound the same. Although this is a normal part of learning Spanish it can be very frustrating. There are certain ways that you can reduce the risk of forgetting words like this and one way is to create a memory palace. If you are unfamiliar with what this is, creating a memory palace is a great way to learn Spanish vocab fast.

Memory Palaces for Vocabulary

Reading Spanish words is not difficult if they are new to you, but when reading vocabulary every day for practice it can get really frustrating because there are so many words that sound similar and so many words that end with the same letter as another word. The biggest issue that you will have is if you can't remember which word comes after the Spanish "consonant + vowel + accent" word because they are also very similar.

This is why it is important to use a memory palace to learn vocabulary for fluency. A memory palace is a strategy that makes learning vocabulary easier because it creates images and pictures in your mind that help you remember every Spanish word correctly. If you are going to learn Spanish for fluency, then you should try to create your own memory palace to get started learning new vocab words for free.

SPANISH PRONUNCIATION

Spanish is usually written with the following letter combinations: a, b, c, ch, d, e, f, g, h (pronounced like an h), *j* (the same as the English y), *k* (pronounced like a k), *l* (a double ll is also used to make a "z" sound; for example: Tengo dos libros — I have two books).

Pronouncing Spanish can be difficult for some people.

The first step is to learn how to pronounce vowels such as "a," "e," "i," "o," and "u." In Spanish, there are five vowels and they are pronounced like the following: (ah-eh-ee-oh-oo). The "e" is usually a softer sound.

The next step after learning how to pronounce vowels is to learn how to say the letters "b," "d," and "g." In the Spanish language, these letters have a soft sound when they are at the beginning of a word. This soft sound is a good thing because this "soft" sound allows you to pronounce the next letter correctly.

After learning how to pronounce the letters "b," "d" and "g," you can now learn how to pronounce letters such as "c," "f" and "j." For example, in Spanish, it is not unusual to hear people say: (KE-ah-fee-ah). This is because the next letter after the vowel is always pronounced like an h. When you are pronouncing Spanish words, it is very important that you remember these rules about pronunciation.

The next way is to learn how to pronounce words with vowels such as "a," "e," and "i". You will notice that when you are saying these vowels, you are not vocalizing the consonant sound that follows.

After learning about how to pronounce vowels, it is now time to learn about how to say the letter "l". In Spanish pronunciation, the letter "l" is pronounced like a light h. The difficult part comes when you try to combine this sound with a vowel. When the letter h comes before a vowel, it makes an l-like sound (for example: Abuelo — Grandfather). Note that it is also possible to pronounce the word like (ah-boo-eh-lo). This word would be pronounced like *ll*.

There is a number of processes to pronounce the letters "e," "i," and "y." You will notice that the letters "e" and "y" have very similar sounds. For example, both words are pronounced: car or cab. The difference between the two words is that in English we do not use the letter e for these two sounds.

In English, we use a vowel i before l (such as: lie or life), whereas in Spanish, they often do not make this distinction when combining both l and y. This means that the Spanish letter y can be a tricky letter to pronounce. It is important to remember that the letter "y" has two sounds: (ee) and (yah).

Now you will learn how to pronounce vowels combined with consonants. It is very important to remember this rule: Never let a vowel follow the consonant. For example, in Spanish, we have two sounds for the word "no." The first sound is "noh" (nah-oh). The second sound is "NWAH" (nwah). You should always pronounce both words as follows: NWAH. Note: when saying the letter "h," remember that it will be pronounced like a soft "h" (like how you say the letters "j" and "g").

After learning how to pronounce consonants, it is time to learn how to pronounce letters. This means that all of the following words will be pronounced the same way as their English counterparts: book, snake, toy, hood. The following words are similar but have only one letter in common—thus, they are pronounced differently: rooster and roofer will both be pronounced roofer in Spanish.

Spanish is different from English not only in pronunciation but also in orthography (spelling). Spanish spelling is more complicated than English spelling. If you get a Spanish dictionary, you can see in the table of contents the spelling for each word as well as the correct pronunciation.

The Spanish alphabet has 28 letters (including the accent marks), which may seem a little difficult to pronounce, but be confident and keep trying. Here is a list of the letters in Spanish alphabetical order: a, b, c, ch, d, e, f, g, h (pronounced like an h), *i* (when it is written by itself it is pronounced like an ee), *j* (the same as the English y), *k* (pronounced like a k), *l* (a double ll is also used to make a "z" sound; for example: Tengo dos libros — I have two books).

The following are some examples of how to say common Spanish phrases correctly.

Spanish Phrases / Spanish Words

- Hello (formal) – Hola.
- How are you? (formal) – Cómo está usted?
- I'm fine, thank you – Estoy bien, gracias.
- Good morning – Buenos días.
- Good afternoon – Buenas tardes.
- Good evening – Buenas noches.
- Good night – Buenas noches
- The weather is good today – El tiempo es bueno hoy.
- How old are you? (formal) –¿Cómo está usted?
- I don't understand – No comprendo/ no entiendo.
- Yes, I'm 21 years old – Sí. Sí, soy 21 años.
- No, I'm 20 – No, soy de 20 años.
- Go away! Leave me alone! Don't talk to me! – Déjame en paz!
- Keep quiet! – Silencio!
- Don't touch me! –¡No te acerques!
- I'm leaving now – Voy a salir ahora.
- Please go away! – Por favor déjame en paz.
- I want to sleep – Quiero dormir.
- What time is it? (formal) –¿Qué hora es?
- I'm going now! – Voy a salir ahora.
- Thank you very much – Gracias mucho.
- Please call me – Llámame por favor.
- See you tomorrow – Hasta mañana, (till tomorrow).
- How long will you stay here for? (formal) – ¿Cuanto tiempo se quedará usted aquí?
- I'll stay here for five years – Me quedaré aquí cinco años.
- My name is ... I am ... years old – Mi nombre es ... Soy de ... años.
- I want to get married – Quiero casarme.
- What's your phone number? (formal) – ¿Cuál es su número telefónico?
- I like you very much. You're my best friend – Te quiero mucho, eres mi mejor amigo.
- How old are you really? (Informal) –¿Cómo está usted realmente?
- I'm three years older than you – Soy tres años más viejo que tú.
- Please take this note to my parents – Por favor lleva este papel a mis padres.
- I like animals – Me gustan los animales.
- What's your dog's name? (formal) – ¿Cómo se llama su perro?

- His name is ... his name is ... his/her name is ... – Se llama ... se llama ... su nombre es ...
- Look! It's raining! – Mira, está lloviendo.
- Leave the money on the table – Deja el dinero sobre la mesa.
- Please write your name – Por favor escribe tu nombre.
- What's your name? (formal) – ¿Cómo se llama?
- We are friends forever – Somos amigos para siempre.
- Hello (informal) – ¡Hola!

Spanish Phrases for answering the telephone:

- Hi ... I am – Hola ... soy ...
- At what time did you leave? –¿A qué hora te vas?
- What time will you be home? – A qué hora llegarás a casa?
- I will be home at five o'clock – Estaré en casa a las cinco.
- What time did you go out last night? – ¿A qué hora saliste anoche?
- I went out at five o'clock in the afternoon – Salí a las cinco de la tarde.
- At five o'clock I'll expect you home – A las cinco de la tarde te espero en casa
- I'll wait for you at home at five o'clock – Te espero en casa a las cinco de la tarde.
- I have to call you back – Tenemos que llamarnos después.
- I'm sorry, can you call me back? – Lo siento, ¿puede devolverme la llamada?
- Sí, tenemos que llamaros después – Yes, we have to call you later.
- Can you call me tomorrow? – ¿Puedes llamarme mañana?
- Can you give me your phone number? –¿Puedes darme tu número de teléfono?

Additional Spanish Phrases

- Something is always happening – Siempre pasa algo.
- Don't say anything to anyone – No digas nada a nadie.
- Do as I say! It isn't nice to say that – ¡Haz lo que te digo! No es agradable decir eso.
- It's already five o'clock – Ya son las cinco.
- I can't talk now please call me back at 3:00 p.m – No puedo hablar ahora por favor llámame a las tres de la tarde.

- There's nothing to do for fun – No hay nada que hacer para divertirse.
- Don't do this without permission – No hagas esto sin permiso.
- Could you please call me back? – ¿Podrías llamarme por favor?
- You can't just do whatever you want – No puedes hacer lo que quieras.
- What do you want? I can't help you – ¿Qué quieres? No te puedo ayudar.
- Where are you going? – ¿Para dónde vas?
- Where is my money? – ¿Dónde está mi dinero?
- I'm already late – Ya estoy atrasado/Voy tarde
- It's better if you don't eat it – Es mejor que no te lo comas.
- It's all right, I'll do it myself – Está bien, lo haré yo mismo.
- Good afternoon everyone! –¡Buenas tardes a todos!
- Let's go to the park! –¡Vamos al parque!
- It's a long story, but I'll tell it to you tomorrow – Es una larga historia, pero te la contaré mañana.
- I'm not very busy today because I have finished my homework – Hoy no estoy muy ocupada/ocupado porque he terminado los deberes.
- Don't worry about it, it doesn't matter because we didn't lose anything in the fire anyway – No te preocupes, no importa porque de todas formas no hemos perdido nada en el incendio.
- It's still good, but it's just too expensive, I can't afford it – Sigue siendo bueno, pero es demasiado caro, no puedo pagarlo.

Example of a Spanish Conversation:

- Alberto: ¿Hola?
- Dante: Hola Alberto.
- Alberto: ¿Cómo estás?
- Dante: Bien gracias, ¿y tú?
- Alberto: Como siempre.
- Dante: ¿Ya estás listo para ir al cine?
- Alberto: Sí, si no es muy tarde.
- Dante: ¡Ah! Es verdad. Bueno, vamos a la biblioteca y allí te encontraré.

The conversation between Alberto and Dante:

- Alberto: Hello?
- Dante: Hi Alberto.
- Alberto: How are you?

- Dante: Fine, thanks, and you?
- Alberto: Just like always.
- Dante: Are you ready to go to the movies?
- Alberto: Yes, but if it's not too late.
- Dante: "Oh!" That's right. Well, we'll go to the library and I will meet you there.

Question sentences in Spanish

- Can you tell me what time it is? (formal) – ¿Puede usted decirme la hora? (formal): ¿Qué hora es?
- What is your name? (formal) – ¿Cómo se llama usted/ustedes?
- What country are you from? – ¿De qué país es usted?
- Where are you from? – ¿De dónde eres?
- What's your sister's/brother's name? – ¿Cómo se llama tu hermana/hermano?
- Where do you live? – ¿Dónde vive usted/ustedes?
- I'm from Mexico – Soy de México
- I'm not sure – No estoy seguro/segura.
- Where is Canada? – ¿Dónde está Canadá?
- I don't understand Spanish – No entiendo español.
- Please speak more slowly – Para favor habla más lento.
- Where is the bathroom? (formal) – ¿Dónde está el baño?
- In which direction is ... – Donde está ...
- Can you tell me where Canada is? (formal) – ¿Puede usted decirme donde está Canadá?
- What is it, please? – ¿Qué es, por favor?
- How much does it cost? – ¿Cuanto cuesta?
- I am not interested in that – No me interesa eso.
- I would like this one – Me gustaría este.
- I'd like the white one – Quiero el blanco, por favor.
- Please hand over me a glass of water – Por favor dame agua tibia (agua estática).
- I want you to listen to me well – Quiero que te hagas una idea de lo que estoy diciendo.
- I'm going to go to the supermarket – Voy al supermercado.
- I'll help you out – Te ayudaré (tú) con esto.
- Please understand me well – Por favor entiendame bien.

- You must tell your father about this – Tienes que contarle a tu padre sobre esto.
- Please don't forget about us – Por favor no nos olvides.
- What is that? –¿Qué es?
- I don't know what that is… – No sé qué es…

FUNDAMENTALS OF THE SPANISH LANGUAGE

T he good news for anybody who speaks English and wants to learn Spanish is that there are many similarities between the two languages, including the fact that both use the Roman alphabet. This helps you build a phonological and phonemic foundation.

Around 30 to 40 percent of all the English words are actually related to a word in Spanish. Due to their similar meanings, appearances, and sounds, the similarities of these words will help you transfer their knowledge about a specific word into this second language.

Other than a few word-order exceptions like noun before an adjective in Spanish and adjective before a noun in English, making sentences in either language use the same sentence structure.

Learning how to write and read will use the same processes as writing mechanics, comprehension, fluency, decoding, and phonemic awareness.

Once students and teachers know about the similarities between these languages, it will save guesswork and time as you learn to transfer your knowledge of English into Spanish.

Phonological and Phonemic Differences

There are a few differences between these languages that could interfere with the correct pronunciation, spelling, or decoding of words.

The main difference between English and Spanish is that Spanish has just five vowel sounds while the English language could have over 14 depending on what region the person is from. This is why people who speak Spanish have problems seeing the difference between vowel phonemes in words such as "sit" and "seat." Both of these phonemes get pronounced differently in the Spanish word **si,** which means yes. This word is pronounced in between these two English phonemes. This can also have an effect on a person's spelling, too. Here are a few examples of the differences between English and Spanish:

Consonants: x, ñ, z, rr, r, j, h, ll, v.

Spanish combinations that get pronounced differently like **güi, güe, gui,** and **gue**.

As an example, the "u" is silent unless it gets written as ü. Because of this, students might not be sure how to correctly pronounce words such as quick, quiet, or queen. Dashes or quotation marks: "Come here," he said. Changes to: Ven aquí, le dijo.

The Spanish language doesn't have these sounds:

- Contractions: weren't, isn't, don't. Basically, no contractions.
- Prefixes/suffixes: -est, -ful, -ness, -ly, under-, over-, un-Endings that don't have vowels: -ts, -ps
- Endings: -s that gets pronounced as "es," "ez," "z," or "s"
- Endings: -ed that gets pronounced as "ted," "ded," "t," or "d"
- Final sounds: gh, ng, ck
- Initial sounds: sk, wr, qu, kn
- Consonant blends: str, spr, scr, sts, sm, sl
- Consonant diagraphs: ph, wh, th, sh
- Vowel diagraphs: oo, aw, au, eigh, ow, ou

Gender and Nouns

The hardest thing for any native English speaker who is trying to learn Spanish is to know the role that gender plays in the language. In the English language, gender isn't important if you are not talking about an animal or person. But in Spanish, every idea, thing, place, or person will have a gender.

If you have studied a romance language or any language that comes from Latin, this might be familiar to you. If you haven't, continue reading to help you learn how gender works within the Spanish language.

The noun's gender is important because the articles and adjectives have to be masculine. An adjective has to match the noun in terms of numbers such as plural or singular and also gender.

Remembering which is Female or Male

There are some rules that you can follow that will help you know whether a noun will be feminine or masculine.

Masculine Nouns

A group that has various genders will always be masculine: five children – cinco niños

Compass direction:

- East – Este
- North – Norte

Months without "el":

- April – Abril
- January – Enero

Weekdays:

- Thursday – Jueves
- Monday – Lunes

Nouns that end in "aje":

- The trip – El viaje
- The voyage – El pasaje

Nouns that "r":

- The motor – El motor

Nouns that are referring to males:

- The man – El hombre
- The father – El padre

Nouns that end in "ma":

- The language – El idioma
- The problem – El problema

Nouns that end in "o":

- The book – El libro
- The boy – El chico

Feminine Nouns

Any noun referring to a female:

- The woman – La mujer
- The mother – La madre

Alphabet: a, b, c – La a, La be, La ce

Nouns that end in "z":

- The light – La luz
- The peace – la paz

Nouns that end in "umbre":

- The tradition – La costumbre

Nouns that end in "tad" or "dad":

- The freedom – La libertad
- The city – La cuidad

Nouns that end in "sion" or "cion":

- The television – La televisión
- The conversation – La conversación

Nouns that end in "a":

- The shirt – La camisa
- The girl – La chica

Exceptions

Every rule will have exceptions, and Spanish isn't any different. You usually have to memorize these exceptions since there isn't any apparent logic. I've listed a few here but this isn't in any way exhaustive:

- La radio = Radio
- La mano = Hand
- El sofá = Couch
- El mapa = Map
- El día = Day

The best way to avoid being always doubtful of yourself is to learn the articles (**unas, unos, una, un, las, los, la, el**) along with the verbs. Articles are what confirm the noun's gender. It is also important to remember that just because you think something might be referring to a male it doesn't mean that the noun will be masculine, such is the case with "the beard" or **la barba**.

Grammar isn't the most exciting part of learning any new language, but it is very necessary. If you don't have a strong grasp of grammar, you won't be able to communicate well, which is usually the main reason we don't learn new languages.

Verb Conjugation

The details of verb conjugation are a lot more complicated in Spanish than it is in English. Conjugating verbs change up the form of the verb in order to provide information about what is going on.

To be able to understand this better, we'll take a look at English verb conjugation and how they differ from Spanish. We will go over the English conjugation first, and then we will go over the Spanish conjugation.

Beginners don't need to worry a lot about "indicative," "auxiliary verb," or "present tense."

This is by no means an exhaustive analysis, but it should give you enough to have a slight grasp on verb conjugation.

Infinitive

In English, the verb's infinitive form is "to talk." This is the basic form of the verb. It doesn't convey any information about the action of the verb. "To talk in public is difficult," is an example of how it can be used in a sentence as a noun.

The same thing holds true in the Spanish language, they can also be used as a noun as they don't convey any information about the action of the verb.

Every Spanish infinitive will end in either –ir, –er, or –ar. **Hablar** is the Spanish word for 'to talk.'

Present-tense indicative verbs

For most verbs in the English language, add an "s" onto the end of it when it is used in a third-person present-tense sentence. There won't be any suffix added to show another subject, just the third person or anyone other than the person who is talking. So, we will say, "they speak, we speak, she speaks, he speaks, you speak, or I speak."

In the Spanish language, there will be different endings that get attached to verbs that show whether the person is first-, second-, or third- in the plural or singular form. For normal verbs, the –ir, –er, or –ar at the end of a word gets replaced with the right ending, such as **ellos hablan** means they talk; **nosotros hablamos** means "we talk"; **ella habla** means "she talks"; **él habla** means "he talks"; **tú hablas** means "you talk"; and **yo hablo** means "I talk." Most of the time, the verb provides enough information that you won't have to show who is performing the action whether it is with a pronoun or noun.

Adjectives

Everyone knows that an adjective is a word that will describe either a pronoun or noun. The biggest difference between an adjective in English and an adjective in Spanish is the placement and agreement.

In this language, the modified noun comes before the adjective, but there are exceptions —which you'll find there are a lot of— for things like numbers that must concur with the noun in gender and number. The noun comes after the adjective used to modify it when we're talking about the English language, and that is always true. This means it doesn't agree. Look at the following sentence and notice how **limpia** is after **persona** but **ocho** is in front of **años.**

"Teníamos que rotar para lavar la cocina, dejar la cocina impecable porque mi mamá era una persona muy limpia, y a los ocho años me dijo: mi hijita, feliz cumpleaños, tienes ocho años y hoy ya puedes participar en la rotación."

This means: "We had to rotate to clean the kitchen, to leave the kitchen impeccable because my mom was a very clean person, and at age eight, she told me: my Little girl, happy birthday, you are eight years old, and today, you can now participate in the rotation."

Adverbs and Adjectives

You remember from elementary school that adverbs can modify other adverbs, adjectives, and verbs while adjectives modify nouns. You will see two adjectives in the following sentences. They are **bonitas** and **mexicanas**. They both modify **tradiciones,** which is a noun. The adverb **muy** modifies the word **bonitas**, which is an adjective.

"Y las tradiciones mexicanas son muy bonitas." This means: "And Mexican traditions are very nice." In the English language, it is common for people to use words like "good" instead of an adverb like "well."

As Adjective

- "George writes good"
- "You should drive slow in a school zone"

As Adverb

- "George writes well"
- "You should drive slowly in a school zone"

In Spanish, you won't typically use adjectives to modify verbs. They normally just use adverbs.

- "George escribe bien"
- "Necesitas manejar lentamente en una zona escolar"

BASIC CONVERSATION

Words

1)

    ✓ Hello means Hola
      Now say it yourself: Hola
      Great!

2)

    ✓ Hi, My Name is means Hola, mi nombre es
      Now say it yourself: Hola, mi nombre es… John
      Great!

3)

    ✓ How are you? means ¿Cómo estás?
      Now say it yourself: ¿Cómo estás?
      Great!

4)

    ✓ Nice to meet you means Mucho gusto
      Now say it yourself: Mucho gusto
      Great!

5)

    ✓ Good, what about you? means Bien, ¿y tú?
      Now say it yourself: Bien, ¿y tú?
      Great!

6)

    ✓ What's the time? means ¿Qué hora es?
      Now say it yourself: ¿Qué hora es?
      Great!

7)

    ✓ Where is? means ¿Dónde está…?
      Now say it yourself: ¿Dónde está…?
      Great!

8)

    ✓ How was your weekend means ¿Qué tal tu fin de semana?
      Now say it yourself: ¿Qué tal tu fin de semana?
      Great!

9)

    ✓ How has your day been? means ¿Qué tal tu día?
      Now say it yourself: ¿Qué tal tu día?
      Great!

10)

    ✓ Where are you from? means ¿De dónde eres?
      Now say it yourself: ¿De dónde eres?
      Great!

11)

    ✓ What's your number? means ¿Cuál es tu número de teléfono?
      Now say it yourself: ¿Cuál es tu número de teléfono?
      Great!

12)

    ✓ You look good today means ¡Te ves bien!
      Now say it yourself: ¡Te ves bien!
      Great!

13)

    ✓ Where is the closest restaurant? means ¿Dónde queda el restaurante más cercano?
      Now say it yourself: ¿Dónde queda el restaurante más cercano?
      Great!

14)

- ✓ What do you do for fun? means ¿Qué tegusta hacer?
  Now say it yourself: ¿Qué te gusta hacer?
  Great!

15)

- ✓ What's your job? means ¿Cuál es tu trabajo?
  Now say it yourself: ¿Cuál es tu trabajo?
  Great!

16)

- ✓ Where do you work? means ¿Dónde trabajas?
  Now say it yourself: ¿Dónde trabajas?
  Great!

17)

- ✓ I need help means Necesito ayuda
  Now say it yourself: Necesito ayuda
  Great!

18)

- ✓ Take care, see you! means ¡Cuídate! Nos vemos
  Now say it yourself: ¡Cuídate! Nos vemos
  Great!

19)

- ✓ Goodbye means Adiós
  Now say it yourself: Adiós
  Great!

20)

- ✓ Please means Por favor

Now say it yourself: Por favor
Great!

21)

✓ Thanks/ Thank you means Gracias
Now say it yourself: Gracias
Great!

22)

✓ Thank you very much means Muchas gracias
Now say it yourself: Muchas gracias
Great!

23)

✓ You're welcome means De nada
Now say it yourself: De nada
Great!

24)

✓ I'm sorry means Lo siento
Now say it yourself: Lo siento
Great!

25)

✓ Excuse me means Permiso
Now say it yourself: Permiso
Great!

26)

✓ Good morning means Buenos días
Now say it yourself: Buenos días
Great!

27)

- ✓ Good night means Buenas noches
  Now say it yourself: Buenas noches
  Great!

28)

- ✓ Good afternoon/ evening means Buenas tardes
  Now say it yourself: Buenas tardes
  Great!

29)

- ✓ See you soon means Nos vemos pronto
  Now say it yourself: Nos vemos pronto
  Great!

30)

- ✓ See you later means Nos vemos luego
  Now say it yourself: Nos vemos luego
  Great!

31)

- ✓ See you tomorrow means Nos vemos mañana
  Now say it yourself: Nos vemos mañana
  Great!

32)

- ✓ Have a nice day means ¡Que tengas buen día!
  Now say it yourself: ¡Que tengas buen día!
  Great!

33)

- ✓ What date is today? means ¿Qué fecha es hoy?
  Now say it yourself: ¿Qué fecha es hoy?
  Great!

34)

    ✓ What's your last name/ surname? means ¿Cuál es tu apellido?
      Now say it yourself: ¿Cuál es tu apellido?
      Great!

35)

    ✓ Do you have a nickname? means ¿Tienes un apodo?
      Now say it yourself: ¿Tienes un apodo?
      Great!

36)

    ✓ What do you do? means ¿A qué te dedicas?
      Now say it yourself: ¿A qué te dedicas?
      Great!

37)

    ✓ What are you doing? means ¿Qué haces?
      Now say it yourself: ¿Qué haces?
      Great!

38)

    ✓ Are you ok? means ¿Estás bien?
      Now say it yourself: ¿Estás bien?
      Great!

39)

    ✓ How do you feel? means ¿Cómo te sientes?
      Now say it yourself: ¿Cómo te sientes?
      Great!

40)

    ✓ Where do you live? means ¿Dónde vives?
      Now say it yourself: ¿Dónde vives?
      Great!

41)

    ✓ Could you please help me? means ¿Podrías ayudarme, por favor?
       Now say it yourself: ¿Podrías ayudarme, por favor?
       Great!

42)

    ✓ May I help you? means ¿Puedovayudarte?
       Now say it yourself: ¿Puedo ayudarte?
       Great!

43)

    ✓ Do you speak English/Spanish? means ¿Hablas inglés/español?
       Now say it yourself: ¿Hablas inglés/español?
       Great!

44)

    ✓ How old are you? means ¿Qué edad tienes?
       Now say it yourself: ¿Qué edad tienes?
       Great!

45)

    ✓ When is your birthday? means ¿Cuándo es tu cumpleaños?
       Now say it yourself: ¿Cuándo es tu cumpleaños?
       Great!

46)

    ✓ Do you like movies or TV series? means ¿Te gustan las películas o las series de televisión?
       Now say it yourself: ¿Te gustan las películas o las series de televisión?
       Great!

47)

    ✓ Where do you study? means ¿Dónde estudias?

Now say it yourself: ¿Dónde estudias?
Great!

48)

   ✓ Would you please repeat? means ¿Puedes repetir, por favor?
Now say it yourself: ¿Puedes repetir, por favor?
Great!

49)

   ✓ What does that mean? means ¿Qué significa…?
Now say it yourself: ¿Qué significa…?
Great!

50)

   ✓ How do you say… means ¿Cómo se dice…?
Now say it yourself: ¿Cómo se dice…?
Great!

51)

   ✓ May I borrow your…? means ¿Podrías prestarme tu…?
Now say it yourself: ¿Podrías prestarme tu…?
Great!

Days, Months and Weather

Days of the week

- Monday is Lunes
- Tuesday is Martes
- Wednesday is Miércoles
- Thursday is Jueves
- Friday is Viernes
- Saturday is Sábado
- Sunday is Domingo

Months

- January is Enero
- February is Febrero
- March is Marzo
- April is Abril
- May is Mayo
- June is Junio
- July is Julio
- August is Agosto
- September is Septiembre
- October is Octubre

- November is Noviembre
- December is Diciembre

Weather and Times of the Day

- Autumn is otoño
- Cloudy is nublado
- Cold is frío
- Evening is tarde
- Fog is neblina
- Freeze is helada
- Fresh is fresco
- Hot is caliente
- Lightning is relámpago
- Midday is mediodía
- Midnight is medianoche
- Moon is luna
- Morning is mañana
- Night is noche
- Rain is lluvia
- Rainy is lluvioso
- Season is estación
- Snow is nieve
- Spring is primavera
- Star is estrella
- Storm is tormenta
- Summer is verano
- Sun is sol
- Sunny is soleado
- Sunrise is amanecer
- Sunset is atardecer
- Thunder is trueno
- Tropical is tropical
- Warmth is calor
- Wind is viento
- Winter is invierno

DEFINITE ARTICLE: THE / EL, LA, LOS, LAS

T he definite article is 'the' in English. It identifies the one out of a group of nouns that you are speaking about. For example, 'give me the pen' means not just any pen but the one that I want. Spanish definite articles operate in much the same way as English but they change depending on the gender of the noun.

Masculine nouns are preceded by 'el'—such as 'el árbol' (the tree) and feminine nouns are preceded by 'la' such as – 'la mesa' (the table).

When this is not true

If the noun starts with a strong 'a' sound the article is 'el'. This happens even if the noun is feminine. For example, 'agua' (water) is feminine, but, when placed with the definite article it is 'el agua.'

This is because, if you were to say 'la agua', the tongue would stumble when trying to pronounce two 'a' sounds so close together. In English, we do the same thing when using 'an' with nouns that begin with vowels. Imagine saying 'a apple', not so easy, huh?

More examples of feminine nouns beginning with 'el':

'el águila' (the eagle), 'el aula' (the classroom), 'el alma' (the soul), 'el arma' (the weapon), 'el hacha' (the axe), 'el hambre' (the hunger).

Plurals

Plural nouns are preceded by 'los' if they are masculine—for example, 'los coches' and 'las' for feminine, 'las plantas.'

Del and al

If your sentence has 'de' + 'el' put them together to form 'del.'

If it has 'a' + 'el' put them together to form 'al.' For example:

'Vamos al parque'—we are going to the park and 'la ventana del edificio'—the window of the building/the building's window.

Spanish/ English Difference: When the article is and is not used

When referring to 'the internet.' It is 'me gusta internet' – I like the internet, not the internet. When referring to monarchs or cities.

For example:

- Felipe, Rey de España' or 'Londres, capital de Reino Unido.

When the article is used 'El,' 'la,' 'los' and 'las' are used when we would use 'the' in English, but they are also used for abstract concepts such as 'love,' 'quality', 'health,' 'nature' ('el amor,' 'la calidad,' 'la salud,' 'la naturaleza,' respectively). We don't do this in English—possibly because most of the time these refer to things you can't see. But just because you can't see them does not mean they are not objects, which is why Spanish speakers still use the article. 'El' and 'los' are also used for days of the week. In English, we would use the preposition 'on.'

For example:

- El sábado juego un partido de fútbol – on Saturday I'll play a football match.

If this event occurs on multiple Saturdays then use the article 'los.'

For example:

- Los Domingo paso tiempo con mi familia – on Sundays I spend time with my family.

For more on days of the week have a look at 'the dates' lesson here.

Indefinite article: A, an (un, una, unos, unas.) The indefinite article is 'a' or 'an' in English and is used to talk about any one of a group. For example, 'give me a pen,' now you don't want one in particular (the pen), any pen will do.

'Un' precedes masculine nouns such as 'un bolígrafo', 'un libro' (a book) while 'una' precedes feminine nouns for example, 'una mesa', 'una bolsa' (a bag).

Spanish/English difference: When to use the indefinite article

'Un' and 'una' can be translated as 'a' in English but there are a couple of important differences:

You don't use the indefinite article:

With professions: For example, 'soy maestra' (I am a teacher) or 'es ingeniero' (He is an engineer). After 'sin' ('without') or 'qué' ('what' or 'how'): For example:

- Sale sin chaqueta
- He goes out without a jacket

- Qué sorpresa la fiesta
- What a surprise the party was

When speaking about something that is not concrete: This is a little tricky — in English, we use 'a' or 'an' for things that are definitely real such as 'there is a cat in the room.' However, we also use it for things that might not be real, such as 'is there a queue at the bank right now?' or 'do you have a pen?'

In Spanish this would be '¿hay cola en el banco ahora mismo? and '¿tienes coche?

The reason why the 'un' or 'una' is omitted is that you can only use it to refer to something that you are sure it exists or used to exist. You don't know whether your friend has a pen or that there is a queue at the bank. For this reason, the indefinite article is hardly ever used in questions or negatives.

How to know when to put 'un' or 'una' in a sentence The Spanish word for number one is 'uno' in masculine and 'una' in feminine, very similar (and indeed identical in feminine) to the indefinite article. For this reason, Spanish speakers often get 'a' and 'one' mixed up when speaking English.

Use this to your advantage. When you say a sentence in Spanish, translate the 'un' or 'una' in your head as 'one.' If the sentence still works in English with the number, then you can use the article in Spanish, if it doesn't work, then leave the article out.

For example:

- Tengo un problema.

- I have a problem or I have one problem.

The sentence still works and so keep 'un.'

- Pásame un libro en la mesa
  Pass me a book on the table, or pass me one book on the table. Still, the sentence works and so keep the 'un.'

- ¿Tienes un móvíl? – Do you have one mobile?
  This really doesn't work and so take out the 'un.'
- ✓ No, no tengo un móvil – No, I don't have one mobile.
  Again it doesn't work, so take out the 'un.'

Plurals

If the items you want are plural then you use 'unos' for masculine and 'unas' for feminine. This can be translated as 'some' in English.

For example:

- Pásame unos libros.
- Pass me some books.

As an alternative to 'unos/unas' you can also use 'algunos/algunas'. Most of the time the two can be used interchangeably, however, there are a few subtle differences.

Unos / unas versus algunos / algunas

Unos: When making an approximation you use 'unos' and not 'algunos'.

For example:

- Hay unas cincuenta sillas en la sala de reuniones.
- There are some fifty chairs in the meeting room.

Algunos: In the case of 'some of', 'algunos de' is far more used that 'unos de'. For example:

- Hay algunos de mis papeles en el estante.
- There are some of my papers on the shelf.

- Algunas de las montañas mas altas existen en Asia.
- Some of the tallest mountains exist in Asia.

Also: if the sentence contrasts with 'none' or 'no one' then, "algunos/as" is more common.

For example:

- Algunas personas les gusta la morcilla
- Some people like blood sausage (as opposed to no one).

- Algunos empleados trabajan durante el fin de semana
- Some employees work at the weekend.

Diminutives and augmentatives

Diminutives

In English we put a 'y' at the end of nouns to emphasize their smallness, such as the words 'doggy' or 'blanky.' Spanish does the same thing. To create a diminutive, drop the '-o' or '-a' from the noun and add '-ito' or '-ita'. Add '-cito' or '-cita' to words not ending in 'o' or 'a.'

For example:

- Perrito – doggy
- Bolsito – little bag
- Mesita – little table
- Cochecito – little car

Augmentatives

Spanish nouns and adjectives can also be changed to imply largeness (and also often 'undesirable'). There are many ways to do this, but, the two most popular endings are: -ón/-ona and -azo/-aza.

For example:

- Copión – Big cheat in exams

- Comilón – Big eater
- Exitazo – Great success
- Perrazo – Big, mean dog
- Portazo – To slam the door

Adjectives

Adjectives in Spanish usually (but not always) go after the noun and match its gender by changing their ending to 'o' or 'a.'

For example: 'la niña alta', or 'el coche blanco.' It is worth noting, that only the colors 'negro' (black), 'blanco' (white), rojo (red) and 'amarillo' (yellow) change depending on the gender of the noun as the others cannot change their endings.

More adjectives don't change their endings. Here is a selection of a few more adjectives that don't change:

- Difícil/fácil – difficult/easy
- Feliz/triste – happy/unhappy (the synonym 'contento,' however, does change gender)
- Fuerte – strong
- Natural – natural
- Optimista/pesimista – optimistic/pessimistic

Plurals

Unlike English, if the noun is plural then the adjective is plural—such as, 'las casas blancas' or 'los perros negros.' This is usually easy to learn as it is perfectly logical.

Nationalities are also, without exception, plural—for example, 'los ingleses' (the English) or 'los alemanes'—(the Germans). Note that nationalities are not capitalized.

Negatives

Spanish speakers hardly ever use prefixes to make adjectives negative (such as 'uninteresting'). Instead they use:

- No "no es común" (it isn't common or it is uncommon).
- Sin "es un problema sin solucionar" (it is an unsolvable problema).

- Poco, this does not mean in this case 'little' or 'few' but rather 'not much' or 'not very.' For example: El hombre es poco inteligente – The man is not very intelligent.

Styles and materials

This is relatively easy. Simply add 'de' and the noun. For example:

"La mesa es de madera" the table is wooden (or literally 'the table is of wood').

This way of speaking means that you can quickly make complicated descriptions without learning a long list of adjectives. Check out these material words:

- De flores – Flowery
- De lunares – Spotted
- De seda – Silky
- De piel – Leather
- De lana – Woolen

Common mistakes: Adjective order

Most of the time adjectives go after the noun but this is not always the case.

Compared to English, Spanish actually has very few adjectives, so Spanish speakers change their position to create a second meaning.

Generally speaking, an adjective placed after the noun classifies the noun in terms of color, size, material or speed and so on, while an adjective before the noun adds emotion.

It is important to note, however, that many before-noun adjectives are not found in everyday speech and are usually only used in poetry and literature. I shall mark when this occurs below.

For example: 'La noche oscura' means 'the dark night' and 'la oscura noche' means 'The creepy night' (poetic term).

Here are some more examples:

Adjectives before and after the noun

- Mi viejo amigo – My old friend

- Mi amigo viejo – My physically old friend

- El triste hombre – The wretched man (poetic term)
- El hombre triste – The sad mad

- La antigua silla – Old-fashioned chair
- La silla antigua – Old chair

- El nuevo libro – Brand new book
- El libro nuevo – Newly issued book

- La pobre mujer – The pitiful woman
- La mujer pobre – The poor (no money) woman

- Mis propios zapatos – My own shoes
- Mis zapatos propios – My appropriate shoes

- Solo un hombre – Only one man
- Un hombre solo – A lonely man

- Un triste viaje – Dreadful trip (poetic term)
- Un viaje triste – A sad trip

- La única estudiente – The only student
- La estudiante única – The unique student

- La gran empresa – The great company
- La empresa grande – The big company

Adjectives that must go before the noun. There are some adjectives that always go before the noun. These are 'mejor' (better), 'peor' (worse), primero (first), 'segundo' (second), 'tercero' (third) and so on.

Buen, mal, gran. When *bueno, malo,* and *grande* go before a masculine noun they drop the last letter.

For example:

- El buen chico.
- The good boy.

- El mal perro.
- The bad dog.

If the noun is feminine, however, you must keep the 'a'.

For example:

- The buena vista.
- The good view.

LEARN FROM WHAT YOU LOVE

There is no point in time where you become ready for material made by native speakers for native speakers. It is certainly not when you complete that set of six Spanish textbooks. This imaginary point in time where you will magically be ready to understand everything doesn't exist. But the truth is that you don't even need to understand half of everything.

If you really want to reach an advanced level of Spanish within a few years, it is absolutely necessary to read, listen, and watch native Spanish materials for multiple hours every day. Although if your goals aren't set on reaching a high level of Spanish in such a short time frame, start with however much time you can commit to every day.

However, it is not recommended to do more than 90 minutes per day of studying the coursebook and reviewing Anki. For this reason, after this rigorous study period is over, we encourage reading, listening, observing and learning from native Spanish materials as much as possible every day.

The 20-Minute Rule

Video games, comics, books, websites, movies, and TV programs all contain everyday Spanish that you can break down and learn from. If you have ever tried to study any of these materials diligently in the past, however, you know how enormous a task it can be. How do you not become overwhelmed by websites where everything is in Spanish? How can you study a TV drama?

How do you keep up the willpower to continue these unsustainable study routines after just two days? The problem gets worse and worse. You can burn all of your initial motivation pushing yourself to break down and learn massive amounts of language until the day comes when you would rather do anything but another day of routine study.

In the case of reading native Spanish materials, you may use a dictionary to look up as many words as you need. Unlike video and audio materials, there's much less context to keep you engaged when there is just text and especially when there are quite a lot of words you don't know.

After the 20 minutes or so have passed, stop and examine your list of repeated words. Break down and learn the meaning of these words and the lines that they are found in by using online dictionaries and grammar resources. Once you have learned the meaning behind these high-frequency words and their respective lines, pick zero, one, or two of what you feel are the most important passages to practice using Anki. For the purposes of this book, one passage can be a single long sentence, a few sentences, or even brief dialogues.

The Power of Context

But why pick just one or two passages to practice using Anki and not three or more passages? There are two main reasons behind this choice. First, the process of creating the Anki cards for just one or two passages already takes a significant amount of time and work. And second, it is to set a strict limit on how much you review through Anki.

Ideally, you want to spend minimal time with Anki so that you can make more time for more reading and listening to native Spanish. And with the help of the 20-Minute Rule, you can easily create more digestible lists of words and contexts to learn from.

Encountering new words, phrases, and grammar points from multiple contexts is how we build upon our understanding of how to use them. It also makes them harder to forget each time we encounter them.

For this reason, you can even pick zero passages to practice with Anki to go straight back to reading and listening. You may want to save Anki for the toughest words and grammar points that you have looked up over and over and still have trouble understanding. Using Anki or even the Goldlist Method to review every single new word or phrase you have learned can severely slow down the time it takes you to reach fluency.

There is an amazing process that slowly blooms as you read, listen to, and mine a single source of native Spanish for vocabulary and sentences.

When you mine passages over and over from a particular subject matter for days and weeks, you will come to know its most commonly used words and phrases. Once you have a strong grasp on the high-frequency words, you will be able to piece together more and more of the meaning of new content from that source as you first hear or see it.

When new words and phrases come from a much larger story or plot that you are highly interested in, all that new information becomes so much more memorable. Almost every line has character to it, and they can become unforgettable. It's the power of context.

Forget the Rest!

Learning everything on your high-frequency word list should be a large enough chunk of work. But if you feel you can handle more, by all means, go through as many lines or sentences as you can before mental fatigue eventually surfaces. That fatigue signals that it's time to take a quick mental break before moving on to new content.

Spanish Is Not Too Fast

Using English subtitles to watch Spanish TV shows, movies, dramas, and videos is an English reading activity with some background noise. You will learn nothing outside a few basic words. You might be tempted to use them to help you focus on the story or relax after an intense study session, but if you choose to use them, native Spanish speakers will always talk too fast for you.

They will always talk too fast unless you take the time each and every day to practice trying to comprehend what they mean. But how can you comprehend them in the beginner and intermediate stages when they use thousands of words that you don't know yet? To answer this question, you must see listening comprehension as a skill. It's a skill that is built through practicing with whatever vocabulary that you do know at the time and relying on context for the words that you do not know.

You will understand the foreign language only by consistently trying to understand the foreign language. You need every chance that you can get to build towards your reading and listening comprehension. Some people like to cite that it takes roughly 10,000 hours of practice to achieve a high level of skill in anything, and this number may or may not be completely accurate. The value of consistent practice, however, is something most of us can agree on.

Listening comprehension is arguably the weakest skill of the average language learner, for they do not receive anywhere close to the amount of comprehensible input required to understand the spoken language as used by native speakers. While audio tracks accompanying language courses are certainly useful, you may quickly find that they do not provide the volume of practice necessary to understand native speakers out in the everyday world.

While subtitles in Spanish are extremely helpful to learning key moments from video materials, allow yourself to just listen for the full 20 minutes before delving into reading the subtitles. Sadly, these subtitles don't come equipped with the native speakers that you encounter in the real world, so think of it as practice in real-time.

Most of us don't have a family that can speak Spanish to us every day for 8-12 hours for 10+ years. You can pay tutors to do just that, but that becomes expensive to do every day for even just one hour a day. Without these adult native speakers constantly around, your ears remain incredibly weak. Listening to and reading native Spanish materials every day and regularly doing the Anki exercises will help to alleviate this problem.

No Subtitles, But How?

Train your ears to listen with your full attention and find the words that are both unknown to you and that are repeated frequently. The moments that you desire to understand the most can also be learned. Simply jot down the video times for later reference and don't press pause.

In case there are irremovable English subtitles in a video, you can block them from view by cutting out and placing a wide and thick but short piece of paper in front of your computer screen.

Keeping English subtitles out can be fairly difficult for some folks. You will be tested. You will need determination and faith to fight against the habit of doing everything in English. If allowed even for a brief moment, you feed the idea that you must understand everything to get the most enjoyment from the material.

This idea, however, is not necessarily true when you consider the enjoyment you gain as you gradually notice yourself being able to understand more and more

Spanish each and every day. Seeing true progress in yourself is a feeling like no other. It is self-empowering.

Start by watching and reading things where the premise is easily understandable. You may want to first choose the material that you have seen before, so you can get used to everything being in Spanish while still being able to follow the plot. Despite how good it may be for listening practice, it can be maddening watching the same episode or movie five or more times within the same week. Watch and read how you normally would in your native language. Once is enough. And if you really enjoy the material, you can always revisit it just like you do in your native language.

Work towards building and maintaining a habit of freely listening and watching without stopping. Do not continually stop to look up words and phrases. Trying new material and getting lost quickly is frustrating, but when you do possess something that you personally find exciting and can understand the gist, that's where learning truly starts to take off. When you finally realize that you do not need to understand everything said and can still enjoy the material that you love, you will know victory.

TIME (TIEMPO)

To talk about the time in Spanish, you just have to know the numbers and a few formulas, because it's not very different from English. These are the basic words you'll need:

- Time – Tiempo
- Hour – Hora
- Minute – Minuto
- Second – Segundo
- Morning – Mañana
- Noon – Mediodía
- Afternoon – Tarde
- Evening – Noche
- Midnight – Medianoche
- Night – Noche
- Sunrise – Amanecer
- Sunset – Atardecer
- Today – Hoy
- Yesterday – Ayer
- Tomorrow – Mañana
- The day before yesterday – Anteayer
- The day after tomorrow – Pasado mañana
- Now – Ahora
- Never – Nunca
- Always – Siempre
- Late – Tarde
- Early – Temprano
- On time – A tiempo/En horario
- Day – Día
- Week – Semana
- Month – Mes
- Year – Año
- Century – Siglo
- Daily – Diario
- Weekly – Semanal
- Monthly – Mensual
- Yearly – Anual

Asking and telling the time (preguntar y decir la hora) to ask for the time, we actually ask what "hour" it is:

✓ What time is it? – ¿Qué hora es?

Another difference with English is that in Spanish we don't have two different words for evening and night:

✓ It's 9 in the evening – Son las nueve de la noche

561

When you write in Spanish, it's quite normal to use the 24-hour clock instead of adding "pm" or "am" to the 12 hour clock:

✓ The meeting is at 4 p.m. – La reunión es a las 16:00

There are different ways of writing the time:

- 16:00
- 16.00
- 16 h
- 4 p. m.

But when you talk in Spanish, you don't normally use the 24-hour clock.

Instead you add de la mañana (in the morning), de la tarde (in the afternoon) or de la noche (in the evening/night) after the time: four a.m. - las cuatro de la mañana

✓ 4 p.m. – las cuatro de la tarde
✓ 8 p.m. – las ocho de la noche

To talk about what time it is, we use the plural conjugation of the verb ser (to be), except for the 1, when we use the singular conjugation:

✓ It's three in the afternoon – Son las tres de la tarde
✓ It's eight o'clock – Son las ocho en punto
✓ It's 1 in the morning – Es la una de la mañana

Here's how to say and write every hour of the day:

00:00 - las doce de la noche / medianoche

01:00 - la una de la mañana

02:00 - las dos de la mañana

03:00 - las tres de la mañana

04:00 - las cuatro de la mañana

05:00 - las cinco de la mañana

06:00 - las seis de la mañana

07:00 - las siete de la mañana

08:00 - las ocho de la mañana

09:00 - las nueve de la mañana

10:00 - las diez de la mañana

11:00 - las once de la mañana

12:00 - las doce del mediodía / el mediodía

13:00 - la una de la tarde

14:00 - las dos de la tarde

15:00 - las tres de la tarde

16:00 - las cuatro de la tarde

17:00 - las cinco de la tarde

18:00 - las seis de la tarde

19:00 - siete de la tarde / siete de la noche

20:00 - ocho de la tarde / ocho de la noche

21:00 - nueve de la noche

22:00 - diez de la noche

23:00 - once de la noche

When you have to write a specific time, you can do it with numbers:

- 16:45
- 13:30
- 21:22

When you're talking, just like in English, you can say the full number or sometimes you can take some 'shortcuts':

- quarter to – menos cuarto/cuarto para…
- ten to – menos diez/diez para…

- five to – menos cinco/cinco para…
- o'clock – en punto
- quarter past – y cuarto
- half past – y media

As you see, it's very similar to English. Examples:

- 14:45 – las tres y cuarto
- 13:30 – la una y media
- 20:15 – las ocho y cuarto
- 17:55 – las seis menos cinco
- 21:50 – las diez menos diez/diez para las once

Exercises:

1) I have to wake up at six a.m. – Tengo que levantarme a las
   ………………………

2) Sunrise will be at a quarter to six – El amanecer será a las seis
   ……………………..

3) Yesterday I was feeling bad – ……………… me sentía mal

4) Today I feel good – ………… me siento bien

5) Tomorrow at half past eight I have a date – Mañana a las ……….. y media tengo una cita

6) When will we see each other? – ¿………………… nos veremos?

Days of the week and months (días de la semana y meses)

These are the days of the week. In Spanish, you don't need to capitalize them:

- Monday – lunes
- Tuesday – martes
- Wednesday – miércoles
- Thursday – jueves
- Friday – viernes
- Saturday – sábado
- Sunday – domingo

And these are the months, which we also don't capitalize:

- January – enero

564

- February – febrero
- March – marzo
- April – abril
- May – mayo
- June – junio
- July – julio
- August – agosto
- September – septiembre
- October – octubre
- November – noviembre
- December – diciembre

Seasons and years

In South America, seasons (estaciones) are the opposite as in North America and Europe. When it's summer in Spain (from June to September), it's winter in South America, and vice versa. The four seasons are the following:

- Summer – verano
- Autumn – otoño
- Winter – invierno
- Spring – primavera

When we're talking about years, remember we don't use a dot nor a comma to mark the thousands: we write 1999 instead of 1.999. Here are some sentences to talk about years:

- I was born in the year 1990 – Nací en el año 1990 (mil novecientos noventa)
- Monet painted his water lilies in the 1920s – Monet pintó sus nenúfares en los años veinte
- Last year I finished college – El año pasado terminé la universidad
- Next year I will get married – El año que viene voy a casarme
- I will move to Europe next year – Me mudaré a Europa el año próximo
- We met some years ago – Nos conocimos hace algunos años
- I can't believe it's almost 2020 – No puedo creer que ya sea casi el 2020 (dos mil veinte)
- Pompeii was destroyed in the year 79 AD – Pompeya fue destruida en el año 79 d. C. (después de Cristo)

- Julius Caesar was born in the year 100 BC – Julio César nació en el año 100 a. C. (antes de Cristo)
- In a couple of centuries, humans will move out to other planets - En un par de siglos, los humanos se mudarán a otros planetas
- I was born in the last century – Nací en el siglo pasado
- It's year 2018 – Es el año 2018

Dates (fechas)

To write a date, remember in Spanish we don't use the month-day-year system, but the day-month-year system, so 12/06/2018 is the 12th of June, and not the 6th of December. To say a full date, you just need to learn the days of the week, the numbers and the months. While in English the ordinal numbers are frequently used to talk about dates, in Spanish we normally use cardinal numbers. Examples:

- Today is Monday, the 7th of January, of year 2018 – Hoy es lunes 7 (siete) de enero del año 2018 (dos mil dieciocho)
- My birthday is on December 12th – Mi cumpleaños es el 12 (doce) de diciembre
- My father was born on February 24th of 1967 – Mi padre nació el 24 (veinticuatro) de febrero de 1967 (mil novecientos sesenta y siete)

We do use the ordinal number for the first day of the month in Spanish:

- Where's the champagne? – ¿Dónde está la champaña?
- It's January 1st already! – ¡Ya es el 1° (primero) de enero!

Age (edad)

In Spanish, we don't say we are a certain amount of years old, but we have years. We use the verb *tener*:

- How old are you? –¿Cuántos años tienes?
- I am 30 years old – Tengo 30 (treinta) años
- I had my first child at 28 – Tuve a mi primer hijo a los 28 (veintiocho) años
- You will go out alone when you're at least 17 years old – Saldrás a bailar solo cuando tengas al menos 17 (diecisiete) años

SUBJECTS

As you might remember from grade school, every sentence has at least one subject—the thing or person who performs the action indicated by the verb.

Determining the Gender

Most of the time, the subject of your sentence will be a noun. Nouns work the same way in Spanish as they do in English—with one major exception. In Spanish, all nouns have an assigned gender, whether the noun represents a person, place, or thing. The gender of a noun is either natural, referring to people who do have an established gender, or grammatical, where gender has been arbitrarily assigned to things or concepts.

Natural Gender

Most nouns in this category come in two versions: masculine and feminine.

Take a look at the following table.

Natural Gender Nouns

Masculine

Feminine

- Doctor (male doctor)
- Doctora (female doctor)

- Estudiante (male student)
- Estudiante (female student)

- Inglés (Englishman)
- Inglesa (Englishwoman)

- Muchacho (boy)
- Muchacha (girl)

- Periodista (male journalist)
- Periodista (female journalist)

- Perro (male dog)
- Perra (female dog)

- Toro (bull)
- Vaca (cow)

There are four basic rules for dealing with natural gender nouns: When a masculine noun ends in –o, substitute an –a to make it feminine. For example, *muchacho* becomes *muchacha*, and *perro* becomes *perra*.

When a masculine noun ends in a consonant, add an/a at the end to make it feminine. For example, *doctor* becomes *doctora*, and *inglés* becomes *inglesa*.

Sometimes nouns have only one gender. For example, there is no feminine noun for hombre, so use mujer; toro becomes vaca. Sometimes the same word may be used for both genders; in these cases, the gender is specified by articles or adjectives.

This rule includes (but is not limited to) words that end in –ista or –e. For example, el periodista becomes la periodista, el estudiante becomes la estudiante, and el modelo becomes la modelo.

Grammatical (Assigned) Gender

Grammatical gender does not follow a logical pattern and must be memorized. You can, however, identify some cases of grammatical gender by looking at the endings.

Masculine Endings

Ending Example English:

Plural

–aje

- ✓ viaje - journey

n/a

–gen

- ✓ origen – origin
- ✓ imagen - image
- ✓ margen - margin

–men

- ✓ examen - exam

n/a

–o

- ✓ libro - book
- ✓ mano - hand

–or

- ✓ doctor - male doctor
- ✓ labor - work

Feminine Endings

Ending example English masculine exceptions:

–a

- ✓ libra - pound
- ✓ mapa – map
  Some abstract nouns, like problema lb.

–ad

- ✓ verdad - truth

n/a

–ed

- ✓ merced - mercy

n/a

–ie

- ✓ serie - series

n/a

–ión

- ✓ religion – religion
  Some concrete nouns, like gorrión (sparrow)

–sis

- ✓ síntesis - synthesis análisis (analysis) , énfasis (emphasis) , éxtasis (ecstasy)

–ud

- ✓ salud - health
- ✓ ataúd - coffin

– umbre

- ✓ costumbre - custom

n/a

Some nouns are feminine even though they end with an –o because they are really abbreviations. For example, foto (photo) is a feminine noun because it is really fotografía (photograph), a noun that ends with an –a.

An "S" for Plural

Making nouns plural is easy because in most cases the concept is the same as in English—just add an –s or an –es. However, there are some variations, so take a look at the following rules:

570

- When the noun ends with an unstressed vowel, just add an –s.
  For example, playa (beach) becomes playas in plural.
- When the noun ends with a consonant other than –s, add an –es.
  For example, flor (flower) becomes flores in plural.
- When the noun ends with a stressed vowel, add an –es.
  For example, iraní (Iranian) becomes iraníes; inglés (Englishman) becomes *ingleses* in plural.
- When the noun ends with an unstressed vowel and –s, don't add anything.
  For example, crisis remains crisis in the plural.

BUILD YOUR OWN SENTENCES

Porks and Recreation

(*Hacer*, *Poder*, and *Querer*)

What's the distinction between "doing" something and "making" something?

In many dialects, they're precisely the same thing. There is no distinction. Most English speakers track down this exceptionally odd. We assume that "making" furthermore, "doing" are two altogether various classifications. By and large, we "make" physical articles, for example, suppers ("they made breakfast"). We "do" activities, like exercise ("I did my activity").

In any case, all things being equal, there's a ton of hybrid. For instance, a "botch" is an activity. So it ought to be "do," shouldn't it? In any case, no, we generally say "I committed an error," not "I did a slip-up."

As another model, on the off chance that you return home to find that everything has been spilled off of your kitchen racks, you would likely be furious that there's a wreck. There are two inquiries you may pose: "Who made this wreck?" or "Who did this?" For Spanish speakers, "to make" and "to do" are precisely the same thing. "Making a wreck" is exactly the same thing as "doing a wreck"; "making supper" is exactly the same thing as "eating." One of our threatening area characters, Sarah, will return to show us this exercise.

Hacer: Do Your Own Dinner

Sarah invests the majority of her energy at her apple shop, *Ser*, where she just frets about being: "Would you say you are a tall individual?"

Be that as it may, when she feels keener on doing or making something, she goes down the road to her café, *Hacer*.

The infinitive *hacer* signifies "to do" or "to make." The syllable-centered sounds like "ser", even though it obviously has a totally unique significance.

(Recollect additionally that the H toward the start is quiet: "ah-SER")

Hacer is a make-your-own feast eatery that Ser oversees. It could be abnormal that you would go to a café and afterward make your own dinner; however, that is the means by which Ser likes to run things. All things considered, the fundamental explanation is for self-centered purposes: She needs others to make nourishment for her. So not at all like at the apple shop, at *Hacer* she isn't exceptionally fussy about who comes in, as long as the visitors will make dinners and give a portion of the food back to Ser herself.

(Think "Ser" or "a Ser," and you'll recollect the way to express *hacer*).

Joel and his companions go to Ser's café on the grounds that they need to make supper for themselves. When they come in, Ser discloses to them that they need to feel free to set up a "hoard" immediately. They're relied upon to plan pigs for supper, yet Sarah consistently calls these pigs "swines."

So she gives out a hoard to every one of her clients: one for Joel, one for the reptile, and one for the pandas to share. Every one of them is relied upon to rub flavors on the hoard and afterward push it into a hoard getting a ready machine that will do the cooking.

Since Joel is childish and hungry, he demands being quick to set up his hoard. He says, "I'll go do my hoard first." The word he utilizes is hago, which sounds similar to "I'll go" (recollect that the *H* is quiet, as usual). This signifies "I do" or "I make."

However, at that point, something unusual occurs: Joel hears a snorting commotion, coming from the heading of the reptile's pig. It appears to be that the reptile's hoard is attempting to say something.

"What did the reptile's hoard say?" asks Joel. Then, at that point, a similar sound starts to come from the pandas' hoard. "What are the swines saying?" This is very disrupting: The pigs appear to talk. In Joel's confounded surge, he articulates "hoard" wrong, leaving out the H and the G, so it seems like "AH-say" and "AH-saying."

The words *hace* and *hacen* are utilized for the reptile and the pandas. *Hace* signifies "it does" or "it makes" (and can likewise be applied to "he" or "she, for example, "she does" or "he makes"). Hacen signifies "they do" or "they make." Obviously, the word *haces* is utilized for "you do" or "you make," so it's what Joel says to Sarah: "You gave us live hoards to cook? What's going on with you?"

To say "what are you doing", Joel says "¿Qué haces?"

However, it's past the point of no return; the swines are as of now locked behind stove-like entryways. Gazing at the swines through the glass, Joel and the pandas all at the same time say, "God help us… " and at precisely the same time, they see the pigs saying exactly the same thing:

"Goodness."

"Did you see that?" yells Joel. "The swines all said exactly the same thing that we did! What's happening with us? What we are doing isn't acceptable." When he says "we are doing," he utilizes the word *hacemos*, which has the focus on syllable "same" (in view of the way that they all said the "same" thing immediately).

The swines vanish into the activities of Hacer's monster hoard planning machines. As they meet a weird destiny, how about we rapidly audit the assortment of words in this scene: *hago* for Joel, *hace* for the reptile, *hacen* for the pandas, haces for *Ser*, and *hacemos* (with the focus on syllable "same") for "we do" or on the other hand "we make."

Hacía

Joel is upset by the idea that he and his companions have sent pigs into a feast getting ready machine while they were as yet alive.

By inspecting the chutes that the pigs were sent through, he can tell that they have probably been coordinated to an enormous machine behind the counter.

At the point when Ser isn't looking, Joel sneaks behind the counter to draw nearer to this machine. It has exceptionally minuscule windows, similar to peep openings, and Joel trusts he can spy into the machine to perceive what's new with the swines: "I need to perceive what I can see."

The focused on the syllable "see" goes with the word hacía, which is the defective past tense for Hacer. Hacía applies to both Joel and the reptile, so it can mean "I was doing," "I was making," "he was doing," "she was making, etc.

In the meantime, different words can be gotten from this word: hacían, hacías, and hacíamos, all of which utilize a similar focused on syllable, "see."

In case you're giving close consideration, you may as of now understand that the action word *Hacer* is an activity action word. All in all, it resembles *Ir*: You normally do it one time, not for a significant stretch of time. The blemished past tense isn't close to as normal as the preterite past tense (which we'll adapt soon).

To illustrate, how about we see what happens when Ser discovers Joel spying through the peep openings. "What are you doing back here?" she requests to know. "You're not approved to come behind the counter. This region is for experienced culinary specialists as it were."

Joel concocts a rationalization: "Yet I AM an accomplished gourmet expert! I used to make supper all when I was a youthful honey bee growing up, in light of the fact that my mom was too sluggish to even consider doing it without anyone else's help."

All the more frequently, obviously, Hacer is viewed as a one-time activity, so the preterite tense is more normal than the hacía tense. We'll gain proficiency with the preterite structures as Joel and his companions track down the pre-arranged swines coming out the opposite finish of the machine.

Red

Review that inside each store, we generally have a current state, a general (flawed) past tense, and a "red" (preterite) past tense.

For instance, in Estar the preterite "red" tense was between the racks, where the reptile and Joel discovered the meat stew cauldron. In Ir, we utilized the specialist's storage room for the preterite tense.

In Hacer, the "red tense" happens at the tablespace of the café, to one side of the passageway. This is the place where the visitors are relied upon to wrap up setting up the swines and afterward eat them.

Joel hears some pounding commotions and takes a gander at the tables. The swines have dropped out of chutes and onto the tables, presently completely cooked and practically prepared to eat, with an apple in each hoard's mouth.

Following the headings, Joel gets some sauce and enhancement, and he goes through around five minutes cautiously brightening the hoard, trusting that it will look pleasant. At the point when he's done with this, supper is prepared to eat!

"Goodness," says Joel, "I did that without anyone else's help? That wasn't hard in any way! Making supper was extremely simple."

Joel's assertion for "I did" (or "I made") is *hice*.

However, at that point, Joel investigates at the reptile. He's astonished to see that albeit the reptile spends a couple of moments tossing the embellishment and sauce onto the hoard, the reptile's hoard by one way or another looks far better than Joel's.

"HE'S SO acceptable at that!" says Joel. "He made his supper much quicker than I."

The word for "he made" (or "she made," or "he did," and so on) is *hizo* (articulated "EEH so").

In the meantime, Ser enters the scene and yells "Make sure to give me a portion of the food!" But as she comes in, she slips on some sauce on the floor, spilling the food that she's holding all around this piece of the eatery.

Joel is furious. "Cut it out!" he yells, in his wicked, formal voice.

"Look what you did! While we were making exceptionally pleasant dinners, you just made a major wreck!" The word for "you did" is hiciste, with the focus on syllable "stop." Shouldn't something be said about the pandas? This is a bit upsetting.

At the point when the pandas' hoard rises out of the chute, the pandas freeze with their mouths hanging open. One of them at last articulates, "Our hoard… it's relaxing!"

Joel takes a gander at the pandas' hoard. It is by all accounts lying unmoving, yet the apple before its mouth is the giveaway: The hoard's breath can be seen on the apple, with buildup musically showing up and blurring on the apple's surface as the hoard breathes in and breathes out.

"See, Ser!" says Joel. "You can see air on the apple before the pandas' hoard's mouth! Something's exceptionally off-base here."

GAMIFY

Calvin: "Hello, stand by a moment! It's mid-year! I'm an extended get-away! I would prefer not to *learn* anything!"

Hobbes: "If no one causes you to do it, it considers fun."

If you've made it past Lesson 4, congrats! You're past where most understudies fail spectacularly. Subsequent to working with many training understudies one-on-one, I have a consistently developing list of effective understudies who adhered to the interaction. They currently talk great conversational Spanish, and many are familiar. Be that as it may, unfortunately, I have a more drawn-out rundown of ex-understudies who all quit before they came to their objectives.

Everyone has their own justification for surrendering:

- ✓ I can't make the time any longer.
- ✓ It's harder than I suspected it would be.
- ✓ I get truly occupied and can presently don't zero in on this.
- ✓ It doesn't appear to merit all the difficulty.

Every one of these reasons shows one thing that these understudies share for all intents and purposes: They lost their adoration for the interaction.

Before you go any further, I need to make one thing clear: No reason is legitimate, period. Try not to gripe that you have no time that you're not shrewd enough, that you have no vacant space left to you. These issues are on the whole nonexistent, and genuine Spanish students have conquered them and some more.

For any individual who is beginning to get baffled or lose their enthusiasm for learning Spanish, here's the truth: The surest method to meet you will probably recapture a youngster-like fixation on it.

Talking about "kid like fixation," here's the greatest (and least legitimate) pardon of all:

"I believe I'm simply excessively old."

In case you're enticed to blame your age, I have news for you. Youngsters are worse than grown-ups at learning second dialects. Controlled examinations over time have exhibited this reality.

Only a couple of models:

Asher and Price, 1967: Three gatherings of understudies were tried on how well they could learn German: rudimentary (4-11), middle school (12-14), and school (18-25). The end: "Both the middle school and school bunches are better than the early age bunch."

Olsen and Samuels, 1973: Adolescents and kids were given short exercises in German elocution. The youths performed better compared to the youngsters.

Fathman, 1975: Non-English-talking kids, ages going from 6-15, were tried on their capacity to learn syntactic constructions of the English language. The more established youngsters scored higher.

Ekstrand, 1976: Immigrants of many ages were tried on their learning of Swedish inside a brief timeframe. The more established understudies performed better compared to the more youthful understudies in all spaces tried.

Snow and Hoefnagel-Höhle, 1978: Three gatherings were chipping away at learning Dutch naturalistically: kids, youths, and grown-ups. More than ten months, the grown-ups and youths performed better compared to the kids.

Ferman and Karni, 2010: Three gatherings of understudies were tried on their capacity to gain proficiency with the morphology of another dialect: 8-year-olds, 12-year-olds, and youthful grown-ups. The grown-ups performed best as a rule, and the 8-year-olds performed most exceedingly awful in all assessments.

However, the fantasy continues.

Truly, it appears to be sensible on a superficial level. All things considered, kids DO appear to learn dialects quicker than grown-ups. Indeed, they appear to learn everything quicker than grown-ups!

Maybe the examinations referenced are unimportant to the real world. Indeed, grown-ups may perform better in "controlled" conditions, yet genuine isn't controlled that way. In everyday living, grown-ups act uniquely in contrast to youngsters.

Youngsters make some simpler memories learning dialects in light of the fact that their ways of life are incredibly unique. Grown-ups have innumerable commitments and pressing factors each day. However, kids have a great time tracking down another test and adhering to it, every day of the week.

We should contemplate the way toward figuring out how to ride a bike. Envision that there are two individuals who are slow off the mark of figuring out how to ride a bike: a 10-year-old kid and her 30-year-old father. The girl is considerably more liable to wind up learning. The father is excessively occupied with different things. In any case, the child REALLY needs to learn. Every last bit of her companions are riding bicycles, and she understands left. She will remain fixed on that a certain something, continually each and every day, until she's prepared to zoom around the area on two wheels like all the cool children.

With language learning, exactly the same thing occurs: Adults and children both say that they "need" to learn, yet the kid is bound to have the concentration and assurance to stick through. In any case, a few grown-ups have kept up with their enthusiasm and industriousness, utilizing a rule that applies to any student of all ages:

Gamification.

Be Young and Be Reckless

Have you at any point seen an 8-year-old playing a computer game for 4 hours in a row?

Pat Flynn, creator of the WSJ hit "Will it fly?" Reports that during a significant stretch of time in his life, he spent a normal of 12 hours out of each day playing "Universe of Warcraft." Once he kept awake for 48 hours in a row due to the habit.

At the point when a youngster tracks down another fixation, regardless of whether it be a Lego set or a snowboard, you realize that he'll spend each waking hour consistently on it on the off chance that he can. His entire world will spin around it. Your psyche will be blown when you perceive how rapidly he aces its subtleties.

Youngsters may even disregard eating and drinking for quite a long time to take part in an invigorating, centered pursuit; they accomplish total stream. Possibly they're headed to arrive at more World of Warcraft achievements than their companions, or perhaps they're longing for some time snowboarding down an incline in the Alps at 65 miles each hour. In any case, nothing else matters. The drive to achievement gives them a high that is more than worth the appetite, thirst, lack of sleep, and wounds.

In any case, stop and think for a minute: This capacity to fixate on one thing isn't limited to kids. Pat Flynn was in school during his World of Warcraft gorging stage.

He remains youngster like in the most ideal manner conceivable, in light of the fact that consistently, he has held this basic expertise:

Tireless spotlight on something energizing.

An excessive number of grown-ups have lost this. Regardless of whether it's computer games or new dialects, we've been molded to have a limited ability to focus outside of earnest work projects. Outer pressing factors cause us subconsciously to scrutinize the manner in which we utilize our time and our consideration. It's awkward to go through four hours attempting to comprehend a ten-page kids' book in Spanish. Toward the rear of our brains, we feel like we're losing valuable time.

All in all, numerous grown-ups have lost their young diligence. We exchange it for stress-based improvements. In the event that a venture isn't critical and squeezing, it subliminally doesn't feel beneficial to invest energy on it.

The arrangement: Don't simply zero in on learning. Zero in on cherishing learning.

Notice the minutes that you get exhausted. Distinguish the pieces of the learning cycle that disappoint you. Then, at that point transform them around by making them into a great test.

- Have you become weary of remembering action word formations? Rather than considering records, envision yourself strolling around an "action word shop" in a memory castle, distinguishing words as you glance around.
- Does articulation disappoint you? Imagine you're a honey bee from another planet, or possibly a bird in a funny cartoon. Be an entertainer, and

get into a different character while you practice. Have a good time judging that individual rather than yourself.

— Are you disappointed with what amount of jargon there is to learn? Rather than retaining considerable arrangements of words, continue to zero in on the fundamental jargon that you've effectively learned. Treat those words as strong milestones to you. Then, at that point learn new words between those milestones, as though shading in the subtleties or coming to an obvious conclusion.

In Lesson 5, we have more jargon to learn than any other time in recent memory. However, the vast majority of that jargon will be in scenes you definitely know, for example, the event congregation and the court.

Try not to breeze over anything. You currently have a strong establishment to expand on, with fundamental jargon coordinated in your memory. Be that as it may, this way will fall on the off chance that you don't keep learning your jargon the same way, playing by the equivalent principles, putting away words in the memory castle regardless of whether you want to recall them without the mental helpers.

Yet, by and by, this all boils down to one guideline. Try not to surge it, don't leave any pieces out, and don't get baffled.

FAMILY MEMBERS- A CHART SHOWING THE MEMBERS OF THE FAMILY

Miembros de la familia

- **Jane:** Buenos días mamá, ¿quién de nuestra familia nos viene a visitar hoy?
- **Jane:** Good morning mom, who from our family is coming to visit us today?

- **Mamá:** Déjame mostrarte a todos en el árbol genealógico, así podrás ver quién nos viene a visitar.
- **Mum:** Let me show you everybody on the genealogical record, so you can see who is coming to visit.

- **Jane:** Está bien, ¡me encantaría ver el árbol genealógico!
- **Jane:** Okay, I'd love to see the family tree!

- **Mamá:** ¿Puedes ver dónde estás, Jane?
- **Mum:** Can you see where you are Jane?

- **Jane:** Sí, estoy en la esquina inferior izquierda debajo de ti y de papá.
- **Jane:** Yes, I'm in the base left corner under you and dad.

- **Mamá:** ¡Correcto! ¿Sabes quiénes son las dos personas encima de mí?
- **Mum:** Correct! Do you know who the two people above me are?

- **Jane:** ¡Son mi abuela y mi abuelo!
- **Jane:** They are my grandma and granddad!

- **Mamá:** Eso es correcto, ellos son mis padres.
- **Mum:** That's right, as they are my parents.

- **Jane:** Me encantará ver a mis abuelos, son muy amables. Mamá, ¿tienes algún hermano o hermana
- **Jane:** I will love to see my grandparents, they are very kind. Mom, do you have any brothers or sisters?

- **Mamá:** Tengo una hermana, tu tía Lucy. Ella está casada con el tío Peter. No tengo ningún hermano.
- **Mum:** I have a sister, your Aunt Lucy. She is married to Uncle Peter. I don't have any brother.

- **Jane:** ¿La tía Lucy y el tío Peter tienen hijos?
- **Jane:** Do aunt Lucy and uncle Peter have any kids?

- **Mamá:** Sí, tienen un hijo llamado Harry. Él es tu primo.
- **Mum:** Yes, they have one child called Harry. He is your cousin.

- **Jane:** ¿La tía Lucy y el tío Peter tienen hijas?
- **Jane:** Do aunt Lucy and uncle Peter have any girls?

- **Mamá:** No, no tienen. Harry es tu único primo. ¿Tienes ganas de verlos hoy?
- **Mum:** No, they don't. Harry is your only cousin. Would you like to see them today?

- **Jane:** Sí, muchas. Nunca he visto a mi primo Harry. Estoy muy emocionada. ¿Qué haremos con ellos
- **Jane:** Yes, of course. I have never seen my cousin Harry. I'm very excited. What are we going to do with them?

- **Mamá:** Tendremos un almuerzo familiar todos juntos, así podremos ponernos al día y disfrutar de nuestro tiempo juntos.

- **Mum:** We will have a family lunch all together, to catch up and enjoy our time together.

- **Jane:** ¡Estoy deseando verlos a tasks! Gracias, mamá, por organizar este almuerzo familiar.
- **Jane:** I am anticipating seeing everybody! Much thanks to you, mum, for getting sorted out the family lunch.

- **Mamá**: De nada, Jane, espero que disfrutes mucho hoy.
- **Mum**: You're gladly received, Jane. I trust you have a good time today.

Extra energy Activities - What do you do in your free time?

Actividades en el tiempo libre

- **Su Lin:** Hola Ivan. No te he visto en años. ¿Cómo estás?

- *Su Lin: Hello Ivan. I have not seen you for ages. How are you?*

- **Ivan:** Oh, hola Su Lin. Estoy bien, sólo un poco cansado.

- *Ivan: Oh, hello Su Lin. I am fine, just a bit tired.*

- **Su Lin:** ¿Qué es lo que te hace estar tan cansado?

- *Su Lin: What is making you so tired?*

- **Ivan:** Es mi nuevo trabajo. Tengo que viajar durante noventa minutos de ida y otros noventa a la vuelta para llegar allí, además de trabajar horas extras. Parece que todo lo que hago es trabajar.

- *Ivan: It is my new job. I have to travel for ninety minutes each way to get there as well as work overtime. All I seem to do is work.*

584

– **Su Lin:** *Por eso no te he visto en el gimnasio.*

– **Su Lin:** *That's why I haven't seen you at the gym.*

– **Ivan:** Hace un mes que no voy al gimnasio ni juego al tenis. Solía ir a nadar los viernes, pero tampoco he tenido tiempo de hacerlo.

– **Ivan:** *I haven't been to the gym or played tennis for a month. I used to go swimming on Fridays, but I haven't had time to do that either.*

– **Su Lin:** ¿Todavía vas a ver a tu hijo jugar al fútbol los domingos?

– **Su Lin:** *Do you still go and watch your son play soccer on Sundays?*

– **Ivan:** La nueva temporada comienza el próximo mes, así que iré a verlo entonces. Ahora trato de pasar los domingos por la mañana en mi jardín.

– **Ivan:** *The new season starts next month, so I will go and watch him then. Now I try to spend Sunday mornings in the garden.*

– **Su Lin:** Suena como si nunca tuvieras tiempo para relajarte.

– **Su Lin:** *It sounds as if you never have time to relax.*

– **Ivan:** Bueno, todavía me gusta cocinar, y ahora también he empezado a cocinar en el horno.

– **Ivan:** *Well, I still like cooking, and I have also now started baking.*

– **Su Lin:** Vaya, mi marido es un inútil en la cocina.

– **Su Lin:** *Wow, my husband is useless in the kitchen.*

– **Ivan:** No soy mal cocinero, pero acabo de empezar a aprender a hornear mi propio pan.

– *Ivan: I'm not a bad cook, but I have just started learning how to bake my own bread.*

– **Su Lin:** Todo lo que mi esposo hace en su tiempo libre es ir al bar o ver la televisión. Bueno, en realidad, no es verdad. A veces ayuda con las tareas domésticas.

– *Su Lin: All my husband does in his free time is go to the pub or watch TV. Actually, that's not true. He does sometimes help with the housework.*

– **Ivan:** Tal vez podrías pedirle que te ayude con la cocina.

– *Ivan: Maybe you could ask him to help you with the cooking.*

– **Su Lin:** Tal vez.
– **Su Lin:** Maybe.

– **Ivan:** A decir verdad, mi esposa está en un club de excursionismo, tal vez a ti y a tu esposo les gustaría eso.

– *Ivan: Actually, my wife is in a hiking club. Maybe you and your husband would like that.*

– **Su Lin:** Lo haría, pero quizás mi esposo lo encuentre aburrido. ¿Puede llamarme tu esposa para darme los detalles?

– *Su Lin: I would, but maybe my husband would find it boring. Can your wife call me with the details?*

– **Ivan:** Claro que sí. Le diré que te llame en cuanto llegue a casa.

– *Ivan: Sure. I will ask her to call you when I get home.*

Fruits - A list of fruit and the difference between Fruit and Veggies

Frutas

– **Sally:** ¡Oye James, mira! ¡Un arbusto de arándanos! Vamos a recoger algunos arándanos.

– *Sally: Hey James, look! A blueberry bush! Let's pick some blueberries.*

– **James:** ¡Oh sí! Me encantan los arándanos. Cortemos algunos. Mi familia recolecta bayas cada verano. Recolectamos arándanos, frambuesas y fresas. Mi madre las usa para hacer mermelada. Es realmente delicioso.

– *James: Oh yeah! I love blueberries. Let's pick some. My family goes berry picking every summer. We pick blueberries, raspberries, and strawberries. My mom uses them to make jam. It's really delicious.*

– **Sally:** Mi madre también hace mermelada. Ella usa melocotón y albaricoque. ¿Los arándanos son tu fruta favorita?

– *Sally: My mom makes jam, too. She makes peach and apricot. Are blueberries your favorite fruit?*

– **James:** ¡A mí me gustan todas las frutas! Pero las manzanas son mis favoritas. ¿Qué frutas te gustan?

– *James: I like all fruits! But apples are my favorite fruit. What fruits do you like?*

587

— **Sally:** Me gustan las frutas cítricas como las naranjas, los pomelos, y las clementinas. Los limones y las limas también son cítricas, pero son muy agrias.

— *Sally: I like citrus fruits, like oranges, grapefruits, and clementines. Lemons and limes are citrus fruits too, but they're too sour.*

— **James:** Oh sí. Esas frutas son buenas.

— *James: Oh, yeah, those fruits are good.*

— **Sally:** ¿Has ido alguna vez a un huerto de manzanas en otoño?

— *Sally: Do you ever go to the apple orchard in the fall?*

— **James:** Sí, a veces voy con mi familia. Recolectamos muchas manzanas. Recogemos manzanas dulces para comer y manzanas agrias para cocinar al horno. ¡Mi madre hornea tartas de manzanas con ellas!

— *James: Yes, sometimes I go with my family. We pick a lot of apples. We pick sweet apples to eat and sour apples for baking. My mom bakes apple pies with them!*

— **Sally:** Me encanta ir al huerto de manzanas. Mi familia tiene un jardín. Cultivamos diferentes tipos de melones.

— *Sally: I love going to the apple orchard. My family has a garden. We grow different kinds of melons.*

— **James:** ¿De qué tipo?

— *James: What kind?*

– **Sally:** Cultivamos sandías, melón de Cantaloupe, y melón dulce. ¡Las sandías se vuelven tan grandes! A veces cultivamos demasiadas, así que se las regalamos a los vecinos.

– *Sally:* We grow watermelons, cantaloupe, and honeydew. The watermelons get so big! Sometimes we grow too many, so we give them to the neighbors.

– **James:** Mi papá quiere cultivar un jardín. Quiere cosechar tomates. ¿Sabías que los tomates son una fruta?

– *James:* My dad wants to cultivate a garden. He wants to grow tomatoes. Did you know that tomato is a fruit?

HOW TO IMPROVE YOUR SPEAKING SKILLS IN SPANISH

Talking is, seemingly, the most troublesome and harrowing piece of learning an unknown dialect. This is on the grounds that, while expressing, your real thoughts are likely heading 1,000,000 distinct bearings. Besides the fact that it is threatening to communicate in an alternate language, yet at the same time you are focused on elocution, sentence structure, formations, manly or feminine, and so forth It may seem like a ton however there are little advances you can take and things you can do to not just move past the nerves and individual limits you might have to keep down, yet additionally drive your speaking capacities forward, past the point that at whatever point anticipated they should be.

Pay attention to Yourself Speak

It might sound senseless yet paying attention to yourself when you talk is a vital viewpoint to working on your talking capacity. This can be exceptionally helpful and significant, particularly toward the start of your Spanish language venture.

From the beginning, you should make it a propensity to pay attention to yourself as you say distinctive Spanish words. Zero in transit your mouth moves and the sounds you make. Make a note of any subtleties that happen as you make a cursory effort of articulating the Spanish words.

At the point when you progress forward to full sentences, make a recording of yourself.

Pay attention to it, as appalling as that might sound. You need to hear what you sound like to know what you need to deal with. How is your elocution?

Do you stagger over explicit action word formations or befuddle the manly/ladylike endings often?

Converse with Yourself

Besides recording yourself occasionally, you can likewise get a great deal of work on communicating in Spanish by talking it as frequently as could be expected—including to yourself! As you go as the day progressed, describe what you're doing in Spanish.

At this point, when you're in the shower, plan out your day's exercises to yourself in Spanish. Have a pet? Converse with them in Spanish!

Work on addressing yourself before a mirror sooner rather than later. This will allow you the opportunity to watch the manner in which your mouth moves as you talk. You will actually want to see any articulation mistakes simpler, and you will end up acquiring certainty when you're completely mindful of what you resemble when you're talking in Spanish.

Recite Out Loud

At the point when you're going through the way toward working on your perusing (like we talked about in the past part), practice your talking by reciting so anyone can hear. Not exclusively can you hear how the words and expressions sound when hung together in a bona fide design—however, you will rapidly recognize which words or sounds trip you up.

You don't need to recite a whole novel for all to hear to get the advantages of this training. Indeed, even zeroing in on little pieces of writings or explicit articulations or sentences will do. In the event that you can discover approaches to work this little propensity into your day-by-day schedule, your certainty when communicating in Spanish will go up and your elocution, syntax, and sentence construction will improve also.

Here are some ways you can work adding so anyone might hear to your ordinary daily practice:

- Write out a few sentences per week that you believe you will utilize a great deal (or that join some syntactic point or jargon words that you're attempting to chip away at) and tape it to within your shower or on the washroom mirror to peruse them each day a couple of times.
- Find a formula to make in Spanish. Peruse the bearings resoundingly to yourself as you head through the means.

- Label various things in your home and put those words into a sentence. For instance, "I like to peruse" (*me gusta scoff*) and tape it to your shelf, or "I need to walk the canine" (*tengo que sacar al perro*) and put it by the canine rope.

Practice Commonly Used Phrases

One approach to guarantee that you're prepared at whatever point you find the opportunity to communicate in Spanish is to be certain that you're knowledgeable in those usually utilized and consistently required expressions. When you have these fundamental, yet essential, express down, you'll have the option to add more to your rundown and your certainty when talking will increment.

For instance, here are a few expressions you might need to be certain you know directly from the beginning when talking in Spanish:

- ¿Qué tal? – What's happening?
- Hola/Buenos días – Hi/Good day
- Adios/Hasta luego – Farewell/Until later
- ¿Cómo estás? – How are you?"
- ¿Dónde está… ? – Where is… ?
- Me llamo/Mi nombre es... – My name is…
- (Muchas) gracias – Thank you (definitely)
- De nada – The pleasure is all mine
- ¿Hablas inglés? – Do you communicate in English?
- Lo siento… – I'm heartbroken…

Expression books and records can be extraordinary assets when securing a functioning reason for talking in Spanish. These will be particularly useful for anybody venturing out to a Spanish-talking country. In the event that you begin dealing with utilizing these and other ordinarily utilized expressions in Spanish, you'll see that your certainty when talking will go up, just as your, generally speaking, conversational capacity.

Communicate in Spanish Every Chance You Get

For clear reasons, having the option to talk with a local Spanish speaker is by a long shot the most profitable approach to work on communicating in Spanish. This, in any case, isn't something that everybody can do consistently. In the event that tracking down a local Spanish-talking discussion accomplice in your space is somewhat troublesome, there are still ways that you can make communicating in Spanish an ordinary and gainful piece of your learning schedule.

Work Your Commonly Used Phrases into your Daily Life

Regardless of whether you don't have a local Spanish-talking companion, who you can rehearse, that doesn't imply that you can't discover others around you to address in Spanish. Take a stab at taking a portion of the expressions we've taken a gander at, or a portion of the others that you've been chipping away at (good tidings, and so forth), and use them with your loved ones.

Regardless of whether they don't get you, they'll be strong on your excursion to learning another dialect. What's more, you might even discover they begin to foster an interest in Spanish of their own!

Utilize the Wonderful Resource That Is the Internet!

There are a couple of sites online that you can use to meet and talk with local Spanish speakers in a type of a language trade. Look at the sites beneath and see what you find.

Taking a Spanish class? Attempt to discover another person in the class who is however persuaded as you may be to make Spanish pieces of their everyday lives. Trade data with them and attempt to set up a week after week Skype call or a period where you can meet to rehearse and communicate in Spanish together.

Make Speaking in Spanish a Habit

We've jabbered about the significance of making a Spanish propensity to be fruitful when learning the language. I'm certain it does not shock anyone that when looking at talking, this little word is coming up once more.

Talking is perhaps the most troublesome aspect of learning a language, and except if you figure out how to make it something you're as OK with as you can be, you'll wind up battling with it for quite a long time.

This is the reason, presently, today, you need to begin figuring out how to function it into your everyday schedule:

- Create a sign that reminds you to communicate in Spanish day by day. This can be something insignificant. For instance, putting on your pot of espresso toward the beginning of the day. This ought to be simply the time that you tell, "OK, self, I will stand up boisterous in Spanish as I plan out the remainder of my day." Or perhaps it's the point at which you're washing the dishes toward the day's end. This activity can be your sign that you need to talk so anyone might hear in Spanish describing the occasions of your day and any plans you have for the end of the week, and so on Interestingly, you discover an action that you do consistently and you make it your "trigger" to advise yourself to talk in Spanish.
- Your sign ought to be inserted into your everyday practice. Make your signal something you do DAILY. This will make it simpler, if not practically unavoidable, to talk in Spanish on a day-in, day-out premise.
- Make your sign simple and deliberate. Particularly towards the beginning, you should configure your login to a greater degree as a "host region" type setting. Thusly, you will have no reason to neglect to start making it a propensity. Assuming you need to utilize brushing your teeth as your sign, tape a couple of Spanish articulations, states, or even inquiries to the mirror as an update. Turning on the espresso pot? Stick a post-it to the counter asking yourself what you will do that day or then again on the off chance that you need to get many things done, and so on
- Make sure your impulse/propensity is not difficult to adopt. Regularly rehearsing in Spanish can be exhausting. Speaking in Spanish constantly can be debilitating. In some cases having a daily signal can seem somewhat monotonous. Therefore, you should try to shake it up as much as you can to make the experience as enjoyable as possible. Some mornings you may well find it hard to be physically active. Today, try to do something

simpler, like utilizing a conversation app on your telephone or simply going over a portion of the expressions and slang for everybody to hear. Interestingly, make sure you are doing something consistently to force yourself to speak Spanish.

- Reward yourself for staying with it! Who doesn't adore a decent compensation for accomplishing something useful? On the off chance that you find that toward the finish of seven days, you've gotten along nicely at communicating in Spanish consistently, why not make it motivation to celebrate? It very well may be anything from an extravagant jug of wine to a night out with your companions. Whatever it is, don't spare a moment to congratulate yourself for all the difficult work you've been doing.

Begin Thinking in Spanish

In the event that your inward exchange is in Spanish, you'll see that it will be a lot simpler to put yourself out there vocally when the opportunity arrives.

HOW TO WRITE IN SPANISH

Composing and talking are basically the same as one another in that they require significantly more dynamic investment from the student. You need to make your own discourse, create your own syntactic mindfulness, and spotlight on seemingly insignificant details like word request and spelling.

Perusing and listening are significant abilities to have and they give essential information (something we've talked about already). Composing and talking, nonetheless, take that information you've gotten and transform it into your very own yield, consequently assisting with hardening the ideas and jargon to you.

Writing in Spanish is a magnificent instrument and will assist with further developing different abilities you've been chipping away at. At the point when you compose, you need to understand what you're composing (practice your perusing). You can recite it for all to hear (practice your talking) and spotlight your elocution and how the words sound (practice your tuning in).

This part will zero in on composition, talking about the advantages, just as certain tips, to guarantee that you're benefiting from this basic expertise.

Advantages of Writing in Spanish

Composing can be monotonous and it's not generally the most agreeable of exercises, particularly when pondering writing in Spanish. It is, in any case, vital expertise to have. We use composing each day, way more frequently than we might even figure it out. Every one of those instant messages and messages you send is composing.

Those updates you put in your telephone or scrawl onto post-it notes?

These simple little methods of composing are certainly where you can start when looking for opportunities to try out this Spanish experience. In the event that you can't find a Spanish conversation partner, you should try to find a pen pal. Perhaps someone from one of your Spanish classes that you can instant message or email back and forth. You can work out your plans for the day or leave updates for yourself in Spanish.

Writing in Spanish is valuable, not just on the grounds that it's something that draws on different spaces of the language that you will need to deal with, yet in addition since it is an everyday part of life. On the off chance that you plan on utilizing your Spanish for work, you'll need to compose messages. In case you're learning Spanish for joy, you'll unquestionably end up needing to meet and speak with local speakers through Facebook, e-mail, WhatsApp, and so on.

How about we investigate ways you can practice and amaze your songwriting skills?

Keep in touch with Other People

As you might have found when we were looking at talking, having an organization of Spanish speakers (or Spanish language students) around you is incredibly advantageous. All things considered, this is additionally obvious when looking at composing. Here are a few hints on how you can make your own Spanish-talking organization.

- If you meet Spanish-talking people while you're voyaging, or while you're in a Spanish class, don't be reluctant to trade contact data. Then, at that point, you can compose to and fro in Spanish.
- Find Spanish language sites and leave remarks - in Spanish. Try not to be modest, all things considered. Indeed, even request that others right your Spanish. You'd be astonished how open and welcoming the language-learning local area can be.

Keep in touch with Yourself

What's that word we continue utilizing when looking at learning Spanish? A propensity? Indeed, who could have imagined, here it returns once more! Making a propensity for writing in Spanish consistently can be the way to progress when dominating this particular ability. A composing propensity can be made by composing seemingly insignificant details in Spanish consistently. This doesn't mean it must be full sentences.

Perhaps it's a daily agenda. Perhaps it's a speedy suggestion to yourself to take care of the gas bill. Whatever it is, writing in Spanish is an extraordinary method to submit jargon to memory and to guarantee that you're utilizing what you've realized consistently.

Keep a Journal

What we're discussing here is only a little journal and everyday propensity for recording a modest bunch of things. Start by composing the day of the week, the month, and so forth to rehearse with that fundamental jargon. Then, at that point, work out three little list items.

How did you respond that day? What beneficial thing occurred (everybody can profit with some sure reflection toward the finish of consistently)? You don't have to record as long as you can remember, just make it a highlight record something in Spanish consistently.

Keep in touch with Yourself Daily Reminders

Do you live in an ocean of post-it notes? Why not make that an ocean of Spanish?

Likewise, do you get yourself composing many updates on your telephone?

Type them out in Spanish. Everybody needs a little assistance monitoring everything that we need to do each day. On the off chance that you begin monitoring those things in Spanish, you as of now have an implicit propensity really taking shape.

Put Your Phone, Calendar, Facebook in Spanish on a superficial level, this tip is something that will assist with your perusing. Be that as it may, on the off chance that you find the additional way to proceed with the Spanish energy, you will actually want to convey this exceptionally valuable device over to assist with your composing abilities. At the point when you're planning for your supper with companions on your schedule record it in Spanish. Setting your caution for the first part of the day? Type in a speedy note to yourself in Spanish helping you to remember anything significant that you're doing that day.

Compose Your Lists in Spanish

This is a superb method to truly try all that jargon you've been examining. Working out your plans for the day in Spanish will help you audit day-by-day errands and family things jargon. Food jargon is something that you will need to be acquainted with, particularly on the off chance that you plan on going to a Spanish-talking nation (having the option to peruse a menu might save you some intriguing encounters you'd prefer not to have). Work out your shopping list in Spanish.

Peruse, Then Write

We've spoken a little about taking notes when perusing. What we didn't say was the amount it will assist with different spaces of your language learning, also.

At the point when you read something in Spanish, you may not understand it, yet you are being presented to an entire slew of valuable, helpful, and essential information - word request, manly/female, action word formations, object pronouns, and so forth

Being acquainted with these things won't just make perusing simpler and talking more normal, yet they will certainly assist your composition with welling.

This doesn't mean it needs to move you on an enthusiastic level. Perhaps it's something that contains one of those precarious action word formations you've been working with or impeccably puts that one jargon word into a setting you believe you would really utilize it in later on. Then, at that point, set aside the effort to work out this piece of text. The most ideal approach to do this, truly, is ordinary pen and paper strategy. This is essentially in light of the fact that it has been demonstrated that the muscle memory that accompanies composing assists the mind with engrossing and hold the data better than just composing it up on a PC or into a "page" on our telephone.

Don't stop with working out that one sentence or expression, in any case.

Odds are they grabbed your eye on purpose. Take what is said in that content and revise it again in the most natural sounding way for you or work out an outline of what was going on around that segment so you can recollect it better later.

This doesn't have to be limited to entries in a book. You can discover a tune you really like or a scene from a movie that really appeals to you. Duplicating or elaborating on things is a smart idea, as it pulls a few different skills simultaneously (reading or tuning or both, and then at the same time composing).

Here are a few thoughts for things you might end up needing to record:

- Song verses

- Passages from a most loved book/sonnet
- Inspirational statements
- Recipes
- Information about things that interest you- - fun realities or measurements, sports wording or clinical terms

Compose, Then Speak

Assuming you need to edit what you've composed, shy of sending it off to another person to check, the most ideal approach to discover any errors is through reciting what you've worked on so anyone can hear. Once you have completed the process of putting together your plan for the day, your journal, or your understandings/responses to the main tune, pause for a minute to recite them for all to hear. This is your opportunity to check for punctuation, spelling, or slang errors.

When perusing your composition, you ought to ask yourself the accompanying inquiries:

- Are my sentences excessively short or uneven? One thing you will see, rapidly, is that in Spanish, sentences will, in general, be longer than we would regularly have in English. Think about your sentence length/style to that of the ones in your valid writings you've been perusing.
- Have I consolidated subtleties or contacts in the right manner, in the right spot?
- Have I focused on the cardinal standard: AGREE (subject/action word, sex, number)?
- Is my statement request right (for example, thing THEN descriptor)?
- Do my thoughts stream together? (Am I utilizing the right connecting words?—see the part beneath.)

Learn "Genuine" Spanish

Perusing the Quijote is a certain something. Composing a book for your companion is another. You will see as you go through your excursion into the Spanish language that, as in English, there is a formal and a casual method of talking or composing.

HOW TO ENHANCE YOUR WRITING

After you've fostered a decent comprehension of Spanish punctuation and linguistic structure, you can start to zero in on fostering your composition—taking it to a higher level. This implies as opposed to composing short, fast notes, and so on, you can stretch out your composition to longer pieces or further developed subjects.

Regardless of you're composing; you can upgrade it by following the means illustrated underneath:

Connectors

These are words that do precisely what you would envision they do—interface. They assist your contemplations with streaming together and keep the cadence and speed of your composing steady. When writing in English, you need to ensure you say more than "and" or "however, while connecting your contemplations together. In Spanish, you will need a reasonable collection of interfacing words you can toss in to zest up your composing a bit.

Here are not many to kick you off:

Connector in Spanish – Connector in English

- Además – Likewise, besides, moreover
- También – As well, too, moreover
- Sin embargo/No obstante – Be that as it may, Nevertheless
- Aunque – In spite of the fact that
- A pesar de que – Regardless of, despite
- Dado que – Since, Given that
- Entonces – Then, at that point
- Así que – So
- En cambio – Though, On the other hand

Sentence Openers

You can't effectively utilize those connectors combining considerations on the off chance that you don't have the foggiest idea of how to begin an idea appropriately. Sentence openers are exceptionally valuable since they help you set up for what you need to say. They give your peruser a thought of what's in store and they cause everything to appear to be more assembled and thoroughly considered.

Beneath you'll discover the absolute most usually utilized and vital sentence openers in Spanish:

Sentence Opener in Spanish – Sentence Opener in English

- A propósito, Por cierto – Coincidentally
- La verdad es que – In all actuality
- En mi opinión – As I would like to think
- Por lo menos – At any rate
- Quizás/Tal vez – Possibly, Perhaps
- Por un lado/Por otro lado – On one hand/On the other hand

We should Talk about Sentences

In English, we like to apply the "KISS" rule to everything- - Keep It Simple Stupid. We like our sentences to be short and exact, to cut to the chase. In Spanish, while this is fine and surprisingly a smart thought at times; by and large, sentences will, in general, be any longer than they are in English - even in conventional composition.

Truly, probably the greatest study Spanish-talking understudies of English get is that their composing is as well "extravagant" and "drawn out." As English-communicating in Spanish students, we can take that standard and flip it around to fit our requirements.

The connectors we referenced before will string together considerations consistently. It's normal to have a sentence that will take up three, four, even five lines of a composed record.

Think about this, for instance. In English, if you somehow happened to compose the accompanying, it would bring about a chiding from any English educator you've at any point had:

"I like going to the seashore, particularly in the late spring, in light of the fact that there are generally many individuals out and the sun is so warm, yet the water is

602

so cold, and it's exceptionally unwinding to sit on a towel with your toes in the sand and read a decent book while you partake in the early evening."

For the most part, in "great" English, you will be advised to split that sentence up to and partition it into more modest, more reasonable pieces—for yourself and for the peruser. In Spanish, however, that development would be okay.

In any case, this is something that our further developed students will need to remember. Particularly when they are truly plunging into writing in Spanish. Toward the start, it's great to take on things in little lumps. This incorporates composing.

The more limited your sentences, the more uncertain you are to commit an error. The less data you attempt to stick into one proclamation, the simpler said data is to deal with.

Toward the start of learning a language, you need to zero in on getting the right contribution as well as making the right yield. On the off chance that you permit yourself such a large number of errors, those missteps will become solidified to you and be harder to address not too far off. That is the reason, in case you're a few seconds ago beginning with Spanish and wanting to handle the specialty of composing, focus on composing accurately, not on composing like a local speaker.

COMMON MISTAKES IN SPANISH AND HOW YOU CAN FIX THEM

There are always certain things that English speakers will struggle with when learning Spanish. These are the little things that are just plain weird to native English speakers. They are challenging for one of two reasons.

- We don't have something similar in English.
- We have something we think is similar in English, but it's actually very different.
- Gender-Remember that in Spanish, every noun and every adjective has a gender-masculine or feminine.
- The Formal and Informal "You"—This is something that changes based on the Spanish—speaking country you're in. The general rule to follow when starting out is:

If you're speaking to someone older than you or someone you would address with a title (Mr., Mrs., Dr., and so on), you'll use the formal you—"usted" for singular or "ustedes" for plural.

These are important to be aware of when starting out on your language-learning journey so you can prevent forming any hard-to-reverse habits early on.

Pronunciation

Let's start out by looking at some of the difficult parts of pronunciation a little more in detail.

Roll Your Rrrrrs!

It's something that not every person can do. Furthermore, it takes a great deal of training to consummate it, yet this is one thing that pretty much every Spaniard will bring up at some time as being something that English-speakers just can't get right.

It's not just the "rr" in words like "perro" or "ahorrar", but also the slight quaver you hear in words like "pero" or "caro". It's nowhere near as long and exaggerated as the "rr" you'll find in the first two words, however, it's still unique relative to the "r" we have in English. It is more liquid and rolls off the tongue somewhat faster.

Try not to Be So Harsh with Your Inter-Vocal Consonants

When a "d" interferes with two vowels, there is a slight change in the way it is articulated. One of the normal mistakes English speakers make is that they continue to articulate perhaps the hard "d" as in "canine."

In the situation that you pay attention to a local Spanish speaker, you'll understand that when they articulate the "d" in words like "task" or "lado," it's to a greater degree a delicate, scarcely recognizable stop. More often than not, in case they're talking rapidly, it will sound more like "to-o" with a little delay in the middle of the two "O's." The tongue actually shoots forward, as it would if the word were articulated gradually and purposely, however in the event that the discourse is liquid, the sound created will be extremely weak.

The equivalent occurs with "b" and "g" in words such "caminaba" and "bodega." In these cases, the consonant is heard somewhat more than the "d" referenced above yet not as brutally as it would be in English articulation, for example, with words like "boat" or "goat."

False Cognates/False Friends

A false cognate (also known as a "false friend") is a word in Spanish that sounds like a word we have in English but has a different meaning than the English word we naturally want to associate it with.

Some of the most common false cognates in Spanish are:

Word in Meaning

What it sounds

- ✓ Embarazada - Embarrassed / Pregnant – Avergonzado/a
- ✓ Actualmente – Actually / Currently – En realidad
- ✓ Molestar – Molest / Bother – Abusar sexualmente
- ✓ Éxito – Exit / Success – Salida
- ✓ Sopa – Soap / Soup – Jabón

- ✓ Delito – Delight / Crime – Delicia
- ✓ Introducir – Introduce / To insert – Presentar

As you can see, mixing up some of these false friends can lead to some very uncomfortable situations and somewhat comical misunderstandings. Being aware of them is definitely a good idea.

Adjective Placement

As a general rule, adjectives in Spanish go after the noun they are describing.

- The red house – La casa roja
- The blue plate – El plato azul

There are, however, a few exceptions to this rule.

Adjectives That Go Before the Noun

There are some adjectives in Spanish that do, actually, go before the noun they are modifying.

1. The first group of adjectives that you will find in front of the noun are those that talk about quantity. They speak to the amount of something.
   a. For example: There are a few people in the house. Hay poca gente en la casa.

2. You may be able to put a descriptive adjective before the noun if you are not trying to differentiate (or single out) the noun you are describing.
   a. For example: If I were to say "The intelligent students" (los estudiantes inteligentes). I'm talking about a specific group of students within an even larger group of not as bright students.
   b. However, if I said "los inteligentes estudiantes," I'm implying that ALL the students are intelligent.

Adjectives That Change Meaning When They Change

Location

There are a handful of adjectives that can go before OR after the noun, but they will change their meaning depending on where you put them.

606

The most common are: Adjective

Meaning before

Meaning after

- ✓ Antiguo – Former, Ex-Old, Ancient
- ✓ Pobre – Poor (as in unfortunate) Poor (as in no money)
- ✓ Gran/Grande – Great, Big, Large
- ✓ Viejo – Old (as in long – old (as in age) standing)
- ✓ Único – Only, Unique

This has just been a quick overview of the basics behind using adjectives in Spanish. At first glance, this very useful part of speech may seem strange and even intimidating to the native English speaker. But the truth is, it's really not all that complicated. It just takes lots of practice and adjusting your mindset a little bit.

Remember—your adjectives need to AGREE (number), AGREE (gender)!

Two Words – One Word

The sets of words that seem to cause beginning-level students the most trouble (and even more advanced students still struggle with this from time to time) are *ser* and *estar* and *por* and *para*. These are pairs of words that mean the same thing in English but have very specific uses in Spanish.

Ser vs Estar-to be

Both of these words mean "to be." I am, you are, he is, etc.

Ser

Ser is used with permanent things-things that won't change or will be very difficult to change (i.e. essential characteristics of something).

Example: I am short (Soy baja – I have been short my whole life and it's not going to change). He is attractive. She is pleasant. They are youthful, yet we are old. These are everything that are utilized to portray characteristics that you would consider to be "extremely durable" about the individual. They won't change—basically not at any point in the near future!

Estar

Estar is used with temporary things. (i.e. a condition).

Example: I am angry (Estoy enfadada – I'm not generally irate; it's simply that this moment, I am!) He is worn out. We are in the store. You are extremely attractive today (assuming you need to stress that somebody looks particularly decent).

Other uses for ser or estar are:

Ser – Estar

- Date or Time (Son las 11:00.)
- Express state or time (Es lunes. Hoy es 8 de noviembre.)
- Condition (La sopa está fría.)
- Place of origin (Soy de los Estados Unidos)
- Location (Estoy en la Estados Unidos. Él es de biblioteca. Ellos están en casa.)
- With progressive tenses
- Express occupation (Estamos hablando ahora – Está estudiando – Somos estudiantes –.)
- To express possession (El libro es de Juan.)
- Express relationship between people (Ella es mi prima. Somos hermanos.)

Por vs Para

Both of these words mean "for." This is very confusing for a lot of English students because they are used in very different ways. They each also have their own, separate meanings as well.

Here's a quick chart to outline the most common uses for these two tricky words.

Por – Para

- Used to show something in process.
- Used to show the "end" of

There's no finality associated with something. There's a sense of it finality with it.

Commonly means or is used to show:

- "Through"

- Indicate destination

- "By"
- Show the purpose of an object

- "On behalf of"
- Indicate the recipient of
- Express gratitude or extend an apology

- "In order to"
- Exchange (including sales)
- Express a deadline
- Express cause or reason

- "During"
- Means of transport

Prepositions

Prepositions are those little words that pack a big punch. They can change the meaning of an entire sentence. It's the difference between saying "the dog is under the table" and "the dog is on the table." One reason why these little words cause so many problems for English-speaking Spanish students is that, while they seem to be the same as the ones we have, there are some very important, key differences to be aware of. To start out with, let's look at the two most commonly confused prepositions:

Spanish – English Examples:

En - In, On, At

- Estoy en la tienda – I'm in the store.
- Está en la mesa – It's on the table.
- Estoy en la casa de un amigo – I'm at a friend's house.

A – To, At (for time)

- Voy a la tienda – I'm going to the store.
- Estaré allí a las tres – I'll be there at 3:00.)

The confusion most commonly happens between "en" and "a," especially when saying "at." It's normal to want to say "Estoy a casa" (I'm at home) because "a" reminds us of "at." However, this is wrong because we are speaking about a location, not a time. The correct way to say the sentence about would be "estoy en casa."

Prepositions with Verbs

There are a lot of cases when we connect certain verbs with certain prepositions. This can be difficult for Spanish-language students because the combinations might be slightly different in Spanish. Here are some of the most notable:

Verb/ Preposition in Spanish - Verb/ Preposition in English

- Enamorarse de – To fall in love with

De (of) vs. With

- Contar con – To count on

Con (with) vs. On

- Soñar con – To dream about

Con (with) vs. About

- Cuidar a – To take care of

A (to) vs. Of

- Preocuparse de – To worry about

De (of) vs. About

- Depender de – To depend on

De (of) vs. On

- Pensar en – To think about

En (on) vs. About

Tener

The verb "tener" is probably one of the most commonly used verbs in Spanish. Meaning "to have," this verb doesn't seem too complicated on the surface. It gets a little tricky, though, when it's used in Spanish in ways we would never think to use it in English. In some cases, *tener* is used in Spanish when an English speaker would naturally want to use "to be." Here are a few of the most notable times that this happens:

Tener Meaning:

- Tener X años – To be X years old
- Tener hambre – To be hungry
- Tener sed – To be thirsty
- Tener sueño – To be sleepy
- Tener miedo – To be scared
- Tener prisa – To be in a hurry
- Tener calor/frío – To be hot/cold
- Tener suerte – To be lucky

The Subjunctive

The subjunctive is one of the most trying aspects of Spanish for the native-English student. This is simply because we believe we don't have it in English. The truth is, we do. We just don't use it as often, we don't use it correctly, or we don't even realize we're using it.

For example, in English, you could say, "I wish I was with you." This may sound fine but the correct way of saying it would be "I wish I were with you."

HOW TO MEMORIZE VOCABULARY AND TENSES

Memorizing is one of those parts of learning a language that seems extremely daunting, especially at the beginning when the lists of words to learn and tenses to become familiar with seem endless. When you put a lot of pressure on yourself to memorize everything, you will often find yourself feeling very overwhelmed, if not discouraged. When a word isn't as easily brought to mind as you would like, it's so tempting to just throw your hands in the air and say, "I just have a horrible memory."

This isn't necessarily the case, though. Remember this: there is no such thing as a bad memory. There are different learning styles. Just because you know someone in your Spanish class who can recite any vocab list a day after seeing it doesn't mean that, because you can't, you lack the ability to. It simply means that you have a different learning style, and you need to find a different way of going about conquering vocabulary and verb tenses.

You may find that not all of them work for you. That's fine!

Vocabulary

Vocabulary is the foundational building block on which the rest of your Spanish language abilities will be built. If you are unable to understand the words, you won't be able to read, write, or speak in Spanish. Some words will be easy to learn whereas others will give you more problems. The important thing to keep in mind is that you have to be patient with yourself.

You are learning vocabulary and you will continue to learn new words throughout your entire language-learning experience. Think about your native language. When you started speaking, you didn't know all the words you know now (obviously). And I'm sure that there are even words that you still hear from time to time that aren't familiar with. Vocabulary develops over time through practice and exposure.

Set Realistic Goals

You cannot expect to sit down in front of a vocabulary list or Spanish dictionary and memorize whatever you see in the span of 20 minutes. Sure, after reading through the list a few times, you might be able to repeat it. But an hour after walking away from your desk, chances are you probably won't remember even half of what you looked at.

A good benchmark goal to set for yourself is to expect to learn 10-15 new words for every hour you spend studying. This doesn't mean that you have to spend one straight hour studying just vocabulary. Break it up into small chunks. Spend 15 minutes every few days with the overall goal of spending one hour a week total on vocab.

Learn Words with Context

While it seems easy and even tempting to simply learn a word a day from a list if you're unable to use that word within a context, what's the point?

Here are a few ideas for how you can learn a word within a larger context: Cluster Words Together

Learning words thematically is a great way to conquer a larger number of new words at one time. If you want to learn how to say "kitchen" why not go ahead and learn how to say the other rooms in your house? If you want to learn how to say "shirt" go ahead and look up how to say "pants," "sweater," and "shoes." The brain has a natural tendency to put information into categories. One way you can use this to help with your Spanish is by selecting a "theme" for each week. One week focus on weather vocab, the next focus on food, and so on and so on.

Learn Sentences

The whole point of learning vocabulary in Spanish is so that you can take those words and use them in a spoken or written form one day. Words learned within an applicable context are more likely to stick in your mind. For example, if you're learning the vocabulary related to weather, why not take the words you're learning and make a sentence to go along with them?

What do you do when it's sunny out? Does it rain a lot where you live? Do you love or hate snow? Create a context around the vocabulary you're learning so that you won't only have an X=Y meaning but an actually applicable significance in your mind.

Avoid Learning Opposites Together

It can be tempting, even seem logical, to learn opposites together. For example, hot and cold. It seems to make sense that these two words would come up together but, if you learn them together, you may experience what is known as vocabulary cross association. This means that when you want to recall the word for cold you may find yourself bringing up the word for hot because they are stored together in your mind in the same place.

One way to avoid this is to apply the techniques we just talked about. When you learn the word for cold, create a word cluster of things that are cold (snow, ice, winter, etc.). Focus on these words one day, and the next move to hot and words you would associate with that word (fire, the sun, summer).

Work Around the Word

As you go through your experience of learning Spanish, you'll come across words that you just can't remember, no matter what you do. They're words that you'll look up a million times, write them out in sentences, put them on flashcards, everything. But they just won't stick in your memory. Or maybe there are words you do know but can't seem to retrieve from your mind when you need to. Don't worry. This isn't the end of the world. There are things you can do to prevent this very common occurrence from holding you back.

Learn Synonyms

It's always useful and beneficial to learn a few words related to a new word you're learning. For example, if you've just seen a movie with your friends, you may want to describe it as "funny," "entertaining," or "hilarious."

Describe the Word You're Trying to Say

It can be frustrating, embarrassing, and discouraging to be in the middle of a conversation and unable to think of a specific word. Every Spanish-language student has had this experience. To get past it, you can use something called "circumlocution." This is the process of describing the word and/or working around it so that the conversation doesn't lose its pace. For example, if you're trying to say that you saw your friend in the "store" but the word for "store" won't come to mind, you can say "the place you buy food/clothes/etc."

Don't Be Afraid to Ask

Analyze New Words as You Learn Them

Learning new words is great. But if you're not paying attention to how those new words are spelled or written you could potentially be missing out on some very useful information. Doing this, however, will help you dedicate the word to memory easier. The thing is, most words have a "root word"—a word around which the rest of the longer word is formed. This is true for nouns, adjectives, and verbs. Being aware of the root word will make the process of learning new words go more smoothly and make it a lot less daunting knowing that you only need to learn one, main word. You can then add the appropriate prefixes or suffixes to change the word to fit your needs.

Im-/In- Prefix

These prefixes are added to adjectives and adverbs to make their opposites Root Word.

- ✓ Capaz – Able
- ✓ Incapaz – Unable

- ✓ Posible – Possible
- ✓ Imposible – Impossible

- ✓ Útil – Useful
- ✓ Inútil – Unuseful

Ante- Prefix

Adding "ante" to the front of the word adds the meaning of "before."

- ✓ Ayer – Yesterday
- ✓ Anteayer – The day before yesterday

- ✓ Mano – Hand
- ✓ Antemano – Beforehand

- ✓ Noche — Night
- ✓ Anteanoche – The night before last night

Re- Prefix

Adding "re" to a verb in Spanish is much like adding "re" to a word in English Root Word

- ✓ Usar – To use
- ✓ Reusar – To reuse

- ✓ Pasar – To pass
- ✓ Repasar – To review (to pass over again)

- ✓ Nacer – To be born
- ✓ Renacer – To be born again

Mal- Prefix

"Mal" is an adjective in Spanish that means "bad." Adding this prefix to the beginning of a verb adds that same meaning to the action.

- ✓ Tratar – To treat
- ✓ Maltratar – To treat someone badly

- ✓ Nutrición – Nutrition
- ✓ Malnutrición – Malnutrition

- ✓ Criado – Raised
- ✓ Malcriado – To be raised badly/ Spoiled

- ✓ Comer – Eat
- ✓ Malcomer – To eat poorly

-mente Suffix

Added to adjectives to turn them into adverbs, much like the "-ly" suffix in English.

- ✓ Difícil – Difficult
- ✓ Difícilmente – With difficulty

- ✓ Lento/a – Slow
- ✓ Lentamente – Slowly

- ✓ Rápido/a – Quick
- ✓ Rápidamente – Quickly

- ✓ Alegre – Happy
- ✓ Alegremente – Happily

-ito/-ita Suffix

This is a diminutive, and when added to nouns means "little."

- ✓ Hermano – Brother
- ✓ Hermanito – Little brother

- ✓ Hermana – Sister
- ✓ Hermanita – Little sister

- ✓ Casa – House
- ✓ Casita – Little house/cottage

- ✓ Mentira – Lie
- ✓ Mentirita – a little lie

-ote/-ota/-on/-ona/-azo/-aza Suffixes

These are augmentatives and function in the exact opposite way of diminutives. When used with a noun, they give the feeling of "large" or "big."

- ✓ Libro – Book
- ✓ Librote – Big book

- ✓ Cabeza – Head
- ✓ Cabezota – Stubborn (Hard headed)

- ✓ Grande – Big
- ✓ Grandote – Very big

-ísimo/-ísima Suffix

These are also augmentative suffixes; however, they are added to adjectives to create the superlative form.

- ✓ Cansado/a – Tired
- ✓ Cansadísimo/a – Extremely tired

- ✓ Temprano – Early
- ✓ Tempranísimo – Very early

- ✓ Barato – Cheap
- ✓ Baratísimo – Extremely cheap

Read to Increase Your Vocabulary

Reading gives you the chance to see new words used in an authentic context. And, of course, make sure you read things that interest you, so you keep your motivation high. This will also help you find and acquire new vocabulary related to topics you enjoy talking about, so are more likely to do so.

Use Visual Representations

Linking a word to a picture or image, and not just the direct English translation, will help to make the word more tangible. It will be easier to remember and you'll begin to work on cutting out the middle translation process that can become a hindrance when you begin reaching higher levels.

Flashcards are a great way to incorporate visual aids into your vocabulary learning process. You can make your own, buy them in shops, or even find them online and print them off. There are even websites that test your vocabulary with the use of virtual flashcards from websites like Spanish Dict.

If you want to be able to take your vocabulary exercises with you on the go, check out these apps that you can download to your phone:

- Memrise
- Duolingo
- FluentU

The only real drawback to visual learning in this way is that you're only working with one word in an isolated situation. To do this, don't just practice with the flashcards, but take the time to write out the words you learn using them and put them into sentences or group them together with other words you've already learned or are in the process of learning.

Pay Attention to the Cognates

It is, of course, very important to be familiar with these. There are, however, true cognates that exist between English and Spanish as well. If a word looks like an English word, take the time to look it up. Is it a false or a true cognate?

True cognates are very easy to remember, for obvious reasons. Here are some examples:

Word in Spanish – Word in English

- Accidente – Accident
- Color – Color
- Opinión – Opinion
- Aceptar – Accept
- Doctor – Doctor
- Necesario – Necessary

CONCLUSION

When you're learning a new language, you'll want to practice it as much as possible. One of the best ways to do this is by finding a partner or three—someone who speaks both of your languages and can help translate and explain things as needed. This offers a far more immersive experience than practicing alone or in groups of only speakers of one language. To make this process even easier, we've assembled for you below some common Spanish language combinations. They're based on where the languages are spoken geographically, which will make them more likely to have people who speak both languages nearby. In addition, the names of the combinations are often based on real places where the two languages are spoken. This may not be the most pronounceable or best-sounding Spanish language combination, but it is genuine and representative.

Combination 1: Spanish-English [Sortable]

- ✓ What you say: "Estoy en una guerra con un guerrero" ("I'm at war with a warrior") [Sortable]
- ✓ Who you say it to: Spanish speakers who know English.

What it means: "I'm at war with a warrior." This is the sequence that we all start with when learning Spanish. It's the first step in the language's grammar and vocabulary, and is called *ser*, *estar*, *hacer* ("to be," "to be in," "to do") in Spanish. It's the most common word in any Spanish-English language combination, and it looks like this: "estoy." There are many variations on this word, but this is the one that often appears first in any Spanish-English language combination. It's the idea behind "I'm at war with a warrior."

Combination 2: English-Spanish [Sortable]

- ✓ What you say: "Estoy aprendiendo inglés con una amiga" ("I'm learning English with a friend.") [Sortable]
- ✓ Who you say it to: Spanish speakers who know English.

What it means: "I'm learning English with a friend." The next step is to combine your languages and create a new language. This is often where people get stuck.

They know what the first and last words are supposed to be, but when they come together, they don't sound right. This is why it's important to have a native speaker nearby to help you out. If you're trying to do this yourself, try switching the order of your language combinations around until they sound correct.

Combination 3: Spanish-French [Sortable]

- ✓ What you say: "¿Qué hace el oso en la boca del guerero?" ("What's the bear doing in the warrior's mouth?") [Sortable]
- ✓ Who you say it to: Spanish speakers who know French.

What it means: "What's the bear doing in the mouth of a warrior?" Another common Spanish language combination is Spanish and French. These two languages often co-exist in Central and South America, but they're also spoken in a large number of communities around the world. Combining them is actually easier than you think, even as an English speaker. You just need to recognize that, despite the extra syllables and consonants involved, the pronunciation between Spanish and French is reasonably similar. You'll notice that some of your words sound worse than others, so if possible pick one that's closer to your native language to begin with—in this case English.

Combination 4: Spanish-German [Sortable]

- ✓ What you say: "¿Habla español el león en la boca del guerero?" ("Does the lion speak Spanish in the mouth of a warrior?") [Sortable]
- ✓ Who you say it to: Spanish speakers who know German.

What it means: "Does the lion speak Spanish in the mouth of a warrior?" Many people are surprised to learn that Spanish and German share many similarities. And while you won't find many fluent speakers of these two languages who can communicate with each other, it is possible for most native speakers to recognize some words, especially when they're spoken clearly. In this case, we have "habla" for "speak" in Spanish, which is also used in German. Combining this with the word for "lion," which is "león," we get a simple sentence that makes sense to a native speaker of Spanish or German.

Combination 5: Spanish-Japanese [Sortable]

- ✓ What you say: "Boca jiwarukokoro-tsukinahito ga aru" ("There's a person who's trying to attack my heart.") [Sortable]

✓ Who you say it to: Japanese speakers who know Spanish.

What it means: "There's a person who's trying to attack my heart." Many native speakers of Spanish and Japanese speak both languages, so it may seem odd that there are no Spanish-Japanese language combinations. If you're interested in learning both languages, this is the place to start. Although they're related as modern languages, this combination works perfectly in the same way as combinations 1-4.

Combination 6: Spanish-Japanese [Sortable]

✓ What you say: "Jigoku no gyakushū" ("Hell's battlefield.") [Sortable]
✓ Who you say it to: Spanish speakers who know Japanese.

What it means: "Hell's battlefield." This is a concrete way of showing how similar Spanish and Japanese are, because they're both based on the Latin alphabet. If you combine these two languages, you'll notice letters that look similar, like "g," which is pronounced "j." The dissimilarity between these two languages is that Spanish has a short vowel sound for that letter (like in English "th" and "ch"), while Japanese has the long vowel sound we have in "b." Since it's pronounced similarly in Spanish and Japanese, you can communicate with one another even though they're not related languages. This is a classic combination that shows how similar many languages are, regardless of their real-world origins.

Combination 7: Spanish-Portuguese [Sortable]

✓ What you say: "O sonhadorengorda no salão" ("The dreamer's fat in the hall.") [Sortable]
✓ Who you say it to: Spanish speakers who know Portuguese.

What it means: "The dreamer's fat in the hall." This is a very common language combination nowadays, especially in Europe. In this case, there are three distinct languages—Spanish, Portuguese and English—but they aren't related at all. In fact, even if you don't actually know what the last word means (it's English for "hall"), you can probably still understand it easily. This is because these languages are all spoken around the world in various countries, and each has a very distinct way of pronouncing sounds. English has it's own language rules, Spanish and Portuguese have their own rules, and the combination of all three allows a native Spanish speaker to speak with a native Portuguese speaker.

Combination 8: Spanish-Russian [Sortable]

✓ What you say: "El riesgo de la torre te hace la historia" ("The tower's risk makes the story.") [Sortable]

CHAPTER 4

SPANISH STORIES

Introduction

Spanish is an important language to know, not just for those who want to visit some Spanish-speaking countries one day, but also for many people living in North America. With so many Spanish speakers around the world, it is essential that people learn the basics and travel to a country where they can practice their newly acquired skills.

But how exactly does one go about learning a new language? If you've ever tried learning a new language by just reading books in your native tongue and making occasional visits to the country where it's spoken, you'll know that this is simply not enough. You need more than a crash course by anyone — you need immersion. You have to live in the country where your new language is spoken and learn from the locals by talking to them.

If you want to study Spanish in a more authentic environment, spend some time traveling around with a native speaker. It's not easy, but it can be very rewarding if you follow these tips:

1. Learn (and practice) vocabulary before your trip

Before going on your trip, get a good book of Spanish words and commit them to memory. It's easier to learn vocabulary if you have a good foundation by which to recognize and memorize them.

You can go for the full Spanish language course, or you can find an electronic dictionary that will allow you to practice as often as you want. The trick is to do it every day. The more often you review your Spanish words, the more likely it is that they will stay with you for longer.

The key is to always keep learning while on your trip, because even though these vocabulary words are useful, they won't get very far if there are no people around who speak them.

2. Play Spanish with locals

Language learning is not just about reading in a textbook or listening to a CD; it's about going out in the world to meet people and speaking to them. Use your

Spanish skills while you travel. Go out for lunch or dinner and try to use as many words as possible when you are ordering food, asking for directions or ordering drinks! In this way, you can practice your Spanish while making new friends and acquaintances wherever you go.

3. Speak with locals whenever possible

When the opportunity presents itself, speak with people in Spanish as frequently as possible. This means that you don't have to be in a classroom or formal setting with other learners. In fact, this is the whole point of immersion. You will learn Spanish much faster if you can speak with native speakers in their native language.

4. Once you've learned some new words, try using them

This is something that many people struggle with when learning foreign languages — and it's one of the key reasons why they fail to become fluent at all. So, it's important that once you do learn some new words, try your best to use them as often as possible and not just in a textbook or on a CD player. You want to learn by doing, and if you only ever practice your Spanish by reading a book, that will never be enough.

5. Keep practicing in the weeks after returning home

The best way to keep learning a language after you have stopped traveling is to keep studying it. This means that even after you've returned from your trip, you should continue learning and practicing as much as possible. This is how you can remain fluent in your new language for years to come.

Adele, La Guardiana del Bosque

Adele, The Guardian of The Forest

Adele es una pequeña niña muy apegada a la naturaleza. Todo lo que es verde o colorido y huele bien le gusta. Para ella, el bosque está vivo y debemos cuidarlo. Cuando ella tiene tiempo, lo ocupa en explorar cada cosa que habita en el bosque. Ella vive de las migajas de los gorriones, recoge unas nueces para las ardillas, y en el verano, riega las flores.

Adele is a little girl who is very close to nature. Everything that is green or colorful and smells good, Adele loves. To her, the forest is alive and we must take care of it. When she has the time, she occupies herself with exploring every little thing that thrives in the forest. She gives crumbs to the sparrows, gathers a few nuts for the squirrels, and, in the summer, she waters the flowers.

Desafortunadamente, no todos son tan gentiles ni cuidadosos con el bosque. Esto hace que Adele se desanime. Ella tiene la impresión de que a nadie le importa. Sus amigos tiran los envoltorios de sus dulces al suelo, ¡y a veces ella encuentra bolsas de basura de sus casas en el bosque!

Algunos incluso se divierten rompiendo algunos árboles jóvenes y pisando las flores silvestres.

Unfortunately, everyone is not as gentle and caring towards the forest. This makes Adele despondent. She is under the impression that nobody cares. Her friends dump their candy wrappers on the ground, and sometimes she finds garbage bags from houses in the forest! Nobody takes care of the forest.

Some even amuse themselves by breaking small young trees and trampling wildflowers.

Hay una cosa de lo que está segura Adele: El bosque está enfermo. Ella se fijó que ciertos árboles no tenían hojas (incluso durante el verano), algunas flores ya no crecían, y había menos animales de los que había antes. Un día, mientras ella estaba caminando por el bosque para ver si todo estaba bien, una criatura de apariencia muy graciosa que no había visto antes se le apareció. ¿Qué era esta criatura?, se preguntaba Adele con asombro. Él era muy pequeño, con un gorro puntiagudo y suave, con voz de niño.

There is one thing Adele is sure about: The forest is ill. She has noticed that certain trees have no leaves (even during the summer), certain flowers do not grow anymore, and there are less animals than there were before. One day, while she was walking through the forest to see if everything was okay, a funny-looking creature that she had never seen before came up to her. What is this strange little person, Adele said to herself in amazement. He was very small, with a little red-pointed bonnet and a very soft, childlike voice.

—"¿Quién eres? ¡Nunca me he encontrado con alguien como tú en el bosque!" preguntó Adele con mucho asombro.

— "Who are you? I have never crossed paths with anyone like you in the forest!" asked Adele with great surprise.

—"¡Hola jovencita! ¡Soy Abou, el Gnomo guardián y estoy orgulloso de serlo!" gritó la pequeña criatura.

— "Hello young lady! I am Abou, the forest warden Gnome and proud to be it!" shouted the little being.

—"¡Un Gnomo! ¡Jamás había visto a un gnomo!" dijo Adele sorprendida.

— "A Gnome! I have never seen a gnome!" said Adele, amazed.

—"Eso es normal. ¡Nosotros nos escondemos cuando los humanos vienen porque caminan sobre nosotros de cualquier manera y destruyen todo! Excepto, raramente, tú. Y por eso que he venido a hablar contigo. ¡Los Gnomos y todo lo demás en el bosque te necesitan!"

— "That is normal. We hide ourselves when the humans come because they walk over us and in any fashion the humans destroy everything! Except, weirdly enough, for you. And that is why I came to talk to you. The Gnomes and everything else in the forest need you!"

—"¿Ah sí? ¿Y por qué, qué está pasando?"

— "Oh, yes? And why, what is happening?"

—"¡El bosque está terriblemente enfermo, Adele! Nos hemos dado cuenta que al bosque no le va bien desde hace algún tiempo. ¡Y un día, Barba Verde, el gran jefe de los árboles, perdió todas sus hojas en medio del verano!"

— "The forest is terribly ill, Adele! We have been noticing that the forest is not doing well at all for a while now. And one day, Green Beard, the great chief of the trees, lost all of its leaves in the middle of the summer!"

—"¿Barba Verde? ¿Estás hablando del gran árbol de roble en medio del bosque?"

— "Green Beard? Are you talking about the large oak tree in the middle of the forest?"

—"Si, ese es Barba Verde. Es el árbol más viejo del bosque, el maestro de todos los árboles y es también uno de nuestros mejores amigos. Está muy enfermo, igual que el bosque. Hay que hacer todo lo necesario para salvarlo".

— "Yes, that is Green Beard. It is the oldest tree in the forest, the master of all other trees and it is one of our best friends. It is very sick, just like the forest. It is absolutely necessary to do something to save it."

—"¿Puedes llevarme a verlo?" preguntó Adele, firme y determinadamente.

— "Can you take me to see it?" asked Adele, firmly and determinedly.

Abou el Gnomo estuvo de acuerdo y partieron a ver a Barba Verde que vivía en medio del bosque. Adele le gustaba mucho el gran árbol — iba ahí a menudo para estudiar para sus exámenes, recostando su espalda en su gran tronco. ¡Pero ella no sabía que Barba Verde podía hablar! Al llegar, ella no podía creer lo que veía. El árbol empezó a sacudir sus ramas y dos grandes ojos y una boca se abrieron sobre el tronco.

Abou the Gnome agreed and they left to meet Green Beard who lived in the middle of the forest. Adele liked the big tree a lot — she went there often to study for exams, leaning back on its immense trunk. But she did not know that Green Beard could talk! Upon arriving, she could not believe her eyes. The tree began to shake its branches and two large eyes as well as a mouth opened on the trunk.

—"Pero qué tal querida Adele, ¿Cómo estás hoy?"

— "Why hello there dear Adele, how are you today?"

Adele estaba totalmente impresionada - ¡un árbol que podía hablar!

Adele was totally impressed — a tree that could talk!

— "Um estoy bien. Pero te ves en mal estado — ya has perdido algunas hojas este verano".

— "Um, I am very good. But you look like you're in a bad state — you've already lost a few leaves this summer."

— "Es cierto. Estoy envejeciendo, sabes. Fui yo quien le dijo a Abou que te buscara. ¡Tú eres una jovencita brillante, sabes! Escucha, es necesario que tú ayudes a mis amigos del bosque porque están enfermos".

— "It's true. I am getting old, you know. It is me that told Abou to go look for you. You are a very bright young lady, you know! Listen here, it is necessary for you to help my friends in the forest because they are ill."

Al escuchar esas palabras, muchas otras criaturitas empezaron a aparecer de todas direcciones. Gnomos, hadas, duendes, enanitos, había cientos de ellos.

Upon hearing those words, many other small beings appeared from every direction. Gnomes, Fairies, Elves, Dwarves, fiery Sprites; there were hundreds of them.

— "¿Sabes cómo cuidar al bosque?" Barba Verde le preguntó.

— "Do you know how to take care of a forest?" Green Beard asked her.

— "Um, Se cómo cuidar el ala de un pajarito, o reparar la patita rota de un zorro, y regar las flores… ¿pero cuidar un bosque? ¿Es difícil, cierto?"

— "Um… I know how to take care of a small bird's wing, or repair the broken paw of a fox, and water the flowers… but take care of a forest? It's difficult, isn't it?"

— "No, verás, es muy simple. Para que el bosque esté en buen estado, es necesario que todos los elementos estén en equilibrio".

— "No, you will see, it is very simple. For a forest to be in good shape, it is necessary that all its elements are in equilibrium."

— "¿Cuáles son los elementos del bosque?" preguntó Adele intrigada.

— "What are the elements in a forest?" asked Adele, who was intrigued.

— "Los cuatro elementos, ¡claro! ¡Fuego, Agua, Aire y Tierra! Los humanos están acabando con los elementos mágicos del bosque. ¡El plástico y la basura apagan al elemento de la Tierra, la suciedad drena al elemento del Agua, el humo contamina al elemento del Aire, y quemar la madera trastorna al elemento de fuego!

— "The four elements, of course! Fire, Water, Air, and Soil! Humans are depleting the magical elements of the forest. Plastic and garbage hinder the element Soil, the dirty drains hinder the element Water, the gas from smoke stacks pollutes the element Air, and burning wood disrupts the element fire!"

— "¿Y qué puedo hacer?"

— "And what can I do?"

— "Los humanos saben también, sin darse cuenta, ¡cómo cuidar a los elementos! Y tú… cuando ayudas, también cuidas a los elementos. Ve con mis amigos, y ellos te ayudarán".

— "Humans know also, without realizing, how to take care of the elements! And you… when you help, you take care of the elements as well. Leave with my friends, they will help you."

Adele se fue, acompañada por los gnomos, hadas y todos los demás. Ellos destaparon drenajes, llenaron los pozos, protegieron los árboles de los leñadores quienes cortaban los árboles jóvenes, y ahuyentaron a los cazadores del bosque que mataban a los animales. Durante todo este tiempo, cuando había ventolera o lloviendo o nevando, Adele hacía todo lo que podía para poder ayudar a revivir a Barba Verde, el Gran Árbol del bosque.

Adele left, accompanied by gnomes, fairies, and all the others. They unblocked the drains, filled up the ponds, protected the trees from woodcutters who cut down trees that were too young, and tripped the hunters of the forest who were killing the animals! During this entire time, when it was windy, raining, or snowing, Adele did everything she could do to help revive Green Beard, the Great Tree in the forest.

El invierno pasó y llegó la primavera. El primer día de primavera, el 21 de marzo, que es el día más mágico del año según Abou, todos los seres se reunieron alrededor de Barba Verde. Gnomos, hadas, duendes, enanitos y otros hicieron un enorme círculo. Ellos empezaron a cantar, y continuaron durante casi tres días seguidos. En el tercer día, la magia llegó. ¡En una de las ramas más altas, apareció un pequeño brote! ¡Barba Verde al fin se había salvado!

The winter passed and the spring finally arrived. The first day of spring, the 21st of March, which is the most magical day of the year according to Abou, all the beings met up around Green Beard. Gnomes, Fairies, Elves, Dwarves, and the others made a huge circle. They began to sing and continued for almost three days in a row. On the third day, the magic arrived. On one of the highest branches, a small bud appeared! Green Beard was finally saved!

¡Así es como Adele se convirtió oficialmente, a los ojos de todo el pueblo, incluso sus amigos, la Gran Guardiana del Bosque!

That is when Adele officially became, in the eyes of the entire town, and even her friends, the Great Guardian of the Forest!

Té Para Dormir – Tea For Sleeping

Es hora de dormir. El sol ya se acostó más allá de las montañas, y la luna salió a iluminar las calles tranquilas. Perros y gatos ya duermen en sus camas, y tan solo grillos y búhos están afuera cantando sus melodías. Niños y niñas en toda la ciudad se ponen sus pijamas, se van a la cama y viajan al mundo de los sueños. Pero, un niño de cinco años muy especial llamado Miguel, no quiere irse a dormir.

It is time to sleep. The sun has already gone down beyond the mountains, and the moon has come out to illuminate the quiet streets. Dogs and cats are already asleep in their beds, and only crickets and owls are outside singing their melodies. Boys and girls all over the city put on their pajamas, go to bed, and travel to the world of dreams. But a very special five-year-old boy named Miguel doesn't want to go to sleep.

"Por favor, Miguel, ponte el pijama y ven a dormir. Es tarde", le dice su mamá a Miguel. Pero el niño sigue jugando y saltando por todo su cuarto. "¡La noche es joven!" se ríe Miguel, "Soy un niño lleno de energía y nunca me voy a cansar. Voy a estar despierto por siempre".

"Please, Miguel, put on your pajamas and come and go to sleep. It's late," his mother tells Miguel. But the boy keeps playing and jumping all over his room. "The night is young!" laughs Miguel, "I am a child full of energy, and I'm never going to get tired. I will be awake forever."

Es cierto que Miguel tiene mucha energía, pero también tiene muy poca paciencia. Es solo un niño, y quiere que todo pase rápido, que todo pase cuando él quiere. Esto puede ser un problema, porque parece que Miguel es grosero y no escucha a su mamá, aun cuando él la quiere mucho.

It is true that Miguel has a lot of energy, but he also has very little patience. He is just a child, and he wants everything to happen quickly: everything to happen when he wants. This can be a problem because it seems like Miguel is rude and that he does not listen to his mother, even though he loves her very much.

Sin embargo, veinte minutos después, sin fallar, Miguel ya está acostado en su cama, con su pijama de dinosaurios. "Mamá, tengo sueño, pero no puedo dormir", se queja el niño mientras da vueltas en su cama una y otra vez. Ese era el problema de Miguel, por mucho que quisiera dormir, no sabía esperar, no se quedaba quieto, y se aburría.

However, twenty minutes later, without fail, Miguel is lying in his bed, in his dinosaur pajamas. "Mom, I'm sleepy, but I can't sleep," complains the boy as he tosses and turns in his bed. That was Miguel's problem; as much as he wanted to sleep, he didn't know how to wait, he didn't stay still, and he got bored.

"Tengo la solución", dice la mamá de Miguel, y le da un vaso, "Este es un té para dormir. Es una receta muy especial que me enseñó tu abuela. Este té es mágico, Miguel. Te ayudará a dormir y… puede ser que te enseñe una pequeña lección". Ese comentario y la mención de algo mágico hace que se despierte la curiosidad del niño. Rápidamente Miguel se toma el té. Justo cuando empezaba a molestarse y aburrirse de estar acostado, por fin se queda dormido.

"I have the solution," says Miguel's mother, and she gives him a glass, "This tea is for sleeping. It is a very special recipe that your grandmother taught me. This tea is magical, Miguel. It will help you sleep and… it might teach you a little lesson." That comment and the mention of something magical awakens the boy's curiosity. Quickly Miguel drinks his tea. Just when he was starting to get annoyed and bored with lying down, he finally fell asleep.

Entonces empiezan los sueños de Miguel. Pero estos no son sueños normales. Su mamá tenía razón, ¡el té es mágico! ¡Es justo como estar despierto! Primero, Miguel abre los ojos y se encuentra en una jungla, pero no está llena de animales normales, ¡Está llena de dinosaurios! Pero no hay que tener miedo, los dinosaurios no atacan. Los dinosaurios más pequeños quieren jugar con Miguel. Tan sólo hay un problema, cuando Miguel corre hacia los dinosaurios, estos desaparecen.

Then Miguel's dreams begin. But these are not normal dreams. His mom was right; the tea is magic! It's just like being awake! First, Miguel opens his eyes and finds himself in a jungle, but it is not full of normal animals; it is full of dinosaurs! But do not be afraid; dinosaurs do not attack. The smallest dinosaurs want to play with Miguel. There is only one problem when Miguel runs towards the dinosaurs, they disappear.

Por ser tan impaciente, a Miguel le parece que pasan horas antes de entender lo que pasa. Cuando corre hacia los dinosaurios ellos desaparecen y vuelven a aparecer mucho más lejos. Pero, cuando Miguel camina con calma hacia ellos, los dinosaurios se acercan. El problema es que cada vez que se acercan, el niño vuelve a perder la paciencia y empieza a correr y… los dinosaurios se van.

Because he is so impatient, it seems to Miguel that it takes hours before he understands what is happening. When he runs towards the dinosaurs, they disappear and reappear much further away. But, when Miguel calmly walks towards them, the dinosaurs come closer. The problem is that every time they get closer, the child loses his patience again and starts running and… the dinosaurs leave.

"¡Es una lección!" exclama finalmente Miguel cuando entiende lo que pasa, "Mi mamá me lo advirtió. Necesito tener paciencia". No es fácil. Miguel tiene que hacer muchos intentos, y fallar muchas veces. Tal vez no se da cuenta de lo importante que son esos ejercicios de paciencia.

Pero finalmente lo logra. Miguel consigue tener paciencia, controlar sus emociones, y cuando los dinosaurios lo alcanzan, por fin pueden jugar juntos. ¡Es la experiencia más maravillosa de todas!

"It is a lesson!" Miguel finally exclaims when he understands what is happening, "My mother warned me. I need to be patient." It is not easy. Miguel has to try many times and fail many times. Maybe he doesn't realize how important these exercises in patience are.

But he finally achieves it. Miguel manages to be patient, control his emotions, and when the dinosaurs reach him, they can finally play together. It is the most wonderful experience of all!

Al día siguiente, Miguel despierta después de haber tenido el mejor sueño de su vida. El niño está muy emocionado, porque ahora entiende que tener paciencia, esperar, y seguir instrucciones le conseguirá grandes premios al final del día.

The next day, Miguel wakes up after having the best dream of his life. The boy is very excited because he now understands that being patient, waiting, and following instructions will get him big rewards at the end of the day

El Retrato De Dorian Gray

EN EL ESTUDIO DEL ARTISTA Basil Hallward, sobre un **caballete,** estaba el **retrato** de un joven de extraordinaria belleza. El artista y su amigo, Lord Henry Wotton, lo veían con admiración.

—Es un hermoso retrato, Basil —dijo Lord Henry—. Es lo mejor que has **pintado.** ¡Debes **exhibirla**!

—Gracias, amigo, pero no pienso exhibirla —respondió el **pintor.**

Lord Henry miró a su amigo con asombro y le preguntó:

—¿Por qué no?

—Porque el cuadro no es mío. Pertenece al joven del retrato. Es muy **apuesto,** inteligente y muy rico, heredó una gran fortuna de su abuelo. Se llama Dorian Gray.

—¿Dorian Gray? —preguntó Lord Henry, **levantando una ceja.**

—Sí, así se llama. No quería decirte su nombre.

—¿Por qué no?

En ese momento la puerta del estudio se abrió y entró el joven Dorian Gray.

Basil sonrió.

Ese día el retrato quedaría terminado.

—Lord Henry, **te presento a** mi modelo.

—**Es un placer conocerte**, Dorian —dijo Lord Henry **estrechando manos.**

—**El placer es mío**, Lord Henry —contestó el joven con entusiasmo.

—Usted **irradia** juventud y prosperidad, Dorian —dijo Lord Henry admirando su rostro y las valiosas **sortijas** que el joven llevaba en los dedos—. ¡La juventud es un tesoro que todos queremos conservar!

—Así es, mi Lord. ¡**La vejez** es un gran **castigo**!

—Sí, Dorian, la vejez es un gran castigo — intervino Basil, mostrándole el retrato—. Pero en este retrato tú serás eternamente joven. ¿**Qué te parece**?

Dorian miró el cuadro impactado y pensó:

"*¡Qué triste! ¡Yo me pondré viejo y feo! ¡Pero en este retrato siempre seré joven y bello! ¿Y si fuera lo contrario? ¿Y si yo fuera joven y bello para siempre y el retrato envejeciera? ¡Daría cualquier cosa por eso! ¡Daría mi **alma**! ¡Sí, mi alma! ¡Quiero ser joven **para siempre**! ¡Daría mi alma **a** cambio de **eso**!*

Basil, al ver que Dorian observaba el retrato en completo silencio le preguntó:

— ¿**Qué pasa** Dorian? ¿Te gusta tu retrato?

—Sí, Basil. Me gusta mucho. Me impactó tanto que **pedí un deseo** —dijo Dorian.

—¿Un deseo? ¿Qué pediste, Dorian? —preguntó Henry con curiosidad.

—Disculpa, Lord Henry, pero es un secreto. Es algo muy personal.

Henry y Basil se miraron **desconcertados**.

—Y ahora, ¡a trabajar! —exclamó Dorian con una **amplia sonrisa** y **enseguida** se sentó en un **taburete** para iniciar su última sesión de modelo.

—Yo, mientras tanto, tomaré una copa de vino —dijo Lord Henry—. ¡**Brindo por** tu retrato Basil y por la vida! La vida buena que debe ser un **constante placer** sin importar nada más —y una gran sonrisa **iluminó su rostro**.

DESPUÉS DE LA LECTURA

VOCABULARIO 1

1-Caballete = easel (wooden frame)

2-El retrato = the portrait

3-Pintado = painted

4-Exhibirla = exhibit it

5-Pintor = painter (artist)

6-Apuesto = handsome

7-Levantando una ceja = raising an eyebrow

8-Te presento a = I present you to (I introduce you to)

9-Es un placer conocerte = It's a pleasure to meet you

10-Estrechando manos = shaking hands

11-El placer es mío = the pleasure is mine

12-Irradia = radiates

13-Sortijas = rings

14-La vejez = old age

15-Castigo = punishment

16-¿Qué te parece? = What do you think?

17-Envejeciera = aged (got older)

18-Alma = soul

19-Para siempre = forever

20-A cambio de = in exchange of (traded for)

21-¿Qué pasa? = What's happening? (What's going on?)

22-Pedí un deseo = I made a wish

23-Desconcertados = disconcerted (bewildered)

24-Amplia sonrisa = broad smile (wide smile)

25-Enseguida = immediately

26-Taburete = stool

27- Brindo por = I cheer for (cheers for)

28-Constante placer = constant pleasure

29 Iluminó su rostro = illuminated his face (lighted his face)

EJERCICIOS

1.-Completa la oración:

a.-En el estudio había un retrato de un joven de extraordinaria _____.

b.-Usted irradia _____, Dorian —dijo Lord Henry.

c.-El cuadro impactó tanto a Dorian que pidió un ____.

.

2.-Indica si es Verdadero o Falso:

a.-Lord Henry era hermano del pintor del cuadro___

b.-Dorian Gray era un pobre viejo __

c.-Para Dorian la vejez era un gran **castigo** __

.

3.-Preguntas de selección múltiple:

Seleccione una única respuesta por cada pregunta:

1.-¿Qué pintó el artista Basil Hallward?

a.-La Mona Lisa.

b.-Un joven de extraordinaria belleza

c.-Un viejo mirando el mar.

d.-Nada, porque no estaba inspirado.

.

2.-¿Quién era Dorian Gray?

a.-Un profesor francés.

b.-Un pobre viejo.

c.-Un joven muy apuesto, inteligente y rico.

d.-Un famoso autor literario.

.

3.-¿Qué deseo pidió Dorian Gray?

a.-Ser joven para siempre.

b.-Ser un famoso pintor.

c.-La paz mundial.

d.-No pidió ningún deseo.

.

4.-¿Qué opinaba Lord Henry de la vida?

a.-Que era aburrida.

b.-Que debía ser un constante placer sin importar nada más.

c.-Que no valía la pena vivir.

d.-No le interesaba el tema.

SOLUCIONES

<u>1.-Completa la oración:</u>

Belleza, juventud, deseo.

<u>2.-Indica si es Verdadero o Falso:</u>

a.-F.

b.-F.

c.-V.

d.-F

.

<u>3.-Preguntas de selección múltiple:</u>

1.-b.

2.-c.

3.-a.

4.-b.

La Apertura del Faro

ESTA AVENTURA COMIENZA una **hermosa noche** en la **Bahía** de Elgor, ubicada en la Isla de los Estados, Argentina.

Un **cañonazo** resonó a bordo del buque Santa Fe. A la vez, el **cielo** se iluminó con la luz del **faro** que por primera vez **resplandecía** para guiar las embarcaciones. Quienes observaron el espectáculo desde la **playa**, ¡aclamaron con entusiasmo!

Luego de la apertura, la tripulación se embarcó en el buque **quedando** sólo en tierra los tres guardianes del faro: Felipe, Vázquez y Moriz. Mientras uno trabajaba en el faro, los otros caminaban por la playa y conversaban llenos de entusiasmo:

—Dime Vázquez, ¿**crees que** el buque parta mañana? —preguntó Felipe, el más joven.

—¡Claro amigo! Por fortuna **culminaron** los trabajos en muy buen momento.

—Sí, ya el faro **está listo** y a partir de hoy todas las noches lo iluminará todo desde lo alto…

—Así es, muchacho, ahora tenemos que trabajar eficientemente para que su luz siempre esté encendida y guie a los barcos.

—¡Qué honor! ¡Ser guardián del faro del Fin del Mundo! —exclamó entusiasmado el joven con una **gran sonrisa**.

—Sí, Felipe, es todo un privilegio. Y ahora, ¡vamos a dormir!

—¡Vamos! En dos horas debo relevar a Moriz.

—Ciertamente, luego me tocará relevarte a las 2 de la mañana. Permaneceré en guardia hasta el amanecer.

LA VISITA DEL CAPITÁN

La noche transcurrió **tranquila**.

El **buque** Santa Fe pertenecía a **la Marina de Guerra** de la República de Argentina. Estaba destinado a la vigilancia de las costas. Sin embargo, en esta oportunidad se utilizó para transportar el material y el personal requerido en la construcción del faro del fin del mundo.

Al día siguiente de la inauguración del faro, el cielo estaba despejado.

Después de desayunar, el comandante del buque, el Capitán Lafayette y a su segundo oficial, fueron al faro a despedirse.

Mientras inspeccionaban las instalaciones del faro, conversaban sobre la **soledad** y **lejanía** de la Isla de los Estados.

—Trabajar en el faro no será fácil —dijo el capitán.

—Sí mi capitán.

—El relevo de los guardianes se hará cada tres meses.

—Afortunadamente para ellos, mi capitán, porque no les afectará el intenso frio del invierno de esta zona.

—Sí —afirmó el capitán, mirando el faro—. Por suerte el faro es un sólido refugio.

En ese momento, los tres guardianes salieron a recibir a los oficiales. El capitán Lafayette se dirigió a Vázquez, el jefe de los guardianes, y preguntó:

—¿Hubo alguna novedad durante la noche?

—Ninguna, mi capitán —respondió Vázquez.

—¿Las lámparas funcionaron perfectamente?

—Sí, capitán.

—¿Y qué tal les pareció la **habitación**?

—Muy **cómoda** y cálida, mi capitán.

—Ahora, señores, revisemos el faro —dijo el capitán.

Siguiendo a Vázquez, subieron la escalera hasta llegar al tope del faro. Desde ahí, contemplaron la espléndida vista antes de inspeccionar el resto del lugar.

Después de esto, el capitán y el segundo oficial **se despidieron** y regresaron al buque. Ese mismo día iniciaron su **largo viaje** de regreso.

DESPUÉS DE LA LECTURA

VOCABULARIO 1

1.-Hermosa noche = beautiful night

2.-Bahía = bay

3.-Cañonazo = cannonshot

4.-Cielo = sky

5.-Faro = lighthouse

6.-Resplandecía = was shining

7.-Playa = beach

8.-Quedando = remaining

9.-¿Crees qué = Do you believe that

10.-Culminaron = culminated

11.-Está listo = It's ready

12.-Gran sonrisa = big smile

13.-Tranquila = peaceful

14.-Buque = warship

15.-Marina de guerra = Navy

16.-Soledad = solitude

17.-Lejanía = distance

18.-Habitación = room

19.-Cómoda = comfortable

20.-Se despidieron = bid farewell

21.-Largo viaje = long journey

EJERCICIOS

1.-Completa el diálogo:

—¿Hubo alguna novedad durante la _____?

—Ninguna, mi _____

—¿Las lámparas funcionaron _____?

—Sí, capitán.

—¿Y qué tal les pareció la _____?

.

2.-Indica si es Verdadero o Falso:

a.-El faro del fin del mundo queda en Alaska __

b.-El faro sirve para iluminar a los barcos __

c.-Los tres guardianes se llamaban Vázquez, Moriz y Fernando __

.

3.-Preguntas de selección múltiple:

Selecciona una única respuesta por cada pregunta:

1.-¿Dónde se construyó el Faro del Fin del Mundo?

a.-Venezuela.

b.-Japón.

c.-Argentina.

d.-Australia.

2.-¿Cuántos guardianes cuidan el faro?

a.-Dos.

b.-Tres.

c.-Cuatro.

d.-Uno.

.

3.-¿Cada cuánto se hará el relevo de los guardianes?

a.-Cada semana.

b.-Cada mes.

c.-Cada dos meses.

d.-Cada tres meses.

.

4.-¿Qué tal le pareció la habitación a Vázquez?

a.-Incómoda y fría.

b.-Muy cómoda y cálida.

c.-Amplia y agradable.

d.-Pequeña y fea.

SOLUCIONES

1.-Completa el diálogo:

a.-Noche.

b.-capitán.

c.-perfectamente.

d.-habitación.

.

2.-Indica si es Verdadero o Falso:

a.-F.

b.-V.

c.-F.

.

3.- **Preguntas de selección múltiple:**

1.-c.

2.-b.

3.-d.

4.-b.

La Casa

CAPÍTULO 1

Miguel y Ana están casados.

MTienen un hijo de tres años y un perro.

Viven en un pequeño apartamento.

Están buscando una nueva casa donde vivir.

Tras mucho buscar, encuentran lo que parece ser un chollo; una fantástica casa a un precio inigualable.

Sin dudarlo, deciden ir a verla.

Conciertan una cita con un agente inmobiliario.

Ese mismo día van a verla.

Miguel y Ana esperan al agente inmobiliario en la puerta principal.

CHAPTER 1

Mike and Anne are married.

They have a three-year-old son and a dog.

They live in a small apartment.

They are looking for a new home to live in.

After much searching, they find what seems to be a bargain; a fantastic house at an unbeatable price.

Without hesitation, they decide to go see it.

They make an appointment with a real estate agent.

They go to see it the very same day.

Mike and Anne are waiting for the estate agent at the main door.

CAPÍTULO 2

—Es la casa de mis sueños —dice Miguel anonadado.

—¡Es una maravilla! —añade Ana.

El agente inmobiliario llega y se añade a la conversación:

—Es una ganga. Aquí pueden vivir muy bien.

El matrimonio mira a su alrededor.

Miguel comenta:

—Parece un vecindario muy tranquilo. Me gusta.

Pero hay algo que preocupa a Ana…

—He oído decir que pasan cosas extrañas en esta casa.

—Habladurías —responde el agente inmobiliario.

CHAPTER 2

"It is the house of my dreams," Mike says dumbfounded.

"It is a wonder!", Anne adds.

The real estate agent arrives and joins in the conversation,

"It's a bargain. You can live very well, here."

The married couple looks around.

Mike remarks,

"It seems like a very quiet neighborhood. I like it."

But there is something Anne is worried about...

"I've heard that strange things happen in this house."

"Gossip, "the real estate agent answers.

CAPÍTULO 3

Los tres entran en la casa para verla por dentro.

Se trata de una casa de una planta.

Tiene cuatro habitaciones con baño propio y armarios empotrados.

También tiene un gran comedor, una sala de estar y una gran cocina.

Toda la casa está amueblada.

Además, tiene un garaje para dos coches y un práctico sótano.

A la pareja les encanta la casa.

—Mañana mismo le damos la paga y señal —dice Miguel.

Pero Ana se fija en un detalle…

—¿Cómo es que una casa tan nueva tiene telarañas?

CHAPTER 3

The trio enters the house to see the inside of it.

It is a one-story house.

It has four en—suite bedrooms and fitted wardrobes.

It has a large dining room, a living room and a great kitchen.

The whole house is furnished.

It also has a garage for two cars and a convenient basement.

The couple loves the house.

"Tomorrow, we'll make a down payment, without fail," Mike says.

But Anne notices something…

How come such a new house has cobwebs?

CAPÍTULO 4

El agente inmobiliario agarra un trapo y la retira.

—Esto no es nada. Es porque la casa está vacía.

—Sí, cariño. En las casas habitadas no entran tantos insectos —añade Miguel.

Ana parece satisfecha con esa respuesta.

El matrimonio se despide del agente inmobiliario.

Se marchan en coche.

Ya en su apartamento Ana y Miguel charlan sobre la casa:

—Estoy tan ilusionado —comenta Miguel.

—Yo también, amor. Pero no sé… hay algo en la casa que me da mal rollo.

—Eso son los nervios, cariño. Vamos a dormir —responde un Miguel.

CHAPTER 4

The real estate agent grabs a rag and removes it.

"This is nothing. It happens because the house is empty."

"Yes, darling. In inhabited houses bugs don't enter," Mike adds.

Anne seems satisfied with that answer.

The married couple says goodbye to the real estate agent.

They drive away.

Back in their apartment Anne and Mike chat about the house,

"I'm so excited," Mike remarks.

"Me too, darling. But, I don't know… there's something in the house that gives me bad vibes…"

"That's because of the excitement, honey. Let's get some sleep," Mike answers.

CAPÍTULO 5

La familia se instala en su nuevo hogar.

La habitación más grande es para la pareja.

Ana utilizará una de las habitaciones como despacho.

Otra habitación será el cuarto de Martín.

Aún queda una habitación libre para invitados.

La pareja está muy ilusionada.

Martín empieza a llorar sin motivo.

Espartaco, el perro, también está ladrando.

Sus padres corren a la habitación.

Martín les dice que no le gusta la casa.

CHAPTER 5

The family settles into their new home.

The largest bedroom is for the couple.

Anne will use one of the rooms as her office.

Another room will be Martin's bedroom.

There is still a spare room for guests.

The couple is very excited.

Martin begins to moan without a reason.

Spartacus, the dog, is barking, too.

His parents run to the room.

Martin tells them that he doesn't like the house.

CAPÍTULO 6

Sus padres le preguntan el porqué.

—¿Por qué no te gusta la casa, hijo?

—Porque hay bichos malos —responde Martín asustado.

Miguel y Ana revisan el cuarto de Martín.

—No te preocupes Martín, todo está bien -dice Miguel.

-Mamá ha limpiado toda la casa -añade Ana.

—¡Venga! Vamos a jugar al jardín —propone Miguel.

Todos salen afuera y pasan una agradable tarde.

Por la noche, Ana prepara la cena.

Después de cenar, ponen a dormir a Martín.

CHAPTER 6

His parents asked him why.

"Why you don't like the house, son?"

"Because there are bad bugs," Martin answers, scared.

Mike and Anne check Martin's room.

"Don't worry, Martin, everything's alright, Mike says.

"Mommy cleaned the whole house," Anne adds.

"Come on! Let's play in the garden," Mike suggests.

They all go out and spend a nice afternoon.

In the evening Anne cooks dinner.

After dinner, they put the children to bed.

CAPÍTULO 7

Ana recoge la mesa y lleva los platos sucios a la cocina.

Mientras, Miguel saca la basura y pasea a Espartaco.

Más tarde, la pareja ve un rato la televisión.

Se hace tarde, así que deciden ir a dormir.

Es medianoche y todo está en silencio.

De repente, Espartaco empieza a ladrar.

Normalmente no ladra tanto.

Miguel decide ir a ver lo que sucede.

Al ver que no pasa nada, Miguel toma una decisión: Mete a Espartaco en el garaje para que no moleste.

CHAPTER 7

Anne clears the table and takes the dirty dishes to the kitchen.

In the meantime, Mike takes out the garbage and walks Spartacus.

Later, the couple watches television for a while.

It's getting late, so the couple decides to go to sleep.

It's midnight and all is quiet.

Suddenly, Spartacus starts barking.

He usually doesn't bark that much.

Mike decides to go see what is happening.

On finding that nothing is happening, Mike makes a decision, He keeps Spartacus in the garage so that he doesn't bother anyone.

CAPÍTULO 8

Miguel vuelve a su habitación.

Ana ya duerme.

Ha sido un día largo y ambos están agotados.

Miguel también se queda dormido rápidamente.

Mientras tanto, en la habitación de Martín…

Una araña sale del armario.

Se acerca a Martín.

La araña sube a la cama y va hasta la cabeza del niño.

Empieza a caminar haciendo círculos por su cara.

CHAPTER 8

Mike returns to his room.

Anne is already sleeping.

It's been a long day and both are exhausted.

Mike also falls asleep quickly.

Meanwhile, in Martin's room...

A spider comes out of the closet.

He approaches Martin.

The spider climbs onto the bed and goes up to the child's head.

It starts walking in circles on his face.

CAPÍTULO 9

A la mañana siguiente, Ana se despierta temprano.

—¿Dónde está Espartaco? —pregunta a su marido.

Miguel, aún medio dormido, le explica lo sucedido.

Al ver la cara de enfadada de Ana le dice:

—Lo hice para que no nos molestase ni a nosotros ni a los vecinos.

Y añade:

—Estaba muy nervioso. Ya puedes sacarlo si quieres.

Ana lo comprende y decide ir a buscar a Espartaco al garaje.

Ana encuentra la puerta del garaje entreabierta.

Espartaco no está allí.

CHAPTER 9

The next morning, Anne wakes up early.

"Where's Spartacus?", she asks her husband.

Mike, still half asleep, tells her what happened.

On seeing Anne's angry face, he says,

"I did it so he didn't bother us, or our neighbors."

And he adds,

"He was very nervous. Now you can take him out if you want."

Anne understands and decides to go and search for Spartacus in the garage.

Anne finds the garage door ajar.

Spartacus is not there.

CAPÍUTLO 10

Ana está preocupada y vuelve a la habitación para decírselo a su marido.

—Espartaco no está allí. ¿Estás seguro de que cerraste bien la puerta del garaje?

—Yo diría que sí —dice Miguel extrañado.

—Pero tampoco estoy muy seguro. Anoche tenía mucho sueño —añade.

—¡Pobre Espartaco! ¿Adónde estará? —pregunta Ana preocupada.

—No te preocupes, seguro que no está lejos —contesta Miguel.

—¡Hay que salir a buscarlo! —dice Ana.

—Sí, ya voy yo. Tú despierta a Martín y prepárale el desayuno.

Miguel sale a buscar a Espartaco.

Busca por todo el vecindario.

CHAPTER 10

Anne is worried and goes back to the room to tell her husband.

"Spartacus is not there. Are you sure you locked the garage door tight?"

"I would say so," Mike says confusedly.

"But I'm not really sure. I was very sleepy," he adds.

"Poor Spartacus! Where can he be?", Anne asks anxiously.

"Do not worry, I'm sure he's not far," Mike says.

"We must look for him!", Anne says.

"Yeah, I'll go. And you wake Martin up and prepare some breakfast for him."

Mike goes out to look for Spartacus.

He looks around the whole neighborhood.

CAPÍTULO 11

Miguel no encuentra a Espartaco.

Cuando vuelve a casa ve a Ana y a Martín en la puerta.

Ana está llorando.

—¿Qué ha pasado? —pregunta Miguel.

—¡Vamos al hospital, ahora! —grita Ana desesperadamente.

Miguel mira a su hijo y se horroriza.

Martín tiene la cara deformada.

Es como si un millón de insectos le hubiesen picado.

Miguel saca rápidamente el coche del garaje.

Los tres van a toda velocidad al hospital.

CHAPTER 11

Mike doesn't find Spartacus.

When he returns home, he sees Anne and Martin at the door.

Anne is crying.

"What happened?", Mike asks.

"Let's go to the hospital, now!", Anne shouts desperately.

Mike looks at his son and is horrified.

Martin's face is contorted.

It is as if a million insects had bitten him.

Mike quickly takes the car out of the garage.

The trio goes at full speed to the hospital.

CAPÍTULO 12

Martín es atendido en el hospital.

El médico les dice que puede tratarse de una reacción alérgica.

Les informa que no es una intoxicación alimentaria.

Dice que su hijo ha sido mordido por un insecto desconocido.

Probablemente ha sido una araña.

El doctor da a Martín un antihistamínico.

El niño empieza a recuperarse.

Cuando la familia vuelve a casa ya es de noche.

Cuando abren la puerta, ven que la casa está patas arriba.

No entran y Miguel llama inmediatamente a la policía.

CHAPTER 12

Martin is treated at the hospital.

The doctor tells them that this may be an allergic reaction.

He informs them that it isn't a case of food poisoning.

He says that their child has been bitten by an unknown insect.

It was probably a spider.

The doctor gives Martin an antihistamine.

The child begins to recover.

When the family return home it's already night.

When they open the door, they see that the house is in a mess.

They don't go in and Mike calls the police immediately.

¿Qué Hora Es?

Hoy es lunes. Lunes por la mañana. El peor día de la semana.

En la clase G23, los estudiantes de español están sentados alrededor de una mesa grande, de una gran mesa. Hay 6 estudiantes. Nadie habla.

Muchos tienen sueño. Probablemente se acostaron tarde anoche y esta mañana se han levantado muy temprano para llegar a clase a las nueve. A nadie le gusta madrugar los lunes por la mañana.

Christina y Carol juegan con sus móviles. Están aburridas.

James ha comprado el periódico El País y está intentando traducir una noticia con la ayuda de un pequeño diccionario de bolsillo.

Anna está haciendo ahora, muy deprisa, los deberes que la profe había mandado el viernes. El fin de semana no ha estudiado nada de español. El sábado salió de marcha con sus amigos. Aprendió una expresión nueva que le gusta mucho: ¡Qué guay! El domingo estaba demasiado cansada para estudiar. Se quedó en casa y vio dos capítulos de Friends. En español, por supuesto. En la televisión española doblan siempre las películas y las series extranjeras.

Charles está durmiendo. Tiene la cabeza sobre la mesa y duerme. El sábado salió con Anna y con otros chicos de la escuela y anoche también salió hasta muy tarde. A Charles le encanta salir por la noche. Ha venido a España a pasárselo bien, a divertirse. Anoche se lo pasó muy bien, pero ahora está hecho polvo.

Rose ha empezado a leer la lección 8 del libro: ¿Cómo es tu ciudad? El viernes terminaron la lección 7 y hoy toca la lección 8. El vocabulario no le parece difícil: barrio, monumentos, calles, tiendas… Pero no hay nada sobre ser y estar.

Rose está un poco decepcionada con las clases de español. Está decepcionada y también está preocupada porque ella quiere hacer el examen del DELE y necesita saber muy bien la gramática. De hecho, se levanta cada día a las cinco de la mañana para estudiar gramática. Sin embargo, después de tres semanas de clase, la profe todavía no ha explicado la diferencia entre ser y estar. Ella no ha venido a Granada para pasárselo bien; ella ha venido a aprender español. Para ella, estudiar español es una cosa seria.

— ¿Qué hora es? —pregunta Rose en voz alta.

— Son las nueve y veinte —responde Christina sin dejar de jugar con el móvil.

— Es raro. Ella nunca llega tarde —comenta James.

— Estará enferma —dice Rose.

Anna la mira. Está sorprendida.

— Perdona, Rose, pero… ¿Has dicho "estará"? ¿Por qué usas el futuro?

Estamos hablando de ahora, del presente…

— Sí, pero se puede usar el futuro para hacer hipótesis, cuando no estamos seguros de algo. Como yo no estoy segura de sí la profe está enferma o no, uso el futuro para indicar que es una posibilidad. También podría decir "quizás está enferma". Es posible, pero no estoy totalmente segura.

— ¡Ah, gracias, no lo sabía! ¡Qué guay! —responde Anna riendo. En realidad, no ha entendido nada, pero no quiere admitirlo delante de Rose, la mejor estudiante de la clase. Para Anna, la gramática española es un rollo.

— ¡Qué guay! —dice también Charles, sin abrir los ojos.

VOCABULARIO 1

1.-Temprano: Early

2.-Nadie: Nobody

3.-Madrugar: To get up very early in the morning.

4.-Diccionario de bolsillo: Pocket dictionary.

5.-(muy) Deprisa: Quickly, in a hurry.

6.-La profe: La profesora = the (female) teacher.

7.-(ir, salir, estar) De marcha: To go party.

8.-Doblar (Una película): To dub (a film).

9.-(estar) Hecho polvo: To be exhausted, very tired, knackered.

10.-Hoy toca la lección 8: Today, itś lesson 8.

11.-Sin embargo: However

12.-En voz alta: Aloud

13.-Riendo (reír): Laughing (to laugh).

14.-(ser) Un rollo: (To be) very boring.

RESUMEN 1

Es lunes por la mañana. La clase de español empieza a las nueve, pero a las nueve y veinte la profesora todavía no ha llegado. Los estudiantes están en clase, sentados alrededor de una gran mesa, esperando.

Preguntas de Comprensión 1

1.-Anna ha estudiado mucho durante el fin de semana.

a.–Verdadero

b.–Falso

2.-Charles tiene sueño.

a.–Verdadero

b.–Falso

3.-Rose está…

a.–Leyendo el periódico.

b.–Jugando con su móvil.

c.-Mirando el libro.

SOLUCIONES 1

1.-b

2.-a

3.-c

2. ¿Estará Enferma?

De repente se abre la puerta de la clase. No, no es la profe. Es Eduardo, otro profesor de español de la escuela.

— ¡Buenos días, chicos!

— ¡Hola! —responden todos.

— ¿Todavía no ha llegado la profe?

— ¡Muy bien! ¿Y tú? —responde Charles, que acaba de despertarse en este momento.

Todos ríen, excepto Charles, que tiene un dolor de cabeza terrible y no entiende nada. A Charles le duele la cabeza cada lunes por la mañana.

— No, todavía no —dice finalmente James.

— ¿Quién es vuestro profesor? —pregunta Eduardo, aunque él sabe muy bien quién es.

— ¡María! —dicen los chicos.

— ¿María Sánchez?

— ¡Sí!

— ¿Una chica rubia, joven, de unos 30 años, delgada y con el pelo largo?

—vuelve a preguntar Eduardo, que quiere estar completamente seguro de que la profe que llega tarde es María.

— ¡Sí! —contestan todos.

— ¡Y muy guapa! —añade Charles.

— ¿Llega a menudo tarde? —vuelve a preguntar Eduardo.

— ¡No! A menudo es puntual. —dice Christina rápidamente, contenta de usar "a menudo" por primera vez, una expresión que ha aprendido jugando con Duolingo en su móvil.

— Ah, muy bien. Bueno, voy a hablar con el director. Él sabrá qué le ha pasado a María.

Cuando Eduardo se va, Rose llama a Anna.

— Anna, ¿has oído? Él también ha usado el futuro para hacer una hipótesis… Ha dicho "él sabrá".

— ¡Ah, sí, es verdad! —le responde Anna, aunque todavía no entiende nada.

Unos segundos después, Eduardo ya está llamando a la puerta del director de la escuela.

— Pablo, buenos días, ¿tienes un minuto? Soy yo, Eduardo…

— Pasa, pasa, Eduardo. ¿Qué sucede?

— No, nada, María… —dice Eduardo, entrando en la oficina.

— ¿Qué le pasa a María?

— Todavía no ha llegado a clase, Pablo. ¡Son casi las diez de la mañana y todavía no ha llegado! He ido yo a hablar con sus estudiantes en nombre de la escuela porque llegar tarde no es profesional, Pablo, no es profesional… No es bueno para la escuela.

— Estará enferma —dice Pablo, sorprendido.

— No creo —contesta Eduardo rápidamente —. Me han dicho los guiris que no es la primera vez que llega tarde…

— ¿En serio? —dice Pablo, preocupado —. Voy a llamarla ahora mismo.

Pablo llama varias veces a María por teléfono, pero nadie contesta.

— Esto no es profesional, Pablo, perdona, pero no es profesional —insiste Eduardo —. Los guiris dirán que esta escuela no es seria.

Pablo no dice nada. Está pensando qué hacer.

— ¿Me puedes hacer un favor, Eduardo? —dice finalmente el director —.

Habla tú con los guiris y diles que María ha tenido un problema personal esta mañana.

— Por supuesto, Pablo, por supuesto. Es una idea excelente.

— Mientras tanto, yo voy a ver quién la puede sustituir.

— Excelente idea, Pablo, excelente idea.

Mientras tanto, los estudiantes de María siguen en clase, esperando.

— ¿Y George? ¿Dónde es George? —pregunta Christina, que todavía no sabe usar los verbos ser y estar correctamente.

— ¡Está! ¿Dónde está George? —la corrige Rose rápidamente.

— ¡Qué raro! —dice James —. George no falta nunca.

— Hace unos días me dijo que le encantaba cómo da clase María; que es la mejor profesora de español que ha tenido… —comenta Christina.

— ¡Ahora recuerdo! —dice Charles de repente —. El sábado por la noche vi a la profe y a George juntos en un bar. ¡Lo había olvidado! Yo estaba tan borracho…

Nadie dice nada, pero todos miran hacia la silla vacía donde George suele sentarse.

VOCABULARIO 2

1.-Acabar de: to have just done something.

2.-A menudo: Often.

3.-Aunque: Although.

4.-Llamando a la puerta: knocking on the door.

5.-Por supuesto: Of course.

6.-Mientras tanto: Meanwhile, in the meantime.

7.-Hace: Ago.

8.-De repente: Suddenly.

9.-Juntos: Together.

10.-(tan) Borracho: (So) drunk.

11.-Donde George suele sentarse: Where George usually sits.

RESUMEN 2

Eduardo dice a Pablo que María todavía no ha llegado a clase. Pablo la llama por teléfono, pero la profesora no contesta. Mientras, en clase, Charles recuerda que vio a George y a María juntos en un bar, el sábado por la noche.

Preguntas de comprensión 2

1.-¿Cómo se llama la profesora de Español?

a.–Eduardo

b.–Rose

c.–María

2.-¿Quién es el director de la escuela?

a.–Pablo

b.–Eduardo

c.–María

3.-¿Con quién salió George el sábado por la noche?

a.–Con María.

b.–Con Anna.

c.–Con Charles

4.-George no está en clase.

a.–Verdadero

b.–Falso

SOLUCIONES 2

1. c

2. a

3. a

4. a

3. Manolo, ¿qué pasa?

Mientras tanto, Pablo, el director de la escuela, estaba intentando encontrar un profesor de español para sustituir urgentemente a María. No era fácil. La mayoría de los profesores estaban ocupados. Buscó en los archivos los currículos de algunos profesores que buscaban trabajo. Llamó por teléfono a cuatro, pero la respuesta era siempre la misma: no puedo, estoy ocupado, estoy enfermo, no tengo tiempo…

La verdad es que Pablo era conocido en la ciudad por pagar muy poco a los profesores que trabajaban para él y nadie quería dar clase en su escuela.

Pablo estaba preocupado. Si no encontraba pronto un nuevo profesor de español, los guiris se quejarían. Quizás cancelarían el curso y le pedirían el dinero que habían pagado. Además, escribirían una opinión muy negativa en la página de Facebook de la escuela. Sería un desastre.

Tenía que hacer algo. Y tenía que hacerlo rápidamente. Pablo empezó a sudar. No tenía calor: tenía miedo.

De repente, tuvo una idea. Una idea excelente, pensó él.

Fue a la recepción. Allí estaba Manolo, el recepcionista, como de costumbre leyendo el Marca. Leía el periódico Marca todos los días. Le gustaba mucho el deporte. Bueno, mejor dicho: le gustaba el fútbol; bueno, tampoco: le gustaba el Real Madrid. El equipo de la capital de España era su pasión. Desde niño. Desde que su padre lo llevó una vez, cuando tenía 8 años, a ver un partido de fútbol en el estadio Santiago Bernabéu. Fue su regalo de cumpleaños. El mejor regalo de cumpleaños de su vida.

— Manolo, ¿qué pasa? —le dijo Pablo al llegar a la recepción.

— Todo tranquilo, jefe. Ningún problema. Algunas personas han llamado, pero no he entendido nada. Hablaban en inglés.

Pablo lo miró unos segundos sin decir nada. Intentaba recordar por qué había contratado como recepcionista de una escuela de idiomas a un hombre que no sabía una palabra de inglés y que solo hablaba de fútbol.

— Entonces, si no tienes nada que hacer, tengo un pequeño trabajito para ti.

— ¿Tengo que ir a comprar tiza otra vez, jefe? ¿Ya se ha terminado?

— No, no es eso.

Unos minutos más tarde, Pablo y Manolo entraban en la clase G23.

— Chicos, hoy María no puede venir a clase. Tiene un problema… un problema personal. Y no puede venir. Eso es… —dijo Pablo, que estaba un poco nervioso. De hecho, estaba sudando.

— ¿Qué le ha pasado?

— ¿Ha tenido un accidente?

— ¿Está enferma?

Los chicos estaban preocupados y querían saber qué le había pasado a su profesora.

— Por el momento no puedo decir nada más, pero este es Manuel —dijo Pablo —. Manuel será hoy vuestro profesor de español.

— ¿El recepcionista? —preguntó Anna, sorprendida.

668

Los chicos se miraron los unos a los otros. Luego miraron a Manolo.

— Manuel es un gran profesional. Puede trabajar en recepción, pero también, como nativo que es, puede dar clase de español sin ningún problema. Solo tenéis que decirle qué lección toca hoy en el libro del curso.

Miércoles, 10 de Julio, por la Tarde

CAPÍTULO 1

sta mañana, cuando me he levantado…

E¿Sabéis qué es lo primero que he hecho esta mañana, en cuanto me he levantado?

No, no me he puesto a ver Facebook. No, tampoco me he puesto a consultar el móvil, ni a ver vídeos en YouTube, ni a ver fotografías en Instagram…

Lo primero que he hecho esta mañana en cuanto me he levantado ha sido mirar por la ventana. Sí, he abierto la ventana de mi dormitorio y he mirado fuera. He mirado hacia el cielo y me he puesto contento. ¿Sabéis por qué me he puesto contento?

Me he puesto contento porque he visto el cielo. He visto un cielo azul precioso, sin nubes. Y a mí el buen tiempo me pone de buen humor. A mí, el buen tiempo siempre me ha puesto de buen humor.

Y entonces, ¿sabéis qué he hecho?

Pues, me he duchado, me he vestido, he desayunado deprisa, me he lavado los dientes, me he afeitado, me he puesto las gafas de sol, he cogido la mochila y he salido de casa.

La verdad es que tendría que haberme quedado a preparar algunas clases y corregir los deberes de mis estudiantes, pero no tenía ganas. Fuera hacía sol, se estaba muy bien y no me apetecía nada quedarme en casa. Al fin y al cabo, en Londres no hace buen tiempo muy a menudo y hay que aprovechar los días de sol.

¿Sabéis dónde he ido? He ido al parque, he ido a dar un paseo por el parque.

¿Solo? Sí, yo solo.

He llamado por teléfono a mi amigo Carlos, pero me ha dicho: "Lo siento, pero es que esta noche he dormido muy poco, no he pegado ojo. El niño ha llorado toda la noche y ahora estoy muy hecho polvo".

La verdad es que a Carlos últimamente lo he visto muy poco. Es mi mejor amigo, pero estos últimos meses apenas nos hemos visto. Hemos quedado un par de veces para ir al cine, pero nada más.

Yo lo entiendo. Es que el pobre ahora no tiene tiempo para nada ni para nadie. Solo tiene tiempo para su mujer y para su hijo. Yo lo entiendo. Carlos se ha casado este año y su mujer ha tenido un hijo recientemente. Así que es normal. Yo lo entiendo.

Luego he llamado a Marta, pero me ha dicho: "¡Ay, perdona, Juan, pero estoy muy cansada! Esta semana he trabajado mucho y me he acostado tarde todas las noches. Estoy muy cansada y hoy quiero quedarme en casa y descansar".

Marta es traductora. Antes era profesora de español, como yo. Ha sido profesora de español muchos años, pero ahora se ha hecho traductora. Creo que ha estudiado un máster en una universidad inglesa, un máster de traducción, y este año se ha puesto a trabajar independientemente, por su cuenta.

Me ha dicho que no le va mal, pero que tiene que trabajar por la noche porque de día no tiene tiempo. Por el día tiene que cuidar de la casa, de su marido y de sus hijos. Así que siempre está cansada. Está cansada y casada.

De hecho, me parece que en los últimos seis meses la he visto solo una o dos veces. Yo lo entiendo. Cambiar de trabajo es muy difícil. No es fácil dejar un trabajo y empezar de cero cuando ya no eres joven, estás casada, tienes una familia...

Luego he escrito mensajes a otros amigos por WhatsApp, pero todos me han dado excusas similares. Elena me ha dicho que su marido se ha puesto enfermo; Antonio se ha excusado diciendo que los padres de su mujer han venido a pasar unos días con ellos y no puede dejarlos solos; Gloria me ha contestado diciendo que le encantaría ir conmigo al parque, si no se hubiera ido de vacaciones con sus dos hijas a Tenerife...

En fin, todos mis amigos me han dado una excusa para no quedar conmigo.

Al final me he visto solo en el parque, rodeado de ardillas, mamás con niños pequeños y parejas de novios jóvenes en busca de rincones solitarios, lejos de la gente...

¿Sabéis qué he hecho? ¿Sabéis qué he hecho en el parque?

Pues, me he puesto a caminar. Sí, he dado un paseo, yo solo.

Me gusta caminar y normalmente me gusta pasear por el parque, pero hoy, hoy tengo que reconocer que me he puesto un poco triste. Me he sentido un poco solo. He pensado: "Todos mis amigos tienen pareja, una mujer, un marido, suegros…" Y me he sentido un poco solo, la verdad.

Luego me he sentado en un banco y me he puesto a leer. He leído un poco en francés. Me gusta leer en francés. El francés me recuerda mi infancia, cuando iba a la escuela y era feliz como solo son felices los niños.

He visto algunas parejas de novios, paseando de la mano, besándose.

Y he escrito. Sí, también he escrito; he escrito un poema. Yo cuando estoy triste escribo poesía. Y hoy en el parque he escrito un poema. No soy muy buen poeta, pero a veces escribo versos.

Y la verdad es que he escrito un libro de poesía. Un libro que…

Bueno, la verdad es que solo lo ha leído mi madre, pero, bueno, de todas formas, puedo decir que, sí, he escrito un libro de poesía y en teoría, al menos en teoría, soy un poeta.

Y después… ¿sabéis qué he hecho después?

He vuelto a casa. Me he levantado del banco donde estaba sentado, he salido del parque y me he puesto a caminar en dirección a mi casa. Mientras caminaba por la calle me sentía un poco solo, un poco triste.

Antes de llegar a casa he pasado por el supermercado y he hecho la compra.

Luego, ya en casa, he puesto todas las cosas en el frigorífico y me he puesto a cocinar.

No he comido mucho. Solo una ensalada porque hoy ha hecho mucho calor y cuando hace calor yo no tengo ganas de comer.

He comido solo, en la mesa de la cocina, y me he vuelto a sentir triste.

Luego he lavado los platos y me he echado un poco en el sofá a dormir la siesta, pero no he pegado ojo. No he podido dormir. Me he puesto a pensar y a pensar y a pensar…

Bueno, total, que no he podido dormir la siesta. No he dormido nada. Cuando estoy preocupado no puedo dormir.

Así, que, bueno, ¿sabéis lo que he hecho?

Tendría que haberme puesto a preparar algunas clases y corregir los deberes de mis estudiantes, pero no tenía ganas, no me apetecía nada.

Entonces, ¿sabéis qué he hecho?

Me he levantado y me he puesto a limpiar.

He descubierto que cuando estás triste, cuando tienes muchos problemas, cuando tienes muchas preocupaciones, lo mejor es limpiar y ordenar la casa.

He descubierto que poner en orden la casa ayuda a poner en orden tus ideas, ayuda a ver las cosas con más claridad y a solucionar los problemas.

Pues eso es lo que he hecho esta tarde. Me he puesto a limpiar y a organizar la casa.

Y ha funcionado. Mi plan ha funcionado porque ahora me siento mejor.

Pero es que, además, he encontrado algo… ¿Sabéis qué he encontrado?

He encontrado algo muy interesante. Algo que me ha gustado mucho. Algo que me ha hecho pensar en el pasado, en mi vida. Algo que me ha traído muchos recuerdos.

Esta noche os contaré lo que he encontrado.

¡Hasta luego!

VOCABULARIO 1

1.-Me he puesto contento: me he alegrado ("ponerse" expresa cambio de humor).

I became happy.

2.-No he pegado ojo: no he podido dormir.

I didn't sleep a wink.

3.-Estoy muy hecho polvo: estoy muy cansado.

I'm knackered; I'm dead beat.

4.-Hemos quedado: hemos acordado vernos, nos hemos puesto de acuerdo para salir juntos ("quedar con alguien" se usa para concertar una cita con alguien).

We've arranged to see each other; we've agreed to meet or go out together at a certain place and time.

5.-Quiero quedarme en casa: no quiero salir de casa ("quedarse en un lugar" indica que permanecemos en el lugar donde estamos, no vamos a ninguna parte).

I want to stay home.

6.-Se ha hecho traductora: ha cambiado de trabajo, de profesión, y ahora es traductora ("hacerse + profesión" expresa cambio de profesión).

She has become a translator.

7.-Trabajar independientemente, por su cuenta: Trabajar o conseguir algo solo, sin ayuda de nadie.

Working freelance; on her own.

8.-Se ha puesto enfermo: ha caído enfermo, se ha enfermado ("ponerse" expresa cambio en el estado de salud).

(He) fell ill; (he) got sick.

9.-Suegros: los padres del marido o de la esposa.

The parents of one's spouse.

10.-Paseando de la mano: caminando juntos, al mismo tiempo que estamos cogiendo la mano de otra persona.

Strolling hand in hand.

11.-Me he echado un poco en el sofá: me he acostado en el sofá (Normalmente se dice "echarse a dormir" la siesta).

I lay down for a while on the couch.

12.-Me he puesto a limpiar: he empezado a limpiar ("ponerse a" indica el inicio de una acción).

I began to clean.

CAPÍTULO 2

Miércoles, 10 de Julio, por la Noche

Ya me he acostado. Todavía no me he dormido, pero ya me he acostado. Ya estoy en la cama. Pero no puedo dormir, no puedo dormir porque hoy… hoy ha sido un día especial. Ha sido un día diferente y yo me he sentido raro. Ha sido un día raro y yo me he sentido también un poco raro.

Me he pasado toda la tarde viendo este álbum de fotografías.

Creo que todavía no os lo he dicho, ¿no? Hoy he encontrado un viejo álbum de fotos, un álbum de fotografías.

He estado toda la tarde limpiando la casa y he encontrado por casualidad este viejo álbum de fotos que ahora tengo en las manos. Un álbum viejo con fotografías viejas, con fotografías antiguas de cuando yo era joven.

Fotografías de hace muchos años, de cuando yo era joven y feliz, de cuando no tenía arrugas en la cara y estaba delgado.

He vuelto al pasado. Ha sido como hacer un viaje en el tiempo. He hecho un viaje en el tiempo al pasado, a mi pasado.

¿Vosotros habéis hecho alguna vez un viaje en el tiempo? ¿Habéis viajado alguna vez al pasado? ¿O al futuro, quizás?

675

Había una película en los años 80 que se llamaba Regreso Al Futuro. ¿La habéis visto? ¿La habéis visto alguna vez? Yo la he visto muchas veces.

Cuatro o cinco veces. Normalmente no veo películas de ciencia ficción, pero Regreso Al Futuro la he visto tres o cuatro veces y me encanta; me encanta la idea de viajar al pasado o al futuro. Me gusta mucho la idea de viajar en el tiempo. Y eso es lo que he hecho hoy: he abierto este álbum de fotos y me he puesto a viajar en el tiempo. He ido al pasado, a los años de mi universidad, a mi infancia, a la casa de mis padres…

Bueno, no sé si todos sabéis qué es un álbum de fotos porque ahora, con Instagram y con Facebook, con Twitter y con todas las redes sociales que han aparecido en los últimos años, ya casi nadie usa álbumes de fotos.

Brexit

Todo empezó un viernes por la mañana. James estaba solo en casa de sus padres.

Aquella mañana se había levantado muy temprano para estudiar. Todavía tenía que hacer dos exámenes. Ese era su último año en la Open University y quería sacar buenas notas.

Después de estudiar se puso a ver una peli española. Fuera llovía y hacía frío. Era el mes de junio, pero en Littleborough, al este de Inglaterra, todavía era invierno.

James se levantó del sofá y se preparó un café con leche en la cocina. James ya no bebía té. Ahora solo bebía café: café con leche, café solo o cortado.

Nada de té. Dejó de beber té cuando leyó en un periódico que a los españoles no les gustaba nada el té.

Desde la cocina oyó a Penélope Cruz que decía: "La fiesta de cumpleaños es en casa de mi madre".

En Twitter se enteró de que los partidarios del Brexit habían ganado el referéndum sobre la Unión Europea. Inglaterra saldría de la UE.

James volvió al salón muy deprisa, con el vaso de café con leche quemándole entre las manos.

—¿Qué? ¿Cómo? ¿Por qué? ¡No puede ser! ¡Es increíble! —dijo James en voz alta y en español.

Cuando estaba solo, James hablaba a menudo en español en voz alta. Lo hacía para practicar porque no conocía a nadie que hablara español.

Littleborough era un pueblo muy pequeño y no era fácil encontrar gente de España o de América Latina. Allí no solían llegar los turistas.

James estaba preocupado. Quizás había escuchado mal. Tal vez no había entendido bien.

Paró el vídeo y lo mandó hacia atrás. Quería volver a escuchar aquella frase otra vez.

Unos minutos después Penélope volvió a decir: "La fiesta de cumpleaños es en casa de mi madre".

James se puso aún más nervioso. Solía ponerse muy nervioso cuando no entendía la gramática del español.

—¡Debe de ser un error! ¡Tiene que ser un error! Todo el mundo sabe que se usa el verbo "estar" para localizar o para situar algo: la casa está lejos, el gato está sobre la mesa, el banco está al final de la calle… ¡está, está, está!

De repente, mientras en el salón él gritaba en español como un loco, la puerta de la calle se abrió y una chica rubia entró en la casa.

Desde el salón, James no la veía, pero sabía quién era. No, no era Penélope Cruz. La chica que acababa de entrar no era morena, ni era española, ni hablaba español y tampoco hablaba inglés con acento extranjero.

— Shut up! Everybody can hear you talking in Spanish to yourself, idiot!

(¡Cállate! ¡Todo el mundo puede oírte hablando en español contigo mismo, idiota!) —le gritó la chica rubia desde la puerta, en un inglés perfecto.

Katie acababa de volver a casa.

VOCABULARIO 1

1.-Universidad Abierta

Open University

2.-Universidad pública de aprendizaje a distancia

A public distance learning university

3.-Quería sacar buenas notas

(He) wanted to get a good grade

4.-Se puso a ver una peli española

(He) started to watch a Spanish film

5.-Dejó de beber té

(He) stopped drinking tea

6.-Penélope Cruz

Famous Spanish actress

7.-Se enteró de que los partidarios del Brexit habían ganado el referéndum sobre la Unión Europea

(He) learnt that Brexit supporters had won the EU referendum

8.-¡No puede ser!

It can´t be!

9.-En voz alta

Aloud

10.-James hablaba a menudo en español en voz alta

James often used to speak aloud

11.-Allí no solían llegar los turistas

Tourists usually didn´t get there

12.-Tal vez

Maybe

13.-Paró el vídeo y lo mandó hacia atrás

(He) stopped the video and rewinded it

14.-Penélope volvió a decir

Penelope said again

15.-James se puso aún más nervioso

James got even more nervous

16.-Solía ponerse muy nervioso

(He) used to get really nervous

17.-Mientras en el salón él gritaba en español como un loco

While he was shouting in Spanish like a mad person

18.-Desde el salón

From the living - room

19.-La chica que acababa de entrar

The girl who had just come in

20.-Le gritó la chica rubia desde la puerta, en un inglés perfecto

The blonde girl shouted at him from the door in a perfect English

21.-Katie acababa de volver a casa

Katie had just come back home

CAPÍTULO 2

The Gipsy Kings

Katie acababa de volver a casa. Venía de trabajar en el supermercado donde estaba de cajera los fines de semana.

— What's wrong with you man? Are you going crazy? (¿Qué te pasa, tío? ¿Te estás volviendo loco?) —le dijo la chica mientras subía las escaleras camino de su dormitorio.

—¡Hola, chica! ¿Qué tal? ¿Qué pasa? ¿Todo bien? ¿Tuviste un buen día en el trabajo? —le contestó James desde el sofá del salón.

Katie no le respondió. Ella no entendía español. Estaba muy cansada de trabajar y solo quería dormir un rato.

No entendía la obsesión de James por el español. Siempre había pensado que su hermano era un poco raro, la verdad, pero ahora, desde que el año pasado fueron a Tenerife de vacaciones con sus padres, estaba mucho peor.

Cuando volvieron a Inglaterra, James se puso a estudiar español. Algo estúpido, según ella, porque todo el mundo sabía hablar inglés y estudiar otros idiomas era, simplemente, una pérdida de tiempo.

Pero, además, el problema era que James se había obsesionado y hacía cosas muy raras.

Dejó de comer pescado con patatas fritas y ahora solo comía paella y bocadillos de tortilla de patatas; también dejó de beber pintas de cerveza en el pub y ahora solo bebía vino tinto y sangría. Dormía la siesta todos los días, escuchaba flamenco, veía corridas de toros en YouTube y siempre llevaba pantalones cortos y camisas de cuadros. Decía que en España los chicos solo llevaban camisas de cuadros del Corte Inglés o de Zara.

Solía ir al gimnasio con una camiseta roja de la selección española de fútbol, el domingo desayunaba churros con chocolate y ahora, además, hablaba en español en voz alta cuando estaba solo.

Katie se acostó vestida en la cama. No tenía ganas de quitarse la ropa. Solo quería dormir un poco. Cerró los ojos…

De repente escuchó un ruido. Un ruido muy fuerte.

¡Boom! ¡Boom! ¡Boom!

Se despertó.

Abrió los ojos.

Escuchó música. Escuchó voces. No entendía nada. Quizás alguien gritaba, tal vez alguien cantaba.

El ruido venía del salón. Alguien había puesto la música muy alta.

Era James que estaba escuchando y cantando una canción típica española: Bamboleo, de los Gipsy Kings, su grupo español favorito.

— James! Shut up! Turn off the music. I want to sleep!

¡James! ¡Cállate! ¡Apaga la música! ¡Quiero dormir! —le gritó Katie desde su dormitorio.

—¡Me llamo Jaime! ¡Mi nombre es Jaime! —dijo él.

— Shut up! Speak English! (¡Cállate! ¡Habla inglés!) —dijo ella, cada vez más enfadada.

—"Bamboleo, bambolea. Porque mi vida yo la prefiero vivir así. Bamboleo, bambolea. Porque mi vida yo la prefiero vivir así" —Respondió James, cantando.

—Katie estaba harta. Su hermano estaba obsesionado con el español. Tenía que hacer algo.

VOCABULARIO 2

1.-Katie acababa de volver a casa

Katie had just arrived home

2.-estaba de cajera

(she) worked at the till

3.-mientras subía las escaleras camino de su dormitorio

while (she) was going upstairs towards her bedroom

4.-un poco raro

A bit strange, a bit weird

5.-se puso a estudiar español

(He) started to learn Spanish

6.-según ella

According to her

7.-una pérdida de tiempo

A waste of time

8.-hacía cosas muy raras

(He) used to do very strange things

9.-Dejó de comer pescado con patatas fritas

He gave up eating fish and chips

10.-pintas de cerveza

Pints of beer

11.-Dormía la siesta

He used to have a nap

12.-los chicos solo llevaban camisas de cuadros

The guys would only wear checked shirts

13.-El Corte Inglés — Zara

Two famous Spanish stores

14.-Solía ir al gimnasio con una camiseta roja de la selección española de fútbol

(He) used to go to the gym wearing a red t—shirt from the Spanish National Football Team.

15.-hablaba en español en voz alta cuando estaba solo

(He) used to speak aloud in Spanish when he was on his own

16.-No tenía ganas de quitarse la ropa

(She) didn´t feel like taking off her clothes

17.-De repente

Suddenly

18.-Un ruido

A noise

19.-Quizás — Tal vez

Maybe

20.-Alguien había puesto la música muy alta

Somebody was playing very loud music

21.-Le gritó Katie

Katie shouted at him

22.-cada vez más enfadada

More and more angry

23.-Katie estaba harta

Katie was fed up

24.-Tenía que hacer algo

She had to do something

CAPÍTULO 3

James Quiere Ser Español

En el pueblo la gente empezaba a hablar mal de James y a cotillear.

Littleborough era un pueblo pequeño y todo el mundo se conocía.

Sus amigas pensaban que James era muy raro. No podía invitarlas a su casa porque se reían de él. A ella le daba vergüenza y se ponía roja como un tomate.

Katie recuerda que un día, mientras estaba en el salón de su casa haciendo los deberes con Sara y con Deborah, dos compañeras de clase, su hermano entró en la habitación bailando flamenco.

Decía que estaba aprendiendo a bailar flamenco con vídeos de YouTube.

Quería ser como Joaquín Cortés. No llevaba camisa, ni camiseta. Iba por toda la casa casi desnudo, dando zapatazos en el suelo y gritando:

¡ole, ole, ole…!

Cuando Sara y Deborah lo vieron, las dos se echaron a reír. Katie se puso roja de vergüenza y casi se echó a llorar.

Desde entonces ninguna de las dos había vuelto a su casa. Cuando las invitaba, solían responder que estaban ocupadas, que tenían muchas cosas que hacer. Luego se miraban y se echaban a reír.

Katie estaba muy enfadada con su hermano, pero la verdad es que eso a James no le importaba mucho. De todas formas, Katie solía enfadarse a menudo y, además, a él Sara y Deborah no le caían bien.

— Could you please stop being silly while my friends are around? People think you are crazy! (Por favor, ¿podrías dejar de hacer el tonto cuando vienen mis amigos? ¡La gente piensa que estás loco!) —le decía Katie.

Pero a James no le importaba lo que pensaba la gente. Le daba igual. Él sabía que en España todos bailaban flamenco. Desde niños. Era algo normal.

Una vez leyó una frase en Facebook que le gustó mucho: "Sigue tus sueños y pasa de la gente".

Ese era su sueño. Soñaba con hablar español muy bien, sin acento, como un español. Quería llegar a ser bilingüe.

Pero no solo quería aprender español: James quería ser español. Sí, quería dejar de ser inglés y hacerse español. Eso es lo que quería.

Quería aprender a bailar flamenco sin camisa, como Joaquín Cortés, y tocar la guitarra como Paco de Lucía; quería tener un bigote muy grande, ponerse a trabajar de camarero en un bar de tapas, estar siempre moreno y tomar el sol en la playa sin quemarse la piel, como los españoles; quería saber cuál era la diferencia entre ser y estar y entender las reglas del subjuntivo. James quería ser español. Punto.

James solía pensar: "Nací en Inglaterra. Mi padre es inglés, mi madre es inglesa. Hablo inglés. Soy rubio, alto, delgado, tengo los ojos azules y la piel muy blanca. Es cierto, parezco inglés. Mi pasaporte dice que soy inglés, pero por dentro yo no me siento inglés. Yo me siento español. No me gusta el té, no bebo cerveza, el porridge me parece asqueroso, odio la Marmite, duermo la siesta, no salgo a la calle en invierno con camisetas de manga corta, quiero bailar flamenco, tocar la guitarra, comer chorizo y patatas bravas... Y además pienso que Gibraltar es español. ¡Yo soy un español encerrado en el cuerpo de un inglés! "

—Uno no es de donde nace, sino de donde se siente. —dijo en voz alta, finalmente.

— What? (¿Qué?) —dijo Katie, que no había entendido nada.

Katie estaba harta. Tenía que hacer algo.

VOCABULARIO 3

1.-Cotillear

To gossip, to nose around

2.-todo el mundo se conocía

Everybody knew each other

3.-se reían de él

They would laugh at them

4.-haciendo los deberes

Doing the homework

5.-Joaquín Cortés

Famous Spanish flamenco dancer

6.-No llevaba camisa

He wasn't wearing any shirt

7.-dando zapatazos en el suelo

Stamping (with his shoes on the floor noisily)

8.-se puso roja de vergüenza

(She) blushed (she was very embarrassed)

9.-a James no le importaba mucho

James didn't care that much

10.-De todas formas

Dejó de Sonreír y Nadie Sabe Por Qué

D e pequeña, Loli era una niña alegre. Lo sabe porque se ha visto en las fotografías que su abuelo guarda en un cajón de su armario, en el dormitorio.

Es un álbum de fotografías viejas, muchas en blanco y negro.

Loli las conoce casi de memoria. Las ha visto muchas veces: su madre de joven, paseando por las ramblas de Barcelona; su abuelo, vestido de soldado cuando hacía el Servicio Militar en Granada; sus padres, saliendo de la iglesia donde acababan de casarse y luego algunas pocas fotos, ya en color, de una niña sonriente que miraba a la cámara con ojos alegres: Dolores o Loli, como la llamaban todos.

De niña, Loli era alegre.

Luego, un día, dejó de sonreír. Nadie recuerda cuándo. Nadie sabe por qué.

La niña que solía estar contenta se volvió una adolescente triste, introvertida, taciturna, seria y silenciosa, que no hablaba con nadie y le gustaba estar sola.

En el álbum de fotos viejas solo hay una fotografía suya de adolescente.

Tiene unos 13 o 14 años. Es una fotografía de la escuela, una de esas fotografías de grupo con los compañeros de clase y con una de las profesoras de aquel año, la Señorita Martina. La Señorita Martina daba clase de español.

Ella, Loli, está en la última fila. Como era una de las chicas más altas de la clase, en las fotografías de grupo solían ponerla detrás de todos: "Loli, tú que eres la más alta, ponte la última, detrás de todos", le solían decir.

Y Loli, sin rechistar, se ponía detrás de todos. No solo era la más alta de la clase, también era la más grande y la más gorda. Por eso la llamaban Elefantona. Era normal. Tan alta y tan gorda, parecía un elefante o, mejor dicho, una elefanta. Una elefanta enorme: una elefantona.

En aquella fotografía en clase de la Señorita Martina, Loli ya no sonríe, ya no mira a la cámara con ojos alegres.

De niña, Loli era alegre. Ya no.

Un día dejó de sonreír. Nadie recuerda cuándo. Nadie sabe por qué.

La niña que solía estar contenta se volvió una adolescente triste, introvertida, taciturna, seria y silenciosa, que no hablaba con nadie y le gustaba estar sola.

VOCABULARIO 1

1.-un cajón: a drawer

2.-un álbum de fotografías: photo album

3.-las ramblas de Barcelona: famous street in Barcelona

4.-el Servicio Militar: compulsory military service

5.-donde acababan de casarse: where they had just got married

6.-De niña: as a little girl

7.-dejó de: (She) stopped or gave up doing something

8.-taciturna: taciturn, reseved, silent

9.-La Señorita Martina daba clase de español: Miss Martina used to teach Spanish

10.-la última fila: the last row

11.-solían ponerla detrás de todos: (They) used to place her behind everybody

12.-le solían decir: (They) used to say to her

13.-sin rechistar: without complaint

14.-Elefantona: pun using the word "elefante" + augmentative suffix "—ona"

15.-(elefante + —ona = elefantona = very big elephant).

16.-Loli ya no sonríe: Loli doesn't smile any more.

2. ¡Hecho, hecho, hecho!

Aquella fotografía suya de adolescente le trajo algunos recuerdos de cuando todavía iba a la escuela. Recordó que no le gustaba ir a clase y que la asignatura que menos le gustaba era el español.

En realidad, ella no quería aprender ningún idioma, pero en aquella época, en Inglaterra, era obligatorio estudiar al menos una lengua extranjera. En su colegio había tres opciones: alemán, francés o español. Ella eligió español porque sus padres eran de España, de Barcelona, y pensó que quizás para ella sería más fácil aprobar.

Se equivocó.

Le aburrían las clases de español y siempre sacaba malas notas.

Era normal. Ella nunca fue una niña muy inteligente y los idiomas no se le daban bien.

Mirando la fotografía, Loli recordó que lo solía pasar fatal en clase de español.

…

"¡Loli, Participio Pasado del verbo hacer!", le dijo la profesora un día, la Señorita Martina.

Loli no sabía qué quería decir, no la entendía. Era normal. Ella nunca entendía a la profesora de español.

"¿Cuál es el Participio Pasado del verbo hacer, Loli?", le volvió a preguntar la profe.

Parecía enfadada. Era normal. Los profesores solían cabrearse a menudo con ella.

"¿El examen es la próxima semana y tú todavía no sabes cuál es el Participio Pasado del verbo hacer?"

No sabía qué decir. Tenía la cabeza baja y miraba su libro.

"Loli, te estoy hablando a ti. ¡Por favor, mírame cuando te hablo!", dijo la profesora alzando la voz.

Sintió la mirada de los otros chicos de la clase. La observaban divertidos.

Loli se puso muy roja.

—¡Yo lo sé, señorita! —dijo Pete, alzando la mano. Pete era uno de los mejores estudiantes de la clase de español.

— ¡Yo también, señorita! —dijo Rose, la chica sabelotodo de la clase. Rose siempre sabía cuál era la respuesta correcta a todas las preguntas de todos los profesores.

Otros chicos alzaron también la mano. Casi toda la clase parecía conocer la respuesta. Seguramente era una pregunta muy fácil, pero ella no sabía qué decir. Era normal. Ella nunca sabía la respuesta a las preguntas de los profesores.

Vicky, la chica sentada a su lado, le dio un golpe con el codo y escribió una palabra con lápiz en su cuaderno: HACIDO. Luego cogió una goma de borrar y la borró rápidamente.

Loli alzó la vista y, mirando a la profesora, dijo con voz temblorosa, casi inaudible: ¡hacido!

Los chicos de la clase se echaron a reír y ella se puso aún más roja.

—¿Cómo? ¿Qué has dicho? —le preguntó la profe, con los ojos muy abiertos.

—¡¡Hacido!! —volvió a decir Loli, ahora un poco más alto, casi gritando.

Los chicos de la clase continuaron riéndose.

La profesora la miraba sin decir nada.

Loli se dio cuenta de que aquella respuesta era la respuesta más estúpida que se le podía ocurrir a alguien. Una respuesta estúpida, típica de una niña estúpida como ella. Y aún más estúpida si se piensa que sus padres eran españoles.

—¿Cómo es posible que todavía no sepas los participios irregulares? ¿Llevas dos años estudiando español y todavía no sabes cuál es el Participio Pasado del verbo hacer? Luego dio media vuelta, fue hacia la pizarra y escribió en letras muy grandes:

HECHO

Vicky le guiñó un ojo a alguien.

Los chicos de la clase se echaron a reír otra vez.

Era normal. Ella nunca fue una niña muy inteligente y los idiomas no se le daban bien.

Lo solía pasar fatal en clase de español.

…

VOCABULARIO 2

1.-la asignatura: subject in school

2.-al menos: at least

3.-aprobar: to pass an exam or a school subject

4.-Se equivocó: (She) was wrong

5.-siempre sacaba malas notas: (She) always got bad marks

6.-los idiomas no se le daban bien: (She) wasn't good at languages

7.-le volvió a preguntar la profe: the teacher asked her again

8.-solían cabrearse a menudo con ella: (They) used to get mad at her often

9.-¡Por favor, mírame cuando te hablo!: Please, look at me when I am talking to you

10.-alzando la voz: raising her voice

11.-Loli se puso muy roja: Loli blushed (Loli went red)

12.-alzando la mano: putting their hands up

13.-sabelotodo: know-it-all

14.-Seguramente: probably, very likely

15.-le dio un golpe con el codo: (She) poked her with her elbow

16.-cogió una goma de borrar y la borró rápidamente: picked up a rubber and erased it quickly

17.-ella se puso aún más roja: (She) went even redder

18.-Los chicos de la clase continuaron riéndose: the kids in the class carried on laughing

19.-Loli se dio cuenta de que: Loli realized that…

20.-aún más estúpida: even more stupid

21.-¿Llevas dos años estudiando español?: have you been studying Spanish for two years?

22.-Vicky le guiñó un ojo a alguien: Vicky winked at somebody

23.-se echaron a reír otra vez: (They) started to laugh again

24.-Lo solía pasar fatal en clase de español: (She) usually had a really hard time in the Spanish class

3. Inútil, tonta, triste

Ya habían pasado más de cinco años desde aquel día en clase de español.

Loli tenía ahora 19 años, pero seguía viviendo en casa de sus padres. No tenía dinero para vivir sola.

Dejó de estudiar en cuanto cumplió los 16, pero nunca encontró trabajo. La gente suele llamar "ni-nis" a este tipo de personas: ni estudian, ni trabajan.

Bueno, en realidad Loli tuvo dos empleos, pero no le duraron mucho tiempo.

Poco después de dejar de estudiar, su madre le encontró un trabajo de niñera.

Tenía que cuidar de los hijos de un matrimonio de abogados que no tenían tiempo para estar en casa durante el día. Parecía un trabajo fácil, pero no le duró mucho tiempo. Los niños tenían miedo de quedarse solos con ella.

Decían que Loli les daba miedo. No se le daban bien los niños.

—Tienes que sonreír más. Eres demasiado seria. Siempre pareces triste. —le dijo su madre.

Luego entró a trabajar de cajera en el supermercado del barrio, pero tampoco se le daba bien. Solía estar muy seria, nunca sonreía y daba miedo a los clientes. De hecho, aunque había dos cajas en el supermercado, los clientes siempre hacían fila en la caja donde ella no trabajaba. La gente pensaba que era muy antipática. A las dos semanas la despidieron.

Cuando llegó a casa y le dijo a su familia que la habían despedido del supermercado, todos se enfadaron con ella.

—You are useless! (¡Eres una inútil!). —le dijo su padre.

—You are stupid! (¡Eres tonta!). —le dijo su hermano.

¡Eres una inútil!

¡Eres tonta!

—You have to smile more. You always look sad (Tienes que sonreír más.

Siempre pareces triste). —le dijo su madre.

Y quizás tenían razón, pensaba ella.

No se le daba bien nada. Nunca tuvo ningún talento especial para nada.

Todo le salía mal. Ni siquiera sabía sonreír.

—What you have to do is to get married. To find somebody who financially supports you. (Tú lo que tienes que hacer es casarte. Encontrar a alguien que te mantenga) —le dijo luego su madre, cuando se quedaron las dos a solas.

Ella no dijo nada. Se fue a la cama, apagó la luz y se echó a llorar.

Un rato después escuchó la voz de su padre en la cocina. Hablaba con su madre.

—Who is she going to marry? Who is going to love her? You will have to find her a boyfriend, otherwise she will be single all her life (¿Con quién se va a casar? ¿Quién la va a querer? Le tendrás tú que buscar un novio, si no se quedará soltera toda la vida).

Según su madre, lo peor que le podía pasar a una mujer era quedarse soltera, que nadie la quisiera como esposa.

Loli tardó un rato en darse cuenta de que sus padres estaban hablando de ella.

VOCABULARIO 3

1.-desde aquel día: since that day

2.-seguía viviendo en casa de sus padres: (She) was still living with her parents

3.-Dejó de estudiar en cuanto cumplió los 16: (She) left school as soon as she was 16

4.-tuvo dos empleos, pero no le duraron mucho tiempo: (She) had two Jobs, but they din´t last her for long

5.-niñera: babysitter

6.-matrimonio de abogados: a married couple (of lawyers)

7.-Los niños tenían miedo de quedarse solos con ella: children were scared of being left alone with her

8.-Decían que Loli les daba miedo: (They) would say she was scary

9.-No se le daban bien los niños: (She) wasn´t good with kids

10.-Tienes que sonreír más: You have to smile more

12.-Siempre pareces triste: You always look sad

13.-entró a trabajar de cajera en el supermercado del barrio: (She) went to work as a cashier in the local supermarket

14.-De hecho: in fact

15.-los clientes siempre hacían fila en la caja donde ella no trabajaba: Customers always queued where she was not working.

Una Noticia Inesperada

No me gusta Londres. Es una ciudad bonita, sí. Tiene todo lo que uno puede querer, cierto. Pero hay algo en esta ciudad que no termina de convencerme.

Me asomo a la ventana, café en mano y miro. Vivo en el quinto piso. La ciudad que se despereza. La ciudad me devuelve la mirada. Aburrida, insulsa.

Antes de seguir, me gustaría presentarme: Me llamo Esteban Faraday y soy inglés. Nadie entiende por qué tomo tanto café. Dicen que tengo los ojos oscuros como una taza de espresso, araño el metro ochenta y vivo en un departamento, en un suburbio de Londres, con mi novia Sarah y mi gato Sherlock.

Hace mucho tiempo que no me pasa nada emocionante. Mi novia me mira y bosteza, ¡mi gato me mira y bosteza! Pero, ¿qué voy a hacer? Creo que no tengo muchas opciones. Además, toda mi vida es tranquila y ordenada. En el fondo no tengo de qué quejarme.

Me siento a trabajar con mi computadora. Esas operaciones en la Bolsa no se van a hacer solas. Miro por la ventana. Parece que va a llover, como siempre.

Mi novia se levanta y conecta la música de su pc con los parlantes de la casa.

Empieza a sonar una canción de Coldplay, su banda preferida. Yo odio esa banda, pero no se lo digo. Se prepara el mismo té Earl Gray de todos los días mientras se viste para ir a su trabajo.

En fin, todo parece indicar que hoy va a ser un día como cualquier otro. Hago click en las pestañas de mis diarios preferidos para leer las noticias. El mundo sigue igual de desastroso que siempre.

Reviso mi correo electrónico. Encuentro lo de siempre: publicidad, ofertas, newsletters a las que estoy suscrito. Abro Facebutt y recorro las novedades: Plane Jane se compró un perro, 154 nuevas fotos del álbum "Vacaciones en el Caribe" de Martin Graymes, Alissa B. se pregunta por qué sigue confiando en el amor y a cuatro personas, incluido su ex-novio, les gusta esto. El resto son fotos de bebés y de gatos. Muchas fotos de bebés y de gatos.

Me distrae el timbre que suena. Es muy extraño a esa hora de la mañana.

Vendrán a entregar algún paquete.

El que toca es el cartero, trae una carta certificada para mí. Esto sí que es una novedad. Firmo en la planilla, despido al cartero y miro el remitente. La carta viene de un despacho de abogados en Buenos Aires.

Hace mucho tiempo que no me pasa nada emocionante

RESUMEN CAPÍTULO 1

Esteban vive en un suburbio de Londres con su novia Sarah y su gato Sherlock. Está aburrido de su vida. Nunca le pasa nada emocionante. Un día recibe una carta misteriosa de Buenos Aires.

SUMMARY CHAPTER 1

Esteban lives in a suburb of London with his girlfriend, Sarah and his cat, Sherlock. He is bored of his life. Nothing exciting ever happens to him. One day he receives a mysterious letter from Buenos Aires.

CAPÍTULO 2

Me preparo una segunda taza de café para leer la carta con atención. Es la primera vez que oigo hablar de la tal tía Paulette, pero al parecer, acaba de morir y me dejó una herencia en Buenos Aires. Una herencia misteriosa.

No dice qué cosa es.

Agradezco entender suficiente español como para leer la carta sin problemas.

En realidad, se lo debo a los mil programas de deportes que miro y escucho en ese idioma. Con el tiempo empecé a entender todo sin subtítulos. Después me animé a ir a clubes de conversación. En uno de esos clubes conocí a Sarah.

Ella no estaba buscando mejorar ningún idioma, sino conocer gente nueva.

No le gustan los idiomas. Siempre dice que con el inglés ya podemos recorrer todo el mundo. Yo estoy de acuerdo, pero igual me gusta aprender. Me gustan los desafíos y las cosas nuevas que estimulan mi cerebro.

Paulette Sterling es (era), al parecer, mi tía por parte de madre. Mi madre, Colette Sterling, murió cuando yo era muy chico y la verdad es que no recuerdo que me haya hablado nunca de ella. Creo que mencionó que tenía una hermana en un país de Sudamérica, pero no lo recuerdo bien.

El día transcurre como uno cualquiera, excepto que no puedo dejar de pensar en esa carta. Al principio decido ignorarla, dejar pasar todo, no responder.

Después de todo, no necesito ninguna herencia. Si es dinero, no lo quiero. No lo necesito. Pero la verdad es que me carcome la curiosidad. ¿Qué será la herencia? ¿Cómo será Buenos Aires?

Con el paso de las horas, lo que al principio parecía una locura, empieza a tener cada vez más sentido. Después de todo puedo seguir con mi trabajo desde allí. Tal vez Sarah quiera tomarse unas vacaciones y venir conmigo.

Por la noche se lo propongo mientras cenamos unas bandejas de comida congelada mirando "Quién quiere ser billonario", quinta edición. La idea no le gusta nada. Pone mala cara desde que menciono la carta. Sostiene que se trata de alguna estafa muy bien planteada y que no tenemos necesidad de ninguna herencia ni de ir a un lugar que le parece lejano y peligroso.

Me irrita su falta de empatía y su poca iniciativa para la aventura. Se lo digo y discutimos. Después de algunos gritos y un par de portazos, en un impulso, abro mi portátil y compro un pasaje solo de ida.

RESUMEN CAPÍTULO 2

La carta viene de una firma de abogados en Buenos Aires.

Esteban heredó algo de una tía. Está entusiasmado con la idea del viaje y un poco enojado con su novia por rechazar la idea de viajar allí. En un impulso, compra un pasaje a Buenos Aires.

SUMMARY CHAPTER 2

The letter comes from a law firm based in Buenos Aires. Esteban has inherited something from an aunt. He is excited about the trip and a little bit mad at his girlfriend for being reluctant about the idea of traveling there. On an impulse, he buys a plane ticket to Buenos Aires.

CAPÍTULO 3

Al día siguiente todo el asunto del pasaje me parece una idea pésima. El día empieza tranquilo como cualquier otro. Decido cancelar el pasaje. Pero cuando estoy a punto de hacerlo, alguien me llama al celular. En la pantalla veo un número desconocido con un prefijo extraño.

Una voz de mujer me habla en un inglés un tanto rudimentario. Suena bastante alterada. Me acomodo mejor en mi asiento y le pido que repita lo que está diciendo.

—Jelou, mai neim is Zoé, Zoé Garcia. Ai guanchu spikgüit Esteban Faraday, ¿hablo con él?

— Sí, claro, soy yo, respondo muy formal, también en inglés. ¿Qué necesita?

La mujer continúa en inglés con evidente dificultad. Se nota que le cuesta bastante.

— Ai guanchu spik por el asunto de la herencia. Es muy importante que vengas a Buenos Aires ya mismo. Chumorrou es la lectura oficial del testamento y si no estás acá, dis can bi a disaster.

En realidad, no estoy prestando demasiada atención a lo que dice. Estoy fascinado con ese acento y el tono melodioso de la voz que escucho del otro lado. Contengo las ganas de reírme y creo que eso se nota en mi voz. La voz del otro lado del teléfono duda, hace un silencio. Parece empezar a comprender lo que pasa.

— No te preocupes, le digo al borde de la carcajada. Hablo español. Te escucho, ¿Por qué es tan importante que yo esté en la lectura del testamento?

La voz del otro lado del teléfono hace un silencio profundo y después de unos segundos que parecen eternos, casi grita:

— Inglés pelotudo, ¡la concha de tu madre! ¿Me estás cargando?

Después parece arrepentirse. Se da cuenta de que lo que dijo fue demasiado. Su reacción me hace gracia y suelto una carcajada al instante. Por suerte ella se ríe también. Siento que la conozco de toda la vida.

La conversación termina amablemente. Me explica que, si no estoy allí, puede perder su lugar de trabajo.

Esa misma tarde preparo una valija y salgo en el último vuelo nocturno.

Me siento una especie de ladrón fugitivo. Noto que, desde que armé la valija, no dejé de sonreír ni un momento.

Una voz de mujer me habla en un inglés un tanto rudimentario.

Suena bastante alterada.

RESUMEN CAPÍTULO 3

Esteban recibe una llamada telefónica. Una mujer le pide que vaya a Buenos Aires a reclamar su herencia. Si no lo hace, ella podría perder su lugar de trabajo. A Esteban le gusta la voz y la actitud de esta mujer. La mujer se llama Zoé. Esteban siente que la conoce de toda la vida.

SUMMARY CHAPTER 3

Esteban receives a phone call. A woman on the other side of the line asks him to go to Buenos Aires to claim his inheritance. Otherwise, she might lose her workplace. Esteban likes the woman. Her name is Zoé. Esteban feels that he has known her all his life.

CAPÍTULO 4

ATERRIZAJE EN BUENOS AIRES

La voz de la megafonía me anuncia que ya estamos a punto de aterrizar. En esta ciudad es cinco horas más temprano que en Londres. Voy a tener que apurarme si quiero llegar a tiempo a la dichosa lectura del testamento.

Al fin se acaba ese viaje interminable. Desde que pongo un pie en el suelo de ese aeropuerto, todo me parece muy caótico e interesante. Nunca había tenido que esperar tanto en la fila para salir de un aeropuerto ni había escuchado a tanta gente hablar de un modo tan particular.

Nadie puede venir a buscarme y yo no conozco a nadie, así que salgo solo del aeropuerto. Tomo un taxi que parece bastante confiable. Ignoro a los taxistas que intentan venderme su recorrido a los gritos. Esto lo aprendí leyendo el blog de viajes de un conocido. El viaje resulta ser bastante caro.

Sospecho que mi origen tiene algo que ver en el precio final que me cobra el taxista. Lo bueno es que, tras un rato en la autopista, con rock nacional a todo volumen, finalmente estoy en el centro de la ciudad.

El taxista para en la puerta de mi hotel. Leo el cartel en la entrada. El cartel dice "Hotel Savoy". Antes de bajarme del taxi pregunto cómo se llama esa canción que suena en la radio. — "Sin disfraz" se llama, pibe. Es una canción de Virus. Le doy las gracias y me pregunta de dónde soy. Quiere seguir charlando conmigo, pero le digo que estoy apurado, lo saludo y bajo del taxi de un salto.

Lo que veo al bajar del taxi me asusta y me encanta. La calle a esa hora de la madrugada está muy transitada. Hay mucho ruido de autos, bocinas, gente que viene y que va.

Me registro en el hotel. La gente de la recepción es muy amable. Intentan hablarme en inglés, pero, amablemente, respondo en castellano. Esto parece gustarles.

Después de completar el registro y pagar una semana por adelantado, subo las cosas a mi habitación y cruzo al bar de enfrente a tomar un merecido café.

En el bar suena Gotan Project. Una pareja se pelea a los gritos en la esquina; otra, se besa apasionadamente. Una chica con rastas en el pelo hace malabarismos en el semáforo, la moza del bar me mira a los ojos y sonríe. Cuando me sirven ese café y doy el primer sorbo, sonrío y pienso que, quizás, una semana en esta ciudad me va a parecer muy poco.

Solo en la Ciudad

sta noche es **Nochevieja**, la última noche del año. Es una noche para pasarlo bien, para estar con los amigos o con la familia, pero Brian no tiene muchos amigos, su familia está lejos y él está solo en la gran ciudad. No es una noche alegre para Brian. Va a estar solo, en casa. Como todas las noches. Como todas las noches desde que María se fue.

Brian está triste, pero ha decidido que esta será la última Nochevieja que pasará solo. De hecho, esta noche será la última noche de su vieja vida y la primera noche de su nueva vida. Brian quiere cambiar su vida completamente. **A partir de** mañana todo será diferente.

"Tengo 25 años y, ¿qué he hecho **hasta ahora**? ¡Nada!" "No tengo amigos, mi familia vive muy lejos, María se fue y no me gusta nada mi trabajo. No me gusta mi trabajo, **tampoco me gustan mis compañeros** de trabajo, ni la oficina donde trabajo. No me gusta levantarme todos los días a las 6 de la mañana, **ni me gusta ir en metro** todos los días a la oficina.

Tardo una hora para ir y una hora para volver. No me gusta **empezar a** trabajar a las 8 de la mañana y **terminar de** trabajar todos los días **a las siete y media** de la tarde; no me gusta comer un sándwich de jamón y queso todos los días, ni me gusta el café de la cantina; tampoco me gusta ir siempre al mismo pub con Robert. No me gusta el pub donde vamos, no me gusta Robert y **cada vez me gusta menos** esta ciudad".

Robert es un compañero de trabajo y su único amigo por el momento. La ciudad es Londres: la gran ciudad a la que llegó hace seis meses desde Glencoe, en Escocia, en busca de empleo y de emociones. La ciudad en la que **se enamoró de** María; la ciudad en la que fue feliz **hasta hace solo unas semanas**. La ciudad que ahora **no soporta,** la ciudad que odia desde que ella se fue y lo abandonó como se abandonan unos zapatos rotos.

Esta noche es Nochevieja y Brian quiere estar solo. Ha terminado de trabajar un poco antes de lo habitual, a las cuatro. Luego ha ido al supermercado para comprar una botella de whisky.

La cajera del supermercado sonríe y le dice *"Happy New Year!"* Ella también **parece** contenta. Es una chica joven, de unos 20 años, un poco baja, pero muy guapa. Parece simpática. Habla inglés con acento extranjero... Quizás sea española, como María, pero no está seguro... La cajera del supermercado lleva un gorro de papa Noel y una camiseta roja con la frase *"Shop and smile before you die!"* Brian también quiere sonreír a la chica y desearle feliz año nuevo, pero ya es demasiado tarde. Ella ya está sonriendo al siguiente cliente de la fila.

"Así es la vida en esta ciudad. Todos corren. Nadie tiene tiempo para nadie". Cuando sale del supermercado, Brian está **más triste que** antes. El acento español de la cajera del supermercado le ha hecho recordar la sonrisa de María. Ahora Brian solo quiere llegar a casa, sentarse en el sofá, abrir la botella de whisky que acaba de comprar, emborracharse, y pensar qué va a hacer el año próximo para cambiar su vida.

"El año próximo va a ser diferente. **Tiene que** ser diferente".

"Tengo 25 años. ¿Qué he hecho hasta ahora? ¡Nada, absolutamente nada!" A Brian **le parece** que su vida no tiene sentido.

Hay **mucha gente** por la calle. Todos parecen contentos. En los pubs y en las tiendas hay mucha gente. Todos parecen tener prisa. Todos van a alguna parte, pero Brian no quiere ver a nadie. Solo quiere **llegar a** casa, abrir la botella de whisky y **tratar de** olvidar.

VOCABULARIO 1

1.-Nochevieja: New Yearś Eve.

2.-Pasarlo bien: To have a good time.

3.-A partir de (mañana): From (tomorrow) on.

*4.-Hasta ahora: **So far.***

5.-Tampoco me gustan mis compañeros: Neither do I like my colleagues at work.

6.-Ni me gusta ir en metro: Nor do I like traveling on the underground.

7.-Empezar a: Start (doing something).

8.-Terminar de: Stop (doing something).

*9.-A las (siete y media): **At (half past seven).***

10.-Cada vez me gusta menos: I like it less and less.

11.-Se enamoró de: (He) fell in love with.

*12.-Hasta hace solo unas semanas: **Until a few weeks ago only.***

13.-No soporta: (He) can't stand.

14.-Ella también parece contenta: She also looks happy.

15.-Más triste que antes: More miserable than before.

16.-Tiene que ser diferente: (It) has to be different.

17.-Le parece que…: It seems to him that…

18.-Hay mucha gente: There are lots of people.

*19.-Llegar a casa: **To get home.***

20.-*Tratar de (olvidar):* **Totry to (forget).**

RESUMEN 1

Brian es un chico joven. Tiene 25 años. Es de un pueblo pequeño en Escocia, pero ahora vive y trabaja en Londres.

Hoy es 31 de diciembre y esta noche es Nochevieja. Normalmente la gente está contenta en Nochevieja, pero Brian está triste. Brian está triste porque su novia, una chica española que se llamaba María, lo abandonó hace unas semanas.

Esta noche Brian se siente muy solo y muy triste. No tiene muchos amigos y su familia está muy lejos. No le gusta su trabajo y no le gusta vivir en Londres.

Brian compra una botella de whisky en el supermercado. Quiere pasar la Nochevieja solo, en casa, bebiendo.

Preguntas de comprensión 1

1.-*¿Dónde vive Brian?*

a.-En Madrid

b.-En Barcelona

c.-En Londres

2.-*¿Brian está soltero o casado?*

a.-Soltero

b.-Casado

3.-*¿Con quién vive Brian?*

a.-Con su novia

b.-Con su familia

c.-Brian vive solo

4.-*La Nochevieja es…*

a.-La noche del 31 de diciembre

b.-El 25 de diciembre

c.-El 6 de enero

5.-¿*Cómo se siente Brian?*

a.-Muy contento

b.-Muy triste

6.-La novia de Brian…

a.-Se llama María y es española.

b.-Se llamaba María y era española.

SOLUCIONES 1

1.-c

2.-a

3.-c

4.-a

5.-b

6.-b

Diez Años Después – Ten Years Later

RESUMEN:

Es mágico relatar el reencuentro de estudiantes, que fueron amigos y no tan amigos en su época de estudios. Diez años después, sin darse cuenta, todavía conservaban recuerdos y momentos que los llevan a reconocerse unos a otros. Todo con sus diferentes habilidades o categorías. Como el caso de Allison que pasó a ser como el eje principal de la ocasión.

Inconscientemente, igual que otros de sus compañeros como Mariana, no tenían el propósito de asistir al aniversario de graduación. Pero coincidieron sin proponérselo en Copos, el café cercano a la escuela, donde Allison fue reconocida por los demás. Resulta que no era tan diferente en su época como lo pensaba, sino que al llegar fue reconocida como 'La Pequeña Allison', así la llamaban, tanto por el señor que atendía el cafetín hasta los demás compañeros. Ellos fueron llegando también evitando presentarse a la fiesta, convirtiéndose esa tarde en un ameno compartir de recuerdos, café, tortas y la mejor risa al compartir exámenes pendientes de diez años atrás.

SUMMARY:

It is magical to narrate the reunion of students that were friends, and not such good friends, in their times of studying. Ten years later, without realizing it, they still held memories and moments that led them to recognize each other. Everyone with their different abilities or categories. Such as the case of Allison that became the main point of the occasion.

Subconsciously, just like some of her other classmates such as Mariana, she had no intention to attend the graduation anniversary. But they happened to meet, unintentionally at Copos, the coffee shop near the school, where Allison was recognized by the others. It turns out she wasn't as different from back then as she thought, but on arriving she was recognized as 'Little Allison'; that's what they used to call her, from the man that worked at the coffee shop to the rest of her classmates. They were arriving, also avoiding going to the party, turning that day into an enjoyable exchange of memories, coffee, cakes, and the best laughter on sharing pending exams from ten years ago.

VOCABULARIO

1.-Grupo - Group

2.-Estudiante - Student

3.-Clásicos - Classics

4.-Deportista - Athlete

5.-Popular - Popular

6.-Artistas - Artists

7.-Categorías - Categories

8.-Colegio - School

9.-Talento - Talent

10.-Pasión - Passion

11.-Invitación - Invitation

12.-Fiesta - Party

13.-Aniversario - Anniversary

14.-Simpático - Nice

15.-Café - Coffee

16.-Pequeña - Little

17.-Famosa - Famous

18.-Galería - Gallery

19.-Reunión - Reunion

20.-Viejos - Old

21.-Compañeros - Classmates

22.-Infancia - Childhood

23.-Joven - Young

24.-Nieto - Grandson

25.-Exámenes - Exams

SPANISH:

Habían pasado ya diez años desde que un grupo muy especial de estudiantes se graduó en 2010. A simple vista, parecían estudiantes normales, pero, por esa misma razón, ellos se creían únicos en el mundo.

Entre ellos estaban los clásicos grupos de deportistas, estudiosos, populares, artistas, y los que no entraban en ninguna de esas categorías. Sin embargo, con el paso de los años, las categorías se tornan borrosas, las amistades se desvanecen y, diez años después, era como si muchos de ellos nunca se conocieron. ¿O sí?

Por ejemplo, y muy buen ejemplo que era, estaba Allison. Ella había llegado al colegio como una niña muy estudiosa, pero aún sin querer tenía talento para el deporte. Su verdadera pasión era el arte, y un poco de éxito la volvió popular. De forma que, amiga de todos, terminó por no ser tan amiga de ninguno. Diez años después, cuando le llegó la invitación a la gran fiesta para celebrar el aniversario de la graduación, decidió no ir. En lugar de ir a la fiesta esa tarde, decidió que en la mañana se pasaría por "Copos", el simpático café que se encontraba cerca de la escuela y el cual visitó casi cada día mientras estudiaba allí, como hacían casi todos en ese entonces.

Allison no se esperaba ser reconocida al entrar al lugar. "Pequeña Allison!" exclamó el dueño del lugar, ahora algo anciano, quien la llamaba así cuando era una niña para diferenciarla de otras estudiantes del mismo nombre. "¡Cuánto me alegra volver a verte! ¿Qué hiciste con tu vida?"

Antes de que Allison pudiera responder, alguien más entró al lugar y dijo en una voz grave, "¿No sabes? La pequeña Allison ahora es una artista famosa. Sus creaciones están en todas las mejores galerías del país". Era Roberto, el simpático chico que cuando Allison lo conoció era capitán del equipo de fútbol y que tanto la había ayudado en los deportes. Sin embargo, su afición por la comida lo había puesto fuera de forma, pero ahora se veía incluso más simpático. "Todo me lo contó un pajarito", Roberto le guiñó el ojo.

"No me llames así!" exclamó otra voz, riendo. Y entonces entró al lugar Mariana. Cuando eran niños, la fortuna de sus padres le aseguró un lugar entre las chicas populares, pero Mariana era una persona peculiar, algo excéntrica, y nunca terminó por encajar entre los demás.

Allison se rio con ellos, y pidió un café. "Y yo que había pensado que era la única con la idea de perderme la reunión para venir aquí" dijo. Como si sus palabras fueran mágicas, más y más de sus viejos compañeros empezaron a llegar al lugar. Allí se encontraban todos los que nunca encajaron, los que se perdían entre los grupos, los que sus amigos habían olvidado, todos los que habían cambiado.

Las horas pasaron mientras los viejos compañeros de clases se saludaban, se abrazaban y se contaban todo lo que había pasado con sus vidas. Entre ellos había un deportista que consiguió éxito y luego lo perdió todo, menos su sonrisa. Había una romántica que estaba trabajando en su tercer divorcio, pero ya tenía una cita planeada. Estaban también los hermanos, que solían ser inseparables cuando niños, pero se encontraron allí por pura casualidad, después de años sin verse.

Todos juntos rieron y revivieron sus recuerdos de la infancia.

Hablaron de sus viejos profesores, y se preguntaron qué pasaría con ellos.

Hablaron de viejos amigos, y viejos enemigos, los amores y peleas de la infancia que ahora se sentían tan inocentes. Tomaron muchas tazas de café y comieron muchos pedazos de tortas. Finalmente, alguien más entró al lugar, pero no estaban seguros de saber quién era.

"Me pareces muy, muy familiar", dijo Allison, "Reconozco tu cara, por alguna razón. Pero me pareces que eres demasiado joven para haber estudiado con nosotros. ¿Me equivoco?" El niño suspiró y les sonrió de forma un poco obligada. "Soy el nieto del profesor Carlos. Me pidió que les entregara esto". El niño, que se parecía muchísimo a su abuelo, le pasó al grupo una carpeta con bastantes hojas que se veían viejas, pero bien guardadas. Luego añadió, "Al parecer les debía esos exámenes desde hace diez años". Todos los viejos amigos rieron entre ellos, y como en los viejos tiempos compararon sus exámenes.

ENGLISH:

It had already been ten years since a very special group of students graduated in 2010. At first sight, they looked like normal students, but, for that same reason, they believed they were unique in the world. Among them were the classic groups of athletes, nerds, populars, artists, and those who didn't fit into any of these categories. However, as the years passed, the categories became blurred, the friendships vanished and, ten years later, it was like some of them had never met. Or did they?

For example, and what a great example she was, there was Allison.

She had arrived at school as a very studious kid, but without meaning to, she had a talent for sports. Her true passion was art, and a little bit of success made her popular. So that, a friend of everyone, she ended up not being such good friends with anyone. Ten years later, when she received the invitation to the big party to celebrate the anniversary of the graduation, she decided not to go. Instead of going to the party that afternoon, she decided that in the morning she would pass by "Copos," the nice coffee shop that was near the school and that she used to visit almost every day while she studied there, just like almost everyone did back then.

Allison wasn't expecting to be recognized upon entering the place.

"Little Allison!" exclaimed the owner of the place, now somewhat elderly, who used to call her that when she was a girl to differentiate her from other students with the same name. "I'm so happy to see you again! What did you do with your life?"

Before Allison could answer, somebody else entered the place and said with a deep voice, "Don't you know? Little Allison is now a famous artist. Her creations are in all the best galleries in the country." It was Roberto, the nice guy who, when Allison met him, was the captain of the football team, and he had helped her a lot with sports. However, his love for food had put him out of shape, but now he looked even nicer. "A little bird told me," Roberto winked.

"Don't call me that!" exclaimed another voice, laughing. And then Mariana entered the place. When they were kids, the fortune of her parents guaranteed her a place among the popular girls, but Mariana was a peculiar person; a bit eccentric, and never ended up fitting in with the others.

Allison laughed along with them and ordered a coffee. "And here I was thinking that I was the only one with the idea of missing the reunion to come here," she said. As if her words were magical, more and more of her old classmates started to arrive at the place. There were all the ones who never fitted in, the ones lost among the groups, the ones forgotten by their friends, all those who had changed.

The hours passed by while the old classmates greeted each other, hugged, and told each other everything that had happened with their lives.

Among them was an athlete that found success, and then lost everything, except for his smile. There was a romantic that was working on her third divorce but already had a date planned. There were also the brothers, the ones that used to be inseparable when they were kids, but met there out of chance, after years without seeing each other.

Everyone laughed and relieved their childhood memories. They talked about their old teachers and wondered what had happened to them.

They talked about old friends, and old enemies, and the loves and fights of their childhood that now felt so innocent. They drank many cups of coffee and ate many slices of cake. Finally, somebody else entered the place, but they weren't sure they knew who he was.

"You look very, very familiar," said Allison, "I recognize your face, for some reason. But you look too young to have studied with us. Am I wrong?" The boy sighed and smiled at them in a way that was a little forced.

"I am the grandson of teacher Carlos. He asked me to give you this," The boy, who looked a lot like his grandfather, passed the group a folder with many pages that looked old but well kept. Then added, "Apparently he owed you these exams from ten years ago." All the old friends laughed with each other, and just like in the old times, they shared their exams.

"El Piloto" – "The Pilot"

RESUMEN:

Cada trabajo o profesión tiene su importancia, aunque algunos parezcan más interesantes, unos más fáciles, y otros más divertidos y llenos de acción, Esta es la historia del piloto de aviones John Thomas. Él tiene más de veinte años en su trabajo; volando los cielos. Algunas veces son viajes muy relajados y tranquilos donde se hace corto el trayecto. Pero otras veces, como en esta ocasión, que decidió no aburrirse y dejar que algunos pasajeros conocieran lo que era la cabina. Mas no para todos los pasajeros fue sorprendente. Como en el caso de la anciana que no era lo que esperaba, o la joven que solo quería que la ayudara con la tarea, o el niño que no quedó muy convencido con las respuestas que le dio John.

Fue John quien tuvo la mayor sorpresa de ver a sus amigos de la infancia como pasajeros y ver que pudo compartir de ese reencuentro durante el viaje hasta que llegaron a tierra firme.

SUMMARY:

Every single job is important in its own right, even though some seem more interesting, some seem easier and others seem more action-packed and fun. This is the story of an airplane pilot called John Thomas. He has worked for more than 20 years, flying the skies. Sometimes, the journeys are very relaxed and calm, which makes them feel shorter than they are. But other times, as on this occasion, the pilot decided he didn't want to get bored, so he invited some of the passengers to visit the cockpit. Not every passenger was surprised. There was an old lady who was a little disappointed, a teenager that simply needed help with her homework, and a little boy that wasn't easily pleased with John's answers.

It was John himself who had the biggest surprise on seeing a couple of childhood friends as his passengers. He saw that he could share a reunion with them during the trip until they all landed back on firm ground.

VOCABULARIO

1.-Piloto - Pilot

2.-Avión – Aeroplane

3.-Profesión - Profession

4.-Exigente - Demanding

5.-Personalidad - Personality

6.-Desafiante - Challenging

7.-Azafata - Stewardess

8.-Cabina - Cockpit

9.-Máquinas - Machines

10.-Armar - Build

11.-Magia - Magic

12.-Incrédulo - Incredulous

13.-Secreto - Secret

14.-Nave - Ship

15.-Aburrimiento - Boredom

16.-Pasajeros - Passengers

17.-Tarea - Homework

18.-Anciana - Old Lady

19.-Volar - Fly

20.-Sorpresa - Surprise

21.-Visita - Visit

22.-Concentrado - Concentrated

23.-Sobresaltado - Startled

24.-Reencuentro - Encounter

SPANISH:

El trabajo de un piloto de avión no es nada fácil. De hecho, es una profesión muy difícil y exigente. No cualquier persona puede convertirse en piloto. Se necesitan años de práctica, trabajo duro y una personalidad segura y valiente. Sin embargo, una vez que un hombre o mujer se convierte en un piloto de avión profesional, todo se vuelve un poco más sencillo. Claro, todos van a pasar por una que otra desafiante aventura que ponga a prueba sus conocimientos y su talento. Pero, la mayoría de los viajes serán algo familiar, agradable y emocionante, casi se podría decir que fáciles. Al menos, eso pensaba el piloto John Thomas.

John había sido un piloto de avión profesional por ya más de veinte años. Le encantaba su trabajo. Amaba estar allá arriba entre las nubes. Amaba tener el control de algo tan grande y complicado como un avión. Pero siempre manejaba el avión con cariño, seguridad y confianza.

Así que, de vez en cuando, cuando era su trabajo hacer un viaje corto, durante un fresco y soleado día de primavera, eso era casi un paseo para John. De hecho, era posible que el hombre se aburriera un poco en estas situaciones. Esto significaba que les decía a las azafatas que, si algún pasajero quisiera visitar la cabina del piloto, eran todos bienvenidos.

La mayoría de las veces sólo niños se acercaban. El primero fue un niño de apenas cuatro años agarrado de la mano de su papá. "¿Cómo se hacen los aviones?" fue la primera pregunta del niño.

"Es mucho trabajo", respondió John con una sonrisa, "Se necesitan a muchos hombres trabajando y máquinas gigantes para armar estos aviones". El piloto creyó que eso sería suficiente para el niño.

Sin embargo, el niño insistió, "¿Sin magia?" preguntó incrédulo. John rio, pero luego se puso muy serio y se inclinó hacia el niño, "Shh, no le digas a nadie nuestro secreto". Eso pareció agradarle al niño, quien dejó escapar una risa y volvió a su asiento con su papá.

Otros niños también visitaron a John el piloto durante ese vuelo.

Unos hermanos, un niño y una niña tenían muchas preguntas. "¿Qué haces si te da sueño? ¿Qué haces si ves un pájaro?" preguntaba el niño, y antes de que John pudiera responder ya la niña estaba haciendo sus propias preguntas, "¿Es posible que choquen dos aviones? ¿De verdad nunca has visto una nave espacial?" No fue fácil responderles, pero definitivamente le quitaron el aburrimiento a John.

Poco después, todo tipo de pasajeros se animaron a visitar la cabina del piloto. Una joven adolescente llegó a la cabina cargando un cuaderno. John se emocionó, pensando que iba a entrevistarlo. Pero, con una sonrisa, la joven admitió, "En realidad necesito ayuda con mi tarea de física. Mis papás no me pudieron ayudar y supuse que un piloto de avión podría". "Oh", suspiró John, "supongo que puedo intentarlo". No sonaba muy convencido, pero luego de un par de minutos ambos se sorprendieron al descubrir que sí pudo ayudarla con un par de cosas.

También una anciana se acercó al piloto. Lo primero que hizo la señora fue reír, "Toda mi vida soñando con volar, con entrar a la cabina del piloto… y no es tan increíble como había imaginado". "¿No?" le preguntó John, algo desconcertado. "No tienes el lugar muy bien decorado", respondió la anciana. "Pero, señora, el avión no es mío en realidad", explicó John. La señora se encogió de hombros, "Podrías traer algunas flores al menos".

La mayor sorpresa vino de última. "John, tienes una última visita", anunció la azafata. "Pasen, pasen, bienvenidos", dijo John, usando su voz formal de piloto, pero sin voltear aún, concentrado en el cielo. Ahí fue cuando llegó la sorpresa. Alguien le quitó su sombrero de la cabeza repentinamente, y entonces John escuchó a alguien decir en tono burlón,

"Si, si, pasen adelante, soy el piloto, bienvenidos a mi silla de piloto".

Inmediatamente John se volteó sobresaltado y exclamó,

"¡Andrés! ¡María!" Saltó de su silla y abrazó a sus amigos. "Sabía que eras tú" exclamó María, abrazando a su viejo amigo del colegio. Los tres amigos intentaron hablar y disfrutar el reencuentro, pero fueron interrumpidos. "John, ya tenemos que prepararnos para el aterrizaje", dijo el copiloto. John suspiró, pero dio otro abrazo a sus viejos amigos que la suerte había puesto en su vuelo y les dijo, "Nos vemos en tierra firme".

ENGLISH:

716

The job of an airplane pilot is not easy. In fact, it is a very difficult and demanding profession. Not just anyone can become a pilot. It takes years of practice, hard work, and a confident and courageous personality.

However, once a man or woman becomes a professional airplane pilot, everything becomes a little easier. Of course, everyone will go through one or another challenging adventure that puts to the test their knowledge and talent. But, most of the trips will be something familiar, enjoyable and exciting, you could almost say easy. At least, that's what pilot John Thomas thought.

John had been a professional airplane pilot for over twenty years. He loved his job. He loved being up there between the clouds. He loved being in control of something as big and complicated as an airplane. But he always handled the plane with love, security and confidence. So once in a while, when it was his job to take a short trip, on a cool sunny spring day, that was almost a stroll for John. In fact, it was possible that the man might get a little bored in these situations. This meant that he was telling the stewardesses that if any passenger wanted to visit the pilot's cockpit, they were all welcome.

Most of the time only children approached. The first was a boy of just four years holding his father's hand. "How do they make planes?" was the boy's first question.

"It's a lot of work," John replied with a smile, "It takes a lot of men working and giant machines to build these planes." The pilot believed that would be enough for the boy. However, the boy insisted, "No magic?" he asked incredulously. John laughed, but then became very serious and leaned towards the boy, "Shh, don't tell anyone our secret."

That seemed to please the boy, who let out a laugh and returned to his seat with his dad.

Other children also visited John the pilot during that flight. Some siblings, a boy and a girl had many questions. "What do you do if you get sleepy? What do you do if you see a bird?" asked the boy, and before John could answer, the girl was already asking her own questions, "Is it possible that two planes crash? Have you really never seen a spaceship?" It wasn't easy to respond to them, but it definitely took John's boredom away.

Soon after, all types of passengers ventured to visit the pilot's cockpit. A young teenager came to the cockpit carrying a notebook. John got excited, thinking she was going to interview him. But, with a smile, the young woman admitted, "Actually, I need help with my physics homework. My parents couldn't help me and I assumed that an airplane pilot could." "Oh!" John sighed, "I guess I can try." He did not sound very convinced, but after a couple of minutes, they were both surprised to discover that he could help her with a couple of things.

An old lady also approached the pilot. The first thing the lady did was laugh, "All my life dreaming of being able to fly in a plane, of entering the pilot's cockpit... and it is not as incredible as I had imagined." "No?" John asked, somewhat bewildered. "You don't have the place very well decorated," replied the old lady. "But, ma'am, the plane is not really mine," explained John. The lady shrugged her shoulders, "You could at least bring some flowers."

The biggest surprise came last. "John, you have one last visit," announced the stewardess. "Come in, come in, welcome," said John, using his formal pilot voice, but not yet turning, concentrated on the sky.

That's when the surprise came. Someone took his hat off his head suddenly, and then John heard someone say in a mocking tone, "Yes, yes, go ahead, I'm the pilot, welcome to my pilot seat."

John immediately turned around startled and exclaimed, "Andrés! Maria!" He jumped out of his chair and hugged his friends. "I knew it was you," exclaimed Maria, hugging her old friend from school. The three friends tried to talk and enjoy the encounter but were interrupted. "John, we have to prepare for landing now," said the co-pilot. John sighed, but gave another hug to his old friends that luck had put on his flight and said,

"See you on the ground."

Las Banderas

En la actualidad las banderas están presentes en todas partes del mundo y se utilizan para identificar a un grupo de personas. Pero no sólo representan países, sino también instituciones, como la Cruz Roja o las Naciones Unidas.

Las primeras banderas probablemente tienen su origen en China, hace 4,000 años, donde los soldados de los ejércitos las usaban para poder seguir a su general.

Las primeras banderas fueron simples palos de madera, pero en el antiguo Imperio Persa, hace 3,000 años, las banderas eran de metal. Algunas monedas antiguas griegas también tienen imágenes de banderas. Igualmente, las personas en Roma utilizaron banderas hace más de 2,000 años. Estas banderas eran de tela, como las que se utilizan hoy.

Las banderas también son importantes para los barcos en el mar.

Generalmente cada barco tiene la bandera de su país. Asimismo, los Juegos Olímpicos tienen una bandera con cinco anillos de cinco colores diferentes que representan a cada continente: África, Asia, Europa, América y Oceanía.

Los equipos de futbol también tienen banderas y los aficionados las usan cuando van a los estadios.

¿Tú cuantas banderas conoces? ¿Cuál es la que te gusta más?

Reading Comprehension Questions:

- ¿Para qué se usan las banderas?
- ¿Cuándo se usaron las banderas por primera vez?
- ¿Cuántos aros tiene la bandera de los Juegos Olímpicos?
- ¿Qué podría suceder si no existieran las banderas?

Discussion:

- ¿Deberían estar prohibidas algunas banderas? Si tu respuesta es afirmativa, ¿cuáles y por qué?

- ¿Debe castigarse el uso de las banderas cuando se considera que faltan al respeto a un país o debe respetarse la libertad de expresión (por ejemplo, cuando se quema o se pisa la bandera de un país en señal de protesta)?

Verbs In Present:

1.-Ser

Las banderas están en todas partes del mundo.

2.-Representar

Las banderas representan a países e instituciones.

3.-Tener

Las banderas tienen su origen en China.

4.-Usar

Los aficionados de los equipos de futbol usan las banderas cuando van a los estadios.

Verbs In Simple Past (Preterite):

1.-Ser

Las primeras banderas fueron simples palos de madera.

2.-Utilizar

Desde hace 2,000 años las personas utilizaron banderas.

Verbs In Imperfect:

1.-Ser

En el Imperio Persa las banderas eran de metal.

2.-Usar

Los soldados usaban banderas para seguir al general.

Keywords:

Institución: es una organización, generalmente del gobierno, que tiene un objetivo o finalidad específicos, por ejemplo, enseñar, dar a conocer la cultura y el deporte o ayudar a distintos grupos de la sociedad.

Aficionado: es una persona que tiene gusto o afición por algo. Por ejemplo, una persona puede ser aficionada al cine o a la lectura. También se usa esta palabra para las personas a las que les gusta un deporte y van a un estadio a apoyar a su equipo. Por último, un aficionado también es el que practica un deporte o actividad por gusto, sin recibir dinero y con un nivel bajo en comparación con un profesional.

DILEMAS ÉTICOS

La ética es una reflexión filosófica acerca de las cosas que son buenas o malas, es decir, acerca de lo que se debe y lo que no se debe hacer.

Comúnmente la gente tiene que resolver dilemas éticos que se presentan en la vida diaria. Aquí hay algunos ejemplos de esos dilemas éticos:

- ¿Debo hacer un donativo a la gente que pide dinero en las calles o no debo ayudarlos porque quizás utilizan el dinero para comprar drogas?
- ¿Debo denunciar a la policía a un vecino que golpea a su esposa o no debo meterme en los asuntos de los demás para evitar problemas?
- ¿Debo obedecer a mi jefe cuando me pide algo que está mal, y conservar mi empleo, o debo desobedecerlo y correr el riesgo de perder mi trabajo?
- ¿Tengo que avisar a la policía si atropellé a alguien accidentalmente con mi coche o sólo debo llamar a la ambulancia y huir del lugar?
- ¿Debo comprar alimentos orgánicos, que son más caros, o debo ahorrar dinero y comprar en los grandes supermercados, donde los alimentos son más baratos, pero quizá no tengan la misma calidad?
- ¿Debo decir una mentira a un vendedor para que no me moleste y no me haga perder el tiempo o debo escucharlo con paciencia y educación, a pesar de que no vaya a comprarle su producto?
- ¿Tengo que votar en las elecciones, aunque ninguno de los candidatos me agrade, o no debo votar si no estoy de acuerdo con ninguno de ellos?

- Si el mesero cometió un error y me trajo un platillo que no pedí, ¿debo pedirle que me traiga el patillo correcto, a pesar de que el restaurante le vaya a cobrar el precio del platillo a él, o debo comer algo que no pedí para no perjudicarlo?
- Si veo a un compañero de la escuela copiar y hacer trampa en el examen, ¿debo decírselo al profesor o debo quedarme callado?

Discussion:

- ¿Sabes por qué la ética es una disciplina filosófica?
- ¿Sabes qué es un deber?
- ¿Sabes qué es la responsabilidad moral?
- ¿Eres responsable sólo de tus actos o también de los actos que alguien pueda realizar como consecuencia de los tuyos?
- ¿Ante quiénes somos responsables moralmente?

Verbs To Express An Obligation Or A Responsibility:

- ¿Debo dar dinero a la gente pobre?
- ¿Debo obedecer a mi jefe cuando me pide algo que está mal?
- ¿Debo decir una mentira piadosa para conseguir un bien mayor?
- ¿Debo denunciar a un amigo o familiar si hace algo malo?
- ¿Tengo que avisar a la policía si atropellé a alguien accidentalmente?
- ¿Tengo que votar en las elecciones cuando los candidatos son malos?
- ¿Tengo que poner los intereses de los demás por encima de los míos?

Keywords:

Dilema: es una situación problemática o difícil de resolver porque ninguna de las posibles soluciones es completamente aceptable o porque tiene consecuencias desagradables. Si elegimos una solución, nos quedamos con la sensación de no hacer lo correcto. Y si elegimos la solución contraria, también nos quedamos con la sensación de no hacer lo correcto.

Donativo: es una ayuda o regalo que se da a la gente necesitada. La ayuda puede ser en dinero o en especie (con productos, como alimentos o ropa).

Alimentos orgánicos: son alimentos que se cultivan y se producen sin utilizar sustancias químicas que dañan la salud o el medio ambiente. Por eso son más caros, aunque también son más saludables.

Votar: significa elegir entre varias opciones disponibles. Por ejemplo, en la política, votar es elegir a una persona para que sea gobernante o representante de la gente. El proceso o el momento en el que las personas votan para elegir a sus gobernantes se conoce como "elecciones".

LOS ANTIGUOS GRIEGOS

¿Sabes quiénes fueron los antiguos griegos? Los primeros griegos llegaron al actual territorio de Grecia desde del centro de Europa, hacia el año 2000 antes de Cristo. Se establecieron en la península Balcánica, donde dominaron a los antiguos pobladores y les impusieron su lengua.

Los antiguos griegos principalmente fueron marineros y se dedicaron al comercio. Navegaban por el Mar Mediterráneo y comerciaban con los pueblos cercanos. También peleaban contra los vecinos que les hacían la guerra, y generalmente los dominaban, porque tenían estrategias de guerra muy avanzadas y utilizaban lanzas, espadas y escudos como armas de guerra.

Los griegos tenían muchos dioses y los adoraban en sus templos. Algunos de estos dioses fueron Zeus, Hera, Poseidón, Ares, Afrodita, Atenea, Apolo y Dioniso. Construyeron hermosos templos para sus dioses, como el Partenón, en honor de la diosa Atenea; crearon hermosas esculturas y escribieron magníficas obras de teatro.

Además, contemplaban la naturaleza, practicaban gimnasia, estudiaban matemáticas, música y filosofía, y tenían grandes sabios y filósofos, como Sócrates, Platón y Aristóteles, entre otros.

Los griegos tenían ciudades independientes y casi siempre rivales entre sí.

Las ciudades más importantes fueron Esparta y Atenas. En Esparta los hombres eran militares que dedicaban su vida al entrenamiento y a la práctica de la guerra. Por el contrario, en Atenas no peleaban en la guerra, porque les gustaba la política y se organizaban en una forma de gobierno llamada democracia, en la que los habitantes tomaban decisiones por votación. En Atenas los niños entraban en la escuela al cumplir siete años, pero en Esparta los niños de esa edad iban a un entrenamiento para convertirse en guerreros.

Además, los antiguos griegos tenían esclavos, y las mujeres no participaban en la vida política. También tenían escuelas públicas, pero los hombres ricos pagaban maestros privados para sus hijos.

Los antiguos griegos tuvieron una influencia extraordinaria en la creación de toda la cultura occidental. Por eso es muy importante conocer su historia.

Reading Comprehension Questions:

- ¿En dónde navegaban los griegos?
- ¿Cuáles fueron las dos principales ciudades griegas?
- ¿Cuál era la principal actividad comercial de los griegos?
- ¿A qué se dedicaban los hombres de Esparta?
- ¿Quiénes pagaban maestros privados para sus hijos?

Discussion:

- ¿Es posible elogiar a los antiguos griegos a pesar de que defendían la esclavitud o relegaban a las mujeres de la vida pública?
- ¿Crees que la democracia, inventada por los griegos, es la mejor forma de gobierno? ¿Por qué sí o por qué no?
- En la antigua Grecia era bien visto al amor erótico entre adolescentes y hombres adultos. ¿Qué opinas de esa costumbre?

Verbs In Simple Past (Preterite):

1.-Llegar

Los primeros griegos llegaron al actual territorio de Grecia desde del centro de Europa.

2.-Establecer (se)

Se establecieron en la península Balcánica.

3.-Dominar

Dominaron a los antiguos pobladores.

4.-Imponer

Les impusieron su lengua.

5.-Ser

Los antiguos griegos fueron marineros.

6.-Dedicar (se)

Se dedicaron al comercio.

7.-Construir

Construyeron hermosos templos.

8.-Crear

Crearon hermosas esculturas.

9.-Escribir

Escribieron magníficas obras de teatro.

10.-Ser

Las ciudades más importantes fueron Esparta y Atenas.

11.-Tener

Los antiguos griegos tuvieron una influencia extraordinaria en la cultura occidental.

Verbs In Imperfect:

1.-Navegar

Los griegos navegaban por el Mar Mediterráneo.

2.-Comerciar

Comerciaban con los pueblos cercanos.

3.-Pelear

Peleaban contra los vecinos que les hacían la guerra.

4.-Dominar

Los griegos dominaban a sus enemigos.

5.-Tener

Tenían estrategias de guerra muy avanzadas.

6.-Utilizar

Utilizaban lanzas, espadas y escudos como armas.

7.-Adorar

Los griegos adoraban a muchos dioses.

8.-Contemplar

Contemplaban la naturaleza.

9.-Practicar

Practicaban gimnasia.

10.-Estudiar

Estudiaban matemáticas y filosofía.

11.-Tener

Tenían grandes sabios y filósofos.

12.-Pelear

En Atenas no peleaban en la guerra.

13.-Organizarse

En Atenas se organizaban de forma democrática.

14.-Tomar

En Atenas tomaban decisiones por votación.

15.-Entrar

Los niños entraban a la escuela a los siete años.

16.-Entrenar

En Esparta los niños entrenaban para la guerra.

17.-Participar

Las mujeres no participaban en la vida política.

18.-Tener

Los griegos tenían escuelas públicas.

19.-Pagar

Los hombres ricos pagaban maestros privados para sus hijos.

Keywords:

Península: es un territorio rodeado de agua por todas partes menos por una relativamente estrecha o delgada, por la cual se une a una extensión de tierra mayor.

EL SENTIDO DE LA VIDA

Alguna vez, al mirarte al espejo y observar que estás envejeciendo, al darte cuenta de que no tienes el trabajo de tus sueños o una buena salud, ¿te has preguntado cuál es el sentido de tu vida? ¿Para qué estás aquí?

A partir de las dolorosas experiencias que vivió en un campo de concentración nazi, el médico Viktor Frankl desarrolló una teoría psicológica para responder a este tipo de preguntas.

Viktor Frankl fue un médico austriaco que durante tres años vivió en un campo de concentración durante la Segunda Guerra Mundial.

Teniendo la visa para emigrar a Estados Unidos en busca de un futuro brillante y prometedor, decidió quedarse en Viena al lado de sus padres y de su joven esposa. Luego, fue llevado, junto con toda su familia, a un campo de concentración.

Frankl sobrevivió a la guerra trabajando doce horas diarias, teniendo como alimento sólo una ración de sopa y un pedazo de pan. Muchas veces quiso terminar con su vida, pero el recuerdo de su esposa y su deseo de volver a verla lo mantuvieron con vida.

Al terminar la guerra, descubrió que sus padres, su hermano y su esposa habían muerto en los campos de concentración. Frankl se encontró completamente solo.

Una Carta Inesperada

Adolfo abre la ventana de su habitación y deja un montón de migas de pan sobre el alféizar. Es ahí donde ha colocado un pequeño comedero, un recipiente de plástico con varias piedras en su interior, para que el viento de la ciudad no se lleve las migas por los aires. También ha colocado un recipiente con agua. Es como si Adolfo tuviera una jaula en la ventana, pero sin barrotes, al aire libre.

Adolfo aspira el aire matinal, huele a otoño. Cuando cierra la ventana, piensa en su soledad y una pequeña lágrima cae por su arrugada mejilla. El hombre se queda ahí, detrás del cristal de la ventana de su habitación, mirando la calle. Son las siete y media y aún hay poca gente por la calle. Desde su ventana, ve al dueño de la papelería recogiendo fardos de periódicos del suelo y a la propietaria de la frutería dando órdenes a un par de chavales jóvenes que ha contratado para que le traigan la fruta fresca al punto de la mañana.

También ve pasar a algún estudiante con su mochila al hombro y a varias personas que suben a sus coches para dirigirse a sus trabajos.

Adolfo conoce ese escenario a la perfección: es el barrio donde nació, donde pasó su juventud, donde crió a sus hijos, donde perdió a su mujer y donde, diariamente, le da de desayunar a una paloma. Le ha puesto de nombre Dorotea y, desde hace un par de meses, no falta ninguna mañana a su cita con las migas de pan que Adolfo le deja en el alféizar de la ventana.

A Adolfo le gusta escuchar el gorjeo de su paloma blanca, ver cómo su buche de ave urbana se le infla de felicidad, o eso cree él, cuando descubre que su desayuno está listo. Cómo la paloma da unas vueltas sobre sí misma antes de lanzarse al comedero. Al otro lado del cristal, Adolfo sonríe y olvida la lágrima que hace tan solo unos minutos caía por su mejilla. Algún día se ha atrevido a sacar su temblorosa mano y acariciar la pequeña cabeza de la paloma. Cuando el pájaro ha terminado de desayunar, alza el vuelo, y Adolfo se retira al salón, donde leerá un libro hasta la hora de salir a dar su paseo.

Pese a la insistencia de sus hijos, Adolfo ha decidido que seguirá viviendo en su casa. No quiere saber nada de residencias. Quiere continuar su vida, aunque sin su esposa sabe que ya nada será lo mismo.

Alicia y Juan, sus hijos, van a verlo siempre que pueden. Alicia es profesora en un colegio a las afueras de la ciudad y Juan trabaja en una oficina de Correos y Telégrafos a unos veinte minutos de la casa de Adolfo. Ambos hijos han sufrido con la repentina muerte de su madre, pero el que peor lo ha pasado ha sido Adolfo. A partir de ese momento, su carácter ha cambiado. Él siempre fue una persona muy animada, con un gran sentido del humor, afable, pero desde la muerte de su esposa se ha vuelto un ser taciturno, huraño y ha envejecido diez años de golpe. Además, y esto es lo que más preocupa a sus hijos, la tensión arterial de su padre ha comenzado a subir y bajar sin motivo, y los niveles de azúcar se le han disparado. Por eso, ambos hijos creen que estaría más cuidado en una residencia. Pero Adolfo se niega.

Así que Alicia y Juan han contratado a una enfermera que va todos los días, por la mañana, sobre las ocho y, tras comprobar su tensión y su nivel de azúcar, le dice si puede irse a dar su paseo o debe quedarse en casa, descansando, hasta que las pastillas le hagan efecto. Lo que no sabe la enfermera es que Adolfo nunca le hace caso y todos los días se da su paseo, sea cual sea su consejo.

— ¿Y porque ese aparato lo diga va a ser verdad? ¡Si yo me encuentro de maravilla! —le dice Adolfo cuando la enfermera asegura que su nivel de azúcar está por las nubes.

Cuando Adolfo escucha el timbre de su casa, permanece quieto en el sillón y continúa leyendo su libro. Sabe que a ese "ding-dong" le va a seguir una vuelta de llave en la cerradura y un "buenos días, señor Adolfo" de la voz de Beatriz, la enfermera.

Los hijos de Adolfo le dieron las llaves de la vivienda cuando, una mañana, el anciano no abrió la puerta y tuvieron que llamar a los bomberos para que forzaran la cerradura. Una vez pudieron acceder a la vivienda, encontraron a su padre tendido en el suelo. Inmediatamente llamaron a una ambulancia y en unos minutos un par de médicos, con un aire de premura y emergencia, sacaban de unos maletines un sinfín de artilugios. A Adolfo le había dado una bajada de tensión, de la cual se recuperó tras los cuidados de los médicos de urgencias, que aconsejaron a los hijos que llevaran a su padre al hospital más cercano para hacerle una revisión a fondo. Desde entonces, la enfermera tiene la llave de casa.

Beatriz es una chica joven que acabó su carrera de enfermería hace un año.

Tal y como están las cosas en el mercado laboral, se siente muy afortunada de tener unos cuantos pacientes a los que visitar a diario. Pero en el fondo a ella le gustaría salir a trabajar al extranjero.

Beatriz, a veces, siente que más que una enfermera es una portera con ese llavero repleto con las llaves de las casas de sus pacientes y bromea a menudo con ellos diciéndoles, mientras mueve el manojo de llaves, un "no se apure que pese a este fajo de llaves no soy San Pedro, sigue usted aquí, en la Tierra, ya habrá tiempo para los cielos". Algunos, los más cascarrabias, le dicen un "estaría mejor allí, soy demasiado viejo y aquí nadie me visita", ante lo que Beatriz hace una mueca de desaprobación y les endosa un "ande, ande, no sea viejo cascarrabias que está usted hecho un chaval".

Siempre que abre la puerta de casa de Adolfo, se le encoge un poco el estómago y mientras ese "buenos días, señor Adolfo" recorre el pasillo de la vivienda, ella mira una por una las habitaciones de la casa empezando por la cocina. Una vez Adolfo le responde el correspondiente "buenos días, Beatriz" ella deja de inspeccionar la vivienda y se dirige sin entretenerse hasta la última puerta del pasillo, donde está el salón.

La noche anterior, Beatriz tan apenas ha dormido media hora. Para sacar un poco más de dinero ha comenzado a acompañar a enfermos en el hospital en el turno de noche. Adolfo le mira a los ojos mientras el aparato de toma de tensión oprime su brazo.

—Deberías irte a dormir —le dice el anciano mientras toca la mano de Beatriz—, se te nota cansada.

Con Beatriz es con la única persona con la que Adolfo es algo más amable.

Tal vez sea porque le recuerda a una antigua novia de juventud o porque realmente Beatriz es un ser que inspira ternura. Sus gestos son delicados, su piel es muy blanca, tiene los ojos claros y su pelo es del color del trigo. Todo esto hace que Beatriz parezca un ángel.

Beatriz le dice que en cuanto acabe su ronda matutina, se irá a casa, a dormir.

—¿Cómo está María? —le pregunta entonces Adolfo.

Suelen hablar de otros pacientes que tiene Beatriz como si fueran conocidos de toda la vida. Adolfo no conoce a la tal María, ni a Rodrigo, ni a Herminio, todos pacientes de Beatriz, pero sabe que María vive a una media hora de su casa y que ha sido operada recientemente de vesícula y que Rodrigo va en una silla de ruedas y requiere una inyección diaria. También sabe que Herminio no anda muy bien de la cabeza.

—Va muy bien, no se preocupe. Ah, por cierto, María me dio ayer unas rosquillas para usted. Son sin azúcar, así que puede comerse unas hoy —dice Beatriz mientras saca un paquete envuelto en papel de aluminio.

—Dale las gracias —dice Adolfo, mientras sonríe y piensa que a su paloma Dorotea esas migas le van a saber a gloria.

En el fondo, son como un grupo de amigos que nunca se han visto y cuyo nexo de unión es Beatriz, la mensajera que les pone al corriente de la vida de los demás. Adolfo es especialmente curioso y le gusta saber los pelos y señales de las vidas de esos otros compañeros de vejez.

Tal vez esto se deba a que Adolfo siempre trabajó de cara al público, en un pequeño comercio de telas, donde se confeccionaban camisas a medida y se arreglaban todo tipo de prendas. Acostumbrado a tratar con la gente, a conocer sus problemas, a dar incluso algunos consejos, esa forma de ser la mantenía años después de haber traspasado el negocio a un comerciante de seda.

RESUMEN CAPÍTULO 1

Adolfo es viudo y se siente muy solo. Todos los días alimenta a una paloma que aparece en su ventana. Le gusta observar al animal. Adolfo tiene dos hijos, pero vive solo. Una enfermera, Beatriz, va a visitarlo todos los días para controlar su salud. Adolfo antes era muy animado, pero desde la muerte de su esposa se ha vuelto muy reservado. La enfermera tiene la llave desde el día que Adolfo perdió el conocimiento y lo encontraron en el suelo de su casa.

Beatriz desea salir a trabajar al extranjero, aunque está muy contenta con sus pacientes y les tiene cariño. Beatriz ha dormido poco porque ha comenzado a trabajar cuidando enfermos en el hospital por las noches. Adolfo es amable con Beatriz porque ella es como un ángel y además le recuerda a una novia de juventud.

Beatriz cuenta a sus pacientes cómo están el resto de ancianos, aunque no se conocen. María, una de las ancianas que cuida, le ha dado un paquete con unas rosquillas para Adolfo y Beatriz se lo ha entregado a Adolfo.

SUMMARY CHAPTER 1

Adolfo is a widower and feels very lonely. Every day, he feeds a dove that appears in his window. He likes to watch the animal. Adolfo has two children but lives alone. A nurse, Beatriz, goes to visit him every day to control his health. Adolfo was very lively before but since the death of his wife, he has become very reserved. The nurse has the key from the day Adolfo lost consciousness and found him on the floor of his house.

Beatriz wants to go to work abroad although she is very happy with her patients and loves them. Beatriz has fallen asleep because she has started to work caring for patients at the hospital at night. Adolfo is kind to Beatriz because she is like an angel and also reminds him of a girlfriend of youth.

Beatriz tells her patients how the rest of the elderly are, even though they do not know each other. Maria, one of the old ladies who Beatriz cares, has given her a package with some doughnuts for Adolfo, and Beatriz has given it to Adolfo.

Una Aventura de WhatsApp

Hoy es lunes, son las seis y cuarto de la mañana y tengo mucho sueño. Aun así, yo me levanto para ir al trabajo. Como todos los días, me ducho, desayuno y me visto. En el portal de casa, saludo al portero «buenos días» y él me responde «hasta luego, Juan». El portero es un hombre muy simpático.

Él es ecuatoriano y su familia vive en Ecuador.

Mi nombre es Juan, soy de España y tengo veintisiete años. Soy profesor de matemáticas en un colegio. Vivo en Madrid, en un piso pequeño en el centro de la ciudad. Me gusta mucho el barrio donde vivo. Mi piso tiene un balcón, donde tengo flores. Madrid es una ciudad muy grande y muy bonita. Hay muchos museos, cines, teatros, plazas y parques. Lo que más me gusta de Madrid es el Parque del Retiro. Lo que menos me gusta de Madrid es el tráfico. Hay muchos coches en Madrid, aunque el transporte público está muy bien. Yo siempre voy al trabajo en metro, me subo en la misma parada, así que todos los días veo a la misma gente.

Hoy, en el metro, encuentro un móvil en un asiento. El teléfono parece nuevo. ¿De quién es?, me pregunto. Examino el móvil y veo que hay muchos mensajes de WhatsApp. Miro hacia los lados para adivinar a quién pertenece.

El vagón de metro está vacío. Estoy solo con un móvil perdido en mis manos.

Voy a encontrar a su dueño: quiero devolver el teléfono.

RESUMEN CAPÍTULO 1

Mi nombre es Juan y vivo en Madrid. Soy profesor de matemáticas en un colegio. Hoy alguien pierde un móvil en el metro. Yo cojo el móvil y veo que hay muchos mensajes de WhatsApp. Decido encontrar al dueño del móvil: quiero devolverlo.

SUMMARY CHAPTER 1

My name is Juan and I live in Madrid. I'm a math teacher at school. Today someone loses a cell phone in the subway. I take the mobile and check that there are many messages from WhatsApp. I decide to find the owner of the mobile: I want to return it.

CAPÍTULO 2

Yo cojo el móvil. La pantalla tiene un fondo azul y varios iconos: el icono del correo electrónico, el icono de llamadas y el icono de WhatsApp. Compruebo que hay muchos mensajes.

Para encontrar a su dueño tengo dos opciones: puedo esperar su propia llamada desde otro teléfono, que me diga dónde está, ir hasta allí y devolver el teléfono, o puedo buscar al dueño yo. Como no me gusta esperar, decido investigar el teléfono. Abro la aplicación de WhatsApp. Pienso que algún contacto me puede dar pistas acerca de su dueño. Miro el estado y el perfil.

Hay una foto, una frase y un nombre. Nombre: Ágata. La frase: «Hoy estoy feliz». Sonrío al leerla y pienso que tal vez la dueña no está feliz porque no tiene su móvil. Me fijo en el perfil. Hay una fotografía de alguien que camina hacia el mar. Al ver el mar, pienso en mis próximas vacaciones en la Costa del Sol, en Málaga. Allí tengo un amigo y todos los veranos estoy quince días con él. Mi amigo se llama Manuel y es andaluz. Yo le conozco desde hace cinco años.

Con estos pocos datos, yo sé que la dueña del móvil se llama Ágata, que dice que hoy está feliz y que le gusta el mar.

Para obtener más pistas, chequeo la galería del móvil y busco una fotografía de Ágata. Sin resultado: la galería está vacía. El móvil es nuevo y no tiene ningún elemento más.

Vuelvo al WhatsApp y leo uno de los chats.

RESUMEN CAPÍTULO 2

Yo cojo el móvil e investigo. En el estado de WhatsApp descubro que Ágata es el nombre de la dueña. De perfil tiene una fotografía con el mar y una frase «Hoy estoy feliz».

Chequeo la galería de fotografías del móvil y está vacía. Abro la aplicación de WhatsApp y leo los mensajes de uno de los chats.

SUMMARY CHAPTER 2

I pick the cell phone up and investigate. In the state of WhatsApp, I discover that Ágata is the name of the owner. In her profile, there is a photograph with the sea and the phrase «I am happy today».

I check the photo gallery of the mobile and it is empty. I open the WhatsApp application and read the messages of one of the chats.

CAPÍTULO 3

Mientras camino hacia el colegio donde trabajo, leo los mensajes del chat entre Ágata y Lorena. Son las ocho y cincuenta minutos y mis clases comienzan a las nueve. Todos los lunes llego tarde.

Ayer 22:54 horas

Lorena: Hola Ágata, ¿qué tal estás?

Ágata: Hola Lorena, yo estoy muy bien, ¿y tú?

Lorena: Ya casi con un pie en la cama. Es un poco tarde, lo sé, pero quiero preguntarte si mañana vas a la biblioteca.

Ágata: Sí, yo voy siempre a la biblioteca después de las clases, tengo mucho que estudiar, el examen de Álgebra es el jueves.

Lorena: Genial, nos vemos allí, en la biblioteca de la Facultad de Ciencias.

Ágata: Claro, nos vemos, llego sobre las cuatro todos los días.

Lorena: Hasta entonces.

Ágata: Hasta luego.

Hoy 6:12 horas

Ágata: Buenos días, Lorena.

Lorena: Buenos días, Ágata.

Ágata: Lorena, quiero pedirte un favor.

Lorena: ¿Cuál?

Ágata: ¿Tú puedes traerme la carpeta roja? La carpeta está en tu casa, tiene unos apuntes que necesito.

Lorena: ¿La carpeta roja?

Ágata: Sí, esa. En la tapa pone "Álgebra" con letras muy grandes. Siempre la olvido. Soy un desastre.

Lorena: Tranquila, yo la llevo y te la doy.

Ágata: Muchas gracias, Lorena.

Lorena: De nada. Un beso.

Ágata: Un beso.

Cuando termino de leer el chat entre Ágata y Lorena, son las nueve y cinco minutos. Estoy en clase. La clase es pequeña. Tiene tres ventanas, quince pupitres, una estantería, mi mesa y una pizarra. También hay una papelera, un armario y una caja con material escolar.

Les digo a los alumnos que se sienten en las sillas. La clase comienza con mi explicación, en la pizarra, de la lección de hoy. Al terminar, les digo a los alumnos que hagan, en silencio, los ejercicios de la página siguiente. Así tengo tiempo de chequear el móvil de Ágata. No hay ningún mensaje más.

De la conversación con Lorena, deduzco que Ágata y Lorena son amigas, que Lorena estudia en la universidad, que el jueves tiene un examen de Álgebra y que hoy, a las cuatro, va a ir a la biblioteca.

Pienso que yo puedo ir a la biblioteca de la universidad, sentarme como uno más y ver si una chica entra con una carpeta roja en cuya tapa pone "Álgebra" con letras muy grandes. Pienso que eso es lo que hago esta tarde.

RESUMEN CAPÍTULO 3

Mientras yo camino hacia el trabajo, leo un chat entre Ágata y Lorena. En el chat pone que, esta tarde, Lorena le lleva a Ágata una carpeta roja a la biblioteca. En la tapa de la carpeta pone "Álgebra" con letras muy grandes.

Mis alumnos están en clase y les explico la lección de hoy. Mientras los alumnos hacen unos ejercicios, yo decido que, esta tarde, también voy a la biblioteca. Allí le devuelvo el móvil a Ágata.

SUMMARY CHAPTER 3

While I am going to work, I read a chat between Ágata and Lorena. In the chat, it says that this afternoon, Lorena takes to Ágata a red folder to the library. At the top of the folder, it says "Álgebra" with very large letters.

My pupils are in class and I explain today's lesson. While the students are doing some questions, I decide that this afternoon, I also go to the library.

There I return the cell phone to Ágata.

CAPÍTULO 4

Cuando mi jornada laboral termina, yo vuelvo a casa. Enchufo el móvil de Ágata y, mientras se carga, me ducho y me cambio de ropa. Quiero pasar desapercibido, parecer un estudiante más en la biblioteca. Abro el armario, miro la ropa y elijo algo informal. Me pongo unos vaqueros, una camiseta blanca y unas deportivas. Me miro en el espejo y, aunque tengo veintisiete años, parezco un chaval de dieciocho. Cojo una carpeta y meto unos pocos folios.

Salgo de casa, camino hasta la estación y subo al metro para ir hasta la biblioteca de la Facultad de Ciencias. La línea seis me lleva hasta la Ciudad Universitaria y luego camino unos diez minutos o un poco más. Hoy es un bonito lunes de mayo. El día está soleado.

Cuando llego a la biblioteca de la Facultad de Ciencias, intento coger un sitio lo más cercano a la entrada para poder ver quién entra y quién lleva una carpeta roja. Los pasos a seguir son sencillos: veo entrar a alguien con una carpeta roja, me fijo en la tapa, si pone "Álgebra" está claro que quien lo lleva es Lorena. La sigo, me siento a su lado y espero el momento en que aparezca otra chica. Luego, dejo el móvil sobre los apuntes de Lorena en un momento de despiste de ella y me marcho.

Con estos pensamientos, me dispongo a observar la puerta de entrada: solo pienso en el color rojo.

RESUMEN CAPÍTULO 4

Cuando termino la jornada laboral, voy a casa y me cambio de ropa para parecer un estudiante. Voy en metro hasta la Ciudad Universitaria. En la biblioteca de la Facultad de Ciencias, cojo un sitio cerca de la entrada para ver si alguien entra con una carpeta roja. El plan consiste en localizar a Ágata cuando Lorena le dé la carpeta y dejar el móvil sobre los apuntes mientras ella está despistada.

SUMMARY CHAPTER 4

When I finish the workday, I go home and change my clothes to look like a student. I go by metro to the University City. In the library of the Faculty of Science, I take a seat near the entrance to see if someone walks in with a red folder. The plan is to locate Ágata when Lorena gives her the folder and leave the mobile on the notes while she is clueless.

CAPÍTULO 5

Son las cuatro y dos minutos. La biblioteca comienza a llenarse de estudiantes. Mientras los estudiantes abren sus libros y sacan sus apuntes, hablan en voz baja para no molestar a los demás. Yo tengo que permanecer muy atento: dos de cada tres estudiantes llevan una carpeta roja. Además, hay varias chicas que llevan una carpeta roja con la palabra "Álgebra" en la tapa.

Es algo normal porque estoy en la Facultad de Ciencias. Cualquiera de ellas puede ser Lorena.

Tengo que pensar otro plan.

No veo otra solución: tengo que hacerme pasar por Ágata, escribir un mensaje a Lorena y preguntar dónde está exactamente. Luego sentarme a su lado disimuladamente.

Ágata (Juan): ¡Hola, Lorena! ¿Cómo estás?

Lorena: ¡Buenas tardes, Ágata! Estoy muy bien. Te espero en la biblioteca.

Ágata (Juan): Genial, yo llego en unos minutos. ¿Hay mucha gente?

Lorena: Sí, hay mucha gente. Se nota que hay exámenes pronto.

Ágata (Juan): Pues guarda un sitio para mí, ¿vale?

Lorena: Claro, sí.

Ágata (Juan): ¿Dónde estás sentada?

Lorena: Estoy donde siempre.

Ágata (Juan): ¿Dónde siempre? ¿Puedes concretar?

Lorena: ¿Te pasa algo, Ágata?

Tengo que pensar qué responder. Ellas siempre se sientan en el mismo sitio, pero yo no sé cuál es ese sitio. Lorena desconfía, tal vez intuye que algo no va bien.

Misterio en la Biblioteca

Lunes, 6 de Abril.

Hoy tengo el día libre, la biblioteca está cerrada. El horario de la sala de investigadores es de martes a sábado, de diez de la mañana a dos de la tarde.

Es ahí donde consulto el libro medieval.

Me despierto tarde y antes de desayunar, me ducho. Mientras desayuno un par de tostadas y un café, pienso en mi investigación. Después de desayunar, me lavo los dientes. Me visto con unos pantalones vaqueros, una camiseta y unas deportivas. Tengo mucho trabajo: ordenar papeles, escribir.

Mis amigos trabajan los lunes. No puedo quedar con nadie. Mejor porque así tengo más tiempo para escribir mi tesis. En casa no hay nadie. Hay mucho silencio las mañanas de los lunes. Mis padres están en el trabajo y mi hermana en el colegio.

En el salón, leo una nota de mi madre: "Por favor, Vicente, ve a la tienda de animales y compra alpiste para Jacinto. Gracias. Mamá".

Jacinto es el nombre de nuestra mascota: un loro de Brasil. Es un loro verde, muy listo. Dice algunas palabras. A veces lo saco de la jaula y me lo pongo sobre el hombro. Entonces parezco un pirata en busca de un tesoro, surco los mares y vivo aventuras. Pero no, soy Vicente, un estudiante de Historia, en pantalón vaquero y un loro brasileño sobre el hombro. Un loro verde, además. El único mar que surco es la carretera que lleva a la biblioteca del Escorial. Pero tampoco es un mar, son cincuenta y un kilómetros de carretera.

Aventuras no tengo. A veces, me aburro.

Voy a la tienda de animales y compro comida para Jacinto. Al volver, compruebo que el móvil está sin batería y lo pongo a recargar. En el mismo momento de encenderlo, recibo un mensaje de WhatsApp. Es de Ana.

Ana: Buenos días, dormilón.

Yo: Hola Ana, ¿cómo estás?

Ana: Bien. Estoy en el trabajo desde las siete de la mañana. Ahora tengo un rato libre. Te escribo para saber qué haces hoy.

Yo: Hoy es lunes… tengo el día libre. ¿Quieres quedar por la tarde?

Ana: ¡Estupendo! Tengo que contarte muchas cosas de mi viaje.

Yo: Genial, soy todo oídos.

Ana: Esta tarde. ¿A las ocho en la cafetería Matilda?

Yo: Sí, perfecto. Nos vemos.

Ana: Hasta luego.

Yo: Que tengas buen día.

Ana: Lo mismo te digo, aunque eso es seguro, hoy es tu día libre ;-) Dejo el móvil sobre la mesa. Pienso en Ana. La conozco desde que empezamos la carrera. Es muy inteligente, simpática y guapa. Por las mañanas, trabaja en el almacén de una empresa de mensajería. Necesita dinero para su viaje. Dentro de un mes se va a Francia. Eso me pone triste.

Me gusta Ana. Puedo ir a verla en verano, si acabo mi tesis. Me merezco unas vacaciones.

Miro el reloj. Son las doce y veinte de la mañana. Es muy tarde. Tengo que madrugar más, pero siempre estoy muy cansado. Me siento en la silla, coloco mis papeles sobre la mesa de trabajo, saco mis apuntes y escribo mi tesis.

Después de comer, salgo a dar un paseo por el parque. Me relaja caminar y ver los árboles. En el parque hay una fuente, unos columpios, muchos árboles. A esta hora tan solo hay unos cuantos deportistas, alguna pareja que pasea, y alguien que escribe una carta. Decido descansar un rato y me siento en un banco. En el suelo, junto al banco, hay un libro. En su portada hay una fotografía. Es la fotografía de una catedral. Miro hacia los lados por si hay alguien cerca, tal vez el dueño del libro, pero no hay nadie. Aunque no tengo tiempo de leer, ni tengo espacio para más libros, decido que me llevo el libro a casa. Mi habitación está muy desordenada y llena de cosas: apuntes, fotografías, documentos. Pienso que esta misma tarde se lo doy a Ana. A ella le gusta leer. Le encanta leer.

Trabajo en mi tesis hasta las ocho. Después, me arreglo para quedar con Ana.

Me pongo mi camiseta preferida, una de los "Guns and Roses", negra. En español significa pistolas y rosas. Salgo de casa y camino por la calle hasta la estación de metro. Me subo al metro y viajo hasta el centro de Madrid. El vagón está lleno de gente a estas horas, no cabe un alfiler. La mayoría, imagino, vuelven de sus trabajos. A veces, los trayectos son largos, y la gente trata de aprovechar el tiempo. Algunos miran las pantallas de sus móviles, o leen un libro o duermen. Llego a mi destino. Veo la figura de Ana a lo lejos y camino más rápido, no me gusta hacerle esperar. Nos saludamos y nos damos dos besos. Dos besos y... un libro.

"¡El nombre de la rosa!" Dice Ana, emocionada. Muchas gracias, Vicente. Es un libro muy bueno. Es de un escritor italiano que se llama Umberto Eco.

Hay una película muy famosa sobre esta historia. ¡Qué bien, me encantan los libros sobre la Edad Media! Dice Ana con una sonrisa en la cara.

No hablo más del libro porque quiero que me cuente cosas sobre su viaje a Francia, pero pienso que La Edad Media me sigue allá donde voy: mi tesis, el libro. Ahora ya no quiero ser pirata, quiero ser caballero medieval, ja, ja, ja.

Seguro que mis padres no aceptan un caballo como mascota.

Ana me cuenta que el día veintitrés de mayo sale su avión. Lo dice tan contenta que pienso que no le importa que yo me quede aquí rodeado de misterios medievales, tan solo. Me dice que viaja con una aerolínea de bajo coste "low-cost" porque no tiene mucho dinero. En la empresa de mensajería no pagan mucho. En París le espera su tía Memé, una hermana de su padre, soltera. Ana habla por los codos, tiene muchos proyectos, muchas ilusiones.

Quiere mejorar su francés y esta es una buena oportunidad. Una beca de la Universidad de la Sorbona. Yo me alegro por ella. Me gustan las personas con inquietudes.

Le digo a Ana que mañana madrugo y que ahora me tengo que ir a casa. Nos despedimos. Llama pronto y quedamos, me dice. Y se aleja.

Camino hacia la estación de metro.

RESUMEN CAPÍTULO 1

Lunes, 6 de Abril.

Vicente es estudiante de Historia y hace su tesis. Todos los días va a la biblioteca del Escorial para consultar un códice medieval. Los lunes la biblioteca está cerrada y Vicente se queda en casa.

En su casa no hay nadie. Sus padres y su hermana están fuera. Por la mañana, Vicente recibe un WhatsApp de Ana y queda con ella por la tarde. A Vicente le gusta Ana. Ana se va a Francia dentro de dos meses.

Vicente quiere acabar su tesis pronto para poder ir a visitarla, pero siempre está muy cansado y duda de que tenga tiempo. Vicente encuentra un libro y como él no tiene tiempo para leer se lo regala a Ana. El libro trata de un misterio medieval.

SUMMARY CHAPTER 1

Monday, 6th of April

Vicente is a student of History and he is doing his thesis. Every day, he goes to the library of Escorial to consult a medieval codex. On Mondays, the library is closed and Vicente stays at home.

There is no one at home. His parents and his sister are out. In the morning, Vicente receives a WhatsApp from Ana and plans to meet her in the evening.

Vicente likes Ana. Ana is leaving to France in two months.

Vicente wants to finish his thesis early so that he can visit her, but he is always very tired and wonders if he has time. Vicente finds a book and because he does not have time to read it, he gives it to Ana as a gift. The book is about medieval mystery.

CAPÍTULO 2

Martes, 7 de Abril

La luz del sol entra por mi ventana y me despierto. Miro mi reloj. Salto de la cama. ¡Son las diez de la mañana! El despertador está roto. Llego tarde a la biblioteca. Tengo sueño.

Desayuno, me ducho y me visto todo lo rápido que puedo. Bajo al garaje y me pongo en marcha. Después de veinte minutos de atascos, por fin estoy en la carretera que lleva al Escorial. Conduzco. Abro la ventanilla del coche para que el aire entre. Brilla el sol y oigo cantar a los pájaros. Huele a flores. El día es maravilloso. Es primavera.

En esta estación del año algunas personas están muy cansadas y solo quieren dormir, astenia primaveral, le llaman. Yo estoy cansado. Llevo meses así, desde que empecé la tesis. Todos los días viajo hasta el Monasterio del Escorial. La distancia entre Madrid, donde vivo, y el Monasterio del Escorial, donde está la biblioteca, es poca, así que conducir mucho no es el motivo de mi cansancio, además las mañanas las paso sentado.

Al final de la carretera, aparece el edificio. El Monasterio de San Lorenzo del Escorial es enorme y muy bonito. También tiene muchos secretos y misterios.

En su gran biblioteca se guardan libros muy especiales. A mí solo me interesa uno. Es del siglo XIV. Es un libro incompleto, sin terminar. ¿Por qué?

Imagino a alguien hace siglos, a un monje. El monje escribe el libro, pero no lo termina. Está cansado como yo. Pero yo tengo que terminar mi tesis. Y para eso tengo dos meses.

Paso los controles de seguridad y llego hasta la biblioteca. Allí está Berta, una mujer mayor encargada de guardar y custodiar la biblioteca. Después de tantos meses, nos conocemos mucho, pero, aun así, todos los días debo mostrarle mi carné de identidad. Ella, todos los días, lee mis datos y me dice lo mismo: te llamas igual que mi gato. Entonces yo sonrío porque también todos los días le escucho pedir el carné de identidad a otros investigadores y decir: te llamas igual que mi canario, o te llamas igual que mi tortuga o te llamas igual que mi iguana. Es un poco rara, pero es una anciana adorable. Su pelo es gris y lo lleva recogido en un moño. El moño se mueve cuando camina, con sus pasos lentos. Las manos le tiemblan cuando me entrega la funda de plástico que contiene el libro. Sé que si no tiene mucho trabajo saca las agujas de tricotar y hace un jersey para su nieto. Siempre llora, un poco, al principio de tricotar. Yo creo que es porque su nieto está lejos, en el extranjero, y le ve poco. Eso me cuenta.

El rato que hablo con Berta es el único momento de distracción, luego me sumerjo en mi tesis hasta las dos del mediodía, que es cuando cierra la sala de los investigadores.

Algún día Berta me despierta porque estoy durmiendo sobre el libro. Me da unos golpes en la espalda y me dice: joven, es hora de cerrar. Entonces yo no sé muy bien dónde estoy. Veo su cara borrosa, muy cerca de la mía. En ese momento, no sé quién es, y pienso que es una bruja medieval, y me asusto.

Me froto los ojos y vuelvo a la realidad. Es Berta, la bibliotecaria. Gracias, Berta, le digo. Necesitas descansar mejor por la noche, no salgas tanto por ahí, me dice como si fuera mi abuela. Anda tómate una café antes de volver a tu casa, me aconseja.

Así lo hago. Luego, conduzco de regreso a casa.

Yo: Buenas tardes, mamá.

Mamá: Buenas tardes, hijo, ¿qué tal hoy?

Yo: Bien, aunque tengo sueño, como siempre.

Mamá: Tal vez tengas astenia primaveral. Me preocupa. Debes ir al médico.

Yo: No tengo tiempo para ir al médico.

Mamá: Sí tienes. Los lunes es el día perfecto, es tu día libre. Ahora mismo llamo al doctor Pérez del Valle y pido una cita.

Yo: Como quieras…

El Secreto del Molino

CAPÍTULO 1

Amelia Plin era una persona con suerte. Un día encontró un anuncio que le cambió la vida.

Hasta entonces, Amelia había trabajado como contable en una librería muy importante. *«Palacios»* era la tienda de libros más grande de la ciudad.

Estaba situada en el centro de Toledo y ocupaba dos pisos de un edificio antiguo. En las estanterías de la librería había todo tipo de libros: novelas, cuentos infantiles, coleccionables de cocina, atlas, enciclopedias, diccionarios, compendios de medicina, incluso había una sección de libros antiguos y descatalogados.

Cualquier libro podía encontrarse en aquella librería maravillosa. Cuando había mucho trabajo, su jefe le pedía que atendiera a los clientes. Poco a poco, el trato con los clientes le ayudó a desarrollar su capacidad de observación. Amelia intuía, por la forma de vestir, por la forma de caminar, por la forma de hablar, qué quería leer cada persona. Cuando en la librería había poco trabajo, Amelia Plin se dedicaba a leer. Sus libros preferidos eran los de aventuras.

El martes veintiuno de febrero del año 1995, Amelia Plin volvía del trabajo hacia su casa. Eran las dos del mediodía y hacía frío, mucho frío.

Normalmente, ella volvía a casa en autobús, pero ese día decidió caminar, pese a las bajas temperaturas. Amelia quería pensar, necesitaba ordenar sus pensamientos. Hacía tres meses que se aburría mucho en el trabajo.

Necesitaba un cambio en su vida. A sus treinta años aún era joven para buscar otro empleo, o incluso para mudarse a otra ciudad. Tenía muchas ganas de vivir las mismas aventuras que leía en los libros.

Cuando llegó al portal de su casa, saludó a Valentina, que en ese momento salía del edificio. Valentina era su vecina del segundo derecha, una anciana adorable, que *hablaba por los codos* y tenía una tortuga. Solía llevar al animal en el bolso, con la cabeza afuera. Amelia sabía que Valentina era una mujer rara, algo excéntrica y no le sorprendió ver que, ese martes de febrero, la tortuga llevaba un gorro de lana. Valentina vestía con pantalones de terciopelo marrón y un largo abrigo azul. Además de excéntrica, Valentina era una mujer entrañable que solía cocinar para Amelia magdalenas y algún caldo para sopa. La anciana trataba a Amelia como a una hija.

Amelia: buenas tardes, doña Valentina. ¿Dónde va a estas horas? ¿No se echa la siesta hoy?

Valentina: buenas tardes, Amelia. Voy a visitar a mi hermana Marisa y a llevarle unos bombones, ya sabes que está recién operada y necesita cariños.

Amelia: muy bien, que tenga buena tarde.

Valentina: querida Amelia, ¿qué te pasa? Te veo preocupada.

Amelia: nada, no se preocupe, estoy cansada, eso es todo.

Valentina: ya sabes que puedes contarme cualquier problema que tengas, ¿verdad?

Amelia: claro que sí, Valentina. Ande, dese prisa o perderá el autobús. Hasta luego.

Valentina: hasta luego.

Valentina era muy intuitiva, por lo que a Amelia no le sorprendió el hecho de que se hubiera dado cuenta de su malestar y preocupación.

Amelia pasó al interior del edifico y, tras encender la luz del rellano, recogió del buzón varias cartas y un papel de propaganda. El papel era uno de esos anuncios que algún comercial deja en el buzón, y que nadie suele leer.

"¿Te apasiona la aventura?

¿Eres una persona observadora?

¿Te gusta la investigación?

No lo dudes más: ven a vernos.

Tenemos un caso para ti.

Escuela de detectives Buenavista.

Teléfono 45443.

Llámanos. Te esperamos."

A pesar de que el folleto era de lo más normal: blanco, con las letras en color granate, escritas en cursiva, y el dibujo de una lupa en la parte izquierda del folleto, algo llamó la atención de Amelia en aquel trozo de papel.

Quizás encontró la solución a su aburrimiento, la respuesta a sus dudas laborales. Amelia miró el anuncio durante varios minutos. Lo leyó una primera vez mientras subía en el ascensor y una segunda y una tercera ya en su casa. Luego, lo dejó sobre la mesa del salón.

Su perro Mimi, un *beagle* inglés, movía el rabo y ladraba de felicidad al ver a su dueña. Mimi era un perro muy cariñoso, inteligente y astuto. Amelia se sentó en el suelo y comenzó a jugar con Mimi. Le acarició su precioso pelo de tres colores: negro, marrón y blanco. Amelia adoraba a su perro.

A Amelia no le cabía ninguna duda de que los perros eran los mejores amigos de los humanos. Mimi le hacía mucha compañía. Amelia Plin era una mujer reservada, aunque era buena confidente. Tenía una buena amiga de la infancia con la que quedaba de vez en cuando a tomar un café y se llamaban por teléfono. Salvo esa amiga de la infancia, Valentina y un hombre que conoció en el parque, no tenía más vida social. Su familia vivía en Madrid y se reunían solo en fechas señaladas: algún cumpleaños, Navidades, Año Nuevo y poco más. Aunque a Amelia Plin le gustaba la soledad, en esos momentos de dudas, echó de menos poder hablar con alguien de sus preocupaciones. Cierto era que podía contarle a Valentina su desgana en el trabajo, pero esos días la anciana solo tenía tiempo para su hermana.

RESUMEN DEL CAPÍTULO 1

Amelia tenía treinta años y quería cambiar de trabajo porque se aburría. Un día encontró en el buzón el anuncio de una escuela de detectives. Amelia guardó el papel, ya que pensó que podía ser la solución a su hastío laboral.

Amelia vivía en Toledo, con su perro. Su familia vivía en Madrid y se veían poco. Tenía poca vida social: una vecina, una amiga de la infancia y un hombre que conoció en el parque.

Su vecina Valentina, una anciana muy intuitiva, era como una madre para ella, pero Amelia no le quería contar nada de su situación laboral porque esos días Valentina estaba preocupada por su hermana, recién operada.

SUMMARY CHAPTER 1

Amelia was thirty years old and wanted to change her job because she was bored of it. One day, she found an advertisement for a detective school in the mailbox. Amelia kept the paper because she thought that it could be the solution to her work boredom. Amelia lived in Toledo, with her dog. Her family lived in Madrid and they didn't see each other very much. She had little social life: a neighbor, a friend from childhood and a man who she met in the park.

Her neighbor Valentina, a very intuitive old woman, was like a mother to her, but Amelia did not want to tell her anything about her work situation because those days, Valentina was worried about her sister, who had surgery.

CAPÍTULO 2

A la mañana siguiente, miércoles, veintidós de febrero, la ciudad estaba llena de nieve. El barrio judío donde vivía era como una pista de esquí. Los montones de nieve se acumulaban en las puertas y varios operarios del ayuntamiento se daban prisa en quitar la nieve con unas palas. Más de media ciudad se quedó ese día en casa, atrapados por la nevada.

Amelia Plin se preparó el desayuno: un café con leche y dos tostadas con mermelada de fresa. Muchos copos de nieve caían desde el cielo y Amelia los miraba, a través de la ventana, mientras desayunaba. Toledo nevado era precioso. Pensó que ese día le vendría muy bien para llamar por teléfono a la escuela de detectives *Buenavista*. Sí, lo tenía decidido: iba a probar suerte.

Amelia marcó el cuatro, cinco, cuatro, cuatro, tres, y esperó los tonos de la línea. Pronto, alguien levantó el auricular.

Escuela Buenavista: buenos días, está usted hablando con Arturo Buenavista, ¿en qué puedo ayudarle?

Amelia: buenos días, mi nombre es Amelia. Le llamo por el anuncio.

Escuela Buenavista: ¿se refiere al anuncio de la escuela? ¿Está usted interesada en formarse como detective?

Amelia: sí, ese anuncio. Lo encontré ayer en mi buzón. Quería información sobre las clases. ¿Me podría comentar en qué consisten sus cursos?

Escuela Buenavista: *verá Amelia…*

Amelia: puedes tratarme de tú, si quieres.

Escuela Buenavista: verás Amelia, lo primero que necesitamos es saber si serías una buena candidata para ser detective. Lo que hacemos es concertar una cita con los futuros estudiantes. Les hacemos una entrevista y, solo si dan el perfil como detectives, es decir, solo si cumplen una serie de requisitos les damos formación.

Amelia: entiendo. ¿Cuál es el precio del curso?

Escuela Buenavista: es un curso intensivo. La cuota es de veinticinco mil pesetas*. No están incluidos los libros ni el material. Los alumnos deben resolver un caso para graduarse. Añadir, Amelia, que todos los alumnos que se graduaron en nuestra escuela han trabajado en menos de medio año. Es una profesión con mucha demanda.

(* La anterior moneda en España era la peseta. El euro entró en vigor en el año 2002) *Amelia*: me parece bien. ¿Cuándo podemos tener la entrevista?

Escuela Buenavista: ¿te va bien mañana, a las siete, en la cafetería La Nube?

Amelia: bien, sí, mañana a las siete. Ahora no recuerdo dónde está la cafetería La Nube. ¿Me podrías indicar dónde está?

Escuela Buenavista: está en la calle Alameda número siete.

Amelia: no conozco esa calle, pero la buscaré. Otra cosa… ¿Cómo te reconoceré?

Escuela Buenavista: buena pregunta, Amelia. No te preocupes por eso, para mí no será difícil reconocerte. Por algo soy profesor en la escuela de detectives, ¿no crees?

Amelia: sí, claro, claro. Entonces, hasta mañana a las siete.

Escuela Buenavista: hasta mañana, Amelia.

Cuando Amelia colgó, se sintió feliz: la llamada, la cita de mañana, todo era emocionante. El resto del día lo ocupó en pensar cómo iba a cambiar su vida si la admitían en la escuela de detectives. Por la noche, de la emoción, no podía dormir y Amelia pasó *la noche en blanco*.

RESUMEN DEL CAPÍTULO 2

Amelia llamó por teléfono a la escuela de detectives *Buenavista*. Arturo le atendió y le dijo que necesitarían concertar una entrevista para saber si Amelia tenía cualidades detectivescas. También le dio explicaciones acerca del precio y duración del curso, así como la necesidad de realizar un trabajo final para graduarse.

Amelia y Arturo quedaron para el día siguiente en la cafetería La Nube, a las siete. Amelia estaba muy emocionada y esa noche no pudo dormir.

SUMMARY CHAPTER 2

Amelia called the Buenavista detective school by phone. Arturo answered and told her that they would need to arrange an interview to see if Amelia had detective qualities. He also gave her explanations about the price and duration of the course, as well as the need to do a final work to graduate.

Amelia and Arturo agreed to meet the next day at La Nube cafeteria, at seven o'clock. Amelia was very excited and that night she could not sleep.

CAPÍTULO 3

Amelia buscó la calle Alameda en un plano de la ciudad y empezó a caminar.

Cuando estaba ya cerca, se sintió algo desorientada y preguntó a un guardia.

Amelia: disculpe, estoy buscando la calle Alameda, ¿me podría indicar dónde está?

Guardia: claro, sigue recto por esta misma calle y al llegar a la segunda bocacalle, gira hacia la derecha. Camina unos cien metros hasta llegar a una plaza. Allí verás la estatua de Don Quijote, y a su izquierda, está la calle Alameda.

Amelia: no sé si le he entendido bien. Entonces, ¿a mano izquierda de la estatua se encuentra la calle Alameda?

Guardia: sí, así es, no tiene pérdida.

Amelia: muchas gracias, agente.

Guardia: de nada, que tengas una buena tarde.

Amelia: igualmente.

Enigma en la Playa

CAPÍTULO 1

Mi nombre es Eduardo y tengo treinta años. Yo soy pintor y vivo en una casa cerca del mar.

La casa está en Remu, un pueblo de la costa valenciana. La casa tiene las paredes de piedra y las ventanas de madera blanca. Hay un jardín con una fuente de agua enfrente de la casa.

La casa pertenece a un señor de Valencia. Yo le pago el alquiler todos los meses. El propietario viene en coche hasta Remu a principios de mes.

Entonces, él me llama al teléfono móvil para cobrar el alquiler.

El dueño habla poco. Parece que siempre tiene prisa. Él viste de gris y siempre lleva gafas de sol. Yo sé poco de su vida. Todos los meses, me dice que él quiere vender la casa pronto. Yo le digo que el próximo invierno, la compro. Él se alegra y me dice que me la vende barata. Parece que tiene mucho interés en venderla.

¡Ojalá yo tenga pronto el dinero! Pero aún tengo que ahorrar.

Es la casa de mis sueños. ¿Por qué digo que es la casa de mis sueños? Pues porque el día que veo el anuncio de esta casa en internet, sencillamente, me enamoro. Es lo que se llama amor a primera vista.

El salón es la habitación que más me gusta. Es muy grande y luminoso. El suelo es de madera y las paredes están forradas de papel. El papel está roto y se despega por las esquinas. En las paredes hay varias fotografías antiguas.

Las fotografías son de sus antepasados. El dueño no quiere llevárselas.

En el centro del salón, hay una mesa de roble con dos candelabros. La mesa tiene cinco sillas de terciopelo azul, muy bonitas. En realidad, falta una. Yo no la encuentro por ningún sitio.

Junto al ventanal hay un piano y una estantería con libros viejos. El dueño tampoco quiere llevarse los libros. El dueño no quiere nada de esta casa.

El jardín también me gusta mucho. En el centro del jardín, hay una fuente, un olivo muy grande y un banco de madera donde yo leo por las tardes.

Por las mañanas, yo pinto cuadros. Mi estudio de pintura está en la buhardilla y tiene una ventana redonda por donde entra mucha luz.

Cuando tengo tiempo libre, me gusta leer, ver películas y caminar por la playa.

Yo veo el mar desde mi estudio. Por esa razón yo adoro esta casa. A veces, yo estoy mucho rato mirando el mar. Me encanta el mar. Me gusta pintarlo en distintas épocas. El mar tiene diferentes colores, según la estación del año.

En primavera, el mar es de color azul intenso. En esos meses, el sol ilumina el agua y parece que el agua brilla. Los primeros turistas empiezan a llegar en primavera, sobre todo en las vacaciones de Semana Santa. Algunas personas se atreven a bañarse, aunque algunos días llueve.

En verano, el mar es de color azul verdoso. Ese color es muy bonito. Durante los meses de verano, el sol brilla con fuerza. Entonces, yo dibujo la playa llena de sombrillas y toallas de colores. Hay familias que veranean en Remu y en la playa hay cubos, palas de juguete, flotadores y pelotas. Ver así la playa produce mucha alegría.

En otoño, el mar es de color gris. Hay pocas personas en la playa. Ya no hay sombrillas de colores, ni tampoco toallas, ni familias, pero hay gente que pasea por la orilla. Algunos cogen conchas y las guardan en sus manos.

En invierno, el agua del mar se oscurece. La arena se vuelve oscura y en el cielo solo hay alguna gaviota. Si yo digo que nadie pasea por la playa en invierno, miento. Todas las mañanas de invierno, un anciano pasea por la orilla. El mar en invierno parece dormido, excepto algún día que parece despertar de repente. El viento vuelve locas a las olas y esos días los pescadores guardan sus barcas y no salen a pescar.

En el pueblo, hay una historia de pescadores ahogados, que no vuelven a sus hogares. Hace años de esa catástrofe, pero en Remu cuando llueve la gente tiene mucho miedo.

Yo vendo mis cuadros en la tienda de Mercedes.

Mercedes es una señora mayor. Ella tiene el pelo blanco y los ojos azules. Le gusta pasear por la playa y comer helados.

En verano es cuando más cuadros vendo. A finales de agosto, la gente quiere llevarse un recuerdo de las vacaciones y compran mis lienzos.

Hoy es quince de septiembre y ya quedan pocas sombrillas en la playa.

RESUMEN CAPÍTULO 1

Eduardo tiene treinta años y él es pintor. Él vive en una casa que está en Remu, un pueblo en la costa de Valencia. La casa es muy grande y muy bonita. A él le encanta la casa y quiere comprarla. Eduardo le dice al dueño que en invierno compra la casa. Él aún no tiene el dinero para comprar la casa. Eduardo pinta el mar en todas las estaciones del año. En su tiempo libre le gusta leer, ver películas y caminar por la playa. Él vende sus cuadros en la tienda de Mercedes.

La gente de Remu tiene miedo a la lluvia porque hay una historia de pescadores ahogados una noche de tormenta.

SUMMARY CHAPTER 1

Eduardo is thirty years old and he is a painter. He lives in a house that is in Remu, a town on the coast of Valencia. The house is very large and very beautiful. He loves the house and wants to buy it. Eduardo tells the owner that in winter he buys the house. He still does not have the money to buy the house. Eduardo paints the sea in all seasons of the year. In his free time, he likes to read, watch movies and walk along the beach. He sells his pictures in Mercedesśhop.

The people of Remu are afraid of the rain because there is a story of drowned fishermen on a stormy night.

CAPÍTULO 2

Mercedes no quiere que yo compre la casa. Ella dice que es demasiado grande para mí solo. Ella asegura que, en el pueblo, hay pisos mucho más bonitos y nuevos. Dice que la casa solo me va a dar problemas. Ella asegura que voy a tener que estar siempre reparándola, que las tuberías son viejas, que las tejas están rotas, que la madera está carcomida.

Y que además hay un rumor. Se dice que la casa está encantada.

Mercedes sabe que no creo en habladurías y no le sorprende que me eche a reír.

—¿No me crees? — dice mientras se pone la mano sobre el pecho, como en un juramento. —Al menos, puedes escuchar lo que se dice acerca de la casa de tus sueños.

—Ahora tengo prisa, doña Mercedes, pero le invito esta tarde a casa a tomar un café y me lo cuenta — le digo mientras coloco mis últimos cuadros en el escaparate.

—Y, ¿qué es eso que corre tanta prisa? — me interroga, mientras limpia con un trapo el mostrador de la tienda.

—Tengo que ir al pueblo de al lado a echar una carta a Correos. La carta es para mi amiga Victoria, que vive en Galicia —le respondo.

—¡Ah sí, tu amiga! — dice remarcando la palabra amiga—, yo pienso que ella tiene que estar aquí contigo porque los novios tienen que verse.

—¡Mercedes! Victoria no es mi novia, es solo una amiga — le digo cansado de que siempre esté con la misma canción—. Entonces, ¿le parece bien hoy a las cinco en mi casa, doña Mercedes?

Mercedes se pasa la mano por la frente como quien quiere alejar una duda o un temor.

—Vas a pensar que soy una vieja miedosa, pero es que esa casa...esa casa...ya sabes — dice sin acabar la frase.

—No, doña Mercedes, no sé qué manía tiene con no venir a mi casa. Yo creo que es momento de visitar mi casa. La espero a las cinco — le digo mientras salgo por la puerta sin dejarle opción a responder.

Conozco bien a Mercedes y ahora la imagino maldiciendo por lo bajo:

"¡condenado chiquillo, te voy a dar un sopapo a ver si me haces caso!"

Mientras camina de un lado a otro de la tienda, y coloca los objetos con cierta brusquedad, porque ella está nerviosa. No quiere venir a mi casa, pero estoy seguro de que esta tarde viene. Mercedes nunca falta a sus citas.

RESUMEN CAPÍTULO 2

Mercedes le aconseja a Eduardo que no compre esa casa porque es muy grande. Además, Mercedes piensa que solo le va a dar problemas porque es vieja y necesita reparaciones. Le dice que él puede encontrar pisos más nuevos en el pueblo. También le dice que hay un rumor sobre la casa: la casa está encantada. Eduardo se ríe porque no cree en rumores.

Mercedes le dice que él debe escuchar la historia. Eduardo no puede escuchar la historia en ese momento, él debe ir al pueblo de al lado a echar una carta para su amiga Victoria. Eduardo le cita a las cinco en su casa para tomar el café y escuchar la historia. Mercedes no quiere ir a la casa porque le da miedo. Eduardo sabe que aun así irá.

SUMMARY CHAPTER 2

Mercedes advises Eduardo not to buy that house because it is too big. In addition, Mercedes thinks that it will only give him problems because the house is old and needs repairs. She tells him that he can find newer flats in the village. She also tells him that there is a rumor about the house: the house is enchanted. Eduardo laughs because he does not believe in rumors.

Mercedes tells him he must listen to the story. Eduardo cannot hear the story at that moment, he must go to a close town to write a letter for his friend Victoria. Eduardo meets her at five in his house to have coffee and listen to the story. Mercedes does not want to go to the house because she is afraid.

Eduardo knows that he will still go.

CAPÍTULO 3

El pueblo de al lado está muy cerca, a unos diez kilómetros. Es más grande que Remu y tiene la oficina de Correos, el centro de salud, una biblioteca y un cine donde ponen películas una vez a la semana.

Cuando yo llego a la puerta de la oficina de Correos, me doy prisa en poner el candado a mi bicicleta. Son las dos y cuarto y, según el horario, la oficina está a punto de cerrar.

Horarios de apertura

De lunes a viernes de 8:30 a 14:30

Sábado de 9:30 a 13:00

Domingo cerrado

Dentro de la oficina de Correos, yo busco la ventanilla de envío de paquetes y me coloco en la fila. Hay tres personas delante de mí.

Mientras espero mi turno para ser atendido, pienso en Victoria. Todas las semanas, suelo escribir a Victoria una carta. Le cuento la vida sencilla que tengo en Remu, que quiero vender muchos cuadros para poder comprar la casa de mis sueños. Ella responde pronto y me cuenta que está feliz trabajando en Lugo, que tiene muchos amigos y se lo pasa bien, aunque no le gusta el clima porque en Lugo hace más frío y llueve más que en Valencia.

El cumpleaños de Victoria es el veintidós de septiembre. Por eso le envío un regalo: una pulsera de conchas de la tienda de Mercedes. Yo sé que le va a gustar mucho porque a ella le encanta el mar, igual que a mí.

Miro el reloj, son las dos y veinticinco. Es mi turno.

La empleada mira su reloj. Antes de que diga que está a punto de cerrar, le doy los buenos días.

Yo: Buenos días.

El Despertar

Arturo se despertó en medio del bosque. Tenía sangre en la cara y estaba tumbado en el suelo.

Intentó ponerse de pie. Al hacerlo, sintió un dolor fuerte que subía por la pierna hasta la rodilla. El mareo le hizo pensar que iba a desmayarse otra vez. Debía intentar caminar o, probablemente, moriría.

La oscuridad de la noche le hacía difícil ver algún objeto que pudiera ser útil. Se arrastró por el suelo hasta llegar a un árbol cercano. Allí, Arturo apoyó la espalda contra el tronco. No era confortable, pero era el único lugar donde descansar y ordenar sus ideas.

Sus ojos comenzaban a acostumbrarse a la oscuridad. Realmente solo uno de ellos podía hacerlo, ya que el otro estaba tan hinchado que le era imposible abrirlo con normalidad.

Vio varias ramas en el suelo. Pensó que sería una buena idea utilizar una de ellas como bastón. Volvió a intentar ponerse en pie y, esta vez, gracias a la ayuda de la rama, logró levantarse.

Al rodear el árbol, distinguió un hueco en uno de los lados del tronco.

Pensó que el agujero era bastante grande como para meterse dentro y resguardarse del frío. Para ello, colocó en el fondo del agujero un montón de hojas con la intención de hacerlo más confortable. Después, se introdujo en el orificio. Desde el interior, clavó en la tierra cinco ramas que había logrado recolectar. Las clavó en sentido vertical, por fuera del agujero, como una valla de protección.

Al poco rato de haberse quedado dormido, un ruido extraño lo despertó. Miró a través de las ramas y vio unos ojos que lo observaban. La cabeza del animal era enorme. En total mediría más de un metro y medio y debía de pesar, al menos, unos setenta kilos. Se fijó un poco más y pudo ver otro par de ojos brillantes y, al lado, otro par más. Una fuerte embestida logró que una de las ramas cayera al suelo dejando una vía libre hacia el hombre.

Entonces, otro de los animales le pisó la pierna herida. El hombre sintió un dolor tan intenso que no pudo evitar gritar. Con ese sonido, los tres jabalíes se alejaron asustados. En la huida, el hombre creyó ver a un zorro que, al parecer, había estado apartado del grupo, como un espectador que observaba la escena.

Cuando volvió la calma, Arturo sacó el brazo para recolocar la rama que el jabalí había tirado al suelo y la hincó en la tierra con fuerza. Estaba temblando, pero esta vez no era de frío, sino de miedo. Tras este suceso, logró dormir un poco antes de que los primeros rayos de sol iluminaran el bosque.

Entretanto, su mente intentaba recordar lo ocurrido durante las horas previas. Recordó los mensajes en el móvil, el trayecto en el coche, el engaño de Aurora, la cita con Rodrigo, la pelea. Todo empezaba a tener sentido.

RESUMEN CAPÍTULO 1

Arturo aparece en el bosque, está herido. Es de noche y todo está oscuro. El hombre intenta ponerse en pie, pero un dolor en su pierna se lo impide. Entonces busca una rama y la utiliza como bastón. Arturo pasa la noche en el interior de un agujero que hay en el tronco de un árbol. Esa misma noche es atacado por unos jabalíes. El hombre grita y los animales huyen. Junto a los jabalíes hay un zorro.

Al despertarse, por la mañana, Arturo empieza a recordar: el viaje en el coche hasta el bosque, el engaño de Aurora, la cita con Rodrigo, la pelea…

SUMMARY CHAPTER 1

Arturo appears in the forest, he is injured. It is nighttime and everything is dark. The man tries to stand up, but a pain in his leg prevents him from doing so. Then, he looks for a branch and he uses it as a walking stick. Arturo spends the night inside the hole that is in a tree's trunk. That night, he is attacked by some boars. The man screams and the animals run away. Next to the boars, there is a fox.

When he wakes up, in the morning, Arturo starts to remember: the trip by car to the forest, Aurora's trickery, the meeting with Rodrigo, the fight…

Aurora

La mañana estaba siendo tranquila en la comisaría. El inspector Ponce revisaba algunos casos pendientes, nada importante. Hacía meses que a la mesa del policía solo llegaban casos de vandalismo, algún robo de vehículos y otras minucias. No parecía que aquella mañana fuera a ser distinta de las demás hasta que, por la puerta de la comisaría, entró una mujer muy nerviosa.

—¡Mi marido ha desaparecido!

—Tranquilícese. Acompáñeme, por favor. Yo soy la oficial Susana García y estoy aquí para ayudarle. Siéntese en esa silla y cuénteme despacio qué ha sucedido —dice la oficial, a la vez que señala una de las sillas del fondo.

—Mi marido no ha venido esta noche a dormir a casa.

—Siéntese aquí. ¿Quiere un vaso de agua? ¿Una tila? —pregunta la oficial mientras trata de calmar a la mujer.

—Sí, un poco de agua, gracias.

—López, ¿puedes traer un vaso de agua para la señora, por favor? —pide a uno de sus compañeros—. Si le parece —habla esta vez mirando directamente a los ojos de la mujer—, yo le haré unas preguntas y usted me las va respondiendo.

—De acuerdo. Y, te lo ruego, no me trates de usted, me pone nerviosa y me hace mayor.

—Por supuesto. No hay problema —accede la oficial de policía—.

Bueno, como ya te he dicho antes, mi nombre es Susana García.

Justo en ese momento, López aparece con un vaso de plástico en una mano y un botellín de agua en la otra. Llena el vaso hasta la mitad y se lo ofrece a la mujer. Esta se lo agradece con una sonrisa y se lo bebe casi de un solo trago.

—Gracias, López. Déjanos solas.

—Si necesitáis cualquier cosa, estoy aquí al lado —dice el agente mientras va camino de su mesa de trabajo.

—Veamos —dice la oficial con intención de retomar la conversación

—, ¿cómo te llamas?

—Me llamo Aurora Riu Montreal.

—Perfecto, Aurora. Y dices que tu marido no ha ido esta noche a dormir a casa, ¿es así?

—En efecto. Así es.

—¿Es la primera vez? Quiero decir, ¿esto había sucedido antes?

—¡Jamás! Ya te he dicho que le ha pasado algo. ¡Estoy segura! —exclama mientras vuelve a llenar el vaso de agua.

—¿Recuerdas cuándo y a qué hora lo viste por última vez, Aurora?

—Fue ayer, serían sobre las cuatro y media de la tarde. Lo sé porque poco antes había terminado el hombre del tiempo de dar la predicción meteorológica en la televisión.

—Entiendo —dice la oficial García mientras anota algo en un cuaderno que está sobre la mesa.

—Yo fui a la cocina, justo entonces su teléfono móvil vibró varias veces —prosigue Aurora con su relato—. Él fue al dormitorio y, al volver, me dijo que tenía que irse. Yo le pregunté adónde iba a esas horas y con quién, pero no me contestó. Se cambió de camisa, cogió las llaves del coche y salió de casa. Esa fue la última vez que lo vi.

—¿A qué se dedica tu marido, Aurora?

—Es transportista. Camionero. Pero últimamente hace repartos con la furgoneta.

—Ajá, comprendo.

—Y, ¿qué te hace sospechar que le ha pasado algo?

—Fui al dormitorio y descubrí que la pistola no estaba en el cajón, entonces intuí que mi marido estaba metido en algo peligroso.

—¿Tu marido tenía un arma?

—Sí, eso parece. La descubrí por casualidad. Fue hace unas pocas semanas, mientras hacía la limpieza en nuestra habitación. Al principio no le di importancia, creí que era para ir protegido en el camión.

—¿Crees que él sería capaz de utilizarla contra alguien? —pregunta la oficial García.

—No lo sé. Imagino que, si está en peligro, sí haría uso de ella, supongo.

—Aurora, ¿hay algo más que quieras contarme?

—Es mi marido. Es un buen hombre, de verdad. Algunas veces transportaba drogas. Él me lo ocultaba, pero yo lo sabía. Pequeñas cantidades, ¿entiendes? No es un narcotraficante. A veces pasa mucho tiempo sin trabajar y necesitamos dinero. Esa era una manera de obtener dinero de una manera fácil —confiesa la mujer llorando—. ¿Crees que lo que le ha pasado tiene que ver con el mundo de las drogas?

—No lo sé, Aurora —responde la oficial moviendo de un lado para otro la cabeza—. ¿Cómo se llama tu marido? Comprobaremos si el arma está registrada a su nombre.

La oficial hace un gesto a su compañero para que se acerque.

—Se llama Arturo Obleas Martos.

—Comprueba estos datos, López —solicita la oficial a su colega a la vez que le entrega una hoja de papel que acaba de arrancar de su cuaderno de notas—. Si encuentras algo, házmelo saber enseguida.

—Ahora mismo —responde él mientras se dirige a su mesa para teclear los datos en el ordenador.

RESUMEN CAPÍTULO 2

Aurora entra muy nerviosa a la comisaría. Quiere denunciar que su marido ha desaparecido. La oficial Susana García interroga a Aurora y descubre que Arturo, el marido de Aurora, recibió un mensaje en su móvil y se fue de casa sin decir a dónde iba. También descubre que Arturo tenía una pistola y que algunas veces traficaba con droga.

SUMMARY CHAPTER 2

Aurora goes into the police station very nervous. She wants to report that her husband was missing. Officer Susana García interrogates Aurora and discovers that Arturo, Aurora's husband, received a message on his mobile phone and he left home without saying where he was going. She also discovers that Arturo had a gun and that he dealt drugs sometimes.

El Cadáver del Puente

CAPÍTULO 1

E l inspector Ponce está en su casa. Son poco más de las tres de la madrugada y él acaba de dormirse. El teléfono suena. La habitación está a oscuras. El hombre enciende la luz de la mesilla y mira a Paula, que aún sigue dormida a su lado. En la pantalla del teléfono ve que se trata de una llamada de Robles.

Si le llama a estas horas es que debe ser algo importante. Se levanta y se dirige al salón para no despertar a la mujer.

—Buenas noches, dime Robles ¿Qué sucede? —dice en un susurro.

—Buenas noches, inspector. Lamento llamar tan tarde, pero ha aparecido un cadáver colgado del puente de Santa Catalina —responde Robles.

—Colgado del puente —repite— ¿Se sabe si tiene signos de violencia?

—No, jefe. Todo apunta a que se trata de un suicidio, pero es muy pronto aún para afirmarlo —argumenta con cautela el policía.

Robles sabe muy bien que al inspector Ponce no le gusta dar nada por sentado hasta que todas las piezas del puzle están perfectamente encajadas. Si no quiere que le deje fuera del caso, debe de andar con cuidado en cada una de las frases y de las hipótesis que formula. Para Ponce todo policía debe ser riguroso, incluso considerándose a sí mismo sospechoso hasta que las pruebas apunten a un verdadero culpable. Una de sus frases preferidas es:

"los hechos nunca hablan por sí solos, somos nosotros quienes les ponemos voz"

—Acabo de llegar a la zona alertado por la llamada de alarma de una mujer.

Vivo cerca de aquí, me pilla muy cerca de casa —continúa informando el agente.

—Pues me avisas tarde, Robles, muy tarde —replica Ponce de mal humor.

—Lo lamento inspector.

766

—No me vengas con lamentos. Me pongo un pantalón y una camiseta y, en cinco minutos, salgo para allí. Que nadie toque nada. ¿Me has oído, Robles?

—Por supuesto inspector.

Cuando el inspector Ponce llega al puente ya hay un puñado de curiosos y un buen número de policías. Nada le pone de peor humor que ser el último en enterarse de un suceso que ocurre en su ciudad.

—¿Ha llegado ya la forense y los de la científica? —pregunta Ponce.

—Aún no, jefe.

—Avísame en cuanto les veas llegar. ¿Me has oído, Robles? En cuanto les veas llegar, ni antes ni después.

—Sí, señor —responde Robles con tono militar cuando considera que Ponce está lo suficientemente lejos como para que no pueda oírle.

El inspector de policía llega al lugar de los hechos a las tres y veintinueve de la madrugada, tan solo quince minutos después de recibir la llamada de su ayudante.

Ponce analiza desde lo alto del puente el cuerpo que sigue suspendido en el aire, colgado de una cuerda que lo sujeta por el cuello. Según le han informado, se trata de un hombre de raza blanca. Delgado y de escasa altura.

El pelo es de color castaño claro y los ojos azules. Viste un traje gris, camisa azul cielo y corbata a rayas. Los zapatos son de piel, de color negro y están adornados con una hebilla plateada en el lateral. En los puños de la camisa lleva unos gemelos con las iniciales L.S.

Raúl Ponce saca su libreta y comienza a anotar cada uno de los detalles que le parecen importantes, los que se ven a simple vista y los que nadie, salvo él, es capaz de percibir.

— Inspector, la forense ya está aquí — avisa obediente Robles.

— Gracias. Voy ahora mismo.

— Buenas noches, monitor Ponce. Menuda nochecita de perros que hace hoy — responde ella sin demostrar que, hace apenas un cuarto de hora, dormía con él en la cama — Diles a tus chicos que se mantengan alejados del perímetro. No quiero que nadie altere la escena.

— Buenas noches, soy el Inspector de policía Raúl Ponce — se presenta — Soy el encargado de llevar a cabo la investigación sobre los hechos que rodean esta muerte.

— Buenas noches, monitor. Aún estoy conmocionada.

— Por supuesto monitor — contesta ella algo recelosa por la insinuación de que sus respuestas pudieran resultar falsas.

— Lo digo porque, a veces, el afán de los testigos por ayudar a la policía falsea sus declaraciones. De una manera no intencionada, por supuesto — aclara el monitor — Vamos a ver, creo que usted fue la que, al observar la existencia de un hombre colgando del puente, llamó a la policía, ¿me equivoco?

— No, monitor. En efecto así fue. Vengo de una *holiday* y de camino a casa he visto algo raro allá abajo — dice la mujer señalando el lugar en el que se encuentra el cuerpo.

—Cuando usted llegó ¿el cuerpo estaba en la misma posición que lo vemos ahora? —interroga a la mujer que enciende de nuevo un cigarrillo.

—Sí, ya le digo que vi cómo una sombra se balanceaba en el andamio, como un péndulo. Igual que se ve ahora. ¡Dios mío! ¡Es una imagen horrible! —consigue decir la testigo mientras se tapa la cara con las manos.

—¿Vio usted algo raro? Alguien corriendo por los alrededores, alguna otra persona por las cercanías, no sé, algo que recuerde y que le haya podido llamar la atención.

—¿Otra persona? No, no vi nada extraño. A estas horas todo está muy solitario — contesta ella recomponiéndose al instante alertada por esta indagación— ¿Por qué me consulta sobre eso? ¿Cree usted que no se trata de un suicidio?

—Aún no sabemos nada, señora. Pero en este trabajo no se puede descartar nunca ninguna hipótesis.

—Pobre hombre —dice ella en voz baja, como sumida en sus propios pensamientos.

—Bueno, de momento esto es todo. Por favor, deje sus datos a mi compañero. Su nombre, apellidos, número de teléfono y dirección. Tal vez tengamos que volver a llamarle para hablar con usted en comisaría. Si recuerda algo, cualquier cosa, por insignificante que le parezca, haga el favor de llamar y preguntar por mí. Esta es mi tarjeta de visita. Ahora puede irse a casa. Gracias por su colaboración.

—De nada inspector, estoy a su disposición para cualquier cosa en la que pueda ayudar —se despide la testigo dando otra calada al cigarrillo.

RESUMEN CAPÍTULO 1

El inspector Ponce recibe una llamada mientras está durmiendo. El agente Robles le informa de que ha aparecido un hombre colgado en el puente de Santa Catalina. El inspector, la policía científica y la forense analizan el cuerpo. Todo apunta a que se trata de un suicidio. Raúl Ponce interroga a la mujer que ha llamado por teléfono a la policía para avisar de la existencia de un cadáver. El cuerpo estaba colgando de la estructura que sujeta el puente que estaba dañado por el último temporal. No parece haber ningún testigo que haya visto nada fuera de lo normal.

SUMMARY CHAPTER 1

Inspector Ponce receives a phone call while he's sleeping. Agent Robles informs him that a man has appeared hanged on Santa Catalina Bridge. The inspector, the scientific police and the coroner analyze the body. Everything indicates that it has been a suicide. Raúl Ponce interrogates the woman who called the police to notify them about the existence of the corpse. The body was hanging from the structure that holds on the bridge which was damaged due to the last storm. No witness seems to have seen anything unusual.

CAPÍTULO 2

Por la mañana, la noticia de la aparición de un hombre colgando del andamio del puente de Santa Catalina aparece en la portada de todos los periódicos digitales. Los teléfonos de la comisaría no paran de sonar. Madres que preguntan por sus hijos que aún no han vuelto a casa tras una noche de juerga, esposas preocupadas por maridos que están de viaje, pero no contestan a las llamadas de teléfono. Todo el mundo quiere saber la identidad del fallecido, unos para poder llorarle una vez confirmada la fatal noticia y otros para respirar aliviados por no ser uno de los suyos.

El inspector Ponce junta a todo el equipo en su despacho. Quiere mantener una reunión de urgencia. Es necesario poner en común la información que tienen hasta el momento y convocar una rueda de prensa. Los periodistas comienzan a hacer especulaciones sobre el caso y la población empieza a alarmarse. Ponce pone al día a sus ayudantes acerca de las últimas novedades. El cadáver ha sido identificado como Luis Solís, un empresario muy conocido en la zona. El señor Solís era dueño de una fábrica de materiales para la construcción fundada por su abuelo en el año mil novecientos veinte. Por suerte, la empresa pudo reabrirse tras la Guerra Civil, pero con la crisis actual no habían corrido la misma suerte, en la actualidad la fábrica estaba al borde de la quiebra. Las deudas contraídas durante los últimos años eran de mucho importe. Además, todos en la ciudad sabían que Luis tampoco estaba pasando por un buen momento personal. Hacía solo dos semanas que su mujer se había presentado en el juzgado para interponer una demanda de divorcio. El perfil psicológico del hombre era el de una persona desesperada y con demasiados problemas que afrontar.

—Parece que la teoría del suicidio se confirma —aventura a decir la sargento de la unidad, sin percatarse de la mirada cortante de Ponce ante una afirmación tan temprana.

—Supongo Sargento que esa afirmación es debida a la investigación que ha llevado a cabo con familia, empleados, socio, amigos y conocidos del finado.

Y que ahora tan amablemente nos va a explicar a todos los aquí presentes —ironiza Ponce.

—Bueno, inspector, yo…

—¿Me quiere decir que aún no ha realizado ninguna pesquisa sargento? —pregunta complacido él.

—En principio todas las evidencias apuntan a que el hombre estaba desesperado —insiste la sargento sin saber cómo arreglar el enfado de su jefe.

—Tenía problemas económicos y familiares, es un caso bastante claro.

—Entonces sargento explique a sus compañeros por qué Luis Solís llevaba más de tres mil euros en la cartera. ¿No le parece una cifra un tanto excesiva para alguien que piensa acabar con su vida? ¿Cree usted que tal vez fuera a sobornar a

San Pedro al llegar al cielo para que le abriera las puertas a pesar de ser un suicida?

Viaje a Singapur

CAPÍTULO 1

Sara prepara su maleta para viajar a Singapur. Le gusta hacer su equipaje con tiempo, por eso, siempre que puede, pide ayuda a su madre, quien le echa una mano con los preparativos antes de cada viaje. Las dos, madre e hija, se llevan realmente bien. Sara tiene mucha práctica en esto de hacer y deshacer equipajes. Es azafata, igual que su madre. Ambas trabajan en una gran compañía aérea, la madre como azafata de tierra y Sara como azafata de vuelo. A pesar de que Sara sabe que para pasar fuera de casa un fin de semana solo necesita una camisa, una blusa y un pantalón vaquero, le gusta pensar que cada viaje es una nueva aventura, por eso prefiere ir bien preparada. Aunque en Singapur el calor es asfixiante en esta época del año, siempre es bueno llevar una chaqueta o un jersey. Por la noche hace más frío.

Pero de todo lo que lleva, lo que más espacio le ocupa es el neceser, nunca pueden faltar las cremas, el cepillo de dientes, el peine y un frasco de colonia o perfume.

—Cariño, llama a casa al llegar a Singapur, por favor —le pide su madre.

—Sí, mamá. No te preocupes. Te prometo que nada más llegar al hotel, te llamo por teléfono.

Las dos mujeres se despiden en el portal de la casa con un abrazo. El taxi espera en la puerta. Se hace tarde.

—Buenas tardes —dice Sara al conductor.

—Buenas tardes. ¿A dónde va? —pregunta el taxista.

—Al aeropuerto, por favor. Mi vuelo sale a las cinco.

—No hay problema. Seguro que llegamos a tiempo, hoy es domingo y a esta hora no hay mucho tráfico.

—Muchas gracias.

—No hay por qué darlas —contesta él con una sonrisa en el rostro mientras pisa el acelerador.

Sara mira a través de la ventanilla y levanta la mano para decir adiós a la figura ya casi borrosa de su madre.

En el aeropuerto, un ir y venir de personas recorre los pasillos. Saluda con la mano a los compañeros de trabajo que están en los mostradores. Les grita ¡buenas tardes! Un saludo al que ellos responden con un alegre ¡hola, Sara!

—Perdón, ¿me deja pasar, por favor? —dice a las personas que esperan en la cola de facturación y que le impiden el paso hacia la sala donde se reúne la tripulación del avión.

—Muchas gracias —les responde cuando estos apartan sus carritos de equipaje.

Cuando por fin consigue llegar a la sala, ya es la hora de subir al avión y comprobar que todo está en orden. Al poco rato, los altavoces anuncian que los pasajeros del vuelo 6739W ya se pueden acercar a la puerta de embarque.

Una vez todos pasan el control, Sara los recibe en la puerta del avión.

—Buenas tardes. Bienvenidos a bordo —les dice.

—Hola, buenas tardes —responden educadamente.

—Que tengan un buen vuelo —les desea con una sonrisa.

—Muchas gracias.

Comprueban la lista de pasajeros. Está todo correcto. Retiran la escalerilla y cierran las puertas del avión. Las azafatas ayudan a colocar los equipajes en su sitio y aconsejan a los pasajeros que se sienten en sus asientos y se abrochen los cinturones. El viaje a Singapur es largo. Mejor estar cómodo.

Tras diez horas de vuelo, por fin se ven los edificios de la ciudad. Los pasajeros vuelven a sus asientos y de nuevo se abrochan sus cinturones de seguridad. En España son las tres de la madrugada, sin embargo, en Singapur ya son las diez de la mañana. Sara solo piensa en llegar al hotel y descansar.

Martín y Teresa le proponen comer en alguno de los restaurantes que tiene la ciudad.

—Vamos, Sara, anímate. Ven a comer con nosotros. Martín promete portarse bien, ja, ja, ja —ríe Teresa.

—Siempre me porto bien, queridas. ¿Alguna queja? —pregunta él mientras guiña un ojo a Sara.

—De acuerdo. Voy al hotel, me ducho, me cambio de ropa y a las doce nos vemos en la recepción. ¿Os parece bien?

—¡Perfecto! —responden a coro los dos.

—Nos vemos en el hall de tu hotel a las doce en punto —confirma Teresa.

Martín y Teresa se alojan en el Hotel Arts, sin embargo, Sara tiene una habitación en el Hotel Embajador. Lo más usual es estar todos juntos en el mismo alojamiento, pero esta vez, por problemas con la reserva, no puede ser así.

En el taxi, camino del hotel, Sara observa la silueta de los enormes edificios que forman un sky-line increíble. Singapur es una ciudad mágica, tiene algo especial. Sara no sabe qué es, pero siente algo distinto, una emoción interior que no es capaz de describir.

Tras pagar y dar las gracias al taxista, recoge su equipaje del maletero del coche. Después se dirige a la recepción donde una chica de rasgos asiáticos, con la melena recogida en una coleta, le atiende de manera muy amable.

—Buenos días. Bienvenida a Singapur. ¿Qué tal el vuelo? —dice la recepcionista, en un correcto español, al observar que Sara va vestida de azafata.

—Buenos días —responde jovial —El vuelo fantástico, muchas gracias.

—¿Tiene reserva en el hotel?

—Sí, a nombre de Sara Tan —se trata de una reserva de mi compañía aérea.

—En efecto, hay una reserva de una habitación doble uso individual para usted. Si es tan amable de darme su pasaporte, por favor —solicita la simpática recepcionista.

—Por supuesto —Sara saca su pasaporte del bolso —aquí lo tiene.

—Gracias.

Después de anotar los datos en el ordenador y rellenar la ficha de entrada, la chica le da una llave electrónica a Sara y le devuelve su documentación.

—Es la habitación número doce, en el primer piso. Al fondo del pasillo está el ascensor. La cena se sirve a las siete y el desayuno es de seis y media a diez de la mañana.

—De acuerdo. Muchas gracias por todo —se despide Sara para dirigirse hacia la dirección indicada.

El botones sube con ella en el ascensor. En unos segundos están en la primera planta. Un cartel indica que su habitación está hacia la derecha. Cuando llegan delante de la puerta que tiene un cartel con el número doce, Sara posa su tarjeta sobre el lector y oye un click que le indica que ya puede acceder al interior. Da una propina al conserje y tras cerrar la puerta se tumba en la cama. De repente siente todo el cansancio. Está agotada. Mira el reloj y recuerda que en breve sus compañeros de trabajo, Teresa y Martín, van a ir a buscarla, así que tiene que darse un poco de prisa.

Pasa más de diez minutos en la ducha. Allí siente cómo el agua templada que le cae por los hombros le reactiva de nuevo. Abre la maleta, coge el vaquero y una de las camisas, y se viste. Peina su larga melena frente al espejo, se aplica algo de maquillaje en la cara, unas gotas de perfume y un poco de carmín en los labios y ya parece otra persona.

Sara es una joven muy atractiva, los hombres se giran a mirarla cuando va por la calle. De hecho, su compañero Martín no deja de tirarle los tejos todo el tiempo y, aunque ella también siente cierta atracción por el chico, hay algo dentro de Sara que le impide dar el paso definitivo para empezar una relación con él.

De inmediato recuerda haber prometido a su madre llamar a casa al llegar a Singapur. Debe de estar preocupada. Sara busca su móvil y marca el número de teléfono con el prefijo internacional. Ahora en España son casi las cinco de la madrugada.

—¿Diga? —se escucha una voz entre somnolienta y angustiada al otro lado del teléfono.

—Mamá, soy yo —contesta Sara de inmediato.

—¡Cariño! ¿Cómo estás? ¿Estás bien?

—Bien, mamá. Estate tranquila. Estoy en el hotel y ahora voy a comer con Teresa y con Martín.

—Ten mucho cuidado, ya sabes que Singapur es una ciudad enorme y…

—¡Mamá! —Le interrumpe Sara —Ya soy mayorcita, y sé cuidarme. Vamos, descansa y duerme un poco. Mañana por la noche sale el vuelo de regreso a Madrid, así que nos vemos en un par de días.

—Muy bien, cariño. Te quiero. Un beso. Cuídate. Y si tienes cualquier problema, ya sabes, me llamas. Más besos.

—Un beso —responde Sara divertida.

Las despedidas de su madre parecen no terminar nunca. Incluso cuando está a punto de colgar el teléfono, sigue oyendo un hilo de voz cargado de precauciones y buenos deseos.

Faltan cinco minutos para las doce. Es hora de bajar al hall del hotel. Nada más abrirse la puerta del ascensor, ve la sonrisa de Martín que ilumina su rostro.

RESUMEN CAPÍTULO 1

Sara es azafata de vuelo y prepara su viaje a Singapur. Ella está muy unida a su madre. Su madre también es azafata, pero de tierra. Sara coge un taxi para ir al aeropuerto. Antes, Sara promete a su madre llamar en cuanto aterrice. El viaje dura diez horas en avión. Martín y Teresa son los compañeros de trabajo de Sara. Los tres jóvenes viajan juntos, pero Sara está en un hotel diferente al de sus amigos. Ella está en el Hotel Embajador. Cuando llegan a Singapur, Sara, Martín y Teresa deciden salir a comer y a visitar la ciudad.

Quedan a las doce en el hall del hotel de Sara. Martín está enamorado de Sara y ella siente cierta atracción por él, pero algo le impide comenzar una relación.

SUMMARY CHAPTER 1

Sara is a flight attendant and she is preparing for her trip to Singapore. She is very close to her mother. Her mother is also a stewardess but on land. Sara takes a taxi to the airport. Before that, Sara promises her mother to phone her as soon as she lands. The trip lasts ten hours by plane. Martin and Teresa are Sara's workmates. The three young people travel together, but Sara stays in a different hotel from her friends. She is at the Hotel Embajador. When they arrive in Singapore, Sara, Martin and Teresa decide to go out to have lunch and visit the city. They are meeting each other at 12 o'clock at Sara's hotel hall. Martin is in love with Sara and she feels a certain attraction for him, but something prevents her from starting a relationship.

CAPÍTULO 2

Los tres jóvenes caminan por las calles de la ciudad, Teresa quiere visitar algunas tiendas de ropa y Martín propone comer en un restaurante que en internet tiene muy buenas críticas.

Para Sara es su primera vez en Singapur, no así para Martín y Teresa, para ellos esta es ya su quinta vez. Recorren a pie el antiguo distrito colonial, pasean por el parque Padang y se adentran en Chinatown. Muy cerca de allí está el restaurante en el que van a comer.

El bullicio de las calles pone de buen humor a los chicos que deciden visitar esa misma tarde el Templo Thian Hock Keng, el más antiguo de Singapur.

Después se acercan al parque de Merlion, donde se encuentra el símbolo de la ciudad, una representación de una criatura mitológica, mitad león, mitad pez.

Desde allí Martín, aficionado a la fotografía, saca unas maravillosas panorámicas de Marina Bay. Con un brillo especial en los ojos, el muchacho le pide a Teresa que le haga una fotografía junto a Sara, él la agarra por la cintura y acerca su mejilla a la de Sara.

—¡Una sonrisa! —exclama Teresa —Muy guapos, los dos. Esta foto va a hacer historia, ja, ja, ja.

Enfermedad y Medicina

n los últimos días, Alejandro ha **presentado** dificultades para **respirar**.

E Tiene 30 años y es un poco extraño que alguien de su edad tenga este **síntoma**. Tal vez, si fuera **fumador**, las cosas **tendrían más sentido**, pero Alejandro nunca ha fumado un **cigarrillo** en su vida. Así que decidió ir a ver a su **médico** para **consultarle**.

Afortunadamente, pudo **programar una cita** para esa misma semana y hacerse revisar. Ya en el **consultorio** del médico, hubo un período de espera considerable antes de que el médico pudiera verlo. Alejandro había llevado un libro para leer en la sala de espera, pero le **resultaba** difícil **concentrarse**, dada su condición. Después de 20 minutos, comenzó a sentir un **dolor de cabeza desgarrador**. **Previendo** tal situación, tenía **analgésicos de venta libre** en su automóvil. Después de ir a buscarlos y de volver rápidamente, **tragó** las **pastillas** con agua del **bebedero** y dio un gran **suspiro de alivio**.

La **enfermera** llamó a Alejandro al consultorio 107 e hizo algunos **procedimientos de rutina**. Le tomó la **presión arterial**, **midió** su **altura** y su **peso** y le preguntó sobre el historial de problemas de **salud** de su familia.

Alejandro tenía la suerte de no tener problemas de salud **hereditarios**. No tenía que preocuparse por **enfermedades cardíacas**, cáncer, diabetes ni artritis. La enfermera también le preguntó sobre todos y cada uno de los **medicamentos actuales** que estaba tomando, pero él respondió que no tomaba ningún medicamento.

Después de registrar la información de Alejandro, la enfermera salió del consultorio y le dijo que el médico estaría con él **en breve**. **Apenas** dos minutos después, se encontró cara a cara con el hombre que podía ayudarle a aliviar su condición en poco tiempo. Ese hombre era el Dr. González y era muy amable. Los dos conversaron sobre el problema respiratorio de Alejandro y Alejandro entró en más detalles sobre su condición.

Experimentaba dolores en el **pecho** durante todo el día, pero no tenía palpitaciones. Tenía un poco de **tos**, pero no **respiración sibilante**. El médico colocó su **estetoscopio** sobre el pecho de Alejandro y le **pidió** que respirara **profundamente** varias veces.

Con unos pocos **asentimientos** breves, parecía que el Dr. González había llegado a un **diagnóstico** final. Era **asma**. Le dijo que era **común** que los adultos, y no solo los niños, **desarrollaran** asma. Un **inhalador frenaría** sus síntomas de inmediato, pero era un medicamento que debía tomar por el resto de su vida para **mantener** los síntomas **a raya**.

Con la **receta** del Dr. González, Alejandro **se dirigió** hacia la **farmacia** para recibir su inhalador. La dejó en el **mostrador de atención al cliente** y luego comenzó a **pasear** por la tienda. **Pasaría algún tiempo** antes de que su receta estuviera lista, por lo que, mientras tanto, examinó los diversos medicamentos que había en los **estantes**. Vio **toneladas** de productos para **tratar resfriados**, **alergias** y **gripe**. Incluso había tratamientos de venta libre para el **estreñimiento** y la diarrea.

El **farmacéutico** llamó a Alejandro, ya era hora de recoger su receta y regresar a casa. Mientras estaba en su automóvil en el **estacionamiento**, Alejandro tomó su primera **dosis** e instantáneamente se sintió mucho mejor.

Le resultaba mucho más fácil respirar y sus dolores en el pecho disminuyeron. Estaba **agradecido** por el **milagro** de la **ciencia** y las medicinas modernas.

A lo largo de la prueba, Alejandro se había puesto a pensar en lo importante que eran para él su salud y su **cuerpo**. Estar en un estado constante de mala salud le **generaría** una muy mala **calidad de vida**. Su **dieta** sería el primer paso para comenzar a hacer mejoras.

VOCABULARIO

1.-enfermedad y medicina = illness and medicine

2.-presentar = to present, to introduce

3.-**respirar** = to breathe

4.-**síntoma** = symptom

5.-**fumador** = smoker

6.-**tener sentido** = to make sense

7.-**cigarrillo** = cigarette

8.-**médico** = doctor

9.-**consultar** = to consult

10.-**programar una cita** = to schedule an appointment

11.-**consultorio** = office, doctor's office

12.-**resultar** = to turn out, to end up

13.-**concentrar** = to concentrate

14.-**dolor de cabeza** = headache

15.-**desgarrador** = excruciating

16.-**prever** = to anticipate

17.-**analgésico** = painkiller

18.-**de venta libre** = over-the-counter

19.-**tragar** = to swallow

20.-**pastilla** = pill

21.-**bebedero** = water fountain

22.-**suspiro de alivio** = sigh of relief

23.-**enfermera** = nurse

24.-**procedimiento de rutina** = routine procedure

25.-**presión arterial** = blood pressure

26.-**medir** = to measure

27.-**altura** = height

28.-**peso** = weight

29.-**salud** = health

30.-**hereditario** = hereditary

31.-**enfermedad cardíaca** = heart disease

32.-**medicamento** = medicine

33.-**actual** = current

34.-**en breve** = shortly

35.-**apenas** = just, barely

36.-**experimentar** = to experience

37.-**pecho** = chest

38.-**tos** = cough

*39.-respiración sibilante = **wheezing***

40.-**estetoscopio** = stethoscope

41.-**pedir** = to ask for

42.-**profundamente** = deeply

*43.-asentimiento = **nod***

44.-**diagnóstico** = diagnosis

45.-**asma** = asthma

46.-**común** = common

47.-**desarrollar** = to develop

48.-**inhalador** = inhaler

49.-**frenar** = to curb

50.-**mantener a raya** = to keep at bay

51.-**receta** = perscription

52.-**dirigirse** = to head towards

53.-**farmacia** = pharmacy

*54.-mostrador de atención al cliente = **customer service desk***

55.-**pasear** = to go for a walk

56.-**pasar algún tiempo** = to spend some time, to pass some time

57.-**estante** = shelf

58.-**tonelada** = ton

59.-**tratar** = to treat

60.-**resfriado** = cold (illness)

61.-**alergia** = allergy

62.-**gripe** = flu

63.-**estreñimiento** = constipation

64.-**farmacéutico** = pharmacist

65.-**estacionamiento** = parking lot

66.-**dosis** = dose

67.-**agradecido** = grateful

68.-**milagro** = miracle

69.-**ciencia** = science

70.-**cuerpo** = body

71.-**generar** = to generate

72.-**calidad de vida** = quality of life

73.-**dieta** = diet

Comprehension Questions

1.-¿Qué tipo de fumador era Alejandro?

a.-Solo fumaba en eventos sociales.

b.-Fumaba un paquete al día.

c.-Sufría de enfisema.

d.-Nunca había fumado un cigarrillo en su vida.

2.-¿Cómo se libró Alejandro de su dolor de cabeza?

a.-El doctor lo curó.

b.-Tomó analgésicos.

c.-Usó un inhalador.

d.-La enfermera le masajeó la frente.

3.-¿Cuál de las siguientes NO se considera una enfermedad grave?

a.-Enfermedad cardíaca

b.-Tos

c.-Diabetes

d.-Cáncer

4.-¿Qué herramienta utiliza un médico para escuchar los sonidos internos de un cuerpo humano o animal?

a.-Prescripción

b.-Estetoscopio

c.-Diagnóstico

d.-Síntomas

5.-¿Qué hace un inhalador?

a.-Mantiene a raya los síntomas del asma.

b.-Evita que el asma se propague a otras personas.

c.-Evita que el asma se convierta en cáncer.

d.-Cura el asma por completo.

ENGLISH TRANSLATION

For the past few days, Alejandro has had some difficulty breathing. He was 30 years old, and it was a bit odd for someone of his age to have this symptom. Maybe if he was a smoker, things would make more sense, but Alejandro has never smoked a cigarette in his life. He decided to go see his doctor about it.

Luckily, he was able to schedule an appointment that very week and get himself checked out. At the doctor's office, there was a considerable waiting period before you could be seen by the physician. Alejandro brought a book to read in the waiting room, but he found it hard to focus for very long, given his condition. After 20 minutes, he started to get a splitting headache. In anticipation of such a scenario, he kept over-the-counter pain relievers in his car. Following a quick trip and back, he washed down the pills with water from the water fountain and took a big sigh of relief.

The nurse called Alejandro back to room 107 and did some routine check-up procedures. She took his blood pressure, measured his height and weight, and asked about his family's history of health problems. Alejandro was fortunate enough to not have any hereditary health issues. There was no heart disease, cancer, diabetes, nor arthritis to worry about. The nurse also asked about any and all current drugs he was taking, but he replied that he doesn't take any medication.

After Alejandro's information was recorded, the nurse left the examination room and told him the doctor would be with him shortly. Just two minutes later, he was finally face to face with the man who could help cure him in no time. Dr. González was his name, and he was as friendly as could be. The two chatted about Alejandro's breathing issue, and Alejandro went into more detail about his condition. Chest pains were occurring throughout the day, but there were no heart palpitations. There was a little coughing but no wheezing. The doctor placed his stethoscope on Alejandro's chest and asked him to take a couple of deep breaths.

With a few subtle nods, it appeared Dr. González had reached a final diagnosis. It was asthma. He said it was common for adults to develop asthma and not just children. An inhaler would immediately curb his symptoms, but it's a medication he would be required to take for the rest of his life to keep his symptoms at bay.

Carrying his prescription from Dr. González, Alejandro headed towards the pharmacy to receive his inhaler. He dropped it off at the customer service desk then started to wander around the store. It would be some time until his prescription was filled, so he browsed the various medicines on the store's shelves. He saw tons of products to treat colds, allergies, and the flu. There were even over-the-counter treatments for constipation and diarrhea.

The pharmacist called out to Alejandro, for it was time to pick up his prescription and head back home. While out in his car in the parking lot, Alejandro took his first dose and instantly felt much better. It became significantly easier to breathe, and his chest pains subsided. He was grateful for the miracle of modern science and medicine.

Throughout the ordeal, it occurred to Alejandro how important his health and body were to him. Being in a constant state of bad health would make for a very poor quality of life. His diet would be the first place to start making improvements.

Mi Familia

Me llamo Juan y mi hermana menor se llama Fabiola. Yo tengo quince años y ella tiene 8 años. Nosotros nacimos en Madrid, pero mi familia no ha vivido aquí todo el tiempo. Mi papá nació en Almería. Él se llama José. A él no le gusta mucho salir de la ciudad de Almería, así que él jamás pensó que él iba a vivir en Madrid.

Mi papá tenía 20 años cuando él viajó a Madrid. Tú te estarás preguntando porque él viajó a Madrid. Por mucho tiempo yo no lo sabía, pero luego mi papá me dijo que él había viajado a Madrid para estudiar en la universidad.

Mi papá estaba estudiando para convertirse en un profesor. Fue en la universidad donde mi papá conoció a mi mamá.

Mi mamá se llama Elsa. Ella nació y vivió en Madrid toda su vida. Al comienzo, ella no quería estudiar en la universidad, pero sus padres la convencieron. Ella estaba estudiando para convertirse en ingeniera. Ella es mayor que mi papá, pero sólo por dos años. Al comienzo, ellos fueron amigos y después ellos se enamoraron y se casaron.

Unos años después nací yo y luego mi hermana. Ahora todos vivimos en el centro de la ciudad de Madrid. Mis primos viven cerca de mi casa. Cuando quiero jugar fútbol con ellos, sólo tengo que pedir permiso a mis padres y caminar dos cuadras. Mi tía siempre nos deja jugar en su patio o también a veces vamos a un campo de fútbol.

Mis abuelos nos visitan de vez en cuando. Ellos siempre nos traen muchos juguetes y regalos. Mi abuela Francisca siempre me da un poco de dinero cada vez que ella viene. Mi abuelo Jorge sabe hacer pasteles, por eso él siempre trae un pastel de chocolate enorme para todos.

Mi perrito, Rayo, es muy juguetón. A él le encanta jugar conmigo y con mi hermana todos los días. Yo lo paseo todos los días después de hacer mi tarea.

Mi papá me ayuda a bañarlo porque si yo no puedo hacerlo sólo. A mi hermana también le encanta jugar con nuestro perrito.

Mi familia tal vez no sea muy grande, pero todos nos queremos y nos ayudamos cuando tenemos problemas. Somos muy felices estando juntos y espero seguir viviendo en esta casa con mi familia por mucho más tiempo.

SUMMARY IN SPANISH

En esta pequeña historia, Juan nos presenta a su familia, compuesta por su hermana, sus padres, sus abuelos y muchos más. Mientras él describe a su familia, él nos cuenta como sobre cómo sus padres se conocieron, qué hace cuando va a la casa de sus primos, y lo que sus abuelos hacen cada vez que ellos vienen a visitarlo. Al final, José nos presenta al último miembro de su familia y él nos cuenta lo que él y su hermana hacen para mantenerlo contento.

SUMMARY IN ENGLISH

In this little story, Juan introduces us to his family, made up of his sister, his parents, his grandparents, and many more. While he describes his family, he tells us about how his parents met, what he does when he goes to his cousins' house, and what his grandparents do every time they come to visit him. In the end, José introduces us to the last member of his family and he tells us what he and his sister do to keep him happy.

VOCABULARIO

1.-Hermana menor = Younger sister

2.-Quince = Fifteen

3.-Ocho= Eight

4.-Nació = He was born

5.-Preguntando = Wondering

6.-Viajando = Traveling

7.-Profesor = Teacher

8.-Ingeniera = Engineer (feminine)

9.-Convencieron = They convinced

10.-Enamoraron = They fell in love

11.-Casaron = They got married

12.-Primos = Cousins

13.-Cuadras = Blocks

14.-Caminar = Walk

15.-Jugar = Play

16.-Patio = Yard

17.-Juguetes = Toys

18.-Pastel de chocolate = Chocolate cake

19.-Perrito = Puppy

20.-Felices = Happy (plural)

Questions

1. ¿Cuántos años tiene Juan?

2. ¿Cuántos años tiene la hermana de Juan?

3. ¿Dónde vive Juan?

4. ¿Dónde nació el papá de Juan?

5. ¿Cuántos años tenía el papá de Juan cuando él se mudó a Madrid?

6. ¿Para qué viajó el papá de Juan a Madrid?

7. ¿Cómo se llama la mamá de Juan?

8. ¿Dónde se conocieron los padres de Juan?

9. ¿Qué hace Juan cada vez que va a la casa de sus primos?

10. ¿Cómo se llaman los abuelos de Juan?

11. ¿Qué es lo que la abuela de Juan siempre le da?

12. ¿Qué es lo que siempre trae el abuelo de Juan?

13. ¿Cómo se llama el perro de Juan?

14. ¿Qué hace la familia de Juan con el perrito?

Answers

1. Juan tiene quince años.

2. La hermana de Juan tiene ocho años.

3. Juan vive en Madrid

4. El papá de Juan nació en Almería

5. El papá de Juan tenía 20 años cuando él se mudó a Madrid

6. El papá de Juan viajo a Madrid para estudiar en la universidad

7. La mamá de Juan se llama Elsa

8. Los padres de Juan se conocieron en la universidad

9. Él juega fútbol en el patio o van a jugar fútbol en un campo deportivo

10. Los abuelos de Juan se llaman Francisca y Jorge

11. La abuela de Juan siempre le da dinero

12. El abuelo de Juan siempre trae un pastel de chocolate

13. El perro de Juan se llama Rayo

14. Ellos juegan con él, lo pasean, y lo bañan.

Mi Mejor Amigo – My Best Friend

Yo me llamo Iván. Yo aún recuerdo cuando conocí a mi mejor amigo. Mi mejor amigo se llama Roberto y hemos sido amigos por casi 10 años.

Nosotros nos conocimos en la escuela secundaria cuando yo tenía 14 años.

Era la primera vez que yo atendía esa escuela. Nunca antes había estudiado en esa escuela. Yo estaba muy nervioso y no quería ir a estudiar. Mis padres me convencieron y me dijeron que todo iba a estar bien. Ellos me dijeron que yo no necesitaba preocuparme y que tal vez iba a hacer nuevos amigos.

No recuerdo exactamente lo que estudié ese primer día de clases, pero sí recuerdo que muchos estudiantes me estaban mirando. Nadie quería hablar conmigo y eso me hacía sentir muy triste. A pesar de todo eso, los profesores fueron muy amables conmigo. Uno de los profesores se dio cuenta que yo estaba sólo y por eso él me ayudó.

El tiempo pasó volando y, sin darme cuenta, ya era la hora del receso.

Muchos estudiantes fueron al comedor para comer y para conversar con sus amigos. Lamentablemente, yo aún no tenía ningún amigo con quien conversar, por eso me senté sólo esperando a terminar mi almuerzo para regresar al salón de clases.

Sin darme cuenta, una persona me sentó junto a mí. Yo no sabía quién era, pero él me dijo que él me había visto cuando yo estaba en camino a la escuela. No entendía lo que él quiso decir con eso, pero él luego me lo explicó.

De seguro ya te habrás dado cuenta que la persona que me habló era Roberto.

Él me explicó que él vivía al frente de mi casa y que él me vio saliendo de mi casa cuando estaba yendo al colegio. Nunca habíamos hablado antes porque nosotros estudiábamos en escuelas diferentes antes de conocernos. Ahora, ambos estudiábamos en la misma escuela y teníamos las mismas clases.

Roberto era un poco diferente a mí. Él era más alto que yo y más fuerte. A él no le gustaba leer mucho, pero le encantaba el deporte. Nosotros también teníamos muchas cosas en común. Una de ellas es que a ambos nos gustaban las películas de acción. A él le gustaban las mismas películas que a mí y también nos gustaban las mismas canciones.

A mí también me encantaba hacer deporte, pero a mí me gustaba el fútbol mientras que a Roberto le gustaba el baloncesto y yo no sabía jugar nada de baloncesto. Después de almorzar, Roberto y yo teníamos un poco de tiempo libre, así que le dije para jugar fútbol. Al principio él me dijo que no quería, pero yo le dije que yo podía enseñarle. A él le gustó jugar conmigo y desde ese entonces, Roberto y yo jugamos fútbol todos los días después de clases.

Después de 10 años, Roberto y yo seguimos siendo buenos amigos. Él todavía vive al frente de mi casa y ambos aún seguimos jugando fútbol, pero ahora sólo los fines de semana.

SUMMARY IN SPANISH

Iván nos cuenta cómo conoció a su mejor amigo, Roberto. Al principio, Iván era el estudiante nuevo de la escuela y nadie quería hablar con él, pero todo cambió durante la hora del almuerzo cuando un muchacho llamado Roberto se acerca a él y le dice que él había visto a Iván antes. Iván y Roberto se dan cuenta que comparten muchas cosas en común y empiezan a ser buenos amigos. Hasta el día de hoy, Iván y Roberto son buenos amigos y siguen jugando fútbol juntos.

SUMMARY IN ENGLISH

Iván tells us how he met his best friend, Roberto. In the beginning, Iván was the new student in his school and nobody wanted to talk to him, but everything changed during lunchtime when a guy named Roberto approaches him and tells him that he had seen Iván before. Iván and Roberto realize that they share many things in common and they begin to be good friends. To this day, Iván and Roberto are very good friends and continue playing soccer together.

VOCABULARIO

1.-mejor amigo = best friend

2.-años = years

3.-secundaria = high school

4.-estudiar = study

5.-padres = parents

6.-preocuparme = worry

7.-amables = friendly (plural)

8.-ayudó = he helped

9.-receso = break

10.-mirando = looking

11.-triste = sad

12.-almuerzo = lunch

13.-persona = person

14.-escuela = school

15.-explicó = explained

16.-profesor = teacher

17.-alto = tall

18.-fuerte = strong

19.-deporte = sport

20.-canciones = songs

21.-fútbol = soccer

22.-baloncesto = basketball

23.-tiempo libre = free time

24.-fines de semana = weekends

Questions

1. ¿Cómo se llama el mejor amigo de Iván?

2. ¿Por cuánto tiempo han sido amigos?

3. ¿Por qué estaba Iván triste durante su primer día de clases?

4. ¿Dónde vivía Roberto?

5. ¿Por qué pudo Roberto decir que él ya había visto a Iván antes de conocerlo?

6. ¿Por qué dice Iván que Roberto era diferente a él?

7. ¿Por qué ellos nunca habían hablado antes?

8. ¿Qué cosas en común tenían Roberto e Iván?

9. ¿Qué deporte le gustaba a Roberto?

10. ¿Qué deporte Roberto aprendió a jugar gracias a Iván?

11. ¿Cuándo juegan fútbol ahora ellos?

Answers

1. El mejor amigo Iván se llama Roberto

2. Ellos han sido amigos por 10 años

3. Iván estaba triste porque él se sentía muy sólo durante su primer día de clases.

4. Roberto vivía al frente de la casa de Iván

5. Porque Roberto había visto a Iván cuando Iván salía de su casa para estudiar

6. Porque Roberto era un poco más alto y fuerte que él, además a él no le gustaba mucho leer

7. Porque ellos estudiaban en escuelas diferentes

8. A ambos les gustaban las películas de acción, las mismas canciones y a ambos les encantaba hacer deporte.

9. A Roberto le gustaba jugar baloncesto.

10. Roberto aprendió a jugar fútbol gracias a Iván

11. Ellos ahora juegan todos los fines de semana.

El Castillo

CAPÍTULO 1 – El detective

Esta es la historia del caso más importante del detective Morgan. El detective Morgan era un hombre muy **alto** y muy **fuerte**. Tenía el pelo negro y un poco largo. El detective trabajaba resolviendo **crímenes** y otros casos. Trabajaba desde hace muchos años en resolver crímenes. Vivía en una ciudad muy **apartada**. Era una ciudad pequeña pero siempre había casos por **resolver**.

Él siempre entraba a trabajar a las 8 de la mañana. Un martes, se levantó de la cama y fue a la cocina. Preparó su café con un nuevo café que había comprado en la nueva tienda de la **esquina**. La nueva tienda de la esquina vendía productos **extranjeros**. A Morgan le gustaba mucho probar **sabores** nuevos y **por eso** siempre compraba allí.

Abrió el armario y sacó una taza para echar el café. Después, abrió la nevera, sacó la leche y la echó en el café. Se sentó en la mesa de la cocina.

Mientras bebía su café, leía el **periódico**. No había nada interesante, como siempre. Las noticias del periódico de la ciudad eran aburridas. Cuando pasó varias páginas, encontró algo:

—¡Vaya! —dijo Morgan con el periódico en la mano— ¡Esto es increíble!

Morgan estaba leyendo el periódico. Leyó un artículo que le interesaba.

El artículo hablaba sobre un **castillo** a las **afueras** de la ciudad. El castillo era un edificio muy **antiguo** y muy grande. El **dueño** del castillo era un señor con muchísimo dinero. Este señor se llamaba Harrison.

—**¡No me lo puedo creer!** —dijo Morgan mientras leía el artículo.

El artículo decía que en el castillo había ocurrido algo. Había ocurrido algo malo. No acabo de leer el artículo ni de beber el café, pero **sonó el teléfono** de su casa.

—*¡Qué casualidad!*

Morgan se levantó y habló con su jefe.

—Buenos días, Morgan.

—Buenos días, jefe. ¿Qué noticias hay?

—Necesito que vengas al **despacho**.

—¿Ha ocurrido algo?

Morgan preguntaba si había ocurrido algo porque era una ciudad tranquila, pero el artículo del periódico era algo importante y **relacionado** con eso.

—Sí, Morgan. ¿Sabes lo que ha ocurrido?

—No, no lo sé.

—Nosotros tampoco. ¿Has leído el artículo del periódico?

—Sí, he leído algo.

—Necesito que vengas al despacho ya. **¡Deprisa!**

—Estoy en camino.

Morgan colgó el teléfono y cogió su **abrigo**. Su abrigo era negro y muy largo, casi le llegaba al **suelo**. Le gustaba porque abrigaba mucho cuando hacía frío en invierno. Salió de su casa y entró en su coche. **Arrancó el coche** y se dirigió al despacho.

El despacho estaba en otra parte de la ciudad, lejos de donde él vivía. Era menos tranquilo y había más gente, pero seguía siendo una zona tranquila.

Morgan **se bajó del coche** y vio la puerta de su despacho. Allí, estaba el **guardia de seguridad**. Le dijo a Morgan:

—Buenos días, señor. Bienvenido.

—Hola, buenos días, gracias —dijo Morgan.

El detective entró en el edificio. Dentro, la gente estaba **nerviosa**.

Trabajaban mucho y muy deprisa. Algo importante estaba pasando seguro.

Morgan subió las escaleras y pasó por varios despachos. Al final, vio su puerta y llegó a ella. En la puerta había un **letrero** con su nombre. Antes de entrar, el jefe lo vio y le dijo:

—¡Morgan, aquí!

El jefe quería que el detective entrase en su despacho, así que entró.

—Siéntate —le dijo el jefe.

Morgan se sentó en la silla del despacho del jefe. El jefe empezó a hablar:

—Vale. Buenos días de nuevo. **Vamos a hablar** sobre este asunto.

—¿Qué asunto? —dijo el detective.

—El periódico ha escrito un artículo, pero todavía no saben qué pasa.

—¿Y usted lo sabe, jefe?

—Sí, por eso te he hecho venir al despacho.

El detective notó que su jefe estaba algo nervioso, pero no preguntó.

Simplemente siguió la conversación.

—Entiendo, ¿qué es lo que ocurre, jefe? ¿Ha ocurrido algo importante?

—Sí, Harrison ha vuelto al castillo.

Morgan se quedó pensando. Eso no era importante. Era algo normal.

Inusual, pero normal. A veces, volvía al castillo y pasaba varios días allí.

Después se iba y dejaba el castillo cerrado.

—Pero jefe, eso es algo normal.

—Sí, es algo normal.

—¿Entonces? No entiendo.

—Siempre que Harrison vuelve al castillo, se vuelve a ir en una semana. Y sigue allí.

El detective Morgan no veía nada raro. ¿Por qué tanto misterio?

—Sigo sin entender nada.

—Han oído **gritos** en el castillo.

—¿Gritos?

—Sí, detective. Seguramente gritos de Harrison. Algo ha pasado en el castillo, o está pasando. No sabemos qué está pasando, pero seguro que nada bueno.

—Si hay gritos, no puede ser nada bueno.

—Exacto, detective. Y queremos que tú vayas al castillo a investigar.

—¿Por qué yo?

—Eres nuestro mejor detective. Queremos que vayas al castillo y resuelvas el asunto. Ten mucho cuidado, puede haber mucho peligro.

El detective Morgan no tenía **miedo**. Era un hombre muy **valiente** y muy **preparado** para este tipo de situaciones. El jefe siguió hablando:

—Coge tu coche y ve al castillo antes de que se haga de noche. Busca a Harrison y vuelve. Queremos saber qué pasa en el castillo.

—Está bien. **¿Desea algo más**, jefe?

—Nada más. Es todo. Coge tu pistola y repito: **ten mucho cuidado**.

—Lo tendré.

Morgan se levantó de la silla y se despidió de su jefe. Salió del despacho, del edificio y entró de nuevo en su coche. Se llevó su abrigo con él. Arrancó el coche y se dirigió al **bosque** cercano. Allí, había una carretera que llevaba al castillo.

ANEXO DEL CAPÍTULO 1

RESUMEN

El detective Morgan trabajaba en una ciudad muy tranquila. Un día, leyó el periódico y había un artículo interesante: había ocurrido algo en el castillo de las afueras. El jefe lo llama por teléfono para ir a trabajar. El jefe le cuenta que el dueño del castillo, Harrison, ha desaparecido y ha habido gritos.

Quiere que Morgan visite el castillo.

VOCABULARIO 1

1.-alto = tall

2.-fuerte = strong

3.-los crímenes = ***crimes***

4.-apartada = remote

5.-resolver = ***solve***

6.-la esquina = ***corner***

7.-extranjeros = ***foreign***

8.-los sabores = taste, flavour

9.-por eso = for that reason, that's why

10.-el periódico = ***newspaper***

11.-el castillo = ***castle***

12.-las afueras = outskirts

13.-antiguo = ancient

14.-el dueño = ***owner***

15.-¡No me lo puedo creer! = ***I can't believe it!***

16.-sonó el teléfono = the telephone rang

17.-¡Qué casualidad! = What a coincidence!

18.-despacho = office

19.-relacionado = related

20.-¡Deprisa! = Quickly!

21.-el abrigo = coat

22.-el suelo = floor

23.-arrancó el coche = started the car

24.-se bajó del coche = got off the car

25.-el guardia de seguridad = security guard

26.-nerviosa = nervous

27.-el letrero = sign

28.-vamos a hablar = we're going to talk

29.-los gritos = screams

30.-el miedo = fear

31.-valiente = brave

32.-preparado = qualified, trained

33.-¿Desea algo más? = Would you like anything else?

34.-ten mucho cuidado = be very careful

35.-bosque = forest

Preguntas de selección múltiple

Seleccione una única respuesta por cada pregunta

1.-La ciudad donde vive el detective es:

a.-Ruidosa

b.-Tranquila

c.-Es una ciudad muy grande

d.-Es una granja

2.-El detective Morgan bebe:

a.-Cerveza

b.-Cacao

c.-Agua

d.-Café

3.-El dueño del castillo:

a.-Vive siempre allí

b.-Lo visita pocas veces

c.-Lo visita muchas veces

d.-Es desconocido

4.-Morgan tiene un despacho propio:

a.-Es correcto

b.-No es correcto

5.-El jefe le dice a Morgan:

a.-Ve a casa

b.-Ve al despacho

c.-Ve al castillo

SOLUCIONES CAPÍTULO 1

1.-a

2.-d

3.-b

4.-a

5.-c

Un Sueño Hecho Realidad

CAPÍTULO 1

Ser madre soltera de una hija pequeña no es fácil. Tengo que tener dos trabajos para poder pagar la renta, comprar los alimentos y proveer para Beth. Algunos días quiero que mi vida fuera diferente, pero, aun así, estoy agradecida por mi hija, y disfruto cada momento que paso con ella. Sí, la disfruto, pero hay veces que se porta mal, como cualquier otra niña de su edad. Hay veces que simplemente quiero dejar que su padre se encargue de ella, porque me es muy difícil disciplinarla.

Being a single mother of a small child is not easy. I have to work two jobs to pay the rent, buy groceries, and provide for Beth. Some days I wish my life were different, but even so, I'm thankful for my daughter and enjoy every moment I spend with her. Yes, I do enjoy being with her, but there are times when she misbehaves, like any other girl her age. There are times when I wish her father would take over her care because it's just so hard for me to discipline her.

Desafortunadamente, su padre está ausente de su vida, y yo tengo que ser papá y mamá a la vez. Tengo que ser el padre que le regaña y cinco minutos después, la madre que le recoge en sus brazos para decirle que está perdonada y que todo está bien. Tengo que dejarla en la escuela por la mañana, trabajar todo el día, recogerla de la escuela, y preparar algo para que comamos mientras que, cansada hasta el alma, intento ayudarla con su tarea.

Es en aquellos momentos en los cuales pienso seriamente en irme de vacaciones.

Unfortunately, her father is absent from her life, and I have to be both father and mother at the same time. I have to be the father who scolds her, and minutes later, the mother who takes her in her arms to tell her that she's forgiven and all is well. I have to drop her off at school every morning, go to work all day, pick her up at school, and make us something to eat while, tired to death, I try to help her with her homework.

Those are the moments when I seriously think about taking a vacation.

Pero irme de vacaciones es solo un sueño— en este momento ni un centavo me sobra. Ya que es noche, acuesto a Beth en su cama y le canto una canción para que se duerma. Cuando veo sus ojos cerrarse, me salgo lentamente de su recamara, regreso a la cocina y me pongo a limpiar y recoger. Cuando por fin termino todo, caigo exhausta en una silla.

But going on a vacation is just a dream— right now I don't have even one extra cent to my name. Since it is nighttime, I lay Beth in her bed and sing her a song to get her to sleep. When I see her eyes close, I back slowly out of her bedroom, return to the kitchen, and begin to clean everything up. When I finally finish, I fall, exhausted, into a chair.

Saco mi teléfono para revisar mis cuentas de redes sociales, y lo primero que veo es una foto de una amiga, con un vaso de vino en la mano, acostada en la arena blanca de una hermosa playa. Sigo desplazando y descubro que tiene una serie de fotos mostrándole correteando en las olas, reposando en una exótica cama de bambú, y el colmo—tomando la máxima foto romántica: besando a su esposo en frente de ondulantes palmeras en el atardecer… Ay…la playa… suspiro con añoranza.

Desplazando la pantalla hacia abajo, veo foto tras foto de gente con vidas perfectas, familias perfectas, y mascotas perfectas, hasta que algo me llama la atención: es un anuncio de una compañía turística, que dice en letras grandes, "¿ESTÁS CANSADA DE LA RUTINA?" Sigo leyendo y me doy cuenta que la compañía turística está rifando un viaje GRATIS a Punta Cana, un destino popular turístico en la República Dominicana.

"TOTALMENTE GRATIS" dice el anuncio, "INCLUYE BOLETOS DE AVION PARA DOS PERSONAS".

I grab my phone to check my social media accounts, and the first thing that I see is a photo of a friend of mine, a glass of wine in her hand, lying on the white sand of a beautiful beach. As I keep scrolling, I see that she has a whole bunch of pictures depicting her running around in the waves, lying on an exotic bamboo bed, and to top it all off— taking the ultimate romantic photo: kissing her husband in front of swaying palm trees at sunset. Oh…the beach… I sigh longingly.

Scrolling further down, I see photo after photo of people with perfect lives, perfect families, and perfect pets, until something catches my eye: it's an advertisement from a tourist company, shouting in large text, "ARE YOU TIRED OF YOUR HUM-DRUM LIFE?" I keep reading and realize that the tour company is raffling off a FREE trip to Punta Cana, a popular destination in the Dominican Republic.

"ABSOLUTELY FREE," says the ad, "INCLUDES PLANE TICKETS FOR TWO PEOPLE."

Inmediatamente me imagino acostada en la arena sobre una toalla, leyendo un libro y tomando una limonada, viendo a mi hija construyendo un castillo de arena mientras la marea baja y sube. Pienso en la paz y tranquilidad de una playa privada, donde el único ruido es el trino ocasional de las gaviotas, lejos de la gente y de la contaminación de mi ciudad. Y sin pensarlo más, busco las instrucciones en el anuncio para participar en la rifa. Las indicaciones son muy simples— solo debo poner "me gusta" a la página de la compañía turística, y compartirla en mi perfil.

Rápidamente hago clic en la página y lleno los requisitos. Ya sé que la probabilidad de ganar probablemente es baja, pero decido darme el lujo de soñar un poco. Cierro la aplicación, me alisto para dormir, y me acuesto en la cama, mis ojos ya cerrándose con sueño. Y esa noche, termino soñando con la playa.

Immediately I imagine myself lying on a towel on the sand, reading a book and sipping lemonade, while watching my daughter build a sandcastle while the tide rises and falls. I think about the peace and the tranquility of a private beach, where the only noise is the occasional calls of seagulls, far away from the people and pollution of my city. And without another thought, I look for the instructions in the ad to participate in the raffle. The directions are simple— I only have to "like" the page and share it on my profile.

I quickly click on the page and complete the requirements. I know there's probably a lousy probability of winning, but I decide to let myself dream a little. I close the application, get ready to go to sleep, and lie down in the bed, my eyes already closing with sleepiness. And that night, I end up dreaming about the beach.

"¿Mamá? ¡Mamá! ¡Ya despiértate!" Mi sueño, que en este momento involucra una conversación muy interesante con un cangrejo en la playa, es interrumpido bruscamente por Beth, quien me empuja y me jala el cabello para despertarme. Abro mis ojos y miro el reloj.

"Mom? Mom! Wake up already!" My dream, which at that moment involves an interesting conversation with a crab, is interrupted abruptly by Beth, who pushes me and pulls my hair to wake me up. I open my eyes and check the clock.

"¿Son las 6:30 a.m.? ¡Ay hija, gracias por despertarme!" (Suelo levantarme todos los días a las seis para tener tiempo para alistar a mi hija y prepararle algo de comer). Beth me mira con ojos de sorpresa típicos de una niña de 6 años y se ríe.

"It's 6:30 a.m.? Oh, hun, thanks for waking me up!" (I usually wake up every day at 6 to have enough time to get my daughter ready and make her something to eat). Beth looks at me with the wide-eyed expression typical of a 6-year-old and laughs.

"¡Mamá! ¡Mira tu pelo!"

"Mom! Look at your hair!"

Me miro en el espejo y me espanto cuando me veo. ¡Qué horror! Y ahora no tengo tiempo para bañarme…

I look in the mirror and jump when I see myself. What a mess! And I don't even have time to take a shower…

Agarro una goma de pelo para sujetarme el cabello mientras bajo las escaleras, corriendo hacia la cocina para preparar un desayuno rápido.

I grab a hair tie and make a ponytail while I run down the stairs, sprinting into the kitchen to whip up a quick breakfast.

"¡Beth! ¡Ya vístete y ven a desayunar!" le llamo, vertiendo cereal en un plato. Beth baja, despeinada y con la blusa puesta al revés, y se sienta en la mesa. Le paso el plato de cereal y una cuchara.

"¡Beth! Get dressed and come eat breakfast!" I call, dumping cereal into a plate. Beth comes down, her hair a mess and her blouse on backward, and sits at the table. I pass her a bowl of cereal and a spoon.

"Ya, come eso tan rápido como puedas, mi amor. Ya nos tenemos que ir".

"Hurry up, eat that as fast as you can, darling. We have to get going."

De repente escucho un tono de mensaje recibido en mi teléfono. Lo reviso mientras como el cereal. Abriendo el buzón, no puedo creerlo cuando veo un mensaje de la compañía turística del anuncio.

"FELICIDADES, CLARA. ERES LA GANADORA DE NUESTRA RIFA DE VACACIONES 2017".

All of a sudden, I hear the tone of "message received" on my phone. I check it while I eat some cereal. Opening my inbox, I can't believe it when I see a message from the tourist company.

"CONGRATULATIONS, CLARA. YOU ARE THE WINNER OF OUR VACATION RAFFLE 2017."

PREGUNTAS CAPÍTULO 1

1.-¿Por qué empieza Clara a pensar en la playa?

a.-ve un anuncio en la televisión acerca de la playa

b.-ve fotos de una amiga en la playa

c.-su hija dice que quiere ir a la playa

2.-¿El viaje gratis de la rifa es para ir a cuál país?

a.-Punta Cana

b.-Dominica

c.-la República Dominicana

3.-¿Con qué sueña Clara?

a.-con la playa

b.-con su novio

c.-con la fiesta

4.-¿Quién despierta a Clara en la mañana?

a.-su esposo

b.-su hija

c.-su teléfono

5.-¿Quién es la ganadora de la rifa?

a.-Beth

b.-Clarissa

c.-Clara

GUÍA DE RESPUESTAS CAPÍTULO 1

Respuestas:

1.-b

2.-c

3.-a

4.-b

5.-c

VOCABULARIO 1

1.-Vino - wine

2.-Acostada - lying down

3.-arena - sand

4.-playa - beach

5.-olas - waves

6.-exótica - exotic

7.-foto - picture/photo

8.-palmeras - palm trees

9.-atardecer - sunset

10.-compañía turística - tourist company

11.-viaje - trip

12.-destino - destination

13.-gratis - free (of charge)

14.-toalla - towel

15.-libro - book

16.-limonada - lemonade

17.-castillo de arena - sand castle

18.-marea - tide

19.-baja - falls (or, goes down)

20.-sube - rises (or, goes up)

21.-paz - peace

22.-tranquilidad - tranquility

23.-privada - private

24.-gaviotas - seagulls

25.-soñar - to dream

UN SUEÑO HECHO REALIDAD

CAPÍTULO 2

RESUMEN

Clara gana la rifa, y planifica tomar sus vacaciones a la playa en el mes de noviembre. Cuando Clara y Beth llegan a Punta Cana, descubren que la playa es un lugar muy hermoso, ¡pero que el agua está un poco fría! Pasan su primer día jugando y relajándose al lado del mar, disfrutando cada momento lejos del ruido y la contaminación de la ciudad.

Clara wins the raffle and plans to take her beach vacation in the month of November. When Clara and Beth get to Punta Cana, they discover that the beach is a very beautiful place, but the water is a bit cold! They spend their first day playing and relaxing by the sea, enjoying every moment far away from the noise and pollution of the city.

David

David tiene 35 años. **Vive** en México, en la ciudad de Guadalajara.

Es **médico**. David es muy **trabajador**. No está **casado**, pero tiene un perro grande de color marrón. El nombre de su perro es Oscar. Ama a su perro, pero a veces **se siente** solo. **A veces**, David trabaja todo el día y llega a la casa tarde por la noche. Oscar le espera por la puerta y siempre está feliz de verle. Su casa es grande, y tiene una cocina grande, tres recamaras, una sala, y dos baños. Es una casa muy grande para una sola persona y un perro. A veces David se siente solo.

David is 35 years old. He lives in Mexico, in the city of Guadalajara.

He is a doctor. David is a very hard worker. He is not married, but he has a big, brown dog. His dog's name is Oscar. He loves his dog, but sometimes he feels lonely. Sometimes, David works all day and arrives home late at night. Oscar waits for him by the door and is always happy to see him. His house is big, and it has a large kitchen, three bedrooms, one living room, and two bathrooms. It is a big house for only one person and a dog. Sometimes David feels lonely.

David **trabaja** mucho. No puede **salir** mucho porque no tiene mucho tiempo. Sin embargo, tiene un amigo a quien ve los **fines de semana**.

El nombre de su amigo es Alan. Alan está casado con Raquel y tienen tres niños: Ana, Sofía, y Miguel. Ellos viven en Guadalajara también. Viven en la misma calle que David, la Calle Linares. Alan y Raquel son **maestros** en una escuela en Guadalajara. Los fines de semana, cenan con David. Cenan, **conversan**, y tocan instrumentos juntos. A veces cenan en la casa de David, y a veces cenan en la casa de Alan y Raquel. Después de comer, David y Alan tocan la guitarra, y Raquel canta. El fin de semana es muy **divertido** para David, porque ve a sus amigos.

David works a lot. He can't go out much because he doesn't have much time. However, he has one friend whom he sees on weekends.

His friend's name is Alan. Alan is married to Raquel and they have three kids: Ana, Sofía, and Miguel. They also live in Guadalajara. They live on the same street as David, Linares Street.

Alan and Raquel are teachers at a school in Guadalajara. On weekends, they eat dinner with David. They eat, talk, and play instruments together. Sometimes they eat at David's house, and sometimes they eat at Alan and Raquel's house. After they eat, David and Alan play the guitar, and Raquel sings. The weekend is fun for David, because he sees his friends.

Esta noche, David, Alan, Raquel, y los niños cenan en la casa de Alan. **Se sientan** en la mesa. Comen hamburguesas, y hablan acerca del trabajo, la familia, y la vida.

Tonight, David, Alan, Raquel, and the children eat dinner at Alan's house. They sit down at the table. They eat hamburgers and talk about work, family, and life.

"David, ¿Te sientes solo a veces?" pregunta Alan.

"David," says Alan, "do you feel lonely sometimes?"

"¿Solo?" David **sonríe**. "Tengo a Oscar. No me siento solo".

"Lonely?" David smiles. "I have Oscar. I don't feel lonely."

"Tu perro es **genial**, pero necesitas **conocer** a más gente", Alan responde. Alan le mira a Raquel. Tienen un **secreto**.

"Your dog is great, but you need to meet more people," Alan replies. Alan looks at Raquel. They have a secret.

"¡Para mí es difícil salir y conocer a más gente, Alan! Tengo a Oscar…"

"It's hard for me to meet people, Alan! I have Oscar…"

De repente alguien toca la puerta. Raquel **se para** y se va de la mesa. Va a la puerta y la abre.

Suddenly someone knocks on the door. Raquel stands up and leaves the table. She goes to the door and opens it.

David mira a Alan. "¡Alan! ¿Quién es?"

David looks at Alan. "Alan! Who is it?"

Una mujer hermosa entra en la casa. ¡David está **sorprendido**!

A beautiful woman enters the house. David is surprised!

"Hola, ¡muchas gracias por invitarme! Mmmm… hamburguesas… ¡que delicioso!" La mujer mira a David. "¡Hola! Soy Karla. ¿**Cómo te llamas**?"

"Hi! Thank you so much for inviting me! Mmm… hamburgers… how delicious!" The woman looks at David. "Hi! I'm Karla. What's your name?"

"Soy David. David Ortiz".

"I'm David. David Ortiz."

"**Mucho gusto**, David". Karla se sienta al lado de David.

"It's nice to meet you, David." Karla sits down next to David.

"**Igualmente**, Karla". David mira a Alan y Raquel. "¿Karla es tu amiga del trabajo?"

"It's nice to meet you too, Karla." David looks at Alan and Raquel. "Is Karla your friend from work?"

"Sí, Karla es nuestra amiga de la escuela. Ella es maestra. Toca el piano y enseña clases de piano. ¡Quizá puede tocar unas canciones con nosotros después de la cena!" dice Raquel. Le pasa un plato y una hamburguesa a Karla.

"Yes, Karla is our friend from school. She is a teacher. She plays piano and teaches the piano class. Maybe after dinner, she can play some songs with us!" says Raquel. She passes Karla a plate and a hamburger.

David sonríe a Karla. "¿En verdad? ¿Eres maestra de piano?"

David smiles at Karla. "Really? You're a piano teacher?"

"Sí, ¿tú tocas el piano?"

"Yes, do you play the piano?"

"No, yo toco la guitarra".

"No, I play the guitar."

Karla y David conversan un buen rato. Pronto, sus hamburguesas están frías. Alan, Raquel, y los niños les miran y sonríen.

Karla and David talk for a long time. Soon, their hamburgers are cold. Alan, Raquel, and the children look at them and smile.

"**Bien hecho**, ¡querido!" Raquel le dice a su esposo. "Están felices".

Raquel y Alan se paran y se van de la mesa. Los niños también se van de la mesa.

"Good job, dear!" Raquel says to her husband. "They are happy."

Raquel and Alan stand up and leave the table. The children also leave the table.

"Los niños tienen sueño". Raquel le dice a David. "Niños— ¡vayan a sus recamaras ahora!"

"The children are sleepy," Raquel tells David. "Children— go to your bedroom now!"

Los niños van a sus recamaras, y Raquel y Alan van también. Karla y David aún conversan en la mesa. Sus hamburguesas frías aún están en sus platos.

The children go to their bedrooms, and Raquel and Alan go too. Karla and David still talk at the table. Their cold hamburgers are still on their plates.

"Karla, ¿**de dónde eres**?" pregunta David.

"Karla, where are you from?" asks David.

"**Yo soy de** Puebla, ¿y tú?"

"I'm from Puebla, and you?"

"Yo soy de Guadalajara. ¡Aún vivo aquí!" Se ríe. "Y… ¿cuántos años tienes?"

"I'm from Guadalajara. I still live here!" He laughs. "And… how old are you?"

"**Tengo 32 años**". Karla sonríe. "¿**Y tú**?"

"I'm 32." Karla smiles. "And you?"

"Tengo 35 años, y me siento un poco solo.

"I'm 35. And I'm a bit lonely."

Karla **se ríe**. "¿Solo? ¿Por qué? ¿No tienes **novia**?"

Karla laughs. "Lonely? Why? Don't you have a girlfriend?"

"Em, no. Tengo a…. Oscar".

"Um, no. I have…Oscar."

"¿Oscar?" Karla está sorprendida. "¿Quién es Oscar?"

"Oscar? Karla is surprised. "Who is Oscar?"

"Oscar es…. ¡mi perro!" David se ríe.

"Oscar is…my dog!" laughs David.

En las siguientes semanas, Karla y David hablan por teléfono, mandan mensajes de texto, y salen a comer juntos. Tocan la guitarra y el piano juntos. A veces, tocan sus instrumentos y cantan en casa de Alan. David ya no se siente solo.

For the next few weeks, Karla and David talk on the phone, text, and go out to eat together. They play the guitar and piano together. Sometimes, they play their instruments and sing at Alan's house. David is not lonely anymore.

Un día, David y Karla van a casa de David. "¡**Quiero presentarte a alguien**!" le dice David a Karla.

One day, David and Karla go to David's house. "I want to introduce you to someone!" David says to Karla.

"¡Ok!" dice Karla. "¿A quién?"

"Ok!" says Karla. "To whom?"

De repente, un perro grande y peludo entra en el cuarto corriendo.

Corre a Karla y ladra. Karla sonríe y mira a David.

Suddenly, a big, furry dog runs into the room. He runs to Karla and barks. Karla smiles and looks at David.

"Karla, este es Oscar, mi perro".

"Karla, this is Oscar, my dog."

"¡Mucho gusto, Oscar! Guau, David, él es un perro lindo".

Oscar quiere jugar. Corre y trae una pelota. Le da la pelota a David.

"Nice to meet you, Oscar! Wow, David, he is a nice dog!"

Oscar wants to play! He runs and brings a ball. He gives the ball to David.

"No, Oscar", dice David, "Estoy **ocupado**". Oscar se acuesta en el piso. Está triste.

"No, Oscar," says David, "I am busy." Oscar lies down on the floor. He is sad.

"Sí, es un perro lindo", David le dice a Karla, "pero creo que está **triste**".

"Yes, he is a nice dog." David tells Karla, "But I think he is sad."

"¿Triste? ¿Por qué?" responde Karla, sorprendida.

"Sad? Why?" responds Karla, surprised.

"Ya no me ve mucho. ¡Siempre estoy contigo!"

"He doesn't see me much anymore. I am always with you!"

Karla se ríe. "Si. Ahora él que se siente solo es Oscar".

Karla laughs. "Yes. Now Oscar is the one who is lonely."

Conclusion

This is one of the findings of a study published by neuroscientists at McGill University. The authors give various reasons that could explain why the auditory mode works so well. One could be because it provides a more natural learning environment, as we are usually able to understand speech better than other sounds. Another reason might be due to the brain's propensity for pattern recognition- it is easier for us to grasp something when we can identify similarities and patterns amongst different things in our environment. In addition, there are many human languages that also use inflections and intonations in sentences - not just syllables or phonetic sounds alone (as in Spanish). This may also help language comprehension via neural pathways established by visual input such as reading.

This study conducted at McGill University was published in the online issue of the Philosophical Transactions of the Royal Society B (2007). Here's how it was done:

The group of researchers recruited four volunteers who were initially native English speakers and were good readers and writers. Then, they taught them to read and write Spanish via auditory-only training. They did this for 7 weeks. Then, the four volunteers were taught to speak Spanish via a different route (the visual route). That is, they learned by reading and writing as well as listening and speaking. After 7 weeks, they compared the two groups (the auditory only vs. both auditory and visual) of four students. Here's what the researchers found:

The auditory-only group has greater reading skills than native speakers of Spanish in both English and Spanish. The results support the claims made by other studies that have shown that this route is more effective than the other route (visual only). This means that people learn better using both routes - the auditory-only and visual-only - not just one or the other when learning a new language.

In general, the results of this study indicate that learning a new language using only one route (auditory, visual or tactile) is inefficient for adults. Learning a new language would be more efficient if you use both routes.

The researchers concluded that learning a new language via the auditory-only route is more effective in terms of helping people learn to read and write than the visual-only route. This applied to English but also to Spanish.

Printed in Great Britain
by Amazon

32179803R00454